DEVELOPMENTAL PSYCHOLOGY
A Life-Span Approach

DEVELOPMENTAL PSYCHOLOGY
A Life-Span Approach

Fifth Edition

Elizabeth B. Hurlock
Lecturer, Consultant, and Author

McGraw-Hill Book Company

New York   St. Louis   San Francisco   Auckland   Bogotá   Hamburg   Johannesburg
London   Madrid   Mexico   Montreal   New Delhi   Panama   Paris   São Paulo
Singapore   Sydney   Tokyo   Toronto

Credits for Chapter-Opening Photographs:

1 Raimondo Borea/Editorial Photocolor Archives
2 Erika Stone
3 Eve Arnold/Magnum Photos
4 Erika Stone
5 Erika Stone
6 Andrew McKeever/Editorial Photocolor Archives
7 Bob S. Smith/Photo Researchers, Inc.
8 Erika Stone
9 Erika Stone
10 Freda Leinwand/Monkmeyer
11 Ginger Chih, 1978/Peter Arnold, Inc.
12 James H. Karales/Peter Arnold, Inc.
13 Irene Bayer/Monkmeyer
14 Irene Bayer/Monkmeyer

Library of Congress Cataloging in Publication Data

Hurlock, Elizabeth Bergner, date
    Developmental psychology.

    Includes bibliographies and index.
    1. Developmental psychology. I. Title. [DNLM:
1. Human development. BF713 H965d]
BF713.H87 1980   155   79-18755
ISBN 0-07-031450-0

DEVELOPMENTAL PSYCHOLOGY: A LIFE-SPAN APPROACH

1 2 3 4 5 6 7 8 9 0   D O D O   8 9 8 7 6 5 4 3 2 1 0

This book was set in Optima by Progressive Typographers. The editors were
Rhona Robbin and David Dunham; the design was done by Caliber Design Planning;
the production supervisor was Leroy A. Young. The photo editor was Inge King.
New drawings were done by Fine Line Illustrations, Inc.
R. R. Donnelley & Sons Company was printer and binder.

To Alexander J. Burke, Jr.,
in appreciation
of his kindness to me

CONTENTS

PREFACE

With the constantly growing volume of research in the area of development at all ages during the life span, bringing this textbook up to date has become increasingly difficult with each revision since it first appeared in 1953. The major task has been to be selective—to include pertinent new material, eliminate dated material, and to cut down on content with which students have become familiar in other courses.

To make this fourth revision a better learning tool for students and a better teaching tool for instructors, several changes have been made. The changes are:

First, many areas that are receiving considerable attention at present, but which are overlooked or touched on only slightly in many other developmental-psychology textbooks, are discussed in enough detail in this revision to emphasize their significance. Among these are discussions of the obstacles scientists encounter in investigating different aspects of development at different age levels; the ethical aspects of scientific research, especially when children and and the elderly are used as subjects; the importance of names, physical attractiveness, clothes, status symbols, alcohol, and drugs to the personal and social adjustments of individuals of different ages; the problems of divorce, widowhood, remarriage, cohabitation, retirement, and unemployment; and interest in death among the elderly.

Second, because of the many favorable comments from instructors and students about the use of boxes in the fourth edition of this text, new boxes have been added in this revision to highlight important facts and to summarize material from different research studies. It is hoped that these boxes, like those in the previous edition, will serve the purposes for which they were intended.

Third, as a result of the rapid growth of interest in middle and old age and the flood of research studies covering all aspects of life at these age levels, the chapters on middle and old age have been markedly expanded to include the most important of these new studies. This has necessitated shortening discussions of the earlier age periods, especially childhood and adolescence, both of which have already been studied in courses devoted to these age levels by many students now enrolled in a course in developmental psychology.

Fourth, more new cartoons have been included in this edition. The reason for this is that cartoons help to make important facts more meaningful and, therefore, easier to remember.

Fifth, more direct quotations from research studies have been given in this than in the previous edition because, when carefully selected, quotations help to highlight certain important facts that might be overlooked if they were summarized or introduced as a part of the text. Because quotations are set off from the remainder of the text, they call to the reader's attention that here is something important enough to read more slowly and carefully than the rest of the material.

Sixth, hazards to development at each age level, first introduced in the fourth edition of this text, have received such favorable comments from both instructors and students that most of them have been retained and new ones have been added. By so doing it is hoped that readers will fully appreciate why it is that variations in development occur at all ages, what are some of the common causes of these variations, and what, with this foreknowledge, might be done to minimize or eliminate the hazards.

Seventh, instead of giving paragraph summaries at the end of each chapter, a common technique used in many college textbooks, fifteen highlights are given. These serve to alert the reader to the important facts in the chapter as a guide for later review. In addition, at the beginning of each chapter there is a list of objectives. They, like the highlights, are designed to alert students to the most important topics discussed in that chapter.

Eighth, many readers, both students and instructors, find constant references within the text of each chapter distracting if not actually annoying. Consequently, references have been used mainly for three purposes: first, to show the source of a quotation; second, to show the source or sources for statements that may seem controversial or dogmatic; and third, to show the source of material used in a box when this material comes from the work of one or several researchers. However, at the end of each chapter there is an extensive bibliography of studies, all of which have been used directly as sources for the subject matter of the chapter or indirectly to influence my point of view or my stated conclusions. As all of the studies have been used for one or both of these purposes, I want to acknowledge my indebtedness to the authors of the books or articles I have used as sources even if I have not quoted directly from their studies or given their points of view.

Ninth, to avoid extensive bibliographies that would confuse the reader about which books or articles could best be used as source material for further information about a particular topic, the bibliographies in this edition have been kept to approximately the same length as in the fourth edition. This was done by eliminating many of the older references unless they were used for one of the three purposes given in the preceding paragraph and by adding new references for the same subject areas. As most of the newer studies refer to the older studies in their introductory sections and in their bibliographies, readers who are interested in tracing the development of an area of research can easily do so through the newer studies.

At this time I wish to express my gratitude to my professional colleagues for their evaluations and criticisms of the fourth edition of this book, which have been invaluable in planning the fifth edition. I also want to say "Thank you very much" to those of my colleagues who read the manuscript for this edition and who provided so many helpful suggestions, most of which have been used.

Elizabeth B. Hurlock

DEVELOPMENTAL PSYCHOLOGY
A Life-Span Approach

CHAPTER ONE
GROWTH AND DECLINE

After reading this chapter, you should be able to:

- Explain the meaning of developmental changes, their goal, and the incentives psychologists have to study them.
- Identify common personal and social attitudes toward developmental changes.
- List the ten most significant facts about developmental changes.
- Tell how the life span of Americans today differs from that of the past and be able to identify the conditions that influence the length of the life span.
- List the different stages in the life span, the labels associated with them, and tell when they normally occur.
- Identify the recent focus of interest in studying the life span and explain the reasons for it.
- Discuss the common obstacles to studying life-span development, the importance of these obstacles, and what attempts are being made to cope with them.
- Explain that there are times of happiness and unhappiness during the life span, talk about what conditions are responsible for these times, and emphasize the impact they have on personal and social adjustments.

Developmental psychology is the branch of psychology that studies intraindividual changes and interindividual changes within these intraindividual changes. Its task, as La Bouvie has pointed out, is "not only description but also explication of age-related changes in behavior in terms of antecedent-consequent relationships" (60).

Some developmental psychologists study developmental change covering the life span from conception to death. By so doing, they attempt to give a complete picture of growth and decline. Others cover only a segment of the life span—childhood, adulthood, or old age. In this book an attempt will be made to cover all segments and show the important developmental changes at different periods during the entire life span.

In the early years, as Siegel has explained, "developmental psychology was preoccupied with ages and stages. Investigators sought to learn the typical age at which various stages of development occurred" (104). The areas in which research was mainly concentrated were those considered significant for human evolutional adaptation. For the most part, research studies were concentrated on preschool and school-age children and on adolescents. Only later did research extend downward, first to birth and then to conception, and later upward, to adulthood, old age, and finally to middle age.

There are two major reasons for the uneven emphasis of developmental psychology. First, the study of a particular period in the developmental pattern has been greatly influenced by the desire to solve some practical problem or problems associated with that period. Research in the area of middle age, for example, is an outgrowth of the realization that good adjustments in the latter years of life depend on how well one has adjusted to the physical and psychological changes that normally occur in the middle years.

Because the focus of interest in developmental psychology has changed over the years, there are gaps in our knowledge of the different developmental phenomena characteristic of the different periods. These gaps are also due in part to difficulties in studying the different patterns of behavior characteristic of a given period, especially difficulties in getting representative samplings of subjects of a given age and in finding a suitable method for the study of behavior patterns.

The second reason for the uneven emphasis is that it is harder to study people at some stages of life than at others. Getting middle-aged and elderly subjects, for example, is far more difficult than getting preschool or school-age children or even adolescents.

Today, developmental psychologists have six major objectives: (1) to find out what are the common and characteristic age changes in appearance, in behavior, in interests, and in goals from one developmental period to another; (2) to find out when these changes occur; (3) to find out what causes them; (4) to find out how they influence behavior; (5) to find out whether they can or cannot be predicted; and (6) to find out whether they are individual or universal.

MEANING OF DEVELOPMENTAL CHANGES

The term *development* means a progressive series of changes that occur as a result of maturation and experience. As Van den Daele has pointed out, "development implies qualitative change" (114). This means that development does not consist merely of adding inches to one's height or of improving one's ability. Instead, it is a complex process of integrating many structures and functions.

Two essentially antagonistic processes in development take place simultaneously throughout life—*growth*, or evolution, and *atrophy*, or involution. Both begin at conception and end at death. In the early years growth predominates, even though atrophic changes occur as early as embryonic life. In the latter part of life, atrophy predominates, though growth does not stop; hair continues to grow, and cells continue to be replaced. With aging, some parts of the body and mind change more than others.

The human being is never static. From conception to death, change is constantly taking place in physical and psychological capacities. As Piaget has explained, structures are "far from being static and given from the start." Instead, a maturing organism undergoes continued and progressive changes in response to experiential conditions, and these result in a complex network of interaction (87).

Even though development is continuous, as Bower has pointed out, in the sense that it is a cyclic process with competences developing, then disappearing, only to appear at a later age, it is not continuous in the sense that it increases constantly but rather in a series of waves with whole segments of development reoccurring repetitively. For example, as Bower has explained, newborns walk, if held, and then this ability disappears only to reappear at eight or ten months of age. He goes on to explain that the "various explanations of repetitive processes in development thus seem to differ depending on the specific repetition to be explained. What all the explanations have in common, however, is that they preserve the assumption that psychologic growth, in spite of its apparent reversals, is a continuous and additive process" (13). When regression to an earlier stage occurs, there is usually a cause for it, as in the regression to awkwardness that occurs with the rapid growth at puberty.

Often the pattern of change resembles a bell-shaped curve, rising abruptly at the start and then flattening out during the middle years, only to decline slowly or abruptly in old age. It is important to recognize that at no time can this pattern be represented by a straight line, though plateau periods of short or long duration may occur in the development of different capacities.

Goal of Developmental Changes

The goal of developmental changes is to enable people to adapt to the environment in which they live. To achieve this goal, self-realization, or, as it is sometimes called, "self-actualization," is essential. However, this goal is never static. It may be considered an urge—the urge to do what one is fitted to do, the urge to become the person, both physically and psychologically, that one wants to be.

How people express this urge depends on the individual's innate abilities and training, not only during the early, formative years of childhood but also as he or she grows older and comes under greater pressures to conform to social expectations.

Because self-realization plays an important role in mental health, people who make good personal and social adjustments must have opportunities to express their interests and desires in ways that give them satisfaction but, at the same time, conform to accepted standards. Lack of these opportunities will result in frustrations and generally negative attitudes toward people and toward life in general.

Studies of Developmental Change

As already stated, studies of developmental changes during childhood and adolescence have

Whether babies achieve the goal of development (self-actualization) depends partly on their innate abilities and partly on the training they receive during the early, formative years of life. (Photo by Erika Stone.)

been far more extensive than studies of changes that occur during the later years. Among the reasons for this uneven emphasis is the fact that the many prevailing traditional beliefs about children and adolescents have acted as a spur to researchers, who have set up studies designed to prove or disprove these beliefs. Traditional beliefs concerning the postadolescent years are less numerous, and have had less impact on the direction of research. Further, developmental changes occurring at middle age were regarded as purely physiological and, therefore, outside the scope of psychological research. Changes occurring in old age affected a relatively small percentage of the population and were thus considered less important than changes that occur during the early years. It is now recognized that changes occurring at any developmental stage are worthy of study.

One important incentive to research about developmental changes has been the nature-nurture controversy which has raged for decades. How important a role maturation based on genetic factors plays in bringing about developmental changes as compared with environmental pressures and experiences has been the focal point of interest, and many research studies have been devoted to trying to find a satisfactory solution to this controversy.

A recent spur to research on developmental changes at all stages has been the emergence of a large number of new theories about the causes and effects of such changes. These theories are not always backed up by adequate evidence, and a great deal of research is motivated by the desire to substantiate or refute material that has widespread acceptance in the field (86). Any new theory can lead to controversy and experimentation, but of all theories, none have provided a more powerful incentive to research than Piaget's developmental theories, especially his theories about cognitive development (87). Other views that have inspired numerous studies are Kohlberg's stages of moral development and Gesell's stages of equilibrium and disequilibrium (99).

Attitudes toward Developmental Changes

Although changes of a physical or psychological nature are constantly taking place, many people are only vaguely aware of them unless they occur abruptly or markedly affect the pattern of their lives. The changes of old age, for example, usually occur at a much slower pace than those of childhood or adolescence. However, they still require readjustments on the part of all individuals. But, when individuals can make these adjustments relatively slowly, they themselves or others may not be conscious of them.

When changes are rapid, on the other hand, the individual is only too well aware of them, as are others. During the puberty growth spurt at the end of childhood and the beginning of adolescence, such comments as "My, how you have grown since I last saw you!" are evidence of how others notice these changes.

Likewise, in senescence, when the downward movement begins to accelerate, the elderly are aware of the fact that their health is "failing" and that their minds are "slipping." Constant readjustment to these changes is necessary in the scheduled pattern of their lives. They must slow down as the incapacities and infirmities of old age catch up with them and they must frequently forgo some of the activities that formerly played important roles in their lives.

There is a tendency for most people to regard the past as better than the present. And even though most children look forward to the day when they will be "teenagers," when that time comes they often long for the carefree days of their childhood. Similarly, many men who look forward to retirement wish, when the mandatory age for retirement arrives, that they could go back to earlier years when their usefulness and prestige were recognized by the social group (25,46,67,121).

When people become aware of the changes taking place in themselves, they develop definite attitudes toward these changes. Whether these attitudes will be favorable or unfavorable depends on a number of factors, the most important of which are described in Box 1-1. How many young children view developmental changes is illustrated in Figure 1-1.

FIGURE 1-1 How many young children view developmental changes. (Hank Ketcham. "Dennis the Menace." Publishers-Hall Syndicate, Oct. 11, 1973. Used by permission.)

"That's what growin' up means, Joey . . . ya just keep gettin' BIGGER and OLDER and BIGGER and OLDER. . . ."

FACTORS INFLUENCING ATTITUDES TOWARD DEVELOPMENTAL CHANGES

Appearance

Changes that improve one's appearance are welcome and lead to favorable attitudes while those that detract from one's appearance are resisted and every possible attempt is made to camouflage them.

Behavior

When behavior changes are disconcerting, as during puberty and senescence, they affect attitudes toward the changes unfavorably. The reverse is true when changes are favorable, as occurs, for example, when the helplessness of babyhood gradually gives way to the independence of childhood.

Cultural Stereotypes

From mass media, people learn cultural stereotypes associated with different ages and they use these stereotypes to judge people of those ages.

Cultural Values

Every culture has certain values associated with different ages. Because maximum productivity is associated with young through early middle-age adulthood in the American culture of today, attitudes toward this age group are more favorable than attitudes toward other ages.

Role Changes

Attitudes toward people of different ages are greatly influenced by the roles they play. When people change their roles to less favorable ones, as in the case of retirement or widowhood, social attitudes toward them are less sympathetic.

Personal Experiences

Personal experiences have a profound effect on an individual's attitude toward developmental changes. Since the authority and prestige of middle-aged executives decreases as they approach retirement, their attitudes toward aging are, for example, unfavorably affected. These attitudes are intensified by unfavorable social attitudes.

SIGNIFICANT FACTS ABOUT DEVELOPMENT

To understand the pattern of development, certain fundamental and predictable facts must be taken into consideration. Each of these facts has important implications, which are explained in the following pages.

Early Foundations Are Critical

The first significant fact about development is that early foundations are critical. Attitudes, habits, and patterns of behavior established during the early years determine to a large extent how successfully individuals will adjust to life as they grow older.

Because early foundations are likely to be persistent, it is important that they be of the kind that will lead to good personal and social adjustments as the individual grows older. As James warned many years ago, "Could the young but realize how quickly they will become mere walking bundles of habits, they would give more heed to their conduct while still in the plastic state" (47). Much the same point of view was expressed by Bijou: "Many child psychologists have said that the preschool years, from about two to five, are among the most important, if not *the* most important, of all the stages of development, and a functional analysis of that stage strongly points to the same conclusion. It is unquestionably the period during which the foundation is laid for the complex behavior structures that are built in a child's lifetime" (10).

White contends that the foundations laid during the first two years of life are the most critical. According to him, the origins of human competence are to be found in a critical period of time between eight and eighteen months. He goes on further to explain that the child's experiences during this time span do more to determine future competence than at any time before or after (117). Erikson claims that babyhood is the period when individuals learn general attitudes of trust or mistrust, depending on how parents gratify their child's needs for food, attention, and love. These attitudes, he maintains, remain more or less persistent throughout life and color the individual's perception of people and situations (35).

Early patterns do tend to persist, but they are not unchangeable. There are three conditions under which change is likely to occur. First, change may come about when the individual receives help and guidance in making the change. Some parents, for example, may succeed in training a child to use the right hand in preference to the left.

Second, change is likely to occur when significant people treat individuals in new and different ways. Children who have been trained to believe that they should be "seen but not heard" can be encouraged to express themselves more freely by a teacher who makes them feel that they have something to contribute to the group.

A third condition that can lead to change exists when there is a strong motivation on the part of individuals themselves to make the change. When behavior is rewarded by social approval, there is little motivation to make a change. When, on the other hand, behavior meets with social disapproval, there will be a strong motivation to change.

Knowing that early foundations tend to persist enables one to predict with a fair degree of accuracy what a child's future development is likely to be. A quiet, introverted child, for example, is not likely to develop into an extrovert, and a child who has little or no interest in school or school activities is not likely to develop into a scholar or a good school citizen.

Environmentalists believe that an optimum environment will result in maximum expression of genetic factors (1). However, it is difficult to provide an optimum environment during the preschool years when development is taking place especially rapidly.

Roles of Maturation and Learning in Development

The second significant fact about development is that maturation and learning play important roles in development. *Maturation* is the unfolding of the individual's inherent traits. In *phylogenetic functions*—functions which are common to the human race, such as creeping, sitting, and walking—development comes from maturation. Learning, in the form of training, is of little advantage, although controlling the environment to reduce opportunities for practice may retard development. Maturation provides the raw material for learning and determines the more general patterns and sequences of behavior.

Learning is development that comes from exercise and effort on the individual's part. In *ontogenetic functions*—those that are specific to the individual, such as writing, driving a car, or swimming—learn-

ing in the form of training is essential. Without it, development would not take place.

Three important facts emerge from our present knowledge of the interrelationship of maturation and learning as the cause of development. First, because human beings are capable of learning, variation is possible. Individual differences in personality, attitudes, interests, and patterns of behavior come not from maturation alone but from maturation *and* learning. Second, maturation sets limits beyond which development cannot progress, even with the most favorable learning methods and the strongest motivation on the part of the learner. Failure may result from either genetic or environmental adversities that reduce the genetic potentials for development. Third, there is a definite "timetable" for learning. The individual cannot learn until ready. "Developmental readiness," or readiness to learn, determines the moment when learning can and should take place. Harris has emphasized the importance of providing an opportunity to learn when the individual is ready: "It is possible, indeed likely, that a person who comes late to his training will never realize the full measure of his potential" (41).

Development Follows a Definite and Predictable Pattern

The third significant fact about development is that it follows a definite and predictable pattern. There are orderly patterns of physical, motor, speech, and intellectual development, for example. The pattern of physical and motor development is shown in Figure 1-2, which illustrates the laws of *developmental direction*—the "cephalocaudal law," which maintains that development spreads over the body from head to foot, and the "proximodistal law," which maintains that development spreads outward from the central axis of the body to the extremities.

Unless environmental conditions prevent it, development will follow a pattern similar for all. Babies creep and crawl, for example, before they walk, and interest in the opposite sex appears only when pubertal changes have taken place (28,106,122). There is no evidence that individuals have their own individual patterns of development, though there is evidence that the rate of development varies from individual to individual.

The importance of this is that it makes it possible to predict what people will do at a given age

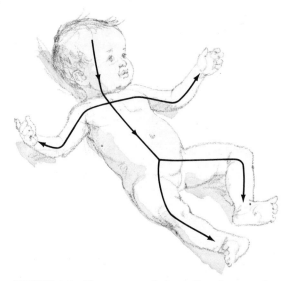

FIGURE 1-2 The pattern of physical and motor development follows the laws of developmental direction, which hold that development proceeds from head to foot and from trunk to extremities. (Adapted from E. L. Vincent and P. C. Martin. *Human psychological development.* New York: Ronald Press, 1961. Used by permission.)

and to plan their education and training to fit into this pattern. If development were not predictable, it would be impossible to plan ahead for any period in the life span. The middle-aged, for example, would not have the foresight to plan for failing health and reduced income as they grow older, and parents would not be able to plan for the training their children will need to fit into adult life.

All Individuals Are Different
The fourth siginificant fact about development is that all individuals are different. As Dobzhansky has emphasized, "Every person is indeed biologically and genetically different from every other," even in the case of identical twins (30). And there is evidence that differences increase rather than decrease as children go from childhood into adolescence and eventually to old age. Neugarten has pointed out that "Adults are not only much more complex than children but they are more different one from another, and increasingly different as they move from youth to extreme old age" (79).

As all individuals are different, no two people can be expected to react in the same manner to the same environmental stimuli. Timid children react differently than aggressive ones, and those who are placid and easygoing are not as upset by family moves as are those who are shy and sensitive.

Because no two individuals ever have identical hereditary endowments or the same environmental experiences, one can never predict with accuracy how people will react to a situation, even when there is ample information about their inherited abilities and even when it is known how the *average* person behaves in similar situations. Nor should one expect the same achievement from people of the same age and intellectual development. Children of the same mental age, for example, will not necessarily be ready to read or do other types of schoolwork at the same time. And, finally, individual differences are significant because they are responsible for individuality in personality makeup. Not only does individuality make people interesting, but it also makes social progress possible.

Each Phase of Development Has Characteristic Behavior
The fifth significant fact about development is that each phase of development has characteristic patterns of behavior. The patterns are marked by periods of *equilibrium,* when individuals adapt easily to environmental demands and, as a result, make good personal and social adjustments, and by periods of *disequilibrium,* when they experience difficulties in adaptation and, as a result, make poor personal and social adjustments.

While it is unquestionably true that some stages of growing up are marked by more difficult behavior than others, there is no stage when the characteristic behavior is not "problem behavior" if it is judged by adult standards. Only when an individual's behavior is atypical for a particular age and leads to poor adjustment may it justly be considered problem behavior. In most instances, such behavior is infantile in that it is characteristic of an earlier age level.

Many of these difficult, unsocial, and often hard-to-understand forms of behavior which appear at different times during the growing-up years will gradually wane and disappear, only to be replaced by other forms of behavior as difficult to understand and live with as the ones that have just been outgrown.

However, it is never safe to assume that all diffi-cult behavior will disappear as the child grows older. Such behavior may be a warning of possible future trouble and should not be disregarded. When it per-sists beyond the age at which it is normally found, dif-ficult behavior suggests that the individual's needs, both personal and social, are not being satisfactorily met.

Even more important, so-called "problem be-havior" does not automatically disappear when chil-dren reach legal maturity. In fact, at every age during the adult years there are periods of equilibrium and disequilibrium, some of which are physical in origin and some of which are environmental or are carry-overs of behavior characteristic of earlier stages. The needless dependency and helplessness of some older people, for example, may readily be a carry-over of dependency developed during the earlier years of life. And the emotional disequilibrium some women ex-perience during menopause may be a carry-over of childish ways of reacting to physical discomforts (102).

Each Phase of Development Has Hazards

The sixth significant fact about development is that each phase of development has its hazards. There is ample evidence that each period in the life span has associated with it certain developmental hazards—whether physical, psychological, or environmental in origin—and these inevitably involve adjustment prob-lems. What these hazards are will be discussed in the chapters dealing with different stages in the develop-mental pattern.

It is essential that persons who are in charge of the training of children be aware of the hazards com-monly associated with each period in the life span. Such awareness may make it possible to prevent or to at least alleviate these hazards. This is true also of the later years, especially middle and old age. It is important because the way in which people cope with these hazards has a great effect on their personal and social adjustments.

Development Is Aided by Stimulation

The seventh significant fact about development is that it is aided by stimulation. While most develop-ment will occur as a result of maturation and environ-mental experiences, much can be done to aid de-velopment so that it will reach its full potential. This can be done by stimulating development through directly encouraging the individual to use an ability which is in the process of developing. Stimulation, it has been found, is especially effective at the time when an ability is normally developing, though it is important at all times.

How important a role stimulation plays has been shown even in the case of children born prema-turely. It has been found that if, instead of keeping these premature infants quiet and ignoring them ex-cept to take care of their physical needs—the usual procedure in American hospitals today—care-givers stimulate them by moving their limbs, turning them into different positions, and talking to them, the pre-mature infants develop faster than unstimulated pre-mature infants. Furthermore, the mortality rate is lower for these infants than for unstimulated prema-ture babies (115). The educational television program "Sesame Street" has stimulated a great interest in reading in preschool children. As a result, children who watch this program regularly are learning to read sooner than nonviewers and, age for age, their read-ing ability is superior (76).

The more often parents talk to their preschool-age children, the sooner the children learn to talk and the stronger their motivation to do so (77). Similarly, stimulation of the muscles during the early years re-sults in earlier and better coordinated motor skills.

Studies of the elderly have revealed that stimu-lation helps to ward off physical and mental decline. Those who remain physically and mentally active in old age show far less physical and mental deteriora-tion than do those who adopt the "rocking-chair phi-losophy" of aging and become so inactive that their physical and mental capacities receive little or no stimulation.

Development Is Affected by Cultural Changes

The eighth significant fact about development is that it is affected by cultural changes. Because an individual's development is molded to conform to cultural standards and ideals, changes in these stan-dards affect the developmental pattern. For example, in the past, standards for patterns of behavior for boys were distinctly different, in most respects, from those considered appropriate for girls. Parents and teach-ers knew they were expected to mold children's behavior to conform to the approved standards. Today, with some adults favoring the traditional sex roles and others the egalitarian sex roles, parents and teachers are often at a loss to know what cultural pattern to use as a standard.

When adults decide that a relaxed and pleasant life-style is more rewarding than just the accumulation of money, and when this cultural value wins the stamp of approval of the social group with which they are identified, this has a marked influence on the pattern of development of interests and behavior of their children throughout the children's lives (9,108). Children brought up in a one-parent home learn to conform to the culturally approved standard of behavior for such homes—standards that differ in many respects from those of two-parent homes (109).

Social Expectations for Every Stage of Development

The ninth significant fact about development is that there are social expectations for every stage of development. Every cultural group expects its members to master certain essential skills and acquire certain approved patterns of behavior at various ages during the life span. Havighurst has labeled them *developmental tasks*. According to him, a developmental task is "a task which arises at or about a certain period in the life of the individual, successful achievement of which leads to happiness and to success with later tasks, while failure leads to unhappiness and difficulty with later tasks." Some tasks arise mainly as a result of physical maturation, such as learning to walk; others develop primarily from the cultural pressures of society, such as learning to read; and still others grow out of the personal values and aspirations of the individual, such as choosing and preparing for a vocation. In most cases, however, developmental tasks arise from these three forces working together (43). The important developmental tasks for different phases in the life span as outlined by Havighurst are shown in Box 1-2.

Purposes of Developmental Tasks Developmental tasks serve three very useful purposes. First, they are guidelines that enable individuals to know what society expects of them at given ages. Parents, for example, can be guided in teaching their young children different skills by the knowledge that society expects the children to master these skills at certain ages and that their adjustments will be greatly influenced by how successfully they do so. Second, developmental tasks motivate individuals to do what the social group

expects them to do at certain ages during their lives. And, finally, developmental tasks show individuals what lies ahead and what they will be expected to do when they reach their next stage of development.

Adjustment to a new situation is always difficult and is always accompanied by varying degrees of emotional tension. However, much of this difficulty and stress can be eliminated if individuals are cognizant of what will come next and gradually prepare for it. Children who absorb social skills needed for the new social life of adolescence will find adjustment to members of the opposite sex easier when they reach adolescence, and young adults will find transition into middle age easier and less stressful if they gradually cultivate leisure-time activities as their parental responsibilities lessen.

Hazards of Developmental Tasks Because developmental tasks play such an important role in setting guidelines for normal development, anything that interferes with their mastery may be regarded as a potential hazard. There are three very common potential hazards related to developmental tasks. The first is inappropriate expectations; either individuals themselves or the social group may expect the development of behavior that is impossible at the time because of physical or psychological limitations.

A second potential hazard is the bypassing of a stage of development as a result of failure to master the tasks for that stage of development. The crises individuals experience when they pass from one stage to another comprise the third common potential hazard arising from developmental tasks. Even though an individual may have mastered the developmental tasks for one stage satisfactorily, having to master a new set of tasks appropriate for the next stage inevitably brings with it tension and stress—conditions that can lead to a crisis. For example, men whose working lives have come to an end often experience a "retirement crisis," in which they feel that the prestige and personal satisfaction associated with the job have also come to an end.

Sooner or later all people become aware that they are expected to master certain developmental tasks at various periods during their lives. Each individual also becomes aware of being "early," "late," or "on time" with regard to these tasks. It is this awareness that affects their own attitudes and behavior as well as the attitudes of others toward them.

Although most people would like to master de-

BOX 1-2

HAVIGHURST'S DEVELOPMENTAL TASKS DURING THE LIFE SPAN

Babyhood and Early Childhood

- Learning to take solid foods
- Learning to walk
- Learning to talk
- Learning to control the elimination of body wastes
- Learning sex differences and sexual modesty
- Getting ready to read
- Learning to distinguish right and wrong and beginning to develop a conscience

Late Childhood

- Learning physical skills necessary for ordinary games
- Building a wholesome attitude toward oneself as a growing organism
- Learning to get along with age-mates
- Beginning to develop appropriate masculine or feminine social roles
- Developing fundamental skills in reading, writing, and calculating
- Developing concepts necessary for everyday living
- Developing a conscience, a sense of morality, and a scale of values
- Developing attitudes toward social groups and institutions
- Achieving personal independence

Adolescence

- Achieving new and more mature relations with age-mates of both sexes
- Achieving a masculine or feminine social role
- Accepting one's physique and using one's body effectively
- Desiring, accepting, and achieving socially responsible behavior
- Achieving emotional independence from parents and other adults

- Preparing for an economic career
- Preparing for marriage and family life
- Acquiring a set of values and an ethical system as a guide to behavior—developing an ideology

Early Adulthood

- Getting started in an occupation
- Selecting a mate
- Learning to live with a marriage partner
- Starting a family
- Rearing children
- Managing a home
- Taking on civic responsibility
- Finding a congenial social group

Middle Age

- Achieving adult civic and social responsibility
- Assisting teenage children to become responsible and happy adults
- Developing adult leisure-time activities
- Relating oneself to one's spouse as a person
- Accepting and adjusting to the physiological changes of middle age
- Reaching and maintaining satisfactory performance in one's occupational career
- Adjusting to aging parents

Old Age

- Adjusting to decreasing physical strength and health
- Adjusting to retirement and reduced income
- Adjusting to death of spouse
- Establishing an explicit affiliation with members of one's age group
- Establishing satisfactory physical living arrangements
- Adapting to social roles in a flexible way

velopmental tasks at the appropriate time, some are unable to do so, while others are ahead of schedule. Box 1-3 gives some of the most important factors that influence mastery of developmental tasks.

Regardless of the cause, there are two serious consequences of failure to master developmental tasks. One is that unfavorable social judgments are inevitable; members of the individual's peer group regard him or her as immature, a label which carries a stigma at any age. This leads to unfavorable self-judgments, which in turn lead to unfavorable concepts of self.

Another consequence is that the foundations for the mastery of later developmental tasks are inadequate. As a result, individuals continue to lag behind their peers, and this increases their feelings of inade-

FACTORS INFLUENCING MASTERY OF DEVELOPMENTAL TASKS

Handicaps to Mastery

- A retarded developmental level
- Lack of opportunity to learn the developmental tasks or lack of guidance in their mastery
- Lack of motivation
- Poor health
- Physical defects
- A low intellectual level

Aids to Mastery

- A normal or accelerated developmental level
- Opportunities to learn the developmental tasks and guidance in mastering them
- Motivation
- Good health and the absence of physical defects
- A high level of intelligence
- Creativity

quacy. Equally serious, they must try to master developmental tasks appropriate for the next stages of development at the same time that they are trying to complete the mastery of the tasks appropriate for the age level from which they have just emerged. Children who are unprepared to enter school will find that their attempts to catch up to their age-mates only intensify their feelings of inadequacy and reinforce judgments of their immaturity.

Traditional Beliefs about People of All Ages

The tenth significant fact about development is that there are traditional beliefs about people of all ages. These beliefs about physical and psychological characteristics affect the judgments of others as well as their self-evaluations (119). In our culture stereotypes relating to old age can lead to unfavorable treatment of people in the later years of their lives. Acceptance of these stereotypes by those who are growing old is responsible for much unhappiness during old age and also is an important factor in physical and mental decline.

In spite of the growing evidence from scientific studies that contradicts many of these stereotypes and

traditional beliefs, the majority of them persist. It has been said that myths are slow to die and that many of them still have "plenty of bounce in them" (78). This is especially true of the traditional beliefs about sex differences and the cultural stereotypes of males and females at all ages (69). So long as they persist, they have a profound influence on the developmental pattern.

THE LIFE SPAN

There are two characteristics of the life span today that distinguish it from the pattern that existed several generations ago. First, the heavy preponderance of young people no longer exists. Instead, as more and more people live to be older, the proportions of individuals at different age levels becomes increasingly similar. It is estimated that, in time, the proportions will be approximately equal. Figure 1-3 shows the proportions of the population of different ages in 1970 and the estimated proportions in the year 2030.

The explanation for this change is that there are fewer children being born today than in the past, due to improved methods of contraception, and that better health and medical care enables more and

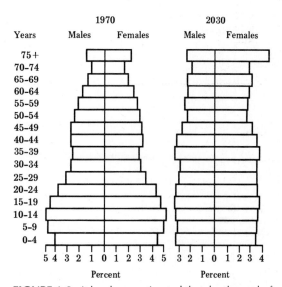

FIGURE 1-3 It has been estimated that, by the end of the present century, the number of Americans in each age level will be approximately equal. (Adapted from Bureau of the Census, National Center for Health Statistics, Washington, D.C., 1977. Used by permission.)

more people to live longer. There is, however, a difference between the sexes in number of people at every age level, with females outnumbering males, especially in the latter years of life (69).

The second characteristic of the life span is that American men and women, on the average, live longer than men and women of any other country and longer than men and women in the United States in past generations. In 1900, for example, the life expectancy for white males was 48.2 years; for white females, it was 51 years. By 1970, the life expectancy for white males had risen to 67.5 years, and for white females it has risen to 74.1 years. For blacks and other minority groups, the life expectancy for both males and females was several years less. It has been estimated that by 1990, 9.4 percent of the entire American population will be over sixty-five years of age (18,82,112).

Many factors influence the length of the life span; the most important of these are given in Box 1-4 (18,36,49,82,84,85,115).

It has never been possible to predict how long a given individual will live. This is just as true today as in the past. However, Scheinfeld has suggested that if three factors are taken into consideration, a general prediction is possible. According to him (96):

How long you, personally, may expect to live depends on these principal influences: First, environment—the way in which you were started off in life and the conditions under which you lived thereafter and live now. Second, your inherited vigor or weakness (as applied both to specific diseases and defects and to general resistance factors), with particular attention to your sex. And, third, luck.

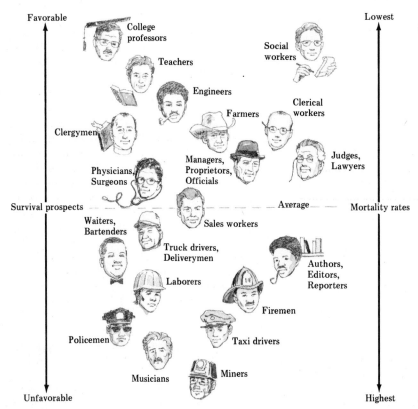

FIGURE 1-4 Longevity in America is related to occupation. (Adapted from A. Scheinfeld. *Your heredity and environment.* Philadelphia: Lippincott, 1965. Used by permission.)

CONDITIONS INFLUENCING LONGEVITY

- *Heredity*. Longevity tends to run in families.
- *Physical Characteristics*. People of average size and body structure tend to live longer than those who are under- or overweight or who are very tall or very short.
- *General Physical Condition*. A good physical condition throughout life, but especially during the growth years of childhood and adolescence, is favorable to longevity.
- *Sex*. Women, as a group, outlive men.
- *Race*. In America, blacks, Puerto Ricans, and other minority-group members have a shorter life expectancy than whites.
- *Geographic Location*. People who live in urban and suburban areas tend to live longer than those who live in rural areas as a result of better health and medical facilities.
- *Socioeconomic Level*. The higher the socioeconomic level, the longer the individual's life span tends to be.
- *Intelligence*. Individuals with high intelligence and those with intellectual interests live longer than the less intelligent.

- *Education*. People who are better educated tend to live longer than those whose education is limited.
- *Smoking and Drinking*. Nonsmokers and nondrinkers tend to live longer than those who smoke and drink excessively.
- *Marital Status*. Those who are or have been married live longer than those who have never been married.
- *Efficiency*. Those who are efficient tend to live longer than the inefficient because they expend less energy in whatever they do.
- *Anxiety*. The tendency to suffer from anxiety due to work, family, economic or other problems leads to hypertension which shortens the life span.
- *Occupation*. The kind of work the individual does affects the length of the life span. See Figure 1-4.
- *Happiness*. People who are reasonably happy and satisfied with the pattern of their lives normally live longer than those who are dissatisfied and unhappy.

Subdivisions of the Life Span

Regardless of how long or how short the total life span is, it is usually subdivided into stages or periods, each of which is characterized by certain behavioral or developmental characteristics. Chronological age (C. A.) is the criterion used for this subdivision. As Fry (37) has explained:

C. A. is only a rough index of biological, psychological, sociological, and cultural aging processes. Yet C. A. continues as the principle criterion for determining age categories on the part of bureaucratic organizations and in a wide variety of research. . . . Cultural age categories are determined on the basis of events in human society which in effect are "social clocks."

Each individual goes through a succession of developmental stages, though at different rates and at slightly different ages (101). However, to quote Fry again, "Age is an index positioning individuals in a developmental sequence" (37).

All cultures divide the life span into periods, although different names are given to the periods and the age levels encompassed by the different stages vary. Even in the American culture there are variations. Erikson, for example, has subdivided the life span into eight stages with the following labels and basic components: *infancy*, the stage of trust versus mistrust; *early childhood*, autonomy versus shame and doubt; *preschool age*, initiative versus guilt; *school age*, industry versus inferiority; *adolescence*, identity versus identity confusion; *young adulthood*, intimacy versus isolation; *adulthood*, generativity versus stagnation; and *senescence*, ego integrity versus despair. As may be seen, Erikson contends that each stage has two possible resolutions, positive and negative. Failure at any stage adversely affects later stages (35).

Today it is customary to subdivide the life span into ten stages or periods, each with certain developmental and behavioral patterns. These are shown in Box 1-5. Not all individuals reach these stages at the same time and not all pass through all of them. Some people die or are killed before they complete the normal life span. But each stage has problems that must be solved before the individual can progress to the

STAGES IN THE LIFE SPAN

- *Prenatal period:* conception to birth
- *Infancy:* birth to the end of the second week
- *Babyhood:* end of the second week to end of the second year
- *Early childhood:* two to six years
- *Late childhood:* six to ten or twelve years
- *Puberty or preadolescence:* ten or twelve to thirteen or fourteen years
- *Adolescence:* thirteen or fourteen to eighteen years
- *Early adulthood:* eighteen to forty years
- *Middle age:* forty to sixty years
- *Old age or senescence:* sixty years to death

next stage. Failure to do so results in immaturity and poor adjustment (43,101). The remaining chapters of this book will discuss in detail the characteristic patterns of behavior for each of these age periods and the reasons for any deviations from the predictable patterns. They will also explain the meanings of the names applied to each of the major periods in the life span.

RECENT FOCUS OF INTEREST IN THE LIFE SPAN

To understand the pattern of development from conception to death, one must have a picture of this that is based on the results of scientific studies, not on traditional beliefs and stereotyped ideas. However, as was pointed out earlier, many obstacles confront the developmental psychologist in the study of the various stages in the life span, and as a result there are gaps in our knowledge. Today there is almost as much scientific interest in the later years of life as there is in the early years, but attempts to study the later years have been blocked, in part at least, by obstacles which are only now being minimized and in some instances eliminated.

Interest in the latter part of the life span is not of recent origin. Hippocrates treated illnesses of old age, and there are also historic references to beauty aids for the elderly and to attempts at rejuvenation (63). However, until the turn of the present century too few

people lived long enough to make the latter part of life a serious problem. Now an increasing percentage of the population lives longer, and this has created many problems for the individuals themselves and for their families, their employers, and society in general.

As a result, two new areas of scientific research have been developed—gerontology and geriatrics. *Gerontology* is the science of aging. It is derived from the Greek *geron,* meaning "old man," and *ology,* meaning "the study of," and it is concerned with all facets of aging. *Geriatrics,* on the other hand, is that branch of medicine concerned with the diseases of old age. It deals with the health of the aged, just as pediatrics deals with the health of infants and children.

The major goal of studies in the area of gerontology is to gather data to disprove traditional beliefs about the aged and to show how they can function successfully in a youth-oriented culture.

To prolong the usefulness and happiness of old people through better health has been the goal of geriatrics. While improvement in the health of old people may and often does add years to their life span, this is of little value unless individuals are able to enjoy and make use of this added time not only for their own enjoyment but also to aid society. The goal of geriatrics is therefore to add life to the years of the elderly, not just years to their lives.

Middle age, until recently one of the least explored periods in the life span, has now come under scientific investigation.

The reason for this is that few problems related to middle age seemed important enough to engage the attention of the psychologist, who was already preoccupied with studies relating to children, adolescents, young adults, and old people.

Not only has there been increasing scientific interest in the latter years of life, but there is also a strong popular interest in the subject, as evidenced by the appearance of many books and articles dealing with the problems of middle and old age.

OBSTACLES IN STUDYING LIFE-SPAN DEVELOPMENT

All studies of the life span are beset by obstacles in varying degrees. The five most common and most serious of these are discussed below.

It is difficult to obtain a large, representative sample of subjects during old age when experimenters have to use, for the most part, those living in institutions—people who, unquestionably, are not representative of the general population. (Photo by Ray Ellis/Photo Researchers.)

Representative Samples of Subjects

The first obstacle scientists encounter in studying development during the life span is securing representative samples of subjects at different age levels, although it is relatively easy to get representative samplings of subjects from among schoolchildren and college students. In the case of newborn infants, however, researchers often meet with strong parental objections. Getting older adolescents and young adults who are not attending school to volunteer as subjects is also difficult because they may not be available for study at any one particular place.

This difficulty increases with advancing age, which is why so many of the studies relating to the latter years of life have been made on men and women living in institutions, people who unquestionably are not representative of the general population.

Recruiting young adults, middle-aged adults, or the elderly as voluntary participants in experiments has likewise been a difficult task, even when they are paid for their time. Many persons shy away from any testing program, partly because of lack of personal interest but mainly because they are afraid they will not do well and, as a result, create an unfavorable impression. Relying on those who are willing to participate may be creating a bias just as using institutional cases does.

Establishing Rapport with Subjects

The second obstacle scientists encounter in studying development during the life span is establishing rapport with subjects at different age levels. There is no guarantee that scientists will be able to elicit the information they are seeking from any group unless they are able to establish rapport with their subjects. Therefore, there is no guarantee that the data they obtain is as accurate or as comprehensive as it might have been had a better relationship existed between subjects and experimenters.

The reason for this is that obtaining information from subjects of any age is extremely difficult because most people resent having a stranger pry into their personal affairs. Even schoolchildren and college students, who often take tests or fill out questionnaires as part of their classroom work, show their resentment by being uncooperative or even by falsifying the information they give. This is even truer of adults of all ages. Their resentment at participating in a scientific study may be partially overcome if they are paid to do so, but they tend to regard the experimenter as an invasion of privacy (91,92).

As a result, it is questionable whether data obtained from many studies is a true picture of the involved individuals' attitudes, feelings, and values. Only when good rapport can be established with the subjects and when there is evidence of cooperation on their part can great confidence be placed in the results of these studies (91,92).

Methodology

The third obstacle scientists encounter in studying development during the life span is securing a satisfactory method. This is because no one method can be used satisfactorily for studying people at all ages or for investigating all areas of development. Some of the methods that must be resorted to, for lack of better ones, are of dubious scientific value.

Because of the wide age range of subjects and the variety of different areas of development that must be studied to give a composite picture, assorted methods have had to be used. Some have been borrowed from medicine, from the physical sciences, and from related social sciences, especially anthropology and sociology. Some have made use of laboratory settings, and others of the naturalistic settings of the home, school, community, or work environment. Some are regarded as reliable, while others, especially the retrospective and introspective techniques, are of questionable value.

Regardless of the method used, most of the studies have been cross-sectional comparisons of the same abilities at different stages of development. As such, they do not give evidence about developmental trends or about intraindividual variability. Nor is it possible, when using cross-sectional comparisons, to assess the relative behavior constellations of individuals at an early age and similar behavior in adult life.

One of the most serious problems connected with the cross-sectional approach is that it is almost impossible to get comparable groups of subjects for study at different age levels. This can bias the result of studies, especially studies of old age. When mental abilities are studied using the cross-sectional approach, mental decline is reported to be far greater than when the same mental abilities are studied using the longitudinal approach. This, in turn, has given scientific backing to the popular belief that mental decline in old age is not only great but also universal.

Another serious problem associated with the cross-sectional approach is that it does not take into consideration cultural changes which always play a major role in the patterns of physical and mental development. This results in a tendency to interpret *any* change that may appear as an age change (34,52).

Cultural changes affect values, among other things. A comparison of adolescents of today with members of the older generation showed that the latter tend to disapprove more strongly of extravagance than adolescents do. This might be interpreted to mean that members of the older generation have become rigid with age. In reality, the difference is one of cultural values. When members of the older generation were growing up, high value was placed on a prudent spending of money and on having a nest egg for the proverbial rainy day. Today, adolescents are growing up in a culture dominated by the philosophy of "keeping up with the Joneses" and of "letting Uncle Sam take care of you when you can't take care of yourself" (59). Because of the rapid change in cultural values taking place at the present time, children often consider their parents' values old-fashioned. See Figure 1-5.

Accuracy of Data Obtained

The fourth obstacle scientists encounter in studying development during the life span is ensuring that the data obtained from the studies will be accurate. Inaccuracies may result when a biased sampling of subjects gives a false picture of the normal developmental pattern at a particular age. This can happen, for example, when institutionalized elderly people are used for the study and the subjects try to present as favorable a picture of themselves as they can and, either consciously or unconsciously, distort their introspective or retrospective reports. It can also occur when the only method available for studying a certain area of development is less than satisfactory.

In the measurement of intelligence it is still questionable if the results are accurate for the first two years of life (65). There is even controversy about the accuracy of intelligence tests for older age levels (27).

FIGURE 1-5 Rapid changes in cultural values make many parental values seem "old-fashioned" to their children. (M. O. Lichty. "Grin and Bear It." Publishers-Hall Syndicate, Nov. 17, 1965. Used by permission.)

"I'm glad we had this man-to-man talk, Pop . . . Some of your ideas were pretty old-fashioned!"

Observational techniques for the study of behavior during the preschool years are questioned for accuracy because of the tendency of observers to draw inferences from their study of children's behavior and speech (40).

Studying well-being, life satisfaction, or happiness is very difficult because only subjective measures can be used. The accuracy of such measures is open to question (22). In the study of fears by means of oral or written checklists, it was found that subjects often do not identify fear as different from anxiety or worry. Furthermore, when parents report their children's fears, they often describe different fears than their children do. In addition, it is impossible to identify the intensity of fears using only a checklist (26).

Even though the longitudinal approach has a methodological advantage over the cross-sectional approach, the problem of accuracy is still ever present. Unless such studies are started when the subjects are very young, information about their earlier lives must be supplied by the subjects themselves or by parents, teachers, and peers, who tend to interpret the data they report in terms of their own attitudes and experiences.

Ethical Aspects of Research

The fifth obstacle scientists encounter in studying development during the life span involves the ethical aspects of research. Today there is a growing trend to take this into account, and it has been a stumbling block to certain kinds of studies, which, in the past, were made without consideration of their fairness to the subjects studied. With the trend nowadays toward considering the rights of subjects, emphasis in being placed on asking their consent to participate in experiments, or, for the very young, the consent of their parents or guardians (15,61). Such consideration also applies to high school and college students; they no longer are expected to take time from their studies to participate in experiments *unless* they are paid to do so. Thus there is a tendency to bias the sampling because only those who need the money or those who feel that the money is worth their while are willing to accommodate the researcher.

Consideration of the rights of subjects is therefore bound to lead to gaps in present-day knowledge of development. Aside from preschool and school-age children, no other group of individuals has been taken greater advantage of by scientific researchers than the institutionalized elderly. Just as preschool and school-age children formerly were not consulted about their willingness to participate in an experiment, so the wishes of the institutionalized elderly were ignored. They were expected to take tests or answer questions, regardless of how they felt about the matter, because they were receiving public assistance. Even in privately supported institutions the inmates were not always consulted.

Such procedures are now regarded as an invasion of privacy and as ethically questionable. As a result, many experimenters are taking into consideration the wishes of those they try to recruit as subjects (89). They are also taking a new attitude toward institutionalized middle-aged people, recognizing their rights to participate or refuse to participate in any research study (12). While these new attitudes toward ethical standards have resulted in fairer treatment of institutionalized middle-aged and older people, they have made it more difficult to get subjects for scientific research among the older age groups.

RESULTS OF OBSTACLES IN STUDYING DEVELOPMENT

The obstacles discussed above have resulted in a paucity of evidence about some areas of development. Of all of the obstacles, the problem of finding a suitable method is probably the most serious. Because of this, relatively few studies of humor at different ages have been made (19). Similarly, few studies of the effects of names and clothes on self-judgments of individuals as well as judgments of individuals by others have been made and, until recently, few of life satisfaction or happiness at different ages during the life span. This leaves gaps in our knowledge of important areas of development at different ages.

This has two serious consequences. First, it tends to lead to a distortion of the picture we have of normal development. For example, lack of adequate evidence about the learning capacities of newborns and about their sensory development encourages acceptance of the traditional belief that they are completely helpless. In time, new evidence may show that newborn infants are less helpless than they appear or than has been formerly accepted as a fact.

Second, lack of adequate information leads to the continued acceptance of traditional beliefs, especially those related to old age. People are conditioned to think unfavorably about this phase of life because of the traditional beliefs associated with it. This affects not only the personal and social adjustments older people make but also the treatment they receive from the social group.

Attempts to Cope with Obstacles

Because of the serious and widespread effects of the obstacles to studying developmental changes, many attempts have been made, with varying degrees of success, to cope with these obstacles. For example, whenever possible animal subjects are being replaced by human subjects for research studies (68). To obtain more representative samplings of subjects at different age levels, especially in the case of middle-aged and old subjects and in the case of the newborn, cooperation has been encouraged by offering guidance and counseling in exchange for participation in research.

To increase the accuracy of the data obtained, research studies are made in naturalistic settings (such as the home, school, or community) whenever possible, rather than in laboratories. Moving pictures and other measuring devices have been substituted for observations by experimenters (80). Even more important, laboratories have been established to train experimenters in observation and in handling children and subjects of other age levels in experimental settings (72, 73, 91, 92). For example, the following suggestions have been made for interviewing children: don't talk down to them or be condescending but treat them as adults; make them feel their answers are important; create a relaxed atmosphere by getting down to their level, relaxing, and putting the children at ease; have patience and allow ample time for response; and explain that other children in the neighborhood and/or over the country are also participating (4).

The problem of methodology is still a thorny one and has been met with only limited success. To date, no satisfactory test has been devised to measure the intellectual development of very young children, and there is growing criticism also of the tests available for the older age levels (27). This obstacle has not yet been successfully dealt with. Because different investigators get different and often conflicting results in their studies, it has been suggested that this obstacle can be overcome by collaboration and coordination of results (8).

A growing number of studies using the longitudinal rather than the cross-sectional approach have been appearing. Some of these cover only small segments of the life span, while others cover large segments. However, they give a picture of developmental changes over a span of years, and when they are combined with other studies covering other age spans, the composite result serves to give a fairly accurate picture of the normal pattern of development. Bijou has commented on how much confidence one can have in the results of these studies (10):

Confidence can be expected to remain high, if after a reasonable period the productions clearly advance basic knowledge of the historical-developmental component of psychological events in the form of the concepts and principles they generate and if they establish new guidelines to applied problems in the form of demonstrated empirical relationships. On the other hand, confidence can be expected to wane, if the field continues to yield products which are peripheral to general psychological theory and offers solutions which turn out to be fads, gimmicks, and verbal prescriptions with only captivating face validities.

By contrast, Skinner (105) has taken a rather dim view about the progress developmental psychologists have made to date. He says:

Why has it been so difficult to be scientific about human behavior? Why have methods that have been so prodigiously successful almost everywhere else failed so ignominiously in this one field? Is it because human behavior presents unusual obstacles to a science? No doubt it does, but I think we are beginning to see how these obstacles may be overcome.

HAPPINESS AND UNHAPPINESS DURING THE LIFE SPAN

Life satisfaction, usually referred to as "happiness," comes from the fulfillment of a need or wish and, as such, is the cause or means of enjoyment. As Alston and Dudley have explained, "Life satisfaction is the ability to enjoy one's experiences, accompanied by a degree of excitement" (3).

According to the definitions of *happiness* given in any standard dictionary, it is a state of well-being and contentment—a pleasurable satisfaction that comes when the individual's needs and wishes are fulfilled. It is not the same as *euphoria,* which implies not only a state of satisfaction but also a buoyancy that is not present in life satisfaction or happiness as it is not only popularly defined but also used by many psychologists. Because happiness is a synonym for life satisfaction and because it is far more widely used than life satisfaction, it will be used throughout this text to imply satisfaction resulting from the fulfillment of needs and wishes.

Because happiness and unhappiness or life satisfactions and dissatisfactions are subjective states, information about them must, of necessity, come from introspections or retrospections or from answers to questionnaires. This is because only the persons involved can say whether they are happy or unhappy or whether they are satisfied or dissatisfied with their lives.

Introspective and retrospective reports, as all psychologists are well aware, are not always accurate. Retrospective reports are especially subject to error because people tend to forget, or to minimize, especially in retrospect, the unhappiness they experienced in some periods of their lives and to exaggerate the unhappiness or the happiness at other periods. In filling out a questionnaire, there is a tendency to give an answer that will put the subject in a favorable light, regardless of the accuracy of the answer.

Because of the many difficulties involved in making long-term longitudinal studies, as was previously pointed out, most studies of happiness and life satisfaction have been made through the use of the cross-sectional approach. The few that have used the longitudinal approach have covered only relatively short periods of the life span, mainly the years of early adulthood and of old age.

Significant Facts about Happiness

Inadequate as are the methods available to date to study happiness, they do give clues to what contributes to the individual's life satisfactions. They also indicate what leads to happiness or unhappiness, not only for different people but also within the same person at different age levels, and what are most likely to be the happy and the unhappy periods in the life span. The results of these studies are summarized below.

Essentials of Happiness There are essentials to happiness, or the state of well-being, contentment, and satisfaction. They are acceptance, affection, and achievement, often called the "three A's of happiness." These are illustrated in Figure 1-6. As Shaver and Freedman have pointed out, "Happiness is more a matter of how you regard your circumstances than of what the circumstances are. . . . It comes from tending one's own garden instead of coveting one's neighbor's" (100).

Acceptance by others is affected by self-acceptance which comes from good personal as well as social adjustments. Shaver and Freedman have further commented, "Happiness has a lot to do with accepting and enjoying what one is and what one has, maintaining a balance between expectations and achievements" (100).

One important contributor to acceptance by others is physical attractiveness. It also affects self-acceptance, achievements, and the affection a person receives from others. Mathes and Kahn have explained (70):

In social exchange physical attractiveness is a positive input and can be used to obtain a variety of good outcomes for the possessor. One of the most frequently obtained outcomes is liking. Attractive people are liked most as friends, dates, sex partners and spouses. Attractive people receive more positive evaluations from others and empathy than unattractive people. Other good outcomes obtained by attractive people include more work from subordinates, greater attitude agreement, better grades, and higher-status spouses. As a result of the many good outcomes obtained by attractive people, it seems likely that they are happier and better adjusted than unattractive people. It is also probable that the liking received from others is reflected in a higher self-esteem.

Affection is a normal accompaniment of acceptance by others. The better accepted people are, the more they can count on the affection of others. That affection is essential to good personal adjustments has been shown in the many studies of emotional deprivation and the devastating effects it has on the individual. These effects, unfortunately, do not always end with childhood. Instead, they are often persistent. As Horn has said, "Someone who experiences a shortage of love in childhood is unhappy then and also develops values that perpetuate unhappiness in later life" (45).

The third A of happiness, *achievement,* relates to reaching a goal one sets for oneself. If this goal is unrealistically high, the result will be failure and the individual will then be dissatisfied and, consequently, unhappy. Then, too, objective success does not necessarily mean subjective success or that the individual who appears to be successful is so. Hard work, competence, and personal sacrifice may achieve money and power, but an executive, with many status symbols, is not necessarily a happy person. Success often reduces chances for individuality and satisfaction of personal needs and desires. Furthermore, an executive may be admired and respected but not loved and may even be feared (81). Achievement without affection will lead to self-dissatisfaction, and this, in turn, will color the individual's outlook on life.

Relative Happiness It is doubtful that such a state as 100 percent happiness or satisfaction or 100 percent unhappiness or dissatisfaction exists. Happiness and satisfaction are relative. At every age level, and at all times during each age level, there are times of happiness and satisfaction and times of unhappiness and dissatisfaction.

If pleasant experiences outweigh the unpleasant, individuals will be satisfied and regard themselves as happy; if unpleasant experiences outweigh the pleasant, they will be dissatisfied and consider themselves unhappy.

Happiness Varies at Different Times in the Life Span Retrospections covering the whole life span or large segments of it reveal the degree of happiness at different ages. Many adults remember puberty and early adolescence as so unhappy that they claim they would not want to return to childhood even if they could. In a study reported by Meltzer and Ludwig, even the adult years were found to vary in degree of happiness, with the subjects describing the years before middle age as happier than those after middle age (75). This is shown in Figure 1-7.

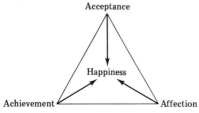

FIGURE 1-6 The "three A's of happiness."

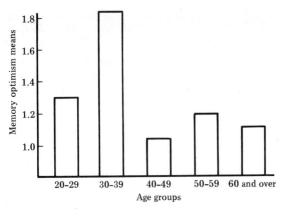

FIGURE 1-7 Age differences in memory optimism, or pleasant memories. (Adapted from H. Meltzer and D. Ludwig. Age differences in memory optimism and pessimism in workers. *Journal of Genetic Psychology*, 1967, **110**, 17–30. Used by permission.)

Happiness at One Age Does Not Guarantee Happiness at Other Ages There is no evidence that once happy always happy, or that once unhappy always unhappy. Happiness and satisfaction at one age may be followed by unhappiness and frustration at the next stage of development and vice versa.

Whether happiness or unhappiness will persist depends to a large extent on how successfully individuals adjust to the new roles and social expectations of each phase in the life span and how their environments enable them to satisfy their needs and desires, especially those for acceptance, affection, and achievement. It is not unusual for a happy child to become a frustrated and unhappy adult or for an unhappy child to develop into a satisfied and relatively happy adult.

At Every Age There Are Sex Differences in Happiness During childhood and adolescence, girls as a group tend to be happier than boys. One of the most important reasons for this is that girls get their greatest satisfaction from interpersonal relationships while boys' greatest satisfaction comes from achievement (39).

During the early years of adulthood, women tend to be happier than men, especially if they are married and feel useful as mothers and wives. Young men, by contrast, tend to be less happy because they are often not able to achieve the success in their occupations that they had hoped for. After forty, the re-verse is true for many women, especially those whose role has been that of homemaker. By contrast, many men become happier and better satisfied with their lives after forty because they feel more successful in their careers than they were when they were younger. Then there is a shift in life satisfactions after sixty or sixty-five. Men rebel against feeling useless while many women feel more useful, either in taking care of retired or ailing husbands or helping with the care of grandchildren (3,107).

At Every Age There Are Obstacles to Happiness Some obstacles to happiness are subjective and some are environmental. Poor health, mental limitations, and unrealistic aspirations are the most common subjective obstacles. It is difficult for people of any age to be satisfied with their lives if they feel they are failures, even if others regard them as successful. Likewise, it is difficult for people to be satisfied with the pattern of their lives if poor health prevents them from doing what they want to do or what their peers are doing.

There may also be environmental obstacles to life satisfactions at any age. For example, children who grow up in a neighborhood where they are discriminated against because of race, religion, socioeconomic status, or any other reason will lack social acceptance, affection from peers, and opportunities to achieve successes in peer-prized activities. Their unhappiness may affect their performance in school and thus jeopardize their chances for success in later life.

Many Factors Influence Happiness At every period in the life span, happiness is influenced by a number of factors. This is in part responsible for the variation in happiness at different ages and also for the fact, discussed above, that happiness at one age does not necessarily guarantee happiness at other ages. The most common and important of the factors are given and briefly explained in Box 1-6.

The relative importance of these factors depends on the individual and the individual's age. Meltzer and Ludwig reported that happiness at different periods in the adult years was remembered as being due to family, marriage, good health, and achievements, while unhappiness was associated with illness, physical injuries, death of a loved one, unsuccessful work experiences, and failure to reach goals (75).

BOX 1-6

FACTORS INFLUENCING HAPPINESS

Health
Good health enables people at all ages to do what they want to do, while poor health or a physical disability is an obstacle to the satisfaction of their wants and needs and, as such, affects their happiness unfavorably.

Physical Attractiveness
Physical attractiveness contributes to social acceptance and affection and often leads to greater achievements than would be possible if the individual were less attractive.

Degree of Autonomy
The greater the autonomy people can achieve, the greater their chances for happiness. This is as true of early childhood as it is of the adult years.

Interactional Opportunities
Outside the Family
Because of the high social value placed on popularity, people at all ages are happier if they have opportunities for social contacts with outsiders than if their social contacts are limited to family members.

Type of Work
The more routine the work and the fewer opportunities for autonomy in it, the less satisfying it will be. This is just as true of chores assigned to children as work in the adult years.

Work Status
Whether in school or in a job, the more successful the person is in the work being done and the more prestige there is associated with it, the greater the satisfaction.

Living Conditions
When the pattern of living enables the person to have interactions with others, either in the family or with friends and neighbors in the community, it adds greatly to life satisfactions.

Material Possessions
It is not material possessions, per se, that influence happiness but the way people feel about them. This is illustrated in Figure 1-8.

Balance between Expectations
and Achievements
If expectations are realistic the person will be satisfied and happy when the goal has been reached.

Emotional Adjustment
Well-adjusted, happy people express negative emotions, such as fear, anger, and jealousy, less often and with less intensity—and with more focus and direction—than do those who are poorly adjusted and unhappy.

Attitude toward an Age Period
How happy people will be at a particular age will be determined partly by their own childhood experiences with other people at that age and partly by cultural stereotypes.

Realism of Self-Concepts
People who believe their abilities to be greater than they actually are are unhappy when they fail to reach their goals. Their unhappiness is intensified by feelings of inadequacy and by the belief that they are misunderstood and mistreated.

Realism of Role Concepts
People tend to romanticize a role they will play at a later age. If the new role does not live up to their expectations, they will be unhappy unless they are willing to accept the realities of the new role. As a group, children and adolescents tend to have more unrealistic role concepts than adults. This contributes to unhappiness at these age levels.

Sears has reported that among men of very high intelligence there is a tendency to regard life satisfactions as coming more from happy family life than from successful achievement in occupations. This conclusion was drawn at an average age of sixty-two, as the men looked back and tried to assess what contributed to their satisfaction at different ages in the adult years (97). The relative importance of factors contributing to life satisfaction—occupation, family life, friendship, richness of cultural life, total service to society and joy in living—is shown in Figure 1-9.

By contrast, for children and adolescents who place high value on popularity and acceptance by peers, such factors as money and status symbols, good health and good looks, and opportunities to play the roles they enjoy add to their life satisfactions more than family life or other factors that contribute to happiness during the adult years (39,45,67).

"Happiness comes from within, my boy . . . from within a safety deposit box full of blue-chip stocks and tax-free investments."

FIGURE 1-8 Happiness comes not from material possessions per se, but from how one feels about them. (George Clark. "The Neighbors." Chicago Tribune–New York News Syndicate, Feb. 19, 1973. Used by permission.)

Importance of Happiness and Unhappiness

The significant fact about the unhappiness that occurs during the life span is that it affects people's attitudes and, in turn, leaves its mark on their personalities. Whether they be schoolchildren, factory workers, housewives, or business executives, their chances of developing their potentials are greatly reduced by their unhappy mental states.

Linn, for example, has reported that older people who remember their childhood as unhappy are dissatisfied and unhappy as adults. Their unhappiness and dissatisfaction not only continue as they grow older but tend to increase rather than decrease (67). It has also been reported that those who, as children, were afraid of being laughed at or punished or of not being attractive and popular tended not only to have unhappy memories of childhood but, even more serious, to suffer from self-derogation as adults (53, 54).

One of the most serious facts about unhappi-

ness is that it may and often does become a habit. And, like all habits, the longer it exists, the more deeply rooted and resistant to change it becomes. That is why, as was pointed out above, people who were unhappy as children are far more likely to be unhappy than happy during their adult years.

Because unhappiness can play such havoc with personal and social adjustments throughout life, an attempt will be made throughout the remainder of this book to discuss the causes of unhappiness at each age level and to suggest what might be done to prevent or to minimize it. In addition, emphasis will be placed on the factors that contribute to happiness at each developmental age and on how they might be strengthened to counteract any unhappiness that is inevitable.

From studies made to date, there is ample evidence that satisfaction and happiness in childhood pave the way for satisfaction and happiness during the remaining years of a person's life. This, however,

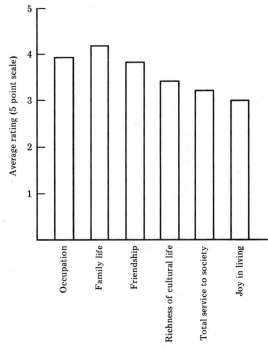

FIGURE 1-9 Average satisfaction achieved in six areas over a lifetime as judged by a group of gifted men at an average age of sixty-two years. (Adapted from R. R. Sears. Sources of life satisfactions of the Terman gifted men. *American Psychologist,* 1977, **32,** 119–128. Used by permission.)

is possible only if the three ingredients of happiness are present. If children learn how to behave in such a way as to encourage others to accept them as friends not only then but as they grow older; if they learn to show affection for others and to expect affection from others with no thought of reciprocation; and if they have realistic concepts of their abilities so that their achievements will come up to their expectations, they can anticipate satisfaction and happiness for the remainder of their lives.

Chapter Highlights

1. Developmental psychology, which studies growth and decline from conception to death, has six major objectives: to find out the common and characteristic age changes; when these changes occur; what causes them; how they influence behavior; whether they can be predicted; and whether they are individual or universal.

2. There are five incentives to studying developmental changes: traditional beliefs, practical problems engendered by these changes, a desire to prove or disprove theories about developmental changes, an attempt to determine the relative importance of nature's and nurture's influence on developmental changes, and a desire to substantiate material accumulated from research or from practical experience.

3. Attitudes toward developmental changes are influenced by the individual's appearance and behavior, by cultural stereotypes, by cultural values, by role changes, and by personal experiences.

4. There are ten significant facts about development: early foundations are critical; maturation and learning are responsible for development; development follows a definite and predictable pattern; all individuals are different; each phase of development has characteristic behavior and hazards; development is aided by stimulation and is affected by cultural changes; there are social expectations for every stage of development; and there are traditional beliefs about individuals at all ages.

5. Even though all individuals are different, they follow definite and predictable patterns of development that are similar for all.

6. Developmental tasks serve three useful purposes: they are guidelines to enable individuals to know what society expects of them; they motivate individuals to do what society expects; and they

show individuals what lies ahead and what will be expected of them later.

7. The three common potential hazards relating to developmental tasks are inappropriate expectations, the bypassing of a stage of development due to failure to master the developmental tasks for that stage, and the crises individuals experience as they pass from one stage of development to another.

8. The life span of today differs from that of the past in two ways: the proportion of individuals at different age levels is becoming increasingly similar, and American men and women, on the average, live longer than those in other countries and longer than did those in America in the past.

9. The life span can be divided into ten periods: prenatal, infancy, babyhood, early childhood, late childhood, puberty, adolescence, early adulthood, middle age, and old age.

10. The recent focus of scientific interest in the life span has been on middle and old age, while the focus of interest was formerly centered on the early years of life.

11. There are many obstacles to studying life-span development, the most common of which are getting representative samples of subjects, establishing rapport with subjects, finding a satisfactory method for studying development at different ages, verifying the accuracy of the data obtained, and conforming to ethical standards regarding research at different age levels.

12. The most difficult and least satisfactorily coped-with obstacles in studying life-span development are finding suitable methods and conforming to ethical standards of research.

13. Because happiness and unhappiness are subjective states, information about them must come from introspective and retrospective reports or from answers to questionnaires, all of which lack scientific accuracy.

14. At all ages there are three essentials of happiness —acceptance, affection, and achievement—all of which must be fulfilled to the individual's satisfaction if happiness is to be attained.

15. The major obstacles to happiness at any age may be subjective or environmental, though the former tend to dominate.

Bibliography

1. Allen, G., and K. D. Pettigrew. Heritability of IQ by social class: Evidence inconclusive. *Science,* 1973, **182**, 1042–1044.
2. Alpaugh, P. A., and J. E. Birren. Are there sex differences in cre-

ativity across the adult life span? *Human Development*, 1975, **18**, 461–465.

3. Alston, J. P., and C. J. Dudley. Age, occupation, and life satisfaction. *Gerontologist*, 1973, **13**, 58–61.

4. APA Monitor report. Tips on interviewing children. *APA Monitor*, 1977, **8**(4), 7.

5. Baumrind, D. From each according to her ability. *School Review*, 1972, **80**, 161–197.

6. Bayley, N. The life span as a frame of reference in psychological research. In D. C. Charles and W. R. Looft (Eds.). *Readings in psychological development through life.* New York: Holt, 1973, Pp. 5–17.

7. Bell, B. D. Cognitive dissonance and life satisfaction of older adults. *Journal of Gerontology*, 1974, **30**, 564–571.

8. Bell, R. Q., and T. W. Hertz. Toward more comparatability and generalability in developmental research. *Child Development*, 1976, **47**, 6–13.

9. Bernard, J. Note on changing life styles, 1970–1974. *Journal of Marriage & the Family*, 1975, **37**, 582–593.

10. Bijou, S. W. Ages, stages, and the naturalization of human development. *American Psychologist*, 1968, **23**, 419–427.

11. Bijou, S. W. Development in the preschool years: A functional analysis. *American Psychologist*, 1975, **30**, 829–837.

12. Borland, D. C. Research on middle age: An assessment. *Gerontologist*, 1978, **18**, 379–386.

13. Bower, T. G. R. Repetitive processes in child development. *Scientific American*, 1976, **235**(5), 38–47.

14. Brody, J. E. Studies asking: "Who's happy?" *The New York Times*, Jan. 16, 1979.

15. Bronfenbrenner, U. Developmental research, public policy, and the ecology of childhood. *Child Development*, 1974, **45**, 1–5.

16. Bronfenbrenner, U. Toward an experimental ecology of human development. *American Psychologist*, 1977, **32**, 513–531.

17. Brooks, J. B., and D. M. Elliott. Prediction of psychological adjustment at age thirty from leisure time activities and satisfactions in childhood. *Human Development*, 1971, **14**, 51–61.

18. Brotman, H. B. Life expectancy: Comparison of national levels in 1900 and 1974 and variations in state levels, 1969–1971. *Gerontologist*, 1977, **17**, 12–22.

19. Browning, R. Why not humor? *APA Monitor*, 1977, **8**(2), 1, 32.

20. Brubaker, T. H., and E. A. Powers. The stereotype of "old": A review and alternative approach. *Journal of Gerontology*, 1976, **31**, 441–447.

21. Bühler, C. The course of human life as a psychological problem. In W. R. Looft (Ed.). *Developmental psychology: A book of readings.* Hinsdale, Ill.: Dryden Press, 1972, Pp. 68–84.

22. Campbell, A. Subjective measures of well-being. *American Psychologist*, 1976, **31**, 117–124.

23. Charlesworth, W. R. Developmental psychology: Does it offer anything distinctive? In W. R. Looft (Ed.). *Developmental psychology: A book of readings.* Hinsdale, Ill.: Dryden Press, 1972, Pp. 1–22.

24. Clemente, F., and W. J. Sauer. Life satisfaction in the United States. *Social Forces*, 1976, **54**, 621–631.

25. Colletto-Pratt, C. Attitudinal predictors of devaluation of old age in a multigenerational sample. *Journal of Gerontology*, 1976, **31**, 193–197.

26. Croake, J. W., and D. E. Hinkle. Methodological problems in the study of fears. *Journal of Psychology*, 1976, **93**, 197–202.

27. Cronbach, L. J. Five decades of public controversy over mental testing. *American Psychologist*, 1975, **30**, 1–14.

28. Denney, N. W. Evidence for developmental changes in categorization criteria for children and adults. *Human Development*, 1974, **17**, 41–53.

29. Dennis, W. (Ed.). *Historical readings in developmental psychology.* New York: Appleton-Century-Crofts, 1972.

30. Dobzhansky, T. Differences are not defects. *Psychology Today*, 1973, **7**(7), 96–101.

31. Donohue, B., and R. G. Ratliff. The effects of reward, punishment, and knowledge of results on children's discrimination learning. *Journal of Genetic Psychology*, 1976, **129**, 97–123.

32. Drevenstedt, J. Perceptions of onsets of young adulthood, middle age and old age. *Journal of Gerontology*, 1976, **31**, 53–57.

33. Edwards, J. N., and D. L. Klemmack. Correlates of life satisfaction: An examination. *Journal of Gerontology*, 1973, **28**, 497–502.

34. Eichorn, D. H. The Berkeley longitudinal studies: Continuities and correlates of behavior. *Canadian Journal of Behavioral Science*, 1973, **5**, 297–320.

35. Erikson, E. H. *Identity and the life cycle. Selected papers.* Psychological Issues Monographs, Vol. 1, No. 1. New York: International Universities Press, 1967.

36. Forbes, W. F. A possible similar pathway between smoking-induced life shortening and natural aging. *Journal of Gerontology*, 1973, **28**, 302–311.

37. Fry, C. L. The ages of adulthood: A question of numbers. *Journal of Gerontology*, 1976, **31**, 170–177.

38. Gagné, R. M. Developmental readiness. In D. C. Charles and W. R. Looft (Eds.). *Readings in psychological development through life.* New York: Holt, 1973, Pp. 139–146.

39. Garai, J. E. Sex differences in mental health. *Genetic Psychology Monographs*, 1970, **81**, 123–142.

40. Gottfried, N. W., and B. Seay. An observational technique for preschool children. *Journal of Genetic Psychology*, 1973, **122**, 263–268.

41. Harris, D. B. The development of potentiality. *Teachers College Record*, 1960, **61**, 423–428.

42. Harry, J. Evolving sources of happiness for men over the life cycle: A structural analysis. *Journal of Marriage & the Family*, 1976, **38**, 289–296.

43. Havighurst, R. J. *Developmental tasks and education.* (3rd ed.) New York: McKay, 1972.

44. Hayflick, L. Biomedical gerontology: Current theories of biological aging. *Gerontologist*, 1974, **14**, 454, 458.

45. Horn, J. Love: The most important ingredient of happiness. *Psychology Today*, 1976, **10**(2), 98–102.

46. Jackson, D. W. Advanced aged adults' reflections of middle age. *Gerontologist*, 1974, **14**, 255–257.

47. James, W. *Talks to teachers on psychology.* New York: Holt, 1899.

48. Jensen, A. R. The meaning of heritability in the behavioral sciences. *Educational Psychologist*, 1975, **1**, 171–183.

49. Jewett, S. P. Longevity and the longevity syndrome. *Gerontologist*, 1973, **13**, 91–99.

50. Johnston, R. B., and P. R. Magrab. *Developmental disorders: Assessment, treatment, and education.* Baltimore, Md.: University Park Press, 1976.

51. Jones, M. C. A report on three growth studies at the University of California. In D. C. Charles and W. R. Looft (Eds.). *Readings*

in psychological development through life. New York: Holt, 1973, Pp. 18–29.

52. Jones, M. C., N. Bayley, J. W. Macfarlane, and M. P. Honzik (Eds.). The course of human development. Waltham, Mass.: Xerox College Publications, 1971.

53. Kaplan, H. B., and A. D. Pokorny. Age-related correlates of self-derogation: Reports of childhood experiences. British Journal of Psychiatry, 1970, 117, 333–354.

54. Kaplan, H. B., and A. D. Pokorny. Sex-related correlates of adult self-derogation: Reports of childhood experiences. Developmental Psychology, 1972, 6, 536.

55. Kilty, K. M., and A. Feld. Attitudes toward aging and toward the needs of older people. Journal of Gerontology, 1976, 31, 586–594.

56. Kinsbourne, M., and P. Caplan. Life-span development of psychological aging. Gerontologist, 1973, 13, 509–510.

57. Knapp, M. R. J. Predicting the dimensions of life satisfaction. Journal of Gerontology, 1976, 31, 595–604.

58. Kobrin, F. E., and G. E. Hendershot. Do family ties reduce mortality? Evidence from the United States, 1966–1968. Journal of Marriage & the Family, 1977, 39, 737–745.

59. Kuhlen, R. G. Age and intelligence: The significance of cultural change in longitudinal vs. cross-sectional findings. In B. L. Neugarten (Ed.). Middle age and aging: A reader in social psychology. Chicago: University of Chicago Press, 1968, Pp. 552–557.

60. LaBouvie, E. W. Descriptive developmental research: Why only time? Journal of Genetic Psychology, 1975, 126, 289–296.

61. Lawrence, S. Panel takes up children as subjects. APA Monitor, 1977, 8(4), 9.

62. Lawton, G. Aging successfully. New York: Columbia University Press, 1951.

63. Leon, F. F. Cicero on geriatrics. Gerontologist, 1963, 3, 128–130.

64. Lesnoff-Caravaglia, G. Senescence and adolescence: Middle-age inventions. Gerontologist, 1974, 14, 98.

65. Lewis, M. Infant intelligence tests: Their use and misuse. Human Development, 1973, 16, 108–118.

66. Liebert, R. M., R. W. Poulos, and G. D. Strauss. Developmental psychology. Englewood Cliffs, N. J.: Prentice-Hall, 1974.

67. Linn, M. W. Perceptions of childhood: Present functioning and past events. Journal of Gerontology, 1973, 28, 202–208.

68. Lowman, R. P. Animal research: Open season on scientists. APA Monitor, 1977, 8(8), 6–7.

69. Maccoby, E. E., and C. N. Jacklin. Myth, reality and shades of gray: What we know and don't know about sex differences. Psychology Today, 1974, 8(7), 109–112.

70. Mathes, E. W., and A. Kahn. Physical attractiveness, happiness, neurotocism, and self-esteem. Journal of Psychology, 1975, 90, 27–30.

71. McCandless, B. R. Life-span models of psychological aging. Gerontologist, 1973, 13, 511–512.

72. McKinsey, M. E. Applying research and training to improve life for the aged. Geriatrics, 1975, 30(12), 80–84.

73. McKinsey, M. E. Training toward understanding the total spectrum of human development. Geriatrics, 1975, 30(11), 120–126.

74. Medley, M. L. Satisfaction with life among persons sixty-five years and older: A causal model. Journal of Gerontology, 1976, 31, 448–455.

75. Meltzer, H., and D. Ludwig. Age differences in memory opti-

mism and pessimism in workers. Journal of Genetic Psychology, 1967, 110, 17–30.

76. Minton, J. H. The impact of Sesame Street on readiness. Sociology of Education, 1975, 48, 141–151.

77. Moerk, E. L. Verbal interactions between children and their mothers during the preschool years. Developmental Psychology, 1975, 11, 788–794.

78. Naffziger, C. C., and K. Naffziger. Development of sex role stereotypes. Family Coordinator, 1974, 23, 251–258.

79. Neugarten, B. L. Continuities and discontinuities of psychological issues into adult life. Human Development, 1969, 12, 121–130.

80. Neuhauser, G. Methods of assessing and recording motor skills and movement patterns. Developmental Medicine & Child Neurology, 1975, 17, 369–386.

81. Neumann, C. P. Success today: Achievement without happiness. Psychosomatics, 1975, 16, 103–106.

82. New York Times report. New population trends transforming U.S. The New York Times, Feb. 6, 1977.

83. Palmore, E. B., and V. Kivett. Change in life satisfaction: A longitudinal study of persons aged 46–70. Journal of Gerontology, 1973, 32, 311–316.

84. Palmore, E. B., and K. Manton. Ageism compared with racism and sexism. Journal of Gerontology, 1973, 28, 363–369.

85. Palmore, E. B., and V. Stone. Predictors of longevity: A follow-up of the aged in Chapel Hill. Gerontologist, 1973, 13, 88–90.

86. Phillips, D. C., and M. E. Kelly. Hierarchical theories of development in education and psychology. Harvard Educational Review, 1975, 45, 351–375.

87. Piaget, J. Piaget's theory. In P. H. Mussen (Ed.), Carmichael's manual of child psychology. (3rd ed.) Vol. 1. New York: Wiley, 1970, Pp. 703–732.

88. Piechowski, M. M. A theoretical and empirical approach to the study of development. Genetic Psychology Monographs, 1975, 92, 231–297.

89. Reich, W. T. Ethical issues related to research involving elderly subjects. Gerontologist, 1978, 18, 326–337.

90. Ridley, J. C., C. A. Bachrach, and D. A. Dawson. Recall and reliability of interview data from older women. Journal of Gerontology, 1979, 34, 99–105.

91. Roodin, P. A., and W. E. Simpson. Effectiveness of social reinforcement as a function of children's familiarity with the experimenter. Journal of Genetic Psychology, 1976, 128, 33–39.

92. Rosenkrantz, A. L., and V. Van de Riet. The influence of prior contact between child subjects and adult experimenters on subsequent child performance. Journal of Genetic Psychology, 1974, 124, 79–90.

93. Salk, L., and R. Kramer. How to raise a human being. New York: Warner Books, 1973.

94. Sameroff, A. J. Early influences on development: Fact or fancy? Merrill-Palmer Quarterly, 1975, 21, 267–294.

95. Scarr-Salapatek, S., and M. L. Williams. The effects of early stimulation on low birth-weight infants. Child Development, 1973, 44, 94–101.

96. Scheinfeld, A. Your heredity and environment. Philadelphia: Lippincott, 1965.

97. Sears, R. R. Sources of life satisfaction of the Terman gifted men. American Psychologist, 1977, 32, 119–128.

98. Sears, R. R., and S. S. Feldman (Eds.). The seven ages of man. Los Altos, Calif.: William Kaufmann, 1973.

99. Senn, M. J. E. Insights on the child development movement in

the United States. *Monographs of the Society for Research in Child Development,* 1975, **40**, (3–4).

100. Shaver, P., and J. Freedman. The pursuit of happiness. *Psychology Today,* 1976, **10**(3), 26–32, 75.

101. Sheehy, G. *Passages: Predictable crises of adult life.* New York: Dutton, 1976.

102. Shulman, N. Life-cycle variations in patterns of close relationships. *Journal of Marriage & the Family,* 1975, **37**, 813–821.

103. Sidana, U. R., R. Singh, and P. Srivatava. Social agents in children's happiness. *Journal of Social Psychology,* 1976, **99**, 289–290.

104. Siegel, A. E. Current issues in research on early development. *Human Development,* 1969, **12**, 86–92.

105. Skinner, B. F. The steep and thorny way to a science of behavior. *American Psychologist,* 1975, **30**, 42–49.

106. Smith, A. C., G. L. Flick, G. S. Ferriss, and A. H. Sellmann. Prediction of developmental outcome at seven years from prenatal, perinatal, and postnatal events. *Child Development,* 1972, **43**, 495–507.

107. Spreitzer, E., and E. E. Snyder. Correlates of life satisfaction among the aged. *Journal of Gerontology,* 1974, **29**, 454–458.

108. Stinnett, N., and C. W. Birdsong. Relationship of personality needs to perceptions concerning alternate life styles. *Journal of Genetic Psychology,* 1976, **128**, 301–302.

109. Stinnett, N., and S. Taylor. Parent-child relationships and perceptions of alternate life styles. *Journal of Genetic Psychology,* 1976, **129**, 105–112.

110. Stone, L. J., and J. Church. Some representative theoretical orientations in developmental psychology. In W. R. Looft (Ed.). *Developmental psychology: A book of readings.* Hinsdale, Ill.: Dryden Press, 1972, Pp. 35–59.

111. Thorson, J. A., L. Whatley, and K. Hancock. Attitudes toward the aged as a function of age and education. *Gerontologist,* 1974, **14**, 316–318.

112. Uhlenberg, P. Changing structure of the older population in the U.S.A. during the twentieth century. *Gerontologist,* 1977, **17**, 197–202.

113. Vaillant, G. E. The climb to maturity: How the best and brightest come of age. *Psychology Today,* 1977, **11**(4), 34–41, 107–110.

114. Van den Daele, L. D. A cook's tour of development. *Journal of Genetic Psychology,* 1976, **128**, 137–143.

115. Watthana-Kastr, S., and P. S. Spiers. Geographic mortality rates and rates of aging—a possible relationship? *Journal of Gerontology,* 1973, **28**, 374–379.

116. Webber, R. L., D. W. Combs, and J. S. Hollingsworth. Variations in value orientations by age in a developing society. *Journal of Gerontology,* 1974, **30**, 676–683.

117. White, B. L. First two years of life found to be most critical. *APA Monitor,* 1976, **7**(4), 4–5.

118. White, S. H. The learning-maturation controversy: Hall to Hull. *Merrill-Palmer Quarterly,* 1968, **14**, 187–196.

119. Whiting, B. B. Folk wisdom and child rearing. *Merrill-Palmer Quarterly,* 1974, **20**, 9–19.

120. Wolk, S., and S. Telleen. Psychological and social correlates of life satisfaction as a function of residential constraint. *Journal of Gerontology,* 1976, **31**, 89–98.

121. Yarrow, M. R., J. D. Campbell, and R. V. Burton. Recollections of childhood: A study of the retrospective method. *Monographs of the Society for Research in Child Development,* 1970, **35**(5).

122. Zender, M. E., and B. F. Zender. Vygotsky's view about the age polarization of child development. *Human Development,* 1974, **17**, 24–40.

CHAPTER TWO
THE PRENATAL PERIOD

After reading this chapter, you should be able to:

- Explain the important characteristics of the prenatal period.
- Describe the ways in which life begins, with emphasis on the preliminary stages.
- Point out why the time of conception and how what happens at that time can have long-lasting effects on development.
- Call attention to the fact that the prenatal period is customarily divided into three subdivisions and summarize the outstanding characteristics of each of them.
- Describe how the attitudes of significant people toward the child-to-be are developed, what conditions influence them, how persistent they are, and what effects they have.
- Summarize the common physical hazards in each subdivision of the prenatal period and the conditions influencing them.
- List the common psychological hazards during the prenatal period and explain why they may be regarded as hazardous.

Early research studies in developmental psychology ignored the prenatal period. Some studies started with the preschool child but most with the school-age child. Later studies extended downward to the time of birth, but it was not until the mid-1940s that developmental psychologists turned their attention to the prenatal period.

By that time it had become apparent that starting the study of development part way along in the life span was like coming into a play or movie after it had started or turning on the TV in the middle of a program. It was recognized that knowing what happens before birth is essential to a complete understanding of the normal pattern of development and to a realization of what can happen to distort this pattern.

Today there is extensive evidence to show how conditions in the prenatal environment can and do affect development before birth. This has justified beginning the study of development from the moment of conception rather than from the time of birth.

Most of the development that takes place before birth has been investigated by physiologists and members of the medical profession, and the results of these studies have been extensively borrowed by developmental psychologists. Their contributions have, for the most part, been to supplement the physiological and physical data with evidence of the effects of psychological states on the pattern of development and the long-term effects of attitudes of significant people.

In this chapter, an attempt will be made to explain the major happenings during the nine months before birth, to emphasize the significance of the moment of conception, and to show what environmental and psychological factors affect the course of development.

CHARACTERISTICS OF THE PRENATAL PERIOD

In spite of the fact that the first developmental period in the life span is next to the shortest of all—the shortest is the period of the newborn or infancy—it is in many respects one of the most, if not *the* most, important period of all. This period, which begins at conception and ends at birth, is approximately 270 to 280 days in length, or nine calendar months.

Although it is relatively short, the prenatal period has six important characteristics, each of which has a lasting effect on development during the life span. They are as follows:

1. The hereditary endowment, which serves as the foundation for later development, is fixed, once and for all, at this time. While favorable or unfavorable conditions both before and after birth may and probably will affect to some extent the physical and psychological traits that make up this hereditary endowment, the changes will be quantitative not qualitative.
2. Favorable conditions in the mother's body can foster the development of hereditary potentials while unfavorable conditions can stunt their development, even to the point of distorting the pattern of future development. At few if any other times in the life span are hereditary potentials so influenced by environmental conditions as they are during the prenatal period.
3. The sex of the newly created individual is fixed at the time of conception and conditions within the mother's body will not affect it, as is true of the hereditary endowment. Except when surgery is used in sex transformation operations, the sex of the individual, determined at the time of conception, will not change. Such operations are rare and only partially successful.
4. Proportionally greater growth and development take place during the prenatal period than at any other time throughout the individual's entire life. During the nine months before birth, the individual grows from a microscopically small cell to an infant who measures approximately twenty inches in length and weighs, on the average, 7 pounds. It has been estimated that weight during this time increases eleven million times. Development is likewise phenomenally rapid. From a cell that is round in shape, all the bodily features, both external and internal, of the human being develop at this time. At birth, the newly born infant can be recognized as human even though many of the external features are proportionally different from those of an older child, an adolescent, or an adult.
5. The prenatal period is a time of many hazards, both physical and psychological. While it cannot be claimed that it is the most hazardous period in the entire life span—many believe that infancy is more hazardous—it certainly is a time when environmental or psychological hazards can have a marked effect on the pattern of later development or may even bring development to an end.
6. The prenatal period is the time when significant people form attitudes toward newly created indi-

viduals. These attitudes will have a marked influence on the way these individuals are treated, especially during their early, formative years. If the attitudes are heavily emotionally weighted, they can and often do play havoc with the mother's homeostasis and, by so doing, upset the conditions in the mother's body that are essential to the normal development of the newly created individual.

HOW LIFE BEGINS

New life begins with the union of a male sex cell and a female sex cell. These sex cells are developed in the reproductive organs, the *gonads.* The male sex cells, the *spermatozoa* (singular: *spermatozoon*), are produced in the male gonads, the *testes,* while the female sex cells, the *ova* (singular: *ovum*), are produced in the female gonads, the *ovaries.*

Male and female sex cells are *similar* in that they contain *chromosomes.* There are twenty-three chromosomes in each mature sex cell, and each chromosome contains *genes,* the true carriers of heredity. A gene is a minute particle which is found in combination with other genes in a stringlike formation within the chromosome. It has been estimated that there are approximately 3,000 genes in each chromosome. These are passed on from parent to offspring (10,53,66).

Male and female sex cells also *differ* in two important ways. First, in the mature ovum there are twenty-three matched chromosomes while in the mature spermatozoon there are twenty-two matched chromosomes and one unmatched chromosome which may be either an X or a Y chromosome. The function of X and Y chromosomes will be discussed later in relation to sex determination.

The second way in which male and female sex cells differ is in the number of preparatory stages of development they pass through before they are ready to produce a new human being. While all sex cells, male or female, must go through preliminary stages of development, male cells go through two preliminary stages—maturation and fertilization—while female cells go through three preliminary stages—maturation, ovulation, and fertilization.

Maturation
Maturation is the process of chromosome reduction through cell division: one chromosome from each pair goes to a subdivided cell, which in turn splits lengthwise and forms two new cells. The mature cell, which contains twenty-three chromosomes, is known as a *haploid cell.* Maturation of sex cells does not occur until sex maturity has been attained, following the onset of puberty in both boys and girls.

In the case of the spermatozoon, there are four new cells, the *spermatids,* each of which is capable of fertilizing an ovum. In the division of the ovum, one chromosome from each pair is pushed outside the cell wall. This new cell is known as a *polar body.* Three polar bodies are formed in the process of division. Unlike the spermatids, the polar bodies cannot be fertilized, while the fourth cell, the *ovum,* can. If, however, the ovum is not fertilized, it disintegrates and passes from the body with the menstrual flow.

Division of the chromosomes during the maturational process is a matter of chance. Any possible combination of chromosomes from the male and female may be found in a new cell after division. It has been estimated that there are 16,777,216 possible combinations of the twenty-three chromosomes from the male and the twenty-three from the female sex cells (66).

Ovulation
Ovulation is a preliminary stage of development limited to the female sex cells. It is the process of escape of one mature ovum during the menstrual cycle. It is believed that the two ovaries alternate in producing a ripe ovum during each menstrual cycle (53,66).

In nonidentical multiple births, two or more mature ova are released from the ovaries. Whether they are released from the same or from both ovaries is still not known nor is it known why more than one mature ovum is released during each menstrual cycle, which is the usual pattern.

After being released from one of the follicles of the ovary, the ovum finds its way to the open end of the Fallopian tube nearest the ovary from which it was released. Once it enters the tube, it is propelled along by a combination of factors: cilia, or hairlike cells which line the tube; fluids composed of estrogen from the ovarian follicle and a mucus from the lining of the tube; and rhythmic, progressive contractions of the walls of the tube. When the length of the menstrual cycle is normal, approximately twenty-eight days, ovulation occurs between the fifth and the twenty-third days of the cycle, with the average on the eleventh day.

Fertilization

Fertilization, which occurs at the time of conception, is the third stage of development preliminary to the beginning of a new life. It normally occurs while the ovum is in the Fallopian tube. More specifically, it is generally believed that fertilization takes place within twelve to thirty-six hours and usually within the first twenty-four hours after the ovum has entered the tube. During coitus, or sexual intercourse, spermatozoa are deposited at the mouth of the uterus. Through strong hormonic attraction, they are drawn into the tubes, where they are aided in making their way up by rhythmic muscular contractions.

After a spermatozoon has penetrated the ovum, the surface of the ovum changes in such a way that no other spermatozoon can enter. After the sperm cell penetrates the wall of the ovum, the nuclei from the two cells approach each other. There is a breakdown in the membrane surrounding each nucleus, and this allows the two nuclei to merge. Thus the species number of chromosomes, forty-six, is restored, with one half coming from the female cell and the other half coming from the male cell.

IMPORTANCE OF CONCEPTION

At the time of conception, four important conditions are determined that influence the individual's later development. What role each of these conditions plays in the individual's development will explain why the time of conception is probably the most important period in the life span.

Hereditary Endowment

The first important happening at the time of conception is the determination of the newly created individual's hereditary endowment. Figure 2-1 shows the contributions to this endowment from both parents and from both maternal and paternal ancestors. Because the hereditary endowment is determined once and for all at the time of conception, its importance is far greater than it would be if it were subject to later change.

The determination of hereditary endowment affects later development in two ways. First, heredity places limits beyond which individuals cannot go. If prenatal and postnatal conditions are favorable, and if people are strongly motivated, they can develop their inherited physical and mental traits to their maximum

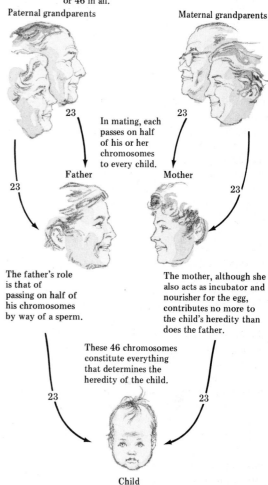

Every man and every woman at conception received 23 chromosomes from each parent or 46 in all.

Paternal grandparents 23

Maternal grandparents 23

In mating, each passes on half of his or her chromosomes to every child.

Father 23   Mother 23

The father's role is that of passing on half of his chromosomes by way of a sperm.

The mother, although she also acts as incubator and nourisher for the egg, contributes no more to the child's heredity than does the father.

These 46 chromosomes constitute everything that determines the heredity of the child.

23   23

Child

FIGURE 2-1 The hereditary process. (Adapted from A. Scheinfeld. *The new you and heredity.* Philadelphia: Lippincott, 1961. Used by permission.)

potential, but they can go no further (10,52,66). Montagu has stressed, "Where we control the environment, we to some extent control heredity. Heredity, it has been said, determines what we *can* do, and environment what we *do* do" (53).

The second important thing about the hereditary endowment is that it is entirely a matter of chance: there is no known way to control the number of chromosomes from the maternal or paternal side that will be passed on to the child. Scheinfeld has pointed out that the birth of a given individual depends on the union of a particular ovum with a particular sperm. The probability that this particular union will occur is only 1 in 300,000,000,000,000 (300 trillion) (66).

Sex

Determination of the individual's sex is the second important happening at the time of conception. Sex depends on the kind of spermatozoon that unites with the ovum.

Two kinds of mature spermatozoa are produced in equal numbers. The first contains twenty-two matched chromosomes plus one X chromosome; the second contains twenty-two matched chromosomes plus one Y chromosome. The X and Y chromosomes are the sex-determining chromosomes. The mature ovum always contains an X chromosome. If it is fertilized by a Y-bearing spermatozoon, the offspring will be a boy; if it is fertilized by an X-bearing spermatozoon, the offspring will be a girl. Figure 2-2 shows how sex is determined.

Once the male and female cells have united, nothing can be done to change the sex of the newly formed individual. Whether this individual is male or female will have a lifelong effect on the individual's patterns of behavior and personality.

There are three reasons why the sex of an individual is important to lifelong development. First, each year children come under increasing cultural pressures from parents, teachers, their peer group, and society at large to develop attitudes and behavior patterns that are considered appropriate for members of their sex. Children who learn to behave in ways that are considered appropriate for their sex are assured of social acceptance. By contrast, children who fail to conform are subjected to criticism and social ostracism.

Second, learning experiences are determined by the individual's sex. In the home, at school, and in play groups, children learn what is considered appropriate for members of their sex. A boy who learns to play girls' games is labeled a "sissy" and girls who prefer boys' games are known as "tomboys."

Third, and perhaps most important of all, is the attitude of parents and other significant family members toward individuals because of their sex. Studies of sex preferences for offspring have revealed that the traditional preference for a boy, especially for the

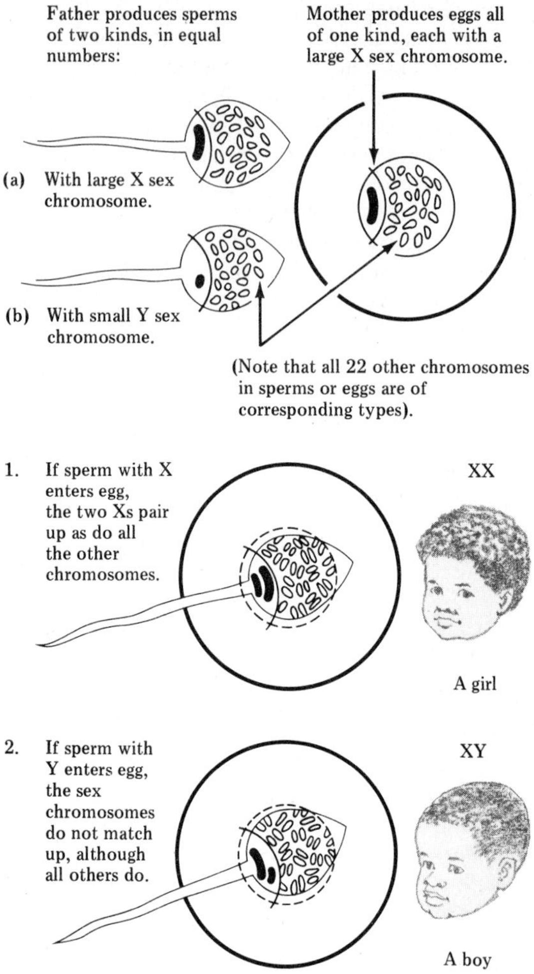

FIGURE 2-2 How sex is determined. (Adapted from A. Scheinfeld. *The new you and heredity.* Philadelphia: Lippincott, 1961. Used by permission.)

firstborn, still persists. Strong preferences for a child of a given sex have marked influences on parents' attitudes, which in turn affect their behavior toward the child and their relationships with the child (31,38).

Number of Offspring

The third important happening at the time of conception or shortly thereafter is the determination of the number of offspring there will be. While most humans are singletons, multiple births also occur. Meredith has reported that 1 out of 80 births is twins,

1 out of every 9,000 is triplets, and 1 out of every 570,000 is quadruplets (47). There are more frequent multiple births among blacks and fewer among Chinese, Japanese, and other Mongoloid-race groups than there are among whites (47,53,65).

When a ripe ovum is fertilized by one spermatozoon, the result will be a *singleton,* unless the fertilized ovum (*zygote*) splits into two or more distinct parts during the early stages of cell cleavage. When this happens, the result will be identical (uniovular) twins, triplets, or other multiple births. If two or more ova are released simultaneously and are fertilized by different spermatozoa, the result will be *nonidentical* (also called *biovular* or *fraternal*) twins, triplets, or other multiple births.

Approximately one-third of all twins are identical. Because the chromosomes and genes of the two or more zygotes from which individuals of nonidentical multiple birth develop are not the same, their mental and physical makeups are different. By contrast, those of identical multiple birth come from the same zygote, and consequently they have the same assortment of chromosomes and genes. Children of identical multiple birth are always of the same sex, while those of nonidentical multiple birth may be of the same or opposite sex.

Effects on Development   Most studies of the effects of multiple birth on development have been limited to twins for the reason that triplets, quadruplets, and other multiple births occur very infrequently and the mortality rates among them are much higher than among twins, thus making studies of them difficult if not impossible.

However, there is reason to assume that the effects of multiple birth on triplets, quadruplets, and other multiples is much the same as on twins though the former feel these effects to a greater extent.

The reason that multiple births affect the pattern of development is not only that there are differences in heredity but that both the prenatal environment and the postnatal environment of singletons are different from those of children of multiple birth. This contributes to different patterns of development, different patterns of behavior, and differences in personality.

Before birth, the singleton has the mother's uterus to itself, and thus development is not affected by crowding, a factor in multiple births that will be discussed more fully in the following chapter.

During the early years, when the foundations of the personality pattern are being laid, twins must share the mother's attention and, consequently, may feel unloved or actually rejected. (Photo by Erika Stone.)

There are also differences in the postnatal environments of singletons and those of multiple birth. While the mother can give her undivided attention to the care of a singleton, those of multiple birth must share it. Thus during the early years, when the foundations of the personality pattern are laid, babies of multiple birth receive less mothering than singletons, and consequently they may feel unloved or actually rejected.

Many parents, especially mothers, feel that children of multiple birth should be dressed alike and share the same friends and engage in the same play activities. This is particularly true when the children are of the same sex. Being subjected to pressures to be alike and being denied opportunities to develop their individualities leaves its mark on their personalities and on their patterns of behavior.

Box 2-1 lists and briefly explains some of the most frequently reported characteristics of twins. It should be apparent that hereditary factors are by no means alone responsible for these characteristics; environmental factors, especially in the form of social pressures, play an even more important role. As Koch has concluded from her extensive studies of twins, "It does seem to me that the play of forces, biological and social, upon twins is rather different in many respects from that which molds singletons" (39).

Long-Term Effects of Twinship   To date, few longitudinal studies of twins have been made. Those that have been made rarely go beyond the tenth year of

BOX 2-1

SOME COMMON CHARACTERISTICS OF TWINS

Developmental Lag

In physical, mental, motor, and speech development, twins tend to lag behind singletons of the same age. Lag in motor and speech development are shown in Figure 2-3. This lag may be due to brain damage or to prematurity but it is more likely to be due to parental overprotectiveness.

Physical Development

Twins tend to be smaller, age for age, than singletons. This is generally due to the fact that they are premature. They also suffer from brain damage and other physical defects more often than singletons.

Mental Development

Mental similarities between identical twins are much greater than between nonidentical twins and this persists into old age. Identical twins also show strong similarities in terms of special abilities, such as musical and artistic aptitudes.

Social Development

Twins tend to compete for adult attention, to imitate each other's speech and behavior, and to depend on each other for companionship during the preschool years. As they grow older, sibling rivalry and competition develop. One twin usually takes on the role of leader, forcing the other into the role of follower. This affects their relationships with other family members and with outsiders.

Personality Development

Many twins have difficulty in developing a sense of personal identity. This is especially true of identical twins and of nonidentical twins of the same sex. Others enjoy the close relationship of twinship and the attention they receive as a result of their similarity in appearance. This leads to self-satisfaction and self-confidence.

Behavior Problems

Behavior problems have been reported to be more common among twins than among singletons of the same ages. It is thought that this is a result of the way twins are treated, both at home and outside the home. Behavior problems have also been reported to be more common among nonidentical than among identical twins. It has been suggested that this is because rivalry is stronger between nonidentical than identical twins.

---

the twins' lives, though cross-sectional studies of twins at different ages have been more frequent. These studies have indicated the following long-term effects.

There is a tendency for the developmental lag in physical development to end before children reach puberty and often much earlier (83). Generally the firstborn twin continues to be larger, brighter, and better adjusted socially throughout the childhood years (80). The smaller the twins at birth, the longer the developmental lag tends to persist (2,3).

The mutual dependency or "twinning relationship" so common among young twins and the one-sided dependency of the smaller on the larger twin generally give way to social relationships similar to those of singletons before the twins enter school. Those who attend day-care centers or preschools tend to abandon these patterns of dependency earlier than twins whose environment is limited to the home

(44). Koch has reported that fraternal twins are more vulnerable to external pressures and to have less support from the twinship relationship than do identical twins not only when they are young but also as they grow older (39). A study of the syntactic abilities of identical and fraternal twins and their siblings has shown that by the time twins are five years old, these abilities are as good as those of their siblings (54).

Ordinal Position

The fourth thing that happens at the time of conception is the establishment of the new child's ordinal position among siblings. While this may change within a year or two after birth, the child's ordinal position remains fairly static from then on. For example, a second-born child may be the "baby of the family" or hold a last-born ordinal position for a year or more after birth but then be replaced by a newly born sibling. Shifting from the "baby-of-the family" position

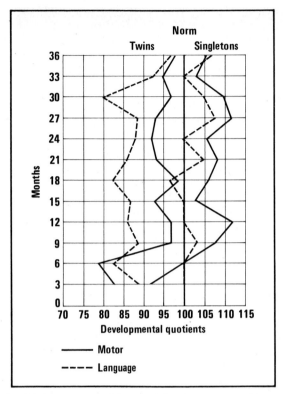

Norm

(Chart axes and labels:)

Twins   Singletons

Months (vertical axis): 36, 33, 30, 27, 24, 21, 18, 15, 12, 9, 6, 3, 0

Developmental quotients (horizontal axis): 70 75 80 85 90 95 100 105 110 115

——— Motor

- - - - Language

FIGURE 2-3 Developmental lag in motor and language development among twins during the first three years of postnatal life. (Adapted from R. J. Dales. Motor and language development of twins during the first three years. *Journal of Genetic Psychology,* 1969, **114,** 263–271. Used by permission.)

to a middle-born's position may be upsetting for a short time, but young children or even babies tend to adjust to these changes.

There is evidence to conclude that it is not ordinal position per se that leaves its mark on the individual's personality and patterns of behavior but rather circumstances in life related to this position—such as the role the individual plays in the family and the treatment he or she receives from significant family members and their attitudes. Since roles, attitudes, and treatment are far more likely to persist than to change, the individual constantly receives reinforcements which, in time, result in firmly established habits.

Forer has described the effects of ordinal position on the individual in the following way (25):

Your place in the family strongly influences how you cope with people and the world. . . . Much of a child's development depends on interactions with siblings. . . . All members of a family force on one another certain patterns of behavior as they interact in meeting their needs. . . . It is in this way . . . that the position in the family leaves an indelible stamp on a person's life style.

Bigner has described specifically how being a second-born or a firstborn in a family affects the child's development. He contends, "A second-born child plays a 'satellite' role in many of his interactions with the older, since the firstborn may act as the natural leader of the siblings in the family constellation" (5).

Box 2-2 gives some of the most common characteristics associated with ordinal position. How ordinal position will affect the individual will depend on a number of conditions, the two most important of which are the sex of the individual and how individuals feel about the roles they are expected to play.

A firstborn girl, for example, who is expected to help with the housework and with the care of young siblings may resent the fact that the boys in the family have fewer domestic duties and are granted privileges and given opportunities denied to her. A second- or later-born boy may resent being "bossed" by an older female sibling or being treated as the "baby of the family" while his female siblings are given more privileges and freedom than he is given.

Some individuals enjoy the role they are expected to play as a result of their ordinal position while others do not. A firstborn child, for example, may resent the pressures of parents to live up to their expectations or having to act as a model for younger siblings. (See Figure 2-4.) On the other hand, the firstborn may derive personal satisfaction from serving as a role model for younger siblings (5).

Long-Term Effects of Ordinal Position Relatively few longitudinal studies have been made of the effects of different ordinal positions. But a few studies of older children, adolescents, and adults of different ordinal positions give clues as to how ordinal position may become a persistent factor in determining the kind of personal and social adjustments the individual will make throughout the life span.

There is evidence that firstborns tend to be brighter and to be higher achievers than their later-born siblings (87,88,89). There is little or no evi-

BOX 2-2

SOME COMMON CHARACTERISTICS ASSOCIATED WITH ORDINAL POSITION

Firstborns

- Behave in a mature way because of association with adults and because they are expected to assume responsibilities.
- Resent having to serve as models for younger siblings and having to assume some of their care.
- Tend to conform to group wishes and pressures and to be suggestible as a carryover of conformity to parental wishes.
- Have feelings of insecurity and resentment as a result of having been displaced as the center of attention by a second-born sibling.
- Lack dominance and aggressiveness as a result of parental overprotectiveness.
- Develop leadership abilities as a result of having to assume responsibilities in the home. But these are often counteracted by tendencies to be "bossy."
- Usually are high achievers or overachievers because of parental pressures and expectations and a desire to win back parental approval if they feel they are being replaced by younger siblings.
- Are often unhappy because of insecurity arising from displacement by younger siblings and resentment at having more duties and responsibilities than younger siblings.

Middle-borns

- Learn to be independent and adventuresome as a result of greater freedom.
- Become resentful or try to emulate the other's behavior when compared unfavorably with an older sibling.
- Resent privileges older siblings are granted.
- Act up and break rules to attract parental attention to themselves and take it away from older or younger siblings.

- Develop a tendency to "boss," ridicule, tease, or even attack younger siblings who get more parental attention.
- Develop the habit of being underachievers as a result of fewer parental expectations and less pressure to achieve.
- Have fewer responsibilities than firstborns—which they often interpret as meaning they are inferior. This then discourages the development of leadership qualities.
- Are plagued by feelings of parental neglect. This then encourages feelings of inadequacy and inferiority which, in turn, encourage development of behavior disorders.
- Turn to outsiders for peer companionship—but this often leads to better social adjustments than those made by firstborns.

Last-borns

- Tend to be willful and demanding as a result of less strict discipline and "spoiling" by family members.
- Have fewer resentments and greater feelings of security as a result of never being displaced by younger siblings.
- Are usually protected by parents from physical or verbal attacks by older siblings and this encourages dependency and irresponsibility.
- Tend to underachieve because of fewer parental expectations and demands.
- Experience good social relationships outside the home and are generally popular but infrequently leaders because of lack of willingness to assume responsibilities.
- Tend to be happy because of attention and "spoiling" from family members during early childhood.

---

dence, on the other hand, that this is due to hereditary difference but rather to environmental conditions that foster the child's intellectual development. Firstborns are not only given more intellectual stimulation than later-borns but they are also given more opportunities to develop their intellectual abilities in school and college (1,70,89). As Zajonc has pointed out, "Parents and psychologists have always regarded firstborn children as different and special and, as a result, have given them greater intellectual stimulation and opportunities to develop their intellectual capacities than their later-born siblings have had" (87).

Because of the greater opportunities they are given and because of the special treatment they receive, firstborns have been found to outnumber later-borns in leadership roles as early as elementary

FIGURE 2-4 Many firstborns resent having to be role models for younger siblings. (Bil Keane. "The-Family Circus." Register and Tribune Syndicate, Oct. 11, 1974. Used by permission.)

PERIODS OF PRENATAL DEVELOPMENT

The prenatal period is ten lunar months of twenty-eight days each in length or nine calendar months. However, the period can and does vary greatly in length, ranging from 180 to 334 days. There are approximately three times as many babies born prematurely as postmaturely.

Meredith has reported that the average length of the prenatal period is 38 weeks or 266 days. However, 70 percent of babies vary from 36 to 40 weeks (252 to 280 days) and 98 percent range from 34 to 42 weeks (238 to 294 days) (47).

Because prenatal development is orderly and predictable, it is possible to give a timetable of the important developments taking place during this period. The prenatal period is generally divided into three stages—the periods of the zygote, of the embryo, and of the fetus—each of which has a predictable length of time and is characterized by specific developments. These developments and the times when they normally occur are outlined in Box 2-3.

Should anything happen to prevent these developments from taking place at the proper time, individuals will suffer handicaps that may plague them for the rest of their lives.

school (56). On the other hand, because of greater overprotectiveness and parental concern about their physical welfare, firstborns tend to be more concerned about their health and to consult doctors more frequently than do later-borns (79). They also tend to be more cautious and take fewer risks as children and as adults than do siblings of other ordinal positions (57).

Several studies of the effects on marital adjustments of ordinal position in the childhood family have revealed that the best marital adjustments were in families where the husbands were the oldest brothers with younger sisters while the poorest adjustments and the greater number of divorces were in families where the husbands were the younger brothers with older sisters and where the wives had, during childhood, learned to be bossy as a result of playing surrogate-mother roles. By contrast, husbands who, as firstborns in their childhood homes, learned to take responsibility made better adjustments to marriage (25,30).

ATTITUDES OF SIGNIFICANT PEOPLE

Until the early 1940s, psychological interest in the prenatal period was concentrated on the physical conditions in the mother's body that might affect development and on the persistence of these effects into postnatal life. The work of Sontag and his associates, for example, called attention to the fact that the mother's emotional state can affect the development of the unborn child (71,72).

Now, however, psychologists are interested in finding out what is responsible for maternal and other family-member attitudes toward the developing child; how persistent these attitudes are; and what effects they have on the relationships of different family members with children during their postnatal lives, especially during the early formative years when the significant people in their world are members of their families. While relatively recent in origin, these studies have revealed the important information summarized below.

TIMETABLE OF PRENATAL DEVELOPMENT

Period of the Zygote (*fertilization to end of second week*)

- The size of the zygote—that of a pinhead—remains unchanged because it has no outside source of nourishment; it is kept alive by yolk in the ovum.
- As the zygote passes down the Fallopian tube to the uterus, it divides many times and separates into an outer and an inner layer.
- The outer layer later develops into the placenta, the umbilical cord, and the amniotic sac, and the inner layer develops into a new human being.
- About ten days after fertilization, the zygote becomes implanted in the uterine wall.

Period of the Embryo (*end of the second week to end of the second lunar month*)

- The embryo develops into a miniature human being.
- Major development occurs, in the head region first and in the extremities last. See Figure 2-5.
- All the essential features of the body, both external and internal, are established.
- The embryo begins to turn in the uterus, and there is spontaneous movement of the limbs.
- The placenta, the umbilical cord, and the amniotic sac develop; these protect and nourish the embryo.
- At the end of the second prenatal month, the embryo weighs, on the average, 1¼ ounces and measures in length 1½ inches.

Period of the Fetus (*end of the second lunar month to birth*)

- Changes occur in the actual or relative size of the parts already formed and in their functioning. No new features appear at this time.
- By the end of the third lunar month, some internal organs are well enough developed to begin to function. Fetal heartbeat can be detected by about the fifteenth week.
- By the end of the fifth lunar month, the different internal organs have assumed positions nearly like the ones they will have in the adult body.
- Nerve cells, present from the third week, increase rapidly in number during the second, third, and fourth lunar months. Whether or not this rapid increase will continue will depend upon conditions within the mother's body such as malnutrition, which adversely affects nerve-cell development—especially during the latter months of the prenatal period.
- Fetal movements usually appear first between eighteen and twenty-two weeks and then increase rapidly up to the end of the ninth lunar month when they slow down because of crowding in the amniotic sac and pressure on the fetal brain as the fetus takes a head-down position in the pelvic region in preparation for birth. These fetal movements are of different kinds—rolling and kicking and short or quick.
- By the end of the seventh lunar month, the fetus is well enough developed to survive, should it be born prematurely.
- By the end of the eighth lunar month the fetal body is completely formed, though smaller than that of a normal, full-term infant.

Origin of Attitudes

Attitudes toward children and parenthood are usually formed early in life, though they may crystallize when the individual knows that he or she will soon become a parent.

Many factors influence the formation of attitudes toward children. First, young people's earlier experiences with children have a marked effect on how they feel about them in general and about their own impending roles as parents. A woman, for example, who had to help care for younger brothers and sisters may have an unfavorable attitude toward chil-

dren, or a woman who grew up as an only child may want many children to make up for the loneliness she felt when she was young.

Second, the experiences of friends, either in the past or at present, color the individual's attitudes. For example, a young man who hears his friends complain about the financial burdens of parenthood may decide that he would rather not have children.

Third, a parent or grandparent who loves children and who pities people who are childless can influence a person's attitudes favorably. Fourth, a person's attitude toward the sex of the unborn child can

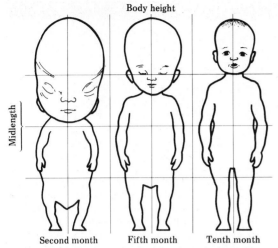

Body height

Midlength

Second month   Fifth month   Tenth month

FIGURE 2-5 Body proportions at the end of different lunar months during the prenatal period. (Adapted from C. Murchison (Ed.). *A handbook of child psychology*. (2d ed.) Worcester, Mass.: Clark University Press, 1933. Used by permission.)

be influenced by stereotyped ideas—that boys are "a handful," for example.

Fifth, the mass media tend to glamorize family life and the parental role. The attitudes of an adult whose own experiences with children have been limited may be profoundly influenced by "family shows" on television.

Conditions Influencing Attitudes

Many conditions affect the attitudes—both favorably and unfavorably—of parents, siblings, and grandparents toward a child. The most commonly reported of these are summarized in Box 2-4.

A careful study of the conditions listed in this box will show that different conditions affect the attitudes of different significant people. For example, the attitudes of siblings are affected by conditions that are different from those of the mother or of the father or of the grandparents—just as the mother's attitudes are affected by conditions different from those of the father, of the siblings, or of the grandparents.

Persistence of Attitudes

Likes, dislikes, prejudices, and attitudes, once formed, tend to persist, though slight changes are possible. The changes that do occur are usually in the form of modifications of existing attitudes; these attitudes become less or more favorable than they originally were. Thus changes in attitudes are *quantitative* rather than *qualitative*. For example, a teenage boy's hero worship of a well-known football player may diminish when he discovers that his idol has faults not readily apparent at first. Similarly, a person's dislike for someone of a different race, religion, or socioeconomic background may mellow somewhat with personal contacts. Such changes are modifications of already-existing attitudes.

There are two reasons for persistence of attitudes. First, attitudes tend to persist because they are based on beliefs the individual considers to be valid and justified. After all, the hero-worshiping teenager contends, his idol certainly must be someone special if he has become a hero to others too.

Siblings and other significant people in the life of the unborn child have reasons for wanting or not wanting the child, and they consider these reasons valid. Hence their attitudes, like those of parents, tend to persist, though they too may be modified.

The second reason for the persistence of attitudes toward a child, formed before the child's birth, are that they are usually highly emotionally toned. And, like all emotional attitudes, they are difficult if not impossible to change. A woman, for example, who as a girl resented having to give up some of the time she wanted to spend with her friends to help with the care of younger siblings, is likely to resent being tied down again with the care of a child, even if it is her own.

Attitudes may appear to change, but there is evidence that they change far less than they may appear to on the surface (37,48,64). This is because most people try to cloak their own unfavorable attitudes toward their children when they realize that social attitudes toward them will be unfavorable if they express in words or actions their unfavorable attitudes toward their own children.

A man, for example, who is upset and resentful at the privations fatherhood brings, may and often will tell others that he is delighted at the prospects of having a child. At home, he may accuse his wife of "being careless" and allowing herself to become pregnant, but, to those outside the home, the camouflage of his true feelings will usually be adequate to make others believe that he is delighted at the prospect of becoming a father and, later, in his role of father.

CONDITIONS AFFECTING ATTITUDES OF SIGNIFICANT PEOPLE

Mother's Attitude

- Love of children
- Desire for companionship
- Desire to please her husband or improve a poor marital relationship
- Desire to be like her friends who have children
- Feelings of inadequacy for the parental role
- Resentment at having to give up a career
- Fear of childbirth or of having a defective child
- Resentment at the physical discomforts and weight gain associated with pregnancy
- Resentment at being overworked or tied down

Father's Attitude

- Desire for a son to carry on the family name or be associated with him in business
- A need to prove his virility to himself and others
- Feelings of inadequacy for the parental role
- Resentment at interference with educational or vocational plans
- Worry about the financial burdens of raising a child
- Resentment at being tied down

Siblings' Attitudes

- Desire for a playmate
- Desire to have as many siblings as their friends
- Fear of losing parental affection and attention
- Fear of having to share a room or toys with the new sibling or having to help care for it
- Desire for sympathy from friends who complain about their own siblings

Grandparents' Attitudes

- Desire for a grandchild to carry on the family name
- Love of children
- Desire to feel useful by helping care for the grandchild
- Fear of being imposed on for financial or other help

When parental attitudes, formed before the baby's birth, are favorable, they tend to be persistent after the baby's birth. This contributes to good parent-child relationships. (Photo by Erika Stone.)

To date, relatively few studies have been made of the persistence of attitudes toward family members, partly because of the problems inherent in making such studies—such as the difficulty of getting accurate reports of attitudes, especially when they are unfavorable—and partly because of the difficulty of following the same group of subjects for a long enough period of time to assess whether their attitudes have persisted or changed over a span of time.

A study by Schaefer and Bayley concentrated on the persistence of maternal behavior toward boys from birth through the preadolescent years. Because behavior is greatly influenced by attitudes, the results of this study help to throw light on the persistence of attitudes. These researchers reported little change in maternal behavior through the years, suggesting that attitudes likewise change little (64).

Effects of Attitudes on Children

The mother's attitude can have an effect on her unborn baby—not through the umbilical cord, which is the only direct connection between the two—but as a result of endocrine changes which can and do occur if the mother-to-be is subjected to severe and prolonged stress which normally accompanies persistently unfavorable attitudes. Favorable attitudes, by contrast, will lead to good body homeostasis and this will favor normal development during the prenatal period.

After birth, the mother's attitudes, most of which were formed before the baby's birth, have an influence because they are reflected in the way the child is treated. For example, a mother who wanted a boy will have a less favorable attitude toward a daughter. If she is disappointed in having a daughter, she may feel guilty and compensate for this by being overprotective and overindulgent of the child. If a later child should be the hoped-for son, either consciously or unconsciously she may show favoritism toward him, and her treatment of her daughter will be colored by rejection.

The attitudes of other family members—the father, siblings, and grandparents—can also affect the child. Before the child's birth they may affect it indirectly through the mother, for example, if family members let her know that they do not welcome the idea of its birth and thus cause her to become nervous and upset. By contrast, favorable attitudes on the part of other family members reinforce the mother's favorable attitudes or lessen any emotional stress she may be under if her own attitude is not favorable.

Like maternal attitudes, the attitudes of other family members tend to persist, though they may change slightly, depending partly on whether the child conforms to their expectations and partly on how he or she treats them. Grandparents, for example, may have favorable attitudes toward very young children but may feel differently about them if, as the children grow older, they treat their grandparents with less respect and less affection.

Effects of Attitudes on Family Relationships

The attitudes of different family members—the foundations of which have generally been laid before a child is born—have a profound influence not only on the child but also on family relationships. This influence may be favorable or unfavorable, depending not on the attitude of one family member but on the attitudes of *all* family members.

If favorable attitudes toward a new baby could be counted on to persist and if unfavorable attitudes could be counted on to become less unfavorable or even favorable, they would not represent a threat to family relationships. Unfortunately, favorable attitudes often become less favorable after the child's birth, and unfavorable attitudes tend to persist, even though they may be so cloaked that they appear to have changed for the better.

Sooner or later children become aware of the way different family members feel about them, and this influences their attitudes toward family members and toward themselves as well. Feeling loved and wanted will motivate a child to behave in a way that will intensify favorable family attitudes and relationships. If, on the other hand, children sense, suspect, or know that they are disappointments to their fathers, a burden to their already overworked mothers, and a nuisance to their siblings, they will show their resentment by behaving in ways that will intensify their unfavorable attitudes and worsen family relationships. This often is the starting point of personality maladjustments and problem behavior that can plague children for years—often throughout life.

HAZARDS DURING THE PRENATAL PERIOD

At no other time during the life span are there more serious hazards to development—or hazards of a more serious nature—than during the relatively short period before birth. These may be physical or psychological. Physical hazards have received more scientific attention because they are more easily recognized.

However, psychological hazards are sometimes as serious as physical hazards since they affect the attitudes of significant people toward the developing child. Furthermore, they often intensify physical hazards.

Physical Hazards

Each of the three major subdivisions of the prenatal period involves particular physical hazards.

While these do not affect all individuals by any means, they do occur with some frequency and can be serious enough to affect the development of the individual throughout life. Davis and Havighurst pointed out many years ago (19):

What happens to the fetus in the womb, and in the process of its birth; the adequacy of its uterine nutrition; its good or ill fortune at birth with regard to infection or injury, all these often prove as important as its heredity.

Box 2-5 gives the common physical hazards associated with each of the prenatal periods.

Conditions Influencing Physical Hazards Certain conditions have been found to increase the likelihood that physical hazards will occur or accentuate them. The first of these conditions is the timing of their appearance. It has been recognized by doctors for many years that if the mother-to-be contracts rubella during the first trimester of pregnancy the chances of developmental irregularities in her unborn child, especially in the form of eye or ear defects or a malformation of the heart, will occur (15).

Heinonen et al. have reported that female hormones, such as estrogens and pregestens, when taken in the early stages of pregnancy may disturb the normal cardiovascular development of the fetus and cause congenital heart diseases. They report that the second and third lunar months, when the heart is developing rapidly, are the most serious times. This is not true if these hormones are taken after the fourth lunar month (32).

The second condition that increases the likelihood of physical hazards is if the condition is intense or greater than is normal. Some conditions that are known to affect the developing child during the prenatal period are described below; others are suspected of affecting development.

Maternal malnutrition can play havoc with normal development, especially the development of the fetal brain (49,53,55). Excessive smoking and drinking are detrimental to normal development, especially during the periods of the embryo and fetus (20,41,46). This is true also of taking drugs (16).

Maternal age has been reported to be a condition that intensifies the possibility of physical hazards during the prenatal period. The reason for this is that as women approach the menopause, they frequently

have endocrine disorders which slow down the development of the embryo and fetus, causing such developmental irregularities as cretinism, Down's syndrome, heart malformations and hydrocephalus, all of which involve physical and mental defects. Figure 2-6 shows how the incidence of Down's syndrome increases as age advances in women. Older women also tend to have smaller babies and to have more complications at birth than do younger women (47, 53,68). While paternal age may likewise cause developmental irregularities or stillbirths, this is likely to happen only when paternal age is over sixty years (61,68).

Certain kinds of *work* are more likely to disturb the prenatal development than others. Chemicals and other hazards faced by women working in such places as hospitals, beauty parlors, and factories may be responsible for the increasing number of birth defects and miscarriages during recent years. As Burnham has pointed out, "The potential damage to the fetus and the possible genetic damage which may occur when pregnant women go to work appears to be an important medical problem" (13).

For reasons as yet unknown, *female* embryos have a better chance of survival than male embryos. For example, for every 100 females lost through mis-

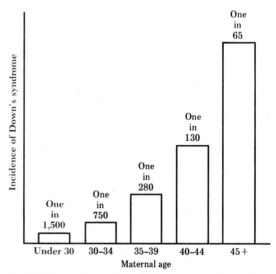

FIGURE 2-6 The relationship between maternal age and Down's syndrome. (Adapted from health statistics from the U.S. Department of Health, Education, and Welfare, Washington, D.C., 1978. Used by permission.)

COMMON PHYSICAL HAZARDS DURING THE PRENATAL PERIOD

Period of the Zygote

Starvation
The zygote will die of starvation if it has too little yolk to keep it alive until it can lodge itself in the uterine wall or if it remains too long in the tube.

Lack of Uterine Preparation
Implantation cannot occur if, as a result of glandular imbalance, the uterine walls are not prepared in time to receive the zygote.

Implantation in the Wrong Place
If the zygote becomes attached to a small fibroid tissue in the uterine wall or to the wall of the Fallopian tube, it cannot get nourishment and will die.

Period of the Embryo

Miscarriages
Falls, emotional shocks, malnutrition, glandular disturbances, vitamin deficiency, and serious diseases, such as pneumonia and diabetes, can cause the embryo to become dislodged from its place in the uterine wall, resulting in a miscarriage. Miscarriages that are due to unfavorable conditions in the prenatal environment are likely to occur between the tenth and eleventh weeks after conception.

Developmental Irregularities
Maternal malnutrition; vitamin and glandular deficiencies; excessive use of drugs, alcohol, and tobacco; and diseases, such as diabetes and German measles, interfere with normal development, especially that of the embryonic brain.

Period of the Fetus

Miscarriages
Miscarriages are always possible up to the fifth month of pregnancy; the most vulnerable time is when the woman's menstrual period would normally occur.

Prematurity
Fetuses who weigh less than 2 pounds 3 ounces have less chance of surviving than heavier fetuses and a greater chance of developing malformations.

Complications of Delivery
Maternal stress affects uterine contractions and is likely to lead to complications during birth.

Developmental Irregularities
Any of the unfavorable environmental conditions present during the period of the embryo will also affect the development of fetal features and retard the whole pattern of fetal development.

---

carriage, 160 males are lost. Developmental irregularities have also been found to be more common among males than among females (53,66).

Multiple births are more hazardous than single births. Fetuses of multiple birth are crowded during the prenatal period, and this inhibits the normal fetal activity essential for development. *Prematurity* is also more likely in the case of multiple births, as is the possibility of developmental irregularities. Because multiple births are more common among blacks than among whites, this may account in part for the higher infant mortality rate and the greater incidence of developmental irregularities among blacks than among whites (47,66).

Long-Term Effects If developmental irregularities are serious and if the embryo or fetus does not miscarry or die at birth or shortly afterward, the indi-

vidual will be deformed in some way. One of the serious aspects of *developmental irregularities* is that they are sometimes not diagnosed as such until months or even years after birth. Epilepsy, cerebral palsy, and mental deficiency, for example, may not show up until babyhood or even early in childhood.

Parents who believe that their baby is normal at birth find it difficult to accept a defective child and often blame themselves for having caused the defect. This leads to strong feelings of guilt and a tendency to overprotect defective children or to refuse to accept the fact that they are as defective as they are.

It is now known that *malnutrition* during pregnancy may damage the developing fetal brain, causing learning difficulties in school, especially reading disabilities. Damage to the fetal brain, whatever the cause, will have effects on the individual's behavior that become more and more apparent as children grow older and are compared with other children of the same age (36,47).

A *chromosomal abnormality,* especially in an X chromosome, has been found to lead to physical abnormalities that can predispose the individual to abnormal behavior if they make it difficult for him or her to adjust to social expectations (11,23).

Studies of the early development of infants of *heroin-addicted mothers* have revealed that, up to the age of two years, their children show behavioral disturbances. How much longer these behavioral disturbances will persist has not yet been determined (82). The long-term effects of *maternal rubella* during pregnancy persist as shown by the fact that children with visual and hearing problems resulting from maternal rubella are delayed in reaching the normal developmental milestones at least until they are eight years old. How much longer this delay will persist has not yet been determined (15).

Studies of the long-term effects of *twinning* have revealed that prenatal crowding, which influences development during that time, carries over into postnatal life and affects patterns of personal and social adjustment (58). Because firstborn twins are likely to be bigger and stronger, they make better academic and social adjustments than their smaller, weaker twins. In addition, smaller twins tend to have lower IQs which account, in part, for their poorer academic performances (39,65). Twins are also usually born prematurely and suffer from the physical and psychological effects of prematurity, some of which are relatively short-lived while others persist throughout life. This will be discussed in detail in the following chapter.

There is no evidence, to date, that moderate *drinking* during pregnancy will have a long-term effect on the developing child; however, excessive drinking that is not decreased after the woman discovers that she is pregnant can have an effect (41). There is, on the other hand, evidence that excessive *smoking,* unless drastically reduced, does have long-term harmful effects (46).

Excessive smoking, not determined in terms of number of cigarettes smoked but rather in terms of nervousness, wakefulness, and irregular maternal heartbeat, has been shown to have some effect on the fetal heart and circulatory systems as well as on other organs. In the early months of life, mortality is greater and average body weight less for babies of mothers who smoke excessively. To date, there is no evidence

of what, if any, long-term effects excessive maternal smoking has on children's intelligence (33,46). In a study of five- to eight-year-olds, children whose mothers smoked excessively during pregnancy were reported to be more hyperactive than children whose mothers smoked moderately or not at all, suggesting that maternal smoking during the prenatal period may be an important contributor to the hyperkinetic syndrome (20).

By the time they are seven years old, children whose mothers smoked excessively during pregnancy have been found to be shorter and generally less well developed than the mean for their age. This is illustrated in Figure 2-7. In addition, they are less well adjusted socially and read less well than children born to nonsmoking or moderately smoking mothers (8,28, 46).

Attempts to Cope with Developmental Irregularities Today two approaches are being used to deal with developmental irregularities. The first consists of *genetic counseling.* This involves a comprehensive and detailed study of the medical history of both the husband and wife to determine if, when, and in what form physical or mental abnormalities have existed in their families. If there are other children already in the family, their medical histories are also studied.

If a study of the medical histories shows or suggests that there is some genetic abnormality in the families of either the husband or the wife, or if another child in the family has some condition stemming from heredity rather than from environmental experiences, the parents are informed of the possibility of having a defective child and are advised to use birth-control techniques to prevent pregnancy. If pregnancy has already begun, they are advised to consider abortion.

The second approach to dealing with developmental irregularities is to use *amniocentesis* if the medical history of a couple suggests the possibility of genetic irregularities or if conditions during pregnancy suggest that the developing fetus may not be normal.

Amniocentesis is a medical procedure which involves the withdrawal of a sample of amniotic fluid from the uterus of a pregnant woman with a needle inserted in the abdomen and guided by ultrasound to ensure that it will not penetrate the body of the developing fetus. The withdrawn fluid contains cells that have been shed by the developing fetus, and

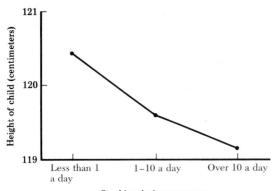

FIGURE 2-7 The relationship of maternal smoking during pregnancy and the height of children up to seven years of age: mean scores for a group of boys and girls. (Adapted from H. Goldstein. Factors influencing the height of seven-year-old children: Results of the National Child Development Study. *Human Biology*, 1971, **43,** 92–111. Used by permission.)

these are then tested for biochemical and chromosomal defects. To date, amniocentesis is the most accurate test to determine the sex of the unborn child though it is rarely used for that purpose.

If tests confirm the geneticist's suspicion that the child will be defective, abortion is usually advised. Amniocentesis is the most accurate test available today to predict any physical or mental abnormalities before birth, and it is being more widely used every year. However, because it is a procedure that can damage the developing fetus or bring on a miscarriage if not properly used, and because relatively few doctors at present are trained in its use, amniocentesis is limited to cases where there is evidence that the child-to-be may be defective. As its use increases, the number of children born with physical or mental defects will, unquestionably, decrease (27).

Psychological Hazards

Like the physical hazards associated with the prenatal period, the psychological hazards can have persistent effects on the individual's development and can influence the postnatal environment and the treatment the child receives from significant people during the early, formative years. The three most important psychological hazards are traditional beliefs about prenatal development, maternal stress during the prenatal period, and unfavorable attitudes toward the unborn child on the part of people who will play significant roles in the child's life.

Traditional Beliefs Perhaps there are more traditional, and more damaging, beliefs about the prenatal developmental period than about any other period in the life span. Such beliefs can and do affect parents' treatment of their children and often have an effect on their attitudes toward each other. See Figure 2-8.

In spite of scientific evidence to the contrary, many people, for example, still believe that it is within their power to control the sex of their offspring. They believe they can do this by intercourse at certain periods during the menstrual cycle, by producing an acid environment in the woman's reproductive organs if a girl is desired and an alkaline environment for a boy, or by artificial insemination after chemically abstracting sperm cells that would produce a child of the desired sex and then implanting them in the woman's reproductive organs (14).

The effects of such a belief are more serious than most people realize. When parents are convinced that they can produce an offspring of the sex

FIGURE 2-8 Acceptance of the traditional belief that the mother's behavior during pregnancy will affect the child's development often leads to husband-wife conflicts. (Drawn by Art Gates. *Atlanta Journal & Constitution*, Oct. 28, 1973. Used by permission.)

"I warned Janet about eating all of those sour pickles!"

they want, they are generally bitterly disappointed when the child turns out to be of the opposite sex. This disappointment may wane and disappear in time, but it frequently leaves its imprint upon the parents' attitudes toward the child. Furthermore, many men feel that it is the woman who has the power to control the sex of the child, and if she does not produce an offspring of the sex her husband wants, his attitude toward her may be seriously affected.

Traditional beliefs about how one can predict the sex of an unborn child likewise lead to resentments and disappointments which are reflected in unfavorable attitudes toward the child, often persisting throughout its life. If, for example, it is believed that doctors can predict with 100 percent accuracy the sex of the unborn child by the heart-beat test or the saliva test, parents are often bitterly disappointed when the child does not turn out to be of the predicted sex. To date, the only known way to predict with high accuracy the sex of an unborn child is by amniocentesis (14).

There are also traditional beliefs about the causes of developmental irregularities. Some of these emphasize heredity, but most stress the role played by maternal impressions. There are two lines of medical evidence to disprove these beliefs about maternal impressions. First, there is evidence that the same types of abnormalities found in humans are also found in the lower animals whose low level of mental development would make them incapable of maternal impressions. Second, there is no direct nervous connection between the mother and the embryo. There are no nerves in the umbilical cord, and thus the mother's thoughts, feelings, and emotions could have no direct influence on the embryo.

Acceptance of these beliefs can lead to strong feelings of guilt on the part of the mother, resentments toward her on the part of the father, and a tendency for the mother to overprotect the child as a form of compensation for the harm she believes she has caused. The more handicapped a child is by a developmental irregularity, the more unfavorable these feelings and attitudes will be.

In the past, *twins* were believed to be caused by evil spirits and thus were feared and rejected by the social group. Today, only the most uncivilized cultures hold such beliefs, although many people still think that it is "animal-like" to have twins and that

twins are less desirable and less acceptable than singletons.

Such unfavorable beliefs will inevitably color the attitudes of family members and also of significant outsiders toward twins. For example, if parents believe that twins always cause trouble in terms of work, expense, family friction, or unfavorable attitudes on the part of relatives, friends, and neighbors, their attitudes toward their twins and their treatment of them will be less favorable than if they were uninfluenced by such beliefs (39,65).

Maternal Stress   The second important psychological hazard associated with the prenatal period is maternal stress—heightened general emotionality over a prolonged period of time. Stress can be the result of fear, anger, grief, jealousy, or envy.

There are many causes of maternal stress during pregnancy, the most common of which are the following: not wanting a child because of marital or economic difficulties or because having a child will interfere with educational or vocational plans; physical discomforts that are severe and frequent enough to make the mother-to-be nervous, irritable, and generally emotionally disturbed; feelings of inadequacy for the parental role; and fears that the child will be physically deformed or mentally deficient—fears that are often heightened by mass-media reports of the frequency of birth defects and of specific causes of birth defects, such as rubella and thalidomide. Some women have fantasies and dreams about giving birth to deformed babies which intensify such fears (26).

Maternal stress affects the developing child both before and after birth. Before birth, severe and persistent glandular imbalance due to stress may result in irregularities in the developing child and complications of delivery or even prematurity. Maternal anxiety affects uterine contractions, with the result that labor lasts longer than normal and the chances of complications are greater because the infant must often be delivered by instruments. Furthermore, anxiety often leads to overeating and excessive weight gain in pregnancy, which further complicates birth.

Sporadic, less severe maternal stress is less likely to lead to developmental irregularities, though it does increase fetal activity. If this increase is slight, the effect is favorable because the fetus will get the exercise necessary for healthy muscular development. If stress leads to excessive fetal activity, however, the fetus will be underweight and nervous to the point where early postnatal adjustments will be seriously affected.

Although relatively few studies have been made of the effects of maternal stress on the child after birth, it has been shown that when prolonged emotional strain affects endocrine balance, anxieties may carry over into the period of the newborn and seriously affect adjustments to postnatal life. The infant may show hyperactivity, which prevents its adjusting to feeding and sleeping patterns, or it may cry excessively (71,72).

It has been noted that newborn infants and young babies who were most active as fetuses show certain motor performances at an earlier age than those who were less active (71,78). On the other hand, excessive fetal activity causes infants to be considerably underweight and often to be slower in acquiring skills postnatally, a result of excessive nervousness. In addition, as Sontag has reported, they often become "hyperactive, irritable, squirming, crying" infants who suffer from a "prenatally produced neurosis" which makes their adjustment to life outside the mother's body difficult (71). Research studies of animals hint that excessive maternal stress can curb masculinity in boys (9).

Prolonged and extreme maternal stress during the period of the fetus frequently causes more illness during the first three years of the child's life than is experienced by children who had a more favorable fetal environment. Children whose mothers were under great stress during pregnancy also show more "free-floating anxiety"; although they can still perform their daily routines, such anxiety has an adverse effect on their ability to learn, to remember, and to reason to their full capacities. As a result, they seem to be less bright than they actually are (71).

Unquestionably one of the most serious effects of maternal stress during pregnancy is on children's postnatal adjustments to family members. Because of their hyperactivity, excessive crying, and other indications of poor adjustment to postnatal life, they are regarded as "difficult" babies. Attitudes of family members toward them are then far less favorable than they would have been had they made better adjustments to postnatal life.

As they grow older, children sense these unfavorable attitudes on the part of family members and later, on the part of peers, teachers, and other out-siders. Feeling unloved and rejected, they often show below average physical development, hyperactivity, lag in developing motor skills and speech, and learning problems. All these lead to poor personal and social adjustments (71,73).

Unfavorable Attitudes on the Part of Significant People The third common psychological hazard during the prenatal period is unfavorable attitudes on the part of significant people in the child's life. This is, in many respects, the most serious and far-reaching in its influence because once attitudes are developed they tend to persist with little if any real change or modification. There is evidence that many unfavorable attitudes toward children begin to develop when their potential arrival becomes known to parents, siblings, relatives, and neighbors. The most common and most serious of these attitudes are listed in Box 2-6.

A careful study of these attitudes may raise the question of why some of them are listed as "unfavorable." For example, on the surface, attitudes toward the child's sex and attitudes influenced by a "dream-child" concept do not seem unfavorable. However, because they are unrealistic, they are likely to lead to disappointment or even resentment which will be expressed in intolerance toward the child or even rejection. If the child is not wanted, or at least not wanted at this time, attitudes are unfavorable from the start, and often little or no attempt is made to cloak them. A father-to-be may blame his wife for being careless and make her feel guilty about not preventing the pregnancy. This will lead to marital friction and resentment toward the child when it is born. If older children do not want the baby, they will show their resentment toward it when it arrives and also toward their parents for having had it. On the basis of observations of the adjustment difficulties that unwanted children experience, Ferreira has commented: "The psychiatric and social implications of these observations suggest a sober reappraisal of the current attitudes toward the unwanted pregnancy" (24).

Unfavorable attitudes toward children of multiple birth are often stronger and more persistent than those toward singletons. These attitudes are intensified when multiple births come unexpectedly and parents have not had time to adjust to them. Even when parents welcome the idea of a multiple birth, their attitudes may become unfavorable when they

BOX 2-6

SOME COMMON UNFAVORABLE ATTITUDES TOWARD AN UNBORN CHILD

Not Wanting the Child

The mother may not want the child because it is illegitimate, because it will interfere with her career, because it will tie her down, or because she is already overworked caring for other children. The father may not want the child because he does not want to be forced to marry the mother, because of the financial burden the child will represent, because he does not want to be tied down, or because he does not want his wife to be preoccupied with child care and neglect him. Siblings may not want the child because they resent the restrictions a baby will place on their activities or because they do not want to share their possessions or their mother's time and attention with the new baby.

Not Wanting the Child at This Time

The parents may not want the child now because it will interfere with their educational and vocational plans, because they feel they are too young and inexperienced to care for a child, because they cannot afford it, or because they do not want to assume parental responsibilities so soon. Grandparents may feel that the young couple cannot afford the baby and may fear that they will have to provide financial and other help.

Preference for a Child of a Particular Sex

The father and the grandparents usually want the firstborn to be a boy; if there are already boys in the family, they may want a girl. The mother may want a boy to please her husband, or she may prefer a girl, who she feels will be more of a companion to her. Siblings generally prefer a child of their own sex, whom they regard as more likely to be a playmate.

Dream-Child Concept

All family members have a dream-child concept that colors their attitudes toward the unborn baby. Parents and grandparents want the baby to be perfect mentally, emotionally, and physically— bright, obedient, beautiful—and siblings want an ideal playmate, one who will do whatever *they* want to do and who will never rival or outstrip them.

Not Wanting Children of Multiple Birth

Many adults, even today, regard multiple births as animal-like or accept the traditional belief that children of multiple birth are doomed to be physical and mental weaklings. Others believe that multiple-birth children make too much work for all family members and dread the added expense for hospital care which is inevitable if they are premature. These unfavorable attitudes are intensified if conditions after birth are similar to those they dreaded before birth.

Wanting to Have a Miscarriage or an Abortion

When a baby is unwanted, regardless of the reason, some women hope they will have a miscarriage or they plan an abortion. If the developing baby's life is ended, either by miscarriage or abortion, women often feel guilty and this unfavorable attitude carries over to any children they may have in the future. Should they decide against an abortion or should there be no miscarriage, they may feel guilty and express their guilt in overprotectiveness and overindulgence of the child they had hoped not to have.

Scorn for the Child

Relatives, friends of the family, and neighbors may have an unfavorable attitude toward the child-to-be because it is illegitimate, because of some stigma in the lives of one or both parents, or because it is the child of an interracial or interreligious marriage. As a result, the parents may become defensive and treat the child in an overprotective or overindulgent way to compensate for these unfavorable attitudes or they may reject the child because they feel embarrassed and ashamed.

are faced with the realities of the babies' care and the expense involved. An anonymous writer, quoted by Scheinfeld, has described such feelings (65).

The Joy (?) of Twins

Drudgery that's double or more
Laundering till your hands are sore;
Tangle of lines with soggy things drying,
Day and night chorus of yelling and crying,
Endless chores and no end of expenses.
Worries that drive you out of your senses,
Everyone bothering you with questions,
Everyone giving you crazy suggestions,
Husband complaining you're no kind of wife,
Everything mixed up in your life.
If I knew whom to blame for twins, I'd sue 'em.
Those who want twins are welcome to 'em.

Chapter Highlights

1. The prenatal period, which extends from conception to birth and is approximately nine months long, has attracted little psychological attention until recently, although it has been extensively investigated by physiologists and members of the medical profession.
2. There are six characteristics of the prenatal period. It is the time when the hereditary endowment and sex of the individual are determined; when conditions in the mother's body can foster or disturb the pattern of prenatal development; when growth and development are proportionally greater than at any other time; when there are many hazards, both physical and psychological; and when significant people form attitudes toward the newly created individual.
3. Before they are ready to produce new individuals, male sex cells must go through two preliminary stages—maturation and fertilization—and female sex cells, three preliminary stages—maturation, ovulation, and fertilization.
4. At the time of conception four things are determined: hereditary endowment and sex—once and for all; whether there will be a single or multiple birth; and what the baby's (or babies') ordinal position in the family will be.
5. The determination of hereditary endowment at the time of conception affects later development in two ways: first, by placing limits beyond

which the individual cannot go and, second, because the hereditary endowment is entirely a matter of chance, it cannot be controlled.
6. The sex of the newly created individual is important for three reasons: first, from early life individuals are molded into the approved cultural stereotype for their sex groups; second, they are denied learning experiences considered inappropriate for their sex groups; and third, attitudes of significant people vary according to which sex group they belong to.
7. The immediate as well as the long-term development of singletons differs from that of individuals of multiple birth.
8. The pattern of development of individuals of different ordinal positions within a family varies greatly—with that of firstborns and last-borns usually more favorable than that of middle-borns.
9. The prenatal period is divided into three subdivisions: the period of the zygote, which extends from conception to the end of the second week; the period of the embryo, which extends from the end of the second week to the end of the second lunar month; and the period of the fetus, which extends from the end of the second lunar month to birth.
10. The period of the embryo is usually regarded as a critical time because the physical features, which are then developing rapidly, can be distorted by unfavorable conditions in the prenatal environment.
11. Attitudes of significant people toward the newly created individual are established during the prenatal period. These attitudes tend to be persistent because they are based on what are regarded as justifiable reasons, and because they are emotionally toned and therefore difficult to change.
12. Of all family attitudes, maternal attitudes are most important because of the close relationship between mother and child during the early, formative years of life.
13. The timing of physical hazards and their intensity are more important in their effects on the individual-to-be's development than the hazards per se.
14. Among the physical hazards of the prenatal period, malnutrition of the mother and certain diseases—such as rubella contacted during the period of the embryo—are usually the most serious because of their long-term effects.
15. The most common and serious among the psychological hazards of the prenatal period are traditional beliefs about conditions that can affect

the unborn child; maternal stress; and unfavorable attitudes toward the child-to-be on the part of significant people.

Bibliography

1. Altus, W. D. Birth order and its sequelae. *Science,* 1966, **151,** 44–49.
2. Babson, S. G., and D. S. Phillips. Growth and development of twins dissimilar in size at birth. *New England Journal of Medicine,* 1973, **289,** 937–940.
3. Backwin, H. Body-weight regulation in twins. *Developmental Medicine & Child Neurology,* 1973, **15,** 178–183.
4. Belmont, L., Z. A. Stein, and M. W. Susser. Comparison of associations of birth order with intelligence test scores and height. *Nature,* 1975, **255,** 54–56.
5. Bigner, J. J. Second-borns' discrimination of sibling role concepts. *Developmental Psychology,* 1974, **10,** 564–573.
6. Bowes, W. A., Y. Brackbill, E. Conway, and A. Steinschneider. The effects of obstetrical medication on fetus and infant. *Monographs of the Society for Research in Child Development,* 1970, **35**(4).
7. Bracken, M. B., M. Hachamovitch, and G. Grossman. The decision to abort and psychological sequelae. *Journal of Nervous & Mental Diseases,* 1974, **158,** 154–162.
8. Brody, J. E. Study finds smoking can imperil fetus. *The New York Times,* Apr. 11, 1970.
9. Brody, J. E. Study hints prenatal stress can curb masculinity. *The New York Times,* Jan. 13, 1972.
10. Brody, J. E. 1976 marks tricentennial of the discovery of sperm. *The New York Times,* Dec. 20, 1975.
11. Brown, W. M. C., W. H. Price, and P. A. Jacobs. Further information on the identity of 47 XYY males. *British Medical Journal,* 1968, **2,** 325–328.
12. Burns, J., J. A. Birkbeck, and D. F. Roberts. Early fetal brain growth. *Human Biology,* 1975, **47,** 511–522.
13. Burnham, D. Rise in birth defects laid to job hazards. *The New York Times,* Mar. 16, 1976.
14. Campbell, C. What happens when we get the manchild pill? *Psychology Today,* 1976, **10**(3), 86–91.
15. Chess, S. The influence of defect on development in children with congenital rubella. *Merrill-Palmer Quarterly,* 1974, **20,** 255–274.
16. Christopher, L. J. Taking drugs during pregnancy. *Developmental Medicine & Child Neurology,* 1978, **20,** 380–383.
17. Copans, S. A. Human prenatal effects: Methodological problems and some suggested solutions. *Merrill-Palmer Quarterly,* 1974, **20,** 43–52.
18. Coursin, D. B. Nutrition and brain development in infants. *Merrill-Palmer Quarterly,* 1972, **18,** 177–202.
19. Davis, A., and R. J. Havighurst. *Father of the man.* Boston: Houghton Mifflin, 1947.
20. Denson, R., J. L. Manson, and M. A. McWatters. Hyperkinesis and maternal smoking. *Canadian Psychiatric Association Journal,* 1975, **20,** 183–187.
21. Dubowitz, V. Fetal movement *in utero. Developmental Medicine & Child Neurology,* 1977, **19,** 239–240.
22. Falbo, T. Does the only child grow up miserable? *Psychology Today,* 1976, **9**(12), 60–65.
23. Ferdon, N. K. Chromosomal abnormalities and antisocial behavior. *Journal of Genetic Psychology,* 1971, **118,** 281–292.
24. Ferreira, A. J. Emotional factors in prenatal environment. *Journal of Nervous & Mental Diseases,* 1965, **141,** 108–118.
25. Forer, L. *The birth order factor.* New York: McKay, 1976.
26. Gillman, R. D. The dreams of pregnant women and maternal adaptation. *American Journal of Orthopsychiatry,* 1968, **38,** 688–692.
27. Golbus, M. S., W. D. Loughman, C. J. Epstein, G. Halbasch, J. D. Stephens, and B. D. Hall. Prenatal genetic diagnosis in 3000 amniocenteses. *New England Journal of Medicine,* 1979, **300,** 157–163.
28. Goldstein, H. Factors influencing the height of seven-year-old children. Results of the National Child Development Study. *Human Biology,* 1971, **43,** 92–111.
29. Graham, H. Smoking in pregnancy: The attitudes of expectant mothers. *Social Science & Medicine,* 1976, **10,** 399–405.
30. Hall, E. Ordinal position and success in engagement and marriage. *Journal of Individual Psychology,* 1965, **21,** 154–158.
31. Hartley, R. E. Children's perceptions of sex preference in four culture groups. *Journal of Marriage & the Family,* 1969, **31,** 380–387.
32. Heinonen, O. P., D. Stone, R. R. Monson, E. B. Hook, and S. Shapiro. Cardiovascular birth defects and antenatal exposure to female sex hormones. *New England Journal of Medicine,* 1977, **296,** 67–70.
33. Hytten, F. E. Smoking in pregnancy. *Developmental Medicine & Child Neurology,* 1973, **15,** 355–357.
34. Jacobs, B. S., and H. A. Moss. Birth order and sex of sibling as determinants of mother-infant interaction. *Child Development,* 1976, **47,** 315–322.
35. Joesting, J., and R. Joesting. Birth order and desired family size. *Journal of Individual Psychology,* 1973, **29,** 34.
36. Kaplan, B. J. Malnutrition and mental deficiency. *Psychological Bulletin,* 1972, **78,** 321–334.
37. Kennelly, J. H., R. Jerauld, H. Wolfe, D. Chester, N. C. Kreger, W. McAlpine, M. Steffa, and M. H. Klaus. Maternal behavior one year after early and extended postpartum contact. *Developmental Medicine & Child Neurology,* 1974, **16,** 172–179.
38. Khatri, A. A., and B. B. Saddiqui. A boy or a girl? Preferences of parents for sex of offspring as perceived by East Indian and American children: A cross-cultural study. *Journal of Marriage & the Family,* 1969, **31,** 388–392.
39. Koch, H. L. *Twins and twin relations.* Chicago: University of Chicago Press, 1966.
40. Lasker, G., and B. Kaplan. Anthropometric variables in the offspring of isonymous matings. *Human Biology,* 1974, **46,** 713–717.
41. Little, R. E., F. A. Schultz, and W. Mandell. Drinking during pregnancy. *Journal of Studies on Alcohol,* 1976, **3,** 375–379.
42. Lytton, H. Do parents create, or respond to, differences in twins? *Developmental Psychology,* 1977, **13,** 456–459.
43. Matheny, A. P. Twins: Concordance for Piagetian-equivalent items derived from the Bayley Mental Test. *Developmental Psychology,* 1975, **11,** 224–227.
44. Matheny, A. P., A. B. Dolan, and R. S. Wilson. Twins: Within-pair similarity on Bayley's Infant Behavior Record. *Journal of Genetic Psychology,* 1976, **128,** 263–270.

45. McClearn, G. E. Genetic influences on behavior and development. In P. H. Mussen (Ed.). *Carmichael's manuel of child psychology*. (3rd ed.) Vol. 1. New York: Wiley, 1970, Pp. 39–76.

46. Meredith, H. V. Relation between tobacco smoking of pregnant women and body size of their progeny: A compilation and synthesis of published studies. *Human Biology*, 1975, **47**, 451–472.

47. Meredith, H. V. Somatic changes during human prenatal life. *Child Development*, 1975, **46**, 603–610.

48. Meyerowitz, J. H. Satisfaction during pregnancy. *Journal of Marriage & the Family*, 1970, **32**, 38–42.

49. Miller, H. C., and K. Hassanein. Fetal malnutrition in white newborn infants: Maternal factors. *Pediatrics*, 1973, **52**, 504–512.

50. Miller, P. Biological and social aspects of language development in twins. *Developmental Medicine & Child Neurology*, 1970, **12**, 741–757.

51. Miller, W. B. Relationship between the intendedness of conception and the wantedness of pregnancy. *Journal of Nervous & Mental Diseases*, 1974, **159**, 396–406.

52. Mitton, J. B. Fertility differentials in modern societies resulting in normalizing selection for height. *Human Biology*, 1975, **47**, 189–201.

53. Montagu, A. *The direction of human development*. New York: Hawthorn, 1970.

54. Munsinger, H., and A. Douglass. The syntactic abilities of identical twins, fraternal twins, and their siblings. *Child Development*, 1976, **47**, 40–50.

55. Naeye, R. L., W. Blanc, and C. Paul. Effects of maternal nutrition on the human fetus. *Pediatrics*, 1973, **52**, 370–371.

56. Neetz, V. M. Birth order and leadership in the elementary school: A cross-cultural study. *Journal of Social Psychology*, 1974, **92**, 143–144.

57. Nisbet, R. E. Birth order and participation in dangerous sports. *Journal of Personality & Social Psychology*, 1968, **8**, 351–353.

58. Ounsted, M. Fetal growth and mental ability. *Developmental Medicine & Child Neurology*, 1970, **12**, 222–224.

59. Paluszny, M., and R. Gibson. Twin interactions in a normal nursery school. *American Journal of Psychiatry*, 1974, **131**, 293–296.

60. Pasamanick, B., and H. Knobloch. Prospective studies on the epidemiology of reproductive casualty: Methods, findings and some implications. *Merrill-Palmer Quarterly*, 1966, **12**, 27–43.

61. Polednak, A. P. Paternal age in relation to selected birth defects. *Human Biology*, 1976, **48**, 727–739.

62. Rosenblatt, P. C., and E. L. Skoogberg. Birth order in cross-cultural perspective. *Developmental Psychology*, 1974, **10**, 48–54.

63. Scarr, S. Environmental bias in twin studies. *Eugenics Quarterly*, 1968, **15**, 34–40.

64. Schaefer, E. S., and N. Bayley. Consistency of maternal behavior from infancy to preadolescence. *Journal of Abnormal & Social Psychology*, 1960, **61**, 1–6.

65. Scheinfeld, A. *Twins and supertwins*. Philadelphia: Lippincott, 1967.

66. Scheinfeld, A. *Heredity in humans*, Rev. Ed. Philadelphia: Lippincott, 1971.

67. Schooler, C. Birth order effects: Not here, not now. *Psychological Bulletin*, 1972, **78**, 161–175.

68. Selvin, S., and J. Garfinkel. Paternal age, maternal age, and birth order and the risk of fetal loss. *Human Biology*, 1976, **48**, 223–230.

69. Senay, E. C., and S. Wexler. Fantasies about the fetus in wanted and unwanted pregnancies. *Journal of Youth & Adolescence*, 1972, **1**, 333–337.

70. Skovholt, T., E. Moore, and F. Wellman. Birth order and academic behavior in first grade. *Psychological Reports*, 1973, **32**, 395–398.

71. Sontag, L. W. Implications of fetal behavior and environment for adult personalities. *Annals of the New York Academy of Sciences*, 1966, **134**, 782–786.

72. Sontag, L. W., W. G. Steele, and M. Lewis. The fetal and maternal cardiac response to environmental stress. *Human Development*, 1969, **12**, 1–9.

73. Stewart, M. A. Hyperactive children. *Scientific American*, 1970, **222**(4), 94–98.

74. Stone, L. J., H. T. Smith, and L. B. Murphy (Eds.). *The competent infant: Research and commentary*. New York: Basic Books, 1975.

75. Tanner, J. M. *Fetus into man: Physical growth from conception to maturity*. Cambridge, Mass.: Harvard University Press, 1978.

76. U.S. News & World Report article. Who stays married longer? *U.S. News & World Report*, Oct. 30, 1972, p. 39.

77. Van den Daele, L. D. Natal influences and twin differences. *Journal of Genetic Psychology*, 1974, **124**, 41–60.

78. Walters, C. E. Prediction of postnatal development from fetal activity. *Child Development*, 1965, **36**, 801–808.

79. Weiner, H. Birth order and illness behavior. *Journal of Individual Psychology*, 1973, **29**, 173–175.

80. Werner, E. E. From birth to latency: Behavior differences in a multiracial group of twins. *Child Development*, 1973, **44**, 438–444.

81. Willerman, L. Activity level and hyperactivity in twins. *Child Development*, 1973, **44**, 288–293.

82. Wilson, G. S., M. M. Desmond, and W. M. Verniaud. Early development of infants of heroin-addicted mothers. *American Journal of Diseases of Children*, 1973, **126**, 457–462.

83. Wilson, R. S. Twins: Mental development in the preschool years. *Developmental Psychology*, 1974, **10**, 580–588.

84. Wilson, R. S. Twins: Patterns of cognitive development as measured on the Wechsler Preschool and Primary Scale of Intelligence. *Developmental Psychology*, 1975, **11**, 126–134.

85. Wilson, R. S. Twins and siblings: Concordance for school age mental development. *Child Development*, 1977, **48**, 211–216.

86. Wolanski, N. The stature of infants and the assortive mating of parents. *Human Biology*, 1974, **46**, 613–619.

87. Zajonc, R. B. Birth order and intelligence: Dumber by the dozen. *Psychology Today*, 1975, **8**(8), 37–43.

88. Zajonc, R. B. Family configuration and intelligence. *Science*, 1976, **192**, 227–236.

89. Zajonc, R. B., and C. B. Markus. Birth order and intellectual development. *Psychological Review*, 1975, **82**, 74–88.

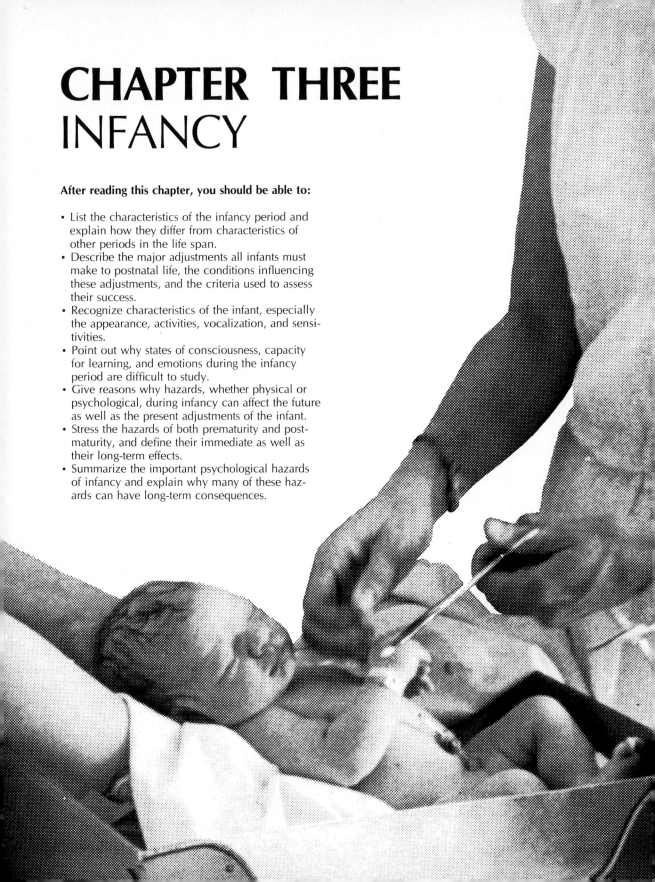

CHAPTER THREE
INFANCY

After reading this chapter, you should be able to:

- List the characteristics of the infancy period and explain how they differ from characteristics of other periods in the life span.
- Describe the major adjustments all infants must make to postnatal life, the conditions influencing these adjustments, and the criteria used to assess their success.
- Recognize characteristics of the infant, especially the appearance, activities, vocalization, and sensitivities.
- Point out why states of consciousness, capacity for learning, and emotions during the infancy period are difficult to study.
- Give reasons why hazards, whether physical or psychological, during infancy can affect the future as well as the present adjustments of the infant.
- Stress the hazards of both prematurity and postmaturity, and define their immediate as well as their long-term effects.
- Summarize the important psychological hazards of infancy and explain why many of these hazards can have long-term consequences.

Infancy, or the period of the newborn, is, according to standard dictionaries, the beginning or the early period of existence as an individual rather than as a parasite in the mother's body. Dictionaries also define an infant as a child in the first period of life.

According to legal standards, an infant is an individual who is a minor until reaching the age of legal maturity, which, in America today, is eighteen years. According to medical terminology, an infant is a young child, but no specific age limits are placed on when the individual ceases to be an infant and becomes a child.

Many psychologists use the word *infant* in much the same way as members of the medical profession do and, like them, fail to set an age limit on infancy. This gives the period an ambiguous status in the life span.

The word *infant* suggests extreme helplessness, and it will be limited in this book to the first few weeks of life. During this period, the newborn's complete helplessness gradually gives way to increasing independence.

the Neonate

CHARACTERISTICS OF INFANCY

Each period in the life span is characterized by certain developmental phenomena that distinguish it from the periods that precede and follow it. While some of these phenomena may be associated with other periods, they appear in a distinctive form during infancy. Following are the five most important characteristics of this period.

Infancy Is the Shortest of All Developmental Periods

Infancy begins with birth and ends when the infant is approximately two weeks old, by far the shortest of all developmental periods. It is the time when the fetus must adjust to life outside the uterine walls of the mother where it has lived for approximately nine months.

According to medical criteria, the adjustment is completed with the fall of the umbilical cord from the navel; according to physiological criteria, it is completed when the infant has regained the weight lost after birth; and according to psychological criteria, it is completed when the infant begins to show signs of

developmental progress in behavior. Although most infants complete this adjustment in two weeks or slightly less, those whose birth has been difficult or premature require more time.

In spite of its shortness, infancy is generally subdivided into two periods: the period of the partunate and the period of the neonate. These are described in Box 3-1. Even in difficult births, it seldom takes more than forty-eight hours for the fetus to emerge from the mother's body. By contrast, it requires approximately two weeks to adjust to the new environment outside the mother's body.

Infancy Is a Time of Radical Adjustments

Although the human life span legally begins at the moment of birth, birth is merely an interruption of the developmental pattern that started at the moment of conception. It is the graduation from an internal to an external environment. Like all graduations, it requires adjustments on the individual's part. It may be easy for some infants to make these adjustments but so difficult for others that they will fail to do so. Miller has commented, "In all the rest of his life, there will never be such a sudden and complete change of locale" (62).

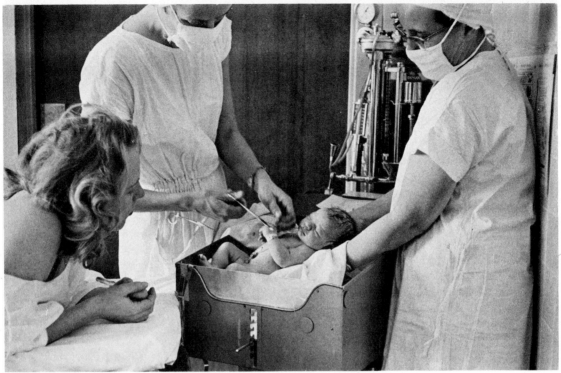

The period of the neonate begins with the cutting and tying of the umbilical cord and extends to approximately the end of the second week of postnatal life. (Photo by Eve Arnold from Magnum Photos.)

Infancy Is a Plateau in Development

The rapid growth and development which took place during the prenatal period suddenly come to a stop with birth. In fact, there is often a slight regression, such as loss of weight and a tendency to be less strong and healthy than at birth. Normally this slight regression lasts for several days to a week, after which the infant begins to improve. By the end of the infancy period, the infant's state of development is usually back to where it was at the time of birth.

The halt in growth and development, characteristic of this plateau, is due to the necessity for making radical adjustments to the postnatal environment. Once these adjustments have been made, infants resume their growth and development.

While a plateau in development during infancy is normal, many parents, especially those of firstborn children, become concerned about it and fear that something is wrong with their child. Consequently,

the infancy plateau may become a psychological hazard, just as it is a potential physical hazard.

Infancy Is a Preview of Later Development

It is not possible to predict with even reasonable accuracy what the individual's future development will be on the basis of the development apparent at birth. However, the newborn's development provides a clue as to what to expect later on. As Bell et al. have said (10):

Newborn behavior is more like a preface to a book than like a table of its contents yet to be unfolded. Further, the preface is itself merely a rough draft undergoing rapid revision. There are some clues to the nature of the book in the preface but these are in code form and taking them as literally prophetic is likely to lead to disappointment.

BOX 3-2

ADJUSTMENTS OF INFANCY

Temperature Changes

There is a constant temperature of 100°F in the uterine sac, while temperatures in the hospital or home may vary from 60 to 70°F.

Breathing

When the umbilical cord is cut, infants must begin to breathe on their own.

Sucking and Swallowing

The infant must now get nourishment by sucking and swallowing, instead of receiving it through the umbilical cord. These reflexes are imperfectly developed at birth, and the infant often gets less nourishment than is needed and thus loses weight.

Elimination

The infant's organs of elimination begin to work soon after birth; formerly, waste products were eliminated through the umbilical cord.

BOX 3-3

INDICATIONS OF THE DIFFICULTY OF ADJUSTMENT TO POSTNATAL LIFE

Loss of Weight

Because of difficulties in adjusting to sucking and swallowing, the newborn infant usually loses weight during the first week of postnatal life.

Disorganized Behavior

For the first day or two of postnatal life, all infants show relatively disorganized behavior, such as irregularities in breathing rate, frequent urinations and defecations, wheezing, and regurgitation. This is due partly to pressure on the brain during birth, which results in a stunned state, and partly to the undeveloped state of the autonomic nervous system, which controls body homeostasis.

Infant Mortality

Even today, the rate of infant mortality during the first two days of postnatal life is high. The causes of infant mortality are many and varied.

Infancy Is a Hazardous Period

Infancy is a hazardous period, both physically and psychologically. Physically, it is hazardous because of the difficulties of making the necessary radical adjustments to the totally new and different environment. The high infant mortality rate is evidence of this.

Psychologically, infancy is hazardous because it is the time when the attitudes of significant people toward the infant are crystallized. Many of these attitudes were established during the prenatal period and may change radically after the infant is born, but some remain relatively unchanged or are strengthened, depending on conditions at birth and on the ease or difficulty with which the infant and the parents adjust.

MAJOR ADJUSTMENTS OF INFANCY

Infants must make four major adjustments before they can resume their developmental progress. If they do not make them quickly, their lives will be threatened. While these adjustments are being made, there is no developmental progress. Instead, the infant remains on a plateau or may even regress to a lower stage of development. These adjustments are described in Box 3-2.

Every newborn infant finds adjustment to postnatal life difficult at first. Some have trouble adjusting to temperature changes and develop colds, which may turn into pneumonia. Others find breathing difficult and must be given oxygen. Most choke when they attempt to suck and swallow, and many regurgitate more than they are able to retain, in which case they get less nourishment than they need to grow or even to retain their birth weight. Few have any real trouble eliminating urine, but many have difficulties with fecal elimination.

Three common indications of the difficulty of adjusting to postnatal life are given in Box 3-3.

CONDITIONS INFLUENCING ADJUSTMENT TO POSTNATAL LIFE

Many conditions influence the success with which infants make the necessary adjustments to postnatal life.

The most important of these, as research to date indicates, are the kind of prenatal environment, the type of birth and experiences associated with it, the length of the gestation period, parental attitudes, and postnatal care. Because of their importance, each of these conditions will be discussed in detail.

Prenatal Environment

The first condition that influences the kind of adjustment infants make to postnatal life is the kind of prenatal environment they had. A healthy prenatal environment will contribute to good adjustments to postnatal life.

On the other hand, there are many kinds of intrauterine disturbance that can and often do cause an infant to be born, as Schwartz has pointed out, "with severe injuries and then be subject to a miserable life" (91). Inadequate prenatal care of the mother, as a result of either poverty or neglect, is often responsible for the development of unfavorable conditions in the intrauterine environment which affect the developing child and lead to complications during childbirth, both of which affect the kind of adjustment the infant makes.

Malnutrition of the mother during pregnancy has been found to be responsible for premature births, stillbirths, and infant mortality during the early days of life. Infants whose mothers suffer from diabetes have more difficulties in adjustment and a higher incidence of mortality than infants whose mothers are nondiabetic (20,60,63).

Unquestionably one of the most important conditions that contribute to difficulties in postnatal adjustment is a prenatal environment characterized by prolonged and intense maternal stress. As was mentioned earlier, this leads to complications during pregnancy and childbirth. Maternal stress also causes the fetus to become hyperactive during the last months of pregnancy, and this condition tends to persist after birth, manifesting itself in feeding difficulties, failure to gain weight, sleep problems, general irritability, distractibility, and a host of other conditions that make adjustment to postnatal life difficult. In commenting on the effects of maternal stress during pregnancy on the infant's later adjustment, Sontag has emphasized (92):

To all intents and purposes, a newborn infant with such a background is a neurotic infant when he is born—the result of an unsatisfactory fetal environ-

---

BOX 3-4

KINDS OF BIRTH

Natural, or Spontaneous, Birth

In a natural birth, the position of the fetus and its size in relation to the mother's reproductive organs allow it to emerge in the normal, head-first position.

Breech Birth

In a breech birth, the buttocks appear first, followed by the legs and finally the head.

Transverse Birth

In a transverse presentation, the fetus is positioned crosswise in the mother's uterus. Instruments must be used for delivery unless the position can be changed before the birth process begins.

Instrument Birth

When the fetus is too large to emerge spontaneously or when its position makes normal birth impossible, instruments must be used to aid in delivery.

Caesarean Section

If x-rays taken during the latter part of pregnancy indicate that complications may result if the infant emerges through the birth canal, the baby is brought into the world through a slit made surgically in the mother's abdominal wall.

---

ment. In this instance, he does not have to wait until childhood for a bad home situation or other cause to make him neurotic. It was done for him before he even saw the light of day.

Kind of Birth

The second condition that influences the kind of adjustment that will be made to postnatal life is the kind of birth the infant experiences. Many traditional beliefs about birth and how it affects the individual's adjustments to life persist even today. For example, there are many beliefs about auspicious and inauspicious times to be born. There is also the belief that the ease or difficulty of birth affects postnatal adjustments and the belief that a premature baby will never be as strong as one born at full term or make as successful an adjustment to life.

Even with our modern medical techniques, birth is a hazardous experience. Jeffcoate has pointed out that the "most hazardous journey made by any individual is through the four inches of the birth canal" (49). Schwartz further emphasized the hazardous nature of birth when he said, "Birth is almost without exception a brutal process which endangers the life and health of the child" (91).

There are five kinds of birth, each with its distinctive characteristics. These are explained in Box 3-4. Figure 3-1 illustrates two of the five—natural (or spontaneous birth) and breech birth.

The infant who has been born spontaneously usually adjusts more quickly and more successfully to the postnatal environment than one whose birth has been difficult enough to require use of instruments or caesarean section.

More hazards are associated with instrument births and caesarean sections than with spontaneous births. The more difficult the birth, the greater the chance of damage and the more severe the damage. Small women show a relatively high stillbirth rate as compared with larger women, often because instruments must be used to aid in delivery. Motor disabilities, paralysis, cerebral palsy, and mental deficiency are frequently reported as aftermaths of difficult births, especially when instruments have had to be used (29,63).

Babies born by caesarean section are the quietest, crying less than those born spontaneously or with the aid of instruments and showing greater lethargy and decreased reactivity. As a result, they normally make better adjustments to their postnatal environment—unless they have had difficulty establishing respiration, which may cause temporary or permanent brain damage. Neonatal deaths are more frequent among those born by caesarean section than among those born spontaneously or with the aid of instruments (8,29).

Experiences Associated with Birth

The third condition that influences the kind of adjustments infants make to postnatal life are experiences associated with birth. Regardless of the kind of birth, two birth experiences have a major effect on postnatal adjustments. They are the extent to which the mother is medicated during the birth process and the ease or difficulty with which the infant establishes respiration.

Infants whose mothers are heavily *medicated*

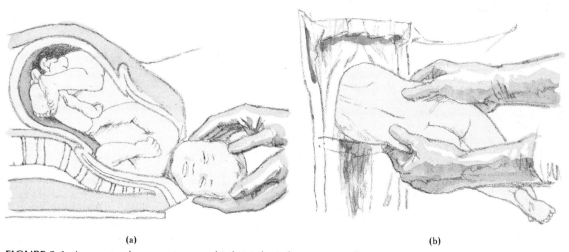

(a)   (b)

FIGURE 3-1 In a natural or spontaneous birth (a) the infant emerges from the mother's body headfirst while in a breech birth (b) the buttocks emerge first and the head last. (Adapted from N. J. Eastman and L. M. Hellman. *Williams obstetrics.* (13th ed). New York: Appleton-Century-Crofts, 1966. Used by permission.)

during labor show drowsiness and disorganized behavior for three or more days after birth, as compared with one or two days for those whose mothers are lightly medicated or receive no medication at all. Furthermore, infants whose mothers are heavily medicated lose more weight and take longer to regain their lost weight than infants whose mothers have less medication (3,53). Federman and Yang, for example, have reported that the effects on the infant's adjustment to postnatal life may persist during the first month after birth (33).

How long the effects of maternal medication will persist and how serious the effects will be will depend to some extent upon the type of medication used. Anesthetics and analgesics can and often do interfere with the immediate adjustments required by newborn infants to sustain life, as in the case of establishing spontaneous respirations, but more persistent effects have not been reported (11). After a careful and complete review of the studies made to date of the effects of pain-relieving drugs administered to mothers during childbirth, Aleksandrowicz has concluded (2):

The evidence to date suggests that drugs administered to the mother for relief of pain during labor and delivery may often produce significant deleterious effects in the newborn to a much greater extent than had been assumed in the past. . . . It is becoming evident that the effect of drugs is not limited to gross physiological signs, such as a delayed onset of respiration, muscular hypotonia, or drowsiness. Recent studies . . . revealed important changes in infants' spontaneous and elicited behavior. . . . It would be an error to dismiss the importance of transient effects because they may well have a significant effect on the interaction of the infant with his environment at points crucial for the development of other functions . . . Summing up, we may say that there is enough evidence to date that obstetric analgesia and anesthesia in any form involves an element of calculated risk to the infant.

The ease or difficulty with which infants start to *breathe* after birth likewise affects their postnatal adjustments. When there is interruption of the oxygen supply to the brain before or during birth—*anoxia*—the infant may die. Infants who live may be temporarily or permanently brain damaged, although this may not be apparent for months or even years after birth.

How serious the consequences will be depends on how severe and how prolonged the oxygen deprivation is (39).

While anoxia may occur in any birth, it is especially likely to occur in *precipitate labor*—labor lasting less than two hours. When this occurs, the infant is introduced to oxygen too suddenly and is not yet ready to start to breathe. How much brain damage there will be and how permanent its effects will be depend largely on how quickly the infant can establish respiration.

Length of Gestation Period

The fourth condition that influences infants' adjustments to postnatal life is the length of the gestation period. Very few infants are born exactly 280 days after conception. Those who arrive ahead of time are known as *prematures*—often referred to in hospitals as "preemies"—while those who arrive late are known as *postmatures*, or *postterm babies*.

Postmaturity occurs less often than in the past because it is now possible to induce labor when x-rays show that the fetus is large enough and well-enough developed to adjust successfully to postnatal life. Induced labor is also used as a means of preventing possible birth complications and birth injuries, especially brain damage, which can result if the fetal head is allowed to grow too large.

In recent years, the number of premature babies has increased. The reason for this is that while it is possible to keep premature babies alive and to prevent miscarriages, medical science has not yet solved the problem of keeping an infant from arriving ahead of schedule.

Many studies of premature infants have used as their major criterion of prematurity low birth weight. It is now recognized that birth weight alone is not enough to determine prematurity. Instead, gestation age, body length, bone ossification, head circumference, irritability, reflex, nutritional state, and neurological assessment are also used (16,17,60,101).

Relatively few studies of prematurity use all of these criteria. In most cases, when infants are 20 or more inches long and weigh 8 or more pounds, they are considered postmature. It they are less than 19 inches long and weigh 5 pounds 8 ounces or less, they are regarded as premature. The more they deviate from the norm for their sex and racial group on the minus side, the more premature they are considered to be. On the other hand, the more they deviate on the plus side, the more postmature they are considered to be.

Unless damaged at birth, the postmature infant usually adjusts more quickly and more successfully to the postnatal environment than the infant born at full term. However, because the chances of birth damage increase as postmaturity increases, the advantages that come from the speed and ease of adjustment are far outweighed by the possibilities of birth damage.

Prematurely born babies usually experience complications in adjusting to the postnatal environment, and these may have a serious effect on future adjustment. Furthermore, every difficulty that the normal, full-term infant faces in adjusting to the new environment is magnified in the case of the premature baby. This will be discussed more fully later in connection with the hazards of infancy.

Parental Attitudes

How quickly and how successfully newborn infants will adjust to postnatal life is greatly influenced by parental attitudes. This is the fifth condition that influences the kind of adjustments infants make to postnatal life.

When parental attitudes are unfavorable, for whatever the reason, they are reflected in treatment of the infant that militates against successful adjustments to postnatal life. By contrast, parents whose attitudes are favorable treat the infant in ways that encourage good adjustment. Parent-infant interactions are not characterized by the emotional tension and nervousness that are normally present when parental attitudes are unfavorable. A relaxed mother, for example, usually produces more milk than one who is tense and nervous, and this helps the infant adjust to a new method of taking nourishment.

While maternal attitudes are, unquestionably, more important than paternal attitudes in determining the newborn infant's adjustment to postnatal life, paternal attitudes cannot be disregarded. Indirectly, they are important because of the effect they have on maternal attitudes. Directly, they are important because of the effect they have on the way fathers handle their newborn infants and on the way they assist in their care after they are brought home from the hospital (40). Fathers who are present during delivery usually have more favorable attitudes toward their children than do those who do not share the childbirth experience with their partners (21).

Parental attitudes toward the newborn infant are influenced by attitudes developed during the prenatal period, by conditions associated with birth, and by the care given the infant after leaving the hospital. Some conditions have a greater effect on maternal attitudes while others have a greater impact on paternal attitudes. These conditions are briefly described in Box 3-5.

Postnatal Care

The sixth influential condition is the kind of postnatal care the newborn receives during the infancy period. For the most part, care during the first three or four days after birth will be by hospital personnel. After that, care will be in the home, usually given by the mother with some assistance from the father, relatives, or paid domestic help brought into the home for a week or more after the mother leaves the hospital.

While the overall quality of the postnatal care is important in determining the kind of adjustments the infant will make to postnatal life, three aspects of this care are especially important. They are the amount of attention infants receive to ensure that their needs will be met satisfactorily and relatively promptly, the amount of stimulation they receive from the time of birth, and the degree of confidence their parents, especially their mothers, have in meeting their needs.

First, newborn infants, accustomed to a stable environment before birth in which their bodily needs were automatically met with no effort on their part, must now depend on the people in their new environment to meet these needs for them. Because of their neurophysiological immaturity, these needs will not necessarily arise at given times. Furthermore, newborns cannot tell those around them what they want or need. All they can do is cry.

In the modern hospital, healthy, normal infants are usually placed in a nursery where they must wait their turn for an overworked nurse to come to them when they cry. As a rule, the nurse will not have time to "mother" them or do anything to stimulate their innate abilities. Furthermore, and more serious, different nurses will be on duty at different times, with the result that an infant must constantly adjust to different kinds of handling. Adjusting to postnatal life is difficult enough for the infant without complicating it with inadequate attention and shifts in the type of attention given. Although the newborn infant usually stays in the hospital only three to four days, these are critical days in the period of postnatal adjustment.

BOX 3-5

CONDITIONS THAT AFFECT PARENTAL ATTITUDES TOWARD THE INFANT

Preparation for Parental Duties

Parents who have had experience in caring for earlier-born children, taken courses given in pre-natal clinics, or baby-sat for older siblings or neighbors' children have more confidence in as-suming the parental role than do those who have lacked any such experiences.

The Childbirth Experience

The mother's attitude toward the infant is more fa-vorable when the childbirth experience has been relatively easy than when it is prolonged, difficult, and followed by physical complications. The father's attitude is also colored by his wife's child-birth experience.

The Mother's Physical Condition after Childbirth

The more quickly a mother recovers after child-birth, the more favorable her attitude toward the infant will be and the more confident she will be of her ability to fulfill her maternal role satisfacto-rily.

Concern about Expenses

When complications arise at childbirth, such as a caesarean operation, prematurity which necessi-tates special nursing care and a prolonged stay in the hospital, or some defect brought on at birth or apparent at birth, parental attitudes will be unfa-vorably affected by concern about the unexpected expenses involved.

Evidence of Defects

If there is a suspicion or actual evidence that the infant is defective in some respect, parental atti-tudes will be colored by disappointment, concern about the future normality of the infant, and the added expense the defect will cost.

The Infant's Postnatal Adjustments

The faster and the better the infant adjusts to the postnatal environment, the more favorable the parents' attitudes will be.

Infantile Crying

Infants who cry excessively and without apparent reason encourage the development of unfavorable attitudes not only on the part of parents but also on the part of all family members.

Parental Resentments against Work, Privations, and Expenses

When parents find that the care of the infant re-quires more work, privations, and expenses than they had anticipated, their attitudes toward the in-fant will be far less favorable than they would have been had they prepared themselves for the condi-tions that parenthood normally imposes.

Concern about Normality

If an infant must remain in the hospital longer than the usual stay, as a result of prematurity, some defect, or poor postnatal adjustments, parents are not only concerned about the infant's normality but also about their ability to care for the infant after leaving the hospital.

Concern about Survival

When an infant must remain in the hospital longer than the usual time and be given special attention, parents become concerned about the infant's sur-vival. If the infant does survive, parents tend to be overprotective when they assume responsibility for its care.

While most normal, full-term infants suffer no serious or lasting effects as a result of this impersonal care, there is evidence that it delays their adjustment to postnatal life (29,80).

The second aspect of postnatal care that influ-ences the infant's adjustments to postnatal life is the type and amount of stimulation given. Because of the little time nurses can devote to each newborn in the hospital nursery, most infants receive minimal stimu-lation during the first few days of their lives. Also, be-cause many parents, especially parents of firstborns, are afraid that handling them will damage them in some way, infants are often deprived at home of the stimulation they formerly had in the uterus from the constant movements of the fetal body. Unfortunately, they are usually handled, rocked, talked to, and in other ways stimulated as little as possible.

There is evidence that this lack of stimulation during the early, critical days of development delays postnatal development. This is especially serious for prematures who remain in the hospital for longer than the average time and who receive little or no stimulation by stroking, rocking, holding, and handling.

When, on the other hand, newborn infants are stimulated, they regain their lost birth weight earlier, they overcome the dazed state characteristic of the first days of postnatal life sooner, and they are more alert and responsive to their new environment. This is true of prematures just as it is of full-term infants (69,78,81,88). As Marcus has explained, "The warmth and affection a mother shows when cuddling her baby apparently does more than demonstrate her love; it may actually stimulate the infant's neurological development. Lack of loving stimulation could contribute to the disabilities often suffered by premature babies" (55).

The third condition associated with postnatal care is the degree of confidence parents, especially mothers, have in performing their parental tasks satisfactorily. Many parents lack confidence in their abilities to take care of their infants once they are released from the hospital. This is especially true of firstborns or infants who are premature or suffer from some physical defect (9).

Recognizing that a mother's self-confidence aids her infant's adjustments to postnatal life, some hospitals are giving the new mother an opportunity to share in the care of her infant through the "rooming-in plan." One of the most difficult problems mothers face, especially in the care of a firstborn, is to know what the infant's different cries mean. Figure 3-2 shows how mothers who have shared in the care of their infants in the hospital are better able to interpret their cries than mothers who have not (41). The greater the mother's confidence in this ability, the better she can care for her infant and the better the infant's postnatal adjustments will be.

CHARACTERISTICS OF THE INFANT

Because some infants are born prematurely and some postmaturely, it is obvious that not all infants will show the same level of physical and mental develop-

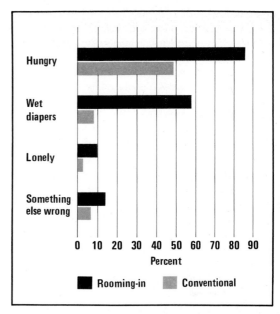

FIGURE 3-2 Comparison of mothers with rooming-in hospital experience with those of conventional hospital experiences in ability to interpret the meaning of their infants' cries. (Adapted from M. Greenberg, I. Rosenberg, and J. Lind. First mothers' rooming-in with their newborns: Its impact upon the mother. *American Journal of Orthopsychiatry*, 1973, **43,** 783–788. Used by permission.)

ment. The following description of the neonate, however, deals with the normal, full-term infant. Exceptions will be noted and explained.

Physical Development
Infants differ greatly in appearance and physiological functions at birth and in their early adjustments after birth.

Size At birth, the average infant weighs 7½ pounds and measures 19½ inches in length. Weight in relation to height is less at birth, on the average, in the more active fetuses than in those who have been less active during the latter part of the fetal period. Boys, on the whole, are slightly longer and heavier than girls. There are marked individual differences, however, in infants of both sexes.

Infantile Features The muscles of the newborn infant are soft, small, and uncontrolled. At the time of birth, less development has taken place in the muscles of the neck and legs than in those of the hands and arms. The bones, like the muscles, are soft and flexible because they are composed chiefly of cartilage or gristle. Because of their softness, they can readily be misshapen. The skin is soft and often blotchy. The flesh is firm and elastic. The skin of white infants becomes lighter as they grow older while that of nonwhites becomes darker (77).

Frequently, soft downy hair is found on the head and back, though the latter soon disappears. The eyes of white newborns are usually a bluish gray, though they gradually change to whatever their permanent color will be. Infants with dark skin have dark brown eyes but they also change, becoming darker in time. Natal teeth occur approximately once in every 2,000 births. They are the "baby" type and are usually lower central incisors.

Physical Proportions The newborn is not a miniature adult. This is illustrated in Figure 3-3. The head is approximately one-fourth of the body length; the adult head, by comparison, is approximately one-seventh of the total body length. The cranial region, the area over the eyes, is proportionally much larger than the rest of the head, while the chin is proportionally much too small. By contrast, the eyes are almost mature in size. The nose is very small and almost flat on the face, while the tiny mouth may look like a slit if the lips are narrow.

The neck is so short that it is almost invisible, and the skin covering it lies in thick folds or creases. In the trunk, the shoulders are narrow, while the abdomen is large and bulging. Proportionally, the arms and legs of the infant are much too short for the head and trunk. The hands and feet are miniature.

Physiological Functions Because of the undeveloped state of the autonomic nervous system at birth, the infant is unable to maintain homeostasis, which is one of the causes of the high mortality rate at this time.

With the birth cry, the lungs are inflated and respiration begins. The respiration rate at first ranges from forty to forty-five breathing movements per minute. By the end of the first week of life, it normally drops to approximately thirty-five per minute and is more stable than it was at first.

FIGURE 3-3 The body proportions of the newborn infant and the adult. (After Stratz, from K. Bühler *Mental development of the child*. New York: Harcourt, Brace, 1930. Used by permission.)

Neonatal heartbeat is more rapid than that of the adult because the infant's heart is small compared with the arteries. When body movements are restricted by means of swaddling the infant's body, there is an increase in stability of the heartbeat. As a result, the infant is quieter, sleeps more, and has a lower heart rate. Even in a healthy infant, the temperature is higher and more variable than in the adult.

Reflex sucking movements occur when the infant is hungry or when the lips are touched. There is an increase in the rate of sucking and in the amount of nutrients consumed with each passing day, partly because of maturation and partly because of learning.

The hunger rhythm does not develop until several weeks after birth. The hunger demands of the newborn are therefore irregular, not only in regard to intervals between feedings but also in regard to amounts. Because the hunger contractions of the infant are more vigorous than those of the adult, the infant experiences real pain when hungry.

Elimination of waste products begins a few hours after birth. Many voidings occur during periods of wakefulness and when the infant is quiet, usually within an hour after feeding. Defecations likewise occur when the infant is awake and quiet, shortly after feeding.

In no physiological function is lack of homeostasis more apparent than in sleep. Neonatal sleep is broken by short waking periods which occur every two or three hours, with fewer and shorter waking periods during the night than during the day. Throughout the neonatal period, there is a general increase in bodily movements during sleep as well as during the time the infant is awake.

There are marked variations in infant posture during sleep. However, the characteristic posture, when prone, is similar to that of the fetus during intrauterine life. By the end of the first month of life, this posture is generally outgrown, owing to the tonus of the baby's musculature.

Activities of the Infant

Movements of the body appear as soon as the fetus emerges from the mother's body. Because of the neurophysiological immaturity of the infant, one could not expect its movements to be coordinated or meaningful. Nor are they related to events in the environment or under the infant's voluntary control. This is one cause of the helplessness of the newborn infant.

In spite of their random, meaningless nature, movements of the infant can be classed, roughly, into two general categories. These are explained in Box 3-6.

Mass Activity Normally, mass activity increases in intensity and frequency with each passing day. Figure 3-4 shows the increases during the first five days after birth. Mass activity also varies during the day. The greatest activity generally occurs early in the morning, when the infant is rested after a relatively long sleep, and is lowest at noon, when it is apt to be fatigued as a result of having been bathed and dressed during the morning.

Its prenatal and birth experiences influence the infant's activity after birth. Infants who have been most active as fetuses tend to be most active during the period of the newborn. A long and difficult labor

or heavy medication of the mother can cause the infant to be relatively inactive for the first few days of life. Infants delivered by caesarean section are usually the least active of all.

The condition of the infant's body has a marked influence on mass activity. Hunger, pain, and general discomfort give rise to great activity, while limited activity follows nursing. When clothing and covers are

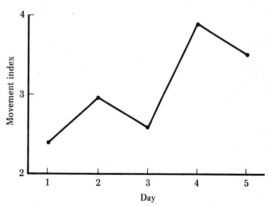

FIGURE 3-4 Increase in mass activity during the first five days of life. (Adapted from W. Kessen, E. J. Williams, and L. P. Williams. Selection and test of response measures in the study of the human newborn. *Child Development*, 1961, **32,** 7–24. Used by permission.)

removed from the infant's body, activity increases. The greatest amount of activity is in the trunk and legs, and the head moves the least. The greatest amount of movement occurs when the infant is awake and crying.

Environmental conditions also influence the amount of neonatal activity. All light is disturbing and becomes increasingly so with added intensity. Sounds likewise produce an increase in the infant's activity.

Reflexes Most of the important reflexes of the body, such as the pupillary reflexes, reflexes of the lips and tongue, sucking, flexion, knee jerk, sneezing, and others, are present at birth. The first reflexes to appear have distinct survival value. The others appear within a few hours or days after birth. With practice, the reflexes become stronger.

Generalized Responses Some of the most common generalized responses which appear during the neonatal period are visual fixation on light; spontaneous eye movements; shedding of tears; feeding responses such as tongue, cheek, and lip movements; sucking of the fingers; yawning; hiccuping; rhythmic mouthing movements; frowning and wrinkling of the brow; turning and lifting the head; turning the trunk; body jerk; hand and arm movements; prancing and kicking; and leg and foot movements. All these are uncoordinated, undefined, and aimless. However, they are important because they are the basis from which skilled, highly coordinated movements will develop as a result of learning.

Vocalization of the Infant

The vocalizations of the newborn infant can be divided into two categories: crying and explosive sounds. During infancy and the early months of babyhood, crying is the dominant form of vocalization. However, from the long-term point of view, explosive sounds are the more important kind of vocalization because speech eventually develops from them.

Crying Normally, crying begins at birth or shortly afterward. Occasionally, in a long and difficult birth, the fetus will cry even while in the uterus. Prebirth cries are rare and dangerous, for there is always the possibility that the fetus will be choked by the fluid in the uterus.

The birth cry is a purely reflex activity which results when air is drawn over the vocal cords, causing them to vibrate. Its purpose is to inflate the lungs, thus making breathing possible, and to supply the blood with sufficient oxygen.

Shortly after birth, the infant's cry shows variations in pitch, intensity, and continuity. Ostwald and Peltzman have reported that the early vocal behavior of newborns is affected by the kind of anesthetic drugs given to their mothers and how quickly the umbilical cord is clamped after delivery (71). Because of the variations that appear in the cries of newborns, it is then possible to tell, within limits, what the infant wants. Ostwald has described the social value of infant crying (70).

The infant cry is the very first piece of human behavior which has social value. It indicates a shift from total silent dependency upon a single being – the pregnant woman —to the possibility of communicating with groups of people in the environment.. . . . Survival of the human species hinges to a certain degree on infants properly emitting and mothers correctly perceiving the cry.

As infants recover from the shock of birth, they are awake more and cry more than they did at first. While crying may occur at any time, it is most frequent and most intense from six in the evening until midnight, as may be seen in Figure 3-5.

Mass activity almost always accompanies the infant's crying. The more vigorous the crying, the more widespread the activity. Bodily activity that accompanies crying is a signal that the infant needs attention. It is thus a form of language.

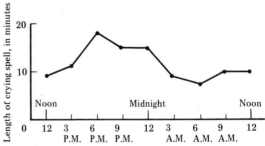

FIGURE 3-5 The characteristic twenty-four-hour pattern of crying during the first ten days of life. (Adapted from J. Bernal. Crying during the first 10 days of life, and maternal responses. *Developmental Medicine & Child Neurology,* 1972, **14,** 362–372. Used by permission.)

Explosive Sounds In addition to crying, the newborn infant occasionally makes explosive sounds similar to heavy breathing. They are uttered without meaning or intent and occur purely by chance whenever the vocal muscles contract. They are commonly called "coos," "gurgles," or "grunts." These are gradually strengthened and develop into babbling, which later develops into speech (70,71).

Sensitivities of the Infant

The best criterion that can be used to determine the presence or absence of sensory capacity is the motor response to sensory stimuli that would normally arise when these sense organs are stimulated. However, it is often difficult to tell whether a motor response is made to a stimulus or whether the reaction is a part of general mass activity. Nor does absence of response necessarily mean absence of sensitivity. It may mean only that the stimulus used was too weak to elicit a response.

An even more serious problem in studying the sensitivities of the infant is finding a suitable method of doing so. To date, for example, no reliable test for color vision in infants has been devised. Consequently, the knowledge of whether infants can see color or whether they are capable of only black-white vision has been determined indirectly from the study of the development of the cones in the eyes of infants who die at birth or shortly afterward. Because the cones are very undeveloped, it is *assumed* that newborn infants are color blind (57).

There is ample evidence that the state of the infant influences reactivity. When infants are dazed by the birth experience, when they are drowsy or asleep, or when they are preoccupied with feeding, they will react differently to sensory stimuli than when their physical condition is better. The intensity of the stimulus likewise has a profound influence on infant's reactivity to different sensory stimuli (5). This explains, in part at least, the variations in the sensory abilities of different infants, just as it explains the variations in the sensory abilities of the same infant from time to time during the infancy period.

While present knowledge of sensory reactions of infants is somewhat limited, it is now believed that infants have a greater capacity for sensory discrimination than formerly was thought. With refinements in experimental techniques and with scientists' increased interest in studying the sensory experiences of newborn infants, more and more knowledge about

this area of development has been accumulating. What is known about the sensory capacities of infants up to the present time is summarized in Box 3-7.

State of Consciousness

Because of the relatively undeveloped state of the most important sense organs—the eyes and the ears—one could not logically expect newborn infants to be keenly aware of what goes on around them. Their awareness is more likely to be "one great blooming, buzzing confusion," as James has described it (48).

As was pointed out earlier, *all* infants experience some disorganization for the first day or two after birth. This would suggest that they are not entirely conscious of what goes on around them. Gradually, as the shock of birth wears off and their sense organs begin to function better, they become more conscious of their surroundings.

The consciousness of the infant is markedly influenced by the depressant effects of drugs used during labor, and these effects persist longer than in adults. Prematurely born infants take longer to adjust to the ordeal of birth than full-term infants whose birth has been difficult. Consequently, it takes them even longer to become conscious of what goes on around them.

Capacity for Learning

To learn, individuals must be aware of what they are expected to do. Furthermore, the brain and nerves must be developed enough to make learning possible. These conditions do not exist in newborn infants, especially during the first few days of postnatal life. Newborn infants are often incapable of even the simplest form of learning—conditioning or learning by association. With the possible exception of the feeding situation, conditioned responses are difficult to elicit. When they do appear, they are unstable and of little permanent value (87,93,97).

Emotions of the Newborn

In view of the incoordination that characterizes the activities of the newborn infant, it would be illogical to expect specific, identifiable emotions to be present at birth. Instead, emotional reactions may be described as states of pleasantness and unpleasantness. The former is characterized by a relaxing of the body and the latter by a tensing of the body.

The outstanding characteristic of the infant's

BOX 3-7

SENSORY CAPACITIES OF INFANTS

Vision

Newborn infants are far from blind but their visual field is only about one-half that of adults because the rods are undeveloped except around the fovea. Color vision is either totally absent or minimal, due to the undeveloped state of the cones. Because of muscle weakness, the infant cannot focus both eyes on the same object simultaneously and, as a result, everything is seen as a blur. There is some evidence that infants respond to differences in brightness but this evidence is inconclusive. The ability to follow a moving object and then move the eyes backward—optic nystagmus—appears during the first week of life for horizontal movements and later for vertical movements.

Hearing

It is believed that hearing is the least developed of all the senses at birth partly because the stoppage of the middle ear with amniotic fluid for several days after birth makes it impossible for sound waves to penetrate to the inner ear where the cells for hearing are located and partly because these cells are only partially developed. Low-frequency tones can be heard sooner than those of high frequency and infants respond sooner to the human voice than to other sounds. Hearing normally improves within the first three or four days after birth, as the amniotic fluid drains from the middle ear. The infant can then determine the direction from which a sound comes and can discriminate pitch and intensity.

Smell

The cells for smell, located in the upper part of the nose, are well developed at birth. That the infant can distinguish odors is shown by crying, head turning, and attempts to withdraw from unpleasant stimuli and by sucking and relaxing the body in response to pleasant stimuli.

Taste

Because taste is markedly influenced by smell and because the cells for taste, located on the surface of the tongue and in the cheek areas, are well developed, the infant's sense of taste is keen. The infant has generally positive reactions—relaxing the body and sucking—in response to sweet stimuli and generally negative responses—crying and squirming—in response to salty, sour, and bitter stimuli.

Organic Sensitivities

Sensitivity to hunger is fully developed at birth and hunger contractions occur within the first day of life. Thirst also appears then.

Skin Sensitivities

The sense organs for touch, pressure, and temperature are well developed at birth and lie close to the surface of the skin. The skin of the newborn's lips is especially sensitive to touch, while the skin on the trunk, thighs, and forearms is less sensitive. Sensitivity to cold is more highly developed than sensitivity to heat. Sensitivity to pain is weak for the first day or two of postnatal life and then improves rapidly. Pain responses develop earlier in the anterior than in the posterior end of the body.

emotional makeup is the complete absence of gradations of responses showing different degrees of intensity. Whatever the stimulus, the resultant emotion is intense and sudden.

Beginnings of Personality

Children are born with characteristic temperamental differences that are reflected in activity rates and sensitivities. It is these differences from which the individual's personality pattern will develop. Individual differences are apparent at birth and are shown in responses to food, in crying, in motor activities, and especially in sleep (28,37).

Personality, like other physical and mental traits, results from the maturation of hereditary traits. Thomas et al. have commented on the importance of the interrelationship between maturation of hereditary traits and experiences in the development of personality thus: "If the two influences are harmonized, one can expect healthy development of the child; if they are dissonant, behavioral problems are almost sure to ensue'' (105).

As early as the neonatal period, a number of factors influence the infant's developing personality. A disturbed prenatal environment, which can result if the mother is subjected to severe or prolonged stress, for example, may cause a modification of the newborn infant's behavior pattern. Such disturbances are especially important if they occur during the latter part of intrauterine life and may cause a state of hyperactivity and irritability in the newborn (92).

There is little evidence that the *birth trauma,* or psychological shock that results when the infant is separated from the mother, has any lasting effects on personality, as Rank claimed (79). There is evidence, however, that infants who are separated from their mothers after birth do not make as good an adjustment to postnatal life as infants who remain with their mothers (114).

There is also evidence that mothers' attitudes toward their infants, which are reflected in their behavior, influence the development of the infants' personalities. For example, if a mother suspects that there is something the matter with the infant, her reaction is likely to be confused and unstable, shifting from day to day or even from hour to hour.

HAZARDS OF INFANCY

In spite of its short duration, infancy is one of the most hazardous periods in the life span. Hazards at this time may be physical, psychological, or both, and they can affect both present and future adjustment. In the case of the plateau in development, the physical adjustments may take place too slowly, thus threatening the infant's life. Psychologically, this plateau is hazardous because it may cause parents to become anxious and fearful about the infant's development, feelings that can persist and lead to overprotectiveness in later years.

Physical Hazards

Some of the physical hazards of infancy are of only temporary significance, while others can affect the individual's entire life pattern. The most serious physical hazards are those relating to an unfavorable prenatal environment, a difficult and complicated birth, a multiple birth, postmaturity, and prematurity, and conditions leading to infant mortality.

Unfavorable Prenatal Environment As a result of unfavorable conditions in the prenatal environment, the infant may have difficulty adjusting to postnatal life. Excessive smoking on the part of the mother, for example, can affect the development of the fetus. Prolonged and intense maternal stress is another important factor, causing the infant to be tense and nervous (60,92).

Difficult and Complicated Birth As was stressed earlier, a difficult or complicated birth frequently results in temporary or permanent brain damage. If the birth requires the use of instruments, as in the case where the fetus is so large that it has to be aided in its passage down the birth canal or if the fetus lies in a foot-first or a transverse position, the chances of brain damage from the use of instruments to aid delivery are always present.

A caesarean section or a precipitate birth, on the other hand, is likely to result in anoxia, a temporary loss of oxygen to the brain. If anoxia is severe, the brain damage will be far greater than if anoxia lasts for only a few seconds. The more complicated the birth and the more damage there is to the brain tissue, the greater the effect on the infant's postnatal life and adjustments.

Severe and persistent brain damage will have adverse effects on all adjustments during infancy and often into childhood or even throughout life. The effects of brain damage are most frequently shown in uncoordinated behavior, hyperactivity, learning difficulties, and emotional problems (72,80).

Multiple Birth Children of multiple birth are usually smaller and weaker than singletons as a result of crowding during the prenatal period, which inhibits fetal movements. These babies tend to be born prematurely, which adds to their adjustment problems.

Postmaturity Postmaturity is hazardous only when the fetus becomes so large that the birth requires the use of instruments or surgery, in which case the hazards are due to the conditions associated with birth rather than to postmaturity per se. One study of babies born more than three weeks after term reported that they experienced neonatal adjustment problems and were also socially maladjusted and required special schooling by the age of seven (92).

Prematurity Prematurity causes more neonatal deaths than any other condition. This will be discussed in more detail in the section on infant mortality. Prematurely born infants are also especially susceptible to brain damage at birth because the skull is not yet developed enough to protect the brain from pressures experienced during birth. Anoxia is another common problem since the premature baby's respiratory mechanism is not fully developed.

The problems of adjustment every newborn infant must face are exaggerated in the prematures. For example, they require nearly three times as much oxygen as full-term infants because their breathing is characterized by jerks and gasps. They often have difficulty in expanding their lungs, and muscular weakness makes breathing difficult (95).

Because sucking and swallowing reflexes are underdeveloped, the premature infant will require special feeding with a medicine dropper or tube. The premature's body temperature is not yet properly controlled, and special equipment is needed to duplicate as nearly as possible the constant temperature of intrauterine life.

Prematurity affects adjustments not only during infancy but also for many years thereafter. Some of these effects are the direct result of the fact that the brain and the nervous system have not had time to develop fully, and others are due to neurological disorders resulting from birth injuries and anoxia, which are especially common among premature infants. Other effects are the indirect result of unfavorable attitudes on the part of significant people in the infant's life.

While few studies of the long-term effects of prematurity have been carried beyond childhood, there is evidence that some of the lag in development experienced by premature children is due to overprotectiveness on the part of parents. Whether this developmental lag persists as the children grow older and parental overprotection is relaxed is still unknown. However, if there has been brain damage, it is likely that such children will continue to lag behind their age group as they grow older. Some of the most common long-term effects of prematurity are listed in Box 3-8.

Another hazard of prematurity that is far too often ignored or overlooked is the staggering cost of keeping the babies alive. A nationwide survey has revealed that the average daily cost in a hospital of premature infants who died was $825 and the total hospital costs $14,236—with a range from $72 to $124,627. For infants who survived, the average daily cost was $450 and the total hospital costs $40,287. However, many survivors cost their parents $88,058. For survivors, the average length of hospitalization was reported to be eighty-nine days. As their conditions improved, the prematures could be transferred from intensive care to regular nurseries, and this lowered the daily and total cost from what it is for those who do not survive. With rising hospital costs, each year the overall cost of prematurity will increase. Add to the charges for special care in hospitals the fees paid to doctors and specialists, the consequences of prematurity as a financial hazard become apparent (76).

Infant Mortality   Unquestionably the most serious of the physical hazards of infancy is infant mortality. The most critical times for death during the period of infancy are the day of birth (when two-thirds of all neonatal deaths occur) and the second and third days after birth. Neonatal deaths have been reported to be most common during the months of June and July but, to date, no satisfactory explanation for this has been given (7). Figure 3-6 shows these peak periods and also the general categories for causes of death during the infancy period.

The causes of infant mortality are numerous and varied. Some neonatal deaths are due to conditions that detrimentally affected the prenatal environment and thus impaired normal development. Some are the result of difficult and complicated births, such as those requiring the use of instruments or caesarean section. Some are the result of brain damage, anoxia, or excessive medication of the mother during labor. And some—but fewer than in the past—are due to unfavorable conditions in the postnatal environment; a radical temperature change may cause pneumonia, for example, or a substitute for the mother's milk may cause diarrhea or other digestive disturbances.

Psychological Hazards

Even though psychological hazards tend to have less effect on the infant's adjustment to postnatal life than physical hazards, they are nonetheless important because of their long-term effects. Psychological scars acquired during infancy can cause the individual lifelong adjustment problems.

Relatively few of the potential psychological hazards of infancy have received more than scanty research attention. However, those that have been stud-

LONG-TERM EFFECTS OF PREMATURITY

Physical Development and Health

Prematures are usually smaller than infants born at full term, and they tend to remain smaller than their age-mates even after the growth spurt of puberty. During the first year of postnatal life they suffer from more illnesses, and more serious illnesses, than full-term infants. The tendency to be "sickly" persists throughout the childhood years. They often have physical defects, especially eye defects resulting from anoxia, a common birth problem of prematures.

Developmental Lag

Until they are two or three years old, prematures often experience a lag in their development as compared with full-term infants. For example, they frequently are slow to sit, stand, walk, and talk.

Sensory Behavior

Prematures are highly sensitive to noises of all types, to colors and to moving objects. Because of this, as they grow older they are more easily distracted than are full-term infants.

Motor Control

Prematures are frequently awkward and have poor posture. Cerebral palsy is also common, a result of brain damage.

Speech Development

Speech is slower to develop in prematures than in those born at full term. Baby talk persists longer, and they have more speech defects, especially stuttering. They also tend to have smaller vocabularies and to make more mistakes in sentence structure.

Intelligence

Prematures as a group have lower IQs than those born at full term, and they have more serious mental defects due to brain injury. Their scores on reading and arithmetic tests tend to be lower, and their grade placement below that which would be normal for their age.

Socialization

Prematures tend to make poorer social adjustments than those born at full term. This persists into adolescence and may be due in part to parental overprotectiveness. They also have more behavior problems at all ages.

Emotional Behavior

Some prematures tend to be emotionally apathetic, but more often they are petulant, irascible, and negativistic. Emotional disorders are common, as are nervous traits, such as irritability, temper outbursts, and thumb sucking.

Deviant Behavior

Infants who have suffered brain damage at birth show, as they grow older, such deviant behavior as accident-proneness, nervous mannerisms, and hyperkinetic, disorganized behavior. If the brain damage is slight and transitory, they may show deviant behavior, especially immature and egocentric behavior. This is due mainly to the overprotectiveness they have been subjected to by anxious parents.

---

ied, even though only superficially, are worth serious consideration.

Traditional Beliefs about Birth There are many traditional beliefs about the effects birth has on the development of children. Difficult births, for example, are believed to result in "difficult children"—those who are hard to handle and whose behavior tends to deviate from that of children born with a minimum of difficulty. For centuries it has been believed that chil-

dren of multiple birth have to be different and inferior to singletons and that prematures are doomed to be physical and mental weaklings.

One of the traditional beliefs about birth that has received considerable scientific attention concerns the effect of time of birth on the future development of the child. While there is little scientific evidence to substantiate the belief that there is a "best time" to be born, there is evidence that, because the mother's health plays an extremely important role

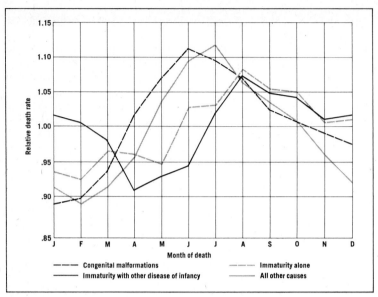

FIGURE 3-6 Relative infant death rate for broad causes of death by month. (Adapted from U.S. Department of Health, Education, and Welfare. Vital Statistics of the United States, 1970.)

during the prenatal period, any unfavorable condition during her pregnancy may and often does prove to be hazardous to her unborn child.

The infant who is conceived during the winter months reaches the critical time in development—the first trimester of the prenatal period—when childhood diseases are most prevalent. If she has not already had it, the mother-to-be may, for example, contract rubella.

A baby who is born within a year after the birth of a sibling is subject to a less favorable prenatal environment than would have been the case had the interval between births been longer. The mother has not had time to recover fully from the previous birth, and such an infant tends to be lethargic at birth which affects postnatal adjustments. Throughout the early years of life, babies born soon after the birth of an older sibling are likely to receive less of their much-needed attention and stimulation because of the other demands on the mother's time (50,108).

There is no reliable evidence, to date, that individuals born at one season of the year or on one day of the week are brighter and achieve greater success in life than those born at other times. There is also no evidence that being born during the so-called "cheerful months" of the year, in the spring or summer, will result in extroverted personality patterns while being born during the so-called "gloomy months," in the fall or winter, will result in introverted personality patterns (7,45,68).

Helplessness To some parents, the helplessness of the newborn infant is appealing while, to most, it is frightening. So long as the infants are in the hospital and under the care of doctors and nurses, parents are not too concerned about their helplessness. However, when they take them home from the hospital and assume the responsibility for their care, infantile helplessness becomes a serious psychological hazard. The reason for this is that parents wonder if they are capable of assuming the care of their newborn babies and this, in turn, makes them nervous and anxious.

Even parents who have had courses in the hospital clinics in the care of babies or who have had some experience in taking care of their babies through the rooming-in plan, often feel insecure and inadequate when they assume full responsibility. Anxiety and insecurity are quickly transmitted to the infants through the way mothers handle them and this affects their postnatal adjustments.

The helplessness of the newborn is more of a psychological hazard in the case of firstborns than of later-born children. By the time parents have had several children, they accept the helplessness of the newborn in a more relaxed way and are not so likely to be disturbed by it as they are for the firstborn infant. Only if the helplessness comes from some unusual condition or is more pronounced than is normal are parents then likely to be concerned. If, for example, a third or fourth child is more helpless than earlier-born siblings because of prematurity, multiple birth, injury during the birth process, or any other cause, parents tend to worry, especially if the infant must have special nursing care in the hospital or remain there longer than the usual time.

Individuality of the Infant To most adults, being different is interpreted as being inferior. When parents steep themselves in child-care literature before the arrival of their first child, or when they set up norms of behavior based on what their earlier-born children did at different ages, they tend to judge a newborn infant in these terms.

If parents remember their earlier-born children as crying very little at night after being taken home from the hospital or having little difficulty in nursing or keeping down their nourishment, they will be concerned if the new infant experiences feeding difficulties or cries every night without apparent reason.

Parental concern is then expressed in their treatment of the infant. This, in turn, affects the infant's adjustments to postnatal life and tends to increase the severity of the problems that concerned the parents. Under such conditions, the infant's individuality becomes a psychological hazard which, unless parents accept individuality as normal, will play havoc with the adjustments made not only during infancy but also as childhood progresses.

Developmental Lag Some infants lag behind the norm in their development during the infancy period. Instead of regaining lost birth weight by the end of the first week or sooner, they may continue to lose weight or rest on a plateau with no improvement at all. Even worse, they may show such a pronounced lag that instead of being allowed to go home with their parents three to four days after birth, as is usual, they are kept

in the hospital and may even have to have special nursing care.

The infants most likely to show developmental lag are those born prematurely or those who were injured at birth. Even a healthy, full-term infant may show developmental lag should there be some minor and temporary illness or should the mother's milk be inadequate and the formula substituted not be suited to the infant's needs.

Regardless of the cause of developmental lag, it is always a source of concern to parents and, as such, affects the way they handle the infant's needs. An anxious, concerned mother will transmit her anxiety by the way she takes care of the infant. Feeling that the infant is too delicate to be handled any more than is absolutely essential, the mother will not stimulate the infant by talking to it, by picking it up and rocking it, or by exercising the arms and legs regularly at different times during the day. Lack of stimulation intensifies the developmental lag and this, in turn, intensifies the unfavorable parental attitudes. Thus a vicious circle is set in motion and the infant becomes the innocent victim.

Plateau in Development Even though a plateau in development is normal immediately after birth, many first-time parents are unaware of this. As a result, they are concerned when their baby seems to be making no progress. Their concern is heightened if the baby regresses from the plateau and has difficulty in keeping down what little nourishment is taken, thus dropping below birth weight.

Should the plateau last only a few days, parental concern wanes and gives way to confidence that all is well. However, it often leaves some psychological obstacles, three of which are common and serious. First, it makes parents believe their infant is delicate and, as a result, should have extra care and attention. This encourages overprotectiveness which, once developed, often persists as a habit. Second, it weakens parents' confidence in their ability to assume full care of the infant after leaving the hospital. If by then the infant has not regained lost birth weight, this lack of confidence is greatly increased. And third, parents feel that they must handle the infant as little as possible and with great care to prevent further loss of weight or failure to gain weight. As a result, they deprive the infant of one of the essentials of development, stimulation of the different areas of the body.

Lack of Stimulation There is increasing scientific evidence that newborn infants need stimulation of different areas of their bodies and of different sense organs if they are to develop as they should. This, of course, is not a "new-fangled idea" because, in the days when babies were born at home, they were picked up, rocked, talked to, and sung to as part of their routine care.

Because it is customary today for babies to be born in hospitals, they are often deprived of the stimulation received by babies born at home or even by those whose mothers have them in their hospital rooms under the rooming-in plan. And, until very recently, premature infants were kept in isolettes or incubators where they received only the minimum of stimulation.

Today there is a gradual increase in the trend to stimulate infants from the time they are born instead of keeping them as quiet as possible. While yet unproved, there is a strong belief that early stimulation helps infants to overcome the dazed state characteristic of the first few days after birth and to remain on a plateau in development for a shorter time than they formerly did. In addition, there is growing evidence that being talked to and having moving objects to look at helps to overcome some of the developmental lag in vision and hearing.

New-Parent Blues States of depression, often called "new-parent blues," are almot universal among new parents. These depressive states tend to be more pronounced in mothers than in fathers and in parents of first babies than in those who have already had one or more children.

In new mothers, depressive states are partly physical and partly psychological. The glandular changes accompanying pregnancy and childbirth, fatigue from labor and childbirth, and the generally weakened condition that persists even after normal childbirth all contribute to maternal states of depression. Also there is concern about the care of a helpless infant, the added expenses, and the changes in the pattern of life. To these conditions may be added the letdown a new mother experiences on going home—after being cared for in the hospital and being the center of attention of family and friends—to assume full the care of the infant and, in addition, to look after the home and older children as well.

While new fathers do not have the glandular changes that contribute to depressive states in mothers, they often experience a letdown after the worry and strain about the welfare of their wives, especially during the last stages of pregnancy and childbirth. The more difficult the pregnancy and the childbirth, the more concern men feel and the more letdown they experience when the baby is born and all is well.

For most fathers, new-parent blues are more psychological than physiological. They are often concerned about the extra expenses they must meet, especially if the mother must give up her job. Many men also are concerned about how the pattern of their lives will change as a result of parenthood and what effect this will have on their marital relationship.

New-parent blues can and often do play havoc with the infant's adjustments to postnatal life. The new baby senses the tensions of the parents, especially of the mother, and this makes it nervous and prone to crying. Many infants cry more after they get home than they did in the hospital. Without question, one of the causes of this is new-parent blues.

Unfavorable Attitudes on the Part of Significant People Even though parents, siblings, and grandparents may have favorable attitudes toward the unborn baby during most of the pregnancy, their feelings may change as the birth draws nearer and they become increasingly aware of the new responsibilities they will have to face.

There are a number of other reasons for the development of unfavorable attitudes toward the infant. Disappointment about the infant's sex and its appearance, its excessive crying and difficulties in taking nourishment, and its extreme helplessness which is often frightening to new parents are just a few of the many reasons. Unfavorable attitudes are often intensified by birth complications, the unexpected arrival of twins or triplets, and the new-parent blues described above.

The mother's attitudes are especially important because they can directly affect the care the baby receives. Moss has pointed out, "The amount of time the infant is awake and crying is a potent modifier of maternal treatment since wakefulness and crying are likely to lead to greater maternal surveillance and contact" (65). Thus the infant's behavior influences the mother's behavior; if this is unfavorable to begin with, it will become increasingly so, with the result that the infant's adjustment problems are worsened.

Attitudes of the father, siblings, grandparents,

Attitudes of parents and siblings toward the infant usually persist as the child grows older. So it is important that the attitudes of significant persons be favorable. (Photo by Erika Stone.)

and other relatives are important not so much for their immediate effects but rather because they are likely to persist beyond the period of infancy when their contacts with the child will increase. This is especially true of the father and siblings.

While any newborn infant may be regarded unfavorably by significant people, the most usual targets for such attitudes are firstborns, those who are damaged at birth, those who are born prematurely, and those of multiple birth. Parents of later-born children are more realistic in their hopes and expectations, and they accept the infant more philosophically. In the case of prematures and those of multiple birth, traditional beliefs are apt to affect attitudes unfavorably.

Names Hartman et al. have emphasized the importance of names given to children (44):

A child's name, like his somatotype, is generally a settled affair when his first breath is drawn, and his future personality must then grow within its shadow. A powerful mesomorphic boy must experience a different world from his puny counterpart; and, similarly, a boy who answers to a unique, peculiar, or feminine name may well have experiences and feelings in growing up that are quite unknown to John or William. We would expect these childhood experiences to be reflected in the subsequent personality. It is plausible, and confirmed by clinic experience, to assume also that some individuals are seriously affected in their adjustment as a result of a peculiar name.

Because it is legally established shortly after birth, a child's name can be classified as one of the important *potential* psychological hazards of infancy. Their names do not become real hazards until children are old enough to respond to how people outside the family react to them (usually during the preschool years). Names become real psychological hazards only if they cause the children embarrassment—or sometimes even humiliation—if their friends think their names are "funny" or regard them as sex-inappropriate.

While it is impossible to predict during infancy how individuals will react to their names as they grow older, certain kinds of names are almost universally hazardous in the American culture of today. The most common of these are listed in Box 3-9.

Because of the potential psychological damage that the infant's name can cause, Allen et al. were correct in saying that "an unfortunate selection may doom him to recurring embarrassment or even unhappiness" (4). McDavid and Harari have warned, a

BOX 3-9

NAMES THAT
ARE POTENTIAL
PSYCHOLOGICAL HAZARDS

- Names that are so common that the individual feels a lack of personal identity
- Names that are so unusual that the individual feels conspicuous
- Names that are used for both sexes and thus are sex-inappropriate
- Names that are associated with comic-strip characters or unpopular characters in television series
- Names that identify the individual with a racial, religious, or ethnic group against which there is prejudice
- Names that are difficult to pronounce or spell
- Names that lend themselves to embarrassing nicknames
- Old-fashioned names

"parent might appropriately think twice before naming his offspring for Greataunt Sophronia" (58).

Chapter Highlights

1. The period of infancy covers approximately the first two weeks of life—the time needed for the newborn to adjust to the new environment outside its mother's body. This period is usually divided into two subdivisions. One is called the *period* of the *partunate,* which lasts from the time the fetus emerges from the mother's body until the umbilical cord has been cut and tied, and the second is called the *period of the neonate,* which lasts from the cutting and tying of the cord until approximately the end of the second week of life.
2. There are five important characteristics of infancy. This is the shortest of all developmental periods; it is a time of radical adjustment, a plateau in development, a preview of later development, and a hazardous period.
3. The newborn infant must make four major adjustments to postnatal life and must make them quickly if it is to survive. These adjustments are to temperature changes, to sucking and swallowing, to breathing, and to elimination.
4. The difficulty of adjustment to postnatal life is shown by loss of weight, disorganized behavior, and infant mortality.

5. The most important conditions influencing the infant's adjustment to postnatal life are prenatal environment, length of the gestation period, kind of birth (normal or otherwise), postnatal care, and parental attitudes.
6. While each newborn infant is different, they all have certain common characteristics such as size, body proportions, lack of body homeostasis, two types of activity, mass and reflex, inability to communicate except through crying, undeveloped sensitivities except for smell and taste, a blurred state of consciousness, a limited capacity for learning, undeveloped emotions, and the beginning of individuality.
7. An unfavorable prenatal environment is as hazardous to normal development in postnatal life as is a difficult and complicated birth.
8. Postmaturity is less hazardous than prematurity because infants born prematurely are not as able to adjust to the radical changes of postnatal life.
9. Infant mortality is an especially serious hazard on the day of birth and on the second and third days after birth.
10. The long-term effects of prematurity are normally less than popularly believed if premature infants are given environmental stimulation and opportunities to overcome the developmental lag that normally accompanies their early birth.
11. Traditional beliefs about birth are serious psychological hazards because they have a profound influence on the way people treat infants.
12. The helplessness of the infant, the plateau in development, and developmental lag—all of which are common among newborn infants—influence the attitudes of significant people and their treatment of the infant.
13. Individuality in infancy can be a serious psychological hazard because most people interpret individuality to mean that the infant is not normal.
14. "New parent blues" and other unfavorable attitudes toward the newborn infant are serious psychological hazards because they are reflected in the way parents treat the infant.
15. Names given to infants are *potential* hazards to good personal and social adjustments because, as they grow older, children may dislike and be embarrassed by their names.

Bibliography

1. Albott, W. L., and J. L. Bruning. Given names: A neglected social variable. *Psychological Record,* 1970, **20,** 527–533.
2. Aleksandrowicz, M. K. The effect of pain-relieving drugs admin-

istered during labor and delivery on the behavior of the newborn: A review. *Merrill-Palmer Quarterly*, 1974, **20**, 121–141.

3. Aleksandrowicz, M. K., and D. R. Aleksandrowicz. "Obstetrical pain-relieving drugs as predictors of infant behavior variability": A reply to Federman and Yang's critique. *Child Development*, 1976, **47**, 297–298.

4. Allen, L., L. Brow, L. Dickinson, and K. C. Pratt. The relation of first-name preference to the frequency in the culture. *Journal of Social Psychology*, 1941, **14**, 279–293.

5. Ashton, R. The influence of state and prandial condition upon the reactivity of the newborn to auditory stimulation. *Journal of Experimental Child Psychology*, 1973, **15**, 315–337.

6. Bagg, C. E., and T. G. Crookes. The responses of neonates to noise, in relation to the personalities of their parents. *Developmental Medicine & Child Neurology*, 1975, **17**, 732–735.

7. Bailar, J., and J. Gurian. The medical significance of date of birth. *Eugenics Quarterly*, 1967, **14**, 89–102.

8. Baird, D. Perinatal mortality. *Developmental Medicine & Child Neurology*, 1970, **12**, 368–369.

9. Bakeman, R., and J. V. Brown. Behavioral dialogues: An approach to the assessment of mother-infant interaction. *Child Development*, 1977, **48**, 195–203.

10. Bell, R. Q., G. M. Weller, and M. F. Waldrop. Newborn and preschooler: Organization of behavior and relations between periods. *Monographs of the Society for Research in Child Development*, 1971, **36**(1 and 2).

11. Bowes, W. A., Y. Brackbill, E. Conway, and A. Steinschneider. The effects of obstetrical medication on fetus and infant. *Monographs of the Society for Research in Child Development*, 1970, **35**(4).

12. Burke, P. M. Swallowing and the organization of sucking in the human newborn. *Child Development*, 1977, **48**, 523–531.

13. Burnham, D. Rise in birth defects laid to job hazards. *The New York Times*, March 14, 1976.

14. Busse, T. V., and J. Helfrich. Changes in first-name popularity across grades. *Journal of Psychology*, 1975, **89**, 281–283.

15. Busse, T. V., and L. Seraydarian. Desirability of first names, ethnicity, and parental education. *Psychological Reports*, 1977, **40**, 739–742.

16. Caputo, D. V., and W. Mandell. Consequences of low birth weight. *Developmental Psychology*, 1970, **3**, 363–383.

17. Caputo, D. V., H. B. Taub, K. M. Goldstein, N. Smith, J. D. Daladck, J. P. Pursner, and R. M. Silberstein. An evaluation of various parameters of maturity at birth as predictors of development at one year of life. *Perceptual & Motor Skills*, 1974, **39**, 631–652.

18. Condon, W. S., and L. W. Sander. Neonate movement as synchronized with adult speech: Interactional participation and language acquisition. *Science*, 1974, **183**, 99–101.

19. Cornell, E. H., and A. W. Gottfried. Intervention with premature human infants. *Child Development*, 1976, **47**, 32–39.

20. Coursin, D. B. Nutrition and brain development in infants. *Merrill-Palmer Quarterly*, 1972, **18**, 177–202.

21. Cronenwett, L. R., and L. L. Newmark. Fathers' responses to childbirth. *Nursing Research*, 1974, **23**, 210–217.

22. Cruise, M. O. A longitudinal study of the growth of low-birth-weight infants: Velocity and distance growth, birth to 3 years. *Pediatrics*, 1973, **51**, 620–628.

23. Darden, D. K., and I. E. Robinson. Mulitdimensional scaling of men's first names: A sociolinguistic approach. *Sociometry*, 1976, **39**, 422–431.

24. Davies, P. A. Low-birth-weight infants: Neurological sequelae and later intelligence. *British Medical Bulletin*, 1975, **31**, 85–91.

25. Davies, P. A., and J. P. M. Tizard. Very low-birth-weight and subsequent neurological defect (with special reference to spastic diplegia). *Developmental Medicine & Child Neurology*, 1975, **17**, 3–17.

26. Desor, J. A., O. Maller, and R. E. Turner. Taste in acceptance of sugars by human infants. *Journal of Comparative & Physiological Psychology*, 1973, **84**, 496–501.

27. De Souza, S. W., R. J. John, B. Richards, and R. D. G. Milner. Fetal distress and birth scores in newborn infants. *Archives of Disease in Childhood*, 1975, **50**, 920–926.

28. Dittrichová, J., K. Paul, and J. Vondráček. Individual differences in infants' sleep. *Developmental Medicine & Child Neurology*, 1976, **18**, 182–188.

29. Eastman, N. J., and L. M. Hellman. *Williams obstetrics*. 13th ed. New York: Appleton-Century-Crofts, 1966.

30. Emde, R. N., T. J. Gaensbaner, and B. H. Suzuki. Quiet sleep and indices of maturation in the newborn. *Perceptual & Motor Skills*, 1973, **36**, 633–634.

31. Engen, T., L. P. Lipsitt, and M. B. Peck. Ability of newborn infants to discriminate sapid substances. *Developmental Psychology*, 1974, **10**, 741–744.

32. Fantz, R. L., and S. B. Miranda. Newborn infant attention to form of contour. *Child Development*, 1975, **46**, 224–228.

33. Federman, E. J., and R. K. Yang. A critique of "obstetrical pain-relieving drugs as predictors of infant behavior variability." *Child Development*, 1976, **47**, 294–296.

34. Fitzgerald, H. E., and S. W. Porges. A decade of infant conditioning and learning research. *Merrill-Palmer Quarterly*, 1971, **17**, 79–119.

35. Flaste, R. When that baby comes, what's in a name? *The New York Times*, Feb. 4, 1977.

36. Francis-Williams, J., and P. A. Davies. Very low-birth-weight and later intelligence. *Developmental Medicine & Child Neurology*, 1974, **16**, 709–728.

37. Gardner, R. W. Individuality in development. In W. R. Looft (Ed.). *Developmental psychology: A book of readings*. Hinsdale, Ill.: Dryden Press, 1972, Pp. 402–414.

38. Goggin, J. E., G. E. Holmes, K. Hassanein, and S. B. Lansky. Observations of postnatal development activity in infants with fetal malnutrition. *Journal of Genetic Psychology*, 1977, **132**, 247–253.

39. Gottfried, A. W. Intellectual consequences of perinatal anoxia. *Psychological Bulletin*, 1973, **80**, 231–242.

40. Greenberg, M., and N. Morris. Engrossment: The newborn's impact upon the father. *American Journal of Orthopsychiatry*, 1974, **44**, 520–531.

41. Greenberg, M., I. Rosenberg, and J. Lind. First mother's rooming-in with their newborns: Its impact upon the mother. *American Journal of Orthopsychiatry*, 1973, **43**, 783–788.

42. Harari, H., and J. W. McDavid. Name stereotypes and teachers' expectations. *Journal of Educational Psychology*, 1973, **65**, 222–225.

43. Hardy, J. B. Birth weight and subsequent physical and intellectual development. *New England Journal of Medicine*, 1973, **289**, 973–974.

44. Hartman, A. A., R. C. Nicolay, and J. Hurley. Unique personal names as a social adjustment factor. *Journal of Social Psychology*, 1968, **75**, 107–110.

45. Hillman, R. W., P. Slater, and M. J. Nelson. Season of birth, parental age, menarchial age, and body form: Some inter-relationships in young women. *Human Biology,* 1970, **42,** 570–580.

46. Horn, J. A rose is a rose is a rosie. *Psychology Today,* 1975, **8**(9), 22–24.

47. Hunt, J. V., and L. Rhodes. Mental development of preterm infants during the first year. *Child Development,* 1977, **48,** 204–210.

48. James, W. *The principles of psychology.* New York: Holt, 1890.

49. Jeffcoate, T. N. A. Prolonged labor. *The Lancet,* 1961, **281,** Pt. 2, 61–67.

50. Karabenick, S. A. On the relationship between personality and birth order. *Psychological Reports,* 1971, **28,** 258.

51. Kearsley, R. B. The newborn's response to auditory stimuli: A demonstration of orienting and defensive behavior. *Child Development,* 1973, **44,** 582–590.

52. Kennell, J. H., R. Jerauld, H. Wolfe, D. Chester, N. G. Kreger, W. McAlpine, M. Steffa, and M. H. Klaus. Maternal behavior one year after early and extended postpartum contact. *Developmental Medicine & Child Neurology,* 1974, **16,** 172–179.

53. Kraemer, H. C., A. F. Korner, and E. B. Thoman. Methodological considerations in evaluating the influence of drugs used during labor and delivery on behavior of the newborn. *Developmental Psychology,* 1972, **6,** 128–134.

54. Lubchenco, L. O., D. T. Searls, and J. V. Brazie. Neonatal mortality rate: Relationship to birth weight and gestational age. *Journal of Pediatrics,* 1972, **81,** 814–822.

55. Marcus, M. Caressing and cuddling helps a baby grow. *Psychology Today,* 1976, **9**(8), 101.

56. Marcus, M. G. The power of a name. *Psychology Today,* 1976, **10**(3), 75–76, 108.

57. Maurer, D. M., and C. E. Maurer. Newborn babies see better than you think. *Psychology Today,* 1976, **10**(3), 85–88.

58. McDavid, J. W., and H. Harari. Stereotyping of names and popularity in grade-school children. *Child Development,* 1966, **37,** 453–459.

59. Mendelson, M. J., and M. M. Haith. The relation between audition and vision in the human newborn. *Monographs of the Society for Research in Child Development,* 1976, **41**(4).

60. Meredith, H. V. Somatic changes during prenatal life. *Child Development,* 1975, **46,** 603–610.

61. Michaelis, R., A. R. Parmelee, E. Stern, and A. Haber. Activity states in premature and term infants. *Developmental Psychobiology,* 1973, **6,** 209–215.

62. Miller, V. L. *The miracle of growth.* Urbana, Ill.: University of Illinois Press, 1950.

63. Montagu, A. *Prenatal influences.* Springfield, Ill.: Charles C Thomas, 1962.

64. Montagu, A. *The direction of human development.* (Rev. ed.) New York: Hawthorn, 1970.

65. Moss, H. A. Methodological issues in studying mother-infant interaction. *American Journal of Orthopsychiatry,* 1965, **35,** 482–486.

66. Natelson, S. E., and M. P. Sayers. The fate of children sustaining severe head trauma during birth. *Pediatrics,* 1973, **51,** 169–174.

67. Nowlis, G. H., and W. Kessen. Human newborns differentiate differing concentrations of sucrose and glucose. *Science,* 1976, **191,** 865–866.

68. Orme, J. E. Ability and season of birth. *British Journal of Psychology,* 1965, **56,** 471–475.

69. Osofsky, J. D., and B. Danzger. Relationships between neonatal characteristics and mother-infant interaction. *Developmental Psychology,* 1974, **10,** 124–130.

70. Ostwald, P. F. The sounds of infancy. *Developmental Medicine & Child Neurology,* 1972, **14,** 350–361.

71. Ostwald, P. F., and P. Peltzman. The cry of the human infant. *Scientific American,* 1974, **230**(3), 84–90.

72. Page, E. W., C. A. Villee, and D. B. Villee. *Human reproduction: The core content of obstetrics, gynecology, and perinatal medicine.* Philadelphia: Saunders, 1972.

73. Palti, H., and B. Adler. Anthrometric measurements of the newborn, sex differences, and correlations between measurements. *Human Biology,* 1975, **47,** 523–530.

74. Parmelee, A. H., C. B. Kopp, and M. Sigman. Selection of developmental assessment techniques for infants at risk. *Merrill-Palmer Quarterly,* 1976, **22,** 177–199.

75. Peoples, D. R., and D. Y. Teller. Color vision and brightness discrimination in two-month-old human infants. *Science,* 1975, **189,** 1102–1103.

76. Pomerance, J. J., C. Tukrainski, T. Ukra, D. H. Henderson, A. H. Nash, and J. L. Meredith. Cost of living for infants weighing 1,000 grams or less at birth. *Pediatrics,* 1978, **61,** 908–910.

77. Post, P. W., A. N. Krauss, S. Waldman, and P. A. M. Auld. Skin reflectance of newborn infants from 25 to 44 weeks gestational age. *Human Biology,* 1976, **48,** 541–557.

78. Powell, L. F. The effect of extra stimulation and maternal involvement on the development of low-birth-weight infants and on maternal behavior. *Child Development,* 1974, **45,** 106–113.

79. Rank, O. *The trauma of birth.* New York: Harcourt, Brace, 1929.

80. Reid, D. E., K. J. Ryan, and K. Benirschke (Eds.). *Principles and management of human reproduction.* Philadelphia: Saunders, 1972.

81. Rice, R. D. Neurophysiological development in premature infants following stimulation. *Developmental Psychology,* 1977, **13,** 69–70.

82. Rich, E. C., R. E. Marshall, and J. J. Volpe. The normal neonatal response to pin-prick. *Developmental Medicine & Child Neurology,* 1974, **16,** 432–434.

83. Richman, N. Individual differences at birth. *Developmental Medicine & Child Neurology,* 1972, **14,** 400–402.

84. Rosenblith, J. F. Relations between neonatal behaviors and those at eight months. *Developmental Psychology,* 1974, **10,** 779–792.

85. Rubin, R. A., C. Rosenblatt, and B. Balow. Psychological and educational sequelae of prematurity. *Pediatrics,* 1973, **52,** 352–363.

86. Sagi, A., and M. L. Hoffman. Empathic distress in the newborn. *Developmental Psychology,* 1976, **12,** 175–176.

87. Sameroff, A. J. Can conditioned responses be established in the newborn infant: 1971? *Developmental Psychology,* 1971, **5,** 1–12.

88. Scarr-Salapatek, S., and M. L. Williams. The effects of early stimulation on low-birth-weight infants. *Child Development,* 1973, **44,** 94–101.

89. Schmidt, K. The effect of continuous stimulation on behavioral sleep in infants. *Merrill-Palmer Quarterly,* 1975, **21,** 77–88.

90. Schonberg, W. B., and D. M. Murphy. The relationship between the uniqueness of a given name and personality. *Journal of Social Psychology*, 1974, **93**, 147–148.

91. Schwartz, P. Birth injuries of the newborn. *Archives of Pediatrics*, 1956, **73**, 429–450.

92. Sontag, L. W. Implications of infant behavior and environment for adult personalities. *Annals of the New York Academy of Sciences*, 1966, **132**, 782–786.

93. Sostek, A. M., A. J. Sameroff, and A. J. Sostek. Evidence for the unconditionability of the Babkin reflex in newborns. *Child Development*, 1972, **43**, 509–519.

94. Spezzano, C., and J. Waterman. The first day of life. *Psychology Today*, 1977, **11**(7), 110–116.

95. Stanley, F. J., and D. Alberman. Infants of very low birth weight: 1. Perinatal factors affecting survival. *Developmental Medicine & Child Neurology*, 1978, **20**, 300–312.

96. St. Clair, K. L. Neonatal assessment procedures: A historical review. *Child Development*, 1978, **49**, 280–292.

97. Stone, L. J., H. T. Smith, and L. B. Murphy (Eds.). *The competent infant: Research and commentary.* New York: Basic, 1973.

98. Stratton, P. M., and K. Connolly. Discrimination by newborns of the intensity, frequency, and temporal characteristics of auditory stimuli. *British Journal of Psychology*, 1973, **64**, 219–232.

99. Tanner, J. M. *Fetus into man: Physical growth from conception to maturity.* Cambridge, Mass.: Harvard University Press, 1978.

100. Tantermannova, M. Smiling in infants. *Child Development*, 1973, **44**, 701–704.

101. Taub, H. B., D. V. Caputo, and K. M. Goldstein. Toward a modification of the indices of neonatal prematurity. *Peceptual & Motor Skills*, 1975, **40**, 43–48.

102. Taub, H. B., K. M. Goldstein, and D. V. Caputo. Indices of neonatal prematurity as discriminators of development in early childhood. *Child Development*, 1977, **48**, 797–805.

103. Thoman, E. B. Sleep and wake behaviors in neonates: Consistencies and consequences. *Merrill-Palmer Quarterly*, 1975, **21**, 295–315.

104. Thoman, E. B., A. F. Korner, and H. V. Kraemer. Individual consistency in behavioral states in neonates. *Developmental Psychology*, 1976, **9**, 271–283.

105. Thomas, A., S. Chess, and H. G. Birch. The origin of personality. *Scientific American*, 1970, **223**(2), 102–109.

106. Tilford, J. A. The relationship between gestational age and adaptive behavior. *Merrill-Palmer Quarterly*, 1976, **22**, 319–326.

107. Turkewitz, G., and S. Creighton. Changes in lateral differentiation of head posture in the human neonate. *Development Psychobiology*, 1975, **8**, 85–89.

108. Waldrop, M. F., and R. Q. Bell. Effects of family size and density on newborn characteristics. *American Journal of Orthopsychiatry*, 1966, **36**, 544–550.

109. Wilder, C. N., and R. J. Baken. Some developmental aspects of infant cry. *Journal of Genetic Psychology*, 1978, **132**, 225–230.

110. Wilson, G. S., M. M. Desmond, and W. M. Verniaud. Early development of infants of herion-addicted mothers. *American Journal of Diseases of Children*, 1973, **126**, 457–462.

111. Yang, R. K., and T. C. Douthitt. Newborn responses to threshold tactile stimulation. *Child Development*, 1974, **45**, 237–242.

112. Yang, R. K., E. J. Federman, and T. C. Douthitt. The characterization of neonatal behavior: A dimensional analysis. *Developmental Psychology*, 1976, **12**, 204–210.

113. Yang, R. K., A. R. Zweig, T. C. Douthitt, and E. J. Federman. Successive relationships between maternal attitudes during pregnancy, analgesic medication during labor and delivery, and newborn behavior. *Developmental Psychology*, 1976, **12**, 6–14.

114. Yarrow, L. J. Research in dimensions of early maternal care. *Merrill-Palmer Quarterly*, 1963, **9**, 101–114.

115. Zelazo, P. R., N. A. Zelazo, and S. Kolb. "Walking" in the newborn. *Science*, 1972, **176**, 314–315.

116. Zweigenhaft, R. L. The other side of unusual first names. *Journal of Social Psychology*, 1977, **103**, 291–302.

CHAPTER FOUR
BABYHOOD

After reading this chapter, you should be able to:

- Define the labels "baby" and "toddler" and understand the characteristics of the babyhood period.
- List the developmental tasks of babyhood and recognize the seriousness of not mastering these tasks when the social group expects them to be mastered.
- Describe the physical, motor, speech, emotional, social, and play developments during babyhood.
- Realize how understanding develops and how this influences moral development and sex-role typing.
- Understand the importance of family relationships to babies' developing self-concepts and to their happiness.
- Recognize the common physical hazards of babyhood and explain what is responsible for them.
- Understand why each area of development can be psychologically hazardous and what the common hazards in each area are.
- Discuss what makes the second year of babyhood less happy than the first.

Babyhood occupies the first two years of life following the brief two-week period of infancy. While babyhood is often referred to as infancy, the label *babyhood* will be used in this book to distinguish it from the extreme helplessness characteristic of the immediate postnatal period.

During the babyhood months, there is a gradual but pronounced decrease in helplessness. This does not mean that helplessness quickly disappears and is replaced by independence. Instead, it means that every day, week, and month the individual becomes more independent so that, when babyhood ends with the second birthday, the individual is a quite different person than when babyhood began.

Because "baby" suggests to many people a helpless individual, it is becoming increasingly common to apply the label *toddler* to the individual during the second year of babyhood. A toddler is a baby who has achieved enough body control to be relatively independent. See Figure 4-1.

CHARACTERISTICS OF BABYHOOD

Certain characteristics of babyhood, while similar to characteristics of other periods in the life span, are of particular importance during the babyhood years. They distinguish babyhood from the periods preceding it and those that follow it. Following are the most important characteristics.

Babyhood is the True Foundation Age

While the whole of childhood, but especially the early years, are generally regarded as the *foundation age*, babyhood is the true foundation period of life because, at this time, many behavior patterns, many attitudes, and many patterns of emotional expression are being established.

Early scientific interest in the importance of these foundations came from the work of Freud, who maintained that personality maladjustments in adulthood had their origins in unfavorable childhood experiences (44). Erikson also contended that "childhood is the scene of man's beginning as man, the place where our particular virtues and vices slowly but clearly develop and make themselves felt." According to Erickson, how babies are treated will determine whether they will develop "basic trust" or "basic distrust"—viewing the world as safe, reliable,

and nurturing or as full of threat, unpredictability, and treachery (38). White contends that the first two years are critical in setting the pattern for personal and social adjustments. As he has pointed out, "Providing a rich social life for a twelve- to fifteen-month-old child is the best thing you can do to guarantee a good mind" (117).

There are four reasons why foundations laid during the babyhood years are important. First, contrary to tradition, children do not outgrow undesirable traits as they grow older. Instead, patterns established early in life persist regardless of whether they are good or bad, harmful or beneficial. Second, if an undesirable pattern of behavior or unfavorable beliefs and attitudes have started to develop, the sooner they can be corrected the easier it will be for the child. Third, because early foundations quickly develop into habits through repetition, they will have a lifelong influence on a child's personal and social adjustments. And, fourth, because learning and experience play dominant roles in development, they can be directed and controlled so that the development will be along lines that will make good personal and social adjustments possible.

Babyhood Is an Age of Rapid Growth and Change

Babies grow rapidly, both physically and psychologically. With this rapid growth comes a change not only in appearance but also in capacities. Babies gradually become less top-heavy than they were at birth and their limbs develop in better proportion to the large head. Changes in body proportions are accompanied by growth in height and weight. While growth is rapid during the entire babyhood period, it is especially so during the first year of babyhood (64).

Intellectual growth and change parallel physical growth and change. Perhaps in no area is change more apparent than in the baby's ability to recognize and respond to people and objects in the environment. Before babyhood has come to an end, babies are able to understand many things and can communicate their needs and wants in ways that others can understand.

Babyhood Is an Age of Decreasing Dependency

The decrease in dependency on others results from the rapid development of body control which

" 'Toddler' means you're too old to be a baby and too young to be a little boy."

FIGURE 4-1 Even young children distinguish between "babies" and "toddlers." (Adapted from Bil Keane. "The Family Circus." *Register and Tribune Syndicate*, April 5, 1977. Used by permission.)

enables babies to sit, stand, and walk and to manipulate objects. The random, mass movements of the infant give way to coordinated movements, which make it possible for babies to do things for themselves which formerly they had to rely upon others to do for them. Independence also increases as babies become able to communicate their needs to others.

With decreased dependency comes a rebellion against being "babied." No longer are babies willing to let others do things for them that they can or believe they can do for themselves. If they are not permitted to try to be independent when they want to be, they protest. This protest takes the form of angry outbursts and crying and soon develops into *negativism* —one of the outstanding characteristics of the closing months of babyhood.

Babyhood Is the Age of Increased Individuality

Perhaps the most significant thing about increased independence is that it permits babies to develop along lines suited to their interests and abilities. As a result, the individuality apparent at birth increases as babyhood draws to a close. Individuality is shown in appearance and in patterns of behavior. Even identical multiple births show individuality.

As individuality increases so does the necessity for treating each baby as an individual. No longer can all babies be expected to thrive on the same food or the same schedules for eating and sleeping. Nor can the same child-training techniques be expected to work equally well for all babies. Most parents discover, even before babies reach the first birthday, that they are individuals and must be treated as such.

Babyhood Is the Beginning of Socialization

The egocentrism, characteristic of the very young baby, quickly gives way to a desire to become a part of the social group. Babies show their desire to become a part of the social group by putting up protests when they are left alone for any length of time and by trying to win the attention of others in any way they can.

One of the ways in which babies show their interest in becoming a part of the social group is by *attachment behavior*. Because they can count on the attention and affection of their mothers or mother substitutes more than on other family members or outsiders, they develop strong emotional ties with their mothers long before babyhood comes to a close. It is from the satisfaction of this attachment behavior that the desire to establish warm and lasting relationships with others develops.

Babyhood Is the Beginning of Sex-Role Typing

Almost from the moment of birth, boys are treated as boys and girls as girls. Boys, for example, are dressed in blue clothes, covered with blue blankets, and live in a room that lacks the frills and ruffles of a girl's room. Toys are selected that are appropriate for boys, and they are told stories about boys and their activities. The same sex-identifying traditions apply to girls.

But while sex-role typing is part of a girl's early training, the pressures on her to be sex-appropriate even as a baby are not as strong as they are on a boy. However, indirectly girls are sex-role typed in babyhood by being permitted to cry and show other signs of "female weakness" which are discouraged in boy babies.

Babyhood Is an Appealing Age

Even though all babies are disproportionate, according to adult standards, they are appealing because of their big heads, protruding abdomens, small, thin limbs, and tiny hands and feet. When they are dressed in baby clothes and wrapped in baby blankets, they become even more appealing.

Older children as well as adults find small babies appealing because of their helplessness and dependency. Gradually, as babies' dependency is replaced by their ability to do things for themselves, and their appearance becomes less appealing as it changes from the small, doll-like body covered with baby garments to a larger, lankier body covered with sturdier, plainer clothes, they become less easy to manage and more resistant to help from others.

Babyhood Is the Beginning of Creativity

Because of their lack of muscle coordination and their inability to control their environment, babies are incapable of doing anything that can be regarded as original or creative. They are learning, however, in these early months of life to develop interests and attitudes that will lay the foundations for later creativity or for conformity to patterns set by others. And this will be largely determined by the treatment they receive from others, especially their parents. Spock (97) puts it this way:

The parent who is introducing babies to the world of inanimate things—or failing to do so—is showing them what fun can be gained by putting a batch of spoons in a saucepan, looking at pictures in a book, dancing to the music of the phonograph. When the parent teaches them in this positive spirit it gives them a sense not only that things are to be enjoyed but also that they will be able to manipulate them successfully. Or if the parent has the opposite attitude, it may teach them that objects are to be suspiciously avoided because playing with them involves some kind of danger or parental wrath.

Babyhood Is a Hazardous Age

While there are hazards at every age during the life span, certain hazards are more common during babyhood than at other ages. Some of these are physical and some psychological.

Among the physical hazards, illnesses and accidents are the most serious because they often lead to permanent disabilities or to death. Since behavior patterns, interests, and attitudes are established during babyhood, serious psychological hazards can result if poor foundations are laid at this time.

DEVELOPMENTAL TASKS OF BABYHOOD

Because the pattern of development is predictable even though different babies reach important landmarks in this pattern at slightly different ages, it is possible to set up standards of social expectations in the form of developmental tasks. All babies, for example, are expected to learn to walk, to take solid foods, to have their organs of elimination under partial control, to achieve reasonable physiological stability (especially in hunger rhythm and sleep), to learn the foundations of speech, and to relate emotionally to their parents and siblings to some extent instead of being completely self-bound, as they were at birth (53). Most of these developmental tasks will not, of course, be completely mastered when babyhood draws to a close, but the foundations for them should be laid.

When babyhood ends, all normal babies have learned to walk, though with varying degrees of proficiency. They have also learned to take solid foods and they have achieved a reasonable degree of physiological stability. The major tasks involving the elimination of body wastes are well under control and will be completely mastered within another year or two.

While most babies have built up a useful vocabulary, can pronounce the words they use reasonably correctly, can comprehend the meaning of simple statements and commands, and can put together several words into meaningful sentences, their ability to communicate with others and to comprehend what others say to them is still on a low level. Much remains to be mastered before they enter school.

The rapid development of the nervous system, the ossification of the bones, and the strengthening of the muscles make it possible for babies to master the developmental tasks of babyhood. However, their success in this regard depends to a large extent upon the opportunities they are given to master them and the help and guidance they receive.

Babies who lag behind their age-mates in mastering the developmental tasks of babyhood will be handicapped when they reach the early childhood years and are expected to master the developmental tasks for these years. A poor foundation in motor skills or in speech, for example, will make it difficult for young children to master the skills in these areas of development. Good mastery of these developmental tasks, by contrast, gives babies the foundations needed for successful mastery of speech, motor skills, and other forms of body control that are essential to becoming a part of the peer group—one of the important developmental tasks of the early childhood years.

PHYSICAL DEVELOPMENT

Babyhood is one of the two periods of rapid growth during the life span; the other comes at puberty. During the first six months of life, growth continues at the rapid rate characteristic of the prenatal period and then begins to slow down. In the second year, the rate of growth decelerates rapidly. During the first year of life, the increase in weight is proportionally greater than the increase in height; during the second year, the reverse is true (36,64,71).

If the rapid growth characteristic of the prenatal and early postnatal periods did not decelerate soon after birth, the child would grow into a giant. It has been estimated that if weight increased at the same rate it did during the first year of life, a child who weighed seven pounds at birth would weigh 230,029 pounds at eleven years of age (69,71).

While the general pattern of growth and development is similar for all babies, there are variations in height, weight, sensory capacities, and other areas of physical development. Some babies start life smaller and less well developed than the norm. This may be due to prematurity or to a poor physical condition resulting from maternal malnutrition, stress, or some other unfavorable condition during the prenatal period. As a result, such babies tend to fall behind their age-mates during the babyhood years.

The pattern of physical growth in babyhood is much the same for boys and girls. However, within the sex groups there are marked variations. Throughout the first year of life, there is little difference in height and weight between black and white babies of comparable economic levels. Differences begin to appear in the second year, however, because black children are, typically, of a more slender build than white children (69).

There are also variations in body size of babies of different socioeconomic levels. Babies whose parents are of the lower socioeconomic levels tend to be smaller, in both weight and height, than those whose parents come from the higher socioeconomic levels. Body build, which begins to be apparent during the second year of life, also contributes to variations in height and weight.

Throughout the babyhood period variations not only continue but become more pronounced. At all times variations in weight are greater than variations in height. This is because variations in weight are dependent partly on body build and partly on eating habits and diets.

However, in spite of variations in physical growth and development, it is possible to get a *general* picture of the pattern of growth and development during the babyhood years. The highlights of this picture are given in Box 4-1.

PHYSIOLOGICAL FUNCTIONS

Babyhood is the time when the fundamental physiological patterns of eating, sleeping, and elimination should be established, even though the habit formation may not be completed when babyhood ends.

Sleep Patterns   During the first year of babyhood, the mean duration of night sleep increases from 8½ hours at three weeks to 10 hours at twelve weeks and then remains constant during the rest of that year. During the first three months, the decline in day sleep is balanced by an increase in night sleep. Throughout the first year, wakefulness-sleep cycles of approximately one hour in length occur in both day and night sleep, with deep sleep lasting only about twenty-three minutes (32,98).

Eating Patterns   From birth until four or five months of age, all eating is in the infantile form of sucking and swallowing. Food, as a result, must be in a liquid form. Chewing generally appears in the developmental pattern a month later than biting. But, like biting, it is in an infantile form and requires much practice before it becomes serviceable.

BOX 4-1

PATTERN OF PHYSICAL DEVELOPMENT DURING BABYHOOD

Weight

At the age of four months, the baby's weight has normally doubled. At one year, babies weigh, on the average, three times as much as they did at birth, or approximately 21 pounds. At the age of two, the typical American baby weighs 25 pounds. Increase in weight during babyhood comes mainly from an increase in fat tissue.

Height

At four months, the baby measures between 23 and 24 inches; at one year, between 28 and 30 inches; and at two years, between 32 and 34 inches.

Physical Proportions

Head growth slows down in babyhood, while trunk and limb growth increases. Thus the baby gradually becomes less top-heavy and appears more slender and less chunky by the end of babyhood. See Figure 4-2.

Bones

The number of bones increases during babyhood. Ossification begins in the early part of the first year, but is not completed until puberty. The fontanel, or soft spot on the skull, has closed in approximately 50 percent of all babies by the age of eighteen months, and in almost all babies by the age of two years.

Muscles and Fat

Muscle fibers are present at birth but in very undeveloped forms. They grow slowly during babyhood and are weak. By contrast, fat tissue develops rapidly during babyhood, due partly to the high fat content of milk, the main ingredient in a baby's diet.

Body Builds

During the second year of life, as body proportions change, babies begin to show tendencies toward characteristic body builds. The three most common forms of body build are *ectomorphic,* which tends to be long and slender, *endomorphic,* which tends to be round and fat, and *mesomorphic* which tends to be heavy, hard, and rectangular.

Teeth

The average baby has four to six of the twenty temporary teeth by the age of one and sixteen by the age of two. The first teeth to cut through are those in the front, the last to appear are the molars. The last four of the temporary teeth usually erupt during the first year of early childhood.

Nervous System

At birth, brain weight is one-eighth of the baby's total weight. Gain in brain weight is greatest during the first two years of life, thus accounting for the baby's top-heavy appearance. The cerebellum, which plays an important role in body balance and postural control, triples in weight during the first year of postnatal life. This is true also for the cerebrum. Immature cells, present at birth, continue to develop after birth but relatively few new cells are formed.

Sense Organ Development

By the age of three months, the eye muscles are well-enough coordinated to enable babies to see things clearly and distinctly and the cones are well-enough developed to enable them to see colors. Hearing develops rapidly during this time. Smell and taste, which are well developed at birth, continue to improve during babyhood. Babies are highly responsive to all skin stimuli because of the thin texture of their skin and because all sense organs relating to touch, pressure, pain, and temperature are present in well-developed forms.

Food dislikes, which begin to develop during the second year, are frequently the result of the prolongation of infantile eating patterns. After being accustomed to food in liquid form, it is difficult for babies to adjust to a semisolid form. This adds to their revolt against the food, even though they may like its taste.

Patterns of Elimination Bowel control begins, on the average, at six months, and bladder control begins

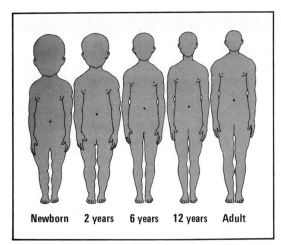

Newborn   2 years   6 years   12 years   Adult

FIGURE 4-2 Changes in body proportions from birth to adulthood. (Adapted from H. Nash. Ascription of maturity to human figure drawings by preschool children. *Journal of Genetic Psychology,* 1973, **122,** 319–328. Used by permission.)

an opportunity to learn how to do so. Until this state of readiness is present, teaching will be of little or no value.

Development of control over the muscles follows a definite and predictable pattern governed by the *laws of developmental direction.* See Figure 1-2. According to these laws, muscle control sweeps over the body from head to foot and from trunk to extremities. This means that the muscles in the head region come under voluntary control first, and those in the leg region last.

The approximate ages at which muscle control appears in the different areas of the body and the usual pattern of development are given in Box 4-2. There are, of course, individual differences in these ages and, to a lesser extent, in the pattern of development.

There is evidence that the age at which babies start to walk is consistent with their total develop-

between the ages of fifteen and sixteen months. In the case of the former, habits of control are established by the end of babyhood, though temporary lapses may be expected when the baby is tired, ill, or emotionally excited. Bladder control, on the other hand, is in a rudimentary state at the close of babyhood. Dryness during the daytime can be expected for a major part of the time except when deviations from the scheduled routine of the day, illness, fatigue, or emotional tension interfere. Dryness at night cannot be achieved in the average child until several years later (14,36,83).

MUSCLE CONTROL

At first, the baby's body is in more or less constant motion similar to the mass activity of the newborn infant. This is true even during sleep. Gradually this random, meaningless movement becomes more coordinated, thus making control of the muscles possible.

Maturation and learning work together in the development of muscle control. As a result of the maturation of the muscles, bones, and nerve structures, and because of the change that takes place in body proportions, babies are able to use their bodies in a coordinated manner. They must, however, be given

Step climbing is one of the important skills developed in babyhood. (Erika Stone.)

BOX 4-2

PATTERN OF MOTOR CONTROL

Head Region

Eye Control

Optic nystagmus, or the response of the eyes to a succession of moving objects, begins about twelve hours after birth; ocular pursuit movements, between the third and fourth weeks; horizontal eye movements, between the second and third months; vertical eye movements, between the third and fourth months; and circular eye movements, several months later.

Smiling

Reflex smiling, or smiling in response to a tactual stimulus, appears during the first week of life; social smiling, or smiling in response to the smile of another person, begins between the third and fourth months.

Head Holding

In a prone position, babies can hold their heads erect at one month; when lying on their backs, at five months; and when held in a sitting position, between four and six months.

Trunk Region

Rolling

Babies can roll from side to back at two months and from back to side at four months; at six months, they can roll over completely.

Sitting

The baby can pull to a sitting position at four months, sit with support at five months, sit without support momentarily at seven months, and sit up without support for ten or more minutes at nine months.

Arm and Hand Region

Hands

Thumb opposition—the working of the thumb in opposition to the fingers—appears in grasping between three and four months and in picking up objects between eight and ten months. This is shown in Figure 4-3.

Arms

The baby can reach for objects by six or seven months and can pick up a small object without random movements by one year.

Leg Region

Shifting of the body by kicking occurs by the end of the second week. Hitching, or moving in a sitting position, appears by six months. Crawling and creeping appear between eight and ten months, and at eleven months babies walk on "all fours." Babies can pull themselves to a standing position at about ten months, stand with support at eleven months, stand without support at one year, walk with support at eleven months or one year, and walk without support at fourteen months.

---

ment. Babies who sit early walk earlier than babies who start to sit later. It is possible to predict with a fair degree of accuracy when babies will start to walk if one knows what their rate of development is in other motor coordinations. A fairly accurate way to predict the age at which babies will start to walk alone is to multiply the age at which they begin to creep by 1½ or the age at which they sit alone by 2 (14).

Babyhood Skills

On the foundations laid through maturation of muscle coordinations, babies begin, before the end of the first year of life, to develop skills—fine coordinations in which the smaller muscles play a major role. To develop skills, however, there are three essentials:

an opportunity for practice, an incentive to learn, and a good model to copy with guidance to ensure that the copying will be correct (1,21). How important imitating a model is has been shown by the fact that, in babies blind from birth, there is a delay in their gross motor development and in the acquisition of skills (1).

Before babyhood is over, babies acquire many skills that are useful to them in their daily activities. At first, they are unable to integrate the different parts of a skill, with the result that the skill is of little value to them (108). With practice integration takes place. None of these skills will be well learned in the relatively short span of babyhood, but they serve as the foundation of skills that will be refined and more com-

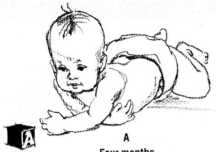

A
Four months
Sees but cannot contact

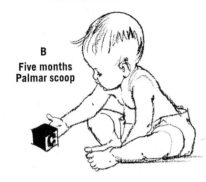

B
Five months
Palmar scoop

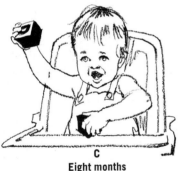

C
Eight months
A cube in each hand

D
Nine months
Pincer grasp perfected

FIGURE 4-3 Pattern of development of hand coordination. (Adapted from E. L. Vincent and P. C. Martin. *Human psychological development.* New York: Ronald, 1961. Used by permission.)

pletely learned as babies emerge into the childhood years.

The skills that all babies can be expected to learn are usually divided into two major categories—hand skills and leg skills. Box 4-3 lists the common hand and leg skills of babyhood and the ages at which these skills are usually acquired.

Because there is a rapid increase in the use of the hands during the early weeks of life, as shown in Figure 4-4, hand coordinations develop rapidly. As each new hand skill develops, it absorbs babies' interests and activities, and they devote much of their waking time to the use of their hands. This further increases their control over them. By contrast, because the major part of babyhood is devoted to developing the ability to walk, leg skills are only in a rudimentary state of development by the end of this period. The new leg skills acquired during babyhood are learned mainly during the last part of the second year.

Beginning of Handedness

Learning to use one hand in preference to the other—*handedness*—is an important aspect of the development of hand skills during babyhood. During

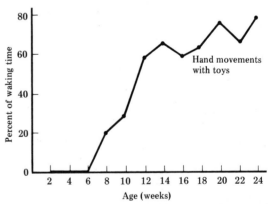

FIGURE 4-4 There is a rapid increase in the use of the hands during the early weeks of babyhood. (Adapted from J. Dittrichová and V. Lápacková. Development of the waking state in the young child. *Child Development,* 1964, **35,** 365–370. Used by permission.)

BOX 4-3

SOME COMMON SKILLS OF BABYHOOD

Hand Skills

Self-feeding

At eight months, most babies can hold their bottles after the nipples have been placed in their mouths; at nine months, they can put the bottle nipples in their mouths and take them out without help. At twelve months, they can drink from a cup when they hold it with both hands, and several months later they can drink from the cup using one hand. At thirteen months, babies begin to feed themselves with a spoon, and a month or two later they can spear food with a fork and carry it to their mouths with much spilling. By their second birthday, most babies can use spoons and forks without too much spilling.

Self-dressing

At the end of the first year most babies can pull off their socks, shoes, caps, and mittens. By the middle of the second year they will attempt to put on caps and mittens, and by the end of babyhood they can pull off all clothes and put on a shirt or dress.

Self-grooming

Self-bathing is limited mainly to running a cloth or sponge over the face and body. Before they are two, most babies try to brush their hair and teeth.

Play Skills

At twelve months, most babies can scribble with a pencil or crayon, and several months later they can throw or roll a ball, open a box, unscrew a lid from a bottle, turn the leaves of a book, build with a few blocks, insert pegs in a pegboard, string large beads, and cut a gash in paper with scissors.

Leg Skills

Babies learn to jump from an elevated position usually by movements resembling walking. They learn to climb stairs first by crawling and creeping. After they can walk alone, they go up and down steps in an upright position, placing one foot on a step and then drawing the other foot up after it. Very few babies are able to ride tricycles at this age and then only when they are held on the seat. They can swim by splashing with their arms and kicking their legs.

---

the early months of life, a baby is *ambidextrous,* with no preference for either hand. By the time they are eight months old, babies who are above average in mental and motor development show a greater degree of hand preference than those who are less well advanced, and this preference is usually for the right hand. However, most babies shift from the use of one hand to the other, depending largely on the position of the person or object they want to reach. If the object is closer to the right hand, that is the hand the baby will use.

Shifting likewise occurs during the second year but not as frequently as during the first. Thus, during babyhood, babies are neither dominantly left- nor dominantly right-handed, though they show, especially in the second year, a tendency to use one hand more than the other (4,73,94).

SPEECH DEVELOPMENT

Speech is a tool for communication. To be able to communicate with others, all individuals must be ca-pable of two separate and distinct functions; the ability to comprehend the meaning of what others are trying to communicate to them and the ability to communicate to others in terms they can comprehend. Communication can be in any form of language—written, spoken, gesticulative, musical and artistic expressions, etc. But for the most part, spoken language is the most efficient because it is least likely to be misunderstood (22,77).

Both aspects of communication—comprehension of what others are trying to communicate and the ability to communicate one's thoughts and feelings to others in terms they can understand—are difficult and not mastered quickly. However, the foundations for both are laid during the babyhood years, though the ability to comprehend is generally greater when babyhood comes to a close than is the ability to speak (11,12,18).

Comprehension

The first task in learning to communicate with others is learning to comprehend what they say. At every age children comprehend the meaning of what others say to them more readily then they can put their own thoughts and feelings into words. This is even truer of babyhood than of the childhood years. The speaker's facial expression, tone of voice, and gestures help babies to understand what is being said to them. Pleasure, anger, and fear, it has been found, can be comprehended as early as the third month of life (12,18).

Until babies are eighteen months old, words must be reinforced with gestures, such as pointing to an object. By the age of two, according to the Terman-Merrill Scale of Intelligence Tests, the average baby should comprehend well enough to respond correctly to two out of six simple commands, such as "Give me the kitty" and "Put the spoon in the cup," when the ojects are within easy reach (105). However, how great the comprehension will be will depend partly upon the baby's own intellectual abilities and partly on how others stimulate and encourage the baby to try to comprehend what they are saying.

Learning to Speak

The second task in learning to communicate with others is learning to speak. Because learning to speak is a long and difficult task and because babies are not mature enough for such difficult and complicated learning during the first year of life, nature provides substitute forms of communication to be used until they are ready to speak. Many babies, during the first and into the second years of their lives, try to make known their needs and wants by these means. These substitute forms of communication are known as "prespeech forms" (6,27).

If the prespeech forms of communication prove to be satisfactory and effective substitutes for speech, motivation to learn to speak will be weakened. Babies will then continue to use the infantile forms of communication even after they are capable of learning to speak.

Prespeech Forms of Communication

Four prespeech forms normally appear in the developmental pattern of learning to talk: crying, babbling, gesturing, and the use of emotional expressions. Crying is the most frequently used form during the early months of life, though from the long-range point of view, babbling is the most important because real speech eventually develops from it.

Crying As Ostwald and Pelzman have pointed out, "Crying is one of the first ways in which the infant is able to communicate with the world at large." While people may not always be accurate in their interpretations of what babies are trying to communicate, their cries are an indication that they are attempting to communicate. In addition, Ostwald and Pelzman have explained that "Crying is one of the first social acts of the infant. It marks a shift on the infant's part from being silently dependent on the mother to being able to communicate with the world at large (77)."

The cries of the newborn infant gradually become differentiated, so that by the third or fourth week of life it is possible to tell what the cry signifies from its tone and intensity and from the bodily movements accompanying it. Pain, for example, is expressed by shrill, loud cries, interrupted by groaning and whimpering. Hunger cries are loud and interrupted by sucking movements. Cries from colic are accompanied by a peculiar, high-pitched scream, with alternate and forceful flexion and extension of the legs. Before they are three months old, most babies have learned that crying is a sure way to get attention.

Crying during the early months of life also serves another useful purpose; it tells whether the baby is normal and healthy or whether there is something wrong. For example, a high-pitched cry of low intensity and long duration often means the baby is suffering from malnutrition or from brain damage (62).

Babbling As the vocal mechanism develops, babies become capable of producing a large number of explosive sounds. Some of these sounds are retained and eventually develop into babbling or lallation. In time, some will form the basis of real speech. The number of sounds produced in babbling gradually increases.

Most babies can, by the time they are six months old, combine certain vowel and consonant sounds such as "ma-ma," "da-da," and "na-na." Babbling begins during the second or third month of life, reaches its peak by the eighth month, and then gradually gives way to real speech. Babbling has completely disappeared by the time babyhood comes to an end (50.)

Gesturing Babies use gestures as a substitute for speech, not as a supplement to speech, as do most older children, adolescents and adults. Even after they are able to say a few words, many babies continue to use gestures, combining them with words to make their sentences. By outstretching their arms and smiling, babies can readily communicate the idea that they want to be picked up. When they push away their plates, at the same time saying "no," it is obvious that they are trying to communicate to others that they do not want the food.

Emotional Expressions Unquestionably one of the most effective prespeech forms of communication is emotional expression. This is because nothing is more expressive than facial gestures, which babies use to communicate their emotional states to others. When babies are happy, for example, they relax their bodies, wave their arms and legs, smile and make cooing sounds as a form of laughter.

Emotional expressions are a useful prespeech form of communication for two reasons. First, because babies have not yet learned to control their emotions, it is easy for others to know, by their facial and bodily expressions, what emotions they are experiencing. Second, babies find it easier to understand what others are trying to communicate to them by their facial expressions than from their words. The words, "I am angry," for example, may mean little or nothing to a baby but an angry expression on someone's face is quickly understood (37,122).

Tasks in Learning to Speak

Learning to speak involves three unrelated and difficult tasks. Babies are learning how to pronounce words, building a vocabulary by associating meanings with words that can be used to communicate meanings to others, and combining words into sentences that are understandable to others. These tasks involve not only control over the vocal mechanism but also the ability to comprehend meanings and to associate them with words which act as symbols for meanings (12,13,33,74). These tasks are explained in Box 4-4.

Because these tasks are far more difficult than may at first be apparent, it is understandable that only the foundation skills involved in speech will be laid. While many babies say words long before babyhood ends, they often do not associate the correct meanings with the words nor are they able to combine the words into meaningful sentences. Learning to

BOX 4-4

TASKS INVOLVED IN LEARNING TO SPEAK

Pronunciation

The baby learns to pronounce words partly by trial and error but mainly by imitating adult speech. Consonants and consonant blends are more difficult for babies to pronounce than vowels and diphthongs. Much of the baby's speech is incomprehensible up to the age of eighteen months, after which there is gradual but marked improvement.

Vocabulary Building

Babies learn the names of people and objects first, and then verbs such as "give" and "take." Just before babyhood ends, they learn a few adjectives such as "nice" and "naughty," as well as a few adverbs. Prepositions, conjunctions, and pronouns are generally not learned until early childhood. Vocabulary increases with age. Figure 4-5 shows how words are learned.

Sentences

The baby's first "sentences," which appear between twelve and eighteen months, generally consist of one word accompanied by a gesture. Gradually more words creep into the sentences, but gestures predominate until well into childhood.

communicate with others by speech is thus a developmental task for the childhood years.

EMOTIONAL BEHAVIOR IN BABYHOOD

At birth, the emotions appear in simple, almost completely undifferentiated forms. With age, emotional responses become less diffuse, less random, and more differentiated, and they can be aroused by a wide variety of stimuli.

There are two distinctive characteristics of babyhood emotions. First, they differ markedly from those of adolescents and adults and often from those of older children. They are, for example, accompanied by behavior responses that are proportionally too great for the stimuli that gave rise to them, espe-

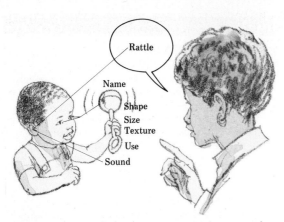

FIGURE 4-5 A baby learns to associate meaning with an object, and then a word becomes a symbol or label for the object. (Adapted from M. E. Breckenridge and E. L. Vincent. *Child development: Physical and psychologic development through adolescence.* (5th ed.) Philadelphia: Saunders, 1965. Used by permission.)

cially in the case of anger and fear. They are brief in duration, though intense while they last. They appear frequently, but are transitory and give way to other emotions when the baby's attention is distracted.

Second, emotions are more easily conditioned during babyhood than at later ages. The reason for this is that because babies' intellectual abilities are limited, they respond easily and quickly to stimuli that have given rise to an emotional response in the past. Sometimes, for example, they may be reluctant to enter a doctor's office if they had an inoculation on their last visit.

Common Emotional Patterns

There are certain emotional patterns that are commonly found among babies. Box 4-5 lists these responses and the usual stimuli that give rise to them (35,55,88,95,111). However, as was pointed out above, since the baby's emotions are especially susceptible to conditioning, there are variations in these patterns as well as in the stimuli that evoke them. Different babies respond emotionally to different stimuli, depending to a certain extent upon their past experiences. For example, babies who are exposed to few people outside the home or who are cared for almost exclusively by members of their families are far more likely to experience a pronounced "shy age" than those who are exposed to many outsiders and who are cared for by grandparents and baby-sitters as well as parents and siblings (79,89,91,95). Figure 4-6 shows the percentage of a group of babies showing fear of strangers at different ages.

Variations in emotional responses begin to appear in babyhood and are influenced by a number of factors, mainly the physical and mental conditions of babies at the time when the stimulus occurs and how successful a given response formerly was in meeting their needs. If, in the past, babies were punished for pulling, biting, or tearing something, they will satisfy their curiosity by a more hands-off approach, merely looking at an object and touching it.

Emotional Dominance In Babyhood

One of the most important variations in emotional responses involves the dominance of pleasant or unpleasant emotions. Some babies experience many more pleasant than unpleasant emotions, while the reverse is true for others, depending mainly on the baby's physical condition and conditions in the environment.

For example, babies who cry from anger or fear more often than they smile or show other pleasant emotions may be sickly or they may live in an environment where they are neglected or treated punitively. By contrast, babies whose dominant emotions are pleasant may be in a better physical condition or

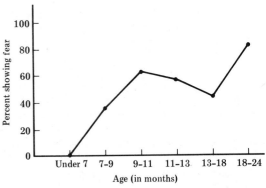

FIGURE 4-6 The development of the fear response: Percentage of a group of babies showing fear of strangers at different ages. (Adapted from S. Scarr and P. Salapatek. Patterns of fear development during infancy. *Merrill-Palmer Quarterly,* 1970, **16,** 53–90. Used by permission.)

BOX 4-5

COMMON EMOTIONAL PATTERNS IN BABYHOOD

Anger

Common stimuli that gives rise to anger in babies are interference with attempted movements, thwarting of some wish, not letting them do what they want to do, and not letting them make themselves understood. Typically, the angry response takes the form of screaming, kicking the legs, waving the arms, and hitting or kicking anything within reach. During the second year, babies may also jump up and down, throw themselves on the floor, and hold their breath.

Fear

The stimuli most likely to arouse fear in babies are loud noises; strange persons, objects, and situations; dark rooms; high places; and animals. Any stimulus which occurs suddenly or unexpectedly or which is different from what the baby is accustomed to gives rise to fear. The typical fear response in babyhood consists of an attempt to withdraw from the frightening stimulus, accompanied by whimpering, crying, temporary holding of the breath, and checking the activity engaged in when the baby became frightened.

Curiosity

Anything new or unusual acts as a stimulus to curiosity, unless the newness is so pronounced that it gives rise to fear. As fear wanes, it is replaced by curiosity. Young babies express curiosity mainly through their facial expressions—tensing the facial muscles, opening the mouth, and protruding the tongue. Later, babies grasp the objects that aroused their curiosity and handle, shake, bang, or suck them.

Joy

Joy is stimulated by physical well-being. By the second or third month of life, babies react to being played with, being tickled, and watching or listening to others. They express their pleasure or joy by smiling, laughing, and moving their arms and legs. When joy is intense, babies coo, gurgle, or even shout with glee, and all bodily movements are intensified.

Affection

Anyone who plays with babies, takes care of their bodily needs, or shows them affection will be a stimulus for their affection. Later, toys and the family pet may also become love objects for them. Typically, babies express their affection by hugging, patting, and kissing the loved object or person.

---

they may live in an environment that stimulates pleasant emotions and in which they are protected from stimuli that would normally give rise to such unpleasant emotions as fear and anger.

At all ages a dominance of the pleasant emotions is a guarantee of better adjustments than a dominance of the unpleasant emotions. At no age is this more true than during babyhood. Babies who experience a dominance of the pleasant emotions are laying the foundations for good personal and social adjustments and for patterns of behavior that will lead to happiness.

DEVELOPMENTS IN SOCIALIZATION

Early social experiences play a dominant role in determining the baby's future social relationships and patterns of behavior toward others. And because the baby's life is centered around the home, it is here that the foundations for later social behavior and attitudes are laid. There is little evidence that people are inherently social or antisocial. Instead, whether they become outer- or inner-bound—extroverted or introverted—depends mainly on their early social experiences.

Studies of the social adjustments of older children and even adolescents show the importance of the social foundations laid in babyhood. There are two reasons for the importance of these early foundations. First, the type of behavior babies show in social situations affects their personal and social adjustments. As Tautermannová has pointed out, "A smiling child is much more likely to provoke intensive maternal feelings and to become a good partner in the relation between him and his mother or other caretakers and to draw more attention of the adult than others who smile less" (104). Passman has explained that when two- to three-year-olds have established an attachment for some object—a favorite toy or a blanket, for example—these "attachment objects, whether animate or inanimate, may serve as anxiety reducers. When a preschooler is accompanied by an attachment object it reduces anxiety in a novel situation and facilitates adjustment to this situation" (82).

The second reason why early social foundations are important is that, once established, they tend to be persistent as children grow older. Children who cried excessively as babies tend to be aggressive and to show other attention-getting behavior. By contrast, friendly, happier babies usually become socially better adjusted as they grow older.

This, of course, does not mean that conditions cannot be changed as babyhood progresses or during the childhood years when it becomes apparent that poor foundations are the cause of poor personal and social adjustments. However, making a change after a pattern of behavior has become habitual is never easy. Nor is there any guarantee that the change will be complete. That is why good social foundations are so important during the babyhood years.

Pattern of Development of Social Behavior

Early social behavior follows a fairly predictable pattern, though variations can and do occur as a result of health or emotional states or because of environmental conditions. At birth, infants are nongregarious in the sense that it makes no difference to them who attends to their physical needs. In fact, young babies can be soothed as well by a hot-water bottle or a soft pillow as by human caresses. But at around the age of six weeks, a true social smile—or a smile in response to a person rather than to a tactile stimulus applied to the lips, which produces a reflex smile—appears, and this is regarded as the beginning of socialization (104).

The pattern of social responses to adults differs from that of social responses to other babies (9,48,59, 81,116). These are described separately in Box 4-6. The first social responses are to adults, while those to other babies appear slightly later.

During the first year of babyhood, babies are in a state of equilibrium which makes them friendly, easy to handle, and pleasant to be with. Around the middle of the second year, equilibrium gives way to

Early social responses to other babies consist mainly of exploring their hair, clothes, and bodies. (Ron Sugiyama/Editorial Photocolor Archives.)

disequilibrium, and babies then become fussy, uncooperative, and difficult to handle. Before babyhood is over, however, equilibrium is restored and babies again exhibit pleasant and social behavior (4).

BEGINNINGS OF INTEREST IN PLAY

There are certain characteristics of babyhood play which are distinctive and which make it different from the play of young children and certainly from the play of older children and adolescents. First, in babyhood play there are no rules or regulations. Consequently, it may be regarded as free, spontaneous play. Babies play how and when they wish without any preparation for, or restrictions on, the way they play.

Second, throughout babyhood, play is more often solitary than social. Even when playing with the mother, as Stone has explained, the baby is "often a plaything, while the mothering one is the player. In time, both the child and the mothering one are mutually players and playthings" (99). When babies are with other babies or with children, there is little interaction or cooperation. Instead, play is "onlooker play" in which babies watch what the others are doing, or "parallel play" in which they play in their own way without regard to what the other is doing.

BOX 4-6

SOCIAL RESPONSES TO ADULTS

Two to Three Months

Babies can distinguish people from inanimate objects and they discover that people supply their needs. They are content to be with people but discontented when left alone. At this age, babies show no preference for any one person.

Four to Five Months

Babies want to be picked up by anyone who approaches them. They react differently to scolding and to smiling faces and to friendly and to angry voices.

Six to Seven Months

Babies differentiate between "friends" and "strangers" by smiling at the former and showing fear in the presence of the latter. This is the beginning of the "shy age." It is also the beginning of the "attachment age"—the time when babies become strongly attached to their mothers or mother-substitutes and show a waning of indiscriminate friendliness.

Eight to Nine Months

The baby attempts to imitate the speech, gestures, and simple acts of others.

Twelve Months

The baby reacts to the warning "no-no."

Sixteen to Eighteen Months

Negativism, in the form of stubborn resistance to requests or demands from adults, is manifested in physical withdrawal or angry outbursts.

Twenty-two to Twenty-four Months

The baby cooperates in a number of routine activities, such as being dressed, fed, and bathed.

SOCIAL RESPONSES TO OTHER BABIES

Four to Five Months

The baby tries to attract the attention of another baby or a child by bouncing up and down, kicking, laughing, or blowing bubbles.

Six to Seven Months

The baby smiles at other babies and shows an interest in their crying

Nine to Thirteen Months

Babies attempt to explore the clothes and hair of other babies, imitate their behavior and vocalizations, and cooperate in the use of toys—although they tend to become upset when other babies take one of their toys.

Thirteen to Eighteen Months

Fighting over toys decreases, and the baby shows more cooperation during play and a willingness to share.

Eighteen to Twenty-four Months

The baby shows more interest in playing with other babies and uses play materials to establish social relationships with them.

When there is any interaction, it consists mainly of grabbing or snatching toys from another baby. There is little or no social give-and-take.

Third, because play is dependent on physical, motor, and intellectual development, the kinds of play depend on the babies' patterns of development in these areas. As these patterns unfold, play becomes more varied and complex.

Fourth, toys and other play equipment per se are less important now than they will be later. This means that babies' play can be carried out with any object that stimulates curiosity and exploration: regular toys are not needed at this period (26,34,85).

And, fifth, babies' play is characterized by much repetition and little variation. The reason for this is that babies lack the skills which make the wider play repertoire of preschoolers and older children possible.

Play Development Follows a Pattern

Play during the babyhood years is greatly influenced by the baby's physical, motor, and mental

BOX 4-7

COMMON PLAY PATTERNS OF BABYHOOD

Sensorimotor Play

This is the earliest form of play and consists of such things as kicking, bouncing, wiggling, moving fingers and toes, climbing, babbling, and rolling.

Exploratory Play

As hand and arm coordinations develop, babies begin to explore their bodies by pulling their hair, sucking their fingers and toes, pushing their fingers in their navels, and manipulating their sex organs. They shake, throw, bang, suck and pull their toys and explore by pulling, banging, and tearing any object within their reach.

Imitative Play

During the second year, babies try to imitate the actions of those around them, such as reading a magazine, sweeping the floor, or writing with a pencil or crayon.

Make-Believe Play

During the second year, most babies endow their toys with the qualities they find they have in real life. Stuffed animals are endowed with the qualities of real animals just as dolls and trucks are treated by the baby as if they were real people or real trucks.

Games

Before babies are a year old, they play such traditional games as peekaboo, pat-a-cake, pigs to market, and hide-and-seek. These are usualy played with parents, grandparents, or older siblings.

Amusements

Babies like to be sung to, talked to, and read to. Most are fascinated by radio and television and enjoy looking at pictures.

development. And because these patterns of development are similar for all babies, the pattern of play is similar and predictable.

For example, at six months babies play with one object at a time. By the time they are nine months, they combine or relate two separate objects in their play and show an interest in similarities among objects. By the time they are two years old, they show evidence of pretending in their play (41).

Different play patterns likewise follow predictable patterns. This is true of manipulative play and play with toys. In playing with toys, babies first explore them and later use them to make things or to supplement their make-believe play (34,41,85).

Regardless of environment and of individual differences, certain patterns of play are found more or less universally (26,34,41). These are given in Box 4-7. Note the relatively small role of toys in these different play patterns.

Value of Play in Babyhood

In spite of the fact that play in babyhood, as is true of play at all ages, is engaged in for pleasure and not for any end result, it makes important contributions to the baby's development. As Bruner has said, "Play is serious business." He further explains that it

provides oppportunities for many forms of learning, two of which are especially important—problem solving and creativity. Without play, the foundations for creativity as well as the foundations for problem solving would not be laid before children developed habits of dealing with their environments in noncreative, stereotyped ways (19).

An equally important contribution of play is the information it gives babies about their environments and the people and things in their environments. As Eckerman and Rheingold have pointed out, "It is through exploration that the infant learns about the world of people as well as of things" (34). Unquestionably, this learning would ultimately take place without play but play hastens the learning and adds to its enjoyment.

One of the most important contributions of play is the enjoyment babies derive from it. Were it not for opportunities for play, equipment to stimulate it, and guidance in how to use the equipment, babies would become bored and spend their time crying for attention. So long as they can amuse themselves part of the time by exploring and other play activities, boredom is warded off and the detrimental effects of crying eliminated.

The ability to amuse themselves and to be self-sufficient, learned in connection with play, carries over into other areas of life as children grow older. The self-confidence that comes with self-sufficiency helps children to cope with the various problems that face them as they grow older.

Then, too, play encourages creativity. While creativity is only in its most rudimentary forms during babyhood, the satisfaction the individual derives from opportunities and encouragement to do things in a creative way provides an incentive to further creativity as the child emerges from the restricted environment of babyhood and has more opportunities to do things in an original way.

While much play in babyhood is solitary, as shown in Box 4-7, some of it is carried out with others, mainly members of the family—siblings, parents, or grandparents. Learning to play with others encourages babies to be cooperative instead of self-bound, an essential to good social relationships when babyhood comes to a close. Like other foundations, if foundations in cooperation are properly laid in babyhood, adjustment to the demands of childhood will be easier to meet successfully.

DEVELOPMENT OF UNDERSTANDING

Because all babies begin life with no comprehension of the meaning of the things they come in contact with in their environment, they must acquire, through maturation and learning, an understanding of what they observe. What meanings babies acquire depends partly on the level of their intelligence and partly on their previous experiences. As new meanings are acquired, babies interpret new experiences in terms of their memories of previous ones. The association of meanings with objects, people, and situations results in the development of *concepts*.

The behavior of normal babies shows that concepts develop rapidly. Babies show recognition of familiar people and objects in their environment through pleasurable responses, just as they regard strange people and objects with fear. At first, they respond to the total situation rather than to any one part of it. As a result, they respond to people, objects, and situations that have elements in common as if they were all one and the same thing.

That is why, as was pointed out earlier, conditioning of the emotions is so easy and so common during babyhood. In his classic experiment, Watson conditioned a baby to fear a rabbit by associating a loud, harsh noise with the rabbit. Later, Watson reported that the baby showed fear of white stuffed animals, a white muff, and even a person in a Santa Claus costume with a flowing white beard (113).

How Understanding Develops

The earliest perceptions of babies come through sensory exploration. They look at, listen to, touch, smell, and taste anything they can. Later, as their muscle coordinations develop, they are able to acquire more meanings through handling whatever is within their reach. Handling causes the attention to be fixed and this gives an opportunity to discover meanings. While babies of about six months of age may be held back in their exploratory behavior by fear of new and strange stimuli, by the end of the first year of life manipulation begins and they try to discover meanings in new and strange objects and situations. Piaget has labeled this the *sensorimotor* stage in conceptual development, lasting from birth to two or three years (84).

Toward the end of babyhood, babies begin to put words together into sentences generally beginning with "who," "what," and "why." While they cannot understand all that is said in explanation, they derive enough meaning from the words they hear and the accompanying demonstration to build on the meanings they already have discovered from sensory exploration and motor manipulation. At no time, however, do babies abandon the simpler forms of discovering meanings, even when they are capable of using more advanced forms.

By the time they are two years old, babies are capable of making simple generalizations based on similar experiences in which they have observed relationships. Their limited knowledge and experience, however, make it difficult for them to distinguish between living and inanimate objects. As a result, they believe that all objects are animate and have the same attributes as living things.

Many of the important concepts needed for adjustment to life are learned in rudimentary form in the babyhood years. As the baby's social horizons broaden during childhood and adolescence, new meanings will be added to the foundations laid at this time. Emotional weighting, characteristic of all concepts, begins to become an important element of the developing concepts during the babyhood years. The

BOX 4-8

SOME IMPORTANT CONCEPTS THAT DEVELOP IN BABYHOOD

Concepts of Space

During the second year, babies rarely reach for objects that are more that twenty inches away, indicating that they are able to estimate distance; the direction of their reach is usually correct.

Concepts of Weight

Concepts of weight are inaccurate during babyhood; babies perceive a small object as light and a large object as heavy.

Concepts of Time

Babies have no idea of how long it takes to eat a meal nor have they any concept of the passage of time. Only when they are on fairly rigid daily schedules do they know morning from afternoon or night.

Concepts of Self

Babies develop *physical* self-concepts by looking at themselves in mirrors and handling the different parts of their bodies. *Psychological* self-concepts develop later and are based mainly on what the significant people in their lives think of them. Before babyhood is over, most babies know that they are either a boy or a girl.

Sex-Role Concepts

By the end of babyhood, most babies have a fairly definite concept of what members of the two sexes are supposed to do and say as well as how they are supposed to look.

Social Concepts

By eight months, the baby responds to the emotions of others, revealed in their facial expressions, though there is little evidence that, even by the end of babyhood, the baby understands exactly what these emotions are.

Concepts of Beauty

Between the ages of six and twenty-four months, babies begin to respond to different colors. They are also apt to say that something is "pretty," for example, and they like music with a definite tune.

Concepts of the Comic

At four months, babies perceive vocal play or babbling as comic, and they enjoy blowing bubbles in their milk and splashing their bath water. At six months, they derive enjoyment from dropping things that are handed to them, and at one year they like to make funny faces. Two-year-olds laugh at their own stunts, such as squeezing through a narrow space.

---

most important concepts that begin to develop during babyhood are given in Box 4-8.

BEGINNINGS OF MORALITY

Babies have no scale of values and no conscience. They are therefore neither moral nor immoral but *nonmoral* in the sense that their behavior is not guided by moral standards. Eventually they will learn moral codes from their parents, and later from their teachers and playmates, as well as the necessity for conforming to these codes.

Learning to behave in a morally approved manner is a long, slow process. However, foundations are laid in babyhood and on these foundations children build moral codes which guide their behavior as they grow older.

Because of their limited intelligence, babies judge the rightness or wrongness of an act in terms of the pleasures or pain it brings them rather than in terms of its good and harmful effects on others. They therefore perceive an act as wrong only when it has some harmful effect on themselves. They have no sense of guilt because they lack definite standards of right and wrong. They do not feel guilty when they take things that belong to others because they have no concept of personal property rights.

The baby is in a stage of moral development which Piaget has called *morality by constraint*—the first of three stages in moral development. This stage lasts until the age of seven or eight years and is characterized by automatic obedience to rules without reasoning or judgment (84).

Role of Discipline in Babyhood

The major purpose of discipline is to teach children what the group with which they are identified regards as right and wrong, and then to see to it that they act in accordance with this knowledge. This is accomplished first by means of external controls over their behavior and later by means of internal controls, when they assume responsibility for their own behavior.

Throughout babyhood, babies must learn to make correct, specific responses to specific situations in the home and in the neighborhood. Acts that are wrong should be wrong at all times, regardless of who is in charge. Otherwise, babies will be confused and will not know what is expected of them.

With strict discipline, involving emphasis on punishment for wrongdoing, even young babies can be forced into a pattern of behavior that makes them less troublesome to their parents during the second year of life when their exploratory behavior and tendency to refuse to comply with parental wishes make them less easy to handle than they were during the first year.

Before babies are punished for wrongdoing, however, they must learn what is right and what is wrong. This they cannot do overnight. Therefore, during babyhood, emphasis should be on the educational aspect of discipline—teaching babies what is right and what is wrong—and on rewarding them with approval and affection when they do what is right rather than on punishment when they do what is wrong. This, of course, does not mean that punishment should not be used. It should be used because of its educational value. If punished by a slight slap on the hand for doing a forbidden thing, the slap tells the baby that this act is wrong and must not be repeated.

Many parents assume that babies cannot understand words of praise and, therefore, they refrain from telling their babies that they have done something good. Although few babies are able to understand what is said in praise, they do understand the accompanying pleasant facial expressions—which are different from those accompanying scolding or other forms of punishment. As a result, they motivate babies to repeat the acts that brought them such favorable responses.

BEGINNINGS OF SEX-ROLE TYPING

Sex-role typing, or learning to play an approved sex role, begins literally at birth. Babies are identified as male or female by the colors of their blankets and wrappers and they are treated as male or as female by family members who emphasize their maleness or femaleness to those who come to see and admire the new baby.

Long before the first year has come to an end, the sex-role typing of babies has extended to the furnishings of their rooms, the clothes they are dressed in—rompers for boys and dresses for girls—the toys they are given to play with and, most important, the way they are treated by parents and other significant people in their lives (119,121). For example, if girl babies, in the second year of their lives, show a tendency to be dependent, this is far more likely to be encouraged than if similar behavior is shown by boy babies. According to the sex-role stereotype of males, independence is appropriate for boys while dependency is appropriate for girls (68).

As is true among older children, more pressure is put on boy babies to look and act in a sex-appropriate manner than on girl babies. Parents may dress girl babies in rompers as they do boys on the grounds that rompers give girls more freedom to move around than dresses. They would never, on the other hand, consider putting a dress on a boy baby.

Similarly, many toys given to girl babies are like those considered appropriate for boy babies, such as engines, carts, and toy automobiles. Boys, on the other hand, would not be given such "sissy" toys as dolls or equipment for the care of dolls (39,40). Also, when stories are told or read to babies during the second year of their lives, care is taken to ensure that those told to boy babies are masculine in theme and characters but less concern is expressed about sex-appropriate stories for girls (39).

If older babies are cared for in day-care centers or are sent to nursery schools, sex-role typing by teachers and other caretakers reinforces the typing begun in the home. As a result, by the time babies emerge into early childhood, the foundations for sex-appropriate behavior have already been laid though the sex-role stereotypes that serve as guidelines for this typing are still largely unfamiliar to babies. They behave in a sex-appropriate or -inappropriate way because they were taught and encouraged to do so without any understanding of the reasons for doing so.

FAMILY RELATIONSHIPS

Because the early environment is limited primarily to the home, family relationships play a dominant role in determining the future pattern of a baby's attitudes toward and behavior in relationships with others. Although this pattern will unquestionably be changed and modified as babies grow older and as their environments broaden, the core of the pattern is likely to remain with little or no modification. That is why early family relationships are so important.

Evidence of Importance of Parent-Child Relationships

Studies of family relationships have revealed that *all* family relationships are important factors in the individual's development. However, during the babyhood years, parent-child relationships are more important than any other family relationships. There are three lines of evidence to show the importance of the parent-child relationship during the babyhood years. They are:

Emotional Deprivation The first evidence of the importance of parent-child relationships is the effect of emotional deprivation during the early years of life. Babies who are institutionalized and thus deprived of normal opportunities to express their love or to be loved by others become quiet, listless, and unresponsive to the smiles and attempts to show affection on the part of others. They show extreme forms of temper, as if seeking attention, and they give the general impression of unhappiness (20,90).

Babies who are neglected or rejected by their parents because they are unwanted, or fail to come up to parental expectations, experience the same effects as do those who are institutionalized. It is not the environment in which they live that is responsible for the effects on their personalities and behavior but the treatment they receive in the environment, mainly the treatment they receive from their mothers (54).

Attachment Behavior A second line of evidence of the importance of parent-child relationships is the presence or absence of attachment behavior.

Attachment behavior means a close, warm, and satisfying relationship of the baby with the mother or a mother-substitute. All babies need, during the first nine or twelve months of life, the continuous care of one person, usually the mother or a satisfactory mother-substitute (2,24,60,72). Such care not only makes them feel secure but shows them the satisfaction they can derive from a close, personal relationship with another person. This lays the foundation for a desire to establish friendships with peers as they grow older and friendly relationships with people outside the home as well as with family members other than the mother or mother-substitute (5,47,109).

How important attachment behavior in babyhood is to the baby's development has been emphasized by the effects of lack of it. When babies are unable, for one reason or another, to establish a close emotional tie to another person, they experience much the same effects as do babies who suffer from emotional deprivation. In addition, they fail to discover the pleasure and security they can derive from close, personal relationships with others and this affects their motivation to try to establish friendships with their peers as they grow older (16,17,120,121).

Different-Sized Families The third evidence of the importance of parent-child relationships is the effect of different-sized families on the early development of babies. Babies from large families, in which the children are closely spaced, have fewer direct contacts with their mothers, who are preoccupied with other responsibilities. As a result, they suffer from some of the usual effects of maternal deprivation—not only lack of opportunities for emotional attachment but also lack of maternal attention and stimulation. Lack of attention and stimulation can and often does cause them to become lethargic and to do less than they are capable of doing.

Important as these three lines of evidence are to emphasize the significance of parent-child relationships during the babyhood years, there is little evidence that satisfying experiences during babyhood will be adequate to compensate for unfavorable parent-child relationships that develop as the child grows older or for the effects of economic privation. Although it is true that the foundations of attitudes, behavior patterns, and personality structure are laid in babyhood, events of childhood and the later years are of great importance in reinforcing or even changing the personality structure tentatively formed in the early years of life.

Changes in Family Relationships

At no time in life do family relationships remain static. Sometimes these relationships change slowly and sometimes rapidly, sometimes for the better and sometimes for the worse. In babyhood, changes are rapid and they tend to be for the worse.

Many conditions are responsible for changes in family relationships but one of the most important is that all members involved in the relationship undergo changes of their own. Davids and Holden (29) have discussed the changes that take place in the mother-child relationship during the early months of the baby's life:

Such changes in maternal characteristics might well be a function of the infant's physical and/or temperamental attributes. That is, whether the infant is healthy or sickly, unusually attractive or obviously handicapped, usually calm and contented or generally fussy and irritable, especially responsive to maternal contacts or somewhat rejecting of her—these are the kinds of infant variables that could well play a prominent role in modifying the mother's attitudes and personality during the first few months after childbirth. Then again, it might be that the infant's physical or emotional makeup has little to do with the mother's changed outlook or behavior. Rather, in certain cases, it might be that changes in the mother's physical condition, or changes in the husband-wife relationship (in either a positive or a negative direction), or changes in the family's socioeconomic situation (for better or worse) are responsible for differences in maternal characteristics found during pregnancy and several months after childbirth.

Normally, family relationships during most of the baby's first year are favorable. It has been said that "everyone loves a baby," and this holds true not only for parents but also for siblings, grandparents, and other relatives. However, before the baby's first birthday, some of this love has been tempered with annoyance, anger, frustration, and other unpleasant emotions, and the baby may have become negativistic in some respects, exhibiting behavior that is in sharp contrast to the docile compliance of early babyhood. With these changes comes a deterioration in the baby's relationships with different family members.

Some of the most common causes of such deterioration are given in Box 4-9.

PERSONALITY DEVELOPMENT IN BABYHOOD

The potentials for personality development are present at birth. As Thomas et al. have emphasized, "Personality is shaped by the constant interplay of temperament and environment" (106). And, because no two individuals have the same physical or mental endowments or the same environmental experiences, no two persons will ever develop identical personality patterns.

Babyhood—The Critical Period in Personality Development

Babyhood is often referred to as a "critical period" in the development of personality because at this time the foundations are laid upon which the adult personality structure will be built.

A number of lines of evidence show how critical a time babyhood is in the development of personality. First, studies of emotional deprivation due either to neglect in the home or to institutionalization have revealed that personality changes are an almost inevitable accompaniment (23,90).

Second, because the baby's environment is limited almost exclusively to the home and because the mother is the most constant companion, the kind of person she is and the kind of relationship they share will have a profound influence on the baby's personality.

Third, there is evidence that functions which are in an active stage of development when something unfavorable occurs in the environment are most subject to damage. For example, when the baby is developing independence, overprotectiveness on the part of the parents is especially harmful (100).

Fourth, sex differences in personality begin to appear as early as the first year of life. There is little evidence that these differences are due to heredity and much evidence that they are the result of environmental pressures, which are different for boys and for girls. These environmental pressures are likely to increase with time, and thus the foundations laid in babyhood will persist (45).

BOX 4-9

COMMON CAUSES OF CHANGES IN FAMILY RELATIONSHIPS DURING BABYHOOD

Dream-Child Concept

If the baby lives up to the dream-child concepts of parents and siblings, in terms of appearance and behavior, family relationships will become increasingly more favorable. If it does not, they will deteriorate.

Degree of Dependency

As complete dependency—one of the most appealing features of babies—decreases, babies become more troublesome and demanding and, as a result, they are less appealing.

Parental Anxiety

Parents may become nervous about how well they are performing their parental roles or they may worry if the new baby behaves differently from their older child or children. Their feelings of anxiety are communicated to the baby who often reacts by becoming resentful and negativistic or by crying excessively. Such behavior makes the baby less appealing.

Child-training Methods

Whether methods of training are permissive or authoritarian will influence parent-child relationships. Corporal punishment, which almost always accompanies authoritarian training, is very damaging to the parent-child relationship.

Maternal Employment

When the mother works outside the home, the care of the baby is often taken over by a person for whom the baby establishes a strong emotional attachment. This the mother is likely to resent. If no emotional attachment is established, the baby is likely to feel neglected and rejected, feelings that lead to resentments and a strained parent-child relationship.

Maternal Overwork

When mothers are overworked, either because of large families or because of carrying an outside job, they tend to be tense, nervous, and irritable when their babies do not behave as they expect them to. This is especially true when babies dawdle over routine activities connected with eating, dressing, or toileting.

Arrival of New Sibling

The arrival of a new sibling may cause the baby to feel displaced and neglected, leading to fussiness, crying, and a tendency to revert to infantile behavior, all of which is upsetting to the family.

Relationships with Older Siblings

Older siblings may begin to think of new babies as a pest when they must be quiet while they nap, share their mother's time and attention with them, and help with their care.

Preference for Certain Family Members

Even before their first birthday, many babies show definite preferences for certain family members—usually the mother or an older sister who has helped with their care. Other family members often resent this and let the babies know how they feel. This tends to intensify the babies' preferences and this, in turn, intensifies family resentments.

Fifth, and most important, genetic studies of the persistence of personality traits over a period of years have revealed that patterns established early in life remain almost unchanged as the child grows older. As Thomas et al. have pointed out, "A child's temperament is not immutable. In the course of his development the environmental circumstances may heighten, diminish or otherwise modify his reactions and behavior" (106).

Changes in the Personality Pattern in Babyhood

Certain personality traits do change, even in the babyhood years. These changes may be either *quantitative,* in that there is a strengthening or weakening of a trait already present, or *qualitative,* in that a socially undesirable trait is replaced by one that is socially more desirable. For the most part, personality changes tend to be quantitative in nature.

Young children who have been shy since babyhood will seek the kind of environment that will encourage development of this trait. At the same time, they avoid situations that would make them feel ill-at-ease or self-conscious. As a result, their shyness tends to become stronger rather than weaker with age.

The core of the personality pattern—the self-concept—remains fundamentally the same. As time goes on, this core becomes less and less flexible. Then a change in personality traits may upset the personality balance. Thus early experiences are extremely important in shaping the personality pattern (78).

HAZARDS IN BABYHOOD

Because babyhood is the foundation age, it is an especially hazardous time. The hazards may be physical, psychological, or both, as is true of infancy. For example, excessive crying is both physically and psychologically damaging to the baby and to the home atmosphere. It leads to gastrointestinal disturbances, regurgitation of food, night waking, and general nervous tension. Furthermore, excessive crying leads to feelings of insecurity which affect the baby's developing personality. In addition, excessive crying affects the baby's relationships with the parents and other family members unfavorably. This, in turn, indirectly affects personality development.

In the first year of babyhood, physical hazards tend to be more numerous and more serious than psychological ones, while the reverse is true during the second year. Both are serious, however, and thus it is important that they be prevented whenever possible and that everything be done to minimize their severity should they occur. For example, certain patterns of maternal responsiveness during the first and fourth quarters of the first year of life can be effective in coping with excessive crying. See Figure 4-7. Since much of the crying that occurs during the first year is social in origin, different forms of social reactions on the part of the mother are most effective in dealing with the crying (7).

Physical Hazards

Physical hazards are serious for all babies but especially for those who are born prematurely; those who suffer from brain damage or other birth defects;

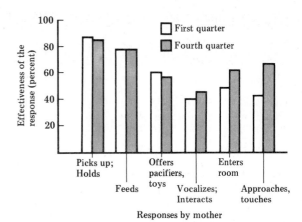

FIGURE 4-7 Effectiveness of various maternal responses to crying in young babies. (Adapted from S. M. Bell and M. D. S. Ainsworth. Infant crying and maternal responsiveness. *Child Development*, 1972, **43,** 1171–1190. Used by permission.)

and those whose physical development and general physical condition at birth are poor.

Mortality Meredith has reported that greater mortality occurs during the first three months of babyhood than later—with approximately two-thirds of all deaths during the first year of life occurring during the first month (71).

During the first year of babyhood, death is usually caused by serious illness while, during the second year, death is more often due to accidents. Throughout babyhood, more boys die than girls (45,71).

Crib Death Apparently normal, healthy babies are sometimes the victims of sudden and unexpected death—referred to in medical circles as *crib death*. Usually crib death occurs after a long period of sleep (76).

To date, medical science has been unable to find the exact cause or causes of crib death. There is some evidence that it is common in babies who experience abnormalities in breathing or who have had some abnormal condition at birth, such as jaundice. It is also more common in babies who have had oxygen therapy during the newborn period (76,110).

More crib death occurs during the first year of babyhood than during the second; and more during the first six months of the first year than in the second six months. There is no evidence, to date, that crib death is more common among boys than among girls, or among babies of lower socioeconomic groups as compared with those of higher groups (110).

Illnesses   While it is true that many deaths during the first few months of postnatal life are due to such illnesses as gastrointestinal or respiratory complications, the number of deaths due to serious illness then declines rapidly because most babies today are given inoculations and vaccinations to immunize them against diseases which, in the past, often proved to be fatal.

However, minor illnesses such as colds and digestive upsets are common. Prompt diagnosis and proper medical care can keep these from causing serious harm, but if they are neglected, as frequently happens in the case of colds, serious disturbances can develop rapidly, especially ear infections.

Even minor illnesses often are psychological as well as physical hazards. The concern parents feel is quickly expressed in their treatment of a sick baby. During the second year of life many babies discover that, when they are ill, they can do much as they please and that all rules of behavior are suspended. This is often the start of behavior problems.

Prolonged illnesses, even though not terminal, can interfere with the normal growth pattern. While most babies, after recovering from an illness, go through a period of "catch up" growth, this is not always so. How much the pattern of growth may be affected by a prolonged illness has, to date, not been determined (102,103).

Accidents   Although accidents are infrequent during the first year of life, owing to the fact that babies are carefully protected in their cribs, play pens, and carriages, they are far more frequent during the second year, when babies can move about more freely and are not as well protected. Some babyhood accidents, such as bruises and scratches, are minor and have no permanent effects. Others, such as blows on the head or cuts, may be serious enough to leave permanent scars or may even be fatal. Even minor accidents, however, leave psychological scars. Babies are often conditioned to fear situations similar to those in which accidents occurred or they develop a generalized timidity as a result of frequent accidents.

Malnutrition   Malnutrition, which may come from inadequate food intake or from an unbalanced diet, can play havoc not only with physical growth but also with mental development. It not only causes stunted growth but also leads to physical defects such as carious teeth, bowed legs, and a tendency to suffer from more or less constant illnesses.

Because the brain grows and develops at such an accelerated rate during babyhood, it can be seriously impaired by malnutrition. The first two years of postnatal life have been called the *critical period* in brain growth because of the marked increase in internal development of the brain cells at this time. As a result, it is the time when the brain is most vulnerable to damage. If babies suffer from malnutrition at this time, there is no evidence that the development that normally would take place will do so later (42,63).

When brain growth and development are impaired, children do not reach their intellectual potentials. Even as they grow older, they are unable to do the intellectual work that they might have done had malnutrition during the critical period of brain development not impaired their chances for normal intellectual development (30,42,107).

Foundations of Obesity   Many parents equate health in babyhood with plumpness and do all they can to see that their babies are chubby. There is evidence that fat babies tend to have obesity problems as they grow older while thin babies do not. This is because the number and size of the fat cells of the body are established early in life.

Medical studies have shown that there are three critical periods of fat-cell development. The first occurs during the three months before birth, the second during the first three years of postnatal life, and the third during the early part of adolescence. If babies are overfed, they are likely to have an obesity problem for the rest of their lives.

The reason for this is that even if children slim down later, they still have the same number of cells capable of storing fat—a built-in potential for becoming obese. Similarly, babies who are fed large amounts of carbohydrates during this critical period of fat-cell development are not only overweight as babies but are more subject to diabetes and heart disease as they grow older. Bottle-fed babies are more likely to be overfed than breast-fed babies, and thus lay the foundation for obesity problems (67,103).

Physiological Habits The foundations of the important physiological habits—eating, sleeping, and eliminating—are established during babyhood, and thus a common physical hazard of this period is the establishment of unfavorable attitudes on the baby's part toward these habits. Box 4-10 gives some of the common hazards that arise in relation to the establishment of physiological habits.

Psychological Hazards

The most serious psychological hazards of babyhood involve the baby's failure to master the developmental task for that age. Mastery of these tasks is important for two reasons. First, the sooner babies gain control over their bodies, the sooner they can become independent of help from others. Second, mastery of these tasks provides the foundations on which mastery of later developmental tasks will be built. The better the mastery of babyhood tasks, the more easily and quickly will the child be able to master the tasks of early childhood.

Most of the serious psychological hazards of babyhood are related, either directly or indirectly, to the failure to master the developmental tasks of babyhood.

Hazards in Motor Development When motor development is delayed, babies will be at a great disadvantage when they begin to play with age-mates. The more they lag behind the group in motor control, the slower they are likely to be in acquiring the skills other children possess. Furthermore, because the desire to be independent makes its appearance early in the second year, babies whose motor development lags behind that of their peers become frustrated when they try to do things for themselves and fail.

Almost as handicapping to good adjustment is parental pressure to achieve motor control and to learn motor skills before maturationally ready to do so. Under such conditions, babies often develop resistant, negativistic attitudes that will stifle their motivation and cause a delay in learning tasks that they otherwise are ready to master.

Speech Hazards Delayed speech, like delayed motor control, is serious in babyhood because, at this age, the foundations are being laid for the development of the tools of communication that will be needed later as social horizons broaden. In early

BOX 4-10

COMMON HAZARDS IN ESTABLISHING PHYSIOLOGICAL HABITS

Eating Habits

Babies who suck for long periods show signs of tenseness. They engage in more nonnutritive sucking (such as thumb-sucking), have more sleep difficulties, and are more restless than those whose sucking periods are shorter. If weaning is delayed, babies are likely to resist new kinds of food and substitute thumb-sucking for the nipple. They will also resist semisolid foods if such foods are introduced too early—not because of their taste but because of their texture.

Sleep Habits

Crying, strenuous play with an adult, or noise can make babies tense and keep them from falling asleep. Sleep schedules that do not meet the requirements of individual babies make them tense and resistant to sleep.

Habits of Elimination

These habits cannot be established until the nerves and muscles have developed adequately. Trying to toilet train babies too early will make them uncooperative about establishing these habits when they are maturationally ready. Delay in toilet training, on the other hand, results in habits of irregularity and lack of motivation on the baby's part. Enuresis—bedwetting—is common when training is not timed according to the baby's developmental readiness.

childhood, when interest in people outside the home begins to awaken, children whose speech lags markedly behind that of other children find themselves in the role of outsiders.

There are a number of reasons for delayed speech, the most common of which are low level of intelligence, lack of stimulation (especially during the first year of life), and multiple births. When parents and other caretakers fail to stimulate babbling and early attempts to speak, most babies lose interest in trying to speak. The result is that their speech is often markedly delayed. By contrast, when babies are encouraged to babble and to learn to say words, their speech development conforms to the normal pattern and is often accelerated (10,86,92). The more novelty there is in the environment, the greater the baby's motivation to vocalize (123).

Delayed speech in babies of multiple birth may be due to the developmental lag characteristic of such babies, or to the fact that these babies usually learn to communicate with one another by prespeech forms and, as a result, lag behind their age-mates in speech development. Twins, it has been reported, are especially susceptible to this hazard (6,12). Refer to Figure 2-3 for a graphic illustration of the effect of twinship on early vocalization.

Baby talk—childish mispronunciations—is frequently regarded as "cute" by parents and relatives, who may permit it to continue or even encourage it by using it themselves. As a result, an incorrect auditory image is developed. Continued mispronunciations of a word results in the formation of a word habit that may be difficult to replace with a habit of correct pronunciation when babies emerge into childhood and discover that their playmates cannot

understand them or ridicule them because they "talk like babies."

Emotional Hazards   There are four common psychological hazards that frequently arise in relation to emotional development during the babyhood years. What these are and why they are hazardous are explained in Box 4-11. It would be impossible to rate these in order of their seriousness as hazards to good personal and social relationships as babies grow older. All are serious if they develop into habits during the babyhood years. On the other hand, if they are recognized and corrected, the chances of their persisting will be greatly decreased.

Social Hazards   The major social hazard of babyhood is lack of opportunity and motivation to learn to become social. This encourages the prolongation of egocentrism, which is characteristic of all babies, and leads to the development of introversion. Being deprived of opportunities for social contacts is detrimental at any age, but it is especially so from the ages of six weeks to six months—the critical time in the development of attitudes which affect the pattern of so-

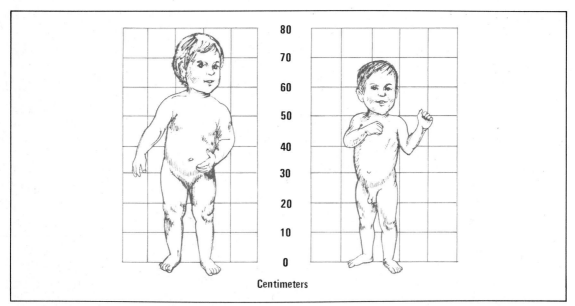

FIGURE 4-8   How emotional deprivation affects the growth of a baby. (Adapted from L. I. Gardner. Deprivation dwarfism. *Scientific American*, 1972, **227**(1), 76–82. Copyright 1972 by Scientific American, Inc. All rights reserved. Used by permission.)

BOX 4-11

COMMON EMOTIONAL HAZARDS OF BABYHOOD

Emotional Deprivation

Babies who are not given the opportunity to experience the normal emotions of babyhood—especially affection, curiosity, and joy—do not thrive physically. If emotional deprivation is severe and prolonged, it inhibits the secretion of the pituitary hormones, including the growth hormone, and this may lead to what has been called "deprivation dwarfism." This is illustrated in Figure 4-8. In addition, emotional deprivation in babyhood often causes babies to be backward in their motor and speech development and they do not learn how to establish social contacts or show affection. They usually become listless, depressed, and apathetic and often develop nervous mannerisms such as thumb-sucking.

Stress

Stress—a prolonged unpleasant emotional state, such as fear or anger—can cause endocrine changes which upset body homeostasis. This, then, is reflected in eating and sleeping difficulties, in nervous mannerisms such as excessive thumb-sucking, and in excessive crying. There are many causes of stress—poor health, parental neglect, and poor environmental conditions that interfere with proper sleeping and eating—but constant and close association with a nervous, tense mother is a particularly important factor.

Too Much Affection

Parents who are oversolicitous or overdemonstrative encourage their babies to focus their attention on themselves and to become self-bound and selfish. Babies thus expect others to show affection for them but they do not reciprocate.

Dominant Emotions

Conditions in the baby's environment encourage the development of certain emotions to the exclusion of others, and these eventually become dominant unless conditions change and the development of other emotions is encouraged. Timidity may persist long after babyhood if a shy or fearful child is exposed to too many strangers or too many frightening situations.

---

cialization. While social attitudes can and do change, many individuals who formed unfavorable social attitudes as babies continue to be socially less well adjusted as they grow older.

Almost as serious a hazard is what Zimbardo et al. have labeled "the social disease called shyness." In a study of college students, 40 percent said they considered themselves to be "shy people." They also explained that their shyness was a carry-over from babyhood when they were subjected to too many strange people and strange caretakers (124).

The long-term effects of shyness which has led Zimbardo et al. to label it a *social disease* are the social problems it gives rise to, especially loneliness, self-consciousness, and unfavorable social evaluations. Shy people are often judged as bored, aloof, condescending or even hostile—judgments that do not contribute to good personal or social adjustments at any age (124).

Play Hazards Play in babyhood is potentially hazardous, both physically and psychologically. Many toys can inflict cuts and bruises or cause the baby to choke on a part that has come loose. The major psychological hazard is that the baby may come to rely too much on the toys themselves for amusement, instead of learning to play in ways that involve interaction with others. Television, used as a built-in babysitter, also discourages the baby from taking an active role in play.

When babies spend most of their play time in being amused by television or by people, they are deprived of opportunities to play with toys in such a way as to experiment in developing new creations with them. While their creations are so simple that they do not in themselves give babies much satisfaction, they do encourage them to be creative.

A play hazard that is often overlooked by parents and other caretakers is the psychological effect of always being a winner. When playing games with adults or older siblings, babies are usually allowed to win. As a result, they find competition with other children difficult as they grow older and are not able to lose graciously.

Hazards in Understanding Even though understanding is in a rudimentary stage of development, it presents one serious psychological hazard. In the development of concepts, it is relatively easy to replace wrong meanings associated with people, objects, or situations with correct meanings. However, all concepts have some emotional weighting, and this is where the potential hazard lies. If, for example, the baby learns to associate sweets with rewards for good behavior and to think of vegetables as a form of punishment, the emotional weighting of these concepts may lead to persistent food likes and dislikes.

Hazards in Morality No one expects babies to be moral in the sense that their behavior conforms to the moral standards of the social group or that they will feel guilt and shame if they fail to do so. However, a serious psychological hazard to future moral development occurs when babies discover that they get more attention when they do things to annoy and antagonize others than when they behave in a more socially approved way.

During babyhood, the patterns of behavior that present the greatest problems for caretakers are dawdling, defiance, and disobedience—the "three D's"

of morality. While not one of these unsocial patterns of behavior is well developed even as babyhood draws to a close, the foundations are often laid at this time. When babies discover that they gain more attention from dawdling, for example, than from doing what they are supposed to do as quickly as they can, they are likely to repeat the dawdling and, by so doing, lay the foundations for the dawdling habit.

Family-Relationship Hazards Because the family constitutes the main social environment, any unfavorable condition in family relationships or in the baby's relationships with different family members leads to psychological hazards with serious and far-reaching consequences. Of the many potential hazards in family relationships, the six that are listed and explained in Box 4-12 are the most common and the most far-reaching in their effects.

Hazards in Personality Development The developing self-concept is in large part a mirror image of what babies believe significant people in their lives think of them. As family relationships deteriorate during the second year of babyhood, self-concepts reflect the unfavorable attitudes babies think family mem-

The dependency of young babies makes them appealing to children as well as to adults. (Erika Stone.)

BOX 4-12

FAMILY-RELATIONSHIP HAZARDS IN BABYHOOD

Separation from Mother

Unless a stable and satisfactory substitute is provided, babies who are separated from their mothers develop feelings of insecurity which are expressed in personality disturbances that may lay the foundation for later maladjustments.

Failure to Develop Attachment Behavior

Babies who fail to establish attachment behavior with their mothers, or some stable mother-substitute, suffer from feelings of insecurity similar to those associated with separation from their mothers. In addition, they do not experience the pleasures that come from close, personal relationships. This handicaps them in establishing friendships as they grow older.

Deterioration in Family Relationships

The deterioration in family relationships that almost always occurs during the second year of life is psychologically hazardous because babies notice that family members have changed attitudes toward them and treat them differently. As a result, they usually feel unloved and rejected—feelings which lead to resentment and insecurity.

Overprotectiveness

Babies who are overprotected and prevented from doing what they are capable of doing become overdependent and afraid to do what other babies of their ages do. This, in time, is likely to lead to abnormal fear of school—*school phobia*—and excessive shyness in the presence of strangers.

Inconsistent Training

Inconsistent child-training methods—which can be the result of permissiveness or of parents' feelings of inadequacy in the parental role—provide poor guidelines for babies. This slows down their learning to behave in approved ways.

Child Abuse

When parents are unhappy in their parental roles or when a frictional relationship exists between them, some babies become the targets of anger and resentment. The babies are either neglected or abused. The second year of life is a more common time for child abuse than the first because babies are more troublesome to their parents and this triggers the outlet of anger, resentment, and other unpleasant emotions engendered in the relationship of the parents.

bers have toward them. They then express these unfavorable self-concepts in aggressive, resentful, negativistic, or withdrawn behavior, all of which make them seem less endearing to family members than they were earlier. The changed attitudes of family members are then reflected in their treatment of the babies. This reinforces the unfavorable self-concepts that the baby is in the process of developing.

HAPPINESS IN BABYHOOD

Normally, the first year of life can be and is one of the happiest of the life span. The dependency of young babies makes them appealing to children as well as to adults. Most children like to play with them, while adults not only want to cuddle and love them but are happy to tolerate their crying and the other disruptions their care brings into their lives.

By contrast, for almost all babies the second year of life is far less happy than the first. There are many reasons for this, the most important of which are given in Box 4-13.

Not all babies, it is important to recognize, have reason to be unhappy as babyhood draws to a close, nor are babies who have one or more reasons for unhappiness *always* unhappy. There are times when they are happy, just as there are times when they are not. Which condition will dominate depends on how many reasons the baby has for being unhappy and how frequently the causes for unhappiness occur. Babies who are neglected or abused by their parents or other caretakers have more reason to be unhappy than those whose parents and caretakers are only occasionally so annoyed by their behavior that they treat them in a punitive way. Generally, most babies have more reason to be unhappy during the second year of life than during the first.

CAUSES OF UNHAPPINESS IN BABYHOOD

Poor Health

Babies who are in poor health, either temporarily or chronically, do not feel up to par and, as a result, tend to be fretful and irritable. Being happy under such conditions is difficult if not impossible.

Teething

Teething causes periodic discomfort, if not actual pain. When in pain or when experiencing discomforts, babies tend to be irritable, fretful, and negativistic. This predisposes them to be unhappy.

Desire for Independence

With increased control over their bodies, most babies resent assistance from others and interference when they are trying to be independent. They show their resentment by being balky or by having temper tantrums.

Increased Need for Attention

As waking time increases, babies want more attention from others. When parents or other caretakers cannot give this attention, babies become angry and fretful. This leads to punitive treatment from parents or other caretakers which babies interpret to mean that they are unloved and unwanted.

Disenchantment with Parenthood

By the baby's second year, it is not uncommon for parents to become somewhat disenchanted with their parental roles. This is especially true of parents who glamorized the parental role before assuming it. Their disenchantment is expressed in lack of warmth in their relationship with the baby —a change in attitude which babies easily sense and resent.

Beginning of Discipline

After babies have had their first birthdays, many parents believe that the time has come to initiate discipline. Initial attempts are usually limited to slaps, spankings, harsh words, and angry facial expressions. After a year of no discipline, it is not surprising that babies interpret this changed parental behavior to mean that they are no longer loved and no longer wanted in the home.

Child Abuse

When parental discipline is characterized by harsh corporal punishment, babies have every reason to feel unloved and unwanted. Even worse, they live in constant dread of abuse from the people who take care of them. Under such conditions, even brief periods of happiness are infrequent.

Increased Sibling Resentment

Many children who at first considered the new babies in their homes "adorable dolls," come to regard them as pests, especially when they are expected to help take care of them, or when the babies take over their possessions, often damaging them. Babies quickly sense how their siblings feel, and this makes them unhappy when they are with them. In large families, where the care of babies is often in the hands of an older female sibling, babies have reason to experience frequent periods of unhappiness because they are aware of how their sisters feel about them and how they resent having to play the role of a surrogate parent.

Chapter Highlights

1. The outstanding characteristics of babyhood, which extends from the end of the second week to the end of the second year of life, are that it is the true foundation age; a time of rapid growth and change and of decreased dependency; a time of increased individuality and the beginning of socialization; a time of sex-role typing and creativity; and a time that is both appealing and hazardous.

2. Babies who lag behind their age-mates in mastering the developmental tasks of babyhood—tasks that make them independent of adult help—are handicapped when they reach the childhood years.

3. Physical growth and development occur at gradually decelerated rates throughout babyhood while development of the physiological functions occurs at a rapid rate.

4. Because muscle control follows the laws of developmental direction, the earliest skills to be learned are the head, arm, and hand skills.

5. To be able to communicate, babies must com-

prehend what others are communicating to them and, in turn, communicate with others. Because of their inability to speak during the major part of babyhood, babies' communications are mainly in prespeech forms—crying, babbling, gestures, and emotional expressions.

6. Babyhood emotions differ from those of older children, adolescents, and adults in that, first, they are accompanied by behavior patterns proportionally too great for the stimuli that give rise to them and, second, they are more easily conditioned than at later ages.

7. Early social foundations are important, first, because the type of behavior babies show in social situations affects their personal and social adjustments and, second, because once established, these patterns tend to persist.

8. Play development follows a pattern that is greatly influenced by the baby's physical, motor, and mental development. This is true of play in general and also of specific play patterns.

9. In babyhood, understanding comes from a combination of sensory exploration, motor manipulation, and, toward the end of babyhood, from answers to questions.

10. Discipline's role in moral development is mainly in the form of punishment for wrong behavior and different forms of approval for socially approved behavior.

11. Sex-role typing begins at birth, though the pressure on boys to look and act in a sex-appropriate way is stronger than the pressure on girls.

12. Evidence of the importance of parent-child relationships in babyhood comes from emotional deprivation, attachment behavior, and the influence of different-sized families.

13. Babyhood is regarded as a critical period in personality development because it is the time when the foundations of adult personality are laid.

14. During the first year of life, physical hazards are more numerous and more serious than psychological hazards while, during the second year, the reverse is true.

15. Unhappiness tends to increase as babyhood draws to a close though, for most babies, it is far less common than happiness.

Bibliography

1. Adelson, E., and S. Fraiberg. Gross motor development in infants blind from birth. *Child Development,* 1974, **45**, 114–126.
2. Ainsworth, M. D. S., S. M. Bell, and D. J. Stayton. Individual differences in the development of some attachment behaviors. *Merrill-Palmer Quarterly,* 1972, **18**, 123–143.
3. Alvy, K. T. Preventing child abuse. *American Psychologist,* 1975, **30**, 921–928.
4. Ames, L. B., and F. L. Ilg. The developmental point of view with special reference to the principle of reciprocal interweaving. *Journal of Genetic Psychology,* 1964, **105**, 195–209.
5. Ban, P. L., and M. Lewis. Mothers and fathers, girls and boys: Attachment behavior in the one-year-old. *Merrill-Palmer Quarterly,* 1974, **20**, 195–204.
6. Bates, E., L. Camaioni, and V. Volterra. The acquisition of performatives prior to speech. *Merrill-Palmer Quarterly,* 1975, **21**, 205–226.
7. Bell, S. M., and M. D. S. Ainsworth. Infant crying and maternal responsiveness. *Child Development,* 1972, **43**, 1171–1190.
8. Birns, B. The emergence and socialization of sex differences in the earliest years. *Merrill-Palmer Quarterly,* 1976, **22**, 229–254.
9. Bischof, N. A. A system approach toward the functional connections of attachment and fear. *Child Development,* 1975, **46**, 801–817.
10. Bloom, K. Social elicitation of infant vocal behavior. *Journal of Experimental Child Psychology,* 1975, **20**, 51–58.
11. Bloom, K. Patterning of infant vocal behavior. *Journal of Experimental Child Psychology,* 1977, **23**, 367–377.
12. Bloom, L., P. Lightbrown, and L. Hood. Structure and variation in child language. *Monographs of the Society for Research in Child Development,* 1975, **40**(2).
13. Braine, M. D. S. Children's first word combinations. *Monographs of the Society for Research in Child Development,* 1976, **41**(1).
14. Breckenridge, M. E., and E. L. Vincent. *Child development: Physical and psychologic development through adolescence.* (5th ed.) Philadelphia: Saunders, 1965.
15. Bretherton, I. Making friends with one-year-olds: An experimental study of infant-stranger interaction. *Merrill-Palmer Quarterly,* 1978, **24**, 29–51.
16. Bronson, W. C. Mother-toddler interaction: A perspective on studying the development of competence. *Merrill-Palmer Quarterly,* 1974, **20**, 275–301.
17. Brooks, J., and M. Lewis. Attachment behavior in thirteen-month-old, opposite-sex twins. *Child Development,* 1974, **45**, 243–247.
18. Brown, R. *The first language: The early stages.* Cambridge, Mass.: Harvard University Press, 1973.
19. Bruner, J. S. Play is serious business. *Psychology Today,* 1975, **8**(8), 81–83.
20. Caldwell, B. M. The effects of psychosocial deprivation on human development in infancy. *Merrill-Palmer Quarterly,* 1970, **16**, 260–277.
21. Chalmers, D. K., and M. E. Rosenbaum. Learning by observing versus learning by doing. *Journal of Educational Psychology,* 1974, **66**, 216–224.
22. Chapanis, A. Interactive human communication. *Scientific American,* 1975, **232**(3), 36–42.
23. Coates, B., E. P. Anderson, and W. W. Hartup. Interrelations in the attachment behavior of human infants. *Developmental Psychology,* 1972, **6**, 218–230.
24. Coates, B., E. P. Anderson, and W. W. Hartup. The stability of attachment behavior in the human infant. *Developmental Psychology,* 1972, **6**, 231–237.

25. Cohen, L. J., and J. J. Campos. Father, mother, and stranger as elicitors of attachment behaviors in infancy. *Developmental Psychology,* 1974, **10**, 146–154.

26. Corter, C., and N. Jamieson. Infants' toy preferences and mothers' predictions. *Developmental Psychology,* 1977, **13**, 413–414.

27. Costello, A. J. Pre-verbal communication. *Journal of Child Psychology & Psychiatry & Allied Disciplines,* 1976, **17**, 351–353.

28. Crawshaw, L. The sudden infant death syndrome: A psychophysiological consideration. *Smith College Studies in Social Work,* 1978, **48**, 132–170.

29. Davids, A., and R. H. Holden. Consistency of maternal attitudes and personality from pregnancy to eight months following childbirth. *Developmental Psychology,* 1970, **2**, 364–366.

30. Dayton, D. H. Early malnutrition and human development. *Children,* 1969, **16**, 210–217.

31. DePalma, D. J., and J. M. Foley (Eds.). *Moral development: Current theory and research.* Hillsdale, N.J.: Lawrence Erlbaum, 1975.

32. Dittrichová, J., and J. Vondracek. Individual differences in infant's sleep. *Developmental Medicine & Child Neurology,* 1978, **18**, 182–188.

33. Doty, D. Infant speech perception. *Human Development,* 1974, **17**, 74–80.

34. Eckerman, C. O., and H. L. Rheingold. Infants' exploratory responses to toys and people. *Developmental Psychology,* 1974, **10**, 255–259.

35. Eckerman, C. O., and J. L. Whatley. Infants' reaction to unfamiliar adults varying in novelty. *Developmental Psychology,* 1975, **11**, 562–566.

36. Eichorn, D. H. Physiological development. In P. H. Mussen (Ed.). *Carmichael's manual of child psychology.* (3rd ed.) Vol. 1. New York: Wiley, 1970, Pp. 157–283.

37. Ekman, P. The universal smile: Face muscles talk every language. *Psychology Today,* 1975, **9**(4), 35–39.

38. Erikson, E. H. *Childhood and society.* (Rev. ed.) New York: Norton, 1964.

39. Etaugh, C., G. Collins, and A. Gersch. Reinforcement of sex-typed behaviors of two-year-old children in a nursery school setting. *Developmental Psychology,* 1975, **11**, 255.

40. Fein, G., D. Johnson, N. Kosson, L. Stork, and L. Wasserman. Sex stereotypes and preferences in the toy choices of 20-month-old boys and girls. *Developmental Psychology,* 1975, **11**, 527–528.

41. Fenson, L., J. Kagan, R. B. Kearsley, and P. R. Zelazo. The developmental progression of manipulative play in the first two years of life. *Child Development,* 1976, **47**, 232–236.

42. Fernstrom, J. D., and R. J. Wurtman. Nutrition and the brain. *Scientific American,* 1974, **230**(2), 84–91.

43. Field, J. The adjustment of reaching behavior to object distance in early infancy. *Child Development,* 1976, **47**, 304–308.

44. Freud, S. *The standard edition of the complete psychological works of Sigmund Freud.* London: Hogarth, 1953–1962. 21 vols.

45. Garai, J. E., and A. Scheinfeld. Sex differences in mental and behavioral traits. *Genetic Psychology Monographs,* 1968, **77**, 169–299.

46. Gardner, L. I. Deprivation dwarfism. *Scientific American,* 1977, **227**(1), 76–82.

47. Gewirtz, J. L. The attachment acquisition process as evidenced in the maternal conditioning of cued infant responding (particularly crying). *Human Development,* 1976, **19**, 143–155.

48. Greenberg, D. J., D. Hillman, and D. Grice. Infant and stranger variables related to stranger anxiety in the first year of life. *Developmental Psychology,* 1973, **9**, 207–212.

49. Hamill, P. V. V., T. A. Drizel, C. L. Johnson, R. B. Reed, and A. F. Roche. *NCHS growth curves for children from birth–18 years.* Hyattsville, Md.: National Center for Health Statistics, U.S. Department of Health, Education, and Welfare, 1977.

50. Hamilton, M. L. Social learning and the transition from babbling to initial words. *Journal of Genetic Psychology,* 1977, **130**, 211–220.

51. Hamilton, M. L., and D. M. Stewart. Peer models and language acquisition. *Merrill-Palmer Quarterly,* 1977, **23**, 45–55.

52. Harrell, J. E., and C. A. Ridley. Substitute child care, maternal employment, and the quality of mother-child interaction. *Journal of Marriage & the Family,* 1975, **37**, 556–564.

53. Havighurst, R. J. *Developmental tasks and education.* (3rd ed.) New York: McKay, 1972.

54. Jacobs, B. S., and H. A. Moss. Birth order and sex of sibling as determinants of mother-infant interaction. *Child Development,* 1976, **47**, 315–322.

55. Jersild, A. T., C. W. Telford, and J. M. Sawrey. *Child psychology.* (7th ed.) Englewood Cliffs, N.J.: Prentice-Hall, 1975.

56. Kagan, J., R. B. Kearsley, and P. R. Zelazo. *Infancy: Its place in human development.* Cambridge, Mass.: Harvard University Press, 1978.

57. Kavanagh, J. F., and J. E. Cutting (Eds.). *The role of speech in language.* Cambridge, Mass.: M.I.T. Press, 1975.

58. Kopp, C. B. Fine motor abilities of infants. *Developmental Medicine & Child Neurology,* 1974, **16**, 629–636.

59. Kotelchuck, M., P. R. Zelazo, J. Kagan, and E. Spelke. Infant reaction to parental separation when left with familiar and unfamiliar adults. *Journal of Genetic Psychology,* 1975, **126**, 255–262.

60. Lamb, M. E. Father-infant and mother-infant interaction in the first year of life. *Child Development,* 1977, **48**, 167–181.

61. Lamb, M. E. A reexamination of the infant social world. *Human Development,* 1977, **20**, 65–85.

62. Lester, B. M. Spectrum analysis of the cry sounds of well-nourished and malnourished infants. *Child Development,* 1976, **47**, 237–241.

63. Lewin, R. Starved brains. *Psychology Today,* 1975, **9**(4), 29–33.

64. Lewis, M. The busy, purposeful world of a baby. *Psychology Today,* 1977, **10**(9), 53–56.

65. Mack, R. W., and J. Ipsen. The height-weight relationship in early childhood. Birth to 48 month correlations in an urban, low-income Negro population. *Human Biology,* 1974, **46**, 21–32.

66. Mack, R. W., and F. E. Johnston. The relationship between growth in infancy and growth in adolescence: Report of a longitudinal study among urban black adolescents. *Human Biology,* 1976, **48**, 693–711.

67. Mack, R. W., and M. E. Kleinhenz. Growth, caloric intake, and activity levels in early infancy: A preliminary report. *Human Biology,* 1974, **46**, 345–354.

68. Marcus, R. E. The child as elicitor of parental sanctions for independent and dependent behavior: A simulation of parent-child interaction. *Developmental Psychology,* 1975, **11**, 443–452.

69. Meredith, H. V. Body size of contemporary groups of one-year-

old infants studied in different parts of the world. *Child Development*, 1970, **41**, 555–600.

70. Meredith, H. V. Relation between tobacco-smoking of pregnant women and body size of their progeny: A compilation and synthesis of published studies. *Human Biology*, 1975, **47**, 451–472.

71. Meredith, H. V. Somatic changes during human postnatal life. *Child Development*, 1975, **46**, 603–610.

72. Messer, S. B., and M. Lewis. Social class and sex differences in the attachment and play behavior of the year-old infant. *Merrill-Palmer Quarterly*, 1972, **18**, 295–306.

73. Miller, E. Handedness and the pattern of human ability. *British Journal of Psychology*, 1971, **62**, 111–112.

74. Moerk, E. L. Piaget's research as applied to the explanation of language development. *Merrill-Palmer Quarterly*, 1975, **21**, 151–169.

75. Mueller, E., and J. Brenner. The origins of social skills and interaction among play-group toddlers. *Child Development*, 1977, **48**, 854–861.

76. Naeye, R. L., R. Fisher, M. Ryser, and P. Whalen. Carotoid body in the sudden infant death syndrome. *Science*, 1976, **191**, 567–569.

77. Ostwald, P. F., and P. Peltzman. The cry of the human infant. *Scientific American*, 1974, **230**(3), 84–90.

78. Papoušek, H., and M. Papoušek. Mirror image and self-recognition in young human infants: A new method of experimental analysis. *Developmental Psychobiology*, 1974, **7**, 149–157.

79. Paradise, E., and F. Curcio. Relationship of cognitive and affective behaviors to fear of strangers in male infants. *Developmental Psychology*, 1974, **10**, 476–483.

80. Parke, R. D., and D. B. Sawin. Fathering: Its major role. *Psychology Today*, 1977, **11**(6), 108–112.

81. Parton, D. A. Learning to imitate in infancy. *Child Development*, 1976, **47**, 14–31.

82. Passman, R. H. Providing attachment objects to facilitate learning and to reduce anxiety: Effects of mothers and security blankets. *Developmental Psychology*, 1977, **13**, 25–28.

83. Peterson, R. A. The natural development of nocturnal bladder control. *Developmental Medicine & Child Neurology*, 1971, **13**, 730–734.

84. Piaget, J. *Psychology and epistemology*. New York: Grossman, 1971.

85. Ramey, C. T., N. W. Finkelstein, and C. O'Brien. Toys and infant behavior in the first year of life. *Journal of Genetic Psychology*, 1976, **129**, 341–342.

86. Roe, K. V. Amount of infant vocalization as a function of age: Some cognitive implications. *Child Development*, 1976, **47**, 936–941.

87. Rosenblith, J. F., and R. Anderson-Huntington. Unexpected deaths in infancy. *Developmental Medicine & Child Neurology*, 1977, **19**, 271.

88. Ross, H. S. The influence of novelty and complexity on exploratory behavior in 12-month-old infants. *Journal of Experimental Child Psychology*, 1974, **17**, 436–451.

89. Ross, H. S. The effects of increasing familiarity on infant's reactions to adult strangers. *Journal of Experimental Child Psychology*, 1975, **20**, 226–239.

90. Rutter, M. Maternal deprivation reconsidered. *Journal of Psychosomatic Research*, 1972, **16**, 241–250.

91. Scarr, S., and P. Salapatek. Patterns of fear development during infancy. *Merrill-Palmer Quarterly*, 1970, **16**, 53–90.

92. Seitz, S., and S. Marcus. Mother-child interactions: A foundation for language development. *Exceptional Children*, 1976, **42**, 445–449.

93. Serafica, F. C. The development of attachment behaviors: An organismic-developmental perspective. *Human Development*, 1978, **21**, 119–140.

94. Seth, G. Eye-hand coordination and ''handedness'': A developmental study of visuo-motor behavior in infancy. *British Journal of Educational Psychology*, 1973, **43**, 35–49.

95. Spelke, E., P. Zelazo, J. Kagan, and M. Kotelchuck. Father interaction and separation protest. *Developmental Psychology*, 1973, **9**, 83–90.

96. Sostek, A. M., T. F. Anders, and A. J. Sostek. Diurnal rhythms in 2–8-week-old infants: Sleep-waking state organization as a function of age and stress. *Psychosomatic Medicine*, 1976, **38**, 250–256.

97. Spock, B. *Raising children in a difficult time*. New York: Norton, 1974.

98. Stern, E., A. H. Parmelee, Y. Akiyama, M. A. Schultz, and W. H. Werner. Sleep cycle characteristics of infants. *Pediatrics*, 1969, **43**, 65–70.

99. Stone, G. P. The play of little children. In R. E. Herron and B. Sutton-Smith (Eds.). *Child's play*. New York: Wiley, 1971, Pp. 4–14.

100. Stone, L. J., and J. Church. *Childhood and adolescence: A psychology of the growing person*. (3rd ed.) New York: Random House, 1973.

101. Stone, L. J., H. F. Smith, and L. B. Murphy (Eds.). *The competent infant: Research and commentary*. New York: Basic Books, 1973.

102. Tanner, J. M. Physical growth. In P. H. Mussen (Ed.). *Carmichael's manual of child psychology*. (3rd ed.) Vol. 1. New York: Wiley, 1970, Pp. 77–165.

103. Tanner, J. M. *Fetus into man: Physical growth from conceptions to maturity*. Cambridge, Mass.: Harvard University Press, 1978.

104. Tautermannová, M. Smiling in infants. *Child Development*, 1973, **44**, 701–704.

105. Terman, L. M., and M. A. Merrill. *Stanford-Binet Intelligence Scale*. Boston: Houghton Mifflin, 1960.

106. Thomas, A., S. Chess, and H. G. Birch. The origin of personality. *Scientific American*, 1970, **223**(2), 102–109.

107. Tizard, J. Early malnutrition, growth and mental development in man. *British Medical Bulletin*, 1974, **30**, 169–174.

108. Todor, J. I. Age differences in integration of components of a motor task. *Perceptual & Motor Skills*, 1975, **41**, 211–215.

109. Tulkin, S. R. Social class differences in attachment behaviors of ten-month-old infants. *Child Development*, 1973, **44**, 171–174.

110. Ubell, E. Crib Death: 10,000 victims in year, cause unknown. *The New York Times*, Jan. 30, 1972.

111. Van Lieshout, C. F. M. Young children's reactions to barriers placed by their mothers. *Child Development*, 1975, **46**, 879–886.

112. Walanski, N. The stature of offspring and the assortive mating of parents. *Human Biology*, 1974, **46**, 613–619.

113. Watson, J. B. *Behaviorism*. New York: People's Institute Publishing Company, 1925.

114. Weisler, A., and R. B. McCall. Exploration and play: Résumé and redirection. *American Psychologist*, 1976, **31**, 492–508.

115. Wenar, C. Executive competence in toddlers: A perspective,

observational study. *Genetic Psychology Monographs,* 1976, **93**, 189–285.

116. White, B. L. Critical influences in the origins of competence. *Merrill-Palmer Quarterly,* 1975, **21**, 243–266.

117. White, B. L. Exploring the origins of human competence. *APA Monitor,* 1976, **7**(4), 4–5.

118. Whiting, G. W. M., T. K. Landauer, and T. M. Jones. Infantile immunization and adult stature. *Child Development,* 1968, **39**, 59–67.

119. Will, J. A., P. A. Self, and N. Dafan. Maternal behavior and perceived sex of infant. *American Journal of Orthopsychiatry,* 1976, **46**, 135–139.

120. Willemsen, E., D. Flaherty, C. Heaton, and G. Ritchey. Attachment behavior of one-year-olds as a function of mother vs. father, sex of child, session and toys. *Genetic Psychology Monographs,* 1974, **90**, 305–324.

121. Williams, T. M. Child rearing practices of young mothers: What we know, how it matters, why it's so little. *American Journal of Orthopsychiatry,* 1974, **44**, 70–75.

122. Wolman, R. N., W. C. Lewis, and M. King. The development of the language of emotions. IV. Bodily referents and the experience of affect. *Journal of Genetic Psychology,* 1972, **121**, 65–81.

123. Zelazo, P. R., J. Kagan, and R. Hartmann. Excitement and boredom as determinants of vocalization in infants. *Journal of Genetic Psychology,* 1975, **126**, 107–117.

124. Zimbardo, P. G., P. A. Pilkonis, and R. M. Norwood. The social disease called shyness. *Psychology Today,* 1975, **8**(12), 68–72.

CHAPTER FIVE
EARLY CHILDHOOD

After reading this chapter, you should be able to:

- Recognize the names that parents, educators, and psychologists use to describe the outstanding characteristics of early childhood.
- Describe the way children continue to master the developmental tasks whose foundations were laid in babyhood.
- Give a brief picture of physical, motor, speech, emotional, social, and play development in early childhood and compare development in these areas with that in babyhood.
- Explain how understanding improves during early childhood and how this affects moral development, sex-role typing, and the kind of interests young children develop.
- Discuss reasons for changes in family relationships during early childhood and point out how these changes contribute to the development of the child's self-concept and individuality.
- Show why the hazards of early childhood can be physical, psychological, or both, and list the most common hazards in each category.
- Explain why early childhood can and should be a happy period and how readily the habit of being either happy or unhappy can be developed at this time.

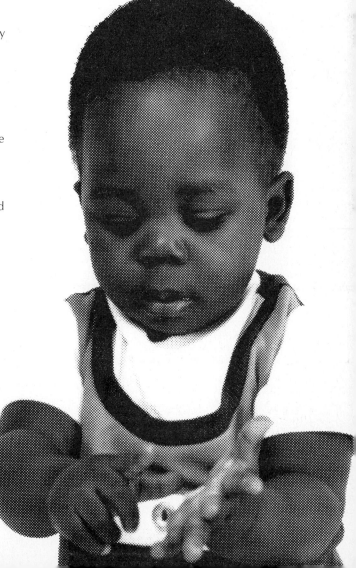

Most people think of childhood as a fairly long period in the life span—a time when the individual is relatively helpless and dependent on others. To children, childhood often seems endless as they wait impatiently for the magic time to come when society will regard them as "grown ups" and no longer as children. Childhood begins when the relative dependency of babyhood is over, at approximately the age of two years, and extends to the time when the child becomes sexually mature, at approximately thirteen years for the average girl and fourteen years for the average boy. After children become sexually mature, they are known as *adolescents*.

During this long period of time—roughly eleven years for girls and twelve years for boys—marked changes take place in the child both physically and psychologically. Because cultural pressures and expectations to learn certain things at one age are different from the pressures and expectations at another age, a child in the early part of childhood is quite different from a child in the latter part of the period.

Today, it is widely recognized that childhood should be subdivided into two separate periods—early and late childhood. Early childhood extends from two to six years, and late childhood extends from six to the time the child becomes sexually mature. Thus early childhood begins at the conclusion of babyhood—the age when dependency is practically a thing of the past and is being replaced by growing independence—and ends at about the time the child enters first grade in school.

This dividing line between early and late childhood is significant for two reasons. First, it is used almost exclusively for American children who, before they reach the compulsory school-entrance age, are treated very differently than they are after they enter school. It is the treatment they receive and the expectations of the social group that influence what this treatment will be that determine when the dividing line between early and late childhood should occur.

The second reason why placing the dividing line between early and late childhood at six years is significant is that it is not influenced by physical but by social factors. There is relatively little difference in the physical growth and development of children before and after they are six years old. The five-year-old, for example, is not radically different from the seven-year-old.

On the other hand, in a culture where the law requires that children must begin their formal education when they reach their sixth birthday, social pressures and social expectations play an important role in determining how children differ before they enter school from those who have already been subjected to school experiences. If formal entrance into school came a year earlier or a year later, the dividing line between early and late childhood would be at five years in the former case, and at seven years in the latter case.

The new pressures and expectations that accompany the child's formal entrance into school result in changes in patterns of behavior, interests, and values. As a result, children become "different" people from what they were earlier. It is this difference in their psychological makeup rather than the difference in their physical makeup that justifies dividing this long span of years into two subdivisions, early and late childhood.

CHARACTERISTICS OF EARLY CHILDHOOD

Just as certain characteristics of babyhood make it a distinctive period in the life span, so certain characteristics of early childhood set it apart from other periods. These characteristics are reflected in the names that parents, educators, and psychologists commonly apply to this period.

Names Used by Parents

Most parents consider early childhood a *problem age* or a *troublesome age*. While babyhood presents problems for parents, most of these center around the baby's physical care. With the dawn of childhood, behavior problems become more frequent and more troublesome than the physical-care problems of babyhood.

The reason that behavior problems dominate the early childhood years is that young children are developing distinctive personalities and are demanding an independence which, in most cases, they are incapable of handling successfully. In addition, young children are often obstinate, stubborn, disobedient, negativistic, and antagonistic. They have frequent temper tantrums, they are often bothered by bad dreams at night and irrational fears during the day, and they suffer from jealousies.

Because of these problems, early childhood seems a less appealing age than babyhood to many parents. The dependency of the baby, so endearing to parents as well as to older siblings, is now replaced by a resistance on the child's part to their help and a tendency to reject demonstrations of their affection. Furthermore, few young children are as cute as babies, which also makes them less appealing.

Parents often refer to early childhood as the *toy age* because young children spend much of their waking time playing with toys. Studies of children's play have revealed that toy play reaches its peak during the early childhood years and then begins to decrease when children reach the school age (11,61).

This, of course, does not mean that interest in playing with toys ends abruptly when the child enters school. Instead, with entrance into first grade, children are encouraged to engage in games and modified forms of sports, none of which require the use of toys. When alone, however, children continue to play with their toys well into the third or even fourth grade.

During the preschool years, nursery schools, kindergartens, day-care centers, and organized play groups all emphasize play which makes use of toys. As a result, whether young children are playing alone or with peers, toys are an important element of their play activities.

Names Used by Educators

Educators refer to the early childhood years as the *preschool age* to distinguish it from the time when children are considered old enough, both physically and mentally, to cope with the work they will be expected to do when they begin their formal schooling. Even when children go to nursery school or kindergarten, they are labeled *preschoolers* rather than *schoolchildren*. In the home, day-care center, nursery school, or kindergarten, the pressures and expectations young children are subjected to are very different from those they will experience when they begin their formal education in the first grade. The early childhood years, either in the home or in a preschool, are a time of preparation.

Names Used by Psychologists

Psychologists use a number of different names to describe the outstanding characteristics of the psychological development of children during the early years of childhood. One of the most commonly applied names is the *pregang age,* the time when children are learning the foundations of social behavior as a preparation for the more highly organized social life they will be required to adjust to when they enter first grade.

Because the major development that occurs during early childhood centers around gaining control over the environment, many psychologists refer to early childhood as the *exploratory age,* a label which implies that children want to know what their environment is, how it works, how it feels, and how they can be a part of it. This includes people as well as inanimate objects. One common way of exploring in early childhood is by asking questions: thus this period is often referred to as the *questioning age.*

At no other time in the life span is imitation of the speech and actions of others more pronounced than it is during early childhood. For this reason, it is also known as the *imitative age.* However, in spite of this tendency, most children show more creativity in their play during early childhood than at any other time in their lives. For that reason, psychologists also regard it as the *creative age.*

DEVELOPMENTAL TASKS OF EARLY CHILDHOOD

Although the foundations of some of the developmental tasks young children are expected to master before they enter school are laid in babyhood, much remains to be learned in the relatively short four-year span of early childhood. Refer to page 10 for a complete list of Havighurst's developmental tasks.

When babyhood ends, all normal babies have learned to walk, though with varying degrees of proficiency; have learned to take solid foods; and have achieved a reasonable degree of physiological stability. The major task of learning to control the elimination of body wastes has been almost completed and will be fully mastered within another year or two.

While most babies have built up a useful vocabulary, have reasonably correct pronunciation of the words they use, can comprehend the meaning of simple statements and commands, and can put together several words into meaningful sentences, their ability to communicate with others and to comprehend what others say to them is still on a low level. Much remains to be mastered before they enter school.

Similarly, they have some simple concepts of social and physical realities, but far too few to meet their needs as their social horizons broaden and as their physical environment expands. Few babies know more than the most elementary facts about sex differences, and even fewer understand the meaning of sexual modesty. It is questionable whether any babies, as they enter early childhood, actually know what is sex-appropriate in appearance, and they have only the most rudimentary understanding of sex-appropriate behavior.

This is equally true of concepts of right and wrong. What knowledge they have is limited to home situations and must be broadened to include concepts of right and wrong in their relationships with people outside the home, especially in the neighborhood, in school, and on the playground.

Even more important, young children must lay the foundations for a conscience as a guide to right and wrong behavior. The conscience serves as a source of motivation for children to do what they know is right and to avoid doing what they know is wrong when they are too old to have the watchful eye of a parent or a parent substitute constantly focused on them.

One of the most important and, for many young children, one of the most difficult of the developmental tasks of early childhood, is learning to relate emotionally to parents, siblings, and other people. The emotional relationships that existed during babyhood must be replaced by more mature ones. The reason for this is that relationships to others in babyhood are based on babyish dependence on others to meet their emotional needs, especially their need for affection. Young children, however, must learn to give as well as to receive affection. In short, they must learn to be outer-bound instead of self-bound (59).

PHYSICAL DEVELOPMENT

Growth during early childhood proceeds at a slow rate as compared with the rapid rate of growth in babyhood. Early childhood is a time of relatively even growth, though there are seasonal variations; July to mid-December is the most favorable time for increases in weight, and April to mid-August is most favorable for height increases (26,86,98,132).

The major aspects of physical development are summarized in Box 5-1. Compare the development that takes place in early childhood with that which takes place in babyhood, as summarized in Box 4-1.

In spite of the predictable pattern described in Box 5-1, there are individual differences in all aspects of physical development. Children of superior intelligence, for example, tend to be taller in early childhood than those of average or below-average intelligence and to shed their temporary teeth sooner. While sex differences in height and weight are not pronounced, ossification of the bones and shedding of the temporary teeth are more advanced, age for age, in girls than in boys. Because children from higher socioeconomic groups tend to be better nourished and receive better prenatal and postnatal care, variations in height, weight, and muscular development are in their favor (26,98,132).

PHYSIOLOGICAL HABITS

During early childhood, the physiological habits whose foundations were laid in babyhood become well established. It is no longer necessary to provide specially prepared foods for young children and they learn to eat their meals at regular times. However, young children's appetites are not as ravenous as they were in babyhood, partly because their growth rate has slowed down and partly because they have now developed marked food likes and dislikes.

There are daily variations in the amount of sleep young children need, depending on such factors as the amount of exercise they had during the day and the kinds of activities they have engaged in. Three-year-olds sleep approximately twelve out of the twenty-four hours. Each successive year during early childhood, the average daily amount of sleep is approximately one-half hour less than in the previous year.

As was pointed out in the preceding chapter, bowel control is generally well established when babyhood ends. By the time the child is three or four years old, bladder control at night should be

BOX 5-1

PHYSICAL DEVELOPMENT IN EARLY CHILDHOOD

Height

The average annual increase in height is three inches. By the age of six, the average child measures 46.6 inches.

Weight

The average annual increase in weight is 3 to 5 pounds. At age six, children should weigh approximately seven times as much as they did at birth. The average girl weighs 48.5 pounds, and the average boy weighs 49 pounds.

Body Proportions

Body proportions change markedly, and the "baby look" disappears. Facial features remain small but the chin becomes more pronounced and the neck elongates. There is a gradual decrease in the stockiness of the trunk, and the body tends to become cone-shaped, with a flattened abdomen, a broader and flatter chest, and shoulders that are broader and more square. The arms and legs lengthen and may become spindly, and the hands and feet grow bigger. Refer to Figure 4-2.

Body Build

Differences in body build become apparent for the first time in early childhood. Some children have an *endomorphic* or flabby, fat body build, some have a *mesomorphic* or sturdy, muscular body build, and some have an *ectomorphic* or relatively thin body build. See Figure 5-1.

Bones and Muscles

The bones ossify at different rates in different parts of the body, following the laws of developmental direction. The muscles become larger, stronger, and heavier, with the result that children look thinner as early childhood progresses, even though they weigh more.

Fat

Children who tend toward endomorphy have more adipose than muscular tissue; those who tend toward mesomorphy have more muscular than adipose tissue; and those with an ectomorphic build have both small muscles and little adipose tissue.

Teeth

During the first four to six months of early childhood, the last four baby teeth—the back molars—erupt. During the last half year of early childhood, the baby teeth begin to be replaced by permanent teeth. The first to come out are the front central incisors—the first baby teeth to appear. When early childhood ends, the child generally has one or two permanent teeth in front and some gaps where permanent teeth will eventually erupt.

achieved. By the time the child is ready to enter school, bladder control should be so complete that even fatigue and emotional tension will not interfere with it.

SKILLS OF EARLY CHILDHOOD

Early childhood is the ideal age to learn skills. There are three reasons for this. First, young children enjoy repetition and are, therefore, willing to repeat an activity until they have acquired the ability to do it well. Second, young children are adventuresome and, as a result, are not held back by fear of hurting themselves or of being ridiculed by peers, as older children often are. And, third, young children learn easily and quickly because their bodies are still very pliable and because they have acquired so few skills that they do not interfere with the acquisition of new ones.

Early childhood may be regarded as the "teachable moment" for acquiring skills (59). If children are not given opportunities to learn skills when they are developmentally ready to do so and when they want to do so because of their growing desire for independence, they will not only lack the necessary foundations for the skills their peers have learned but they will lack the motivation to learn skills when they are eventually given an opportunity to do so.

Typical Skills of Early Childhood

What skills young children will learn depends partly upon their maturational readiness but mainly upon the opportunities they are given to learn and the guidance they receive in mastering these skills

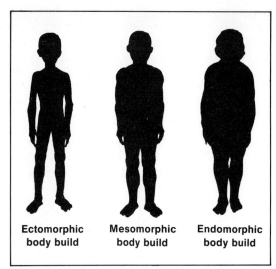

| Ectomorphic | Mesomorphic | Endomorphic |
| body build | body build | body build |

FIGURE 5-1 Types of body build in children.

quickly and efficiently. Children from poor environments, it has been reported, generally master skills earlier and in larger numbers than children from more favored environments, not because they are maturationally more advanced but because their parents are too busy to wait on them when it is no longer necessary (19,27,30).

There are sex differences in the kinds of skills children learn. Early in childhood, boys come under pressure to learn play skills that are culturally approved for members of their own sex and to avoid mastering those which are considered more appropriate for girls. They are, for example, encouraged to learn skills involved in ball play, just as girls are encouraged to learn skills related to homemaking.

In spite of variations, all young children learn certain common skills, though the time they learn them may vary somewhat and the proficiency with which they learn them may be different. These common skills can be divided into two major categories: hand skills and leg skills.

Hand Skills Self-feeding and dressing skills, begun in babyhood, are perfected in early childhood. The greatest improvement in dressing skills generally comes between the ages of 1½ and 3½ years. Brushing the hair and bathing are skills which can be acquired easily in early childhood. By the time children reach kindergarten age, they should be able to bathe

and dress themselves with a fair degree of proficiency, to tie their shoelaces and to comb their hair with little or no assistance.

Between the ages of five and six, most children can become proficient in throwing and catching balls. They can use scissors and can mold with clay, make cookies, and sew. Using crayons, pencils, and paints, young children are able to color outlined pictures, draw or paint pictures of their own, and make a recognizable drawing of a man.

Leg Skills Once young children have learned to walk, they turn their attention to learning other movements requiring the use of their legs. They learn to hop, skip, gallop, and jump by the time they are five or six years old. Climbing skills are likewise well established in early childhood. Between the ages of three and four, tricycling and swimming can be learned. Other leg skills acquired by young children include jumping rope, balancing on rails or on the top of a wall, roller skating, ice skating (on double-runners), and dancing.

Handedness

Early childhood may be regarded as a critical period in the establishment of handedness. The reason is that, during this period, children abandon, to a large extent, the tendency to shift from the use of one hand to the use of the other and begin to concentrate on learning skills with one hand as the dominant hand and the other as the auxiliary or helping hand.

There is evidence that handedness—or the tendency to use one hand in preference to the other —is not firmly established until sometime between the ages of three and six years (60). This, of course, does not mean that children cannot change the dominant hand if they want to do so. For example, should first-graders discover that it is a handicap to use their left hand when they are trying to imitate the model of right-handed writing the teacher puts on the chalkboard, they can change to using the right hand as the dominant hand if their motivation to do so is strong enough. However, with each passing year, the habit of using one hand as the dominant hand in preference to the other hand becomes more firmly established. As a result, changing handedness becomes increasingly difficult.

There is evidence, though not substantiated by research studies, that children who attend preschools —nursery schools or kindergartens—or who are cared for in day-care centers or day camps during the summer months, are less likely to develop left-handed tendencies than children whose early childhood years are spent mainly in the home and with neighborhood play groups.

The reason for this is that, in preschools and child-care centers, teachers and other caretakers are advised to encourage children to use their right hands and are expected to teach new hand skills in such a way that children who are still somewhat ambidextrous will find the use of their right hands relatively easy and far less confusing than they will by the time they reach first grade. Not all preschools or child-care centers emphasize the encouragement of right-handedness but many more do than those which ignore this aspect of guidance. By contrast, many parents believe that handedness is a hereditary trait and, as a result, when they see their children using their left hands, they assume that they are *naturally* left-handed and do nothing to encourage them to learn new skills with their right hands as the dominant ones.

Because many of the hand skills young children learn cannot be carried out with one hand but require the use of both hands, both hands must be trained to carry out the skill. However, few skills require that both hands play equally important roles in carrying out the skills. Consequently, in teaching young children new hand skills emphasis should be placed on the movements made by the dominant hand and those by the auxiliary hand. These movements are often quite different. In the case of crayoning, for example, the dominant hand uses the crayon and the auxiliary hand holds the paper in place so the child can crayon a figure on it. In buttoning a garment, most of the movements of pushing the button through the hole are done by the dominant hand while the movements made by the auxiliary hand consist mainly of holding the garment in such a way that the button will be close enough to the buttonhole to be inserted into it.

IMPROVEMENTS IN SPEECH DURING EARLY CHILDHOOD

By the time children are two years old, most of the prespeech forms of communication they found so useful during babyhood have been abandoned. Young children no longer babble, and their crying is greatly curtailed. They may use gestures, but mainly as supplements to speech—to emphasize the meaning of the words they use—rather than as substitutes for speech. However, they continue to communicate with others by emotional expressions which, on the whole, are less subject to social disapproval and less likely to be judged as "babyish" than other prespeech forms (13). (Refer to pages 88–89 for a more complete discussion of prespeech forms of communication.)

During early childhood, there is a strong motivation on the part of most children to learn to speak. There are two reasons for this. First, learning to speak is an essential tool in socialization. Children who can communicate easily with their peers make better social contacts and are more readily accepted as members of the peer group than children whose ability to communicate is limited. Young children attending preschools will be handicapped both socially and educationally unless they speak as well as their classmates.

Second, learning to speak is a tool in achieving independence. Children who cannot make known their wants and needs, or who cannot make themselves understood, are likely to be treated as babies and fail to achieve the independence they want and feel capable of handling successfully. If children cannot tell their parents or other caretakers that they want to try to cut their own meat or brush their own hair, the adults are likely to continue these tasks on the assumption that the children are too young to be interested in mastering them. This keeps the child from becoming self-reliant and independent.

To improve communication, children must master two major tasks, both of which, as was pointed out in the preceding chapter, are essential elements of learning to speak. They must, first, improve their ability to comprehend what others are saying to them and, second, they must improve their own speech so that others can comprehend what they are trying to communicate to them. While parents and other caretakers usually put more emphasis on learning to speak, the task of improving comprehension is, indirectly, taken care of by children themselves because of their strong motivation to communicate as a tool for social belonging.

Improvement in Comprehension

To be able to communicate with others, children must understand what others say to them. Otherwise their speech will be unrelated to what others have said to them and this will jeopardize their social contacts. The importance of comprehension of what others say is well illustrated in the case of bilingual children whose dominant language is different from that of their playmates. Because they cannot understand what their playmates are saying, they become socially isolated (45).

Comprehension is greatly influenced by how attentively children *listen* to what is said to them. Listening to the radio and to what is said on television has proved to be helpful in this regard because it encourages attentive listening. In addition, if people speak slowly and distinctly to young children, using words they have reason to believe the child understands, this will likewise encourage attentive listening. By contrast, when people speak rapidly to young children, using difficult and unfamiliar words and complex sentences, children become confused and discouraged because they cannot understand what is being said. This discourages them from trying to be attentive listeners (106,124,137).

Improvement in Speech Skills

Early childhood is normally a time when rapid strides are made in the major tasks of learning to speak—building up a vocabulary, mastering pronunciation, and combining words into sentences. Box 5-2 describes how these tasks are mastered. Compare the pattern of speech development in early childhood with that in babyhood, as outlined in Box 4-4.

There is evidence that young children of today speak better than young children of past generations. McCarthy (95) has suggested the reason for this improvement:

Several possibilities account for this. Among those I would list are the advent of radio and television, fewer foreign-born and bilingual children, the rise of nursery schools affording more opportunities for language stimulation outside the home for formerly underprivileged groups of children, more leisure time for parents to spend with their children, reduced amount of time that children are cared for by nursemaids of limited verbal ability, better economic conditions allowing parents even in lower income brackets to provide more stimulating environments for their children, and finally the somewhat greater tendency for children to be treated more permissively and to find greater acceptance in the modern home.

BOX 5-2

TASKS INVOLVED IN LEARNING TO SPEAK IN EARLY CHILDHOOD

Pronunciation of Words

Certain sounds and sound combinations are especially difficult for a young child to learn to pronounce, such as the consonants *z, w, d, s,* and *g* and the consonant combinations *st, str, dr,* and *fl.* Listening to radio and television can be an aid in learning correct pronunciation.

Vocabulary Building

Young children's vocabularies increase rapidly as they learn new words and new meanings for old words. Figure 5-2 shows the rapid increase in vocabulary during early childhood. In vocabulary building, young children learn a general vocabulary of words, such as "good" and "bad," "give" and "take," as well as many words with specific usage, such as numbers and the names of colors.

Forming Sentences

Three- or four-word sentences are used as early as two years of age and commonly at three. Many of these sentences are incomplete, consisting mainly of nouns and lacking verbs, prepositions, and conjunctions. After age three, the child forms six- to eight-word sentences containing all parts of speech.

There are two lines of evidence that have served to explain the most important reasons for the fact that today's young children speak better than children, age for age, did in the past.

First, parents of today, especially mothers, talk more to their children partly because they have more free time to do so owing to smaller families and more labor-saving devices in the home, and partly because they recognize how important it is to give young children opportunities to talk and to encourage them to do so (63,101,123). Because girls spend more time in the home than do boys, who play more with neighborhood children, mothers talk more to their daughters than to their sons. This may and probably does explain, in part at least, the better speech development of girls than of boys during the preschool years (15).

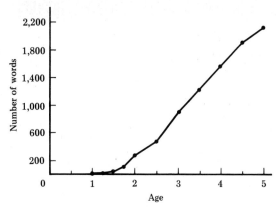

FIGURE 5-2 Vocabulary increases rapidly during early childhood. (Adapted from L. P. Lipsitt. Learning processes of human newborns. *Merrill-Palmer Quarterly,* 1966, **12,** 45–71. Used by permission.)

Second, the more contacts young children have with their peers, the more encouragement they have to talk, and the more models they have to imitate (53, 56). However, this does not guarantee that qualitatively their speech will be better. In talking to peers, young children can and often do pick up mispronunciations of words and incorrect grammatical structures.

Content of Speech

At first, the speech of young children is egocentric in the sense that they talk mainly about themselves, their interests, their families, and their possessions. Toward the end of early childhood, socialized speech begins and children talk about other people as well as about themselves. But much of this early socialized speech is unsocial in that it is heavily weighted with criticism of others, and it may take the form of tattling or complaining. Most young children also make unkind, derogatory comments about other people, and about their actions and their possessions. They also engage in name-calling, especially when they are angry. Boasting, primarily about material possessions, is very common at this age.

As the size of the play group becomes larger, children's speech becomes more social and less egocentric. They become less critical, they ask fewer questions, and they give more commands. There is evidence that small social groupings are more favorable for the development of speech in young children than large social groupings (75,77,92,117).

The most frequent topics of conversation among young children are themselves and their activities. When a second person is the subject of a remark, the remark is generally a command for that person to do something. Topics such as personal likes and dislikes, clothes, where one lives, and matters of everyday routine predominate in the young child's conversation.

Regardless of what young children talk about, they more often put their words into questions than into statements of fact. Meyer and Shane (99), from extensive studies of young children's questions, have come to the conclusion that

Question-asking behavior follows Piaget's model of cognitive development. It reflects the logic of their thinking processes. At the preoperational stage, the child's questions concerning physical causality reflect largely undifferentiated cognitive structures in which the child's concerns with motivations and intentions are not separated from the causal explanations. When the child moves into the concrete operations stage, his questioning behavior reflects a higher level of differentiation: thus the questions separate physical causality from psychological causality. The question-asking behaviors of children at the level of concrete operations are initially concerned with physical causality and then shift to a diverse number of categories.

Amount of Talking

Early childhood is popularly known as the *chatterbox age.* The reason for this is that, once they are able to speak with ease, many young children talk incessantly. Other children, by contrast, are relatively silent—the nontalkers or "Silent Sams."

How much young children talk depends upon a number of factors, the most important of which are listed in Box 5-3.

EMOTIONS OF EARLY CHILDHOOD

Emotions are especially intense during early childhood. This is a time of disequilibrium when children are "out of focus" in the sense that they are easily aroused to emotional outbursts and, as a result, are difficult to live with and guide. While this is true of

FACTORS INFLUENCING HOW MUCH YOUNG CHILDREN TALK

Intelligence

The brighter the child, the more quickly speech skills will be mastered and, consequently, the ability to talk.

Type of Discipline

Children who grow up in homes where discipline tends to be permissive, talk more than those whose parents are authoritarian and who believe that "children should be seen but not heard."

Ordinal Position

Firstborn children are encouraged to talk more than their later-born siblings and their parents have more time to talk to them.

Family Size

Only-children are encouraged to talk more than children from large families and their parents have more time to talk to them. In large families, the discipline is likely to be authoritarian and this prevents children from talking as much as they would like to.

Socioeconomic Status

In lower-class families, family activities tend to be less organized than those in middle- and upper-class families. There is also less conversation among the family members and less encouragement for the child to talk.

Racial Status

The poorer quality of speech and of conversational skills of many young black children may be due in part to the fact that they have grown up in homes where the father is absent, or where family life is disorganized because there are many children, or because the mother must work outside the home.

Bilingualism

While young children from bilingual homes may talk as much at home as children from monolingual homes, their speech is usually very limited when they are with members of their peer group or with adults outside the home.

Sex-Role Typing

As early as the preschool years, there are effects of sex-role typing on children's speech. Boys are expected to talk less than girls, but what they say, and how they say it, is expected to be different. Boasting and criticizing others, for example, are considered more appropriate for boys than for girls, while the reverse is true of tattling.

---

the major part of early childhood, it is especially true of children aged 2½ to 3½ and 5½ to 6½ (2).

Although any emotion may be "heightened" in the sense that it occurs more frequently and more intensely than is normal for that particular individual, heightened emotionality in early childhood is characterized by temper tantrums, intense fears, and unreasonable outbursts of jealousy. Part of the intense emotionality of children at this age may be traced to fatigue due to strenuous and prolonged play, rebellion against taking naps, and the fact that they may eat too little.

Much of the heightened emotionality characteristic of this age is psychological rather than physiological in origin. Most young children feel that they are capable of doing more than their parents will permit them to do and revolt against the restrictions placed upon them. In addition, they become angry when they find they are incapable of doing what they think they can do easily and successfully. Even more important, children whose parents expect them to measure up to unrealistically high standards will experience more emotional tension than children whose parents are more realistic in their expectations.

Common Emotional Patterns

Young children experience most of the emotions normally experienced by adults. However, the stimuli that give rise to them and the ways in which children express these emotions are markedly different. Box 5-4 gives the common emotional patterns of early childhood.

Note that the fear-related emotional patterns— worry, anxiety, and embarrassment—are not listed. They normally do not become important emotions until late childhood, when contacts with peers and

BOX 5-4

COMMON EMOTIONS OF EARLY CHILDHOOD

Anger

The most common causes of anger in young children are conflicts over playthings, the thwarting of wishes, and vigorous attacks from another child. Children express anger through temper tantrums, characterized by crying, screaming, stamping, kicking, jumping up and down, or striking.

Fear

Conditioning, imitation, and memories of unpleasant experiences play important roles in arousing fears, as do stories, pictures, radio and television programs, and movies with frightening elements. At first, a child's response to fear is panic; later, responses become more specific and include running away and hiding, crying, and avoiding frightening situations.

Jealousy

Young children become jealous when they think parental interest and attention are shifting toward someone else in the family, usually a new sibling. Young children may openly express their jealousy or they may show it by reverting to infantile behavior, such as bed-wetting, pretending to be ill, or being generally naughty. All such behavior is a bid for attention.

Curiosity

Children are curious about anything new that they see and also about their own bodies and the bodies of others. Their first responses to curiosity take the form of sensorimotor exploration; later, as a result of social pressures and punishment, they respond by asking questions.

Envy

Young children often become envious of the abilities or material possessions of another child. They express their envy in different ways, the most common of which is complaining about what they themselves have, by verbalizing wishes to have what the other has (see Figure 5-3), or by appropriating the objects they envy.

Joy

Young children derive joy from such things as a sense of physical well-being, incongruous situations, sudden or unexpected noises, slight calamities, playing pranks on others, and accomplishing what seem to them to be difficult tasks. They express their joy by smiling and laughing, clapping their hands, jumping up and down, or hugging the object or person that has made them happy.

Grief

Young children are saddened by the loss of anything they love or that is important to them, whether it be a person, a pet, or an inanimate object, such as a toy. Typically, they express their grief by crying and by losing interest in their normal activities, including eating.

Affection

Young children learn to love the things—people, pets, or objects—that give them pleasure. They express their affection verbally as they grow older but, while they are still young, they express it physically by hugging, patting, and kissing the object of their affection.

---

adults outside the home become more frequent and more pronounced than they were in early childhood.

Variations in Emotional Patterns

Many factors influence the intensity and frequency of emotions in early childhood. Emotions are intense at certain *ages* and less so at others. Temper tantrums, for example, reach their peak of severity between the ages of two and four, after which they become shorter in duration and give way to sulking, brooding, and whining. Fear follows much the same pattern, partly because young children realize that there is nothing frightening about situations they formerly feared and partly because of social pressures that make them feel that they must conceal their fears. By contrast, jealousy begins around the age of two and increases as the child grows older.

Young children vary greatly in amount of curiosity and in the way they express it. *Bright* children, it has been found, are more active in exploring their environment and ask more questions than those of lower intellectual levels (76).

FIGURE 5-3 Children learn at an early age to express their envy. (Bil Keane. "The Family Circus." *Register and Tribune Syndicate*, July 21, 1972. Used by permission.)

"I wish you'd buy us a swing like THEIRS!"

Sex differences in emotions come mainly from social pressures to express emotions in sex-appropriate ways. Because temper tantrums are considered more sex-appropriate for boys than for girls, boys throughout early childhood have more tantrums, and more violent tantrums, than girls. On the other hand, fear, jealousy, and affection are considered less sex-appropriate for boys than for girls, and thus girls express these emotions more strongly than boys (16, 42).

Family size influences the frequency and intensity of jealousy and envy. Jealousy is more common in small families, where there are two or three children, than in larger families, where none of the children can receive much attention from their parents. Envy, on the other hand, is more common in large than in small families; the larger the family, the fewer material possessions the children will have and, therefore, the more likely they are to envy one another's things. *Firstborn* children display jealousy more often and more violently than their later-born siblings.

The *social environment* of the home plays an important role in the frequency and intensity of the young child's anger. For example, temper tantrums are more frequent in homes where there are many guests or where there are more than two adults. Similarly, the child with siblings has more temper outbursts than the only child. The kind of *discipline* and the *child-training* methods used also influence the frequency and intensity of the child's angry outbursts. The more authoritarian the parents are, the more likely the child is to respond with anger.

SOCIALIZATION IN EARLY CHILDHOOD

One of the important developmental tasks of early childhood is acquiring the preliminary training and experience needed to become a member of a "gang" in late childhood. Thus early childhood is often called the *pregang age*. The foundations for socialization are laid as the number of contacts young children have with their peers increases with each passing year. Not only do they play more with other children, but they also talk more with them (93,103). This is illustrated in Figure 5-4.

The *kind* of social contacts young children have is more important than the number of such contacts. If young children enjoy their contacts with others, even if they are only occasional, their attitudes toward future social contacts will be more favorable

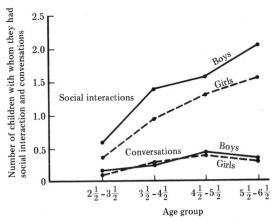

FIGURE 5-4 Children play more with, and talk more to, other children as they grow older. (Adapted from H. R. Marshall. Relations between home experiences and children's use of language in play interactions with peers. *Psychological Monographs*, 1961, **75**(5). Used by permission.)

than if they have more frequent social contacts of a less favorable kind. Children who prefer interacting with people to interacting with objects develop more social know-how and, as a result, are more popular than those who have limited social interactions (67).

The advantages young children take of the opportunities offered them for social contacts will be greatly influenced by how pleasurable their past social contacts have been. As a general rule, during the preschool years, children find social contacts with members of their own sex more pleasurable than those with members of the opposite sex (41,81).

Patterns of Early Socialization

Between the ages of two and three years, children show a decided interest in watching other children and they attempt to make social contacts with them. This is known as *parallel play,* play in which young children play independently *beside* other children rather than *with* them. If any contacts are made with other children, they tend to be frictional rather than cooperative. Parallel play is the earliest form of social activity young children have with their peers.

Following this comes *associative play,* in which children engage in similar, if not identical, activities with other children. As social contacts increase, young children engage in *cooperative play,* play in which they are a part of the group and interact with group members.

Even after children begin to play with other children, they often play the role of *onlooker,* watching other children at play but making no real attempt to play with them. From this onlooker experience, young children learn how others make social contacts and what their behavior is in social situations.

By the time young children are four years old, if they have had these preliminary socializing experiences, they usually understand the rudiments of team play, they are conscious of the opinions of others, and they try to gain attention by showing off. In the remaining years of early childhood, they then polish off the rough edges of their social behavior and learn new patterns of behavior that will make acceptance by the peer group more assured.

Early Forms of Behavior in Social Situations

The most important forms of social behavior necessary for successful social adjustment appear and begin to develop at this time. In the early years of childhood, these forms are not developed well enough to enable the child to get along successfully with others at all times. However, this is a crucial stage in development because it is at this time that the basic social attitudes and the patterns of social behavior are established. In a longitudinal study of a group of young children, Waldrop and Halverson reported that those children who, at age 2½ years, were friendly and socially active continued to be so when they reached the age of 7½ years. They concluded that "Sociability at 2½ years was predictive of sociability at 7½ years (138).

The different forms of behavior in social situations during the early childhood years are given in Box 5-5. Note that many of these patterns appear to be unsocial or even antisocial rather than social. However, each of these apparently unsocial or antisocial patterns of behavior is important as a learning experience that will enable young children to know what the social group approves and disapproves and what it will and will not tolerate.

Companions in Early Childhood

At all ages, companions may be of three different kinds. What they are and what role they play in the socialization of young children are explained in Box 5-6.

In early childhood, companions are mainly associates and playmates. While young children may refer to some of their favorite playmates as their "friends," few play the role of friends during the early childhood years.

During the first year or two of early childhood, when contacts with others are mainly in parallel or associative play, children's companions are primarily associates. Later, when they engage in cooperative play, their companions become their playmates. At this time, many young children have one or more favorite playmates with whom they not only play but with whom they also communicate their feelings, emotions, interests, and even their aspirations for the future. These children then play the role of friends as well as of playmates. Only as early childhood draws to a close and the egocentric speech of young children gradually becomes more socialized does this happen.

In the selection of companions, children prefer other children of their own ages and levels of development who can do what they are able to do. Chil-

BOX 5-5

SOCIAL AND UNSOCIAL BEHAVIOR PATTERNS

Social Patterns

Imitation

To identify themselves with the group, children imitate the attitudes and behavior of a person whom they especially admire and want to be like.

Rivalry

The desire to excel or outdo others is apparent as early as the fourth year. It begins at home and later develops in play with children outside the home.

Cooperation

By the end of the third year, cooperative play and group activities begin to develop and increase in both frequency and duration as the child's opportunities for play with other children increase.

Sympathy

Because sympathy requires an understanding of the feelings and emotions of others, it appears only occasionally before the third year. The more play contacts the child has, the sooner sympathy will develop.

Empathy

Like sympathy, empathy requires an understanding of the feelings and emotions of others but, in addition, it requires the ability to imagine oneself in the place of the other person. Relatively few children are able to do this until early childhood ends.

Social Approval

As early childhood draws to a close, peer approval becomes more important than adult approval. Young children find that naughty and disturbing behavior is a way of winning peer approval.

Sharing

Young children discover, from experiences with others, that one way to win social approval is to share what they have—especially toys—with others. Generosity then gradually replaces selfishness.

Attachment Behavior

Young children who, as babies, discovered the satisfaction that comes from warm, close, personal associations with others, gradually attach their affection to people outside the home, such as a nursery school teacher, or to some inanimate object, such as a favorite toy or even a blanket. These then become what are known as *attachment objects*.

Unsocial Patterns

Negativism

Negativism, or resistance to adult authority, reaches its peak between three and four years of age and then declines. Physical resistance gradually gives way to verbal resistance and pretending not to hear or understand requests.

Aggressiveness

Aggressiveness increases between the ages of two and four and then declines. Physical attacks begin to be replaced by verbal attacks in the form of name-calling, tattling, or blaming others.

Ascendant Behavior

Ascendant behavior, or "bossiness," begins around the age of three and increases as opportunities for social contacts increase. Girls tend to be bossier than boys.

Selfishness

While young children's social horizons are limited mainly to the home, they are often selfish and egocentric. As their social horizons broaden, selfishness gradually wanes but generosity is still very undeveloped.

Egocentrism

Like selfishness, egocentrism is gradually replaced by an interest in and concern for others. How soon this change will occur will depend on how many contacts young children have with people outside the home and how anxious they are to win their acceptance.

Destructiveness

A common accompaniment of temper outbursts in young children is destroying anything within their reach, whether their own or someone else's possessions. The angrier they are, the more widespread their destructiveness.

Sex Antagonism

Until they are four years old, boys and girls play together harmoniously. After that, boys come under social pressures that lead them to shun play activities that might be regarded as "sissyish." Many engage in aggressive behavior which antagonizes girls.

Prejudice

Most preschool children show a preference for playmates of their own race, but they seldom refuse to play with children of another race. (See Figure 5-5). Racial prejudice begins sooner than religious or socioeconomic prejudice, but later than sex prejudice.

CATEGORIES OF COMPANIONS

Associates

Associates are people who satisfy an individual's companionship needs by being in the same environment where they can be watched and listened to. There is no direct interaction between the individual and the associates. At any age, associates can be of either sex and of any age. Adults, for example, enjoy watching and listening to children just as children enjoy watching and listening to adults.

Playmates

Playmates are people with whom individuals engage in pleasurable activities. Their age and sex are, on the whole, less important than the interests and skills they have in common with the individual for whom they serve in this role. Children prefer playmates of their own sex.

Friends

Friends are not only congenial playmates, but they are also people with whom the individual can communicate by exchanging ideas and confidences and by asking or giving advice. Throughout childhood and adolescence, the most congenial and most satisfactory friends are those of the individual's own sex and level of development, who have similar interests and values.

FIGURE 5-5 Among preschool children, there is little refusal to play with children of another race. (Hank Ketcham. "Dennis the Menace." *Publishers-Hall Syndicate,* Jan. 6, 1970. Used by permission.)

"Me 'n' Jackson are exactly the same age. Only he's different. He's LEFT-HANDED!"

Young children often find elderly people to be congenial playmates because they engage in pleasurable activities with them. (Raimondo Borea/Editorial Photocolor Archives.)

dren younger or older may serve as associates but they are not satisfactory playmates because their play is on a different level.

Young children give little consideration to the traits of those they associate with. In fact, some traits they find unacceptable in playmates, such as foolhardiness and cutting up, they find amusing in associates and may even envy them for their "nerve." However, when it comes to selecting playmates and, later, friends, the traits of these individuals become very important.

Not only do they want playmates who have the play skills they admire but they want their playmates to be good sports, cooperative, generous, unselfish, honest, and loyal. These qualities are even more important in the children they select as friends (50). Because young children are relatively unaware of socioeconomic differences, and even less of racial differences, these factors are of little importance in young children's choice of their companions (6,97).

Substitute Companions

When companionship needs are not met, either because of geographic isolation or because the only other children available are of different ages or levels of development or have different interests and values, young children often try to fill their needs by substituting imaginary playmates or by treating a pet as if it were a real person (111).

Most young children, at some time or other, have *pets*—dogs, cats, hamsters, white rats, goldfish, birds, etc.—but the ones that meet their needs for companionship best are dogs and cats because they can play with these animals as if they were people. This they cannot do with birds, hamsters, goldfish, and other common pets (85). See Figure 5-6.

Less common as substitute companions are *imaginary playmates*—children who are a product of the child's imagination. Lonely children create playmates in their imagination and play with them as if they were real playmates. These imaginary playmates have the qualities children would like real playmates to have and play as their creators want them to play. Because young children's vivid imaginations are not held in check by reasoning ability, they actually believe that their imaginary playmates are real children and treat them as such (90,91,111).

Leaders in Early Childhood

In early childhood, leaders are characteristically larger, more intelligent, and slightly older than the other members of the play group. The fact that they are older and more intelligent makes it possible for them to offer suggestions for play which the other children, because of their habitual reliance upon adult suggestions, are willing to follow. In addition, bigger children have an advantage over smaller ones in that children tend to respect size as a result of their habits of obedience to adult requests.

There are two types of leaders in early childhood. Most are tyrannical bosses who show little consideration for the wishes of others. If the tyranny becomes too great, the leader loses status and is replaced by another. Some leaders in early childhood

FIGURE 5-6 If pets are to serve as substitute companions, children must be able to play with them and show affection for them. (Adapted from Bil Keane. "The Family Circus." *Register and Tribune Syndicate,* Oct. 17, 1973. Used by permission.)

1973, The Register and Tribune Syndicate

"Fish aren't very good pets. They're too hard to hug."

are "diplomats," who lead others by indirect and artful suggestions or by bargaining. Girls at this age frequently assume the role of leadership in groups containing boys.

PLAY IN EARLY CHILDHOOD

Early childhood is often called the *toy stage* because, at this time, most play makes use of toys in one form or another. As early childhood draws to a close, children no longer endow their toys with the qualities associated with the people, animals, or other objects they represent. As a result, they begin to lose interest in playing with toys and, as they reach school age, regard them as "babyish" and want to play more "grown-up" games.

Many people, even today, regard children's play as a waste of time and feel that their time could be better spent in learning something useful that will prepare them for adult life. Bruner, on the other hand, contends that play in childhood is "serious business" that makes important contributions to development during the early years of childhood. As he explains: "We now know that play is serious business, in-

Television watching is one of the most popular play activities of early childhood. (Erika Stone.)

sex than for the other. This influences the kind of play equipment they use and the way they play with it. Boys are more aware than girls of the sex appropriateness of toys. Boys also, throughout early childhood, show a wider range of play interests than girls (32, 147).

The amount of *play equipment* children have and the amount of *space* they have to play in—both of which are influenced to a large extent by the *socioeconomic status* of the family—also influence the pattern of their play. The type of play equipment children have likewise influences the pattern of their play. The more that toys and other play equipment can be manipulated, the better children like them and the more they play with them (48,113,131).

Well-developed *motor skills* encourage children to engage in games and constructions while poor motor skills encourage them to devote their play time to amusements (118). Children who are *popular* with their peers want to play more with other children while those who lack social acceptance or enjoy only marginal acceptance are forced to play alone most of the time (118).

Creative children spend much of their play time doing something original with their toys and play equipment while noncreative children follow a pattern set by others (131). The more *guidance* children receive in their play, the greater the variety of play activities they engage in, and the greater the enjoyment they derive from these activities. How much guidance children receive in their play is influenced by the *socioeconomic status* of the family. The higher the socioeconomic status, the more guidance children are likely to receive. This is especially so in the books and comics they are given to read and the television programs they are permitted to watch (140).

Play Patterns of Early Childhood

In spite of variations, certain patterns of play are found almost nationwide among children of preschool age in the American culture of today. The most common of these are given in Box 5-7 (7,20,112,127, 140).

It is important to note that not all of these play patterns are equally popular at all times during the early childhood years. Toys, for example, become increasingly unimportant as early childhood draws to a close. And interest in games increases as early childhood comes to an end and becomes one of the dominant play interests of late childhood.

deed the principle business of childhood. It is the vehicle of improvisation and combination, the first carrier of rule systems through which a world of cultural restraints replaces the operation of childish impulse'' (11).

Variations in Play Interests

The play interests of young children conform more or less closely to a pattern which is markedly influenced by their maturational readiness for certain forms of play and by the environment in which they are growing up. However, there are variations in this pattern. Highly *intelligent* children, for example, show a preference for dramatic play and creative activities and for books which inform rather than merely amuse. In their constructions, they make more complicated and original designs than children who are less bright (121).

Even in the preschool years, children become aware of the fact that certain kinds of play and certain kinds of toys are considered more appropriate for one

BOX 5-7

PLAY PATTERNS OF EARLY CHILDHOOD

Toy Play

In the early part of this period, play with toys is the dominant form of play. However, interest in playing with toys begins to lag somewhat toward the end of early childhood as children are no longer able to imagine that their toys have the living qualities they associated with them earlier. Furthermore, as their interest in group play increases, they find toy play, which is mostly solitary play, less enjoyable.

Dramatizations

At around age three, children's dramatizations consist of playing with toys in ways that imitate life experiences. Later, children play make-believe games with their friends—cops and robbers, Indians, or storekeeper—many of which are based on stories that have been read to them or on movies and television shows they have seen.

Constructions

Young children make many things with blocks, sand, mud, clay, beads, paints, paste, scissors, and crayons. Most of their constructions are in imitation of what they see in daily life or on the movie and television screens. As early childhood draws to a close, young children often introduce creativity into their constructions, using as foundations what they have seen in daily life.

Games

During the fourth year the child begins to prefer games played with peers to those played with adults. These games can have any number of players and involve few rules. Games that test skills, such as throwing and catching balls, are also popular.

Reading

The young child likes to be read to and to look at pictures in books or comics. Fairy tales, nursery rhymes, and stories about animals and everyday occurrences have special appeal.

Movies, Radio, and Television

Most young children attend movies infrequently, but they do like cartoons, movies about animals, and home movies of family members. They also enjoy listening to the radio, but are especially fond of watching television. They like programs meant for older children as well as those aimed at the preschooler. Since they watch in the security of their own homes, they are not usually upset by frightening elements in the programs.

DEVELOPMENT OF UNDERSTANDING

With increased intellectual abilities, especially the abilities to reason and to see relationships, with increased ability to explore their environments because of greater motor coordinations and controls, and with increased ability to ask questions in words others can understand, young children's understanding of people, objects, and situations increases rapidly. This increase in understanding comes from new meanings being associated with meanings learned during babyhood.

Young children now begin to notice details that formerly escaped their attention. As a result, they are not so apt to confuse objects, situations or people that have elements in common as they formerly did. Their concepts thus become more specific and meaningful to them. Piaget has called this the *preoperational stage* of thinking, a stage which extends from about two or three years of age until children are seven or eight years old (109).

How long and difficult a mental process children must contend with in the development of understanding has been emphasized by Bernstein's study of how children learn about sex and birth. According to this study, there are six levels of understanding, extending from three or four years of age until children are twelve or thirteen years old. During early childhood, their understanding is limited to where babies come from and how they are manufactured by people. As late childhood draws to a close, most children understand the physical causality of conception and birth (5).

Common Categories of Concepts

Children develop many of the same concepts because of common learning experiences. Other concepts are individual and depend upon the learning

COMMON CATEGORIES OF CONCEPTS THAT DEVELOP DURING EARLY CHILDHOOD

Life

Children tend to ascribe living qualities to inanimate objects—dolls and stuffed animals, for example. Adults may encourage this by pointing out similarities between animate and inanimate objects, such as a cloud formation that resembles a dog or a horse.

Death

Young children tend to associate death with anything that goes away, but they are usually unable to comprehend the finality of death.

Bodily Functions

Young children, as a group, have very inaccurate concepts of bodily functions and of birth. This is true even when they enter school though, in time, these faulty concepts are corrected through teachings in hygiene and sex education classes.

Space

Four-year-olds can judge short distances accurately but the ability to judge long distances does not develop until late childhood. By the use of cues they understand, they learn to judge right and left accurately. See Figure 5-7.

Weight

Before children learn that different materials have different weights—which does not occur much before the school age—they estimate weight almost exclusively in terms of size.

Numbers

Children who attend nursery school or kindergarten usually understand numbers up to 5, but have only vague concepts about numbers higher than that.

Time

Young children have no idea of the duration of time—how long an hour is, for example—nor can they estimate time in terms of their own activities. Most four- or five-year-olds know the day of the week, and by the age of six they know the month, season, and year.

Self

By the time they are three, most young children know their sex, their full names, and the names of the different parts of their bodies. When they start to play with other children, their self-concepts begin to include facts about their abilities and their race but not about their socioeconomic levels.

Sex Roles

Clear concepts of appropriate sex roles are developed by the time boys are five years old but, for girls, these concepts are less clear because the approved sex role for girls is not as clearly defined as for boys.

Social Awareness

Before early childhood ends, most children are able to form definite opinions about others—whether a person is "nice" or "mean," "smart" or "dumb," for example.

Beauty

Most young children prefer music with a definite tune or rhythm and they like simple designs and bright, gaudy colors.

Comic

Among the things most often perceived as comic by young children are funny faces made by themselves or by others, socially inappropriate behavior, and the antics of domestic animals. Play on words likewise appeals to them as "funny."

opportunities of the particular child. For example, a young child who has traveled to other countries will develop concepts of people and patterns of life unlike those of a child whose experiences have been more limited.

Box 5-8 shows the important categories of concepts that commonly develop during early childhood. Not all children, it is important to understand, develop all of these concepts nor do they develop them to the same degree. Furthermore, it is important to realize that even when there are differences in the concepts children develop in their preschool years, many

© 1975 The Register
and Tribune Syndicate

"This is my WRITE hand 'cause I write with it."

FIGURE 5-7 Young children use as cues to right and left what they do with their hands. (Adapted from Bil Keane. "The Family Circus." *Register and Tribune Syndicate,* Feb. 12, 1975. Used by permission.)

of these differences will be overcome when they go to school and are subjected to similar learning experiences. Children, for example, who learn during the preschool years that babies are brought by storks or in a doctor's satchel will, when they take courses in hygiene or sex education in school, learn the scientific facts about procreation and birth which will enable them to develop concepts of procreation and birth similar to those of their peers.

MORAL DEVELOPMENT IN EARLY CHILDHOOD

Moral development in early childhood is on a low level. The reason for this is that young children's intellectual development has not yet reached the point where they can learn or apply abstract principles of right and wrong. Neither do they have the necessary motivation to adhere to rules and regulations because they do not understand how these benefit them as well as members of the social group.

Because of their inability to comprehend the whys and wherefores of moral standards, young children must learn moral behavior in specific situations. They merely learn *how* to act without knowing *why*

they do so. And because the retention of young children, even those who are very bright, tends to be poor, learning how to behave in a socially approved way is a long, difficult process. Children may be told not to do something one day but, by the next day or even the day after that, they may have forgotten what they were told not to do. Thus what may appear to adults to be willful disobedience is often only a case of forgetting.

Early childhood has been characterized by what Piaget has called "morality by constraint." In this stage of moral development, children obey rules automatically, without using reason or judgment, and they regard adults in authority as omnipotent. They also judge all acts as right or wrong in terms of their consequences rather than in terms of the motivations behind them. According to the way young children view a matter, a "wrong" act results in punishment, which is dealt with either by other human beings or by natural or supernatural factors (109).

Kohlberg has elaborated on and extended Piaget's stages of moral development during the early childhood years to include two stages of this first level which he has labeled "preconventional morality." In the first stage, children are obedience- and punishment-oriented in the sense that they judge acts as right or wrong in terms of the physical consequences of these acts. In the second stage, children conform to social expectations in the hope of gaining rewards (74).

As early childhood comes to an end, habits of obedience should be established, provided children have had consistent discipline. However, young children have not yet developed consciences and, as a result, they do not feel guilty or ashamed if caught doing something they know is wrong. Instead, they may be frightened at the prospect of punishment or they may try to rationalize their acts in the hope of escaping punishment.

Discipline in Early Childhood

Discipline is society's way of teaching children the moral behavior approved by the social group. Its goal is to let children know what behavior is approved and what is disapproved and to motivate them to behave in accordance with these standards.

In discipline, there are three essential elements: rules and laws which serve as guidelines for approved behavior, punishment for willful violation of rules and laws, and rewards for behavior or attempts to behave

BOX 5-9

TYPES OF DISCIPLINE USED IN EARLY CHILDHOOD

Authoritarian Discipline

This is the traditional form of discipline and is based on the old saying that "to spare the rod means spoiling the child." In authoritarian discipline, parents and other caretakers establish rules and inform children that they are expected to abide by them. No attempt is made to explain to the children why they must conform nor are children given opportunities to express their opinions about the fairness or the reasonableness of the rules. If children fail to conform to the rules, they are subjected to corporal punishment, often harsh and cruel, which is supposed to act as a deterrent to future rule breaking. Their reason for breaking the rule is not taken into consideration. It is assumed that they knew the rule and willfully violated it. Nor is it considered necessary to reward them for complying with a rule. This is regarded as their duty and any reward given, it is believed, might encourage children to expect to be bribed to do what society regards as their duty.

Permissive Discipline

Permissive discipline developed as a revolt against the authoritarian discipline many adults had been subjected to during their own childhoods. The philosophy behind this type of disciplinary technique was that children would learn from the conse-

quences of their acts how to behave in a socially approved way. Consequently, they were not taught rules, they were not punished for willful breaking of rules, nor were they rewarded for behaving in a socially approved way. There is a tendency on the part of many adults today to abandon this form of discipline on the grounds that it fails to fulfill all three of the essential elements of discipline.

Democratic Discipline

Today there is a growing tendency to favor discipline based on democratic principles. These principles emphasize the rights of the child to know why rules are made and to have an opportunity to express their opinions if they believe a rule is unfair. Blind obedience is not expected even when children are very young. Attempts are made to have children understand the meaning of the rules and the reasons the social group expects them to abide by them. Instead of corporal punishment, in democratic discipline an attempt is made to make the punishment "fit the crime" in the sense that the punishment is related to the misdeed. Appreciation for attempts to conform to social expectations as spelled out in rules is shown by rewards, mainly in the form of praise and social recognition.

---

in a socially approved way. During the early childhood years, major emphasis should be placed on the educational aspects of discipline and punishment given only when there is evidence that children not only know what is expected of them but when they willfully violate these expectations. To increase young children's motivations to learn to behave in a socially approved manner, rewards serve the purpose of reinforcing the motivations.

Today, there are three methods in common use for disciplining children and adolescents. The labels attached to these methods and the common characteristics of each are given and explained in Box 5-9.

Regardless of the kind of discipline used, almost all young children are punished at some time. Common forms of *punishment* in use today include corporal punishment in the form of slaps, spankings

and beatings; isolating children in their rooms; sending them to bed, often without food; making them sit in a chair in the corner so everyone can see them in disgrace; withholding privileges, such as watching a favorite TV program; threatening to leave them or to cease to love them; comparing a child unfavorably with siblings; and nagging and harping on their misdemeanors. After a decade or more when spanking was frowned upon as a form of "cruel punishment," there is some evidence that there is a swing back to its use.

Rewards in the form of toys, candy, or being taken somewhere or given a special treat are used, somewhat sparingly, by parents of young children, even by those who favor democratic discipline. They are afraid they will spoil the child, or they regard the reward as a form of bribery, which they have been told is a bad disciplinary technique. Omission of the use of rewards deprives young children of a powerful reinforcer of their motivation to learn to behave in a socially approved way.

Studies of the effects of discipline on young children have shown that children are affected differently by the different types of discipline they receive (39,78). The common effects of discipline on children's behavior, attitudes, and personalities are given in Box 5-10.

Childhood Misdemeanors

Misdemeanors—mild forms of breaking of rules or misbehavior—are very common during the preschool years. This is one of the reasons why young children are regarded as "troublesome" and why they are said to be in states of disequilibrium.

There are three common causes of misdemeanors during the early childhood years. First, young children may misbehave due to ignorance of the fact that their behavior is disapproved by the social group. They may have been told what a rule is but they may have forgotten it or they may not understand all the different situations the rule applies to. They may, for example, understand that it is wrong to take the material possessions of others—toys, candy, money, etc.—but they do not associate cheating—taking another person's work—as a form of stealing.

Second, many young children learn that willful disobedience of a minor sort will generally bring them more attention than good behavior. Thus, children who feel that they are being ignored may misbehave in the hopes of gaining the attention of others. And, third, boredom may be responsible for much misbehavior during the years of early childhood. It is a case of "idle hands getting into mischief." When young children have too little to occupy their time and attention, they want to "stir up some excitement," just as bored teenagers often do. Or they may want to test adult authority to see how much they can get away with without being punished.

While young children engage in every conceivable kind of misdemeanor, the most common forms are capriciousness ("orneriness"), thumb-sucking, bed-wetting, boisterous attempts to get attention, temper tantrums, lying, destructiveness, cheating in games, and dawdling. Most of these are associated with immaturity and appear less and less frequently as the child grows older.

BOX 5-10

EFFECTS OF DISCIPLINE ON YOUNG CHILDREN

Effects on Behavior

Children of permissive parents become selfish, disregard the rights of others, and are aggressive and unsocial. Those who are subjected to strict, authoritarian training are overly obedient in the presence of adults but aggressive in peer relationships. Children brought up under democratic discipline learn to restrain behavior they know is wrong, and they are more considerate of the rights of others.

Effects on Attitudes

Children whose parents are either authoritarian or permissive tend to resent those in authority. In the former case, they feel they have been treated unfairly; in the latter case, they feel their parents should have warned them that not all adults will accept undisciplined behavior. Democratic discipline may lead to temporary anger, but not to resentment. The attitudes formed as a result of child-training methods tend to become generalized, to spread to all persons in authority, and to persist.

Effects on Personality

The more physical punishment is used, the more likely the child is to become sullen, obstinate, and negativistic. This results in poor personal and social adjustments, which are also characteristic of children brought up permissively. Those brought up with democratic discipline make the best personal and social adjustments.

COMMON INTERESTS IN EARLY CHILDHOOD

Some interests are almost universal among young children in the American culture today. These include interest in religion, in the human body, in self, in sex, and in clothes.

Interest in Religion

Religious beliefs are, for the most part, meaningless to young children although they may show some interest in religious observances. However, be-

"I'm gonna say my prayers, Daddy. Is there anything you want?"

FIGURE 5-8 For most young children, prayers are "begging rituals" in which they ask God to do something for them. (Adapted from Bil Keane. "The Family Circus." *Register and Tribune Syndicate,* Feb. 6, 1978. Used by permission.)

cause so many of the things that mystify children, such as birth, death, growth and the elements, are explained in religious terms, their curiosity about religious matters is great and they ask many questions relating to religion. Young children accept the answers to their questions without doubting as older children and adolescents often do.

The religious concepts of young children are realistic in the sense that they interpret what they hear and see in terms of what they already know. To them, for example, God is a man who wears clothes different from the clothes of the people they know and who has a flowing white beard and long white hair. They accept what they have been taught, namely, that God is all-knowing, all-powerful and a "watcher" who observes what people do and punishes them if they do bad things but is kind and merciful to those who try to be good. To young children, angels are men and women with white wings, and heaven is a place where every human wish is gratified.

Throughout early childhood, interest in religion is egocentric. Prayer, for example, is a way of gaining

one's desires. To many young children, God is a person who can and will do things for others and who requires no more than good behavior as payment. See Figure 5-8. The egocentrism of religion in early childhood is best illustrated by young children's attitudes toward Christmas. This is a day they think of as when Santa Claus will bring them all the things they asked for rather than as a time to celebrate Christ's birth.

Early childhood has been called the *fairy-tale stage* of religious belief. This is because young children endow all their beliefs with an element of unreality. That is why religious stories and the pageantry of religious services has such a strong appeal for them. Even home religious observances inspire awe and reverence in young children and add to their desire to participate in these observances.

Interest in the Human Body

Young children become interested in the exterior of the body before the interior. However, before early childhood comes to an end, most young children have an absorbing interest in the interiors of their bodies and want to know not only where their hearts, lungs, brains, etc., are but also what they do. They are also curious about elimination and where the products coming from their bodies originated.

When young children recognize anatomical differences between boys and girls, men and women, they want to know what these differences mean and what causes them. They are curious about germs, how they cause the body to become sick, and how medicine can drive the germs out of the body and make the person well. When a person dies, young children are curious about the body and how it gets to heaven.

Young children express their interest in the body by commenting on the various parts and by asking questions about them. As this is usually not enough to satisfy their curiosity, they examine different parts of their bodies and the bodies of their playmates. Nothing fascinates them more than the processes of elimination, which they watch with curiosity whenever they go to the toilet.

Unlike adolescents and even some adults, interest in the human body among young children is largely objective. While it is true that they want to know about their bodies, their interest in them is impersonal in the sense that they do not think of their bodies as their bodies per se but rather as *things* that have strange and curiosity-provoking ways of functioning. Even in the case of eliminations, young children's attitudes tend to be matter-of-fact, impersonal, and unconcerned (44,82).

Interest in Self

After the helpless days of babyhood are over, it is not surprising that many young children carry over an interest in themselves engendered during the time when their helplessness necessitated their being waited on and catered to by others. This *egocentrism* of early childhood is especially pronounced in the first year or two before children begin to play with other children—the age of parallel play, as was explained earlier. Once young children begin to play with their peers, interest in self gradually gives way to increased interest in peers and their activities.

Many parents, caretakers, and other adults encourage egocentrism in young children without realizing that they are doing so. This they do by talking to children about themselves, their possessions, and their activities; by asking them questions relating to themselves and their activities; by commenting on their toys, clothes, and other possessions; by praising or commenting on their play achievements, such as crayoned pictures or block constructions; or by asking them what they want to be or do when they are grown up. Indirectly, parents and other adults encourage egocentrism in young children by not letting them share in adult work activities, such as making beds or clearing the table after a meal, and by suggesting instead that they go off to play with their toys or watch TV.

There are many ways young children show their great interest in self. Some of the most common ways are looking at themselves in mirrors, examining the different parts of their bodies and their clothes, asking questions about themselves, comparing their possessions and achievements with those of their playmates, boasting about their achievements and possessions, or cutting up to attract attention.

While all young children tend to be egocentric, there are certain ones whose environments encourage greater egocentrism than is found in the average child of the same age level. Boys tend to be more egocentric than girls, partly because they sense they are often parental favorites, and partly because they are given more privileges. Also, their misbehavior is frequently overlooked more than misbehavior by girls of the same age. Children who are attractive looking, bright and alert, or are handicapped are usually in the spotlight of attention at home. This encourages them to think about themselves more than about others. Within a family group, firstborns, only-children, or last-borns in large families are likely to be encouraged to be egocentric by the treatment they receive. Constant reinforcement of treatment that encourages egocentrism during the preschool years results in habits of egocentrism which many children have firmly established by the time they enter first grade and are anxious to become members of a play gang.

Interest in Sex

Young children are extremely curious about where babies come from and ask many questions about this matter. Some children believe that babies come from heaven, but most believe that they come from a hospital or a store or that a stork brings them.

Many children show their interest in sex by talking about it to their playmates when adults are not present, by looking at pictures of adult men and women in amorous poses, by engaging in sex play with members of their own sex or of the opposite sex, and by masturbating. However, because many parents regard sex play and masturbation as naughty, if not actually wicked, such activities are usually carried out in private.

Interest in Clothes

Young children have little interest in their appearance, whether they are clean or dirty, sloppy or well-groomed, but they do have a strong interest in their clothes. The reason for this is that, at an early age, they discover that their clothing attracts attention. Adults, they find, make favorable comments about their clothes and their playmates often admire them or envy them because of their clothes.

While young children are interested in their clothes in general, they are especially interested in clothes that others will see. For example, people outside the family will see their sweaters, coats, shoes, dresses, etc., while only family members are likely to see their pajamas or bedroom slippers.

In their different clothes, the focal point of childish interest is on newness of a garment, its color and ornamentation, its similarity to that of their playmates, and its sex-appropriateness. Long before early childhood comes to an end, most young children are well aware of the sex-appropriateness of clothes and want to be sure that their clothes conform to the approved styles for their sex group. Boys, for example, regard being dressed up as a sign of a sissy and, for that reason, they prefer play clothes to dressy clothes.

It is popularly believed that girls, as a group, are far more clothes-conscious than boys, as a group. This is not true in early childhood any more than it is at other age levels. Boys' interests in clothes are different from girls' interests but there is little evidence of differences in intensity of interest. Boys, for example, may be more interested in the sex-appropriateness of their clothes than girls, who tend to be more interested in the color and newness of their clothes.

SEX-ROLE TYPING IN EARLY CHILDHOOD

While some of the foundations of sex-role typing are laid as babyhood draws to a close, the major part of these foundations is laid during early childhood. That is why early childhood is often referred to as a *critical age* in sex-role typing.

During this stage in the developmental pattern, two important aspects of sex-role typing are expected to be mastered: learning how to play the appropriate sex role and accepting the fact that they must adopt and conform to the approved sex-role stereotype if they want to win favorable social judgments and, in turn, social acceptance. Failure to do so will handicap children in their adjustment to the peer gangs that play such an important role in the social life of the older child.

Learning Sex-Role Stereotypes

Sex-role stereotypes are constellations of meanings associated with members of the male and members of the female sex. These meanings relate to the approved appearance and body build of the individual; the approved type of clothing, speech, and behavior; the approved way to behave in relation to members of the other sex; and the approved way to earn a living during the adult years (144).

Until shortly after World War I, the approved stereotypes for male and female sex roles were clearly defined and not subject to change or modification. They were stereotypes handed down from generation to generation because each generation found that behavior conforming to these stereotypes brought the greatest good and the greatest satisfaction to members of the two sexes as well as to society. These stereotypes are today called *traditional sex-role stereotypes*.

Gradually, since the end of World War I but with greater speed since World War II, these stereotypes have been changing. Instead of marked differences in the roles of the two sexes, as prescribed by the traditional sex-role stereotypes, modifications have made the two roles more similar than different. Instead of being different, it began to be recognized that members of the two sexes were more similar than different and, as a result, should play roles that are more similar than different. These stereotypes are called the *egalitarian sex-role stereotypes*.

Whether young children will learn traditional or egalitarian sex-role stereotypes will depend on the pressures and opportunities given in the home. If parents play traditional roles and if they believe that their children will make better social adjustments and be happier if they learn to play these roles, they will present models of traditional sex roles in their own behavior and select stories, TV programs, and other mass media that emphasize the traditional roles. Only if their contacts outside the home, in nursery school, kindergarten, day-care center, or in the homes of playmates show them patterns of the egalitarian sex roles will they know that there is any sex role except that depicted in the traditional sex-role stereotypes they learn at home.

In learning sex-role stereotypes, whether traditional or egalitarian, young children do not learn all aspects of the stereotypes at one time. Instead, the stereotypes are built up gradually as new meanings are added and interrelated to old meanings in the constellation of meanings.

While different children may learn sex-role stereotypes in different ways, the usual pattern is fairly predictable. They learn first that some children are girls and others are boys, that some adults are women and some are men. At the same time, they learn that they themselves are female or male. Then they learn that certain possessions—clothes, toys, books, and play equipment—are regarded as appropriate for one sex while others are regarded as appropriate for the other sex. They discover that certain personality characteristics and patterns of behavior are associated with one sex while others are associated with the other sex. Gradually, they learn that males play certain roles in childhood as well as in adulthood while females play other roles. By the time early childhood draws to a close, most young children have fairly well developed sex-role stereotypes (79,144).

Agencies of Sex-Role Typing

Learning sex-role stereotypes does not guarantee *sex-role typing*. Young children must learn to behave in accordance with the patterns outlined in the stereotypes. This they do partly by imitation but more by *direct* training in which they are shown how to imitate a model—and are either encouraged to do so or reproved for failure to do so.

In addition to direct methods of sex-role typing, young children are subjected to *indirect* methods. They are kept from having opportunities to learn to behave in what those responsible for their training regard as sex-inappropriate behavior. Girls, for example, are not given boys' play equipment or toys; and if they do play with the toys of their brothers or male peers, they are often given female-appropriate toys and encouraged to play with them rather than with those regarded as inappropriate for their sex.

In early childhood, parents and other family members are the main agencies of sex-role typing. Should young children go to preschools or be cared for at day-care centers, the teachers and other caretakers will play important roles in their sex-role typing. Bernstein has explained how this is done: "Sexism starts with kindergarten activities in which little girls are directed to the housekeeping corner, while boys are steered toward blocks and trucks. . . . Schools thus provide a shrinking of alternatives instead of an expansion" (5).

Outside the schoolroom, Bernstein has further explained, sex-role typing likewise goes on. Recreations for boys and girls are strongly differentiated. Boys, for example, are given balls and bats and are shown how to use them, while girls are expected to spend their outdoor recreational time on such sex-approved games as jacks and jumping rope (5).

Another important agency of sex-role typing in early childhood comes from the mass media. The stories read to children, the comics they look at, and the TV shows and commercials they see all contribute to their typing. However, these play a less important role in the typing process than do the people in the child's life. This is because parents, older siblings, caretakers, and teachers can show their approval or disapproval of the child's behavior. This acts as a motivation to conform to the sex-role stereotypes the group with which the young child is identified considers appropriate. This motivation to conform is absent in the mass media.

By the time early childhood draws to a close, most children are well typed. They not only know what the social group considers appropriate for members of their sex but they have also learned to accept and act in accordance with this stereotype. Girls, have already learned to think of boys as stronger, brighter, and more able than they are, while boys have learned to think of girls as less able to play as they want to play and, as a result, stop playing with them (35,96,144).

While both boys and girls are well sex-role typed by the time early childhood ends, boys tend to be better typed than girls. There are two reasons for this. First, the stereotype of the male is more clearly defined than the stereotype of the female, with the result that it is easier for boys to know exactly what constitutes a male than for girls to know what the social group regards as "feminine." Second, because more stigmas are associated with a "sissy" than with a "tomboy," more pressure is put on boys to learn the male sex role than on girls to learn the female sex role. Not until girls approach puberty is the social pressure to be feminine as great as the social pressure to be masculine (31,68,144).

FAMILY RELATIONSHIPS IN EARLY CHILDHOOD

Even when young children begin to play with other children outside the home, the family remains the most important socializing influence. Not only are there more contacts with family members than with other people, but the contacts are closer, warmer, and more emotionally tinged than contacts with those outside the home. These close family relationships exert a greater influence over the child than do any other social influences. However, how much influence different family members have depends on their individual relationship with the child.

In general, young children's attitudes toward people, things, and life in general are patterned by their home life. Although no one method of child training can guarantee good or poor adjustments, whether personal or social, there is evidence that children brought up in democratic homes generally make better adjustments to outsiders than children from permissive or authoritarian homes.

The ordinal position of the child likewise influences the type of adjustments the child will make. Firstborns usually make better social adjustments than their later-born siblings, though not necessarily better personal adjustments.

Perhaps the most important condition influencing the kind of adjustments young children will make, both personal and social, is the type of parent-child

CONDITIONS CONTRIBUTING TO CHANGED PARENT-CHILD RELATIONSHIPS

Changes in the Child

When soft, cuddly babies become more independent and self-sufficient, they tend to be rebellious, mischievous, self-assertive, exploratory—constantly into everything—demanding of attention, and refusing to do what they are told to do. Even in looks they are less appealing then they were as babies.

Changes in Parental Attitudes

As young children become more independent, parents feel that they need less care and attention than they did when they were babies. But even though young children want to be independent, they often resent not having the attention they had become accustomed to during babyhood.

Parental Concept of a "Good" Child

When young children do not come up to parental expectations, parents often become critical and punitive. Children react to this treatment by being even more negativistic and troublesome.

Childish Concept of a "Good" Parent

To most young children, "good" parents are at their beck and call, willing to do what they want when they want it. When parents fail to conform to this concept, children resent it and this weakens the affection children have for their parents. See Figure 5-9.

Parental Preferences

Because mothers spend more time with young children than fathers, and because they better understand troublesome behavior, many young children prefer their mothers and show it plainly. If fathers resent this and show their resentment by being critical of young children and their behavior, it further widens the gap between them. Should little boys show a preference for their fathers, many mothers resent this, feeling that as they are the ones who have assumed greater responsibility for the care of the children, they should be the favorites.

Preference for Outsiders

When young children go to nursery school or kindergarten or when they are placed in a child-care center, they sometimes develop a preference for a teacher or caretaker. Many parents feel hurt and resentful, thus widening the gap between them and their children.

---

relationship there is during the early childhood years. Of less significance are sibling relationships and relationships with relatives, especially grandparents. The influence comes from the closeness of the relationship the child has with a specific family member. When, for example, young children feel closer to one parent than to the other, they imitate the attitudes, emotions, and behavior patterns of that parent.

Parent-Child Relationships

Changes in parent-child relationships, which began during the second year of babyhood, continue throughout early childhood, usually at a more rapid rate. Many conditions are responsible for these changes, the most common and most important of which are given in Box 5-11.

Because young children depend more on their parents for feelings of security and for happiness than on anyone else, poor relationships with their parents have a devastating effect. This is especially true when the poor relationship is with the mother, the parent on whom most young children are especially dependent.

Not only is a poor relationship with parents serious because it undermines feelings of security but it is especially serious if it is broken, due to death or divorce. Children who are deprived of the parent on whom they have depended for security since birth are likely to experience severe emotional trauma when this source of security is removed. Some of the emotional trauma can be eased if the missing parent is replaced by a stepparent, or if the child is adopted into a two-parent family where a satisfactory relationship can be established (71,139).

Sibling Relationships

The pleasant relationship between babies and their siblings starts to deteriorate during the second year of life and, by the time babies become young

"Why CAN'T you play cards with us, Mommy? Grandma always does."

FIGURE 5-9 When parental behavior does not come up to children's expectations, it leads to unfavorable parent-child relationships. (Bil Keane. "The Family Circus." *Register and Tribune Syndicate*, Jan. 10, 1966. Used by permission.)

children, the relationship is often frictional. This frictional relationship not only plays havoc with the home climate but it also has a detrimental effect on the young child's self-concept. Young children are made to feel inadequate, especially if their achievements are criticized and ridiculed by their older siblings.

Not all sibling relationships are frictional, and those that are, are not frictional all of the time. Consequently, sibling relationships can be and often are important aids to the young child's personal and social development.

From their siblings, for example, young children learn to evaluate their own behavior as others do, and to think of themselves as others think of them. Older siblings serve as role models to imitate and, by so doing, young children learn not only the socially approved behavior patterns of the group with which they are identified but also those which are considered appropriate for their sex.

Whether the siblings are older or younger, they

contribute emotional security and teach young children how to show affection for others. Furthermore, all children learn, in a family where there are siblings, to play certain roles, depending on their sex, their ordinal position in the family, and the age difference between them and their siblings. This is an important aid to their socialization because, in the peer group, they will be expected to play a specific role, whether that of leader or follower.

Even sibling quarrels provide a valuable learning experience for young children. From these quarrels, they discover what other children will and will not tolerate, and learn how to be good losers as well as gracious winners (21). While only-children are spared sibling quarrels and have the undivided attention of their parents, they are deprived of the social learning experiences young children have with siblings. As a result, only-children often have difficulty in making good social adjustments during the gang age of late childhood (34).

Relationships with Relatives

How relationships with relatives affect young children's personal and social adjustments depends upon two conditions. The first is the frequency of contacts. If families live in different communities or in different states or countries, the contacts between young children and their relatives will be infrequent. The second condition is the role relatives play in the young child's life. In the case of cousins, for example, the role will be that of playmate. In the case of grandmothers, on the other hand, the role is likely to be that of caretaker or surrogate mother.

Because many families today live in areas remote from other family members, young children's relationships with their relatives are often infrequent and brief. They may see them for some family celebration, such as Christmas, Thanksgiving, or a grandparent's birthday. Of all relatives, the most frequent contacts are those between the child and the maternal grandmother because it is she who is most often called on to help in an emergency, or to look after the young child if the parents are unable to get or afford a baby-sitter when they want to be away from home (110).

So long as the relationship young children have with their relatives is that of playmates, it will tend to be pleasant, though there may be occasional quarrels with cousins just as there are with siblings. On the other hand, if the relative is given authority over the children in the absence of their own parents, the chances are that the relationship will be far from pleasant for all concerned. The reason is that relatives rarely do things exactly as parents do, whether it be preparation of food or rules about going to bed. Young children, accustomed to a stable pattern of living, find changes upsetting and they resent the person who makes these changes necessary. As a result, their relationships with these relatives tend to be frictional and, hence, unpleasant.

Unpleasant relationships between young children and their relatives have two common consequences. First, they condition children to want to avoid contacts with these relatives. Children who object to the way their grandmothers take care of them during their parents' absence are conditioned to want to avoid their grandmothers, even for such festive occasions as Thanksgiving at the grandmother's home. Second, when young children have unpleasant experiences with one relative, they are likely to be conditioned to want to avoid all relatives of the same age level. A child who has a frictional relationship with one cousin, for example, is likely to want to avoid all cousins, even those with whom former relationships have not been frictional and may even have been pleasant.

PERSONALITY DEVELOPMENT IN EARLY CHILDHOOD

The personality pattern, the foundations of which were laid in babyhood, begins to take form in early childhood. Because parents, siblings, and other relatives constitute the social world of young children, how they feel about them and how they treat them are important factors in shaping self-concepts—the core of the personality pattern. That is why Glasner has said that the child's self-concept is "formed within the womb of family relationships" (46).

As early childhood progresses, young children have more and more contacts with peers either in the neighborhood or in a preschool or child-care center. The attitudes of their peers and the way their peers treat them then begin to have an effect on their self-concepts, an effect which may reinforce the effect of family members or may contradict and counteract some of the family influences (43,73).

These early peer attitudes, like attitudes on the part of significant family members, are important be-cause, once the foundations for the self-concept are·laid, they are far less likely to change than to remain stable. Furthermore, because both family members and peers get into the habit of thinking of young children in a certain way—as kind and helpful or as troublesome show-offs, for example—they are far less likely to change their attitudes than to continue to think of them in the same way (54).

Conditions Shaping the Self-Concept in Early Childhood

Because the environment of young children is limited, to a large extent, to their homes and to family members, it is not surprising that many conditions within the family are responsible for shaping the self-concept during the early childhood years. The general relationships of young children with their families are important but, of these, *parental attitudes* stand out as especially important. How parents feel about their children's appearances, their abilities, and their achievements have a marked influence on how the children feel about themselves.

The *child-training* method used in the home is important in shaping the young child's developing concept of self. Strict, authoritarian discipline, accompanied by frequent and harsh corporal punishment, tends to build up resentments against all persons in authority and create feelings of martyrdom—feelings which can and often do develop into a martyr complex.

The *aspirations* parents have for their children play an important role in their developing self-concepts. When their aspirations are unrealistically high, children are doomed to failure. Regardless of how children react, failure leaves an indelible mark on their self-concepts and lays the foundations for feelings of inferiority and inadequacy.

The *ordinal position* of children in a family has an effect on their developing personalities. This influence may be explained in part by the fact that each child in a family learns to play a specific role, in part by differences in the child-training methods used by parents with different children, and in part by the successes and failures children have in their competition with their siblings.

Even though young children are infrequently aware of *minority-group* identification, those who have such an awareness are influenced unfavorably if their peers neglect or reject them. As was pointed out earlier, young children tend to show a preference for playmates of their own race and to neglect, though not discriminate against, those of other racial groups (3).

As Inselberg and Burke have pointed out, as early as the late preschool years "appropriate *sex-role identification* in boys is associated with favorable personality characteristics." Boys with masculine physiques are more successful in interacting with other boys, and this reinforces overt masculine behavior, which in turn leads their peers to judge their actions as sex-appropriate (64).

Environmental insecurity, whether due to death, divorce, separation, or social mobility, affects young children's self-concepts unfavorably because they feel insecure and different from their peers. Children whose parents are upwardly mobile, it has been reported, may learn to be independent and ambitious, but they tend to become nervous, tense, and anxious, and highly competitive and aggressive in their peer relationships (65).

Increase in Individuality

Individuality, which is apparent at birth and becomes increasingly more so in babyhood, is one of the outstanding characteristics of young children. By the time early childhood is over and children are ready to enter school, the patterns of their personalities can be readily distinguished. Some children are leaders and some are followers; some are despotic while others are meek; some are sociable while others are solitary; some like to show off and be the center of attention while others prefer to shun the limelight; and some are egocentric to the point where they think only about themselves while others are conformers, trying to be like members of the group.

Thomas et al. have identified three personality syndromes among young children: There are "easy children," who are well adjusted both physically and psychologically; "difficult children," who are irregular in bodily functions, intense in their reactions, and slow to adapt to change; and "slow-to-warm-up children," who have a low activity level and do not adapt quickly. These syndromes show up in children's characteristic adjustive behavior during the preschool years (133).

Individuality is greatly influenced by early social experiences outside the home. When these experiences are unfavorable, children are likely to become unsocial in their relationships with people and to compensate in unsocial ways, such as spending their

playtime watching television and imagining themselves as martyrs who are picked on by others.

HAZARDS OF EARLY CHILDHOOD

Like the hazards of babyhood, those of early childhood can be physical, psychological, or both. Poor nutrition, for example, may stunt physical and mental growth, just as excessive family friction can lead to stress, which can also stunt growth. However, the psychological hazards of early childhood are more numerous than the physical hazards and are more damaging to the child's personal and social adjustments.

Physical Hazards

The physical hazards of early childhood have psychological as well as physical repercussions, especially such hazards as illness, accidents, and awkwardness.

Mortality Deaths start to decline rapidly in the latter part of babyhood and decline even more rapidly during early childhood. Deaths in early childhood are more often the result of accidents than of illness, and because boys have more accidents than girls, deaths in early childhood are more frequent among boys than among girls.

Illness Young children are highly susceptible to all kinds of illness, though respiratory illnesses are the most common. While most illnesses are physiological in origin, some are psychosomatic and result from family tensions.

Because of the "wonder drugs" and widespread immunization available today, children's illnesses are shorter in duration and less severe than in the past and are far less likely to result in permanent physical defects. However, they are psychologically damaging for two reasons. First, children who are sick for an extended period of time fall behind in their learning of skills needed for play with their peers. As a result, they find they are misfits in the play group when they are able to rejoin it. Second, if parents consider the illness a family calamity and blame children for the expense and inconvenience the illness has caused, it will make children tense and nervous. This will not only tend to prolong the illness but it will also damage parent-child relationships.

Accidents Most young children experience cuts, bruises, infections, burns, broken bones, strained muscles, or similar minor disturbances resulting from accidents. Others have more serious accidents that disable them temporarily or permanently. As was pointed out above, boys have more accidents than girls, and the accidents tend to be more serious.

Although most accidents in early childhood are not fatal, many of them leave permanent physical or psychological scars. Many *disabilities* of childhood, for example, are the result of accidents. A disability can cause young children to develop feelings of inferiority and martyrdom that permanently distort their personality patterns. Even if an accident leaves no permanent physical scar, it can make young children fearful and timid to the point where these feelings will predominate in their adjustments to life.

Unattractiveness As early childhood progresses, children become increasingly unattractive, reaching a low point as they emerge into late childhood. There are a number of reasons for this. First, as the body changes shape, children begin to look skinny and gawky; second, their hair becomes coarser and less manageable, and this gives them an unkempt appearance; third, there are gaps in the mouth where baby teeth have fallen out and the permanent teeth which have erupted seem proportionally too large; and, fourth, young children care more about having a good time than about keeping neat and clean. The result is that they frequently look dirty and ill-groomed.

Regardless of the individual's age, people react positively to those who are attractive looking and negatively to those who are unattractive. As one preschooler explained, "People like you if you are pretty" while another said, "You're nice to pretty people" (22). The less attractive appearance of young children added to their changed behavior makes them less appealing to their parents and other adults than they were when they were babies. This many young children interpret as rejection and bitterly resent it. Even in the peer group, attractiveness is a social advantage, especially for girls. It may be a social disadvantage for boys, especially as they approach the gang age of late childhood (129).

Awkwardness As Dare and Gordon have explained, "Children are not by nature clumsy and, once the toddler stage has passed, the grace of movement of the average child is something to be admired. So the child whose movements are awkward and incoordinate presents an unhappy contrast" (18).

While awkwardness in early childhood may be due to brain damage at birth, to mental deficiency, or to some other physical cause, it is far more likely to be due to the fact that children are hampered by overprotective parents, by fears engendered by accidents or warnings to "be careful," by environmental obstacles, or by lack of opportunity to practice. As a result, motor development is delayed and children give the impression of being "awkward" as compared with their age-mates (27).

Children who are awkward due to delay in their motor development cannot keep up with their age-mates and, as a result, they are left out of their play. They soon come to think that their age-mates are better than they—a feeling which, in time, may become generalized and develop into an inferiority complex.

Obesity Young children who are 20 percent or more above the norm for their ages and body builds are regarded, medically, as "obese." Children with endomorphic body builds tend, as a group, to have more problems with obesity than do those with mesomorphic or ectomorphic builds.

Obesity is always a hazard and this is just as true of early childhood as of any other age. First, it is a health hazard. Like people of any age, obese children are far more likely to develop diabetes and to experience heart and blood-pressure problems than are those whose weight is more nearly normal. Second, obesity is a hazard to attractiveness. While chubby babies may be regarded as "cute," plump, overstuffed young children are not only not regarded as "cute" but, more seriously, they are likely to be scorned by their peers and labeled "Fatty." In addition, obesity is a hazard in early childhood because it is the time when eating habits are being established. If young children are encouraged to overeat, if they are praised and rewarded for their "clean plates," and if they are permitted to overindulge in carbohydrates and what is commonly known as "junk food"—food that fills one up but has little nutrient value—the chances are that the habit will become a life-long one that will lead to an obesity problem that will plague them throughout life (86).

Left-Handedness As Herron has pointed out, "Throughout history, the left hand has had a bad press'' (60). There is no physical reason why it is better to be right-handed than left-handed but, because approximately 90 percent of all Americans are right-handed, being left-handed makes the individual different, and, throughout the childhood and adolescent years, being different is usually interpreted as being inferior (57).

There are other reasons why being left-handed is regarded as a hazard during the early childhood years. When young children attempt to learn a skill from a right-handed person, they are likely to become confused about how to imitate the model. This confusion tends to worsen as children grow older and as skills play a more important role in their lives.

Left-handedness can affect children's educational success and, later, their vocational success or their social adjustments. Self-conscious adolescents, for example, may shun social situations in which eating with their left hands would embarrass them and make them feel conspicuous.

Many parents, believing that left-handedness is a hazard, try to force their left-handed children to use their right hands. This can also be hazardous because it emphasizes their difference, which they often interpret as inferiority, especially when parents use punitive approaches to force them to use their right hands. Ames and Ilg (2) have sounded a word of caution about putting too much pressure on the young child to learn to use the right hand in preference to the left. According to them:

If nature is working out something so complex, it seems obvious that, in all probability, best results will be obtained if parents do not interfere with the child's natural expression of handedness other than, perhaps, to present objects nearest to his right hand.

Psychological Hazards

Every major area of the child's behavioral development has associated with it potential hazards which can affect personal and social adjustments adversely. The most common of these are discussed below.

Speech Hazards Because speech is a tool for communication and because communication is essential to social belonging, children who, unlike their age-mates, cannot communicate with others, will be socially handicapped, and this will lead to feelings of inadequacy and inferiority.

Four common hazards are associated with the communicative ability of young children. First, people cannot expect young children to comprehend what they are saying if they use words children do not understand, if they use pronunciations that are unfamiliar to children, or if they speak too fast. Children's failure to listen is an even more common cause of failure to comprehend. Because most young children are egocentric and more interested in what they want to say to others than in what others are saying to them, they often do not listen attentively enough to comprehend what is being said. As a result, their speech is unrelated to what others are saying and this jeopardizes their social contacts.

Second, when the quality of young children's speech is so poor that what they say is unintelligible, their ability to communicate with others is even more jeopardized than if they had not listened to what was being said to them. In early childhood, poor speech quality may be due to mispronunciations of words or grammatical errors, often the result of imitating a poor model, to speech defects such as stuttering, lisping, or slurring, or to bilingualism (9,10).

Third, bilingualism is a serious handicap to the social development of young children. Children who speak a foreign language in their homes and know only a few words in English cannot communicate with their age-mates in play, nor can they comprehend what their age-mates are trying to communicate to them. While this may not be a serious hazard to socialization in the first year or two of early childhood, when most play with age-mates is either parallel or associative play, when children want to engage in cooperative play, it becomes such a serious handicap that bilingual children often withdraw from the social group. By the time they enter first grade and begin to learn English, their age-mates have already laid the foundations for social activities and have learned social skills. The bilingual child, as a result, does not fit into the group (45).

The fourth serious speech hazard in early childhood, and in many respects the most serious one, concerns the content of young children's speech. While many people will overlook poor speech, assuming that young children will learn to speak more correctly as they grow older, people are far less likely to be tolerant if the speech of young children is largely egocentric and if the comments they do make about others are critical and derogatory. Because young children derive temporary ego-satisfaction from hurting others, they are likely to get into the habit of speaking in an unsocial way. This, in time, will play havoc with their social adjustments (21).

Emotional Hazards The major emotional hazard of early childhood is the dominance of the unpleasant emotions, especially anger. If young children experience too many of the unpleasant emotions and too few of the pleasant ones, it will distort their outlook on life and encourage the development of an unpleasant disposition. In addition, children soon acquire a facial expression that makes them look surly, sullen, or generally disagreeable—a condition that contributes to the decline of their appealingness.

Almost as great a hazard to good personal and social adjustments in early childhood is the inability to establish the *empathic complex*—an emotional linkage between an individual and significant people. There are two common reasons for inability to establish the empathic complex. First, children who, as babies, never experienced attachment behavior because of lack of opportunity to have a warm and stable relationship with the mother or a mother-substitute, fail to realize the pleasure they could derive from such relationships. As a result, they do not try to establish warm, friendly relationships with others, either adults or peers, during the early childhood years. The second reason for children's inability to establish the empathic complex is that those who do not receive affection from others are likely to become self-bound, and this prevents them from having an emotional exchange with others.

Another serious hazard to good emotional development is the development of too strong an affection for one person—usually the mother—because this makes children feel insecure and anxious whenever the loved person's behavior seems threatening—as in the case of reproval for misbehavior, or when the loved one pays attention to another person. Both the inability to establish emotional linkages with others and development of an emotional overdependence on one person make it difficult for young children to establish friendly relationships with their peers.

Failure to become emotionally attached to toys or other inanimate objects, such as blankets, often leads to feelings of insecurity in new strange situations. As Passman has pointed out, "Attachment objects, whether animate or inanimate, may serve as anxiety reducers" (108). This is especially true of children who are just emerging from babyhood and who,

as yet, have had only limited experiences outside the home. When preschoolers are accompanied by attachment objects, whether a favorite toy or a blanket, for example, it reduces anxiety in a new situation and facilitates their adjustment to the new situations (108).

Social Hazards There are a number of common hazards to good social adjustments in early childhood, five of which are especially common and especially serious. First, if young children's speech or behavior makes them unpopular with their peers, not only will they be lonely but, even more important, they will be deprived of opportunities to learn to behave in a peer-approved manner. Their socially unacceptable speech or behavior may readily become habitual and their chances of winning social acceptance will then worsen as time goes on.

Second, children who are placed under strong pressures to play in a sex-appropriate way may overdo it and make themselves obnoxious to their peers. Young boys, for example, may try to be so masculine and aggressive in their play that they antagonize their peers and, as a result, are rejected by the peer group.

As a result of the treatment they receive from their age-mates, young children may and often do develop unhealthy social attitudes. (Sybil Shelton/ Monkmeyer.)

Third, as a result of the treatment they receive from their age-mates, young children may and often do develop unhealthy social attitudes. Young children who have unfavorable early social experiences because of their race or sex, or because they are younger than the other children, may readily come to the conclusion that they do not like people. As a result, they shun contacts with people outside the home and, to some extent, even in the home. By so doing they not only deprive themselves of pleasant social experiences but also of opportunities to learn to behave in a social way.

The fourth social hazard of early childhood is the use of imaginary companions and pets to compensate for lack of real companions. Having an imaginary companion is a temporary solution to the lonely-child problem but it does little to socialize young children. They are likely to acquire the habit of dominating their age-mates, which is possible with an imaginary playmate but usually not possible with a real one. When they discover that the technique that worked so successfully with imaginary playmates

"I'm lonely!"

FIGURE 5-10 Children who spend too much time in social play do not learn to be self-sufficient and to enjoy solitary play, regardless of how much play equipment they have to amuse themselves. (Adapted from Bil Keane. "The Family Circus." *Register and Tribune Syndicate*, July 2, 1974. Used by permission.)

does not work with real children, they are likely to become maladjusted members of the group (111).

While pets meet the social needs of a child to some extent, they lack the socializing influence that the child should have. A pet that is considered suitable for a young child is usually so docile that it will take *any* treatment from the child without protest. This encourages the child to be aggressive in relationships with the pet. As was stressed earlier, in order for a child to be an accepted member of the play group, aggressive reactions must give way to friendly, affectionate ones.

A fifth hazard in the social development of young children is parental encouragement to spend proportionally too much time with other children and proportionally too little time alone. When young children become accustomed to having playmates readily available at all times for them to play with, as often happens when they are placed in a child-care center or spend the major part of the day in a nursery school or kindergarten, they fail to develop the ability to amuse themselves when alone and, as a result, feel lonely and deserted. See Figure 5-10, which shows that, no matter how many toys and how much play equipment a young child may have, loneliness occurs whenever the child is away from other children.

Play Hazards When children lack playmates, either because of geographic isolation or because they are not accepted by the children who are available for them to play with, they are forced to engage in solitary forms of play. A certain amount of solitary play is beneficial because it teaches young children to be self-sufficient. As Moore et al. have said, "Solitary play is a normal and probably functionally beneficial activity rather than an indicant of poor social adjustment" (102). On the other hand, because socialization in early childhood comes mainly through play with peers, children who have few playmates are deprived of opportunities to learn to be social.

Equally serious is the fact that, because most young children enjoy watching television more than other forms of solitary play, children who lack playmates often spend proportionally too much of their playtime in front of the television screen. Studies of television watching by young children recognize that it has some beneficial effects, such as increase in knowledge and broadening of interests. On the other hand, there is evidence of the harmful effects, such as too little exercise, nervous tension, sleeplessness, nightmares, increased aggressiveness in play with other children, and acceptance of patterns of unsocial behavior as the norm. This is especially true when parents exercise little or no control over the programs their children watch (104,140). Furthermore, while many parents claim that television watching is not harmful to young children because they do not "understand what they see," they fail to realize that children are less critical than adults and therefore are more influenced by what they see on the screen than adults are. They may not understand what a particular program is about, but they often have a distorted impression or misconception of what they have seen. Thus even a harmless program can be harmful to the young child. Even more important, young children remember details of frightening programs better than those of programs that arouse less fear, which reinforces their harmful effects.

Toys can present another play hazard in early childhood. Toys that offer little opportunity for creativity, such as fully equipped doll houses or sets of soldiers, will stifle the child's creative urge. The child's creativity can also be stifled if parents or nursery school teachers provide too much supervision and direction concerning the use of toys. Children who are given too many toys that encourage aggressive play, such as toy guns or soldiers, are likely to develop aggressive patterns of behavior which they carry over into real-life situations (135).

Hazards in Concept Development There are three common hazards in concept development during the early childhood years. The first is *inaccuracy in understanding*. Because of their limited experience with people and things, because of their limited vocabularies which make it difficult for them to comprehend accurately the meaning of what is said to them, and because of their limited opportunities to learn correct meanings from authoritative sources, such as books or adults with correct information, it is understandable that many of the concepts young children learn are inaccurate or actually faulty. This is especially true when they learn meanings from peers or from adults whose knowledge is limited if not actually faulty.

The seriousness of inaccuracies in concepts learned during the early childhood years is that they often become strongly entrenched beliefs before their inaccuracies are detected by adults. In G. Stanley Hall's classic study, "Contents of Children's Minds on Entering School," Hall and his co-workers found that many first-grade children had inaccurate concepts of everyday objects and experiences. One of their most quoted examples is the belief of many city children that butterflies are flies made of butter (52).

Just because early concepts are inaccurate does not mean that they cannot be corrected. They can be and they usually are. However, like all relearning, learning new meanings to replace faulty ones takes time that might better be spent on learning new meanings. Children, for example, who must learn, after they enter school, what butterflies actually are to replace their earlier-learned concepts could spend their learning time to greater advantage in learning something new.

The second common hazard in concept development in early childhood is the development of *concepts below the level of those of their peers*. If this happens, it can greatly affect children's personal and social adjustments. When, for example, young children have limited opportunities to associate with people outside the home, they do not develop the social concepts that would enable them to understand people better. As a result, they often say things that seem rude and tactless and their behavior tends to annoy and antagonize others.

The *emotional weighting* of concepts can present a third and even more serious hazard. When, for example, young children build up concepts of Christmas around Santa Claus, with its pleasurable emotional weighting, they will be resistant to changing their concepts of Christmas when they discover that there is no Santa Claus. Even worse, they will feel that they have been duped by those who told them about Santa Claus, and they will feel that Christmas means little to them now (17).

Moral Hazards There are four common hazards in moral development during early childhood. First, inconsistent discipline slows down the process of learning to conform to social expectations. When different people have different rules relating to the same behavior, such as where children may play with their toys, children are understandably confused about why what they did yesterday is regarded as wrong today. They are also confused and annoyed when they are punished severely for an act today which, yesterday, went unpunished or was only mildly reproved. This encourages them to be sly and to lie if threatened by punishment.

Second, if children are not reprimanded for misdemeanors and if they are permitted to get temporary satisfaction from the admiration and envy of their peers when they misbehave, this is likely to encourage them to persist in their misbehavior. As Glueck pointed out, it is possible to spot potential delinquents at two or three years of age, not just by their behavior but, even more important, by their attitudes toward their misbehavior (47).

Third, too much emphasis on punishment for misbehavior and too little emphasis on rewards for good behavior can lead to unfavorable attitudes toward those in authority. Children who are punished more often than they are rewarded are less apt to be repentant than to be angry, rebellious, and determined to "get even" with the person who punished them. There are only three justifications for the use of punishment in early childhood. First, only when there is no other way to communicate a prohibition to a child; second, only when punishment can be given while the forbidden act is being carried out; and third, it must be a rare event to be effective or otherwise it desensitizes the child to the whole purpose of punishment.

Fourth, and most serious of all from the long-term point of view, young children who are subjected to authoritarian discipline, which puts major emphasis on external controls, are not encouraged to develop the internal controls over their behavior that form the foundations for the later development of a conscience. Development of these internal controls must begin early. It is best accomplished through democratic discipline, which encourages the child to *want* to learn to conform to group expectations.

Hazards in Sex-Role Typing   There are three common and serious hazards in sex-role typing during the early childhood years. First, if children do not learn the sex-role stereotypes commonly accepted by their peers, whether they be traditional or egalitarian, they will view behavior differently than their peers do. While this may not be serious during the first few years of early childhood, it becomes increasingly so as early childhood draws to a close and children are ready to enter school. A boy, for example, who has learned egalitarian sex-role stereotypes at home is likely to discover that the peer group regards him as a "sissy" when he plays with girls or enjoys playing with girls' toys or engaging in girls' games.

Second, when girls are trained to conform to the traditional stereotypes for members of their sex, they learn, indirectly, from these stereotypes that members of the female sex are regarded as inferior physically and psychologically to members of the male sex. This lays the foundations for inferiority complexes which stifle girls' motivations to do what they are capable of doing.

And, third, failure to sex-role type young children can be a social handicap to both boys and girls. If young children do not learn to behave according to the accepted stereotypes for their sex groups, they will find themselves social misfits in any group where their peers have been sex-role typed to the point where they expect all members of their sex group to behave according to the pattern they have learned to accept as the correct pattern.

Family-Relationship Hazards   Deterioration in any human relationship is hazardous to good personal and social adjustments. This is especially so in the case of the relationships between young children and their parents—the most significant people in every young child's life.

The conditions that bring about deterioration in the parent-child relationship are those that normally give young children feelings of security and of belonging. When these conditions deteriorate, it plays havoc with their feelings of security and belonging. Because these conditions are different for boys and girls, they will be discussed separately.

Girls who feel that their parents prefer the boys in the family will resent their parents and also their brothers. This resentment may grow as early childhood draws to a close if a girl's brothers, who have learned that sex-appropriate behavior involves not playing with girls or with girls' toys, adopt an attitude of smug superiority.

For boys the major threat to parent-child relationships during early childhood is the lack of a father to identify with or the lack of emotional warmth between father and son, which encourages continuation of children's identifications with their mothers and the acquisition of interests and behavior patterns which may cause their peers to regard them as "sissies."

Other threats to good parent-child relationships in early childhood are working mothers and stepparents. When mothers work outside the home, the care of the children must be turned over to relatives or paid caretakers or they must be sent to a day-care center. If children are happy in their new environment and like their caretakers, mothers may resent it. Should children be unhappy, on the other hand, they will resent their mothers' not taking care of them and this will make the mothers feel guilty about neglecting their parental roles.

How parent-children relationships are affected by stepparents depends largely on how young children feel about their stepparents. As a rule, young children prefer their stepfathers to their stepmothers because stepfathers play the "fun" role with the children while stepmothers play the caretaker and disciplinarian roles (146).

An often overlooked family hazard in early childhood is sibling quarreling, which can be caused by jealousy or by differences in interests among siblings. Quarreling among siblings is serious because it can deprive them of companionship at an age when their social world is limited mainly to the family and when the rudiments of social behavior should be learned. Equally important, sibling quarreling can become such a habitual pattern of adjustment to peers that children will carry it to the play group. This can jeopardize their chances for making friends, which they need to fill the companionship gap created by poor sibling relationships that have developed in the home.

Deterioration in relationships with relatives comes when relatives are expected to play the roles of surrogate parents. So long as they play "fun" roles with children, all will be well. But, when they are given control over the children and are permitted to discipline them, there is a rapid decline in the pleasant relationships that otherwise might have existed. This is especially true of young children's relationships with their grandmothers, the most common surrogate parents among their relatives.

An occasional but very serious family-relationship hazard during early childhood is *child abuse*. This may take forms varying from mild abuse in the form of slaps to such serious abuse as to lead to the permanent disability or death of the child.

While there are no statistics, to date, to show what family members are most responsible for child abuse, there is some evidence that it is more common among male than female relatives with fathers and stepfathers the usual offenders. When the care of young children is turned over to older siblings, especially when mothers work outside the home, older brothers more often abuse their younger siblings than do older sisters. Child abuse is also not uncommon when the care of young children is turned over to paid caretakers, especially male caretakers. This is more likely to occur when the caretakers are high school students than adults (1).

Personality Hazards The most serious personality hazard during early childhood is the development of an unfavorable self-concept. Unfavorable self-concepts may be due to the treatment young children receive from family members and peers, they may be due to unrealistic aspirations which cause young children to think of themselves as failures because they do not reach the goals they have been encouraged by their parents to set for themselves, or they may be due to persistent egocentrism. Young children who continue to be self-bound after their age-mates have started to become more social, and to think of others rather than of themselves, discover that social attitudes toward them are unfavorable. As a result, their attitudes toward self become unfavorable.

Whatever their cause, unfavorable self-concepts develop easily during early childhood. Once developed, they are hard to overcome. Unfortunately, far too many parents either fail to recognize that young children are developing unfavorable self-concepts or they believe that the children will "outgrow" these unfavorable self-concepts as they grow older and as their social horizons broaden.

The seriousness of unfavorable sef-concepts is that they tend to be persistent. Genetic studies of the same children over a period of time have shown that their personality patterns tend to remain persistently uniform. It is possible, however, during the early childhood years to eliminate habits and attitudes which predispose children to act in a socially unacceptable manner (133).

Certain aspects of the personality pattern do change during early childhood as a result of advancing maturity, experience, and the social and cultural environments in which the children live. Factors within themselves, such as emotional pressures or identification with another person, may also be responsible for the changes. Difficult children, for example, may become more tractable just as happy, contented children may develop into sullen ones as they grow older.

Changes, however, are usually quantitative rather than qualitative; for example, an undesirable trait is more likely to worsen than to disappear and be replaced by a new one. As Emmerich has pointed out, "Salient personality dimensions have high stability from ages 3 to 5, supporting the view that personality differences arise early in life and are maintained in essentially their original form" (28).

HAPPINESS IN EARLY CHILDHOOD

Early childhood can and should be a happy period in life, and it is important that it be so. Otherwise, the habit of being unhappy can readily develop. Once it does, it will be hard to change.

As is true of every age, happiness in early childhood depends partly on what happens to children—such as the loss of friends and the break-up of the family—and partly on conditions within themselves, such as physical defects that prevent them from doing what their age-mates do or the failure to reach goals they set for themselves.

Because young children spend most of their time at home, their happiness depends mainly on how the different members of their families treat them and on what they believe family members think of them. Not until the latter part of early childhood are young children's contacts with people outside the home frequent enough, close enough, or prolonged enough to have any appreciable influence on their happiness. It is thus the family's responsiblity to see that their children have the three A's of happiness—acceptance by others, affection and achievements which will encourage children to like and accept themselves.

Certain basic wants and needs must be fulfilled if young children are to be happy. Box 5-12 gives some of the most important conditions that contribute to happiness during the years of early childhood.

Chapter Highlights

1. Eary childhood, which extends from two to six years, is labeled by parents as the *problem,* the *troublesome,* or the *toy* age; by educators as the *preschool* age; and by psychologists as the *pre-gang,* the *exploratory,* or the *questioning* age.
2. Physical development proceeds at a slow rate in early childhood but the physiological habits, whose foundations were laid in babyhood, become well-established.
3. Early childhood is regarded as the *teachable mo-*

BOX 5-12

SOME IMPORTANT CONDITIONS CONTRIBUTING TO HAPPINESS IN EARLY CHILDHOOD

- Good health, which enables young children to enjoy whatever they undertake and to carry it out successfully.
- A stimulating environment in which children have opportunities to use their abilities to the maximum.
- Parental acceptance of annoying childish behavior and parental guidance in learning to behave in a socially more acceptable way.
- A disciplinary policy that is well planned and consistently carried out. This lets young children know what is expected of them and prevents them from feeling that they are unfairly punished.
- Developmentally appropriate expressions of affection, such as showing pride in young children's achievements and spending time with them, doing things they want to do.
- Realistic aspirations, in accordance with their capacities, so that children have a reasonable chance of making a success of what they undertake, thus fostering favorable self-concepts.
- Encouragement of creativity in play and avoidance of ridicule or unnecessary criticism which dampen young children's enthusiasm to try to be creative.
- Acceptance by siblings and playmates, so that children will develop favorable attitudes toward social activities. This can be encouraged by guidance in how to get along with other people and by good home models to imitate.
- A prevailing atmosphere of cheerfulness and happiness in the home so that children will learn to make their contributions to maintaining this atmosphere.
- Achievements in activities important to the child and valued by the group with which the child is identified.

ment for acquiring skills because children enjoy the repetition essential to learning skills; they are adventuresome and like to try new things; and they have few already-learned skills to interfere with the acquisition of new ones.

4. Speech development advances rapidly during early childhood as seen in improvement in comprehension as well as in the different speech skills. This has a strong impact on the amount of talking young children do and the content of their speech.

5. While emotional development follows a predictable pattern, there are variations in this pattern due to intelligence, sex, family size, child training, and other conditions.

6. Early childhood is the *pregang age*—the time when the foundations of social development, characteristic of the *gang age* of late childhood, are laid. It is also a time when companions play an important role in the socialization process.

7. Play in early childhood is greatly influenced by the motor skills children have acquired, the degree of popularity they enjoy among their age-mates, the guidance they receive in learning different patterns of play, and the socioeconomic status of their families.

8. Inaccuracies in understanding are common in early childhood because many childish concepts are learned with inadequate guidance and because children are often encouraged to view life unrealistically to make it seem more exciting and colorful.

9. Early childhood is characterized by *morality by constraint*—a time when children learn, through punishment and praise, to obey rules automatically. It is also the time when discipline differs, with some children subjected to authoritarian discipline while others are brought up by permissive or democratic discipline.

10. The common interests of early childhood include interest in religion, in the human body, in self, in sex, and in clothes.

11. Early childhood is often referred to as the *critical age* in sex-role typing because, at this time, the important aspects of sex-role typing are mastered, especially learning the meaning of sex-role stereotypes and accepting and playing the sex role approved for members of their sex.

12. Different family relationships—parent-child, sibling, and relationships with relatives—play roles of different degrees of importance in the socialization of young children and in their developing self-concepts.

13. The important physical hazards of early childhood include mortality, illnesses, accidents, unattractiveness, obesity, and left-handedness.

14. Among the most important psychological hazards of early childhood are unsocial content of speech, inability to establish the empathic complex, failure to learn social adjustments due to lack of guidance, preference for imaginary companions or pets, too much emphasis on amusements and too little on active play, unfavorable emotional weighting of concepts, inconsistent discipline or discipline that relies too much on punishment, failure to be sex-role typed in accordance with the approved pattern of the social group, deterioration in family relationships, and unfavorable self-concepts.

15. Happiness in early childhood depends more on what happens to children in the home than outside the home.

Bibliography

1. Alvy, K. T. Preventing child abuse. *American Psychologist*, 1975, **30**, 921–928.
2. Ames, L. B., and F. L. Ilg. The developmental point of view with special reference to the principle of reciprocal interweaving. *Journal of Genetic Psychology*, 1964, **105**, 195–209.
3. Ballard, B., and H. R. Keller. Development of racial awareness: Task consistency, reliability and validity. *Journal of Genetic Psychology*, 1976, **129**, 3–11.
4. Berndt, T. J., and E. G. Berndt. Children's use of motive and intentionality in person perception and moral judgment. *Child Development*, 1975, **46**, 904–912.
5. Bernstein, A. C. How children learn about sex and birth. *Psychology Today*, 1976, **9**(8), 31–35, 66.
6. Best, D. L., S. C. Smith, D. J. Graves, and J. E. Williams. The modification of racial bias in preschool children. *Journal of Experimental Child Psychology*, 1975, **20**, 193–205.
7. Bettelheim, B. *The uses of enchantment: The meaning and importance of fairy tales.* New York: Knopf, 1976.
8. Blank, M. Cognitive functions of language in the preschool years. *Developmental Psychology*, 1974, **10**, 229–245.
9. Bloom, L., P. Lightbrown, and L. Hood. Structure and variation in child language. *Monographs of the Society for Research in Child Development*, 1975, **40**(2).
10. Braine, M. D. S. Children's first word combinations. *Monographs of the Society for Research in Child Development*, 1976, **41**(1).
11. Bruner, J. S. Play is serious business. *Psychology Today*, 1975, **8**(8), 80–83.
12. Bruner, J. S., A. Jolly, and K. Sylva (Eds.). *Play: Its role in development and evolution.* New York: Library of Human Behavior, 1977.
13. Buck, R. Nonverbal communication of affect in children. *Journal of Personality & Social Psychology*, 1975, **31**, 644–653.
14. Burnett, C. N., and E. W. Johnson. Development of gait in childhood. *Developmental Medicine & Child Neurology*, 1971, **13**, 207–215.
15. Cherry, L., and M. Lewis. Mothers and two-year-olds: A study of sex-differentiated aspects of verbal interaction. *Developmental Psychology*, 1976, **12**, 278–282.
16. Croake, J. W. Fears of children. *Human Development*, 1969, **12**, 239–247.
17. Cummins, S., N. Gams, and L. Zusne. Another note on Santa Claus. *Perceptual & Motor Skills*, 1971, **32**, 510.

18. Dare, M. T., and N. Gordon. Clumsy children: A disorder of perception and motor organisation. *Developmental Medicine & Child Neurology,* 1970, **12**, 178–185.

19. Denckla, M. B. Development of motor coordination in normal children. *Developmental Medicine & Child Neurology,* 1974, **16**, 729–741.

20. Denzin, N. K. Play, games and interaction: The contexts of childhood socialization. *Sociological Quarterly,* 1975, **16**, 458–478.

21. Deutsch, F. Observational and sociometric measures of peer popularity and their relationship to egocentric communication in female preschoolers. *Developmental Psychology,* 1974, **10**, 745–747.

22. Dion, K. K. Young children's stereotyping of facial attractiveness. *Developmental Psychology,* 1973, **9**, 183–188.

23. Dorman, L. Assertive behavior and cognitive performance in preschool children. *Journal of Genetic Psychology,* 1973, **123**, 155–162.

24. Drabman, R., and R. Spitalnik. Social isolation as a punishment procedure: A controlled study. *Journal of Experimental Child Psychology,* 1973, **16**, 236–249.

25. Edelsky, C. The acquisition of communicative competence: Recognition of linguistic correlates of sex roles. *Merrill-Palmer Quarterly,* 1976, **22**, 47–59.

26. Eichorn, D. H. Physiological development. In P. H. Mussen (Ed.). *Carmichael's manual of child psychology.* (3rd ed.) Vol. 1. New York: Wiley, 1970, Pp. 157–283.

27. Ely, K. P., A. Healey, and G. L. Smidt. Mothers' expectations of their child's accomplishment of certain gross motor skills. *Developmental Medicine & Child Neurology,* 1972, **14**, 621–625.

28. Emmerich, W. Continuity and stability in early social development. II. Teacher ratings. *Child Development,* 1966, **37**, 17–27.

29. Endsley, R. C., and S. A. Clarey. Answering young children's questions as a determinant of their question-asking behavior. *Developmental Psychology,* 1975, **11**, 863.

30. Etaugh, C. Effects of maternal employment on children: A review of recent research. *Merrill-Palmer Quarterly,* 1974, **20**, 71–98.

31. Fagot, B. I. Sex differences in toddlers' behavior and parental reactions. *Developmental Psychology,* 1974, **10**, 554–558.

32. Fagot, B. I., and I. Litman. Stability of sex roles and play interests from preschool to elementary school. *Journal of Psychology,* 1975, **89**, 285–292.

33. Fairchild, L., and W. M. Erwin. Physical punishment by parent figures as a model of aggressive behavior in children. *Journal of Genetic Psychology,* 1977, **130**, 279–284.

34. Falbo, T. Does the only child grow up miserable? *Psychology Today,* 1976, **9**(12), 60–65.

35. Fischer, P. L., and J. V. Torney. Influence of children's stories on dependency: A sex-typed behavior. *Developmental Psychology,* 1976, **12**, 489–490.

36. Fish, M. C., and E. E. Loehfelm. Verbal approval: A neglected educational resource. *Teachers College Record,* 1975, **76**, 493–498.

37. Flaste, R. In youngsters' books, the stereotype of old age. *The New York Times,* Jan. 7, 1977.

38. Ford, F. R., and J. Herrick. Family rules: Family life styles. *American Journal of Orthopsychiatry,* 1974, **44**, 61–69.

39. Forehand, R., M. W. Roberts, D. M. Dolleys, S. A. Hobbs, and P. A. Resick. An examination of disciplinary procedures with children. *Journal of Experimental Child Psychology,* 1976, **21**, 109–120.

40. Fouts, G., and P. Liikanen. The effects of age and developmental level on imitation in children. *Child Development,* 1975, **46**, 555–558.

41. Galejs, I. Social interaction of preschool children. *Home Economics Research Journal,* 1974, **2**, 153–159.

42. Garai, J. E., and A. Scheinfeld. Sex differences in behavioral and mental traits. *Genetic Psychology Monograph,* 1968, **77**, 169–299.

43. Gecas, V., J. W. Calonico, and D. L. Thomas. The development of self-concept in the child: Mirror theory versus model theory. *Journal of Social Psychology,* 1974, **92**, 67–76.

44. Gellert, E. Children's conceptions of the content and function of the human body. *Genetic Psychology Monographs,* 1962, **65**, 293–405.

45. Genosce, F., G. R. Tucker, and W. E. Lambert. Communication skills of bilingual children. *Child Development,* 1976, **47**, 1010–1014.

46. Glasner, Rabbi S. Family religion as a matrix of personal growth. *Marriage & Family Living,* 1961, **23**, 291–293.

47. Glueck, E. T. A more discriminative instrument for the identification of potential delinquents at school entrance. *Journal of Criminal Law, Criminology & Police Science,* 1966, **56**, 27–30.

48. Gramza, A. F. Responses to manipulability of a play object. *Psychological Reports,* 1976, **38**, 1109–1110.

49. Grant, W. W., A. N. Boelsche, and D. Zin. Developmental patterns of two motor functions. *Developmental Medicine & Child Neurology,* 1973, **15**, 171–177.

50. Guilford, J. S. Maturation of values in young children. *Journal of Genetic Psychology,* 1974, **124**, 241–248.

51. Gutkin, D. C. Maternal discipline and children's judgments of moral intentionality. *Journal of Genetic Psychology,* 1975, **127**, 55–61.

52. Hall, G. S. The contents of children's minds on entering school. *Pedagogical Seminary,* 1891, **1**, 139–173.

53. Hallahan, D. P., J. M. Kauffman, and C. S. Mueller. Behavioral observation and teacher rating correlates of motor and vocal behavior in preschoolers. *Journal of Genetic Psychology,* 1975, **126**, 45–52.

54. Halverson, C. F., and M. F. Waldrop. Relations between preschool activity and aspects of intellectual and social behavior at age 7½. *Developmental Psychology,* 1976, **12**, 107–112.

55. Hamill, P. V. V., T. A. Drizel, C. L. Johnson, R. B. Reed, and A. F. Roche. *NCHS growth curves for children from birth–18 years.* Hyattsville, Md.: National Center for Health Statistics, U.S. Department of Health, Education, and Welfare, 1977.

56. Hamilton, M. L., and D. M. Stewart. Peer models and language acquisition. *Merrill-Palmer Quarterly,* 1977, **23**, 45–55.

57. Hardyck, C., R. Goldman, and L. Petrinovich. Handedness and sex, race, and age. *Human Biology,* 1975, **47**, 369–375.

58. Haskett, C. J. The exploratory nature of children's social relations. *Merrill-Palmer Quarterly,* 1977, **23**, 101–113.

59. Havighurst, R. J. *Developmental tasks and education.* (3rd ed.) New York: McKay, 1972.

60. Herron, J. Southpaws: How different are they? *Psychology Today,* 1976, **9**(10), 50–56.

61. Herron, R. E., and B. Sutton-Smith (Eds.). *Child's play.* New York: Wiley, 1971.

62. Hogan, J. C., and R. Hogan: Organization of early skilled action: Some comments. *Child Development,* 1975, **46**, 233–236.

63. Holzman, M. The verbal environment provided by mothers for their very young children. *Merrill-Palmer Quarterly,* 1974, **20**, 31–42.

64. Inselberg, R. M., and L. Burke. Social and psychological correlates of masculinity in young boys. *Merrill-Palmer Quarterly,* 1973, **19**, 41–47.

65. Jacobs, R. A. Mobility pains: A family in transition. *Family Life Coordinator,* 1969, **18**, 129–134.

66. Jakobson, R. Verbal communication. *Scientific American,* 1972, **227**(3), 73–80.

67. Jennings, K. B. People versus object orientation, social behavior, and intellectual activities in preschool children. *Developmental Psychology,* 1975, **11**, 511–519.

68. Jennings, S. A. Effects of sex-typing in children's stories on preference and recall. *Child Development,* 1975, **46**, 220–223.

69. Jensen, L. C., and A. M. Rytting. Changing children's beliefs about punishment. *British Journal of Social & Clinical Psychology,* 1975, **14**, 91–92.

70. Johnson, E. G. The development of color knowledge in preschool children. *Child Development,* 1977, **48**, 308–311.

71. Jones, A. P., and R. G. Demaree. Family disruption, social indices, and problem behavior: A preliminary study. *Journal of Marriage & the Family,* 1975, **37**, 497–502.

72. Katz, P. A. Perception of racial cues in preschool children: A new look. *Developmental Psychology,* 1973, **8**, 295–299.

73. Kirchner, E. P., and S. I. Vondracek. Perceived sources of esteem in early childhood. *Journal of Genetic Psychology,* 1975, **126**, 169–176.

74. Kohlberg, L. *Stages in the development of moral thought and action.* New York: Holt, 1969.

75. Krauss, R. M., and S. Glucksberg. Social and nonsocial speech. *Scientific American,* 1977, **236**(2), 100–105.

76. Kreitler, S., E. Zigler, and H. Kreitler. The nature of curiosity in children. *Journal of School Psychology,* 1975, **13**, 185–200.

77. Kuczaj, S. A., and P. M. Maratsos. What children *can* say before they *will. Merrill-Palmer Quarterly,* 1975, **21**, 89–111.

78. Kuhn, D. Short-term longitudinal evidence for the sequentiality of Kohlberg's early stages of moral judgment. *Developmental Psychology,* 1976, **12**, 162–166.

79. Kuhn, D., S. C. Nash, and L. Brucken. Sex-role concepts of two- and three-year-olds. *Child Development,* 1978, **49,** 445–451.

80. Lamb, M. E. Interactions between two-year-olds and their mothers and fathers. *Psychological Reports,* 1976, **38**, 447–450.

81. Langlois, J. H., N. W. Gottfried, and B. Seay. The influence of sex of peer on the social behavior of preschool children. *Developmental Psychology,* 1973, **8**, 93–98.

82. Lerner, R. M., and E. Gellert. Body build identification, preference, and aversion in children. *Developmental Psychology,* 1969, **1**, 456–462.

83. Lerner, R. M., and C. Schroeder. Racial attitudes in young white children: A methodological analysis. *Journal of Genetic Psychology,* 1975, **127**, 3–12.

84. Levine, L. E., and M. L. Hoffman. Empathy and cooperation in four-year-olds. *Developmental Psychology,* 1975, **11**, 533–534.

85. Levinson, B. M. *Pets and human development.* Springfield, Ill.: Charles C Thomas, 1972.

86. Lohman, T. G., R. A. Boileau, and B. H. Massey. Prediction of lean body mass in young boys from skinfold thickness and body weight. *Human Biology,* 1975, **47**, 245–262.

87. Longstreth, L. E., G. V. Longstreth, C. Ramirez, and G. Fernandez. The ubiquity of big brother. *Child Development,* 1975, **46**, 769–772.

88. Looft, W. R. Animistic thought in children: Understanding of "living" across its associated attributes. *Journal of Genetic Psychology,* 1974, **124**, 235–240.

89. Lynn, D. B., and A. DeP. Cross. Parent preferences of preschool children. *Journal of Marriage & the Family,* 1974, **36**, 555–559.

90. Manosevitz, M., S. Fling, and N. M. Prentice. Imaginary companions in young children: Relationships with intelligence, creativity and waiting ability. *Journal of Child Psychology & Psychiatry & Allied Disciplines,* 1977, **18**, 73–78.

91. Manosevitz, M., N. M. Prentice, and F. Wilson. Individual and family correlates of imaginary companions in preschool children. *Developmental Psychology,* 1973, **8**, 72–79.

92. Maratsos, M. P. Nonegocentric communication abilities in preschool children. *Child Development,* 1973, **44**, 697–700.

93. Marshall, H. R. Relations between home experiences and children's use of language in play interactions with peers. *Psychological Monographs,* 1961, **75**(5).

94. Maurer, A. Corporal punishment. *American Psychologist,* 1974, **29**, 614–626.

95. McCarthy, D. Language development. *Monographs of the Society for Research in Child Development,* 1965, **25**(3), 5–14.

96. McGhee, P. E., and P. Grodzitsky. Sex-role identification among preschool children. *Journal of Psychology,* 1973, **84**, 189–193.

97. McGuire, J. M. Aggression and sociometric status with preschool children. *Sociometry,* 1973, **36**, 542–549.

98. Meredith, H. V. Somatic changes during human postnatal life. *Child Development,* 1975, **46**, 603–610.

99. Meyer, W. J., and J. Shane. The form and function of children's questions. *Journal of Genetic Psychology,* 1973, **123**, 285–296.

100. Moerk, E. L. Piaget's research as applied to the explanation of language development. *Merrill-Palmer Quarterly,* 1975, **21**, 151–169.

101. Moerk, E. L. Verbal interactions between children and their mothers during the preschool years. *Developmental Psychology,* 1975, **11**, 788–794.

102. Moore, N. V., C. M. Evertson, and J. E. Brophy. Solitary play: Some functional reconsiderations. *Developmental Psychology,* 1974, **10**, 830–834.

103. Mueller, E., M. Bleier, J. Krakoco, T. T. Hegedus, and P. Cournoyer. The development of peer verbal interaction among two-year-old boys. *Child Development,* 1977, **48**, 284–287.

104. Murray, J. P. Television and violence: Implications of the Surgeon General's Research Program. *American Psychologist,* 1973, **28**, 472–478.

105. Nelson, G. K. Concomitant effects of visual, motor, and verbal experiences in young children's concept development. *Journal of Educational Psychology,* 1976, **68**, 466–473.

106. Nelson, N. W. Comprehension of spoken language by normal children as a function of speaking rate, sentence difficulty, and listener age and sex. *Child Development,* 1976, **47**, 299–303.

107. Nolan, J. D., J. P. Galst, and M. A. White. Sex bias on children's television programs. *Journal of Psychology,* 1977, **96**, 197–204.

108. Passman, R. H. Providing attachment objects to facilitate learning and reduce stress: Effects of mothers and security blankets. *Developmental Psychology*, 1977, **13**, 25–28.

109. Piaget, J. *Psychology and epistemology*. New York: Grossman, 1971.

110. Pieper, E. Grandparents can help. *The Exceptional Parent*, 1976, **6**(2), 6–10.

111. Pines, M. The invisible playmate. *Psychology Today*, 1978, **12**(4), 38–42, 106.

112. Pulaski, M. A. The rich rewards of make believe. *Psychology Today*, 1974, **7**(8), 68–74.

113. Rabinowitz, F. M., B. E. Moely, N. Finkel, and S. McClinton. The effects of toy novelty and social interaction on exploratory behavior of preschool children. *Child Development*, 1975, **46**, 286–289.

114. Richmond, B. P., and G. P. Weiner. Cooperation and competition among young children as a function of ethnic grouping, grade, sex, and reward conditions. *Journal of Educational Psychology*, 1973, **64**, 329–334.

115. Rosenbloom, L., and M. E. Horton. The maturation of fine prehension in young children. *Developmental Medicine & Child Neurology*, 1971, **13**, 3–8.

116. Rubin, K. H. Relation between social participation and role-taking skill in preschool children. *Psychological Reports*, 1976, **39**, 823–826.

117. Rubin, K. H. Social interaction and communicative egocentrism in preschoolers, *Journal of Genetic Psychology*, 1976, **129**, 121–124.

118. Rubin, K. H., and T. L. Maioni. Play preference and its relationship to egocentrism, popularity and classification skills in preschoolers. *Merrill-Palmer Quarterly*, 1975, **21**, 171–179.

119. Rubin, K. H., T. L. Maioni, and M. Harnung. Free play behaviors in middle- and lower-class preschoolers. Parten and Piaget revisited. *Child Development*, 1976, **47**, 414–419.

120. Rubin, K. H., K. S. Watson, and T. W. Jambor. Free-play behaviors in preschoolers and kindergarten children. *Child Development*, 1978, **49**, 534–536.

121. Scheffler, R. Z. The child from five to six: A longitudinal study of fantasy change. *Genetic Psychology Monographs*, 1975, **92**, 19–56.

122. Schleifer, M., and V. I. Douglas. Effects of training on the moral judgment of young children. *Journal of Personality & Social Psychology*, 1973, **28**, 62–68.

123. Seitz, S., and S. Marcus. Mother-child interactions: A foundation for language development. *Exceptional Children*, 1976, **42**, 445–449.

124. Shatz, M., and R. Gelman. The development of communication skills: Modifications in the speech of young children as a function of listeners. *Monographs of the Society for Research in Child Development*, 1973, **38**(5).

125. Sheehan, R. Young children's contact with the elderly. *Journal of Gerontology*, 1978, **33**, 567–574.

126. Sherman, L. W. An ecological study of glee in small groups of preschool children. *Child Development*, 1975, **46**, 53–61.

127. Singer, J. L. Fantasy: The foundation of serenity. *Psychology Today*, 1976, **10**(2), 32–34, 37.

128. Smith, P. K. A longitudinal study of social participation in preschool children: Solitary and parallel play reexamined. *Developmental Psychology*, 1978, **14**, 517–523.

129. Styczynski, L. E., and J. H. Langlois. The effects of familiarity on behavioral stereotypes associated with physical attractiveness in young children. *Child Development*, 1977, **48**, 1137–1141.

130. Suppes, P. The semantics of children's language. *American Psychologist*, 1974, **29**, 103–114.

131. Switzky, H. N., H. C. Haywood, and R. Isett. Exploration, curiosity, and play in young children: Effects of stimulus complexity. *Developmental Psychology*, 1974, **10**, 321–329.

132. Tanner, J. M. *Fetus into man: Physical growth from conception to maturity*. Cambridge, Mass.: Harvard University Press, 1978.

133. Thomas, A., S. Chess, and H. G. Birch. The origin of personality. *Scientific American*, 1970, **223**(2), 102–109.

134. Tierney, M. C., and K. H. Rubin. Egocentrism and conformity in childhood. *Journal of Genetic Psychology*, 1975, **126**, 209–215.

135. Turner, C. W., and D. Goldsmith. Effects of toy guns and airplanes on children's antisocial free play behavior. *Journal of Experimental Child Psychology*, 1976, **21**, 303–315.

136. Turnure, J. E., and J. E. Rynders. Effectiveness of manual guidance, modeling, and trial-and-error learning procedures in the acquisition of new behavior. *Merrill-Palmer Quarterly*, 1973, **19**, 49–65.

137. Vincent-Smith, L., D. Bricker, and W. Bricker. Acquisition of receptive vocabulary in the toddler-age child. *Child Development*, 1974, **45**, 189–193.

138. Waldrop, M. F., and C. F. Halverson. Intensive and extensive peer behavior: Longitudinal and cross-sectional analysis. *Child Development*, 1974, **45**, 19–26.

139. Wallerstein, J. S., and J. B. Kelly. The effects of parental divorce: Experiences of the preschool child. *Journal of the American Academy of Child Psychiatry*, 1975, **14**, 600–616.

140. Wells, L. Television versus books for preschoolers. *Child Study Journal*, 1974, **4**, 93–100.

141. White, E., B. Elsom, and R. Prawat. Children's conceptions of death. *Child Development*, 1978, **49**, 307–310.

142. White, W. F., and S. Human. Relationship of self-concepts of three-, four-, and five-year-old children with mother, father, and teacher percepts. *Journal of Psychology*, 1976, **92**, 191–194.

143. Whiteman, M. Children's conceptions of psychological causality as related to subjective responsibility, conservation, and language. *Journal of Genetic Psychology*, 1976, **128**, 215–226.

144. Williams, J. E., S. M. Bennett, and D. L. Best. Awareness and expression of sex stereotypes in young children. *Developmental Psychology*, 1975, **11**, 635–642.

145. Williams, J. E., D. L. Best, and D. A. Boswell. The measurement of children's racial attitudes in the early school years. *Child Development*, 1975, **46**, 494–500.

146. Wilson, K. L., L. A. Zurcher, D. C. McAdams, and R. L. Curtis. Stepfathers and stepchildren: An exploratory analysis from two national surveys. *Journal of Marriage & the Family*, 1975, **37**, 526–536.

147. Wolf, T. M. Response consequences to televised modeled sex-inappropriate play behavior. *Journal of Genetic Psychology*, 1975, **127**, 35–44.

148. Yarrow, M. R., and C. Z. Waxler. Dimensions and correlates of prosocial behavior in young children. *Child Development*, 1976, **47**, 118–125.

CHAPTER SIX
LATE CHILDHOOD

After reading this chapter, you should be able to:

- List common names used by parents, educators, and psychologists as indicators of the important characteristics of the late childhood years.
- Describe the patterns of physical, motor, speech, and emotional development in late childhood and recognize the advancement in these areas since early childhood.
- Explain new social groupings in late childhood and point out their influence on children's play interests and activities.
- Stress the influence of increased understanding on moral attitudes and behavior in late childhood and on children's interests.
- Point out the effects of sex-role typing and family relationships on older children's real and ideal self-concepts.
- Briefly describe the hazards of late childhood that are carry-overs of those from early childhood and those that may develop as a result of new conditions in the lives of older children.
- Discuss the new conditions in the lives of older children that influence the degree of happiness they experience.

Late childhood extends from the age of six years to the time the individual becomes sexually mature. At both its beginning and end, late childhood is marked by conditions that profoundly affect a child's personal and social adjustments.

The beginning of late childhood is marked by the child's entrance into first grade—compulsory at six years in America today. For most young children, this is a major change in the pattern of their lives, even when they have had a year or more of experience in some preschool situation. While adjusting to the new demands and expectations of first grade, most children are in a state of disequilibrium; they are emotionally disturbed and, as a result, difficult to live and work with. Entrance into first grade is a milestone in every child's life, therefore it is responsible for many of the changes that take place in attitudes, values, and behavior.

During the last year or two of childhood, marked physical changes take place and these, also, are responsible for changes in attitudes, values, and behavior as this period draws to a close and children prepare, physically and psychologically, for adolescence. The physical changes that take place at the close of childhood bring about a state of disequilibrium in which the accustomed pattern of life is disturbed and there is a temporary upset until adjustments to the changes can be made.

Although it is possible to mark off the beginning of late childhood fairly accurately, one cannot be so precise about the time this period comes to an end because sexual maturity—the criterion used to divide childhood from adolescence—comes at varying ages.

This is because there are marked variations in the ages at which boys and girls become sexually mature. As a result, some children have a longer-than-average late childhood, while for others it is shorter than average. For the average American girl, late childhood extends from six to thirteen, a span of seven years; for boys, it extends from six to fourteen, a span of eight years.

CHARACTERISTICS OF LATE CHILDHOOD

Parents, educators, and psychologists apply various names to late childhood and these names reflect the important characteristics of the period.

Names Used by Parents To many parents, late childhood is the *troublesome age*—the time when children are no longer willing to do what they are told to do and when they are more influenced by their peers than by their parents and other family members.

Because most older children, especially boys, are careless and irresponsible about their clothes and other material possessions, parents regard late childhood as the *sloppy age*—the time when children tend to be careless and slovenly about their appearance and when their rooms are so cluttered that it is almost impossible to get into them. Even when there are strict family rules about grooming and care of possessions, few older children adhere to these rules unless parents demand that they do so and threaten them with punishment.

In families where there are brothers and sisters, it is common for the boys of the family to pick on the girls and to ridicule them—a pattern of behavior that comes from their association with peers outside the home. When girls retaliate, quarrels ensue in which there is much name-calling or actual physical attacks. Because of this common pattern of behavior in families where there are siblings of both sexes, late childhood is regarded by many parents as the *quarrelsome age*—the time when family fights are common and when the emotional climate of the home is far from pleasant for all family members.

Name Used by Educators Educators call late childhood the *elementary school age*. It is the time when the child is expected to acquire the rudiments of knowledge that are considered essential for successful adjustment to adult life. It is also the time when the child is expected to learn certain essential skills, both curricular and extracurricular.

Educators also regard late childhood as a *critical period* in the achievement drive—a time when children form the habit of being achievers, underachievers or overachievers. Once formed, habits of working below, above, or up to one's capacity tend to persist into adulthood. It has been reported that the level of achievement behavior in childhood is highly correlated with achievement behavior in adulthood (76). See Figure 6-1.

When children develop the habit of working up to their capacities in school or under or above their capacities, the habit becomes persistent and tends to spread to all areas of the child's life, not to academic

"Junior flunked all subjects . . . I think the kid's developing a life-style, dear."

FIGURE 6-1 Underachievement will become persistent if it gives the child satisfaction. (Adapted from Lichty and Wagner. "Grin and Bear It." *Publishers-Hall Syndicate,* June 30, 1974. Used by permission.)

work alone. Because girls discover, long before their elementary-school days are over, that doing better academically than the boys in their class is regarded as sex-inappropriate, they begin to develop the habit of working below their capacities. In time, this habit of

underachievement spreads to all areas of their lives in which their achievements are compared with those of boys. The "motive to avoid success," so characteristic of many females in the American culture, is well established by the time girls reach the fifth or sixth grades of elementary school (129).

Names Used by Psychologists To the psychologist, late childhood is the *gang age*—the time when children's major concern is acceptance by their age-mates and membership in a gang, especially a gang with prestige in the eyes of their age-mates. Because of this absorbing concern, children are willing to conform to group-approved standards in terms of appearance, speech, and behavior. This has led psychologists to label late childhood as the *age of conformity.* How important conformity to gang-approved standards is to older children has been explained thus by Church and Stone (28):

For a 7- or 8-year old the worst "sin" is to be in any way different from other children. . . . He apes the dress and mannerisms of older children and subscribes to the group code, even when it runs

To the psychologist, late childhood is the "gang age"—the time when children's major concern is acceptance by their age-mates and membership in a gang. (Andrew McKeever from Editorial Photocolor Archives.)

sharply counter to his own, his family's, and the school's.

Recent studies of creativity have shown that older children, if unhampered by environmental restraints, by criticism, or by ridicule from adults or peers, will turn their energies into creative activities. As a result, psychologists label late childhood the *creative age,* the time in the life span when it will be determined whether children will become conformists or producers of new and original work. While the foundations for creative expressions are laid in early childhood, the ability to use these foundations for original activities is generally not well developed before children reach the late childhood years (140).

Late childhood is frequently called the *play age* by psychologists, not because more time is devoted to play than at any other age—which would be impossible after the child enters school—but rather because there is an overlapping of play activities characteristic of the younger years and those characteristic of adolescence. It is thus the breadth of play interests and activities rather than the time spent in play that is responsible for giving the name *play age* to late childhood.

DEVELOPMENTAL TASKS OF LATE CHILDHOOD

To achieve a place in the social group, older children must accomplish the developmental tasks that society expects them to master at this time. Failure to do so will result in immature patterns of behavior, which will militate against acceptance in the peer group and in an inability to keep up with their age-mates who have mastered these developmental tasks (69). See page 10 for a list of the developmental tasks of late childhood.

No longer is the mastery of developmental tasks the sole responsibility of parents, as it was during the preschool years. It now becomes the responsibility also of the child's teachers and, to a lesser extent, the peer group. For example, developing fundamental skills in reading, writing, and calculating and developing attitudes toward social groups and institutions becomes as much the responsibility of teachers as of parents. Although parents can help to lay the foundation of the child's learning to get along

with age-mates, being a member of the peer group provides the major part of this learning experience.

Because boys mature sexually later than girls and, as a result, have a slightly longer childhood, it is logical to assume that they would master the developmental tasks of late childhood better than girls and therefore be more mature. There is little evidence that this is the case. In fact, evidence points to the greater maturity of girls of the same ages. The reason for this is that girls have more adult guidance and supervision than boys, which provides them with better opportunities to master the developmental tasks (69).

PHYSICAL DEVELOPMENT IN LATE CHILDHOOD

Late childhood is a period of slow and relatively uniform growth until the changes of puberty begin, approximately two years before the child becomes sexually mature, at which time growth speeds up markedly. Box 6-1 shows the important physical changes that take place before the puberty growth spurts begin. Compare these physical changes with those of babyhood (Box 4-1) and of early childhood (Box 5-1).

Physical growth follows a predictable pattern, although variations do occur. *Body build* affects both height and weight in late childhood. The ectomorph, who has a long, slender body, can be expected to weigh less than a mesomorph, who has a heavier body. Children with mesomorphic builds grow faster than those with ectomorphic or endomorphic builds and reach puberty sooner (141).

Good *health* and good *nutrition* are important factors in the child's growth and development. The better the health and nutrition, the larger children tend to be, age for age, as compared with those whose nutrition and health are poor. Children who were *immunized* against disease during the early years of life grow larger than those who were not immunized (153). *Emotional tension* likewise affects physical growth. Placid children grow faster than those who are emotionally disturbed, though emotional disturbance has a greater effect on weight than on height (141).

Bright children tend to be taller and heavier than those who are average or below average in *intelligence.* However, when very bright children are compared with their less bright siblings, this differ-

BOX 6-1

PHYSICAL DEVELOPMENT IN LATE CHILDHOOD

Height

The annual increase in height is 2 to 3 inches. The average eleven-year-old girl is 58 inches tall, and the average boy of the same age is 57.5 inches tall. See Figure 6-2.

Weight

Weight increases are more variable than height increases, ranging from 3 to 5 or more pounds annually. The average eleven-year-old girl weighs 88.5 pounds, and the average boy of the same age weighs 85.5 pounds. See Figure 6-3.

Body Proportions

Although the head is still proportionally too large for the rest of the body, some of the facial disproportions disappear as the mouth and jaw become larger, the forehead broadens and flattens, the lips fill out, the nose becomes larger and acquires more shape. The trunk elongates and becomes slimmer, the neck becomes longer, the chest broadens, the abdomen flattens, the arms and legs lengthen (although they appear spindly and shapeless because of undeveloped musculature), and the hands and feet grow larger, but at a slow rate.

Homeliness

The body disproportions, so pronounced during late childhood, are primarily responsible for the increase in homeliness at this time. In addition, careless grooming and a tendency to wear clothes like those of peers, regardless of their becomingness, contribute to homeliness.

Muscle-Fat Ratio

During late childhood, fat tissue develops more rapidly than muscle tissue which has a marked growth spurt beginning at puberty. Children of endomorphic builds have conspicuously more fat than muscle tissue while the reverse is true of those of mesomorphic builds. Ectomorphs do not have a predominance of either, and this accounts for their tendency to look scrawny.

Teeth

By the onset of puberty, a child normally has twenty-eight of the thirty-two permanent teeth. The last four, the wisdom teeth, erupt during adolescence.

---

ence ceases to exist. As Laycock and Caylor have explained, "The gifted child probably comes from a home where all the children grow bigger" because of better nutrition and health care (82).

Sex differences in physical growth, relatively slight in earlier years, become more pronounced in late childhood. Because boys begin their puberty growth spurt approximately a year later than girls, they tend to be slightly shorter and lighter in weight than girls of the same age until they too become sexually mature. Girls also get their permanent teeth slightly earlier than boys, while boys' heads and faces grow larger than girls'.

To date, no foolproof method has been devised to predict the adult height of children during the late childhood years. Adult height is determined, to some extent, by parental stature, but it is also affected by how long children grow and at what rate during the years preceding puberty (21,109).

SKILLS OF LATE CHILDHOOD

At the beginning of late childhood, children have a remarkably large repertoire of skills that they learned during the preschool years. What skills older children learn depends partly on their environment, partly on the opportunities given them for learning, partly on their body builds, and partly on what is in vogue among their age-mates.

Marked sex differences, for example, exist not only in play skills at this age but also in the level of perfection of these skills. Girls, as a rule, surpass boys in skills involving finer muscles, such as painting, sewing, weaving, and hammering, while boys are superior to girls in skills involving the grosser muscles, such as throwing a basketball, kicking a soccer ball long distances, and doing broad jumps (39).

The socioeconomic status of the family likewise has a marked influence on the number and kind

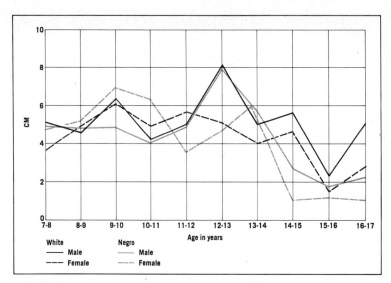

FIGURE 6-2 Growth in height during late childhood and early adolescence. Note the slow rate of growth in childhood and the rapid rate at puberty. (Adapted from W. M. Krogman. Growth of head, face, trunk, and limbs in Philadelphia white and Negro children of elementary and high school age. *Monographs of the Society for Research in Child Development,* 1970, **35**(3). Used by permission.)

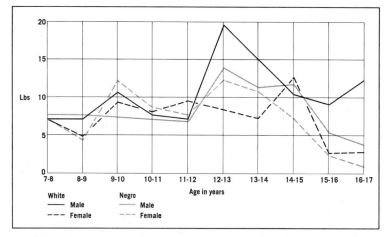

FIGURE 6-3 Growth in weight during late childhood and early adolescence. (Adapted from W. M. Krogman. Growth of head, face, trunk, and limbs in Philadelphia white and Negro children of elementary and high school age. *Monographs of the Society for Research in Child Development,* 1970, **35**(3). Used by permission.)

of skills children learn. Children from the upper socioeconomic levels tend, as a whole, to have fewer skills, age for age, than those of lower levels. Also, the skills they learn are more concentrated in the areas of self-help and social-help skills, while those of children of the middle and upper socioeconomic levels are more concentrated in the category of play skills.

Categories of Skills of Late Childhood

The skills of late childhood can be divided roughly into four categories: self-help skills, social-help skills, school skills, and play skills. What these different categories mean is explained in Box 6-2. Not all categories are equally important throughout the years of late childhood. Play skills, for example, are more important to children during the early part of late childhood than they are when they approach puberty. Then interest in active play wanes and is replaced by interest in amusements (39).

However, it is important to note that all the different skills of late childhood contribute either directly or indirectly to children's socialization (34). Although social-help skills learned in the home, such as dusting and doing dishes, will not help children directly to make better adjustments to their peers in school and in the neighborhood, indirectly they help them by teaching them to be cooperative—a trait that will contribute greatly to their acceptance by the peer group.

Handedness

By the time they reach late childhood, most children are so predominantly right- or left-handed that changing handedness is far from easy (66,145). As was pointed out in the discussion on changing handedness in the chapter on early childhood, doing so even then must be with caution and only under certain conditions.

Many left-handed children become *ambidextrous* during late childhood in that they use both hands, though there is a tendency to favor the left hand. As they learn new skills, both play and school skills, they often discover that it is easier for them to learn by following the right-handed model than by trying to adapt the right-handed model to the use of the left hand. Consequently, some of their skills are carried out predominantly with the right while others are carried out with the left hand.

Because of the difficulties involved in changing handedness, once skills have been well learned, rela-

CATEGORIES OF LATE-CHILDHOOD SKILLS

Self-Help Skills

Older children should be able to eat, dress, bathe, and groom themselves with almost as much speed and adeptness as an adult, and these skills should not require the conscious attention that was necessary in early childhood.

Social-Help Skills

Skills in this category relate to helping others. At home, they include making beds, dusting, and sweeping; at school, they include emptying wastebaskets and washing chalkboards; and in the play group, they include helping to construct a tree house or lay out a baseball diamond.

School Skills

At school, the child develops the skills needed in writing, drawing, painting, clay modeling, dancing, crayoning, sewing, cooking, and woodworking.

Play Skills

The older child learns such skills as throwing and catching balls, riding a bicycle, skating, and swimming in connection with play.

tively few children who are left-handed when late childhood begins change to the use of their right hands later. Knowing how difficult and emotionally disturbing it is to change handedness at this age, elementary-school teachers do not insist that children replace left-handed skills with right-handed skills. Instead, they encourage left-handers to learn new skills with their right hands and only when a child shows a strong desire to change from the use of the left to the use of the right hand does the teacher help or encourage the child to do so. Instead, most teachers encourage left-handers to become ambidextrous.

SPEECH IMPROVEMENT IN LATE CHILDHOOD

As children's social horizons broaden, they discover that speech is an essential tool for gaining acceptance in a group. This gives them a strong incentive to speak better. They also discover that the simpler forms of communication, such as crying and gesturing, are socially unacceptable. This gives them an added incentive to improve their speech. Perhaps most important of all, they discover that comprehension of what others say is essential to communication. If they fail to understand what others are saying to them, they not only cannot communicate but, even more serious, they are likely to say something totally unrelated to what their peers are talking about and, as a result, they are not acceptable to the peer group (6,79,150).

Help in improving speech in late childhood comes from four sources. First, parents from middle and upper socioeconomic groups may feel that speech is especially important and thus motivate their children to speak better by correcting faulty pronunciation and grammatical errors and by encouraging them to participate in general family conversations. Second, radio and television provide good models for speech for older children, as they do for children during the preschool years. They also encourage attentive listening on the part of older children and, as is true of younger children, this results in an improvement in the ability to comprehend what others are saying. Third, after children learn to read, they add to their vocabularies and become familiar with correct sentence formation. And, fourth, after they start school, mispronounced words and wrong meanings associated with words are usually quickly corrected by their teachers.

Areas of Improvement

In spite of the fact that all children are given similar opportunities to improve their speech in school, there are marked variations in the improvements made. There are also variations in the amount of improvement that takes place in the different tasks involved in learning to speak. An analysis of these tasks will show where the improvement occurs.

Vocabulary Building   Throughout late childhood, children's general vocabularies grow by leaps and bounds. From their studies in school, their reading, their conversations with others, and their exposure to radio and television, they build up vocabularies which they use in their speech and writing. This is known as a "general vocabulary" because it is composed of words in general use, not those of such lim-

ited meanings that they can be used only in a specific context.

It has been estimated that average first-graders know between 20,000 and 24,000 words, or 5 to 6 percent of the words in a standard dictionary. By the time they are in the sixth grade, most children know approximately 50,000 words (85).

Not only do older children learn many new words but they also learn new meanings for old words. This further enlarges their vocabularies. Children from better-educated families, as a rule, increase their vocabularies more than those from families in which the parents have less education. Girls, age for age, usually build up larger vocabularies than boys (120).

In addition to learning words in a general vocabulary, children build up "special vocabularies"—vocabularies made up of words with special meanings and limited uses. Box 6-3 gives the most common of the special vocabularies learned by older children.

Sex differences are marked in these special vocabularies. Girls have larger color vocabularies than boys because of their greater interest in clothes and in activities involving the use of color—decorating a dollhouse, for example. Boys, on the other hand, have larger and rougher slang-word and swear-word vocabularies than girls because they regard such words as signs of masculinity, while girls have larger secret vocabularies. *Socioeconomic* differences in slang-word and swear-word vocabularies are apparent in both sex groups with boys and girls from the lower socioeconomic groups using such words more frequently, and using more offensive words, than those of the same ages from higher socioeconomic groups. Children of both sexes in the lower socioeconomic groups also have larger money vocabularies because they are more apt to run errands for their mothers and thus become accustomed to handling money.

Pronunciation   Errors in pronunciation are less common at this age than earlier. A new word may be incorrectly pronounced the first time it is used, but after hearing the correct pronunciation once or twice, children are generally able to pronounce it correctly. This, however, is less true of children of the lower socioeconomic groups who hear more mispronunciations in their homes than children from more favored

SPECIAL VOCABULARIES OF LATE CHILDHOOD

Etiquette Vocabulary

By the end of the first grade, children who have had training at home in using such words as "please" and "thank you," have as large etiquette vocabularies as those of the adults in their environments.

Color Vocabulary

Children learn the names of all the common colors and many of the less common ones shortly after they enter school and begin to have formal training in art.

Number Vocabulary

From their study of arithmetic at school, children learn the names and meaning of numbers.

Money Vocabulary

Both in school and at home, older children learn the names of the different coins and they understand the value of the various denominations of bills.

Time Vocabulary

The time vocabularies of older children are as large as those of adults with whom they come in contact but their understanding of time words is sometimes incorrect.

Slang-Word and Swear-Word Vocabularies

Children learn slang words and swear words from older siblings and from the older children in the neighborhood. Using such words makes them feel "grown-up" and they soon discover that, in addition, the use of such words has great attention value. See Figure 6-4.

Secret Vocabularies

Children use secret vocabularies to communicate with their intimate friends. These can be *written*, consisting of codes formed by symbols or the substitution of one letter for another; *verbal*, consisting of distortions of words—pig Latin, for example; or *kinetic*, consisting of gestures and the use of fingers to communicate words. Most children start to use one or more of these forms at the time they enter the third grade, and their use reaches a peak just before puberty.

---

home environments, and it is even less true of children from bilingual homes.

Forming Sentences The six-year-old child should have command of nearly every kind of sentence structure. From six until the age of nine or ten, the length of sentences will increase. These long sentences are generally rambling and loosely knit. Gradually, after the age of nine, the child begins to use shorter and more compact sentences.

Improvement in Comprehension

With increased interest in group-belonging comes an increased interest in desire to communicate with group members. Children soon learn that meaningful communication cannot be achieved unless they understand the meaning of what others are saying to them. This provides the necessary incentive to improve their comprehension.

Improved comprehension is also aided by training in concentration in school. Children soon discover that they must pay attention to what is going on in class—what both the teacher and their classmates say—if they are to get along reasonably well with their lessons. In some schools, failure to concentrate is punished by having to stay after school or having to do extra work.

As is true of younger children, concentration is improved by listening to the radio and watching television, and this, in turn, improves comprehension. In addition, older children do not hesitate to ask questions about a word, a phrase, or even a sentence that is meaningless to them.

Perhaps the most important aid to improved comprehension comes from the shift that normally takes place from egocentric to socialized speech. So long as children are talking about themselves, they are thinking about themselves. This militates against

"NOW HERE'S A WORD THAT'S *GUARANTEED* TO MAKE EVERBODY STOP TALKIN' AND *LOOK* AT YOU."

FIGURE 6-4 Swearing by children is often used as a way of attracting attention. (Adapted from Hank Ketcham. ''Dennis the Menace.'' *Field Newspaper Syndicate*, March 25, 1976. Used by permission.)

their paying close attention to what others say. When, on the other hand, their speech becomes more socialized, there is a greater incentive to pay attention to what others say and, as a result, comprehension is greatly increased (6).

Content of Speech

Just when children will shift from egocentric to socialized speech will depend not so much upon their age as upon their personalities, the number of social contacts they have had, the satisfaction they have derived from these contacts, and the size of the group to which they are speaking. The larger the group, other conditions being equal, the more socialized the speech. Also, when children are with their contemporaries, their speech is generally less egocentric than when they are with adults. Many adults encourage egocentric speech in children, while their contemporaries not only discourage it but disregard those who persist in talking about themselves (7,132).

Although children may talk about anything, their favorite topics of conversation, when with their

peers, are their own experiences, their homes and families, games, sports, movies, television programs, their gang activities, sex, sex organs and functions, and the daring of a contemporary that led to an accident. When the child is with an adult, it is the latter who usually determines the topic of conversation (7).

When older children talk about themselves, it is usually in the form of *boasting*. They boast about anything related to themselves but generally less about their material possessions—a common form of boasting in young children—than about their superior skills and achievements. Boasting, as a rule, is very common between the ages of nine and twelve years, especially among boys.

Older children also like to criticize and make fun of other people. Sometimes they criticize people openly, and sometimes behind their backs. When criticizing adults, children generally put their criticisms in the form of a suggestion or a complaint, such as ''Why don't you do so-and-so?'' or ''You won't let me do what my friends do.'' Criticism of other children frequently takes the form of name-calling, teasing, or making derogatory comments.

How much improvement there will be in the content of older children's speech and in the way they present what they have to say will depend not so much on their intelligence as on the level of their socialization. Children who are popular have a strong incentive to improve the quality of their speech. They learn, from personal experience, that words can hurt and that the popular children are those whose speech adds to the enjoyment of their contact with their peers.

Amount of Talking

The *chatterbox stage*, characteristic of early childhood, is gradually replaced by more control and selection of speech. No longer do children talk just for the sake of talking, regardless of whether others pay attention to what they say, as they did in early childhood. Instead, they use speech as a form of communication, not as a form of verbal exercise.

There is progressively less and less talking as late childhood continues. As first, when children enter school, they often continue the meaningless chattering they engaged in during the preschool years. However, they soon discover that this is no longer permitted—they may speak only when the teacher gives them permission to do so.

Within the peer group, older children also discover that endless talking annoys their peers and that it is a quick way to lose social acceptance. In addition, they discover that their peers also want an opportunity to talk and resent their trying to dominate a conversation.

Some older children talk less than they would like to because they have been ridiculed by peers for their "funny pronunciation," if they are bilinguals, or because they have been scorned by peers because of the unsocial content of their speech. Others have discovered that if they try to dominate a conversation it will lead to social rejection so they curb their desire to talk.

Throughout the late childhood years, girls talk more, age for age, than boys, and children from the upper socioeconomic groups talk more than those from the lower groups. Boys discover that too much talking is regarded as sex-inappropriate while children from the lower socioeconomic groups are afraid of being ridiculed because of the poor quality of their speech.

Normally, as childhood draws to a close, children talk increasingly less. This is not because they are afraid they will be criticized or ridiculed for what they say, but it is, rather, a part of the withdrawal syndrome that is characteristic of the puberty period. This will be discussed in detail in the following chapter.

EMOTIONS AND EMOTIONAL EXPRESSIONS IN LATE CHILDHOOD

Older children soon discover that expression of emotions, especially of the unpleasant emotions is socially unacceptable to their age-mates. They learn that their age-mates regard temper outbursts as babyish, withdrawal reactions to fear as cowardly, and hurting others in jealousy as poor sportsmanship. As a result, older children acquire a strong incentive to learn to control the outward expressions of their emotions.

At home, however, there is not the same strong incentive to control the emotions. As a result, children frequently express their emotions as forcibly as they did when they were younger. Under such circumstances, it is not surprising that parents criticize or punish them for "not acting their age."

Characteristically, emotional expressions in late childhood are pleasant ones. The child giggles or laughs uproariously; squirms, twitches, or even rolls on the floor; and in general shows a release of pent-up animal spirits. Even though these emotional expressions are immature by adult standards, they indicate that the child is happy and making good adjustments.

Not all emotionality at this age, however, is of a pleasant sort. Numerous outbursts of temper occur, and the child suffers from anxiety and feelings of frustration. Girls often dissolve into tears or have temper outbursts reminiscent of their preschool days; boys are more likely to express their annoyances or anxieties by being sullen and sulky.

Common Emotional Patterns of Late Childhood

The common emotional patterns of late childhood are similar to those of early childhood. See Box 5-4 for a listing and brief description of these emotional patterns.

However, the common emotional patterns of late childhood differ from those of early childhood in two respects. First, they differ in the kind of situation that gives rise to them and, second, they differ in the form of emotional expression. These changes are the result of broadened experience and learning rather than of maturation.

From experience, children discover how others feel about various forms of emotional expression. In their desire to win social approval, they then try to curb the forms of expression they have found are socially unacceptable. As they grow older, children begin to express their anger in moodiness, sulkiness, and general orneriness. Temper tantrums become less frequent because older children have discovered that they are considered babyish.

Just as there are differences in the ways older children express their emotions, so there are differences in the kind of situation that gives rise to them. Older children are far more likely to become angry when a person makes a derogatory comment about them than are younger children who do not completely understand the meaning of the derogatory comment. Similarly, young children's curiosity is aroused by anything new and different. To an older child, the new and different must be pronounced or it will not arouse curiosity (97).

As is true of younger children, there are variations in the common emotions older children experience and in the way they express these emotions. Children who are popular tend to be less anxious and less jealous than those who are less popular. Boys, at every age, express the emotions that are regarded as sex-appropriate, such as anger and curiosity, more overtly than girls, while girls are likely to experience more fears, worries, and feelings of affection than boys—emotions that are regarded as sex-appropriate for them.

Periods of Heightened Emotionality

There are times during late childhood when children experience frequent and intense emotions. Because these emotions tend to be more unpleasant than pleasant, periods of heightened emotionality become periods of disequilibrium—times when children are out of focus and difficult to live with.

Heightened emotionality in late childhood may come from physical or environmental causes or from both. When children are ill or tired, they are likely to be irritable, fretful, and generally difficult. Just before childhood ends, when the sex organs begin to function, heightened emotionality is normally at its peak. This will be discussed in detail in the following chapter.

Environmental causes of heightened emotionality are also common and serious in late childhood. Because adjustments to new situations are always upsetting for children, heightened emotionality is almost universal at the time when children enter school. Any marked change in the pattern of the older child's life, as when the home is broken by death or by divorce, inevitably leads to heightened emotionality.

Generally, however, late childhood is a period of relative emotional calm which lasts until the puberty growth spurt begins. There are several reasons for this. First, the roles older children are expected to play are well defined and children know how to play them; second, games and sports provide a ready outlet for pent-up emotional energy; and, finally, because of improvement in their skills, older children are less frustrated in their attempts to accomplish various tasks than they were when they were younger.

Beginnings of Emotional Catharsis

As children learn to curb the external expressions of their emotions, they discover that, in doing so, they become nervous, tense, and ready to fly off the handle in a temper outburst at the slightest provocation. They are said to be in a "bad mood" or in a "bad humor."

Because the pent-up emotional state is unpleas-

ant for children, they discover, more often by trial-and-error than by guidance, that they can clear their systems of this pent-up state by strenuous play, by a hearty laugh, or even by crying. Clearing the system of pent-up emotional energy—*emotional catharsis*—once discovered, becomes a new way for older children to handle their emotional expressions to conform to social expectations.

While many forms of catharsis may work, older children discover, more through trial-and-error than through guidance, that some work better than others and some are more socially approved than others.

While crying, for example, may release pent-up emotional energy, it usually has as its side effect a depressed feeling which seems to sap the individual's energy. In addition, children discover that crying is considered babyish. Even when they cry in private, the redness of their eyes proclaims to others that they have been crying. Laughing and playing strenuously, on the other hand, do not have unpleasant side effects nor do they arouse social disapproval. As a result, before childhood comes to an end, most older children have discovered a form of emotional catharsis that meets their needs and helps them to cope with the control of their emotions which the social group expects of them.

Some children who have close, intimate friends discover before childhood comes to an end that it helps greatly to discuss with their friends the situations that give rise to unpleasant emotions—their frustrations, fears, jealousies, and griefs. By so doing, they get a new perspective on their emotional problems, with the result that the situations that gave rise to their emotions either are eliminated or minimized. They have discovered, in this way, the value of *mental* catharsis which, when combined with *physical* catharsis, enables them to learn to express their emotions in socially approved ways and with minimum physical or emotional stress (77).

SOCIAL GROUPINGS AND SOCIAL BEHAVIOR IN LATE CHILDHOOD

Late childhood is often referred to as the "gang age" because it is characterized by interest in peer activities, an increasingly strong desire to be an accepted member of a gang, and discontent when children are not with their friends. Older children are no longer satisfied to play at home alone or with siblings or to do things with family members. They want to be with their peers and they are lonely and dissatisfied when they are not with them.

Even one or two friends are not enough for older children. They want to be with the gang, because only then will there be a sufficient number of individuals to play the games and sports they now enjoy and to give excitement to their play. From the time children enter school until puberty, the desire to be with and to be accepted by the gang becomes increasingly strong. This is just as true of girls as it is of boys.

Characteristics of Children's Gangs

Most people think of gangs as groups of hoodlums or mischief-makers because of the popular association of the term with juvenile delinquents. As used by child psychologists and sociologists, *children's* gangs are markedly different from *adolescent* gangs. For that reason, when speaking of gangs in childhood, it is customary to refer to them as *children's gangs* to distinguish them from adolescent gangs.

There are many ways in which children's gangs differ from adolescent gangs, four of which are especially common and important. First, the major purpose of children's gangs is to have fun; they are primarily play groups. By contrast, the major purpose of adolescent gangs is to cause trouble for others in retaliation for real or imagined slights on the part of the social group. Second, children's gangs are made up of children who are popular with their peers, while adolescent gangs are composed of those who have failed to gain peer acceptance and, as a result, band together in the desire to vent their revenge on those who have failed to accept them. Third, children's gangs rarely have members of both sexes, while adolescent gangs are more often composed of members of both sexes than members of one sex. And, fourth, children's gangs are composed of children of the same age and level of development whose interests and abilities are similar, while adolescent gangs are composed of individuals of different age levels and whose abilities and interests are not necessarily similar except that they all want to seek revenge on those who have refused to accept them.

Box 6-4 gives the outstanding characteristics of children's gangs. The most important of these characteristics is that gangs are social groups formed by children themselves, not by adults; that their major purpose is to have fun, not to engage in mischief or other

---

BOX 6-4

CHARACTERISTICS OF CHILDREN'S GANGS

- Children's gangs are play groups.
- To belong to a gang, a child must be invited.
- Members of a gang are of the same sex.
- At first gangs consist of three or four members, but this number increases as children grow older and become interested in sports.
- Boys' gangs more often engage in socially unacceptable behavior than girls' gangs.
- Popular gang activities include games and sports, going to the movies, and getting together to talk or eat.
- The gang has a central meeting place, usually away from the watchful eyes of adults.
- Most gangs have insignia of belonging; the members may wear similar clothes, for example.
- The gang leader represents the gang's ideal and is superior in most respects to the other members.

---

forms of unsocial behavior; that they satisfy the social needs of older children; and, most important of all, that they are an important socializing agency in late childhood. While not all gangs have all of the characteristics listed in Box 6-4, they all serve the purpose of socializing children.

Effects of Gang Belonging

Figure 6-5 shows some of the most important ways in which belonging to a children's gang helps to socialize children. This comes primarily from conforming to the patterns of behavior, the values, and the attitudes of gang members (35). Unsure of their status and often afraid that they will be rejected by the gang unless they conform wholeheartedly to its standards, many older children bend over backward to be like their gang-mates in dress, behavior, and opinions, even when this means going against parental standards. It is upon this slavish conformity that socialization in late childhood is based (30,132). While conformity to peers persists throughout the latter childhood years, it usually reaches a peak between the ages of ten and eleven (135).

Group belonging is not without some unfavorable effects on children, four of which are very com-

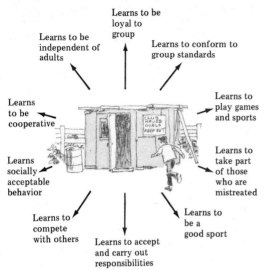

Learns to be loyal to group

Learns to be independent of adults

Learns to conform to group standards

Learns to be cooperative

Learns to play games and sports

Learns socially acceptable behavior

Learns to take part of those who are mistreated

Learns to compete with others

Learns to accept and carry out responsibilities

Learns to be a good sport

FIGURE 6-5 Some ways in which gang belonging leads to improved socialization in late childhood.

mon and serious enough to be considered detrimental to the socialization process. First, gang belonging often results in friction with parents and a rejection of parental standards. In addition to being more influenced by gang members than by parents, many older children spend more of their time with their gangs than with their families and, in so doing, they fail to carry their load of home work or family responsibilities. When parents object to this, parent-child friction develops and, with it, a weakening of the emotional ties between them.

The second common unfavorable effect of gang belonging is the development of antagonism between the sexes. While children's gangs, as was pointed out earlier, are usually made up of members of the same sex, some older children may prefer a member of the opposite sex as a friend and may find some of the play activities of the opposite sex more enjoyable than the play activities considered appropriate for the individual's sex. Some boys prefer the friendship of girls but, fearing unfavorable attitudes on the part of their fellow gang members, they do not want to be seen playing with girls.

The more usual pattern, however, is for antipathy toward members of the opposite sex to reach a high point just before puberty, at which time girls' attitudes toward boys are more emotionally toned than

boys' attitudes toward girls. There is reason to believe that the unfavorable attitude of girls toward boys at this age stems partly from their resentment at the greater freedom boys are permitted and partly from the fact that, as girls reach puberty, the greater social maturity that accompanies their early sexual maturity makes the typical behavior of boys of their own age seem immature.

The third common unfavorable effect of gang belonging is the tendency of older children to develop prejudices against those who are different. At first, prejudice does not take the form of discrimination and refusal to associate with children who are different but tends rather to show preference for those who are similar. Also, discrimination is based on racial differences and later, as children approach puberty, on religious and socioeconomic differences (49,78,98,156).

The fourth and, in most respects, the most detrimental effect of gang belonging is on the way older children treat non-gang members. Once older children have formed a gang, they are often cruel to those whom they do not regard as their friends. Much of the secrecy that surrounds gangs is designed to keep out children the members do not want as friends. The tendency to be cruel and callous toward all who are not gang-mates generally reaches a peak around the eleventh year.

While any child may have difficulty making friends and being accepted by a gang, children who are new to a neighborhood or a school have an especially difficult problem. It is the new children who must initiate the contacts if they want to have friends. This they do by trying to talk to or play with members of one of the already-formed gangs, by observing and imitating their play, and by trying to attract their attention.

At first, newcomers are usually ignored or rebuffed. If they are willing to try again and again, they may succeed in getting one or more members of the gang interested in them and, through this contact, they may eventually win a place in the gang.

Companions in Late Childhood

Companions in late childhood, as is true of early childhood, may be associates, playmates, or friends. Refer to Box 5-6 for a description of these three categories. Older children, unlike younger, are rarely satisfied with associates. To fill their social needs, companions must play the role of playmate or friend. While older children may have a closer relationship with some of the gang members than with others, they regard them all as "friends," though they also fill the role of playmates.

Boys tend to have more extensive peer relationships than girls. They prefer to play with groups rather than with one or two other boys. By contrast, girls' social relationships are more intensive in the sense that they play more with one or two girls than with a group (148).

Many factors influence older children's choice of friends. As a rule, they choose those they perceive as similar to themselves and those who meet their needs. Because physical attractiveness affects first impressions, children tend to select as playmates and friends those who are attractive looking (29,37).

Propinquity in the school or neighborhood is important because older children are limited to a relatively small area from which to select their companions. There is a strong tendency for older children to choose their companions from their own grades in school. And, at all times, companions of their own sex are selected rather than companions of the opposite sex.

Personality traits are important in the choice of companions, whether they play the role of playmates or friends. Older children value cheerfulness, friendliness, cooperativeness, kindness, honesty, generosity, even temperedness, and good sportsmanship in their playmates as well as in their friends. As childhood draws to a close, children show a preference for companions with similar socioeconomic, racial and religious backgrounds. This is especially true in the case of friends (15,16,38).

Treatment of Companions Unfavorable treatment of other children is not limited to those who are not members of a gang. Within every gang there is a great deal of fighting among its members. Often children in a gang are not on speaking terms with some of their playmates or friends. Many of these quarrels are made up and friendly relationships are reestablished; others are not.

When children quarrel with a gang-mate, there is a tendency for the group to refuse to play with the child with whom the group has quarreled. Sometimes this quarrel is only temporary and play relationships are soon reestablished. At other times, the strained relationship persists and the child who is the target of the gang's antagonism is made to feel unwelcome as a playmate and, as a result, may be dropped from the gang.

Much the same pattern is found in children's friendships. As a result, these friendships are rarely static. Children shift from best friend to enemy, from casual acquaintance to close friendship, quickly and often for little reason. Quarreling, bossiness, disloyalty, underhandedness, conceit, and incompatibility are the reasons most often given by children for changing friends. However, as children grow older, their friendships become more stable. Children who are popular have been found to change their friends almost as often as unpopular children. Girls, at all ages in late childhood, are slightly more stable in their friendships than boys (23,56).

Sociometric Status

Before late childhood draws to a close, most children are aware not only of their own *sociometric status*—the status they enjoy in the social group—but also of the sociometric status of their age-mates. They know that some are well accepted and liked by their age-mates while others are only marginally accepted and still others are either rejected or voluntarily withdraw from their age-mates. They also know how they themselves rate with their age-mates, though there is a tendency on the part of many children to exaggerate their social acceptance and to minimize their social rejection.

The degree of acceptance children enjoy is influenced, to some extent, by the child-training methods used by their parents. Children from democratic homes tend, on the whole, to be better liked and better accepted than those from homes where authoritarian or permissive child-training methods are used (4). Attractive children are generally better accepted than their less attractive age-mates. The reason for this is that people tend to attribute more favorable traits and fewer antisocial traits to those who are attractive than to those who are less attractive (1,37).

Social skills and social competence likewise contribute to the sociometric status of older children. As Gottman et al. have explained, "Popular children are more knowledgeable about how to make friends" (56). An experiment in which children were coached in social skills for friendship making showed that the coached group made a distinct improvement over the control group that did not receive this coaching (114). This is shown in Figure 6-6.

The ordinal position of a child within a family

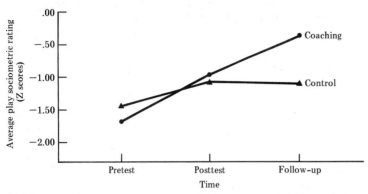

FIGURE 6-6 The effect of coaching children in social skills on their peer acceptance. (Adapted from S. Oden and S. R. Ashley. Coaching children in social skills for friendship making. *Child Development,* 1977, **48,** 495–506. Used by permission.)

likewise affects social acceptance. Later-born children, it has been reported, tend to be better accepted by their age-mates than their first-born siblings (104). This may be explained by the fact that as ordinal position in a family increases, children have more siblings

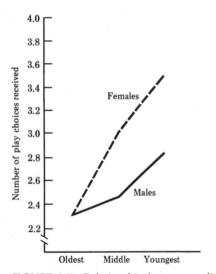

FIGURE 6-7 Relationship between ordinal position in the family and peer popularity as determined by number of play choices received by children of different ordinal positions. (Adapted from N. Miller and G. Maruyama. Ordinal position and peer popularity. *Journal of Personality & Social Psychology,* 1976, **33,** 123–131. Used by permission.)

to learn to adjust to. The relationship between ordinal position and social acceptance is shown in Figure 6-7.

Once children's sociometric status in a group has been established, it tends to remain constant. By the fifth or sixth grade, the chances of changing one's sociometric status in the same group become increasingly slim (23). There are two reasons for this. First, children get into the habit of behaving in certain ways and, once established, these habits tend to persist. Children, for example, can readily develop the habit of being generous if their generosity is encouraged by parents and appreciated by peers. As a result, they will be liked by their age-mates. Second, children acquire reputations which persist and affect the judgments their age-mates make of them. When children acquire the reputation of being poor sports or of being immature, the reputation not only spreads to all group members but tends to persist, even when children change the behavior pattern that has led to an unfavorable reputation.

Leaders in Late Childhood

Children who are chosen by their peers for leadership roles in late childhood closely approximate the group's ideal. They are not only liked by the majority of the members of their gangs but they have many of the qualities most admired by group members.

Because much of the time older children spend with their age-mates is spent in playing games and sports, children whose skills in these areas are superior to those of the other gang members have a very good chance of being chosen as the leaders. However, skills alone are not enough. Children who play leadership roles must also have personality traits admired by the gang, such as good sportsmanship, cooperativeness, generosity, and honesty.

Unlike leaders during the preschool years, leaders in late childhood who use authoritarian and despotic techniques soon lose their leadership roles. Older children deeply resent being "bossed" by their playmates, just as they resent being "bossed" by their parents and teachers.

When the leadership role does not meet the child's needs or the needs of the group members, there is a shift to other leaders. If, on the other hand, children can play leadership roles to the satisfaction of group members and to their own satisfaction, there will be a persistence of leadership. Persistence enables children to learn the technique of leadership and to gain confidence in their abilities to carry out this role satisfactorily. Furthermore, if they gain the reputation among their gang-mates of being "good" leaders, they are likely to be chosen for other leadership roles. Children who play leadership roles in games and sports to the satisfaction of group members have a very good chance of being selected as class presidents or for other leadership roles unrelated to games and sports (74).

PLAY INTERESTS AND ACTIVITIES IN LATE CHILDHOOD

Because older children go to school and many have home duties, they have less time for play than they did during the preschool years. However, in the American culture of today, play is regarded as so important to children's physical and psychological development that all children, regardless of the socioeconomic status of their families, are given time and opportunities to play and encouragement to do so. In discussing the socializing effect of play, Lever has said, "During play children develop numerous social skills that enable them to enjoy group membership in the community of peers" (86).

While all older children play, how they play is more of an individual matter than it was during the early childhood years. The play activities of older children and the amount of time they devote to these activities will depend on how popular they are and whether or not they belong to gangs. Children who lack acceptance in a gang are forced to spend much of their playtime in solitary activities, such as making things or amusing themselves by watching television, listening to the radio, or reading.

During late childhood, both boys and girls are keenly aware of the sex-appropriateness of different types of play, and they shun play activities that they know are regarded as inappropriate for their sex, regardless of personal preference.

Bright children, especially as they grow older, are more solitary than social in their play, and they participate in fewer activities that involve strenuous physical play than children who are less bright. The kind of neighborhood in which the child lives also determines what opportunities there will be for play.

Regardless of these variations, for most children play becomes less active as childhood progresses, and such amusements as movies, radio, television, and reading gain in popularity. This shift is due partly to increased schoolwork and partly to additional home duties.

Constructive Play

Making things just for the fun of it, with little thought given to their eventual use, is a popular form of play among older children. Construction with wood and tools appeals to boys, while girls prefer finer types of construction, such as sewing, drawing, painting, clay modeling, and jewelry making.

Drawing, painting, and clay modeling gradually decrease in popularity as childhood advances, not so much because older children lose interest in these activities, but rather because they feel self-conscious if they are criticized by their classmates and teachers. Many children, however, enjoy these activities at home, in private, where they are less likely to be criticized or ridiculed for them. The drawings that older children do make are likely to be cartoons of their teachers, their classmates, or people in the news. This kind of drawing is generally done during school hours, when they are bored.

Singing is another form of creative play that older children enjoy. In most cases, they do not like to sing at school, during the music period when their singing is likely to be criticized, but rather with their friends when they are away from the listening ears of teachers and parents. Few boys make any serious attempt to sing well; they derive their fun just from making a noise or from making up a silly version of a song they already know.

Exploring

Like younger children, older children like to satisfy their curiosity about anything new and different by exploring it. However, unlike younger children, older children are not satisfied with exploring toys and objects in their immediate environment. Instead, they want to go beyond their own homes and neighborhoods and explore new areas.

For example, an old, shut-up house, or a new house under construction, will intrigue them. If they are city children, they will want to explore country environments and, if they live in the country, they will want to explore city environments.

Because exploring in late childhood can best be done with others, rather than alone, as is true of the exploratory behavior of babies and young children, exploring in late childhood becomes a popular gang activity. This, however, is truer of boys than of girls because girls are usually restricted in where they can go and what they can do.

The popularity of exploring as a play activity has resulted in its being included in many of the recreational activities of organized groups, such as the Boy Scouts and the Girl Scouts, the ''Y's,'' and church groups. However, in such groups older children explore under direction and supervision, not freely as they do when exploring is a gang activity. In the former, there is usually an adult to guide and direct the exploring while, in the latter, children explore in any way that gives them enjoyment.

Collecting

Collecting as a form of play increases as childhood progresses. The reason for this is that it serves as a source of envy and prestige among the child's gang-mates as well as giving pleasure to the collector.

At first, older children, as is true of younger ones, collect anything that attracts their attention—rocks, bottle caps, baseball cards, marbles, sea shells, etc. Gradually they become more selective in their collections, concentrating on things that are pretty and different from those collected by age-mates. However, regardless of personal interests and preferences, older children concentrate on things that will give them prestige in the eyes of their friends and they

try to get as large a number of these prestigious items as possible (149).

Another way in which collecting among older children differs from that of younger children is that older children arrange the items they collect in some systematic way—in specially labeled envelopes or boxes, for example—so that they can easily be displayed to their age-mates. By contrast, younger children, once they have had the pleasure of collecting items that attract their attention and interest, carry them home, put them in a drawer or box, and usually forget them. They do not show them off to age-mates nor do they make any attempt to keep them in systematic ways.

Games and Sports

Older children are no longer satisfied to play the simple, undifferentiated types of games of early childhood. Instead, they want to play the games of older children, such as basketball, football, baseball, and hockey. By the time children are ten years old, their games are largely competitive in spirit, with interest concentrated on skill and excellence rather than on merely having fun.

During late childhood, most children who belong to gangs start to play indoor games when the weather is too poor to allow them to play outdoors. Many of these are games they played with family members when they were younger, while others, such as simple card games and craps, they learn from older siblings or from watching adults play them. Boys prefer games with an element of gambling.

In late childhood, major emphasis is put on the sex-appropriateness of the games and sports children engage in (105). Lever has made an analysis of the sex differences in the games older children play and has concluded that there are six major differences. First, boys play outdoors more than girls, partly because of their greater interest in sports; second, boys play in larger groups than girls; third, boys' play occurs in more mixed-age groups than girls' play; fourth, girls more often play predominantly male games than boys play girls' games; fifth, boys play competitive games more often than girls do; and sixth, boys' games last longer than girls' games.

As Lever has pointed out, these differences in play result in different social skills and, as a result, different capacities are developed. This, Lever emphasized, is a major force in the development and perpet-

SOME FAVORITE AMUSEMENTS OF LATE CHILDHOOD

Reading

Older children prefer books and the children's magazines that stress adventure and in which they may read about a heroic person with whom they can identify. They prefer pleasant settings and the positive group interactions of middle-class people to stark settings and negative group interactions of inner-city people. Above all, they want their stories to have happy endings.

Comic Books and Comic Strips

Regardless of intellectual level, almost all children enjoy comic books and comic strips, whether humorous or adventure-oriented. Their appeal comes from the fact that they are amusing, exciting, easy to read, and a stimulus to the child's imagination.

Movies

Movie attendance is one of the favorite gang activities of late childhood, although some children attend alone or with family members. They enjoy cartoons, adventure movies, and movies about animals.

Radio and Television

Radio is less popular than television among older children, although they do enjoy listening to music or tuning into a sports event that is not presented on television. Watching television is one of the favorite amusements of most older children. They enjoy cartoon shows and other programs geared toward their age level, as well as many adult shows. As Leifer et al. have pointed out, "television is not only entertainment for children, it is also an important socializer of them" (84).

Daydreaming or Fantasizing

Children who are lonely at home and who have few playmates or friends often amuse themselves by daydreaming. Typically, they imagine themselves as "conquering heroes" in their daydream world and, thus, compensate for the lack of companionship and attention they get in daily life.

---

uation of differential abilities between the sexes and helps perpetuate the traditional sex roles (86).

Amusements

When older children are not with their gang-mates—in the evenings, on holidays, or when recovering from an illness—they spend what time they have free from schoolwork and from home responsibilities amusing themselves by reading, looking at comics, listening to the radio, watching television, or daydreaming. The most popular amusements of late childhood are described in Box 6-5.

Because amusements are, for the most part, a solitary form of play, individual preferences are more apparent than in group-play activities, where the child's preferences are overshadowed by those of the group. Regardless of individual preferences, there are predictable age differences; children show a preference for more serious reading and less interest in comic books as they grow older, for example. Sex difference in amusements, especially reading, television watching, and movie going, are even more marked

than in other forms of play. Children of the lower socioeconomic groups spend more time watching television than those of the middle and upper groups and less time reading. The more popular children are, the less they will daydream and the more they will prefer amusements that can be carried out as group activities, such as going to the movies or watching television. There are also changes in the relative popularity of different forms of amusement with age. Daydreaming or fantasizing, for example, becomes more popular as childhood progresses. There are two common reasons for this. First, older children, as a result of many duties and responsibilities, have less energy than they had earlier, and daydreaming is an effortless form of amusement. Second, as they accumulate more information about different matters, they have more bases on which to build their daydreams. As Pulaski has explained: "Children must have content in order to fantasize. . . . Much of this material comes from stories adults read to children, and now television provides additional content for today's fantasizers" (122).

As children grow older, television often loses some of its earlier appeal. This is partly because programs are designed mainly for preschoolers and adults, with little available of interest for older children, and partly because they cannot watch television while studying or doing household chores. Their interest in radio increases because they can listen while doing other things and because there are more programs, especially musical programs, of interest to them than are available on television.

INCREASE IN UNDERSTANDING IN LATE CHILDHOOD

As their world expands with their entrance into school, so do children's interests. And with this broadening of interests comes an understanding of people and things which formerly had little or no meaning. Children now enter what Piaget has called the "stage of concrete operations" in thinking, a time when the vague and nebulous concepts of early childhood become specific and concrete (116).

Children associate new meanings with old concepts on the basis of what they learn after starting school. In addition, they derive new meanings from the mass media, especially movies, radio, and television. In building up social concepts, for example, they associate cultural stereotypes with people of different racial, religious, sex, or socioeconomic groups —stereotypes which, for the most part, they have learned from the mass media.

As children read textbooks in school and consult encyclopedias and other sources of information, they not only learn new meanings for old concepts but they also correct faulty meanings associated with old concepts. Their own experiences likewise give them meanings for their concepts. Children's own experiences with illness, for example, color their concepts of illness (25).

In the development of concepts, emotional weightings are added as well as new meanings. Sometimes these emotional weightings are new and sometimes they are reinforcements of former emotional weightings. From their religious teachings at home or in Sunday school, for example, children may associate pleasant emotional weightings with death. Later, as they watch movies or television shows involving death or see pictures of dead people in magazines or newspapers, they may develop quite different

concepts and different emotional weighting to these concepts as they are colored by these vicarious experiences. As Barclay has explained (10):

The way that life is lived today children are exposed continually to ersatz examples of death on television which are either cold, bloodless, and unmourned, or violently reacted to in the most melodramatic manner possible. At the same time, news programs, newspapers and picture magazines show them graphic evidences of real death and of real reactions to it—some stricken, some apparently emotionless, a few smirkingly self-conscious. .... If the child is upset by death in a movie or television show, his parents reassure him that the upsetting incident was just "make believe." But he knows that at other times and other places it is surely real.

Because older children's experiences are more varied than those of preschoolers, it is understandable that their concepts change in different directions and become increasingly more varied. However, certain concepts are commonly found among older children in the American culture of today. The concepts that change most and the new ones most commonly developed in late childhood are given in Box 6-6. Compare these concepts with those of early childhood, given in Box 5-8.

MORAL ATTITUDES AND BEHAVIOR IN LATE CHILDHOOD

When early childhood comes to an end, children's moral concepts are no longer as narrow and specific as they were earlier. Instead, older children gradually generalize their moral concepts so that they refer to *any* situation rather than to specific situations. In addition, older children discover that the social group attaches different degrees of seriousness to different acts. This knowledge is then incorporated in their moral concepts.

Between the ages of five and twelve, as Piaget has explained, children's concepts of justice change. Their rigid and inflexible notions of right and wrong, learned from parents, become modified and they begin to take into account the specific circumstances surrounding a moral violation. Thus, according to Piaget, moral relativism replaces moral inflexibility. For example, to a five-year-old lying is always bad, while an older child realizes that in some situations a

BOX 6-6

COMMON CATEGORIES OF CONCEPTS IN LATE CHILDHOOD

Life

While some older children find it difficult to understand that many things that move—a river, for example—are not alive, they become increasingly aware that movement is not the sole criterion of life.

Death

Children who experience the death of a family member or pet have a good understanding of the meaning of death, and the emotional weighting of their concepts of death is colored by the reactions of those around them.

Life after Death

Concepts of life after death depend mainly on the religious instruction children receive and on what their friends believe.

Bodily Functions

Until children begin to study hygiene in elementary school, many of their concepts about bodily functions are inaccurate and incomplete. This is especially true of internal bodily functions. See Figure 6-8.

Space

By using scales and rulers, children learn the meaning of ounces, pounds, inches, feet, and even miles. From reports of space exploration in the mass media, they develop concepts about outer space.

Numbers

Numbers take on new meanings as older children use money and work out arithmetic problems. By the time they are nine or ten years old, children understand number concepts to 1,000 and beyond.

Causality

Concepts of physical causality usually develop earlier than concepts of psychological causality. Children know, for example, what causes rain or snow earlier than what causes people to become angry.

Money

Children being to understand the value of various coins and bills when they start to use money. Opportunities to use money vary markedly and are greater in the lower socioeconomic-status families than in the upper.

Time

The rigid schedule of the school day enables children to develop concepts of what they can accomplish in a given period of time. Social studies in school and mass media help them to develop concepts of historical time.

Self

Children's concepts of themselves become clarified when they see themselves through the eyes of their teachers and classmates and when they compare their abilities and achievements with those of their peers.

Sex Roles

Not only do boys and girls develop clear concepts of approved sex roles, but before childhood is over they may also learn that the male role is apt to be considered more prestigious than the female role.

Social Roles

Older children are aware of their peers' social, religious, racial, and socioeconomic status and they accept cultural stereotypes and adult attitudes toward these statuses. This leads to group consciousness and, in many cases, to social prejudice.

Beauty

Older children tend to judge beauty in terms of group standards rather than according to their own aesthetic standards. What the group regards as beautiful or ugly, they accept as their own concepts.

The Comical

Older children's concepts of the comical are based partly on what they have observed others to perceive as funny and partly on what they themselves can comprehend, as in the case of riddles.

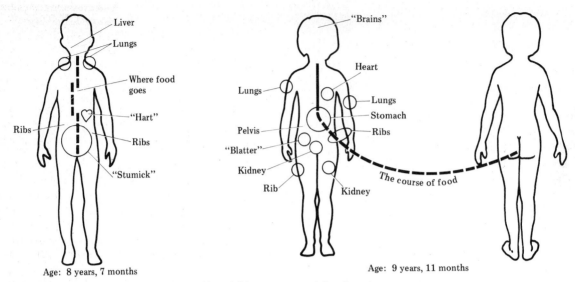

FIGURE 6-8 Some examples of the older child's concepts of the digestive process and of the location of different bodily organs. (Adapted from E. Gellert. Children's conceptions of the content and function of the human body. *Genetic Psychology Monographs*, 1962, **65**, 293–405. Used by permission.)

lie is justified and, therefore, not necessarily bad (116).

Kohlberg has elaborated on Piaget's theory and has labeled late childhood the second level of moral development, the level of *conventional morality,* or morality of conventional rules and conformity. In the first stage of this level, which Kohlberg has called *good boy morality,* children conform to rules to win the approval of others and to maintain good relationships. In the second stage, Kohlberg contends that if the social group accepts rules as appropriate for all group members, they should conform to them to avoid social disapproval and censure (81).

Development of Moral Codes

Moral codes develop from generalized moral concepts. In late childhood, as is true of the early adolescent years, moral codes are greatly influenced by the moral standards of the groups with which older children are identified. This does not, of course, mean that they abandon family moral codes in favor of the code of the gang with which they are identified. Rather, it means that if older children must make a choice, they will go along with the gang's standards *while they are with the gang* as a means of maintaining their status in the gang.

As children reach the end of childhood, their moral codes gradually approach those of the adults with whom they are associated and their behavior conforms more closely to the standards set up by these adults. Children with high IQs, it has been reported, tend to be more mature in their moral judgments than those of lower intellectual levels, and girls tend to form more mature moral judgments than boys (143,148).

Role of Discipline in Moral Development

Discipline plays an important role in the development of a moral code. In spite of the child's need for discipline, it becomes a serious problem with older children. Continuing use of the disciplinary techniques that proved to be effective when the child was younger is likely to lead to strong resentments on the part of the older child. If discipline is to fill its role as a developmental need, it must be suited to the child's level of development. Box 6-7 gives the essentials of effective discipline for older children.

ESSENTIALS OF DISCIPLINE FOR OLDER CHILDREN

Aid in Building a Moral Code

In the case of the older child, the teaching of right and wrong should emphasize the reasons why certain patterns of behavior are acceptable while others are not, and it should be directed toward helping the child broaden specific concepts into more generalized, abstract ones.

Rewards

Rewards, such as praise or a special treat for handling a difficult situation well, have a strong educational value if they show children that they have behaved correctly and they also motivate children to repeat the approved behavior. However, if they are to be effective, rewards must be appropriate to the child's age and level of development.

Punishment

Like rewards, punishment must be developmentally appropriate and administered fairly; otherwise, it may arouse resentment on the child's part. Punishment must also motivate the child to conform to social expectations in the future.

Consistency

Good discipline is always consistent. What is right today is right tomorrow and the next day. A wrong act should receive the same punishment every time it is repeated, and a right act the same reward.

Development of Conscience

The kind of discipline used also plays an important role in the development of conscience—one of the important developmental tasks of late childhood. The term *conscience* means a conditioned anxiety response to certain kinds of situations and actions which has been built up by associating certain acts with punishment. It is an "internalized policeman" which motivates children to do what they know is right and thus avoid punishment (42).

Guilt is a "special kind of negative self-evaluation that occurs when an individual acknowledges that his behavior is at variance with a given moral value to which he feels obligated to conform." *Shame*, by contrast, is an "unpleasant emotional reaction of an individual to an actual or presumed negative judgment of himself by others, resulting in self-depreciation vis-à-vis the group." Shame thus relies on external sanctions alone, though it may be accompanied by guilt. Guilt, by contrast, relies on *both* internal and external sanctions (42).

Misdemeanors in Late Childhood

Like those of younger children, some of the misdemeanors of older children are due to ignorance of what is expected of them or to a misunderstanding of the rules. Some are the result of children's testing of authority and their attempts to assert their independence. Most, however, are the result of children's conformity to gang misbehavior. To maintain their position in a gang, children discover that they must do what the rest of the gang does regardless of how they feel about such behavior.

The misdemeanors of late childhood are dependent upon the rules children break. And, because there are no universal rules either in the home or in the school for all American children, there are no universal misdemeanors in childhood in the American culture of today. Furthermore, because home rules are different from school rules, home misdemeanors are different from school misdemeanors. Box 6-8 lists some of the most commonly reported misdemeanors of late childhood.

As children grow older, they tend to violate more rules both at home and in school than they did when they were younger. At home this is due, in part, to the fact that older children want to assert their independence and, in part, to the fact that they often regard rules as unfair, especially if they differ from the home rules their gang-mates are expected to abide by, and the punishment they receive for violating them unjust.

Increased misbehavior at school may be explained by the fact that older children like school less than they did when they were younger; that they almost always like their teachers less than they did in the early grades; that they find some school subjects boring and, as a result, "cut up" instead of concentrating on these subjects; and that older children are often less well accepted by their classmates than they

COMMON MISDEMEANORS OF LATE CHILDHOOD

Home Misdemeanors

- Fighting with siblings
- Breaking possessions of other family members
- Being rude to adult family members
- Dawdling over routine activities
- Neglecting home responsibilities
- Lying
- Being sneaky
- Pilfering things belonging to other family members
- Spilling things intentionally

School Misdemeanors (See Figure 6-9)

- Stealing
- Cheating
- Lying
- Using vulgar and obscene language
- Destroying school property and materials
- Being truant
- Annoying other children by teasing them, bullying them, and creating a disturbance
- Reading comic books or chewing gum during school hours
- Whispering, clowning, or being boisterous in class
- Fighting with classmates
- The use of drugs, especially marijuana, on the school grounds

were in the earlier grades or than they had hoped to be. Regardless of the cause, misdemeanors often are an outgrowth of boredom (101).

As childhood draws to a close, misdemeanors generally become fewer (36). This may be due in part to greater maturity, both physical and psychological, but it is more often due to the lack of energy characteristic of the growth spurt that accompanies the early part of puberty. Many prepubescents simply do not have the energy to "cut up" or to get into mischief.

At home, in school, and in the neighborhood, boys break more rules than girls. There are two reasons for this sex difference: First, boys are given more freedom than girls and are less often punished for misbehavior on the grounds that "boys will be

boys''; and second, boys feel that they must defy rules to show their masculinity and thus win peer approval.

INTERESTS IN LATE CHILDHOOD

Because of differences in abilities and experiences, the interests of older children vary more than those of younger children. Although each child will develop certain individual interests, every child in a particular culture develops other interests that are almost universally found among children of that culture. Box 6-9 summarizes the interests that are common among children in this country.

Effects of Interests

The interests older children develop have a powerful influence on their behavior, not only during childhood but also as they grow older. That is why the development of wholesome interests suited to children's abilities and needs is too important to be left to chance, as it so often is. Many parents and teachers feel that most childish interests are merely whims—passing interests though they may be strong while they last. Consequently, they tend to take them lightly and assume that children will "outgrow" these interests as they become older and have broader experiences.

Nuckols and Banducci, in a study of children's knowledge of different vocations and their perceptions of vocations based on the knowledge they have, whether favorable or unfavorable, have come to the conclusion that children's perceptions of different vocations are the foundations for their interest or lack of interest in these vocations. This, they emphasize, is important because "vital decisions which may potentially affect an entire lifetime are predicated upon the occupational images to which one subscribes" (113).

Some of the most important ways in which interests, established during the late childhood years, affect children are as follows. First, they influence the form and intensity of aspirations. A girl, for example, who is interested in matters of health or in the functioning of the human body, may aspire to be a nurse or a doctor when she grows up, while a boy who has a strong interest in sports may want to become a professional athlete or an athletic coach.

Second, interests can and do serve as a strong motivating force. Children who are interested in being as autonomous as their age-mates will strive

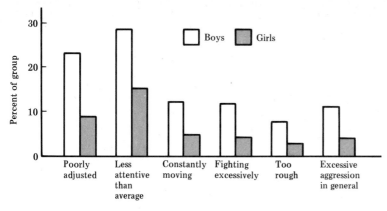

FIGURE 6-9 Percent of boys and girls, six to eleven years of age, found in a nationwide sample to commit different kinds of school misdemeanors. (Adapted from J. Roberts and J. T. Bird. *Behavior patterns of children in school: United States*. Rockville, Md.: U.S. Department of Health, Education, and Welfare, 1972. Used by permission.)

hard to be mature in their behavior in the hopes of winning the autonomy they crave.

Third, achievements are always influenced by the kind and intensity of the individual's interests. The child who is interested in mathematics, for example, will work hard to get good grades in that subject, while the child who lacks interest in math will likely become an underachiever in this area.

Fourth, interests established in childhood often become lifetime interests. This is because interests lead to satisfaction. Children are likely to repeat activities related to their interests and thus these interests become habitual and may persist throughout life. Interest in painting or music in adulthood, for example, usually originated during childhood.

SEX-ROLE TYPING IN LATE CHILDHOOD

Sex-role typing, which began shortly after birth, now continues with new agencies playing important roles in the typing process. Among the new forces that play significant roles in the sex-typing process, teachers and school subjects are important because of the prestige children attach to the teacher role (83). The different mass media likewise play important roles in sex-role typing of children. As Nolan et al. have explained, "Children are covertly taught on television

that boys are more significant persons than girls" (112). In the books they read, either in school or for pleasure, when men and women are shown holding the same job, males are typically pictured as directing the task (70). When mothers work outside the home, it affects girls' vocational aspirations and influences what girls think women should do (8).

Unquestionably the most important force in sex-role typing during the late childhood years comes from peer pressures. As was stressed earlier in this chapter, children must conform wholeheartedly to the beliefs, values, and patterns of behavior of the peer group if they want to be accepted members of children's gangs. This means that they must accept the sex-role stereotype of their gang-mates as a guide for their own behavior and they must accept the attitudes of their gang-mates toward their own and the opposite sex. Even more important, they must behave as their gang-mates consider appropriate, whether this be to treat members of the other sex as inferior or to lower their levels of aspiration if their gang-mates believe they are aspiring too high for their sex group.

By the time children enter school, they have been sex-role typed according to the standard—traditional or egalitarian—accepted in their homes. However, after they come in contact with their age-mates in school and after the new forces in typing, described above, begin to be effective, they may change

BOX 6-9

SOME COMMON INTERESTS OF LATE CHILDHOOD

Appearance

Older children are interested in their looks only if they are so homely or so different in appearance from their age-mates that they feel conspicuous.

Clothes

Older children are interested in new clothing, but it must be like that worn by their friends. They also have definite color preferences in clothing.

Names and Nicknames

First names are of interest to older children only when they are different from their friends' names or when they feel conspicuous because of them. As family names and middle names are infrequently used, children are interested in them only if the names identify them with racial or religious groups against which there is prejudice. When they become aware of the fact that the nicknames their age-mates give them are reflections of their judgments, they do not want nicknames that imply ridicule.

Religion

Older children who attend Sunday school may have less interest in it than they did earlier, although they still enjoy seeing their friends. However, they often become skeptical about religious teaching and about the efficacy of prayer.

The Human Body

Because they are unable to observe most bodily functions directly, older children try to satisfy their curiosity about what goes on inside their bodies by asking questions, reading books, or looking at illustrations.

Health

Only when children are ill or have a chronic illness, such as asthma, are they interested in health. Boys, especially, regard such interest as a sign of a sissy.

Sex

Older children want to know more details about the relations between the sexes, the father's role in reproduction, and the birth process. They try to get such information from books or from their friends with whom they exchange "dirty" stories and jokes.

School

Typically, children are enthusiastic about school at first. By the end of the second grade, many develop bored, antagonistic, and critical attitudes toward the academic work though they may still like the nonacademic aspects of school. Their attitudes are greatly influenced by how interesting the teachers make the material they are expected to learn and how they view this material in terms of future occupations.

Future Vocation

Early interest in their future vocations is centered on jobs children regard as glamorous, exciting, and prestigious, or which embody activities or uniforms that are important to them at that time. See Figure 6-10. They give little consideration to their capacities for these jobs.

Status Symbols

As children develop a growing realization of the importance of socioeconomic status, they become interested in visible symbols of the socioeconomic status of their families, such as cars or large houses.

Autonomy

How much autonomy older children are interested in having depends mainly on how much their friends have. If they have as much or more than their friends, they are usually satisfied.

---

from egalitarian to traditional roles or vice versa. Because the forces outside the home that play important roles in the typing process remain relatively stable, there is little change in typing after the second grade, especially in the case of boys (91).

Effects of Sex-Role Typing

Sex-role typing influences in important ways both the behavior and self-evaluations of children. In appearance, clothing and even in mannerisms, children try to create the impression of sex-appropriate-

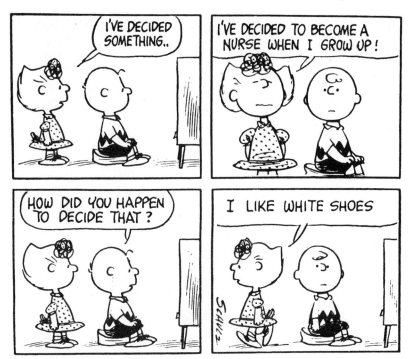

FIGURE 6-10 The child's vocational choice is based on what is important to the child at that time. (Adapted from Charles Schulz. "Peanuts." *United Features Syndicate,* 1970. Used by permission.)

ness (125). By the time children reach second grade, they are well aware of what is regarded as a sex-appropriate appearance (60).

Even as preschoolers, children discover that certain forms of play—games and sports as well as amusements in the form of books, comics, and television programs—are considered more appropriate for boys than for girls. While girls continue, throughout childhood, to play some of the games, read some of the comics and books and watch some of the television programs that are considered appropriate for boys, boys rarely engage in any form of play that is labeled "girls' play."

Even before they have completed first grade, most children learn to aspire to what the social group regards as sex-appropriate. Boys, for example, are expected to aspire higher academically and vocationally than girls. This means that they learn to expect higher grades in school than girls; to go further in their educational careers than girls; and to have a wider selection of more prestigious vocations to choose from than girls (11,68,71). As Bacon and

Lerner have pointed out, "Girls develop strong vocational role stereotypes at an early age. By the second grade, girls perceive that certain vocations are only appropriate for males and others are only appropriate for females" (8).

Because girls learn to aspire lower than their capacities would justify, it is not surprising that their *achievements* often fall short of their abilities. In schoolwork, in play, and in other activities in which boys are also involved, girls are generally underachievers. Soon the habit of working below their capacities develops and girls in general become underachievers (11,93).

Sex antagonism, as was explained earlier, is an outgrowth of sex-role typing. When boys are encouraged to believe that they are superior to girls, it leads to a derogatory attitude toward members of the female sex. This may be shown in attempts to avoid members of the female sex, in treatment of girls as inferiors, or in a tendency to make derogatory comments about girls and their achievements.

In the development of *interests,* regardless of

the area in which these interests are, children are expected to develop only those interests that are regarded as sex-appropriate. This is encouraged by exposing them to areas in which interests are appropriate for their sex group—as in the case of such sports as football and baseball, where boys are taken to games by their fathers while girls are not encouraged to even watch them on TV because they are not considered appropriate. Instead, girls are encouraged to watch swimming and diving—activities considered more appropriate for them.

Perhaps in no area does sex-role typing play a more important part than in *self-evaluation*. Children evaluate themselves in terms of what they believe significant people in their lives think of them. If parents, teachers, or peers regard girls as inferior to boys and the roles and achievements of girls as less important than those of boys, it is not surprising that boys tend to overvalue themselves while girls tend to undervalue themselves. In these tendencies lay the foundations for masculine superiority complexes and feminine inferiority complexes.

CHANGES IN FAMILY RELATIONSHIPS IN LATE CHILDHOOD

The deterioration in family relationships, which began during the latter part of babyhood and continued through early childhood, becomes increasingly detrimental to children's development as late childhood progresses. It is also responsible for much of the feelings of insecurity and the unhappiness that older children experience.

Many conditions are responsible for deterioration in family relationships in the closing years of childhood. Some of these are carry-overs of earlier conditions and some are new, arising from situations characteristic of this period in the life span. The conditions contributing to changed parent-child relationships in early childhood, given in Box 5-11, still exert their influence in late childhood. In addition, new conditions develop that contribute to the deterioration in family relationships. These are described in Box 6-10.

There are, of course, times of peace and harmony in the home. And there are times when older children show real affection for, and interest in, their siblings, even to the point of helping in the care of younger brothers or sisters and following the advice

There are times when an older child shows real interest in and affection for a younger sibling. (Photo by Erika Stone.)

and pattern of behavior set by older siblings. But these favorable relationships are outweighed in number and frequency by less favorable ones.

Similarly, there are times when older children are on the best of terms with their parents and relatives and even seem to enjoy family gatherings. However, they more frequently show a definite preference for their own friends and a critical, resentful attitude toward their parents and relatives. The more pronounced these unfavorable attitudes and behavior patterns are, the more family relationships will deteriorate.

Effects of Family Relationships in Late Childhood

The far-reaching effects of older children's relationships with their families are apparent in many areas of their lives. The most important of these are discussed below.

First, children's work in school and their attitudes toward school are greatly influenced by their relationships with family members. Wholesome,

BOX 6-10

COMMON CONDITIONS CONTRIBUTING TO DETERIORATION IN FAMILY RELATIONSHIPS IN LATE CHILDHOOD

Attitudes toward Parenthood

Parents who perceive their roles unfavorably and feel that the time, effort, and money expended on their children are unappreciated tend to have poor relationships with their children.

Parental Expectations

By the time children enter school, many parents have high expectations about the quality of their schoolwork and the amount of responsibility they will assume in the home. When children fail to meet these expectations, parents often criticize, nag, and punish.

Child-Training Methods

Authoritarian child training, commonly used in large families, and permissive discipline, used mainly in small families, both lead to friction in the home and feelings of resentment on the child's part. Democratic discipline fosters good family relationships.

Socioeconomic Status

If children feel that their homes and possessions compare unfavorably with those of their peers, they often blame their parents and the parents tend to resent this bitterly.

Parental Occupations

How peers feel about their fathers' occupations influences children's feelings both about the occupation and about their fathers. If their mothers work outside the home, children's attitudes toward their mothers are colored partly by how their friends feel about women working outside the home and partly by how many home responsibilities they are expected to assume.

Changed Attitudes toward Parents

From contacts with their friends' parents and as a result of what they read in books or see on television or in the movies, children build up concepts of an ideal mother and father. If their own parents fall short of these ideals, as they invariably do, they are likely to become critical of them and compare them unfavorably with the parents of their friends.

Sibling Friction

Older siblings frequently criticize the appearance and behavior of the younger child, who, in turn, likes to tease and bully even younger siblings. If parents attempt to put a stop to this, they are accused of playing favorites. The children may then gang up against them and the sibling whom they regard as the parental pet.

Changed Attitudes toward Relatives

Older children enjoy being with relatives less than they did when they were younger and tend to regard them as "too old" or "too bossy." When they are expected to be a part of a family gathering, they often put up a protest and claim that family gatherings "bore" them. Relatives resent these attitudes and frequently reprove the children.

Stepparents

Older children who remember a real parent who is no longer in the home usually resent a stepparent and show it by critical, negativistic, and generally troublesome behavior. This leads to friction in the home.

---

happy family relationships lead to motivation to achieve, while unwholesome, unhappy relationships cause emotional tension which usually has a detrimental effect on a child's abilities to concentrate and to learn.

Second, family relationships affect social adjustments outside the home. When family relationships are favorable, children's social adjustments to people outside the home are better than when family relationships are stressful.

Third, role-playing in the home sets the pattern for role-playing outside the home. The reason for this is that the roles children learn to play in the home and the kind of relationships they have with their siblings form the basis for their relationships with peers outside the home. This, in turn, influences children's patterns of behavior toward their peers.

Fourth, the type of child-training method used in the home influences the role-playing of older children. When authoritarian child-training methods are employed in the home, children learn to be followers —often discontented followers as they are in their relationships with their parents. Democratic child-training methods, on the other hand, encourage the development of leadership ability.

Fifth, home training is responsible for sex-role typing. What sex-role stereotypes children learn and how well they learn to perform them outside the home is greatly influenced by the home training they have received.

Sixth, children's aspirations and achievements in different areas of their lives are greatly influenced by their parents' attitudes. Firstborn and only children usually come under more pressure to achieve than later-born children and are given more aid and encouragement to achieve the goals their parents set for them or that their parents encourage them to set for themselves.

Seventh, whether children will be creative or conformists in their behavior is greatly influenced by their home training. Democratic child-training methods encourage creativity, while authoritarian methods tend to foster conformity.

Eighth, in no area of development do family realtionships play a more important role than in children's developing personalities. What older children think of themselves is a direct reflection of what they *believe* different family members think of them—as judged by the way they are treated by members of the family.

PERSONALITY CHANGES IN LATE CHILDHOOD

As children's social horizons broaden when they enter school, new factors begin to influence the development of their personalities. As a result, they must frequently revise their self-concepts. Since until now they have seen themselves almost exclusively through the eyes of their parents, it is not surprising if their self-concepts are biased. Now they see themselves as their teachers, their classmates, and their neighbors see them. Even their parents react differently to them now and this helps to shatter the foundations upon which their self-concepts were based (106).

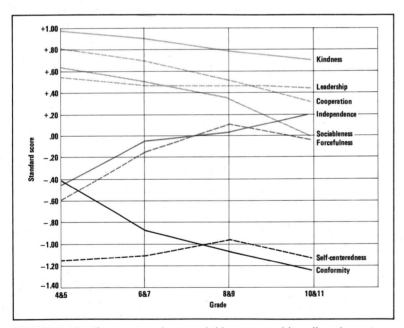

FIGURE 6-11 Changes in values as children grow older affect the traits they admire in others. (Adapted from W. Emmerich. Developmental trends in evaluations of single traits. *Child Development,* 1974, **45,** 172–193. Used by permission.)

Not only are there changes in the self-concept in late childhood, but there are also changes in the traits older children value and admire in others as well as in themselves. These changes are illustrated in Figure 6-11. Note, for example, how conformity falls in value as children progress through the grades in school and how independence and forcefulness increase (40).

Factors Affecting Self-Concepts in Late Childhood

Many of the factors that influenced self-concepts in early childhood continue to do so as the child grows older. Refer to Chapter 5 for a discussion of these factors under the heading, "Personality Development in Early Childhood."

Even though the social environment of older children has broadened, family relationships continue to exert a marked influence on their developing personalities. The quality of their relationships with their parents, siblings, and relatives—and the way older children feel about the child-training methods used in their homes—all play a role in determining what sort of individuals they will become.

Ordinal position is even more important now than it was in early childhood because the children's attitudes toward the roles associated with their positions in the family have a greater effect on the way they feel about themselves than they formerly did. Firstborns, for example, who are now expected to help with the care of younger siblings may feel either self-important or martyred. Only-children may become increasingly dependent or increasingly more mature than children with siblings, depending on how their parents treat them (44).

When children from minority groups enter school, they become more aware of prejudice against them than they had been before. This gradually builds up a feeling of inferiority which may be expressed in poor social adjustments and antisocial behavior, both of which may color the child's outlook on life.

An unstable home environment has less effect on the personality development of older children than on that of younger children, while an unstable social environment has a greater effect. When geographic or upward or downward social mobility brings radical changes in the social world of older children, this affects them in much the same way that instability in the home environment affected them when they were younger. A feeling of rootlessness and of not belonging makes them insecure. This encourages overconforming and a curbing of individuality.

A number of new factors influence the self-concept when older children enter school and when, as a result, the patterns of their lives change. All of these factors are related, either directly or indirectly, to the new environmental conditions that are part of their expanded social horizons. Box 6-11 lists these new factors.

Development of Ideal Self-Concepts

As childhood draws to a close, children begin to hero-worship characters in history or in fiction, on the stage or on the screen, or in the world of sports or national affairs. They then form concepts of the *ideal self,* the kind of person they would like to be. At first, the ideal self-concept is patterned along the lines set by parents, teachers, and others from their immediate environments. Later, as their horizons broaden, people they do not know but have heard of or read about form the nucleus for this ideal self. From these many sources, older children build ego-ideals which, as Van den Daele has pointed out, "serve as a general internalized standard of the self's behavior" (146).

This ego-ideal includes traits admired by the group. Because the two sexes are widely separated at this age, it is not surprising that boys and girls admire different personality traits.

Search for Identity

As children enter late childhood and become interested in gang membership, they are obsessed with the belief that they must conform to the standards of appearance, speech, and behavior set by their gangs. In the fear that they will lose what acceptance they are able to gain from members of a gang they want to be identified with, they conform and often become overconformists.

While conformity gives children the satisfaction of security in peer relationships, it fails to give them ego satisfaction. Sooner or later they begin to feel that they are cut from the same pattern as their age-mates and that they lack individuality and any sense of identity.

The search for identity begins in the latter part of childhood and reaches a crisis stage in adolescence. As explained by Erikson: "Identity" means a sense of being able to function as a separate person but with a close relationship to others. It means being one of a group but, at the same time, having charac-

BOX 6-11

FACTORS AFFECTING THE SELF-CONCEPT IN LATE CHILDHOOD

Physical Condition

Poor health or physical defects that cut children off from play with their peers make them feel inferior and martyred.

Body Build

Children who are overweight or very small for their ages may be unable to keep pace with their peers and, as a result, they develop feelings of inferiority.

Names and Nicknames

Names which cause children to be ridiculed, or which suggest minority-group status, can lead to feelings of inferiority. Nicknames that make fun of a physical or personality trait lead to feelings of inferiority, martyrdom, and resentment.

Socioeconomic Status

If children feel that they have better homes, better clothes, and better play equipment than their age-mates, they will feel superior. If, on the other hand, they sense that their socioeconomic status is inferior to that of their age-mates it is likely to lead to feelings of inferiority.

School Environment

Competent, understanding teachers do much to bring about good adjustment in their pupils, while teachers who use discipline that children consider unfair or that otherwise antagonize them have the opposite influence.

Social Acceptance

Acceptance or the lack of it on the part of peers influences the child's personality through its effect on the self-concept. Very popular children and isolates are especially affected, and others less so.

Success and Failure

Success in the tasks the child sets out to achieve leads to a feeling of confidence and self-acceptance, while failure makes for a feeling of inadequacy. The more prestigious the activity, the greater the effect of success or failure on the self-concept. Repeated failures have a damaging effect on a child's personality.

Sex

Girls recognize that the sex roles they are expected to play are inferior to male roles, and this realization results in a corresponding decrease in self-evaluation. They incorporate society's evaluations of their roles as inferior and so value themselves less.

Intelligence

Children's personalities are adversely affected if their intelligence deviates markedly from the norm. Children who are duller than average sense their inferiority and the rejectant attitude of their group. As a result, they may become shy, introverted, or apathetic—or they may become aggressive toward those who reject them. Children with very high IQs also are likely to have poor self-concepts. This is due partly to the fact that adults expect too much of them and the children, as a result, feel that they are failures, and partly to unfavorable peer attitudes because they often become smug and intolerant toward those less bright than themselves.

---

teristics that stand out from the group and identify the bearer of these characteristics as an individual (41).

To achieve a sense of identity, children must have an inner assurance that they are able to function independently. Until they get this feeling of assurance, they are insecure. To cope with this problem, older children try to cut parental apron strings and associate themselves emotionally with their peers. It is not until they reach the adolescent years that they are capable of coping successfully with the identity problem.

HAZARDS OF LATE CHILDHOOD

Some of the common hazards of late childhood are carry-overs from earlier years, though they often take new forms. Others are new, arising from changes in the child's life pattern after entering school.

As is true of earlier ages, the hazards of late childhood are both physical and psychological. However, during late childhood the psychological repercussions of many of the physical hazards are especially serious, and major emphasis will be placed on these.

Physical Hazards

As a result of new medical techniques for diagnosing, preventing, and treating illnesses, mortality during late childhood occurs much less frequently than in the past. However, accidents still cause death among older children.

While many of the physical hazards of the earlier years persist into late childhood, their effects on the child's physical well-being tend to be less severe and less far-reaching than they were earlier. On the other hand, their psychological effects are greater and more persistent. The major physical hazards of late childhood are discussed below.

Illness Since vaccines against most childhood diseases are now available, older children suffer mainly from occasional colds and stomach upsets which rarely have any lasting physical effects.

The psychological effects of illness in late childhood, however, can be serious. Illness upsets the body's homeostasis, which in turn makes children irritable, demanding, and difficult to live with. If they are sick for a long period, their schoolwork may suffer and they may fall behind their peers in the learning of play skills. Equally serious, parents may become intolerant in their attitudes toward the illnesses, complaining about the extra work and the expense the illnesses entail.

While most illnesses of late childhood are real, some are imaginary or "faked." Sooner or later most children learn that when they are ill they are not expected to carry out their usual activities, home discipline is relaxed, and they receive more attention than usual. As result, they may feign illness—or actually believe they are ill—as a way of avoiding an unpleasant task or situation. If this tactic works, they will repeat it and thus lay the foundations for a proneness to imaginary illness.

Obesity Obesity in older children may be due to a glandular condition but it is far more often due to overeating, especially of the carbohydrates. Studies of fat children have revealed that they eat faster, take bigger bites and are more likely to clean their plates and ask for second or even third helpings than their more slender age-mates (95).

Regardless of its cause, obesity in older children is a physical hazard not only to their health—obese children are more prone to diabetes, for example, than their more slender age-mates—but to their socialization. Obese children lose out in active play and, as a result, they miss opportunities to acquire the skills so essential to social success. In addition, their playmates often tease and taunt them, calling them "Fatso" or other names that make them feel inferior or martyred.

Sex-Inappropriate Body Build Girls with masculine body builds and boys with girlish physiques are likely to be ridiculed by their peers and pitied by adults. This leads to personal and social maladjustment, though more so for boys than for girls. By contrast, a sex-appropriate body build aids good adjustment. In speaking about boys, Biller and Borstelmann have explained (17):

The tall and husky or mesomorphic boy may, even without the encouragement of parents, find success easier in masculine activities so that he is seen by others, and consequently learns to see himself, as very masculine. The frail ectomorph or pudgy endomorph may find such success difficult so that he may be seen by others, and learn to see himself, as unmasculine.

Accidents Even when accidents leave no permanent physical scar, they can and often do, leave psychological scars. Older children, like younger, who experience more than their share of accidents, usually learn to be more cautious. In time, this may lead to timidity concerning all physical activities and may even spread to other areas of behavior. When this happens it develops into a generalized shyness that affects social relationships, schoolwork, and personalities (19).

Physical Disabilities Many physical disabilities are the aftereffect of an accident and thus are more common among boys than girls. The seriousness of the aftereffect depends on the degree of the disability and on the way others treat the child, especially members of the peer group. While some children may show marked sympathy and consideration for a disabled child, others may ignore, reject, or even ridicule such a child.

Most disabled children become inhibited and ill at ease in social situations. As a result, they make poor social adjustments and this, in turn, affects their personal adjustments (147). It has been reported that there are more cases of problem behavior among children with minor physical anomalies than among those who lack these problems (62).

It is not uncommon for children to discover that a physical handicap is a way of avoiding unpleasant situations. As a result, they may develop an imaginary handicap or even pretend that a real handicap is more disabling than it actually is. This is a form of imaginary invalidism, discussed above.

Awkwardness As older children begin to compare themselves with their age-mates, they often discover that their awkwardness and clumsiness prevent them from doing what their playmates do or from keeping pace with them in play. As a result, they start to think of themselves as inferior to their playmates and as martyrs.

Because motor skills play such an important role in children's play and at school, clumsy children find themselves in many situations where their awkwardness is apparent to themselves and to others. This reinforces their feelings of inadequacy which, in time, lay the foundations for an inferiority complex.

Homeliness Unlike adolescents or adults who develop feelings of personal inadequacy when they know they are considered unattractive, most homely children are relatively unconcerned about their appearance unless it is so unattractive as to elicit unfavorable peer comments or to lead to rejection by peers.

However, homeliness can be and often is a hazard if other people react unfavorably and communicate their feelings by the way they treat homely children. Because older children, as a group, are less appealing than babies or even young children, adults tend to be more critical of them and less tolerant of their normal, but often annoying, behavior. Older children interpret this as rejection, an interpretation that can have a harmful effect on their developing self-concepts.

By contrast, teachers tend to evaluate the academic work of attractive children more favorably than they do that of less attractive children and to give them higher grades than they deserve (126). In school, as Clifford has pointed out, "Attractive children have a sizable advantage over unattractive ones" (29).

Physical attractiveness is also important in social situations. On the whole, attractive children are better liked by their age-mates than those who are less attractive and they tend to be selected more often for leadership roles. Physical attractiveness is especially important for geographically or socially mobile children because they make better first impressions than those who are less attractive and this facilitates social acceptance (82).

Psychological Hazards

The psychological hazards of late childhood are mainly the ones that affect children's social adjustments, around which the major developmental tasks of this period are centered. Thus they have a powerful influence on children's personal adjustments and on their developing personalities. The most important psychological hazards of late childhood are given and briefly explained in Box 6-12.

Effects of Psychological Hazards Children who are less well accepted by their peers than they would like to be, may, and often do, become dissatisfied with themselves and envy those who are more popular. Many personality maladjustments begin in this way, usually early in school, when children first begin to compare themselves with their age-mates and to consider their own achievements in the light of the achievements of their age-mates.

Among the common signs of future trouble, stemming from personal dissatisfaction, are habitual withdrawal, excessive excitability, excessive resentment against authority, chronic depression, self-enhancement through derogation of others, diffuse hyperactivity, excessive egocentrism, and chronic anxiety or emotional "deadening."

Children who are dissatisfied with themselves commonly use defense mechanisms such as rationalization to explain their shortcomings or projection of blame on others; they may also resort to escape mechanisms, especially daydreaming and imaginary illness. Although these may alleviate unhappiness temporarily, they are only stopgap measures. With each passing year the child will have to use such mechanisms more frequently and in more exag-

BOX 6-12

PSYCHOLOGICAL HAZARDS OF LATE CHILDHOOD

Speech Hazards

There are four common speech hazards in late childhood: (1) A smaller-than-average vocabulary handicaps children in their schoolwork as well as in their communications with others. (2) Speech errors, such as mispronunciations and grammatical mistakes, and speech defects, such as stuttering or lisping, may make children so self-conscious that they will speak only when necessary. (3) Children who have difficulty speaking the language used in their school environment may be handicapped in their efforts to communicate and may be made to feel that they are "different." (4) Egocentric speech, critical and derogatory comments, and boasting antagonize their peers.

Emotional Hazards

Children are considered immature by both age-mates and adults if they continue to show unacceptable patterns of emotional expression, such as temper tantrums, and if such unpleasant emotions as anger and jealousy are so dominant that children are disagreeable and unpleasant to be with.

Social Hazards

There are five types of children whose adjustments are affected by social hazards. First, children who are rejected or neglected by their peer group are deprived of opportunities to learn to be social. Second, voluntary isolates who have little in common with their peer group come to think of themselves as "different" and to feel that they have no chance for acceptance. Third, geographically or socially mobile children who find acceptance by already-formed gangs difficult. Fourth, children against whom there is group prejudice because of their race or religion. And, fifth, followers who want to be leaders become resentful and disgruntled group members.

Play Hazards

Children who lack social acceptance are deprived of opportunities to learn the games and sports essential to gang belonging. Children who are discouraged from fantasizing because it is a "waste of time," or from creative activities in their play, develop the habit of being rigid conformists.

Conceptual Hazards

Children who have idealized self-concepts are usually dissatisfied with themselves as they are and with the way others treat them. When their social concepts are based on stereotypes, they tend to become prejudiced and discriminatory in their treatment of others. Because such concepts are emotionally weighted, they are likely to persist and to continue to affect children's social adjustments unfavorably.

Moral Hazards

Six hazards are commonly associated with the development of moral attitudes and behavior in late childhood: (1) the development of a moral code based on peer or mass-media concepts of right and wrong which may not coincide with adult codes; (2) a failure to develop a conscience as an inner control over behavior; (3) inconsistent discipline which leaves children unsure of what they are expected to do; (4) physical punishment which serves as a model of aggressiveness in children; (5) finding peer approval of misbehavior so satisfying that such behavior becomes habitual; and (6) intolerance of the wrongdoings of others.

Hazards Associated with Interests

There are two common hazards associated with childhood interests: first, being uninterested in the things age-mates regard as important and, second, developing unfavorable attitudes toward interests that would be valuable to them, as in the case of health or school.

Hazards in Sex-Role Typing

There are two common hazards in sex-role typing in late childhood: failure to learn the elements of the sex roles their age-mates regard as appropriate, and unwillingness to play the approved sex roles. The first hazard is likely to develop when children grow up in homes where parents play sex roles that differ from those of their age-mates' parents, and the second, when boys are expected to play egalitarian roles and girls, traditional ones.

Family-Relationship Hazards

Friction with family members has two serious effects: it weakens family ties and it leads to a habitual unfavorable pattern of adjustment to people and problems which is carried outside the home.

Hazards in Personality Development

There are two serious hazards in personality development in late childhood. First, the development of an unfavorable self-concept, which leads to self-rejection and, second, the carry-over from early childhood of egocentrism. Egocentrism is serious because it gives children a false sense of their importance.

"I believe it's called 'cookie jar diplomacy.'"

FIGURE 6-12 The child who craves social acceptance by peers may try to "buy" it. (George Clark. "The Neighbors." *Chicago Tribune-New York News Syndicate*, July 21, 1972. Used by permission.)

gerated forms. In time they may lose their effectiveness and cease to work altogether.

Maladjustment stemming from lack of acceptance by the social group tends to persist. Shy, retiring, self-effacing children, for example, continue their characteristic patterns of behavior even though they know such behavior lessens their chances of acceptance.

Some children who are unhappy and dissatisfied with themselves because of lack of social acceptance take matters into their own hands and try to "buy" their way into the group. See Figure 6-12. While this may produce the desired results temporarily, it rarely results in permanent acceptance.

Attempts to Cope with Lack of Social Acceptance
Because of the psychological damage of persistent lack of social acceptance, clinicians and educators are now trying to find ways to help children who are experiencing such difficulties. However, making unacceptable children more acceptable to their age-mates is difficult for three reasons.

First, children may have acquired the reputation of being a "bully," a "crybaby," or a "tattler," and this reputation is likely to cling.

Second, by the time children reach first grade, the patterns of behavior that make them unpopular with their age-mates are so much a part of their personalities that changing them is difficult and rarely satisfactory.

Third, the way children treat other children will determine their reaction to these children. If, for example, they are bossy and domineering, other children will resent them and such attitudes are hard to change.

This, of course, does not mean that there is no hope for children who are poorly accepted by their peers. With guidance, they can acquire socially acceptable patterns of behavior. They can, for example, learn to say pleasant things instead of unpleasant ones, to talk about things other than themselves, and to consider the wishes of the group, rather than just their own wishes.

Equally important, children must learn that what makes them acceptable to their peers at one age does not guarantee acceptance later. Consequently, they must be willing to change their patterns of behavior to conform to those of the group as its members become more socially mature.

HAPPINESS IN LATE CHILDHOOD

Late childhood can and should be a happy period in the life span. While it cannot be a completely carefree time, since the child is expected to assume added responsibilities in school and at home, success in handling these responsibilities, especially those which significant people consider important, will add to, instead of detract from, happiness.

Many factors contribute to the happiness of older children. Some of these were also important factors in early childhood, though now they affect children differently because their interests and patterns of life have changed and because they want to spend increasingly more time with their age-mates.

Because most of their skills have improved greatly, older children are less dependent than they formerly were. Now they can do many things for themselves without relying on help from others. Similarly, speech skills have developed to the point where children no longer experience the frustration of not understanding what others are talking about or of not being understood when they try to communicate with others.

Unless some unusual condition exists in the family life of older children, they will have ample opportunity for play and the equipment needed for play as their age-mates play. If they enjoy reasonable social acceptance, their play can be a source of daily happiness.

As school begins to occupy an increasingly large part of the time of older children, how they feel about school can be a source of happiness or unhappiness. Children who do well academically, who get along well with their teachers and classmates, and who enjoy learning new things will have an added reason to be happy.

Even though older children spend increasingly more time outside the home than in it, the home climate and the relationships they have with different family members are two vitally important factors in their happiness. If older children have a warm, affectionate relationship with their families, even though there may be occasional friction and occasional punishment for intentional misbehavior, they will feel that their families love them and treat them fairly. Their happiness will be greatly increased if the home climate is relaxed and cheerful.

While happiness in the closing years of childhood will not guarantee happiness for the remainder of life, the conditions that contribute to happiness then will likewise contribute to happiness as the child grows older. Even though new values are used in the selection of friends in adolescence and adulthood, the individual who learned to be socially acceptable to others when young has a foundation on which to build new patterns of behavior to conform to the new values.

Similarly, children who have learned to see themselves realistically, and whose failures either motivate them to find better ways of achieving their goals or cause them to modify their aspirations in accordance with their capacities, will, as they grow older, be spared the unhappiness that comes from repeated failures and the feelings of inadequacy and inferiority that accompany them. This is just as true in the case of social failures as in the case of academic or business failures.

When it is apparent that one or more of the three A's of happiness—achievement, acceptance by others, and affection from others—are not present in a child's life, this should be regarded as a danger signal of future trouble. If an individual is not happy at a time when conditions are favorable to happiness, it suggests that the child is poorly equipped to face later periods when conditions will be less favorable.

Chapter Highlights

1. Late childhood, which extends from six years until children become sexually mature at approximately age thirteen for girls and fourteen for boys, is labeled by parents as the "troublesome," "sloppy," or "quarrelsome" age; by educators as the "elementary-school" age; and by psychologists as the "gang age," the "age of conformity," or the "age of creativity."

2. Physical growth, which is at a slow and relatively even rate in late childhood, is influenced by health, nutrition, immunization, sex, and intelligence.

3. The skills of late childhood can be categorized roughly into four major groups: self-help skills, social-help skills, school skills, and play skills. All of these are influenced, to some extent, by the development of handedness.

4. While all areas of speech—pronunciation, vocabulary, and sentence structure—improve rapidly during late childhood, as does comprehension, the content of speech tends to deteriorate.

5. Older children learn to control the overt expressions of their emotions and to use emotional catharsis to clear their systems of the pent-up emotionality caused by social pressures to control their emotions.

6. Late childhood is called the "gang age" because older children are interested in activities with their peers and want to belong to a gang, which expects them to conform to the patterns of behavior and to the values and interests of its members. As gang members, children often reject parental standards, develop an antagonistic attitude toward members of the opposite sex, and become prejudiced against all who are non-gang members.

7. The sociometric status of older children varies from popular to that of social isolate. Once a child's status is established in the social group, it is difficult to change—whether the status is that of leader, follower, or social isolate.

8. The play interests of older children and the amount of time they devote to play depends

more on the degree of social acceptance they enjoy than on any other condition.

9. There is a rapid increase in understanding and in the accuracy of concepts during late childhood, partly as a result of increased intelligence and partly as a result of increased learning opportunities.

10. In late childhood, most children develop moral codes influenced by the moral standards of the groups with which they are identified, and a conscience which guides their behavior in place of the external controls needed when they were younger. In spite of this, home, school, and neighborhood misdemeanors are common.

11. The interests of older children are broader than those of younger children and include many new subjects. Among these are names, clothes, the human body, sex, school, future vocations, status symbols, and autonomy.

12. Sex-role typing in late childhood influences children's appearance, behavior, aspirations, achievements, interests, attitudes toward members of the opposite sex, and self-evaluation.

13. The deterioration in family relationships, characteristic of late childhood, affects children's personal and social adjustments and has a strong impact on their personalities through its effect on their self-evaluation. This is especially serious when the gap between their ideal and real self-concepts is large, because it acts as an obstacle in their search for identity.

14. Among the new physical hazards of late childhood are obesity, a sex-inappropriate body build, a tendency to be accident-prone, awkwardness, and homeliness. The new psychological hazards are mainly those that affect children's social adjustments because they lead to unfavorable self-evaluations and social evaluations.

15. While happiness in late childhood does not guarantee lifetime happiness, the conditions that contribute to happiness will continue to do so as children grow older. This is especially true if the three A's of happiness—acceptance, affection, and achievement—are fulfilled.

Bibliography

1. Adams, G. R., and J. C. LaVoie. The effect of students' sex, conduct and facial attractiveness on teacher expectancy. *Education*, 1974, **95**, 76–83.

2. Adams, R. E., and R. H. Passman. Effects of intensities of punishment upon children's subsequent moral judgments of behavior. *Developmental Psychology*, 1977, **13**, 408–412.

3. Allan, G. Sibling solidarity. *Journal of Marriage & the Family*, 1977, **39**, 177–184.

4. Armentrout, J. A. Sociometric classroom popularity and children's reports of parental child-rearing behaviors. *Psychological Reports*, 1972, **30**, 261–262.

5. Asbury, C. A. Selected factors influencing over- and underachievement in young school age children. *Review of Educational Research*, 1974, **44**, 409–428.

6. Asher, S. R., and S. L. Oden. Children's failure to communicate: An assessment of comparison and egocentrism explanations. *Developmental Psychology*, 1976, **12,** 132–139.

7. Attoy, E. Measurement of egocentrism in children's communication. *Developmental Psychology*, 1975, **11**, 392.

8. Bacon, C., and R. M. Lerner. Effects of maternal employment status on the development of vocational-role perception in females. *Journal of Genetic Psychology*, 1975, **126**, 187–193.

9. Baird, J. T., and J. Roberts. *Relationships among parent ratings of behavioral characteristics of children.* Rockville, Md.: National Center for Health Statistics, U.S. Department of Health, Education, and Welfare, 1972.

10. Barclay, D. Questions of life and death. *The New York Times*, July 15, 1962.

11. Barnett, R. C. Sex differences in occupational preference and occupational prestige. *Journal of Counseling Psychology*, 1975, **22**, 35–38.

12. Barton, K., T. E. Dielmand, and R. B. Cattell. Child raising practices and achievement in school. *Journal of Genetic Psychology*, 1974, **124**, 155–165.

13. Bauer, D. H. An exploratory study of developmental changes in children's fears. *Journal of Child Psychology & Psychiatry & Allied Disciplines*, 1976, **17**, 69–74.

14. Bernstein, J. The elementary school: Training ground for sex-role stereotypes. *Personnel & Guidance Journal*, 1972, **51,** 97–103.

15. Bigelow, B. J. Children's friendship expectations: A cognitive-developmental study. *Child Development*, 1977, **48**, 246–253.

16. Bigelow, B. J., and J. J. LaGaupa. Children's written descriptions of friendship: A multidimensional analysis. *Developmental Psychology*, 1975, **11**, 857–858.

17. Biller, H. B., and L. J. Borstelmann. Masculine development: An integrative review. *Merrill-Palmer Quarterly*, 1967, **13**, 253–294.

18. Bixenstine, V. E., M. S. DeCorte, and B. A. Bixenstine. Conformity to peer-sponsored misconduct in four grade levels. *Developmental Psychology*, 1976, **12**, 226–236.

19. Block, J. R. Attention future: A test that tells who is accident-prone. *Psychology Today*, 1975, **9**(1), 84–85.

20. Bowerman, C. S., and R. M. Dobash. Structural variations in inter-sibling affect. *Journal of Marriage & the Family*, 1974, **36**, 48–54.

21. Brook, C. G. B. Prediction of adult stature. *Developmental Medicine & Child Neurology*, 1977, **19**, 78–80.

22. Burger, G. K., R. E. Lamp, and D. Rogers. Developmental trends in children's perceptions of parental child-rearing behavior. *Developmental Psychology*, 1975, **11**, 391.

23. Busk, P. L., R. C. Ford, and J. L. Schulman. Stability of sociometric responses in classrooms. *Journal of Genetic Psychology*, 1973, **123**, 64–84.

24. Busse, T. B., and J. Helfrich. Changes in first name popularity across grades. *Journal of Psychology*, 1975, **89**, 281–283.

25. Campbell, J. D. Illness is a point of view: The development of children's concepts of illness. *Child Development*, 1975, **46**, 92–100.

26. Cavior, N., and D. A. Lombardi. Developmental aspects of judgment of physical attractiveness in children. *Developmental Psychology*, 1973, **8**, 67–71.

27. Chang, T. S. Self-concepts, academic achievement, and teachers' ratings. *Psychology in the Schools*, 1976, **13**, 111–113.

28. Church, J., and L. J. Stone. The early school years. *Children*, 1960, **7**, 113–114.

29 Clifford, M. M. Physical attractiveness and academic performance. *Child Study Journal*, 1975, **5**, 201–209.

30. Cohen, R., R. Bornstein, and R. C. Sherman. Conformity behavior of children as a function of group make-up and task ambiguity. *Developmental Psychology*, 1973, **9**, 129–131.

31. Cohen S. J. Drug use, misuse, and abuse incidents among elementary school children. *Drug Education*, 1976, **6**, 247–253.

32. Condry, J., and M. L. Siman. Characteristics of peer- and adult-oriented children. *Journal of Marriage & the Family*, 1974, **36,** 543–554.

33. Day, L. G. The development of the God complex: A symbolic interaction approach. *Journal of Psychology & Theology*, 1975, **3**, 172–178.

34. Denckla, M. B. Development of motor co-ordination in normal children. *Developmental Medicine & Child Neurology*, 1974, **16**, 729–741.

35. Denzin, N. K. Play, games, and interaction: The contexts of childhood socialization. *Sociological Quarterly*, 1975, **6**, 458–478.

36. Dinkmeyer, D., and D. Dinkmeyer, Jr. Logical consequences: A key to the reduction of disciplinary problems. *Phi Delta Kappan*, 1976, **57**, 664–666.

37. Dion, K. K., and E. Berscheid. Physical attractiveness and peer perception among children. *Sociometry*, 1974, **37**, 1–12.

38. Duck, S. W. Personality similarity and friendship choice: Similarity of what, when? *Journal of Personality*, 1973, **41**, 543–558.

39. Eckert, H. M. Variability in skill acquisition. *Child Development*, 1974, **45**, 487–489.

40. Emmerich, W. Developmental trends in evaluations of single traits. *Child Development*, 1974, **45**, 172–183.

41. Erikson, E. H. *Childhood and society*. (Rev. ed.) New York: Norton, 1964.

42. Eysenck, H. J. The development of moral values in children. VII. The contribution of learning theory. *British Journal of Educational Psychology*, 1960, **30**, 11–21.

43. Fairchild, L., and W. M. Erwin. Physical punishment by parent figures as a model of aggressive behavior in children. *Journal of Genetic Psychology*, 1977, **130**, 279–284.

44. Falbo, T. Does the only child grow up miserable? *Psychology Today*, 1976, **9**(12), 60–65.

45. Fein, D., S. O'Neill, C. Frank, and K. McC. Velit. Sex differences in preadolescent self-esteem. *Journal of Psychology*, 1975, **90**, 179–183.

46. Fein, D., and G. M. Stein. Immanent punishment and reward in six- and nine-year-old children. *Journal of Genetic Psychology*, 1977, **131**, 91–96.

47. Foot, H. C., A. J. Chapman, and J. R. Smith. Friendship and social responsiveness in boys and girls. *Journal of Personality & Social Psychology*, 1977, **35**, 401–411.

48. Formanek, R. When children ask about death. *Elementary School Journal*, 1974, **75**, 92–97.

49. Fox, D. J., and V. B. Jordon. Racial preference and identification of black, American Chinese and white children. *Genetic Psychology Monographs*, 1973, **88**, 229–286.

50. Freeman, N. Children's drawings: Cognitive aspects. *Journal of Child Psychology & Psychiatry & Allied Disciplines*, 1976, **16**, 345–350.

51. Garrett, C. S., P. L. Ein, and L. Themaine. The development of gender stereotyping of adult occupations in elementary school children. *Child Development*, 1977, **48**, 507–512.

52. Genesee, F., G. R. Tucker, and W. E. Lambert. Communication skills of bilingual children. *Child Development*, 1975, **46**, 1010–1014.

53. Gingrich, D. D. Sex, grade level, and religious-educational environment as factors in peer conformity. *Journal of Genetic Psychology*, 1973, **123**, 321–328.

54. Gordon, D. A., and R. D. Young. School phobia: A discussion of aetiology, treatment and evaluation. *Psychological Reports*, 1976, **39**, 783–804.

55. Gorn, G. J., M. E. Goldberg, and R. N. Kanungo. The role of educational television in changing intergroup attitudes of children. *Child Development*, 1976, **47**, 277–280.

56. Gottman, J., J. Gonso, and B. Rasmussen. Social interaction, social competence, and friendship in children. *Child Development*, 1975, **46**, 709–718.

57. Gottman, J. M. Toward a definition of social isolation in children. *Child Development*, 1977, **48**, 513–517.

58. Greenberg, B. S., and B. Reeves. Children and the perceived reality of television. *Journal of Social Issues*, 1976, **32**(4), 86–97.

59. Haddad, N. F., J. C. McCullers, and J. D. Moran. Satiation and the detrimental effects of material rewards. *Child Development*, 1976, **47**, 547–550.

60. Haley, E. G., and N. J. Hendrickson. Children's preferences for clothing and hair styles. *Home Economics Research Journal*, 1974, **2**(3), 176–193.

61. Halperin, M. S. First-grade teachers' goals and children's developing perceptions of school. *Journal of Educational Psychology*, 1976, **68**, 636–648.

62. Halverson, C. F., and J. B. Victor. Minor physical anomalies and problem behavior in elementary school children. *Child Development*, 1976, **47**, 281–285.

63. Hamill, P. V. V., T. A. Drizel, C. L. Johnson, R. B. Reed, and A. F. Roche. *NCHS growth curves for children from birth–18 years*. Hyattsville, Md.: National Center for Health Statistics, U.S. Department of Health, Education, and Welfare, 1977.

64. Hamilton, M. Ideal sex roles for children and acceptance of variation from stereotypic sex roles. *Adolescence*, 1977, **12**, 89–96.

65. Hanspie, R., C. Susanne, and F. Alexander. A mixed longitudinal study of the growth in height and weight of asthmatic children. *Human Biology*, 1976, **48**, 271–283.

66. Hardyck, C., R. Goldman, and l. Petrinovich. Handedness and sex, race, and age. *Human Biology*, 1975, **47**, 369–375.

67. Harris, S., P. Mussen, and E. Rutherford. Some cognitive, behavioral, and personality correlates of maturity of moral judgment. *Journal of Genetic Psychology*, 1976, **128**, 123–135.

68. Harris, S. R. Sex typing in girls' career choices: A challenge to counselors. *Personnel & Guidance Journal*, 1974, **23**, 128–133.

69. Havighurst, R. J. *Developmental tasks and education*. (3rd ed.) New York: McKay, 1972.

70. Heshusius-Gilsdorf, L., and D. L. Gilsdorf. Girls are females, boys are males: A content analysis of career materials. *Personnel & Guidance Journal*, 1975, **54**, 206–211.

71. Hewitt, L. S. Age and sex differences in the vocational aspirations of elementary school children. *Journal of Social Psychology*, 1975, **96**, 173–177.

72. Higgins, E. T. Social class differences in verbal communicative accuracy: A question of "Which question?" *Psychological Bulletin*, 1976, **83**, 695–714.

73. Horrocks, J. E., and M. C. Mussman. Developmental trends in wishes, confidence, and the sense of personal control from childhood to middle maturity. *Journal of Psychology*, 1973, **84**, 241–252.

74. Isaacs, A. F. Giftedness and leadership. *Gifted Child Quarterly*, 1973, **17**, 103–112.

75. Johns, J. L. Reading preferences of intermediate-grade students in urban settings. *Reading World*, 1974, **14**, 51–63.

76. Kagan, J. The child in the family. *Daedalus*, 1977, **106**(2), 33–56.

77. Kaplan, R. M. The cathartic value of self-expression: Testing catharsis, dissonance, and interference explanations. *Journal of Social Psychology*, 1975, **97**, 195–208.

78. Katz, P. A., I. Katz, and S. Cohen. White children's attitudes toward Blacks and the physically handicapped. A developmental study. *Journal of Educational Psychology*, 1976, **68**, 20–24.

79. Kessel, F. S. The role of syntax in children's comprehension from ages six to twelve. *Monographs of the Society for Research in Child Development*, 1976, **35**(6).

80. Kleck, R. E., S. A. Richardson, and L. Ronald. Physical appearance cues and interpersonal attraction in children. *Child Development*, 1974, **45**, 305–310.

81. Kohlberg, L. *Stages in the development of moral thought and action*. New York: Holt, Rinehart and Winston, 1969.

82. Laycock, F., and J. S. Caylor. Physique of gifted children and their less gifted siblings. *Child Development*, 1964, **35**, 63–74.

83. Lee, P. C., and N. B. Gropper. Sex-role culture and educational practice. *Harvard Educational Review*, 1974, **44**, 369–410.

84. Leifer, A. D., N. J. Gordon, and S. B. Graves. Children's television: More than mere entertainment. *Harvard Educational Review*, 1974, **44**, 213–245.

85. Lenneburg, E. H., and E. Lenneberg (Eds.). *Foundations of language development: A multidisciplinary approach*. New York: Academic Press, 1975.

86. Lever, J. Sex differences in the complexity of children's play and games. *American Sociological Review*, 1978, **43**, 471–483.

87. Levinsohn, F. H. Happy endings: TV's kindly offering. *School Review*, 1975, **84**, 109–115.

88. Lieberman, J. N. *Playfulness: Its relation to imagination and creativity*. New York: Academic Press, 1977.

89. Long, L. H. Does migration interfere with children's progress in school? *Sociology of Education*, 1975, **48**, 369–381.

90. Ludwig, D. J., T. Weber, and D. Iben. Letters to God: A study of children's religious concepts. *Journal of Psychology & Theology*, 1974, **2**, 31–35.

91. Lynch, J. Equal opportunity or lip service? Sex-role stereotyping in the schools. *Elementary School Journal*, 1975, **76**, 20–23.

92. Mabe, P. A., and J. E. Williams. Relation of racial attitudes to sociometric choices among second grade children. *Psychological Reports*, 1975, **37**, 547–554.

93. Manes, A. L., and P. Melnyk. Televised models of female achievement. *Journal of Applied Social Psychology*, 1974, **4**, 365–374.

94. Marantz, S. A., and A. F. Mansfield. Maternal employment and the development of sex-role stereotyping in five- to eleven-year-old girls. *Child Development*, 1977, **48**, 668–673.

95. Marston, A. R., P. London, and L. M. Cooper. A note on the eating behavior of children varying in weight. *Journal of Child Psychology & Psychiatry & Allied Disciplines*, 1976, **17**, 221–224.

96. Martindale, C. What makes creative people different? *Psychology Today*, 1975, **9**(2), 44–50.

97. Maw, W. H., and E. W. Maw. Social adjustment and curiosity of fifth-grade children. *Journal of Psychology*, 1975, **90**, 137–145.

98. Maykovich, M. K. Correlates of racial prejudice. *Journal of Personality & Social Psychology*, 1975, **32**, 1014–1020.

99. McGhee, P. E. Development of children's ability to create joking relationships. *Child Development*, 1974, **45**, 552–556.

100. McGhee, P. E. Moral development and children's appreciation of humor. *Developmental Psychology*, 1974, **10**, 514–533.

101. McKinney, J. D. Teacher perceptions of the classroom behavior of reflective and impulsive children. *Psychology in the Schools*, 1975, **12**, 348–352.

102. McMillan, J. H. Factors affecting the development of pupil attitudes toward school subjects. *Psychology in the Schools*, 1976, **13**, 322–325.

103. Melear, J. D. Children's conceptions of death. *Journal of Genetic Psychology*, 1973, **123**, 359–360.

104. Miller, N., and G. Maruyama. Ordinal position and peer popularity. *Journal of Personality & Social Psychology*, 1976, **33**, 123–131.

105. Montemayer, R. Children's performance in a game and their attraction to it as a function of sex-typed labels. *Child Development*, 1974, **45**, 152–156.

106. Montemayer, R., and M. Eisen. The development of self-conceptions from childhood to adolescence. *Developmental Psychology*, 1977, **13**, 314–319.

107. Morris, L. W., C. S. Finkelstein, and W. R. Fisher. Components of school anxiety: Developmental trends and sex differences. *Journal of Genetic Psychology*, 1976, **128**, 49–57.

108. Morrow, L. A nation without last names. *Time*, July 11, 1977, P. 40.

109. Mueller, W. H. Parent-child correlations for stature and weight among school-aged children: A review of 24 studies. *Human Biology*, 1976, **48**, 379–397.

110. Mukerji, R. TV's impact on children: A checkerboard scene. *Phi Delta Kappan*, 1976, **67**, 316–321.

111. Naffziger, C. C., and K. Naffziger. Development of sex-role stereotypes. *Family Coordinator*, 1974, **23**, 251–258.

112. Nolan, J. D., J. P. Galst, and M. A. White. Sex bias and children's television programs. *Journal of Psychology*, 1977, **96**, 197–204.

113. Nuckols, T. E., and R. Banducci. Knowledge of occupations—is it important in occupational choice? *Journal of Counseling Psychology*, 1974, **21**, 191–195.

114. Oden, S., and S. R. Asher. Coaching children in social skills for friendship making. *Child Development*, 1977, **48**, 495–506.

115. Perloff, R. M. Some antecedents of children's sex-role stereotypes. *Psychological Reports*, 1977, **40**, 463–466.

116. Piaget, J. *Science of education and psychology of the child*. New York: Orion Press, 1970.

117. Pieper, E. Grandparents can help. *The Exceptional Parent,* 1976, **6**(2), 6–10.

118. Pitts, V. P. *Concept development and the development of the God complex in the child: A bibliography.* Schenectady, N.Y.: Character Research Press, 1977.

119. Porter, C. S. Grade school children's perceptions of their internal body parts. *Nursing Research,* 1974, **23**, 384–391.

120. Prawat, R. S., and H. Jones. A longitudinal study of language development in children at different levels of cognitive development. *Merrill-Palmer Quarterly,* 1977, **23**, 115–120.

121. Prentice, N. M., and R. E. Fathman. Joking riddles: A developmental index of children's humor. *Developmental Psychology,* 1975, **11**, 200–216.

122. Pulaski, M. A. S. The rich rewards of make-believe. *Psychology Today,* 1974, **7**(8), 68–74.

123. *Reader's Digest* report. What TV does to kids. *Reader's Digest,* June 1977, Pp. 81–84.

124. Redl, F. Disruptive behavior in the classroom. *School Review,* 1975, **83**, 569–594.

125. Rekers, G. A., H. D. Amaro-Plotkin, and B. P. Low. Sex-typed mannerisms in normal boys and girls as a function of sex and age. *Child Development,* 1977, **48**, 275–278.

126. Rich, J. Effects of children's physical attractiveness on teachers' evaluations. *Journal of Educational Psychology,* 1975, **67**, 599–609.

127. Roberts, J., and J. T. Baird. *Behavior patterns of children in school.* Rockville, Md: Public Health Service, U.S. Department of Health, Education, and Welfare, 1972.

128. Robinson, W. P. Boredom at school. *British Journal of Educational Psychology,* 1975, **45**, 141–152.

129. Romen, N. The motive to avoid success and its effect on performance in school-age males and females. *Developmental Psychology,* 1975, **11**, 689–699.

130. Rossiter, J. R., and T. S. Robertson. Children's television viewing: An examination of parent-child consensus. *Sociometry,* 1975, **38**, 308–326.

131. Salva, J., R. Algozzine, and J. B. Sheare. Attractiveness and school achievement. *Journal of School Psychology,* 1977, **15**, 60–67.

132. Schachten, F. F., R. E. Marquis, S. A. Ganger, and R. M. McCaffery. Socialized speech. I. A proposed resolution of the controversy. *Journal of Genetic Psychology,* 1977, **130**, 305–321.

133. Scheresky, R. F. Occupational roles are sex-typed by six- to ten-year-old children. *Psychology in the Schools,* 1977, **14**, 220–224.

134. Shores, R. E., P. Hester, and P. S. Strain. The effects of amount and type of teacher-child interaction on child-child interaction during free play. *Psychology in the Schools,* 1976, **13**, 171–175.

135. Sigston, A., and D. G. White. Conformity in children as a function of age level. *British Journal of Social & Clinical Psychology,* 1974, **14**, 313–314.

136. Singer, J. L. Fantasy: The foundation of serenity. *Psychology Today,* 1976, **10**(2), 32–34, 37.

137. Sinnott, J. D., and B. M. Ross. Comparison of aggression and incongruity as factors in children's judgment of humor. *Journal of Genetic Psychology,* 1976, **128**, 241–249.

138. Skidgell, A. C., S. L. Witryol, and P. J. Wirzbicki. The effect of novelty-familiarity levels on material reward preference of first-grade children. *Journal of Genetic Psychology,* 1976, **128**, 291–297.

139. Stenner, A. J., and W. G. Katzenmayer. Self-concept, ability, and achievement in a sample of sixth-grade students. *Journal of Educational Research,* 1976, **69**, 270–273.

140. Sussman, G., and J. Justman. Characteristics of preadolescent boys judged creative by their teachers. *Gifted Child Quarterly,* 1975, **19**, 210–216.

141. Tanner, J. M. *Fetus into man: Physical growth from conception to maturity.* Cambridge, Mass.: Harvard University Press, 1978.

142. Trowbridge, N. Self-concept and IQ in elementary school children. *California Journal of Educational Research,* 1974, **25**, 37–49.

143. Turiel, E. A comparative analysis of moral knowledge and moral judgment in males and females. *Journal of Personality,* 1976, **44**, 195–208.

144. *U.S. News & World Report* article. TV violence and children. *U.S. News & World Report,* July 4, 1977, P. 74.

145. Van Camp, S. S., and M. B. Bixley. Eye and hand dominance in kindergarten and first-grade children. *Merrill-Palmer Quarterly,* 1977, **23**, 129–139.

146. Van den Daele, L. A developmental study of the ego-ideal. *Genetic Psychology Monographs,* 1968, **78**, 191–256.

147. Waldrop, M. F., R. Q. Bell, and G. D. Goering. Minor physical anomalies and inhibited behavior in elementary school girls. *Journal of Child Psychology & Psychiatry & Allied Disciplines,* 1976, **17**, 113–122.

148. Waldrop, M. F., and C. F. Halverson. Intensive and extensive peer behavior: Longitudinal and cross-sectional analysis. *Child Development,* 1975, **46**, 19–26.

149. Walls, R. T., R. A. Moxley, and S. P. Gulkus. Collection preferences of children. *Child Development,* 1975, **46**, 783–785.

150. Welkowitz, J., G. Cariffe, and S. Feldstein. Conversational congruence as a criterion of socialization in children. *Child Development,* 1976, **47**, 269–272.

151. White, E., B. Elsom, and R. Prawat. Children's conceptions of death. *Child Development,* 1978, **49**, 307–310.

152. Whiteman, M. Children's conceptions of psychological causality as related to subjective responsibility, conversation, and language. *Journal of Genetic Psychology,* 1976, **128**, 215–226.

153. Whiting, G. W. M., T. K. Landauer, and T. M. Jones. Infantile immunization and adult stature. *Child Development,* 1968, **39**, 59–67.

154. Wilson, K. L., L. A. Zurcher, D. C. McAdams, and R. L. Curtis. Stepfathers and stepchildren: An exploratory analysis from two national surveys. *Journal of Marriage & the Family,* 1975, **37**, 526–536.

155. Zeligs, R. *Children's experience with death.* Springfield, Ill.: Charles C Thomas, 1974.

156. Zimmerman, B. J., and G. H. Brody. Race and modeling influences on the interpersonal play patterns of boys. *Journal of Educational Psychology,* 1975, **67**, 591–598.

157. Zweigenhaft, R. L. The other side of unusual first names. *Journal of Social Psychology,* 1977, **103**, 291–302.

CHAPTER SEVEN
PUBERTY

After reading this chapter, you should be able to:

- Describe what the three stages of puberty are and what parts of childhood and adolescence they overlap.
- Recognize what criteria are used to determine the different stages of puberty, the ages at which puberty normally occurs in boys and girls in the American culture of today, and what causes it.
- Understand what the pubescent growth spurt is and its normal pattern.
- List and explain the four major categories of body changes during puberty and the effects they have on the individual's physical and psychological well-being.
- Identify the different forms deviant maturing can take and describe their effects on personal and social adjustments.
- Discuss the two major sources of concern pubescent children experience and explain how these concerns affect their personal and social adjustments.
- List the major physical and psychological hazards of puberty and explain the effects, both immediate and long-term, of each.
- Define what stages of puberty are likely to be the most unhappy and the seriousness of unhappiness during this period in the life span.

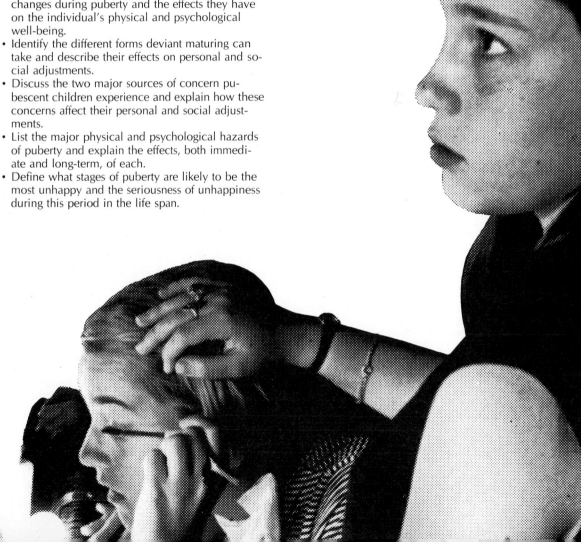

P uberty is the period in the developmental span when the child changes from an asexual to a sexual being. As Root has explained, "Puberty is that stage in development during which maturation of the sexual apparatus occurs and reproductive capacity is attained. It is accompanied by changes in somatic growth and psychological perspective" (74).

The word *puberty* is derived from the Latin word *pubertas,* which means "age of manhood." It refers to the physical rather than the behavioral changes which occur when the individual becomes sexually mature and is capable of producing offspring.

Most primitive people have, for centuries, recognized puberty as a time of importance in the life span of every individual. It is customary for them to observe various rites in recognition of the fact that, as their bodies change, children are emerging from childhood into maturity. After successfully passing the tests that are a significant part of all puberty rites, boys and girls are granted the rights and privileges of adulthood and are expected to assume the responsibilities that accompany that state.

Among the ancient Greeks, puberty was recognized as a time of physical as well as behavioral changes. Aristotle wrote in his *Historia Animalium:*

For the most part males begin to produce sperm when 14 years have been completed. At the same time pubic hair begins to appear. . . . At the same time in females a swelling of the breasts begins and the menses begin to flow and this fluid resembles fresh blood. . . . In the majority the menses are first noticed after the breasts have grown to the height of two fingers' breadth.

Of even greater significance was Aristotle's emphasis on behavioral changes. He described pubescent girls as being irritable, passionate, ardent, and in need of constant surveillance because of their developing sexual impulses.

In the American culture of today, as is true of most civilized cultures, the formal rites of puberty to mark the transition from childhood to adolescence have been abandoned except for the bar mitzvah for Jewish boys. However, scientists of today have been able to pinpoint the cause of puberty changes, and extensive studies of behavior during this period have revealed what behavioral changes can normally be expected to occur.

On the basis of present-day knowledge, social expectations have developed which, in the form of developmental tasks, act as guidelines for parents and teachers to know what to expect of children as they progress through this period of metamorphosis. Children likewise become aware that they are entering a new phase in their lives and, like it is with all adjustments to new social expectations, most of them find puberty a difficult period in their lives.

CHARACTERISTICS OF PUBERTY

Puberty is a unique and distinctive period and is characterized by certain developmental changes that occur at no other time in the life span. The most important of these are discussed below.

Puberty Is an Overlapping Period

Puberty must be regarded as an overlapping period because it encompasses the closing years of childhood and the beginning years of adolescence, as shown in Figure 7-1. Until they are sexually mature, children are known as "pubescents" or "pubescent children." After they become sexually mature, they are known as "adolescents" or "young adolescents."

Puberty Is a Short Period

Considering the many and extensive changes that take place inside the body as well as externally, puberty is a relatively short period, lasting from two to four years. Children who pass through puberty in two years or less are regarded as "rapid maturers," while those who require three to four years to complete the transformation into adults are regarded as "slow maturers." Girls, as a group, tend to mature more rapidly than boys, as a group, but there are marked variations within each sex group.

Puberty Is Divided into Stages

In spite of the fact that puberty is a relatively short period in the life span, it is customary to subdivide it into three stages—the prepubescent stage, the pubescent stage, and the postpubescent stage. When each of these three stages normally occurs and its characteristics are described in Box 7-1.

BOX 7-1

STAGES OF PUBERTY

Prepubescent Stage

This stage overlaps the closing year or two of childhood when the child is regarded as a "prepubescent"—one who is no longer a child but not yet an adolescent. During the prepubescent (or "maturing") stage, the secondary sex characteristics begin to appear but the reproductive organs are not yet fully developed.

Pubescent Stage

This stage occurs at the dividing line between childhood and adolescence; the time when the criteria of sexual maturity appear—the menarche in girls and the first nocturnal emissions in boys. During the pubescent (or "mature") stage, the secondary sex characteristics continue to develop and cells are produced in the sex organs.

Postpubescent Stage

This stage overlaps the first year or two of adolescence. During this stage, the secondary sex characteristics become well developed and the sex organs begin to function in a mature manner.

The latter is usually referred to as the "baby growth spurt."

The rapid growth and development that occur during puberty are generally referred to as the "adolescent growth spurt." More correctly, it is the "puberty growth spurt" because it precedes slightly or occurs simultaneously with the other changes of puberty. This growth spurt lasts for a year or two before children become sexually mature and continues for six months to a year afterward. Thus the entire period of rapid growth lasts for almost three years, slightly longer than the "baby growth spurt" which lasts for less than a year and a half.

The rapid changes that take place during puberty lead to confusion, to feelings of inadequacy and insecurity, and in many cases to unfavorable behavior. In discussing these changes, Dunbar has said (16):

During this period the developing child experiences changes in body, changes in status including appearance and clothes, possessions and range of choice, and changes in attitude toward sex and the opposite sex, all of which by necessity involve a changed child-parent relationship and changes in the rules and regulations to which the youngster is subjected.

Puberty Is a Negative Phase

Many years ago, Charlotte Bühler labeled puberty the *negative phase* (5). The term *phase* suggests a period of short duration; *negative* suggests that the individual takes an "anti" attitude toward life or seems to be losing some of the good qualities previously developed.

There is evidence that negative attitudes and behavior are characteristic mainly of the early part of

Puberty Is a Time of Rapid Growth and Change

Puberty is one of the two periods in the life span that are characterized by rapid growth and marked changes in body proportions. The other is the prenatal period and the first half of the first year of life.

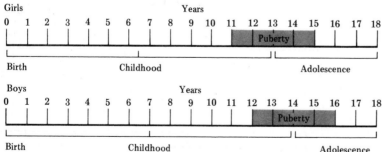

FIGURE 7-1 Puberty overlaps the end of childhood and the beginning of adolescence.

puberty and that the worst of the negative phase is over when the individual becomes sexually mature. There is also evidence that the behavior characteristic of the ''negative phase'' of puberty is more pronounced in girls than in boys (66,80).

Puberty Occurs at a Variable Age

Puberty can occur at any time between the ages of five or six and nineteen years. However, the average girl in the American culture of today becomes sexually mature at thirteen and the average boy, a year later. There are also variations in the amount of time needed to complete the transformation process of puberty. These range from two to four years with girls, on the average, requiring slightly less time than boys.

Variations in the age at which puberty occurs and in the time needed to complete the transformation process of puberty create many personal as well as social problems for both boys and girls. It is the variations in timing of puberty rather than the changes associated with it that make puberty one of the most difficult, even though one of the shortest, periods in the life span.

CRITERIA OF PUBERTY

The criteria most often used to determine the onset of puberty and to pinpoint a particular stage of puberty that the child has reached are the menarche, nocturnal emissions, evidence derived from chemical analysis of the urine and x-rays of bone development.

The *menarche,* or the first menstruation, is commonly used as a criterion of sexual maturity among girls, but it is neither the first nor the last of the physical changes that occur during puberty. When the menarche occurs, the sex organs and secondary sex characteristics have all started to develop, but none of them have yet reached a state of maturity. The menarche is more correctly considered a midpoint in puberty (21,66).

Among boys, a popularly used criterion of puberty is *nocturnal emissions.* During sleep, the penis sometimes becomes erect, and semen, or the fluid containing sperm cells, is released. This is a normal way for the male reproductive organ to rid itself of excessive amounts of semen. However, not all boys experience this phenomenon, and not all realize what it is. Furthermore, nocturnal emissions, like the menarche, occur after some puberty development has

taken place and therefore cannot be used as an accurate criterion of the onset of puberty.

Chemical analysis of the first urine passed by boys in the morning has proved to be an effective technique for determining sexual maturity, as has analysis of girls' urine to see whether the female gonadotropic hormone, estrogen, is present. However, the practical difficulty of obtaining specimens of the early-morning urine of boys and girls limits the use of this method.

X-rays of different parts of the body, but especially the hands and knees, during the preadolescent growth spurt can reveal whether puberty has begun and the rate at which puberty is progressing. To date, this has proved to be the most dependable method of determining sexual maturity, though it, like the chemical analysis of early-morning urine, involves certain practical difficulties that make its widespread use unfeasible (65,71).

CAUSES OF PUBERTY

Until the turn of the present century, the cause or causes of the physical changes that occur at puberty remained a mystery. With the growth of research in the field of endocrinology, medical science has been able to pinpoint the exact causes of these changes though, to date, endocrinologists have been unable to explain the variations in the age of puberty and in the time needed to complete the changes of puberty.

At the present time, it is known that about five years before children become sexually mature, there is a small excretion of the sex hormones in both boys and girls. The amount of hormones excreted increases as time passes, and this eventually leads to the maturing of the structure and function of the sex organs.

It has been established that there is a close relationship between the pituitary gland, located at the base of the brain, and the gonads, or sex glands. The male gonads are the *testes,* and the female gonads are the *ovaries.* The roles they play in bringing about the changes of puberty are described in Box 7-2.

AGE OF PUBERTY

In the American culture of today, approximately 50 percent of all girls mature between 12.5 and 14.5 years, with the average maturing at 13. Figure 7-2 shows the ages of menarche. The average boy be-

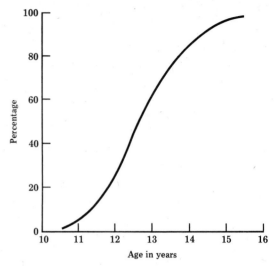

FIGURE 7-2 Percentage of girls whose menstrual periods had started at different ages, according to a nationwide survey. (Adapted from B. MacMahon. *Age at menarche: United States.* Rockville, Md.: National Center for Health Statistics, U. S. Department of Health, Education, and Welfare, 1973. Used by permission.)

BOX 7-2

CONDITIONS RESPONSIBLE FOR PUBERTY CHANGES

Role of the Pituitary Gland

The pituitary gland produces two hormones: the *growth* hormone, which is influential in determining the individual's size, and the *gonadotropic* hormone, which stimulates the gonads to increased activity. Just before puberty, there is a gradual increase in the amount of the gonadotropic hormone and an increased sensitivity of the gonads to this hormone; this initiates puberty changes.

Role of the Gonads

With the growth and development of the gonads, the sex organs—the primary sex characteristics—increase in size and become functionally mature, and the secondary sex characteristics, such as pubic hair, develop.

Interaction of the Pituitary Gland and the Gonads

The hormones produced by the gonads, which have been stimulated by the gonadotropic hormone produced by the pituitary gland, act in turn on this gland and cause a gradual reduction in the amount of growth hormone produced, thus stopping the growth process. The interaction between the gonadotropic hormone and the gonads continues throughout the individual's reproductive life, gradually decreasing as women approach the menopause and men approach the climacteric.

comes sexually mature between the ages of 14 and 16.5, with 50 percent of all boys maturing between 14 and 15.5 years. The remaining 50 percent in each sex group is about evenly divided between those who mature earlier and those who mature later than average—the *early maturers* and the *late maturers* (9,21, 85,87).

Between the ages of twelve and fourteen, differences between the sexes are especially marked, with many more girls having become mature than boys. This difference is reflected in the larger and more mature bodies of the girls and in their more mature, more aggressive, and more sex-conscious behavior.

There is evidence that boys and girls in the United States are reaching puberty earlier now than in past generations. This is true also in Europe and especially in the Scandinavian countries. The explanation for this is better health, better prenatal and postnatal medical care, and better nutrition (80,84).

The total time needed to become sexually mature is approximately three years for girls and two to four years for boys. Boys show less uniformity in this process than girls. Approximately one to two years are required for the preliminary changes from an asexual to a sexual state, the prepubescent stage, and one to two years for the changes to be completed after the individual's sex organs have become mature.

Children who are slow in starting to mature— the late maturers—usually mature more rapidly, once they get started, than the average child and often even more rapidly than those who entered puberty earlier than the average. *Fast maturers* have greater spurts of rapid growth, their periods of accelerated and halted growth come abruptly, and they attain adult proportions very quickly. There is an early development of the sex organs and the secondary sex characteristics, and the osseous development comes earlier than the average (83,85).

Slow maturers, by contrast, have less intense periods of accelerated growth, their growth is more even and gradual, and it continues for a longer time. The sex organs and secondary sex characteristics develop later than average and the osseous development is also late (82,85).

Individual differences in age and rate of maturing are more common than similarities, even among children in the same family. As Johnston has pointed out, "The time clock which governs the developmental process in children is an individual one" (35).

THE PUBERTY GROWTH SPURT

The puberty growth spurt for girls begins between 8.5 and 11.5 years, with a peak coming, on the average, at 12.5 years. From then on, the rate of growth slows down until growth gradually comes to a standstill between seventeen and eighteen years. Boys experience a similar pattern of rapid growth except that their growth spurt starts later and continues for a longer time. For boys, the growth spurt starts between 10.5 and 14.5 years, reaches a peak between 14.5 and 15.5 years, and is then followed by a gradual decline until twenty or twenty-one years, when growth is completed. Increases in height, weight, and strength come at approximately the same time (82, 88). Figure 7-3 shows the onset, the apex, and the end of the puberty growth spurt for boys and girls.

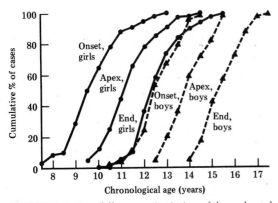

FIGURE 7-3 Sex differences in timing of the pubertal growth spurt. (Adapted from M. S. Faust. Somatic development of adolescent girls. *Monographs of the Society for Research in Child Development,* 1977, **42**(1). Used by permission.)

The rapid growth and development that occur during puberty depend partly on hereditary factors, as they influence the endocrine glands, and partly on environmental factors, of which nutrition has been found to be the most important. Poor nutrition in childhood causes a diminished production of the growth hormone. Good nutrition, on the other hand, speeds up the production of this hormone. Emotional disturbances can affect growth by causing an overproduction of the adrenal steroids, which have an adverse effect on the growth hormone.

When the growth spurt of puberty is interfered with by illness, poor nutrition, or prolonged emotional tension, there will be delayed fusion of the bones and children will not attain their full height. However, if such disturbances are detected in time and corrected, growth can be speeded up to three or four times its normal rate and continue at that rate until children reach their hereditary potentials (69, 84). At the present time, there is no completely reliable way of predicting adult height from the percentage of adult height reached when the secondary sex characteristics begin to develop, or at any other time during the puberty growth spurt (63).

BODY CHANGES AT PUBERTY

During the puberty growth spurt, four important physical changes occur which transform the child's body into that of an adult: changes in body size, changes in body proportions, the development of the primary sex characteristics, and the development of the secondary sex characteristics.

Changes in Body Size

The first major physical change at puberty is change in body size in terms of height and weight. Among girls, the average annual increase in the year preceding the menarche is 3 inches, though a 5- to 6-inch increase is not unusual. Two years preceding the menarche, the average increase is 2.5 inches, making a total increase of 5.5 inches in the two years preceding the menarche. After the menarche, the rate of growth slows down to about 1 inch a year, coming to a standstill at around eighteen years.

For boys, the onset of the period of rapid growth in height comes, on the average, at 12.8 years and ends, on the average, at 15.3 years, with a peak occurring at fourteen years. The greatest increase in height comes in the year following the onset of puberty. After that, growth decelerates and continues at a slow rate until the age of twenty or twenty-one. Because of this longer growth period, boys achieve greater height by the time they are mature than girls do. Refer to Figure 6-2.

Weight gain during puberty comes not only from an increase in fat but also from an increase in bone and muscle tissue. Thus, even though pubescent boys and girls gain weight rapidly, they often look thin and scrawny. Girls experience the greatest weight gain just before and just after the menarche. Only slight increases in weight occur after that. For boys, the maximum gain in weight comes a year or two later than for girls and reaches its peak at sixteen years, after which the gain is small. Refer to Figure 6-3.

It is not uncommon for both boys and girls to go through a fat period during puberty. Between the ages of ten and twelve, at or near the onset of the growth spurt, children tend to accumulate fat on the abdomen, around the nipples, in the hips and thighs, and in the cheeks, neck, and jaw. This fat usually disappears after pubertal maturing and rapid growth in height are well started, though it may remain for two more years during the early part of puberty (24,84).

Changes in Body Proportions

The second major physical change at puberty is change in body proportions. Certain areas of the body which, in the early years of life were proportionally much too small, now become proportionally too big because they reach their mature size sooner than other areas. This is particularly apparent in the nose, feet, and hands. It is not until the latter part of adolescence that the body attains adult proportions in all areas, although the most pronounced changes take place before puberty is over.

The thin, long *trunk* of the older child begins to broaden at the hips and shoulders, and a waistline develops. This appears high at first because the legs grow proportionately more than the trunk. As the trunk lengthens, the waistline drops, thus giving the body adult proportions. The broadness of the hips and shoulders is influenced by the age of maturing. Boys who mature early usually have broader hips than boys who mature late and girls who mature late have slightly broader hips than early-maturing girls.

Just before puberty, the *legs* are disproportionately long in relation to the trunk and continue to be

so until the child is approximately fifteen. In late-maturing children, the leg growth continues for a longer time than in early maturers. The result is that the late maturer is a long-legged individual at maturity, while the early maturer is short-legged. The legs of the early maturer tend to be stocky, while those of the late maturer are generally slender.

Much the same pattern occurs in the *arms,* whose growth precedes the rapid spurt of growth in the trunk, thus making them seem disproportionately long. As is true of leg growth, the growth of the arms is affected by the age of maturing. Early maturers tend to have shorter arms than late maturers, just as the early maturer is shorter-legged than the late maturer. Not until the growth of the arms and legs is nearly complete do they seem to be in the right proportion to the hands and feet, both of which reach their mature size early in puberty. Figure 7-4 shows the changes in body proportions of boys and girls after they have completed the puberty growth spurt.

Primary Sex Characteristics

The third major physical change at puberty is the growth and development of the primary sex characteristics, the sex organs. In the case of the *male,* the gonads or testes, which are located in the scrotum, or sac, outside the body, are only approximately 10 percent of their mature size at the age of fourteen years. Then there is a rapid growth for a year or two, after which growth slows down; the testes are fully developed by the age of twenty or twenty-one.

Shortly after the rapid growth of the testes begins, the growth of the penis accelerates markedly. The first growth is in length, followed by a gradual increase in circumference.

When the *male* reproductive organs have become mature in function, *nocturnal emissions* generally begin to occur, usually when the boy is having a sexually exciting dream, when he has a full bladder or is constipated, when he is wearing tight pajamas, or when he is too warmly covered. Many boys are unaware of what is taking place until they see the telltale spot on their bedclothes or pajamas.

All parts of the *female* reproductive apparatus grow during puberty, though at different rates. The uterus of the average eleven- or twelve-year-old girl, for example, weighs 5.3 grams; by the age of sixteen, the average weight is 43 grams. The Fallopian tubes, ovaries, and vagina also grow rapidly at this time.

The first real indication that a girl's reproduc-

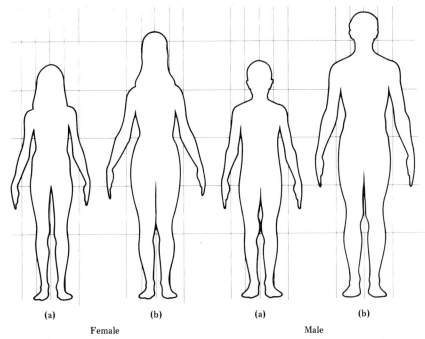

(a)	(b)	(a)	(b)
Female		Male	

FIGURE 7-4 Changes in body proportions of boys and girls (a) before and (b) after puberty changes have been completed. (Adapted from J. M. Tanner. *Growing up. Scientific American,* 1973, **229**(3), 35–43. Used by permission.)

tive mechanism is becoming mature is the *menarche,* or first menstrual flow. This is the beginning of a series of periodic discharges of blood, mucus, and broken-down cell tissue from the uterus that will occur approximately every twenty-eight days until the girl reaches the menopause, in the late forties or early fifties.

The girl's menstrual periods generally occur at very irregular intervals and vary markedly in length for the first year or so. This period is known as the *stage of adolescent sterility.* During this time ovulation, or the ripening and release of a ripe ovum from a follicle in the ovary, does not occur, and the girl is therefore sterile. Even after several menstrual periods, it is questionable whether the girl's sex mechanism is mature enough to make conception possible.

The puberty fat period in girls, which usually levels off between sixteen and eighteen years, coincides with the period of adolescent sterility. At this time there is rapid growth in length in the uterus and in the weight of the ovaries (24).

Secondary Sex Characteristics

The fourth major physical change at puberty is the development of the secondary sex characteristics. These are the physical features which distinguish males from females and which make members of one sex appealing to members of the other sex. They are unrelated to reproduction though indirectly they are related by making males appealing to females and vice versa. That is why they are called "secondary" as compared with the sex organs proper which are called "primary" sex characteristics because they are directly related to reproduction. As long as the body remains childlike in appearance, there is no "sex appeal." This, however, changes when the secondary sex characteristics appear.

As puberty progresses, boys and girls become increasingly dissimilar in appearance. This change is caused by the gradual development of the secondary sex characteristics which, like other developments at puberty, follows a predictable pattern.

The pattern of development of several of the

BOX 7-3

IMPORTANT SECONDARY SEX CHARACTERISTICS

Boys

Hair
Pubic hair appears about one year after the testes and penis have started to increase in size. Axillary and facial hair appear when the pubic hair has almost completed its growth, as does body hair. At first, all hair is scanty, lightly pigmented, and fine in texture. Later it becomes darker, coarser, more luxuriant, and slightly kinky.

Skin
The skin becomes coarser, less transparent, and sallow in color, and the pores enlarge.

Glands
The sebaceous, or oil-producing, glands in the skin enlarge and become more active, which may cause acne. The apocrine glands in the armpits start to function, and perspiration increases as puberty progresses.

Muscles
The muscles increase markedly in size and strength, thus giving shape to the arms, legs, and shoulders.

Voice
Voice changes begin after some pubic hair has appeared. The voice first becomes husky and later drops in pitch, increases in volume, and acquires a pleasanter tone. Voice breaks are common when maturing is rapid.

Breast Knots
Slight knobs around the male mammary glands appear between the ages of twelve and fourteen. These last for several weeks and then decrease in number and size.

Girls

Hips
The hips become wider and rounder as a result of the enlargement of the pelvic bone and the development of subcutaneous fat.

Breasts
Shortly after the hips start to enlarge, the breasts begin to develop. The nipples enlarge and protrude and, as the mammary glands develop, the breasts become larger and rounder.

Hair
Pubic hair appears after hip and breast development is well under way. Axillary hair begins to appear after the menarche, as does facial hair. Body hair appears on the limbs late in puberty. All hair except facial hair is straight and lightly pigmented at first and then becomes more luxuriant, coarser, darker, and slightly kinky.

Skin
The skin becomes coarser, thicker, and slightly sallow, and the pores enlarge.

Glands
The sebaceous and apocrine glands become more active as puberty progresses. Clogging of the sebaceous glands can cause acne, while the apocrine glands in the armpits produce perspiration, which is especially heavy and pungent just before and during the menstrual period.

Muscles
The muscles increase in size and strength, especially in the middle of puberty and toward the end, thus giving shape to the shoulders, arms, and legs.

Voice
The voice becomes fuller and more melodious. Huskiness and breaks in the voice are rare among girls.

important secondary sex characteristics, in relation to growth in height, and several primary sex characteristics are shown in Figure 7-5, which diagrams the sequence of events at puberty for boys and girls, and indicates the range of ages at which these developments take place. The secondary sex characteristics of boys and girls are summarized in Box 7-3.

EFFECTS OF PUBERTY CHANGES

The physical changes of puberty affect every area of the body, both externally and internally, and thus it is not surprising that they also affect the pubescent's physical and psychological well-being. Even though these effects are normally only temporary, they are se-

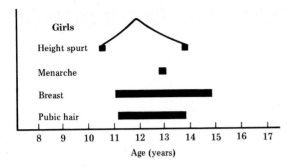

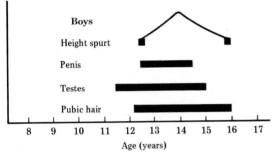

FIGURE 7-5 Sequence of events of puberty for girls and boys and predictable patterns of development of the secondary sex characteristics. (Adapted from W. A. Marshall and J. M. Tanner. Variations in the pattern of pubertal changes in boys. *Archives of Disease in Childhood*, 1970, **45,** 13–23. Used by permission.)

vere enough while they last to bring about a change in habitual patterns of behavior, attitudes, and personality.

Effects on Physical Well-Being

Rapid growth and body changes are likely to be accompanied by fatigue, listlessness, and other unfavorable symptoms. These discomforts are frequently made worse by an increase in duties and responsibilities, just at the time when the individual is least able to cope with them successfully.

Digestive disturbances are frequent, and appetite is finicky. The prepubescent child is upset by glandular changes and changes in the size and position of the internal organs. These changes interfere with the normal functions of digestion. Anemia is common at this period, not because of marked changes in blood chemistry, but because of erratic eating habits, which in turn increase the already-present tendency to be tired and listless.

During the early menstrual periods, girls frequently experience headaches, backaches, cramps, and abdominal pain, accompanied by fainting, vomiting, skin irritations, and even swelling of the legs and ankles. As a result, they feel tired, depressed, and irritable at the time of their periods. As menstruation becomes more regular, the physical and psychological disturbances which accompany its early appearances tend to diminish.

Headaches, backaches, and a general feeling of achiness occur at other times between menstruation. Both boys and girls suffer intermittently from these discomforts, their frequency and severity depending to a large extent upon how rapidly the pubescent changes are occurring and upon how healthy the individuals were when puberty began.

While puberty may be regarded as a "sickly age," when the individual is not up to par, relatively few diseases are characteristic of this period. If pubescent children were actually ill, they would be treated with more sympathy and understanding than they usually are; less would be expected of them, and much of their unsocial behavior would be understood and tolerated, which it rarely is.

Effects on Attitudes and Behavior

It is understandable that the widespread effects of puberty on children's physical well-being would also affect their attitudes and behavior. However, there is evidence that the changes in attitudes and behavior that occur at this time are more the result of social than of glandular changes, though the glandular changes unquestionably play some role through their influence on body homeostasis. The less sympathy and understanding the pubescent child receives from parents, siblings, teachers, and peers and the greater the social expectations at this time, the greater the psychological effects of the physical changes.

The most common, serious, and persistent of puberty changes on attitudes and behavior are given in Box 7-4. Although all children exhibit some of these attitudes and behavior patterns, they are more marked before sexual maturity is attained, or during what Bühler has called the "negative phase" (5).

Girls, as a general rule, are more seriously affected by puberty than boys, partly because they usually mature more rapidly than boys and partly because more social restrictions begin to be placed on their behavior, just at a time when they are trying to free themselves from such restrictions. More (59) has

BOX 7-4

COMMON EFFECTS OF PUBERTY CHANGES ON ATTITUDES AND BEHAVIOR

Desire for Isolation

When puberty changes begin, children usually withdraw from peer and family activities and often quarrel with peers and family members. They spend much time in daydreaming about how misunderstood and mistreated they are and in experimenting with sex through masturbation. Part of this withdrawal syndrome includes refusal to communicate with others.

Boredom

Pubescent children are bored with the play they formerly enjoyed, with schoolwork, with social activities, and with life in general. As a result, they do as little work as they can, thus developing the habit of underachieving. This habit is accentuated by not feeling up to par physically.

Incoordination

Rapid and uneven growth affects habitual patterns of coordination, and the pubescent child is clumsy and awkward for a time. As growth slows down, coordination gradually improves.

Social Antagonism

The pubescent child is often uncooperative, disagreeable, and antagonistic. Open hostility between the sexes, expressed in constant criticism and derogatory comments, is common at this age.

As puberty progresses, the child becomes friendlier, more cooperative, and more tolerant of others.

Heightened Emotionality

Moodiness, sulkiness, temper outbursts, and a tendency to cry at the slightest provocation are characteristic of the early part of puberty. It is a time of worry, anxiety, and irritability, as may be seen in Figure 7-6. Depression, irritability, and negative moods are especially common during the premenstrual and early menstrual periods of girls. As pubescent children become more mature physically, they become less tense and exhibit more mature emotional behavior.

Loss of Self-Confidence

The pubescent child, formerly so self-assured, becomes lacking in self-confidence and fearful of failure. This is due partly to lowered physical resistance and partly to the constant criticism of adults and peers. Many boys and girls emerge from puberty with the foundations of an inferiority complex.

Excessive Modesty

The bodily changes that take place during puberty cause the child to become excessively modest for fear that others will notice these changes and comment on them unfavorably.

---

discussed the reason why boys are not as greatly affected by puberty changes as girls:

Puberty appears to have been a more gradual affair. It did not burst on them with the rapidity of development that the girls experienced. The impulses aroused may have been just as strong or stronger for the male but he had more chance to adjust to them as they grew.

Because they reach puberty earlier, girls show signs of disruptive behavior sooner than boys do. However, girls' behavior stabilizes earlier than that of boys, and they begin to act more as they did before the onset of puberty, just as boys will do later.

How seriously puberty changes will affect behavior will be greatly influenced by the ability and

willingness of pubescent children to communicate their concerns and anxieties to others and, in that way, get a new and better perspective on them. As Dunbar has explained, "The affective reaction to change is largely determined by the capacity to communicate. . . . Communication is a means of coping with anxiety which inevitably accompanies stress" (16). Pubescent children who find it difficult or impossible to communicate with others exhibit more negative behavior than those who can and will communicate.

The psychological effects of puberty are also complicated by the social expectations of parents, teachers, and other adults. Boys and girls are expected to act according to certain standards appropriate for their ages. They find this relatively easy if

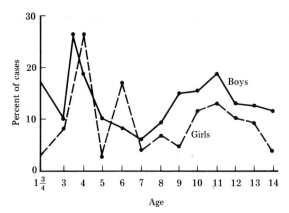

FIGURE 7-6 Irritability tends to increase early in puberty and then to decline. (Adapted from J. Macfarlane, L. Allen, and M. P. Honzik. *A developmental study of the behavior problems of normal children between twenty-one months and fourteen years.* Berkeley: University of California Press, 1954. Used by permission.)

their behavior patterns are at the appropriate developmental levels. However, children who are maturationally unready to fulfill the social expectations for their ages are likely to have problems.

EFFECTS OF DEVIANT MATURING

Children who are most affected by the physical changes that normally occur at puberty are the deviant maturers. A *deviant maturer* is one whose sexual maturation deviates by a year or more from the norm for the individual's sex group, in the time at which sexual maturation occurs, or by a year or more from the norm for the individual's sex group in the time needed to complete the maturation process. Children who mature sexually earlier than their sex group are called "early maturers" while those who mature sexually later than their sex group are called "late maturers." When children require less than the normal time for their sex group to complete the maturational process they are known as "rapid maturers" while those who need more than the normal time are called "slow maturers."

Early versus Late Maturers

For *boys,* early maturing is advantageous, especially in the area of sports, from which they derive much of their prestige and status in the peer group. It is from the ranks of the early maturers that most of the leaders in boys' groups come, and this gives them added prestige in the eyes of girls also.

By contrast, boys who are late maturers tend to be restless, tense, rebellious, and attention-seeking. Because of these unsocial patterns of behavior, they are less popular with both peers and adults and are far less often selected for leadership roles by their peers than early maturers are. In commenting on the disadvantages of late maturing for boys, Weatherley has pointed out the following problems (95).

The later maturer must cope with the developmental demands of the junior high and high school period with the liability of a relatively small, immature appearing physical stature. His appearance is likely to call out in others at least mild reactions of derogation and the expectation that he is capable of only ineffectual, immature behavior. Such reactions constitute a kind of social environment which is conducive to feelings of inadequacy, insecurity and defensive "small-boy" behavior. Such behavior once initiated may well be self-sustaining, since it is likely to only intensify the negative environmental reactions which gave rise to it in the first place.

Early maturing is less advantageous to *girls* than it is to boys. Early-maturing girls are more grown-up and sophisticated in their behavior, but their appearance and actions may lead to a reputation of being "sexually promiscuous." In addition, early-maturing girls are more out of step with their peers than early-maturing boys, and this adds to their social problems. In commenting on the social problems the early-maturing girl is confronted with, Jones and Mussen have pointed out (39):

The early-maturing girl quite naturally has interests in boys and in social usages and activities more mature than those of her chronological age group. But the males of her own age are unreceptive, for while she is physiologically a year or two out of step with the girls in her class, she is three or four years out of step with the boys—a vast and terrifying degree of developmental distance.

Girls who are late maturers are less damaged psychologically than late-maturing boys. They are less likely to engage in status-seeking behavior than boys, though they are concerned about their normalcy, which they reflect in shy, retiring, diffident be-

BOX 7-5

COMMON CONCERNS ABOUT NORMALCY DURING PUBERTY

Boys' Concerns

Nocturnal Emissions
If the boy has not been told about nocturnal emissions, his first such experience is likely to be traumatic.

Secondary Sex Characteristics
Boys are disturbed mainly by the slow growth of facial hair, the huskiness and cracking that accompany voice changes, and the slow development and strengthening of their muscles.

Lack of Interest in Girls
When they see older or sexually mature boys showing an interest in girls and in dating, boys wonder whether they are normal because they have no such interests.

Girls' Concerns

The Menarche
Even with some foreknowledge, the menarche is often a traumatic experience, especially if accompanied by vomiting and cramps. Many girls wonder whether they will "bleed to death."

Menstruation
Many girls wonder whether the cramps, headaches, and backaches they often experience during their periods are normal.

Secondary Sex Characteristics
Because the breasts have a conical shape when they begin to develop, girls wonder whether they will eventually be normal in appearance. They also worry about whether their hips will be too large for the rest of their bodies and whether the down on their faces will turn into a beard or mustache.

Lack of Sex Appeal
Many girls worry if they are unable to attract the attention and win the favor of boys.

Concerns of Boys and Girls

Sex Organs
Pubescent children often fear that their enlarged sex organs will show through their clothing or that the menstrual discharge and nocturnal emissions will leave telltale signs on their clothing.

Body Disproportions
Large hands, feet, and noses; long and lanky arms and legs; small shoulders and perhaps a receding chin, all characteristics of early puberty, make pubescent children wonder whether they will ever look like normal people.

Awkwardness
Because all children become awkward and clumsy to some extent during puberty, they are likely to worry because they believe they are losing skills acquired earlier. Their concerns are heightened if they are ridiculed or reproved for their awkwardness.

Age of Maturing
Earlier maturers may feel like misfits, while those who are slow to mature are embarrassed by their undeveloped bodies and concerned about their lack of interest in the things that absorb their more mature age-mates.

Masturbation
Tension and discomfort in the developing sex organs often lead the pubescent to handle them. Most children have been told that masturbation is wrong, and they feel guilty and ashamed. Their concern is heightened if they have heard old wives' tales—that masturbation leads to insanity, for example.

havior. Because this is considered sex appropriate behavior for girls, it is not as damaging to their reputations as similar behavior in boys would be.

A study of social attitudes among members of the peer group toward early- and late-maturing boys and girls revealed that early-maturing boys were mentioned much more often in the school newspaper than late maturers, while the reverse was true for girls (37).

Rapid versus Slow Maturers

Rapid maturers face certain problems that slow maturers are spared. All of the common effects of puberty changes on attitudes and behavior, as explained in Box 7-4, tend to be exaggerated in rapid maturers. For example, incoordination as shown in clumsiness and awkwardness of behavior is exaggerated in rapid maturers because their bodies change in size so rapidly that they do not have time to learn to control them. By contrast, changes in body size in slow maturers come so slowly that children have time to learn to control their bodies and, as a result, they do not show the pronounced awkwardness and clumsiness so characteristic of rapid maturers.

Similarly, because rapid maturing tends to sap energy, rapid-maturing children become lethargic and perform below their potentials in whatever they do. As a result, they tend to become underachievers, a tendency which can and often does become habitual during the puberty years (73). Unless steps are taken to correct it, after the worst impact of puberty changes has passed, it is likely to become persistent and the child becomes a lifelong underachiever.

The speed of sexual maturing affects attitudes unfavorably mainly when children are slow maturers. While rapid maturers may be temporarily emotionally disturbed by their awkwardness and clumsiness and while periods of heightened emotionality may occur more frequently and more intensely in rapid than in slow maturers, rapid maturers have no cause for concern about whether they will ever turn into adults. They can almost see themselves doing so from one day to another.

By contrast, slow maturers are plagued by the fear that they will never turn into adults and by the constant reminders of how much more like adults their peers seem to be. They experience the same problems that late maturers experience because they lag behind their age-mates and, as a result, are treated by both adults and age-mates as if they were younger than they actually are.

SOURCES OF CONCERN

One of the developmental tasks of growing up is that of accepting the newly developed body and recognizing that nature has endowed the individual with certain physical characteristics that the individual can do little to change. Many children enter puberty with childhood ideals of what they will look like when they are grown up. Because these ideals rarely take into consideration the realities of the child's physical endowment, they must be markedly revised.

Furthermore, most children enter puberty with little foreknowledge of the time needed to mature or the pattern that maturing takes. As a result, they may become deeply concerned as they watch their bodies change, often so slowly that they wonder whether they will ever grow up. The pubescent child's

concern about the developing body is heightened by growing realization of the important role appearance plays in social acceptance.

Different children worry about different parts of their bodies. Usually they consider one physical characteristic to be particularly homely, out of proportion, or sexually inappropriate and magnify its seriousness out of all reasonable proportion. Girls, as a rule, are more concerned about their physical appearance than boys.

While the concerns of pubescent children are myriad, in general they can be divided into two major categories: first, concerns about whether certain physical characteristics are normal and, second, concerns about whether they are sexually appropriate.

Concerns about Normalcy

As Havighurst has pointed out, "It is a rare youngster who is never worried during this period with the question: Am I normal?" (34). Because boys and girls are very conscious of every change that takes place in their bodies and because they have definite ideas about how they would like to look, they become concerned if they feel that they are unattractive or that their appearance is sexually inappropriate.

Since boys and girls undergo very different changes in appearance during puberty, they are naturally concerned about the normalcy of different physical characteristics. Some concerns, however, are shared by all pubescents. Box 7-5 gives the usual concerns of boys and of girls as well as those common to both sexes.

Concerns about Sex-Appropriateness

From early childhood, boys and girls are sex-typed to the point where they have a definite stereotype of "masculine" and "feminine" people. From movies, television programs they watch, and the books they read, as well as from their observations of adults, pubescent children build up a clear concept of what constitutes masculine and feminine appearance and behavior.

While every pubescent child will have individual concerns about sex-appropriateness, there are certain concerns that are almost universal in the American culture of today.

Concern about Size The sudden increase in size that occurs during the pubertal growth spurt is likely to disturb girls because they are afraid their size will

By the time they reach puberty, girls have a clear and well-defined concept of a "feminine" woman. Through beauty aids, many try to conform to this concept. (Bob S. Smith from Photo Researchers, Inc.)

Boys are often disturbed by the slow growth of facial hair. (Jean B. Hollyman from Photo Researchers, Inc.)

make them unattractive to boys. Boys, on the other hand, become disturbed when they see girls of their own age literally towering over them.

Concern about Weight Children frequently gain weight during the early part of puberty, and this is a source of great concern. In our culture, fat is considered unattractive, and the overweight girl who compares herself with movie stars and cover girls, for example, may be very distressed by her own appearance.

For a boy, fat is considered sexually inappropriate, especially on the thighs, around the waist, and in the mammary region. While this generally disappears as puberty progresses, it may affect personality development unfavorably for many years.

Concern about Genitalia There is a widespread belief that small male genitalia means lack of normal sexual development. When a boy's penis is developing, he is greatly concerned about its thinness. Because growth in circumference normally follows growth in length, boys may and often do feel for months that they are not developing normally and they are concerned about whether they will be sexually inadequate.

Concern about Secondary Sex Characteristics Any secondary sex characteristic that is not well developed is sure to be a source of concern. For example, until the breasts become curved and filled out as a result of the development of the mammary glands and subcutaneous tissue, the girl worries that they are unfeminine in appearance. Broad hips are regarded as sexually inappropriate for both sexes, but especially so for boys, and can also be a source of concern during the early stages of puberty.

Secondary sex characteristics that are late in developing are likely to be the source of greatest concern, especially those which differentiate the two sexes most clearly. In the case of boys, facial hair, the development of large muscles in the shoulder and arm regions, and voice changes come late in puberty. As the boy watches hair appear on other areas of his body but not on his face, he wonders whether he will always have the smooth skin of a girl and anxiously awaits the time when he can begin to shave. The breast knots, which develop early in puberty and then gradually disappear, add to his concern about his sex-inappropriate appearance.

Typically, a feminine woman is supposed to have a beautiful complexion. As puberty progresses, acne usually gets worse rather than better, and facial hair is darker and more profuse than in the early stages of puberty, which frequently alarms the girl.

HAZARDS OF PUBERTY

The hazards of puberty are generally serious mainly in terms of their long-range consequences. This contrasts with the earlier stages of development, when the hazards themselves tend to be more important than their long-term effects.

As is true of late childhood, the psychological hazards of puberty are more numerous and more far-reaching in their effects than the physical ones. Furthermore, only a small percentage of pubescent children are affected by the physical hazards, while *all* are affected by the psychological ones, though to varying degrees.

Physical Hazards

Even though most pubescent children do not feel up to par physically, actual illness is less common during this period than at earlier ages. Mortality also occurs infrequently among pubescent children. Since they rarely suffer from illnesses severe enough to lead to death and since they are so inactive and socially withdrawn that accidents—a common cause of death in the years preceding and following puberty—are infrequent, there is less likelihood of mortality at this time than in the earlier or even the postpubescent years. Actually, many deaths reported as due to accidents are the result of suicide which pubescent children may attempt if they become severely depressed.

The major physical hazards of puberty are due to slight or major malfunctioning of the endocrine glands that control the puberty growth spurt and the sexual changes that take place at this time. Box 7-6 describes the effect of glandular malfunctioning on development.

Psychological Hazards

There are many psychological hazards of puberty, the long-term effects of which are even more important than the immediate effects. It is this that makes the psychological hazards so serious. Some of the most important of the psychological hazards of puberty are discussed below.

Unfavorable Self-Concepts Few children pass through puberty without developing unfavorable self-concepts. This is true even of those who, earlier, had good opinions of themselves and who, as a result, had enough self-confidence to play leadership roles in their peer groups.

There are many reasons for the development of unfavorable self-concepts during puberty, some of which may be personal in origin and some environmental. Almost all pubescents have unrealistic concepts about what their appearance and abilities will be when they are grown up, concepts that often trace their origin to childhood days when the ideal self-concept is being formed. As pubescents watch their bodies change and as they observe their awkward behavior and their tendencies toward obesity, they become increasingly disillusioned because what they observe is so far removed from what they had anticipated. This affects their self-concepts unfavorably (86,96).

Because pubescents tend to be unsocial if not actually antisocial in their behavior, the treatment they receive from others is affected by this. As a result, pubescents do not enjoy the social acceptance they may have had earlier, nor does it come up to their hopes and expectations. Unfavorable treatment from others seriously affects self-concepts, causing them to be colored by negative attitudes toward self.

When children develop unfavorable self-concepts, it is soon revealed in their behavior. They either become withdrawn from others, contributing little in actions or speech to the group, or they become aggressive and defensive, retaliating for what they regard as unfair treatment. Regardless of what form of expression their unfavorable self-concepts take, pubescent children's behavior is such that it increases what unfavorable social attitudes toward them already existed.

Like most of the psychological hazards of puberty, the long-term effects of unfavorable self-concepts are even more serious than the immediate effects. Children who develop unfavorable self-concepts at puberty are far more likely to reinforce these unfavorable self-concepts with their unsocial behavior than they are to improve them. As a result, the foundations for an inferiority complex are laid and, unless remedial steps are taken to correct it, it will likely become persistent and color the quality of the individual's behavior throughout the remainder of the life span.

Underachievement With rapid physical growth comes a sapping of energy. This leads to a disinclination to work and to attitudes of boredom toward any activities that require effort on the individual's part. While underachievement often begins around the fourth or fifth grade in school, when early enchantment with school gives way to disenchantment, it generally reaches its peak during puberty (73).

As girls accept the cultural stereotype about themselves, they realize that it is not regarded as "feminine" to be achievers, especially when their achievements surpass those of boys. This encourages girls to work below their capacities and increases the tendency to be underachievers caused by the sapping of physical strength which is a normal accompaniment of the rapid physical changes of puberty.

Once the tendency to work below one's capacities develops, it is likely to become habitual as it is reinforced, month after month, by the sapping of physical energy during the rapid growth period of puberty and by the cultural pressures on girls not to surpass boys in their achievements. As a result, many pubescents grow up to be underachievers, not only academically but also vocationally. They develop attitudes toward themselves and their abilities that reinforce their lack of motivation to try to do what they are capable of. Many enter adult life as general underachievers, a tendency to work below their capacities and potentials in whatever they undertake because they learned patterns of behavior and attitudes in puberty which have become habitual. Unless remedial steps are taken to correct them, they will lead to lifelong underachievement.

Lack of Preparation for Puberty Changes As Thomas has said, "Rare is the child who even partially understands the basic nature of the changes taking place in him and in his peers" (86). When pubescent children are not informed about or are psychologically unprepared for both the physical and psychological changes that take place at puberty, undergoing these changes may be a traumatic experience. As a result, they are likely to develop unfavorable attitudes toward these changes—attitudes that are more apt to persist than to disappear. There are many reasons why children are often unprepared for puberty. Parents, for example, may lack adequate knowledge or they may be held back by modesty and embarrassment. Or, the gap that often develops between pubescent children and their parents prevents them from asking questions about the changes that are taking place in their bodies. In addition, to avoid embarrassment, pubescent children may pretend that they already know all they need to know. In that way they rebuff parental attempts to give them the information they want.

Unless the school gives courses in sex hygiene or provides information about puberty in connection with a physical hygiene course, children will not get the information they want at school nor will they be likely to turn to a teacher for help. This is partly because of embarrassment and partly because their attitudes toward school and toward teachers are more likely to be unfavorable than favorable at this time. They are also unlikely to turn to their classmates or friends for information, even if those classmates are better informed than they are. Pride keeps most pubescent children from admitting that they know less than their friends know (89).

Regardless of the reason for inadequate preparation for puberty, it is a serious psychological hazard, especially in the case of early or late maturers. The reason for this is that it encourages them to think that something is wrong or that their development is so abnormal that they will never again look like their peers.

Being different is always a concern to children and young adolescents. The more they deviate in ways that are apparent to all, the more concerned they become and the more likely they are to feel abnormal and, consequently, inferior. The section on deviant maturing as a psychological hazard will explain this in more detail and stress its long-term effects.

Acceptance of Changed Bodies One of the important developmental tasks of puberty is acceptance of the changed body. Few pubescents are able to do this. As a result, they are dissatisfied with their appearance. Knowing how important appearance is in social acceptance, they often blame it for their less-than-hoped-for acceptance.

There are many reasons why pubescent boys and girls are dissatisfied with their changed bodies and find it difficult to accept them. Two, however, are so common that they are almost universal. First, almost all children build up an ideal physical self-concept based on concepts from different sources of the ideal individual of their sex group. Few pubescents ever even remotely approach this ideal physique in real life. Under such conditions, they are dissatisfied with their looks and find it difficult to be self-acceptant.

Second, traditional beliefs about a sex-appropriate appearance tend to color pubescent children's attitudes in ways that interfere with their acceptance of their own changed bodies. For example, since being flat-chested is generally considered unattractive and unfeminine in women, pubescent girls whose breasts are developing slowly may not only become concerned about their femininity but also are likely to become self-rejectant. In the same way, boys who ac-

cept the traditional belief that well-developed genitalia are a sign of masculinity become concerned and self-rejectant when their penises are long and thin before their final development has been completed.

Acceptance of Socially Approved Sex Roles Like acceptance of the changed body, acceptance of the sex roles pubescents are expected to play as near-adults is one of the major developmental tasks of this age level. Throughout childhood, strong pressure is put on boys to play the socially approved masculine sex role which, in most social groups, is the traditional role which emphasizes the superiority of members of the male sex.

Because of the advantages and prestige associated with the traditional male sex role, most boys are not only willing but also eager to play it. As was pointed out in the preceding chapter, before late childhood is over most boys have not only accepted the stereotype of the traditional male but they have been sex-role typed to the point where their behavior closely conforms to this stereotype. Consequently, during puberty, acceptance of the sex role they are expected to play as near-adults presents no real problem for pubescent boys and, consequently, cannot be regarded as a psychological hazard for them.

This, however, is by no means true of girls. Having been far less strictly sex-role typed during childhood then boys, and having a somewhat blurred concept of the sex role they will be expected to play as adults, girls are now confronted with the problem of accepting the traditional stereotype of the female and of behaving in a manner that conforms to this stereotype.

For some pubescent girls, this presents few problems because they, like boys, have learned to play the traditional sex role throughout the childhood years. For other girls, by contrast, this may be a major psychological hazard to good personal and social adjustments. Not only do they prefer the egalitarian to the traditional sex role but they have, at home and to some extent in the play group, learned to play this role. Being expected, at puberty, to accept a role that is less to their liking and less prestigious than the role they have played through childhood is a psychological hazard for them.

For many pubescent girls, the psychological hazard of acceptance of the traditional female sex role is intensified by the periodic discomforts they suffer at the time of their menstrual periods. While not all girls are subject to these discomforts, most are during the early months of puberty, while the sex organs are still only partially developed and therefore unready to function in rhythmic manner as they will later.

The realization that boys are not subject to periodic discomforts similar to those they experience at the times of their menstrual periods intensifies the resistance of many girls to accept the traditional female sex role. Unfavorable attitudes toward menstruation are often intensified by the unfavorable social attitudes of older women who often refer to it as the "curse" and who emphasize the role it plays in the traditional female sex role.

It has been reported that, unfortunately, the unfavorable attitudes toward menstruation, developed at puberty, often continue throughout life (21,80). As a result, they cause women to become even more depressed at the time of their menstrual periods than would be justified on the basis of the discomforts involved. For example, attempts at suicide among women occur more frequently during menstrual periods than at other times (90).

Deviations in Sexual Maturing   Unquestionably one of the most serious psychological hazards during puberty is a deviation in the age at which sexual maturing occurs or in the time needed for the maturing. This hazard, of course, affects only those children who are deviant enough from their age-mates in this aspect of their development to be recognized by them as "different."

As is true of the late childhood years, it is difficult for pubescent children to be acceptant about anything that makes them different and thus, in their view, inferior. As Thomas has explained (86):

Not only are these children "different" from their peers and, therefore, liable to be ostracized, but they suffer through academic, social, and physical activities that are not geared to meet their unique needs and abilities. As such, these experiences only serve to heighten their sense of "differentness."

Deviations in sexual maturing, regardless of what form they take, are a potential psychological hazard. Children who deviate from their age-mates in sexual maturing feel that there is something wrong with them. They are concerned about their normalcy and about their future normalcy. If, for example, children deviate from their age-mates in height at puberty, they worry about their adult height. As Onat has pointed out (63):

The future mature height of a child becomes a real problem in those who grow at unusual rates and develop sexually at unusual ages. Rapid growers or early maturers may become anxious that they will be abnormally tall adults. On the other hand, slow growers may worry that they will be short adults or remain sexually underdeveloped.

Early maturers, Schonfeld has said, have "distinct social advantages in most cultures over late-maturing youths, but youths who mature 'too early' may manifest personality difficulties" (76). These difficulties come from the fact that early maturers, who look older than they actually are, are usually expected to act in accordance with their appearance rather than in accordance with their chronological age. If they fail to do so, they are criticized and this leads to resentments as well as feelings of inadequacy and inferiority. Studies of school dropouts have suggested that early maturing is a common cause of dropping out. The reason for this is that teachers, like parents, tend to expect more of early maturers than they are capable of and, as a result, early maturers often see school as hostile and rejecting (87). There is no question about the fact that all the normal effects of puberty—heightened emotionality, awkwardness, and so forth—are accentuated in early maturers. This intensifies their feelings of inferiority.

Late maturers, who look younger than they are, may be treated accordingly by friends and adults. This makes them doubt their ability to do what their age-mates do. *Slow maturers* have more time to adjust to the physical changes of puberty than rapid maturers or those who mature at a normal rate. But concern about whether they will ever grow up counteracts this favorable effect and encourages their belief that they are inferior to their age-mates. In the case of boys, as Thomas has explained, this may and often does lead to the "locker room" syndrome. According to him, "In our culture where athletic prowess is often as important, and sometimes more important, than academic and creative achievement, a student's self-image is shaped by his perception of his physical ability in relation to his classmates" (86). Being weaker and less well developed than they causes those who lag behind their age-mates in sexual maturing to feel inferior.

Serious as the immediate effects of deviant sexual maturing are to children's personal and social adjustments, the *long-term effects* are even more serious. Studies have documented what these long-term effects on behavior are, some of which will be discussed in detail below.

In the case of slow maturers, damage results from the fact that they have longer than average time during which to develop the undesirable patterns of behavior associated with puberty, although this need not necessarily be permanently handicapping.

Some, it is true, may develop into habitual daydreamers; some may develop a hypercritical, frictional attitude toward others; and some may develop into restless people who find it difficult to concentrate on any task. But if their desire for social acceptance is strong enough and if they are able to achieve a reasonable amount of social acceptance, they will be sufficiently motivated to break these habits and replace them with more socially acceptable patterns of behavior.

Not all those who deviate from the norm—the early and late maturers—are damaged permanently by this. Some, in fact, benefit, not only during puberty, but in later years as well. Although studies of the long-term effects on behavior have so far been limited to boys, evidence from these studies and knowledge of the effects of reinforcement through repetition enable us to hazard a guess concerning what the long-term effects on girls might be.

Early-maturing boys normally become socially active and popular, holding leadership roles in the peer group. They have assets that are valued in the peer group, and as a result of repetition, these develop into habitual patterns of behavior. Follow-up studies of subjects into middle and early old age have shown these patterns of behavior to be persistent. As a result, the early maturers are more successful vocationally and socially as adults, just as they were during adolescence. Their success stems from the fact that they make better impressions on others than the normal or late maturers.

By contrast, middle-aged men who were late maturers were found to cling to the "little-boy" patterns of behavior which caused them to be unpopular when they were younger. Thus late maturers tend to be less active socially, less successful in business, and less likely to be selected for leadership roles than might be expected on the basis of their abilities (2,38, 77).

Speculation about the long-term effects of deviant maturing on girls leads one to believe that early maturers who were embarrassed about being larger than their contemporaries and who often developed aggressive patterns of behavior to attract the attention of boys will continue to show similar patterns of behavior as adult women. Late maturers, by contrast, who were better adjusted personally and socially in adolescence, are likely to continue to be so during adulthood, unless conditions unrelated to sexual maturing interfere with this pattern.

UNHAPPINESS AT PUBERTY

The "three A's of happiness," acceptance, affection, and achievement, discussed in detail in Chapter 1, are often violated during the puberty years. Hence it is questionable whether any pubescent child is or can be really happy or even partially satisfied with life under such conditions.

The first essential of happiness is *acceptance*, both self-acceptance and social acceptance. To be satisfied with their lives to the point that they can consider themselves happy, pubescents must not only like and accept themselves but must also feel that they are accepted by others. The more they can like and accept themselves, the happier they will be. Similarly, the more people there are whom they want to like and accept them, the more satisfied they are with their status in the social group.

It is difficult for pubescent children to be self-acceptant when they are anxious and concerned about their changing bodies and dissatisfied with their appearance. Furthermore, the realization of the increasingly important role that appearance plays in social acceptance adds to their worries. The more concerned pubescent children are about social acceptance, the more concerned they will be about their appearance. Girls tend to worry more about their looks than boys because they realize that appearance plays a more important role in their social acceptance than it does in boys'.

Studies of pubescent children who are dissatisfied with their looks have pinpointed the areas of greatest concern. Girls, for example, want to have a good figure. Boys want to be tall, since they associate this with masculinity, and very tall girls want to be shorter to conform to the stereotype for their sex. Boys want to be heavier than they are, and girls want to be lighter. Boys want broader shoulders and thicker arms and legs, while girls want smaller hips and waists, thinner arms and legs, and larger busts. Boys are usually dissatisfied with their chins—they want more prominent ones—while girls and boys both wish their noses were less prominent and better shaped (6,41). As Calden et al. have pointed out, "Females desire changes from the waist down and wish for smallness and petiteness of body parts (except for bust). Males are dissatisfied with body dimensions from the waist up, desiring bigness of body parts" (6).

Concern about the role of appearance in social acceptance is not the only cause of unhappiness during puberty. The behavior of most pubescents is so unsocial that parents, teachers, siblings, and peers—the most significant people in their lives—may be rejectant in their attitudes toward them. Even worse, their temper outbursts and restlessness create the impression that they are not acting their ages—an impression that further jeopardizes their social acceptance and, consequently, their self-acceptance.

The second essential of happiness is *affection* from others. Because affection from and acceptance by others go hand in hand, pubescents whose attitudes toward family members and friends are critical and derogatory, and whose behavior in social situations is egocentric and unsocial, do not receive the affection they formerly did. While they may try to create the impression that they do not care, or that the affection of others means little to them, this is not the case. Pubescents crave affection, just as children do, and often they want more affection than they formerly did because they are unhappy and dissatisfied with themselves and with life in general.

The third essential of happiness, *achievement,* likewise is at such a low level at this age that it makes little or no contribution to the pubescent child's happiness. As was stressed earlier in discussing hazards during the puberty years, underachievement is common. This is partly the result of the disinclination to work caused by lowered physical resistance and strength and partly because of girls' acceptance of the traditional sex-role stereotype of female achievement below that of males.

When their achievements fall short of their potentials, most pubescents realize it and feel guilty and ashamed. When, for example, their school grades take a plunge, as they often do during the puberty years, pubescents are aware of the fact that they can do and have done better work than they are now

doing. If parents and teachers criticize and reprimand them for their lack of achievements, this adds to the feelings of guilt they experience and affects detrimentally their happiness.

Variations in Unhappiness at Puberty

Not all phases of puberty are unhappy to the same degree. The early part, the so-called "negative phase," is usually the most unhappy. After sexual maturing occurs and growth slows down, pubescent children have more energy. This results in better achievements and better social relationships—thus making possible better social acceptance and greater affection from others.

Furthermore, pubescents are less concerned about their appearance as puberty progresses because they realize that many of the conditions that worried them were only temporary. As they more closely approximate their self-ideals in appearance and in personality, and as they become more sex-appropriate in appearance, some of their anxieties wane. Even more important, they learn that there are ways in which they can improve their appearance—girls may try dieting or they may experiment with different hairstyles, for example—and thus increase their chances for social acceptance and, with it, affection from others.

Seriousness of Unhappiness at Puberty

Because puberty is a short period in the total life span, being unhappy at this time may seem relatively unimportant. This, however, is not the case. There are two reasons for this. First, a pattern of unhappiness established at this time may be reinforced to the point where it will become habitual and persist long after puberty has ended. Second, conditions that contribute to unhappiness at puberty are likely to be persistent unless remedial steps are taken to change them. For example, unless children are encouraged to develop a more realistic ideal self-concept, they will continue to be self-rejectant year after year as they see how far below their ideal they are and what little progress they are making in reaching this ideal.

Because unhappiness at any age is serious, especially if it persists long enough to become habitual, it is important to keep the unhappiness of pubescent children at a minimum. Parents and teachers can do this by making sure that pubescents are as healthy as possible, by telling them what they want and need to know about the maturing process so that they will not imagine that there is something seriously wrong with them if they deviate in any way from their peers, by helping them to improve their appearance, by lightening the work load during periods of rapid growth, by overlooking drops in the quality of their work at such times, by encouraging them to aspire realistically so that they will not be disappointed in their achievements, and by accepting their moodiness and orneriness as only a temporary condition.

Children usually look forward to the time when they will be grown up, and this attitude can be maintained if steps are taken to prevent unhappiness from developing during puberty. This is important for the pubescent child's mental health, but even more important, it increases the child's motivation to learn adult patterns of behavior.

The developmental tasks of adolescence are difficult, and learning them is a long, laborious task at best. A strong motivation to do so, resulting from happy anticipation of achieving adult status in society, will go a long way toward easing the burden of these tasks and toward guaranteeing a successful end result.

Chapter Highlights

1. In spite of the fact that puberty is a short period that overlaps the end of childhood and the beginning of adolescence, it is a time of rapid growth and change. It occurs at different ages for boys and girls and for individuals within each sex group.
2. There are three stages of puberty—the prepubescent, the pubescent, and the postpubescent.
3. The criteria most often used to determine the onset of puberty are the menarche, or first menstruation, in girls, and nocturnal emissions in boys.
4. Puberty is caused by hormonal changes which, because they are not controllable to date, come at variable times. The average age for girls is thirteen years, and for boys, fourteen to fourteen and a half years. The time needed to complete the puberty changes ranges from two to four years.
5. The puberty growth spurt—the time when puberty changes are taking place most rapidly—is variable because it is influenced partly by hereditary factors and partly by environmental factors, such as nutrition, health, and emotional stress.
6. There are four major body changes at puberty—changes in body size, changes in body propor-

tions, development of the primary sex characteristics, and development of the secondary sex characteristics.
7. The most rapid growth in body size comes during the year or two before the sex organs begin to function and then tapers off.
8. Changes in body proportions are influenced by the age of sexual maturing.
9. The primary sex characteristics—the sex organs—grow and develop rapidly during puberty and become functionally mature in approximately the middle of puberty.
10. The secondary sex characteristics—the physical features that distinguish males from females—develop according to predictable patterns but, by the end of puberty, all of these patterns are at their mature or near-mature levels.
11. Puberty changes affect physical well-being as well as attitudes and behavior. Because these effects tend to be unfavorable, especially during the early part of puberty, puberty is sometimes called the "negative phase."
12. Deviant sexual maturing, whether the deviation is in the age at which sexual maturing occurs or in the time needed to complete the sexual and bodily changes, has a profound influence on the attitudes, behavior patterns and self-concepts of boys and girls. Of the different forms of deviant maturing, late and slow maturing have, on the whole, more unfavorable effects than early and rapid maturing.
13. The two major concerns characteristic of puberty relate to normalcy and sex-appropriateness.
14. The physical hazards of puberty are minor compared with the psychological hazards. The most common of the latter are the tendency to develop unfavorable self-concepts; to become underachievers; unwillingness to accept changed bodies or socially approved sex roles; and deviant sexual maturing.
15. Because the three A's of happiness—acceptance, affection, and achievement—are often violated during these years, puberty tends to be one of the most unhappy periods of the life span. This is serious because unhappiness can and often does become habitual.

Bibliography

1. Adams, J. F. (Ed.). *Understanding adolescence: Current developments in adolescent psychology.* (2nd ed.) Boston: Allyn & Bacon, 1973.
2. Ames, R. Physical maturing among boys as related to adult social behavior. *California Journal of Educational Research,* 1957, **8**, 69–75.

3. Bojlen, K., and M. W. Bentzon. The influence of climate and nutrition on age at menarche: A historical review and a modern hypothesis. *Human Biology*, 1968, **40**, 69–85.

4. Brŏzek, J. (Ed.). Physical growth and body composition. *Monographs of the Society for Research in Child Development*, 1970, **35**(7).

5. Bühler, C. *Das seeleben der jungendlichen*. Stuttgart: Gustav Fischer Verlag, 1927.

6. Calden, G., R. M. Lundy, and R. J. Schlater. Sex differences in body concepts. *Journal of Consulting Psychology*, 1959, **23**, 378.

7. Clarke, A. E., and D. N. Ruble. Young adolescents' beliefs concerning menstruation. *Child Development*, 1978, **49**, 231–234.

8. Corboz, R. J. Psychological aspects of retarded puberty. *Adolescence*, 1966, **1**, 141–143.

9. Damon, A., and C. J. Bajema. Age at menarche: Accuracy of recall after thirty-nine years. *Human Biology*, 1974, **46**, 381–384.

10. Damon, A., S. T. Damon, R. B. Reed, and I. Valadian. Age at menarche of mothers and daughters with a note on accuracy of recall. *Human Biology*, 1969, **41**, 161–175.

11. Delong, G. Inquiry into pre- and early-adolescent interests. *Adolescence*, 1975, **10**, 187–190.

12. Diers, C. J. Historical trends in the age at menarche and menopause. *Psychological Reports*, 1974, **34**, 931–937.

13. Dreyer, A. S., V. Hulac, and D. Rigler. Differential adjustment to pubescence and cognitive style patterns. *Developmental Psychology*, 1971, **4**, 456–462.

14. Duffy, R. J. Description and perception of frequency of breaks (voice breaks) in adolescent female speakers. *Language & Speech*, 1970, **13**, 151–161.

15. Duffy, R. J. Fundamental frequency characteristics of adolescent females. *Language & Speech*, 1970, **13**, 14–34.

16. Dunbar, F. Homeostasis during puberty. *American Journal of Psychiatry*, 1958, **114**, 673–682.

17. Eichorn, D. H. Physiological development. In P. H. Mussen (Ed.). *Carmichael's manual of child psychology* (3rd ed.). Vol. 1. New York: Wiley, 1970, Pp. 157–283.

18. Ellis, J. D., A. V. Carron, and D. A. Bailey. Physical performance in boys from 10 through 16 years. *Human Biology*, 1975, **47**, 263–281.

19. Faterson, H. F., and H. A. Witkin. Longitudinal study of development of the body concept. *Developmental Psychology*, 1970, **2**, 429–438.

20. Faust, M. S. Developmental maturity as a determinant in prestige of adolescent girls. *Child Development*, 1960, **31**, 173–184.

21. Faust, M. S. Somatic development of adolescent girls. *Monographs of the Society for Research in Child Development*, 1977, **42**(1).

22. Frisancho, A. R., S. M. Gam, and C. G. Rothman. Age at menarche: A new method of prediction and retrospective assessment based on hand x-rays. *Human Biology*, 1969, **41**, 42–50.

23. Frisch, R. E. Weight at menarche: Similarity for well-nourished and undernourished girls at differing ages, and evidence for historical constancy. *Pediatrics*, 1972, **50**, 445–450.

24. Frisch, R. E. Fatness in girls from menarche to age 18 years, with a nomogram. *Human Biology*, 1976, **48**, 353–359.

25. Frisch, R. E., and R. Revelle. The height and weight of adolescent boys and girls at the time of peak velocity of growth in height and weight. Longitudinal data. *Human Biology*, 1969, **41**, 536–559.

26. Frisch, R. E., and R. Revelle. The height and weight of boys and girls at the time of initiation of the adolescent growth spurt in height and weight and the relationship to menarche. *Human Biology*, 1971, **43**, 140–159.

27. Frisch, R. E., R. Revelle, and S. Cook. Height, weight, and age at menarche and the "critical weight" hypothesis. *Science*, 1971, **174**, 1148–1149.

28. Fulton, C. D., and A. W. Hubbard. Effect of puberty on reaction and movement times. *Research Quarterly*, 1975, **46**, 335–344.

29. Golub, S. The effect of premenstrual anxiety and depression on cognitive function. *Journal of Personality & Social Psychology*, 1976, **34**, 99–104.

30. Hamill, P. V. V., T. A. Drizel, C. L. Johnson, R. B. Reed, and A. F. Roche. *NCHS growth curves for children from birth to 18 years*. Hyattsville, Md.: National Center for Health Statistics, U.S. Department of Health, Education, and Welfare, 1977.

31. Harms, E. Puberty: physical and mental. *Adolescence*, 1966, **1**, 293–296.

32. Harper, J. F., and J. K. Collins. The effects of early or late maturation on the prestige of the adolescent girl. *Australian & New Zealand Journal of Sociology*, 1972, **8**, 83–88.

33. Hart, M., and C. A. Samoff. The impact of the menarche: A study of two stages of organization. *Journal of the American Academy of Child Psychiatry*, 1971, **10**, 257–271.

34. Havighurst, R. J. *Developmental tasks and education*. (3rd ed.) New York: McKay, 1972.

35. Johnston, F. E. Individual variations in the rate of skeletal maturation between five and eighteen years. *Child Development*, 1964, **35**, 75–80

36. Johnston, F. E. Control of age at menarche. *Human Biology*, 1974, **46**, 159–171.

37. Jones, M. C. A study of socialization patterns at the high school level. *Journal of Genetic Psychology*, 1958, **93**, 87–111.

38. Jones, M. C. Psychological correlates of somatic development. *Child Development*, 1965, **36**, 899–911.

39. Jones, M. C., and P. H. Mussen. Self-conceptions, motivations, and interpersonal attitudes of early- and late-maturing girls. *Child Development*, 1958, **29**, 491–501.

40. Joseph, W. Voice growth measurements in male adolescence. *Journal of Research in Music Education*, 1969, **17**, 423–426.

41. Jourard, S. M., and P. F. Secord. Body-cathexis and the ideal female figure. *Journal of Abnormal & Social Psychology*, 1955, **50**, 243–246.

42. Koeske, R. K., and G. F. Koeske. An attributional approach to moods and the menstrual cycle. *Journal of Personality & Social Psychology*, 1975, **31**, 473–478.

43. Krogman, W. M. Growth of head, face, trunk and limbs in Philadelphia white and Negro children of elementary and high school age. *Monographs of the Society for Research in Child Development*, 1970, **35**(3).

44. Kulin, H. E. The physiology of adolescence in man. *Human Biology*, 1974, **46**, 133–144.

45. Lamphiear, D. E., and H. J. Montoye. Muscular strength and body size. *Human Biology*, 1976, **48**, 147–160.

46. Lewis, V. G., J. Money, and N. A. Bobrow. Psychologic study of boys with short stature, retarded osseous growth, and normal age of pubertal onset. *Adolescence*, 1973, **8**, 445–454.

47. Litt, I. F., and M. I. Cohen. Age at menarche: A changing pattern and its relationship to ethnic origin and delinquency. *Journal of Pediatrics*, 1973, **82**, 288–289.

48. MacMahon, B. *Age at menarche: United States.* Rockville, Md: National Center for Health Statistics, U. S. Department of Health, Education, and Welfare. 1973.

49. Malino, R. M. Adolescent changes in size, build, composition, and performance. *Human Biology,* 1974, **46,** 117–131.

50. Marshall, W. A., and J. M. Tanner. Variations in pattern of pubertal changes in girls. *Archives of Disease in Childhood,* 1969, **44,** 201–203.

51. Marshall, W. A., and J. M. Tanner. Variations in the pattern of pubertal changes in boys. *Archives of Disease in Childhood,* 1970, **45,** 13–23.

52. Masterson, J. G. True precocious puberty. *Annals of the New York Academy of Sciences,* 1967, **142,** 778–782.

53. Meredith, H. V. Body size of contemporary youth in different parts of the world. *Monographs of the Society for Research in Child Development,* 1969, **34**(7).

54. Meredith, H. V. Somatic changes during human postnatal life. *Child Development,* 1975, **46,** 603–610.

55. Miller, A. C. Role of physical attractiveness in impression formation. *Psychonomic Science,* 1970, **19,** 241–243.

56. Money, J., and R. R. Clopper. Psychosocial and psychosexual aspects of errors of pubertal onset and development. *Human Biology,* 1974, **46,** 173–181.

57. Money, J., and A. A. Erhardt. *Man and woman: Boy and girl. Differentiation and dimorphism of gender identity from conception to maturity.* Baltimore, Md.: Johns Hopkins Press, 1973.

58. Money, J., and G. Wolff. Late puberty, retarded growth and reversible hyposamatotropinism (psychological dwarfism). *Adolescence,* 1974, **9,** 121–134.

59. More, D. M. Developmental concordance and discordance during puberty and early adolescence. *Monographs of the Society for Research in Child Development,* 1953, **18,** 1–128.

60. Muuss, R. E. Adolescent development and the secular trend. *Adolescence,* 1970, **5,** 267–284.

61. Muuss, R. E. Puberty rites in primitive and modern societies. *Adolescence,* 1970, **5,** 109–128.

62. Newton, M., and M. Issekutz-Wolsku. The rate of female maturation. *Gerontologia,* 1969, **15,** 328–331.

63. Onat, T. Prediction of adult height of girls based on the present age of adult height at onset of secondary sex characteristics, at chronological age, and skeletal age. *Human Biology,* 1975, **47,** 117–130.

64. Onat, T., and B. Erfem. Adolescent female height velocity: Relationships to body measurements, sexual and skeletal maturity. *Human Biology,* 1974, **46,** 199–217.

65. Onat, T., and E. Numan-Cobeci. Sesamed bones of the hand: Relationship to growth, skeletal and sexual development. *Human Biology,* 1976, **48,** 559–576.

66. Parker, E. *The seven ages of woman.* Baltimore, Md.: Johns Hopkins Press, 1960.

67. Poppleton, P. K. The secular trend in puberty: Has stability been achieved? *British Journal of Educational Psychology,* 1966, **36,** 95–100.

68. Poppleton, P. K. Puberty, family size, and the educational progress of girls. *British Journal of Educational Psychology,* 1968, **38,** 286–292.

69. Prader, A., J. M. Tanner, and G. E. Von Hamack. Catch-up growth following illness or starvation. *Journal of Pediatrics,* 1963, **62,** 646–659.

70. Rakoff, A. E. Menstrual disorders of the adolescent. *Annals of the New York Academy of Sciences,* 1967, **142,** 801–806.

71. Roche, A. F., and G. H. Davila. The reliability of assessments of the maturity of individual hand-wrist bones. *Human Biology,* 1976, **48,** 585–597.

72. Roche, A. F., N. Y. French, and G. H. Davila. Areola size during pubescence. *Human Biology,* 1971, **43,** 210–223.

73. Romer, N. The motive to avoid success and its effects on performance in school-age males and females. *Developmental Psychology,* 1975, **11,** 689–699.

74. Root, A. W. Endocrinology of puberty: I. Normal sexual maturation. *Journal of Pediatrics,* 1973, **83,** 1–19.

75. Root, A. W. Endocrinology of puberty: II. Aberrations of sexual maturation. *Journal of Pediatrics,* 1973, **83,** 187–200.

76. Schonfeld, W. A. The body and the body image in adolescents. In G. Caplan and S. Lebovici (Eds.). *Adolescence: Psychosocial perspectives.* New York: Basic Books, 1969, Pp. 27–53.

77. Sears, R. R. Sources of life satisfaction of the Terman gifted men. *American Psychologist,* 1977, **32,** 119–128.

78. Shaffer, D. Suicide in childhood and early adolescence. *Journal of Child Psychology & Psychiatry & Allied Disciplines,* 1974, **15,** 275–291.

79. Sigurjonsdotter, T. J., and A. B. Haynes. Precocious puberty. *American Journal of Diseases of Children,* 1968, **115,** 309–321.

80. Sommer, B. B. *Puberty and adolescence.* New York: Oxford University Press, 1978.

81. Sullivan, W. Boys and girls are now maturing earlier. *The New York Times,* Jan. 24, 1971.

82. Tanner, J. M. Physical growth. In P. H. Mussen (Ed.). *Carmichael's manual of child psychology* (3rd ed.). Vol. 1. New York: Wiley, 1970, Pp. 77–155.

83. Tanner, J. M. Sequence, tempo, and individual variation in the growth and development of boys and girls aged twelve to sixteen. *Daedalus,* 1971, **100,** 907–930.

84. Tanner, J. M. Growing up. *Scientific American,* 1973, **229**(3), 35–43.

85. Tanner, J. M. *Fetus into man: Physical growth from conception to maturity.* Cambridge, Mass.: Harvard University Press, 1978.

86. Thomas, J. K. Adolescent endocrinology for counselors of adolescents. *Adolescence,* 1973, **8,** 394–406.

87. Thomas, W. D. Maturation age: Another dropout factor? *Canadian Counsellor,* 1972, **6,** 275–277.

88. Thompson, G. W., F. Popovich, and D. L. Anderson. Maximum growth changes in mandibular length, stature and weight, *Human Biology,* 1976, **48,** 285–293.

89. Thornburg, H. D. Educating the preadolescent about sex. *Family Coordinator,* 1974, **23,** 35–39.

90. Tonks, C. M., P. H. Rack, and M. J. Rose. Attempted suicide and the menstrual cycle. *Journal of Psychosomatic Research,* 1968, **11,** 319–323.

91. Valisk, J. A. The seasonal rhythm of the menarche: A review. *Human Biology,* 1965, **37,** 75–90.

92. Verinis, J. S., and S. Roll. Primary and secondary male characteristics: The hairiness and large penis stereotypes. *Psychological Reports,* 1970, **26,** 123–126.

93. Villee, D. B. *Human endocrinology.* Philadelphia: Saunders, 1975.

94. Waber, D. P. Sex differences in cognition: A function of maturation rate? *Science,* 1976, **192,** 572–574.

95. Weatherley, D. Self-perceived rate of physical maturation and

personality in late adolescence. *Child Development,* 1964, **35,** 1197–1210.

96. Weiland, R. G., J. C. Cohen, E. M. Zorn, and M. C. Hallberg. Correlation of growth, pubertal staging, growth hormone, gonadotropins, and testosterone levels during the pubertal growth spurt in males. *Journal of Pediatrics,* 1971, **79,** 999.

97. Whisant, L., and L. Zegans. A study of attitudes toward menarche in white middle-class American adolescent girls. *American Journal of Psychiatry,* 1975, **132,** 809–814.

98. Wolanski, N., and M. Pyzuk. A new graphic method for the evaluation of sexual maturity in girls. *Developmental Medicine & Child Neurology,* 1971, **13,** 590–596.

CHAPTER EIGHT
ADOLESCENCE

After reading this chapter, you should be able to:

- Understand the timing of adolescence, its subdivisions, its outstanding characteristics, and the developmental tasks of this period.
- List and briefly explain the physical, emotional, and social changes at this age and the characteristic interests of adolescents in the American culture of today.
- Explain why changes in morality occur during adolescence and their effects on adolescent attitudes and behavior.
- Describe the changes in sex interests, sex behavior, and sex roles that are characteristic of American adolescents of today.
- Point out why family relationships tend to deteriorate in adolescence and when and why this deterioration normally ends.
- Give reasons why adolescents attempt to improve their personalities and the consequences of these attempts.
- Verify that physical hazards are less numerous and less important than psychological hazards during adolescence and give some examples from each category to illustrate this point.
- Emphasize that normally *all* adolescence is not an unhappy age, only the early part of this period.

The term *adolescence* comes from the Latin word *adolescere,* meaning "to grow" or "to grow to maturity." Primitive peoples—as was true also in earlier civilizations—do not consider puberty and adolescence to be distinct periods in the life span; the child is regarded as an adult when capable of reproduction.

As it is used today, the term *adolescence* has a broader meaning. It includes mental, emotional, and social maturity as well as physical maturity. This point of view has been expressed by Piaget (121) when he said:

Psychologically, adolescence is the age when the individual becomes integrated into the society of adults, the age when the child no longer feels that he is below the level of his elders but equal, at least in rights. . . . This integration into adult society has many affective aspects, more or less linked with puberty. . . . It also includes very profound intellectual changes. . . . These intellectual transformations typical of the adolescent's thinking enable him not only to achieve his integration into the social relationships of adults, which is, in fact, the most general characteristic of this period of development.

Legally, in the United States today, the individual is regarded as an adult at age eighteen, instead of twenty-one, as formerly. The prolongation of adolescence, after the individual has become sexually mature and before being given the rights as well as the responsibilities of adulthood, has resulted in a generation gap between what is popularly regarded as the youth culture and the adult culture. The youth culture emphasizes immediacy and obliviousness to adult responsibilities. It has its own social hierarchy, its own beliefs, its own fashions of appearance, its own values, and its own standards of behavior.

The youth culture in the American society of today prides itself on being different from the adult culture. Conformity to the standards of the youth culture has had two profound and serious effects. First, it causes alienation and protest against the adult culture and second, it is a poor preparation for entrance into the adult society marked by adult values. Adolescents who must conform to the standards of the youth culture if they want to be accepted by their peers learn standards of behavior and values which they will have to revise before they are accepted by the adult culture. The sloppy appearance in clothes and hair

styles, for example, which is the approved standard by today's youth culture, is not acceptable in the adult culture and must be drastically revised if the adolescent, upon reaching legal maturity, wants to become a part of the adult culture (18,82).

THE ADOLESCENT YEARS

It is customary to regard adolescence as beginning when children become sexually mature and ending when they reach the age of legal maturity. However, studies of changes in behavior, attitudes, and values throughout adolescence have revealed not only that these changes are more rapid in the early than in the latter part of adolescence but also that the behavior, attitudes, and values in the early part of the period are markedly different from those in the latter part. As a result, it has become a widespread practice to divide adolescence into two subdivisions, *early* and *late* adolescence.

The dividing line between early and late adolescence is somewhat arbitrarily placed at around seventeen years; the age when the average adolescent enters the senior year of high school. When adolescents become seniors at school, they are usually recognized by their parents as nearly grown up and on the verge of entering the adult world of work, of going to college, or of receiving vocational training of some kind. Their status in school likewise makes them conscious of the responsibilities they have never before been expected to assume as they take their place as "seniors" in school. Awareness of this new and formally recognized status, both at home and in school, motivates most adolescents to behave in a more mature manner.

Because boys mature, on the average, later than girls, they have a shorter period of early adolescence, although they are regarded as adults when they reach eighteen, just as girls are. As a result, they frequently seem more immature for their age than girls. However, as they are accorded, along with girls, a more mature status in the home and school, they usually settle down quickly and show a maturity of behavior which is in marked contrast to that of the younger adolescent.

Early adolescence extends roughly from thirteen to sixteen or seventeen years, and late adolescence covers the period from then until eighteen, the age of legal maturity. Late adolescence is thus a very short period.

Early adolescence is usually referred to as the "teens," sometimes even the "terrible teens." Although older adolescents are, strictly speaking, "teenagers" until they reach twenty years of age, the label *teenager*, which has become popularly associated with the characteristic pattern of behavior of young adolescents, is rarely applied to older adolescents. Instead, they are usually referred to "young men" and "young women"—or even "youths"—indicating that society recognizes a maturity of behavior not found during the early years of adolescence (101).

CHARACTERISTICS OF ADOLESCENCE

As is true of every important period during the life span, adolescence has certain characteristics that distinguish it from the periods that preceded it and the periods that will follow it. What these characteristics are will be explained briefly below.

Adolescence Is an Important Period

While all periods in the life span are important, some are more important than others because of their immediate effects on attitudes and behavior, whereas others are significant because of their long-term effects. Adolescence is one of the periods when both the immediate effects and long-term effects are important. Some periods are important for their physical and some for their psychological effects. Adolescence is important for both.

In discussing the physical effects of adolescence, Tanner has said (156):

For the majority of young persons, the years from twelve to sixteen are the most eventful ones of their lives so far as their growth and development is concerned. Admittedly, during fetal life and the first year or two after birth developments occurred still faster, and a sympathetic environment was probably even more crucial, but the subject himself was not the fascinated, charmed, or horrified spectator that watches the developments, or lack of developments, of adolescence.

Accompanying these rapid and important physical developments, especially during the early adolescent period, rapid mental developments occur.

These give rise to the need for mental adjustments and the necessity for establishing new attitudes, values and interests.

Adolescence Is a Transitional Period

Transition does not mean a break with or a change from what has gone before but rather a passage from one stage of development to another. This means that what has happened before will leave its mark on what happens now and in the future. Children, when they go from childhood to adulthood, must "put away childish things" and they must also learn new patterns of behavior and attitudes to replace those they have abandoned.

However, it is important to realize that what happened earlier has left its mark and will influence these new patterns of behavior and attitudes. As Osterrieth has explained, "The psychic structure of the adolescent has its roots in childhood and many of its characteristics that are generally considered as typical of adolescence appear and are already present during late childhood" (118). The physical changes that take place during the early years of adolescence affect the individual's behavioral level and lead to reevaluations and a shifting adjustment of values.

During any transitional period, the individual's status is vague and there is confusion about the roles the individual is expected to play. The adolescent, at this time, is neither a child nor an adult. If adolescents behave like children, they are told to "act their age." If they try to act like adults, they are often accused of being "too big for their britches" and are reproved for their attempts to act like adults. On the other hand, the ambiguous status of today's adolescents is advantageous in that it gives them time to try out different lifestyles and decide what patterns of behavior, values, and attitudes meet their needs best (58).

Adolescence Is a Period of Change

The rate of change in attitudes and behavior during adolescence parallels the rate of physical change. During early adolescence, when physical changes are rapid, changes in attitudes and behavior are also rapid. As physical changes slow down, so do attitudinal and behavioral changes.

There are five almost universal concomitants of the changes that occur during adolescence. The first is heightened emotionality, the intensity of which depends on the rate at which the physical and psychological changes are taking place. Because these changes normally occur more rapidly during early adolescence, heightened emotionality is generally more pronounced in early than in late adolescence.

Second, the rapid changes that accompany sexual maturing make young adolescents unsure of themselves, of their capacities, and of their interests. They have strong feelings of instability which are often intensified by the ambiguous treatment they receive from parents and teachers.

Third, changes in their bodies, their interests, and in the roles the social group expects them to play create new problems. To young adolescents, these may seem more numerous and less easily solved than any they have had to face before. Until they have solved their problems to their satisfaction, they will be preoccupied with them and with themselves.

Fourth, as interests and behavior patterns change, so do values. What was important to them as children seems less important to them now that they are near-adults. For example, most adolescents no longer think that a large number of friends is a more important indication of popularity than friends of the type that are admired and respected by their peers. They now recognize quality as more important than quantity.

Fifth, most adolescents are ambivalent about changes. While they want and demand independence, they often dread the responsibilities that go with independence and question their ability to cope with these responsibilities.

Adolescence Is a Problem Age

While every age has its problems, those of adolescence are often especially difficult for boys and girls to cope with. There are two reasons for this. First, throughout childhood, their problems were met and solved, in part at least, by parents and teachers. As a result, many adolescents are inexperienced in coping with problems alone. Second, because adolescents want to feel that they are independent, they demand the right of coping with their own problems, rebuffing attempts on the part of parents and teachers to help them.

Because of their inability to cope with problems alone as well as they believe they can, many adolescents find that the solutions do not always come up to their expectations. As Anna Freud has explained, "Many failures, often with tragic consequences in these respects, are due not to the individual's incapacity as such but merely to the fact that

such demands are made on him at a time in life when all his energies are engaged otherwise, namely, in trying to solve the major problem created for him by normal sexual growth and development" (50).

Adolescence Is a Time of Search for Identity

Throughout the gang age of late childhood, conformity to group standards is far more important to older children than individuality. As was pointed out earlier, in dress, speech, and behavior older children want to be as nearly like their gang-mates as possible. Any deviation from the group standard is likely to be a threat to group belonging (17).

In the early years of adolescence, conformity to the group is still important to boys and girls. Gradually, they begin to crave identity and are no longer satisfied to be like their peers in every respect, as they were earlier.

However, the ambiguous status of the adolescent in the American culture of today presents a dilemma that greatly contributes to the adolescent "identity crisis" or the problem of ego-identity. As Erikson has explained (42):

The identity the adolescent seeks to clarify is who he is, what his role in society is to be. Is he a child or is he an adult? Does he have it in him to be someday a husband and father? . . . Can he feel self-confident in spite of the fact that his race or religious or national background makes him a person some people look down upon? Overall, will he be a success or a failure?

Erikson has further explained how this search for identity affects the adolescent's behavior (42):

In their search for a new sense of continuity and sameness, adolescents have to refight many of the battles of earlier years, even though to do so they must artificially appoint perfectly well-meaning people to play the roles of adversaries; and they are ever ready to install lasting idols and ideals as guardians of a final identity. The integration now taking place in the form of ego identity is more than the sum of childhood identifications.

One of the ways adolescents try to establish themselves as individuals is by the use of status symbols in the form of cars, clothes, and other readily observable material possessions. They hope, in this way, to attract attention to themselves and to be recognized as individuals while, at the same time, maintaining their identity with the peer group. The importance of status symbols in adolescence will be discussed in detail later in the chapter.

Adolescence Is a Dreaded Age

As Majeres has pointed out, "Many popular beliefs about adolescents have definite evaluative connotations and, unfortunately, many of them are negative (101). Acceptance of the cultural stereotype of teenagers as sloppy, unreliable individuals who are inclined toward destructiveness and antisocial behavior has led many adults who must guide and supervise the lives of young adolescents to dread this responsibility and to be unsympathetic in their attitudes toward, and treatment of, normal adolescent behavior.

Popular stereotypes have also influenced the self-concepts and attitudes of adolescents toward themselves. As Anthony has explained, in speaking about the cultural stereotypes of adolescents, "The stereotypes have also functioned as mirrors held up to the adolescent by society reflecting an image of himself that the adolescent gradually comes to regard as authentic and according to which he shapes his behavior" (4). The acceptance of this stereotype and the belief that adults have poor opinions of them make the transition into adulthood difficult. By so doing, it leads to much friction with their parents and places a barrier between them and their parents which prevents them from turning to their parents for help in solving their problems.

Adolescence Is a Time of Unrealism

Adolescents have a tendency to look at life through rose-tinted glasses. They see themselves and others as they would like them to be rather than as they are. This is especially true of adolescent aspirations. These unrealistic aspirations, not only for themselves but also for their families and friends, are, in part, responsible for the heightened emotionality characteristic of early adolescence. The more unrealistic their aspirations are, the more angry, hurt, and disappointed they will be when they feel that others have let them down or that they have not lived up to the goals they set for themselves (135).

With increased personal and social experiences, and with increased ability to think rationally, older adolescents see themselves, their families and

friends, and life in general in a more realistic way. As a result, they suffer less from disappointment and disillusionment than they did when they were younger. This is one of the conditions that contributes to the greater happiness of the older adolescent (6).

As adolescence draws to a close, it is not uncommon for both boys and girls to be plagued by overidealism of the single, carefree life that they will soon give up as they achieve the status of adults. Feeling that this period of their lives is happier than what they will face in adulthood, with its demands and responsibilities, there is a tendency to glamourize adolescence and to feel that a happy, carefree age has been lost forever (75).

Adolescence Is the Threshold of Adulthood

As adolescents approach legal maturity, they are anxious to shed the stereotype of teenagers and to create the impression that they are near-adults. Dressing and acting like adults, they discover, are not always enough. So, they begin to concentrate on behavior that is associated with the adult status—smoking, drinking, using drugs, and engaging in sex, for example. They believe that this behavior will create the image they desire.

DEVELOPMENTAL TASKS OF ADOLESCENCE

All the developmental tasks of adolescence are focused on overcoming childish attitudes and behavior patterns and preparing for adulthood. See page 10 for a list of these tasks (63).

The developmental tasks of adolescence require a major change in the child's habitual attitudes and patterns of behavior. Consequently, few boys and girls can be expected to master them during the years of early adolescence. This is especially true of late maturers. The most that can be hoped is that the young adolescent will lay foundations on which to build adult attitudes and behavior patterns.

A brief survey of the important developmental tasks of adolescence will serve to illustrate the extent of the changes that must be made and the problems that arise from these changes. Fundamentally, the necessity for mastering the developmental tasks in the relatively short time that American adolescents have, as a result of lowering the age of legal maturity to eighteen, is the reason for much of the stress that plagues many adolescents.

It may be and often is difficult for adolescents to accept their physiques if, from earliest childhood, they have a glamourized concept of what they wanted to look like when they are grown up. It takes time to revise this concept and to learn ways to improve their appearance so that it will conform more to their earlier ideals.

Acceptance of the adult-approved sex role is not too difficult for boys; they have been encouraged in this direction since early childhood. But for girls, who as children were permitted or even encouraged to play an egalitarian role, learning what the adult-approved feminine role is and accepting it is often a major task requiring many years of adjustment.

Because of the antagonism toward members of the opposite sex that often develops during late childhood and puberty, learning new relationships with members of the opposite sex actually means starting from scratch to discover what they are like and how to get along with them. Even developing new, more mature relationships with age-mates of the same sex may not be easy.

Achieving emotional independence from parents and other adults would seem, for the independence-conscious adolescent, to be an easy developmental task. However, emotional independence is not the same as independence of behavior. Many adolescents who want to be independent want and need the security that emotional dependence on their parents or some other adults gives. This is especially true for adolescents whose status in the peer group is insecure or who lack a close tie with a member of the peer group.

Economic independence cannot be achieved until adolescents choose an occupation and prepare for it. If they select an occupation that requires a long period of training, there can be no assurance of economic independence even when they reach legal adulthood. They may have to remain economically dependent for several years until their training for their chosen vocations has been completed.

Schools and colleges put emphasis on developing intellectual skills and concepts necessary for civic competence. However, few adolescents are able to use these skills and concepts in practical situations. Those who are active in the extracurricular affairs of their schools and colleges get such practice,

but those who are not active in this way—because they must take after-school jobs or because they are not accepted by their peers—are deprived of this opportunity.

Schools and colleges also try to build values that are in harmony with those held by adults; parents contribute to this development. When, however, the adult-fostered values clash with peer values, adolescents must choose the latter if they want the peer acceptance on which their social life depends.

Closely related to the problem of developing values in harmony with those of the adult world the adolescent is about to enter is the task of developing socially responsible behavior. Most adolescents want to be accepted by their peers, but they often gain this acceptance at the expense of behavior that adults consider socially irresponsible. If, for example, it is the "thing to do" to cheat or to help a friend during an examination, the adolescent must choose between adult and peer standards of socially responsible behavior.

The trend toward earlier marriages has made preparation for marriage one of the most important developmental tasks of the adolescent years. While the gradual relaxing of social taboos on sexual behavior has gone a long way toward preparing adolescents of today for the sexual aspects of marriage, they receive little preparation—at home, in school, or in college—for the other aspects of marriage, and even less preparation for the duties and responsibilities of family life. This lack of preparation is responsible for one of the major pieces of "unfinished business" which the adolescent carries into adulthood.

PHYSICAL CHANGES DURING ADOLESCENCE

Growth is far from complete when puberty ends, nor is it entirely complete at the end of early adolescence. However, there is a slackening of the pace of growth, and there is more marked internal than external development. This cannot be so readily observed or identified as growth in height and weight or the development of the secondary sex characteristics. Box 8-1 gives the important external and internal bodily changes that take place during adolescence and the ages at which these changes normally occur.

BOX 8-1

BODY CHANGES DURING ADOLESCENCE

External Changes

Height

The average girl reaches her mature height between the ages of seventeen and eighteen and the average boy, a year or so later. Refer to Figure 6-2. Boys and girls who were immunized during babyhood are usually taller, age for age, than those who were not immunized and who, as a result, suffered from more illnessses that tended to stunt their growth.

Weight

Weight changes follow a timetable similar to that for height changes, with weight now distributed over areas of the body where previously there was little or no fat.

Body Proportions

The various parts of the body gradually come into proportion. For example, the trunk broadens and lengthens, and thus the limbs no longer seem too long.

Sex Organs

Both male and female sex organs reach their mature size in late adolescence, but are not mature in function until several years later.

Secondary Sex Characteristics

The major secondary sex characteristics are at a mature level of development by late adolescence.

Internal Changes

Digestive System

The stomach becomes longer and less tubular, the intestines grow in length and circumference, the muscles in the stomach and intestinal walls become thicker and stronger, the liver increases in weight, and the esophagus becomes longer.

Circulatory System

The heart grows rapidly during adolescence; by the age of seventeen or eighteen, it is twelve times as heavy as it was at birth. The length and thickness of the walls of the blood vessels increase and reach a mature level when the heart does.

Respiratory System

The lung capacity of girls is almost at a mature level at age seventeen; boys reach this level several years later.

Endocrine System

The increased activity of the gonads at puberty results in a temporary imbalance of the whole endocrine system in early adolescence. The sex glands develop rapidly and become functional, though they do not reach their mature size until late adolescence or early adulthood.

Body Tissues

The skeleton stops growing at an average age of eighteen. Tissues, other than bone, continue to develop after the bones have reached their mature size. This is especially true of muscle tissue.

Variations in Physical Changes

As is true at all ages, there are individual differences in physical changes. *Sex* differences are especially apparent. Even though boys start their growth spurt later than girls, their growth continues longer, with the result that, at maturity, they are usually taller than girls. Because boys' muscles grow larger than girls' muscles, at all ages after puberty boys surpass girls in strength, and this superiority increases with age.

Individual differences are also influenced by *age of maturing*. Late maturers tend to have slightly broader shoulders than those who mature early. The legs of early-maturing boys and girls tend to be stocky; those of late maturers tend to be more slender. Early-maturing girls weigh more, are taller, and have greater weight for their height than do late-maturing girls (3). Figure 8-1 shows the effect of age of maturing of girls on body proportions when their growth is completed.

Effects of Physical Changes

As physical changes slow down, the awkwardness of puberty and early adolescence generally disappear. This is because older adolescents have had time to gain control of their enlarged bodies. They are

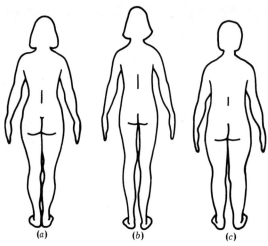

FIGURE 8-1 Three eighteen-year-old girls who matured at different ages and at different rates. (a) Accelerated growth; (b) retarded growth; (c) irregular growth. (Adapted from N. Bayley. Individual patterns of development. *Child Development,* 1956, **27,** 45–74. Used by permission.)

also motivated to use their newly acquired strength and this further helps them to overcome any awkwardness that appeared earlier.

Because strength follows growth in muscle size, boys generally show their greatest increase in strength after age fourteen, while girls show improvement up to this age and then lag, owing more to changes in interests than to lack of capacity. Girls generally attain their maximum strength at about seventeen, while boys do not attain their maximum strength until they are twenty-one or twenty-two (102).

Concerns about Physical Changes

Few adolescents experience *body-cathexis* or satisfaction with their bodies. However, they do experience more dissatisfaction with some parts of their bodies than with other parts. This failure to experience body-cathexis is one of the causes of unfavorable self-concepts and lack of self-esteem during the adolescent years (100).

Dion et al. have explained why satisfaction with the physical changes that take place as children's bodies are transformed into adult bodies is so important. According to them, "A person's physical appearance, along with his sexual identity, is the per-

sonal characteristic most obvious and accessible to others in social interactions" (36). While clothing and beauty aids can be used to hide the physical features the adolescent dislikes, and to enhance those the adolescent regards as attractive, they alone are not enough to guarantee body-cathexis.

Some of the concerns adolescents have about their bodies are carry-overs of concerns they experienced during puberty and which, in the early years of adolescence, are based on conditions that still prevail. Concern about *normalcy,* for example, will persist until the physical changes on the surface of the body have been completed and adolescents can be sure that their bodies conform to the norms for their sex groups. Similarly, concern about sex-appropriateness, so all-prevading in puberty, continues until the primary and secondary sex characteristics have completed their growth and development and, thus, give adolescents an opportunity to see if their bodies conform to the cultural standard of sex-appropriateness.

Awareness of social reactions to different *body builds* leads to concern in adolescents whose changing bodies fail to conform to the culturally approved standards. Knowing that social reactions to endomorphic builds in both boys and girls are less favorable than they are to ectomorphic and mesomorphic builds leads to concern on the part of adolescents whose body builds tend toward endomorphy (156, 157).

For many girls, *menstruation* is a serious concern. This is because they suffer physical discomforts such as cramps, weight gain, headaches, backaches, swollen ankles, and breast tenderness and experience emotional changes, such as mood swings, depression, restlessness, depression, and a tendency to cry without apparent reason.

Because menstruation is commonly referred to as "the curse," it is not surprising that this unfavorable social reaction will color girls' attitudes. Furthermore, knowing that boys do not experience any such form of physical discomfort also colors girls' attitudes unfavorably and encourages them to believe that they are martyrs (119).

Acne and other skin eruptions are a source of concern to both boys and girls. With the increase in the severity of acne, there is an increase in concern. This concern is often as great for boys as for girls because they realize that acne mars their chances for physical attractiveness and because they cannot use cosmetics to cover it up as girls can (126). Figure 8-2

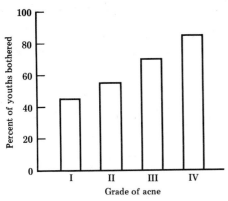

FIGURE 8-2 Percentages of boys and girls, twelve to seventeen years of age, who said they were bothered "some" or "a lot" by their acne conditions graded by medical standards.

Grade I—Sparse to profuse comedones with little or no inflammatory reaction.

Grade II—Acne usually confined to face and consists of comedones and superficial small postular lesions at the folicular orifice.

Grade III—This grade of acne represents a true disease rather than a cosmetic change. It is characterized by comedones and small pustules, and there is a tendency for deeper inflamed lesions to develop.

Grade IV—The face and neck may be severely involved, with extensive lesions on the upper trunk. There may also be some extension up into the scalp on the posterior neck.

(Adapted from J. Roberts and J. Ludford. *Skin conditions of youth.* Rockville, Md.: National Center for Health Statistics, U.S. Department of Health, Education, and Welfare, 1976. Used by permission.)

shows how boys' and girls' concern about acne increases during the adolescent years according to the severity of the acne.

The tendency toward *obesity* that plagues most pubescent boys and girls continues to be a source of concern during the early adolescent years. In most cases, however, with increase in height and with efforts to control their appetites and the eating of "junk food," most older adolescents start to slim down and look less obese than they did during the puberty fat period (19,52). In addition, careful selection of clothing helps to create the illusion that they are more slender than they actually are.

It is unusual for adolescents, boys or girls, not to be concerned about their *physical attractiveness.*

As was explained earlier, few are satisfied with their appearance and many are concerned about what they can do to improve it.

The reason for concern comes from realization of the role attractiveness plays in social relationships. Adolescents realize, even more than children do, that people treat those who are attractive more favorably than they do those who are less attractive. They are also aware of the important role attractiveness plays in choice for leadership. Consequently, when they feel that they are less attractive than they had hoped to be when their growth was complete or nearly complete, they are concerned about what they can do to improve their looks. Few adolescents escape being "looks-conscious" to the point where they spend proportionally more time and thought on how to improve their looks than most adults consider justified (1,13,25).

EMOTIONALITY DURING ADOLESCENCE

Traditionally, adolescence has been thought of as a period of "storm and stress"—a time of heightened emotional tension resulting from the physical and glandular changes that are taking place. While it is true that growth continues through the early years of adolescence, it does so at a progressively slower rate. What growth is taking place is primarily a completion of the pattern already set at puberty. It is necessary, therefore, to look for other explanations of the emotional tension so characteristic of this age.

The explanations are to be found in the social conditions that surround the adolescent of today. Adolescent emotionality can be attributed mainly to the fact that boys and girls come under social pressures and face new conditions for which they received little if any preparation during childhood (136).

Not all adolescents, by any means, go through a period of exaggerated storm and stress. True, most of them do experience emotional instability from time to time, which is a logical consequence of the necessity of making adjustments to new patterns of behavior and to new social expectations. For example, problems related to romance are very real at this time. While the romance is moving along smoothly, adolescents are happy, but they become despondent when things begin to go wrong. Similarly, with the end of their schooling in sight, adolescents begin to worry about their future.

While adolescent emotions are often intense, uncontrolled, and seemingly irrational, there is generally an improvement in emotional behavior with each passing year. Fourteen-year-olds, Gesell et al. have reported, are often irritable, are easily excited, and "explode" emotionally instead of trying to control their feelings. Sixteen-year-olds, by contrast, say they "don't believe in worrying." Thus the storm and stress of this period lessens as early adolescence draws to a close (53).

Emotional Patterns in Adolescence

The emotional patterns of adolescence, while similar to those of childhood (see Box 5-4), differ in the stimuli that give rise to the emotions and, even more important, in the degree of control the individuals exercise over the expression of their emotions. For example, being treated "like a child" or being treated "unfairly" is more likely to make the adolescent angry than anything else.

Instead of having temper tantrums, however, adolescents express their anger by sulking, refusing to speak, or loudly criticizing those who angered them. Adolescents also become envious of those with more material possessions. While they may not complain and feel sorry for themselves, as children do, they are likely to take a part-time job to earn money for the material possessions they crave or even drop out of school to get these things.

Emotional Maturity

Boys and girls are said to have achieved emotional maturity if, by the end of adolescence, they do not "blow up" emotionally when others are present, but wait for a convenient time and place to let off emotional steam in a socially acceptable manner. Another important indication of emotional maturity is that the individual assesses a situation critically before responding to it emotionally instead of reacting to it unthinkingly, as would a child or an immature person. This results in adolescents ignoring many stimuli that would have caused emotional outbursts when they were younger. Finally, emotionally mature adolescents are stable in their emotional responses and they do not swing from one emotion or mood to another, as they did earlier.

To achieve emotional maturity, adolescents must learn to get a perspective on situations which otherwise would lead to emotional reactions. They can do this best by discussing their problems with others. Their willingness to disclose their attitudes, feelings, and personal problems is influenced partly by how secure they feel in their social relationships, partly by how much they like the "target person" (the person to whom they are willing to make the disclosure), and by how much the target person is willing to disclose to them.

In addition, if adolescents are to achieve emotional maturity, they must learn to use *emotional catharsis* to clear their systems of pent-up emotional energy. This they can do by strenuous physical exercise, in play or work, by laughing or by crying. While all of these provide an outlet for pent-up emotional energy that accompanies control over emotional expressions, social attitudes toward crying are unfavorable, as they are toward laughing, unless the laughter is held in check and occurs only when the social group approves.

SOCIAL CHANGES DURING ADOLESCENCE

One of the most difficult developmental tasks of adolescence relates to social adjustments. These adjustments must be made to members of the opposite sex in a relationship that never existed before and to adults outside the family and school environments.

To achieve the goal of adult patterns of socialization, the adolescent must make many new adjustments, the most important—and, in many respects, the most difficult—of which are those to the increased influence of the peer group, changes in social behavior, new social groupings, new values in friendship selection, new values in social acceptance and rejection, and new values in the selection of leaders (56).

Increased Peer-Group Influence

Because adolescents spend most of their time outside the home with members of the peer group, it is understandable that peers would have a greater influence on adolescent attitudes, speech, interests, appearance, and behavior than the family has. Most adolescents, for example, discover that if they wear the same type of clothes as popular group members wear, their chances of acceptance are enhanced (96,

109). Similarly, if members of the peer group experiment with alcohol, drugs, or tobacco, adolescents are likely to do the same, regardless of how they feel about these matters.

Horrocks and Benimoff (67) have explained peer-group influence in adolescence in this way:

The peer group is the adolescent's real world, providing him a stage upon which to try out himself and others. It is in the peer group that he continues to formulate and revise his concept of self; it is here that he is evaluated by others who are presumably his equals and who are unable to impose upon him the adult world sanctions from which he is typically struggling to free himself. The peer group offers the adolescent a world in which he may socialize in a climate where the values that count are those that are set, not by adults, but by others of his own age. Thus, it is in the society of his peers that the adolescent finds support for his efforts at emancipation and it is there that he can find a world that enables him to assume leadership if his worth as a person is such that he can assert leadership. In addition, of course, the peer group is the major recreational outlet of the teenager. For all these reasons it would seem of vital importance to the adolescent that his peer group contain a certain number of friends who can accept him and upon whom he can depend.

As adolescence progresses, peer-group influence begins to wane. There are two reasons for this. First, most adolescents want to become individuals in their own right and to be recognized as such. The search for identity, discussed earlier in this chapter, weakens the influence of the peer group on the adolescent. The second reason for waning of peer-group influence is the result of the adolescent's choice of peers as companions. No longer are adolescents interested in large group activities, as was true during their childhood days. In adolescence there is a tendency to narrow down friendships to smaller numbers though most adolescents want to belong to larger social groups for social activities. Because these social activities are less meaningful to adolescents than close, personal friendships, the influence of the larger social group becomes less pronounced than the influence of friends.

Changes in Social Behavior

Of all the changes that take place in social attitudes and behavior, the most pronounced is in the area of heterosexual relationships. In a short period of time, adolescents make the radical shift from disliking members of the opposite sex to preferring their companionship to that of members of their own sex. Social activities, whether with members of the same sex or with the opposite sex, usually reach their peak during the high-school years.

As a result of broader opportunities for social participation, *social insight* improves among older adolescents. They are now able to judge members of the opposite sex as well as members of their own sex better than they could when they were younger. As a result, they make better adjustments in social situations and they quarrel less.

The greater the social participation of adolescents, the greater their *social competency*, as seen in their ability to dance, to carry on conversations, to play sports and games that are popular with age-mates, and to behave correctly in different social situations. As a result, they gain self-confidence which is expressed in poise and ease in social situations.

Whether *prejudice* and *discrimination* will increase or decrease during adolescence will be greatly influenced by the environment in which adolescents find themselves and by the attitudes and behavior of their friends and associates. Because adolescents, as a group, tend to be more "choosey" in the selection of associates and friends than they were as children, they find adolescents of different racial, religious, or socioeconomic backgrounds less congenial than those with similar backgrounds. However, they are more likely to ignore those they find uncongenial than to treat them in a way that expresses their feelings of superiority, as older children do (120).

New Social Groupings

The gangs of childhood gradually break up at puberty and during early adolescence as the individual's interests shift from the strenuous play activities of childhood to the less strenuous and more formal social activities of adolescence. In their place come new social groupings. The social groupings of boys, as a rule, are larger and more loosely knit while those of girls are smaller and more sharply defined. The most common social groupings during adolescence are described in Box 8-2.

There are changes in some of these social groupings as adolescence progresses. Interest in *organized groups*, whose activities are planned and to a

BOX 8-2

ADOLESCENT SOCIAL GROUPINGS

Close Friends

The adolescent usually has two or three close friends, or confidants. They are of the same sex and have similar interests and abilities. Close friends have a marked influence on one another, though they may quarrel occasionally.

Cliques

Cliques are usually made up of groups of close friends. At first they consist of members of the same sex, but later include both boys and girls.

Crowds

Crowds, made up of cliques and groups of close friends, develop as interest in parties and dating grows. Because crowds are large, there is less congeniality of interest among the members and thus a greater social distance between them.

Organized Groups

Adult-directed youth groups are established by schools and community organizations to meet the social needs of adolescents who belong to no cliques or crowds. Many adolescents who join such groups feel regimented and lose interest in them by the time they are sixteen or seventeen.

Gangs

Adolescents who belong to no cliques or crowds and who gain little satisfaction from organized groups may join a gang. Gang members are usually of the same sex, and their main interest is to compensate for peer rejection through antisocial behavior.

are in contact with people of all ages, most of whom have friends and families of their own outside their jobs. Unless noncollege older adolescents have friends from their school days who live and work near enough to make contacts possible, they may find themselves limited to a few friends connected with their work and out of touch with any group large enough to form a crowd.

By contrast, the influence of the *gang* tends to increase as adolescence progresses (113). This influence is often expressed in violent behavior committed by gang members. As Friedman et al. have explained (51):

The authority with which the street gang influences its members represents nearly absolute control of the group over the behavior of the individual. It probably takes relatively few exemplary incidents to convince all of the members that they must either submit to the gang's decisions or face more personally destructive consequences.

New Values in Selection of Friends

Adolescents no longer select their friends on the basis of ready availability at school or in the neighborhood, as they did during childhood, and the enjoyment of the same activities is not such an important factor in friendship selection. Adolescents want as friends those whose interests and values are similar to theirs, who understand them and make them feel secure, and in whom they can confide problems and discuss matters they feel they cannot share with parents or teachers. Figure 8-3 shows how self-disclosure increases in importance as adolescence progresses.

In a study of what adolescents want in their friends, Joseph has pointed out that most adolescents claim they want "someone to be trusted, someone to talk to, someone who is dependable" (73). Because of these changed values, childhood friends will not necessarily be friends in adolescence.

Nor are adolescents interested only in friends of their own sex. Interest in the opposite sex becomes increasingly stronger as adolescence progresses. As a result, by the end of adolescence there is often a preference for friends of the opposite sex, though both boys and girls continue to have a few intimate friends of their own sex with whom they associate constantly.

To most young adolescents, popularity means having a large number of friends. As they grow older,

large extent controlled by adults, wanes rapidly as independence-conscious adolescents resent being told what to do. Only if the control of the activities of these groups is turned over to them, with minimum of adult advice and interference, will interest continue.

Crowds tend to disintegrate in late adolescence and are replaced by loosely associated groups of couples. This is especially true of adolescents who go to work at the completion of high school. At work they

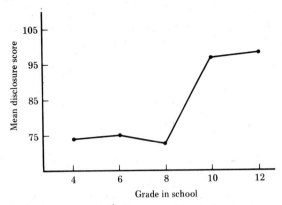

FIGURE 8-3 Self-disclosure to friends becomes an important value used in the selection of friends during adolescence. (Adapted from W. H. Rivenbark. Self-disclosure patterns among adolescents. *Psychological Reports*, 1971, **28,** 35–42. Used by permission.)

the *kind* of friends they have becomes more important than the number. However, adolescent values regarding the "right" kind of friends tend to change from one year to another, depending on the values of the group with which they are identified at that time.

Because adolescents know what they want in their friends, they insist upon the right to select them without adult interference. This often leads to two consequences that interfere with the stability of adolescent friendships. First, as a result of their inexperience—especially with members of the opposite sex—they may choose friends who turn out to be less congenial than they had thought they would be; quarreling often occurs then and friendships are broken.

Second, as in other areas of their lives, adolescents tend to be unrealistic concerning the standards they set up for their friends. They then become critical of them if they do not come up to these standards and try to reform them. This again usually leads to quarreling and the break-up of friendships. In time, most adolescents become more realistic about other people, just as they do about themselves. As a result, they are less critical and more acceptant of their friends.

New Values in Social Acceptance

Just as adolescents have new values concerning their friends, so they have new values concerning acceptable or unacceptable members of different peer groups, such as cliques, crowds, or gangs, for example. These values are based largely on peer-group values which are used to judge members of the group. Adolescents soon discover that they are judged by the same standards by which they judge others.

No one trait or characteristic pattern of behavior will guarantee social acceptance during adolescence. Instead, acceptance depends upon a constellation of traits and behavior patterns—the *acceptance syndrome*—all of which make adolescents fun to be with and add to the prestige of the clique or crowd with which they are identified.

Similarly, no one trait or behavior pattern alienates adolescents from their peers. Instead, there is a grouping of traits—the *alienation syndrome*—that makes others dislike and reject them. Some of the common elements of the acceptance and alienation syndromes in adolescence are given and briefly explained in Box 8-3.

New Values in Selection of Leaders

Because adolescents feel that the leaders of their peer groups represent them in the eyes of society, they therefore want leaders of superior ability who will be admired and respected by others and who, in turn, will reflect favorably on them. Because there are so many different kinds of groups in adolescence—athletic, social, intellectual, religious, and class or community groups—the leader of one group will not necessarily have the ability to be the leader of another. Leadership is now a function of the situation as it is in adult life.

In general, however, adolescents expect their leaders to have certain qualities. While a good physique, in and of itself, does not makes leaders, it gives them prestige and, at the same time, contributes favorably to their self-concepts. The adolescent leader is in excellent health and thus is energetic and eager to do things, both of which contribute to the quality of initiative.

The clothes-conscious adolescent expects leaders to be attractive and well groomed. The characteristic leader will also be slightly above average in intelligence, academic achievement, and level of maturity.

As a rule, leaders in adolescent social activities come from families of higher socioeconomic status than nonleaders. This not only gives them prestige in the eyes of their peers but also makes possible better dressing and grooming, the possession of social

BOX 8-3

CONDITIONS CONTRIBUTING TO ACCEPTANCE AND REJECTION IN ADOLESCENCE

Acceptance Syndrome

- A favorable first impression as a result of an attractive appearance, poise, and cheerfulness
- A reputation as a good sport and one who is fun to be with
- Appearance that conforms to that of peers
- Social behavior characterized by cooperativeness, responsibility, resourcefulness, interest in others, tact, and good manners
- Maturity, especially in terms of emotional control and willingness to conform to rules and regulations
- Personality traits that contribute to good social adjustments, such as truthfulness, sincerity, unselfishness, and extroversion
- A socioeconomic status that is equal to, or slightly above, that of the other group members and a good relationship with family members
- Geographic proximity to the group which permits frequent contacts and participation in group activities

Alienation Syndrome

- An unfavorable first impression as a result of an unattractive appearance or an aloof, self-centered attitude
- A reputation as a poor sport
- Appearance that does not conform to group standards of physical attractiveness or grooming
- Social behavior characterized by showing off, teasing and bullying others, bossiness, uncooperativeness, and lack of tact
- Lack of maturity, especially in the areas of emotional control, poise, self-confidence, and tact
- Personality traits that irritate others, such as selfishness, stubbornness, resentfulness, nervousness and irritability
- A socioeconomic status below that of the group and poor relationships with family members
- Geographic isolation from the peer group or inability to participate in group activities due to family responsibilities or a part-time job

know-how, opportunities for entertaining, and participation in group activities.

Because leaders, as a rule, are more active participants in social life than nonleaders, they develop social insight and self-insight. They can judge themselves realistically and can size up the interests and wishes of the members of the groups they lead. Leaders are not "self-bound" in the sense that they are so concerned with their personal interests and problems that they cannot direct their energies outward and concern themselves with the interests and problems of the other members of their groups.

Perhaps the most important single factor that contributes to leadership is personality. Leaders have been found to be more responsible, more extroverted, more energetic, more resourceful, and more able to take initiative than nonleaders. They are emotionally stable, well-adjusted, happy individuals with few neurotic tendencies (66,107).

SOME ADOLESCENT INTERESTS

There is no such thing as a universal adolescent interest in the American culture of today. The reason for

this is that the interests of adolescents depend upon their sex, their intelligence, the environment in which they live, the opportunities they have had for developing interests, what their peers are interested in, their status in the social group, their innate abilities, the interests of their families, and many other factors. Since girls are expected to behave in a feminine way and boys in a masculine way, it is not surprising that girls' interests during adolescence are usually very different from boys' interests.

As adolescence progresses, many of the interests that were carried over from childhood wane and are replaced by more mature interests. Also, because of the greater responsibilities older adolescents are expected to assume and the consequent decrease in time to spend as they wish, many older adolescents are forced to limit the range of their interests. This is especially true of recreational interests.

Furthermore, with experience most adolescents acquire a different and more mature sense of values. This is reflected in a shift in emphasis on different interests. Interests that were of major importance in early adolescence, such as clothes and appearance, become less important, while interest in a career now

RECREATIONAL INTERESTS OF ADOLESCENTS

Games and Sports

Organized games and sports lose their appeal as adolescence progresses, and the adolescent begins to prefer spectator sports. Games requiring intellectual skill, such as card games, increase in popularity.

Relaxing

Adolescents enjoy relaxing and talking with their friends. They often eat while gossiping and exchanging jokes, and older adolescents may smoke, drink, or take drugs.

Traveling

The adolescent enjoys traveling during vacations and may want to go farther and farther away from home. Parental affluence and youth hostels make travel possible for many adolescents.

Hobbies

Because hobbies are, for the most part, solitary recreational activities, unpopular adolescents are more interested in hobbies than popular ones. Many pursue useful hobbies; girls may make their own clothes, and boys enjoy repairing radios, bicycles, or cars.

Dancing

Although many boys have little interest in dancing, they, like girls, try to become good dancers because it is an important part of dating.

Reading

Because adolescents have limited time for recreational reading, they tend to prefer magazines to books. As adolescence progresses, comic books and comic strips lose some of their appeal, and newspapers gain in popularity.

Movies

Going to the movies is a favorite clique activity and later a popular dating activity. Girls prefer romantic movies, while boys like those dealing with adventure.

Radio and Records

Adolescents enjoy listening to the radio while studying or engaging in solitary forms of amusement. Programs of popular music are the favorites. They also enjoy listening to records.

Television

Television watching loses some of its appeal as adolescence progresses, partly because the adolescent becomes increasingly critical of the programs and partly because the adolescent cannot study or read and watch television simultaneously. Figure 8-4 shows how television program preferences are influenced by those with whom the adolescent views the program (23).

Daydreaming

In a typical adolescent daydream, adolescents see themselves as conquering heroes gaining prestige in the eyes of the peer group by their achievements. Daydreaming is a popular recreation among all adolescents when they are bored or lonely.

becomes dominant. Experience also helps older adolescents to evaluate their interests more critically and to know which are really important. As a result of this critical evaluation, older adolescents tend to stabilize their interests and carry them into adulthood.

In spite of variations, certain adolescent interests are fairly universal in the American culture of today, though they may vary from one part of the country to another and with the different social classes within each area. All young adolescents possess these interests to a greater or lesser extent, and they all have certain specific interests that fall within the different categories, the most important of which are recreational interests, social interests, personal interests, educational interests, vocational interests, religious interests, and interest in status symbols.

Recreational Interests

As adolescence progresses, there is a breaking away from recreations that require much expenditure of energy and the development of a preference for recreations in which the adolescent is a passive spectator. In early adolescence, there is a carry-over of some of the play activities of the early years and the introduction of new and more mature forms of recreation. Gradually, the childish forms of play disappear,

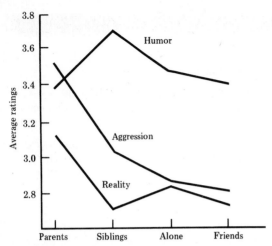

FIGURE 8-4 Adolescent television program preferences are influenced by those with whom the adolescent views the program. (Adapted from S. H. Chaffee and A. R. Tims. Interpersonal factors in adolescent television use. *Journal of Social Issues*, 1976, **32**(4), 98–115. Used by permission.)

and when early adolescence comes to a close, the individual's recreational pattern is much the same as it will be during the latter part of adolescence and the early years of adulthood.

Because of the pressures of schoolwork, home duties, extracurricular activities, and after-school or weekend jobs, most adolescents have far less time for recreation than they did when they were younger. As a result, they select the kinds of activities that they enjoy most or in which they excel. This limits the number of their activities.

The number of recreations adolescents engage in is also greatly influenced by how popular they are. Because many of the recreations of adolescents require participants from the peer group, the adolescent who does not belong to a clique and who has few friends is forced to concentrate on solitary forms of recreation. Box 8-4 describes the favorite recreations of adolescents. Compare these with the play activities of early and late childhood.

Social Interests

Social interests depend partly on what opportunities adolescents have to develop such interests and partly on how popular they are with members of the peer group. An adolescent whose family's socio-economic status is low, for example, will have fewer opportunities to develop an interest in parties and dancing than adolescents from more favorable home backgrounds. Similarly, an adolescent who is unpopular will have a limited repertoire of social interests. However, certain social interests are almost universal among American adolescents of today, seven of which are described in Box 8-5.

Personal Interests

Interest in themselves is the strongest interest young adolescents have, partly because they realize that their social acceptance is markedly influenced by their general appearance, and partly because they know the social group judges them in terms of their material possessions, independence, and school and social affiliations, as well as the amount of spending money they have. These are "status symbols" that will enhance young adolescents' prestige in the eyes of peers and hence increase their chances for greater social acceptance.

Interest in Appearance Interest in appearance covers not only clothes but personal adornment, grooming, attractive and sex-appropriate physical features. Cross and Cross have explained why appearance is so important that it becomes a dominant personal interest. According to them, "Beauty and physical attractiveness are of great practical importance for human beings. Social acceptance, popularity, mate selection and careers are all affected by an individual's physical attractiveness" (29). Kernan has emphasized the social value of appearance in this way: "As children develop, the appearance they present—especially to their peers—is a strong indication of their interest in socialization" (83). The reason is that it is a proof of their togetherness with their peers.

Interest in Clothes Because their personal and social adjustments are greatly influenced by their age-mates' attitudes toward their clothes, most adolescents are anxious to conform to what the group approves of in the matter of dress. As Ryan has pointed out, "One of the primary requirements of clothing for the young adolescent is that their clothing meets the approval of the peer group" (137).

While boys claim not to be interested in clothes, grooming, or appearance, their behavior indicates that their interest is greater than they will

BOX 8-5

COMMON SOCIAL INTERESTS OF ADOLESCENTS

Parties

Interest in parties with members of the opposite sex first manifests itself at about age thirteen or fourteen. Girls enjoy parties more than boys throughout adolescence.

Drinking

Drinking on dates or at parties becomes increasingly more popular as adolescence progresses. Girls rarely drink with members of their own sex, as boys do.

Drugs

While far from universal, the use of drugs is a popular clique and party activity, beginning in early adolescence. Many adolescents try drugs because it is the "thing to do," although few become addicts.

Conversations

All adolescents derive a sense of security from getting together with a group of peers and talking about the things that interest or disturb them. Such get-togethers provide an opportunity to blow off emotional steam and get a new perspective on their problems.

Helping Others

Many young adolescents are sincerely interested in trying to help people they feel have been misunderstood, mistreated, or oppressed. As adolescence progresses, this interest wanes for two reasons. First, adolescents start to feel that there is nothing they can do to right these wrongs and, second, they feel that their attempts are often unappreciated.

World Affairs

Through courses in school and the mass media, adolescents often develop an interest in government, politics, and world affairs. They express this interest mainly through reading and discussions with their peers, teachers, and parents.

Criticism and Reform

Almost all young adolescents, but especially girls, become critical and attempt to reform their parents, peers, schools, and communities. Their criticisms are generally destructive rather than constructive, and their suggestions for reform are usually impractical.

---

admit. Like girls, they recognize that appearance plays an important role in social acceptance. This interest is heightened when they reach the end of their schooling and prepare to enter the world of work. They realize that an attractive appearance facilitates their getting and holding a job.

Interest in Achievements Achievements bring personal satisfaction as well as social recognition. That is why achievements, whether in sports, school work, or social activities become such a strong interest as adolescence progresses.

However, if achievements are to bring satisfaction to adolescents, they must be in areas that are important to their peers and carry prestige in the eyes of the peer group. If their peers are interested in academic success, for example, good grades will be a satisfactory achievement. If, on the other hand, little prestige is associated with good grades and much

prestige with athletic success, academic achievements will bring little satisfaction to the adolescent (129, 167).

Adolescents tend to aspire unrealistically high. Therefore they often do not get the satisfaction from their achievements that they would get if their aspirations were more realistic. When they fail to reach their goals, their achievements bring them little satisfaction.

Interest in Independence A strong desire for independence develops in early adolescence and reaches a peak as this period draws to a close. This leads to many clashes with parents and other adults in authority. Because girls are expected to conform more to parental wishes than boys are, they rebel more against home restraints. Much of the radicalism of young adolescents can be traced to their attempts to think and act independently. If, however, adult authority is relaxed gradually, so that adolescents can see themselves reaching their goals, there is far less rebellion with its accompanying friction (8,49).

Interest in Money   Every adolescent sooner or later discovers that money is the key to independence. As long as parents pay their bills and give them spending money, parents can control adolescents' behavior. When, on the other hand, adolescents have money they have earned themselves, they can enjoy independence. Interest in money therefore becomes an important element in independence. This interest centers mainly on how to earn the most money possible, regardless of the kind of work done.

Educational Interests

Typically, *young adolescents* complain about school in general and about restrictions, homework, required courses, food in the cafeteria, and the way the school is run. They are critical of their teachers and the way they teach. This is the "thing to do." Young adolescents who want to be popular with their peers must avoid creating the impression that they are "brains." This is even more important for girls than for boys because less prestige is associated with academic achievement among girls than among boys. However, in spite of their stated attitudes, most young adolescents get along well both academically and socially in school and they secretly like it.

The attitudes of *older adolescents* toward education are greatly influenced by their vocational interests. If they are aspiring to occupations which require education beyond high school, they will regard education as a stepping-stone. They will be interested in the courses they feel will be useful to them in their chosen field of work. As is true of the younger adolescent, the older adolescent considers success in sports and social life as important as academic work as a stepping-stone to future success. Many factors influence the younger as well as the older adolescent's attitude toward education; the most important of these are given in Box 8-6.

There are three types of adolescents who have little interest in education and who usually dislike school. They are, first, adolescents whose parents have unrealistically high aspirations for their academic, athletic, or social achievements and who are constantly prodding them to come up to these goals (82). The second type are those who find little acceptance among their classmates and who, as a

FIGURE 8-5   For many adolescents, interest in school subjects is influenced by how relevant they perceive the subject to be. (George Clark. "The Neighbors." Chicago Tribune-New York News Syndicate, Dec. 6, 1965. Used by permission.)

"I can guess YOUR question, Bivins. How can the study of ancient conquests help you make a buck?"

result, feel that they are missing out on the fun their age-mates are having in extracurricular activities (11). Third, early maturers who feel conspicuously large among their classmates and who, because they look older than they actually are, are often expected to do better academic work than they are capable of (33).

Adolescents who have little interest in education usually show their lack of interest in the following ways. They become *underachievers,* working below their capacities in all school subjects or in the subjects they lack interest in. Others who are disinterested in education become truants and try to gain parental permission to withdraw from school before the legal age for leaving. Still others become dropouts as soon as they reach the legal age of school leaving, regardless of whether they have finished the present grade. This is especially true of early maturers who find school not only uninteresting but often a humiliating experience.

Vocational Interests

Boys and girls of high school age begin to think seriously about their futures. Boys are usually more seriously concerned about an occupation than girls, many of whom regard a job as just a stopgap until marriage (70).

Boys, typically, want glamorous and exciting jobs, regardless of the ability required or the chances that such jobs will be available for them. They also want jobs with high prestige, even if they pay less than those with lower prestige. Many boys from low-status families hope to achieve higher social status through their occupations. Girls, as a rule, show a preference for occupations with greater security and less demand on their time. In their vocational choices, they usually stress service to others, such as teaching or nursing (124).

By late adolescence, interest in a life career has often become a source of great concern. At this time, as Thomas has explained, adolescents learn to distinguish between vocational choice, vocational preference, and vocational aspirations (158). Older adolescents are concerned about what they would like to do and what they are capable of doing. The more they hear and talk about different lines of work, the less sure they are of what they would like to do. They are also concerned about how they can get the kind of jobs they want.

Furthermore, older adolescents have a growing realization of how much it costs to live and they also know what young people, just out of school, can expect to earn. As a result of this greater realism, they approach the choice of their careers with a more practical and more realistic attitude than they had when they were younger.

During childhood and early adolescence, many boys and girls judge different lines of work, such as law and medicine, in terms of the stereotypes presented in the mass media. As near-adults, they begin to judge them in terms of their abilities and of the time and money required for training for these lines of work. While prestige is still an important factor in vocational selection, the older adolescent is more concerned about the autonomy, authority, and security the occupation will give (115).

Because their attitudes toward vocations have gradually become more realistic, most adolescents change their minds often about their future occupations. They are in an "exploratory stage" and may take after-school or summer jobs in fields they think might interest them as a lifetime career. This experience gives them more information on which to base their final decisions.

Religious Interests

Contrary to popular opinion, adolescents of today are interested in religion and feel that it plays an important role in their lives. They talk about religion, take courses in it in school and in college, visit churches of different denominations, and join various religious cults.

Many boys and girls begin to question the religious concepts and beliefs of their childhood and this has led adolescence to be called the *period of religious doubt.* However, Wagner maintains that what is often interpreted as "religious doubt" is, in reality, *religious questioning.* According to him (170):

Many adolescents investigate their religion as a source of emotional and intellectual stimulation. Youngsters want to learn their religion on an intellectual basis rather than by blind acceptance. They question religion not because they want to become agnostic or atheistic, but because they want to accept religion in a way that is meaningful to them—based on their desire to be independent and free to make their own decisions.

On the other hand, adolescents now attend church, Sunday school, and church social events far less than adolescents of previous generations. This suggests that many of them are disillusioned with organized religion, but not uninterested in religion per se. Jones has explained, "There is more a decrease in enthusiasm and in positive feeling *for* the church than an increase in antagonism *against* it." He say further that the change in interest in religion in adolescence reflects not a lack of belief but "a disillusionment with the church establishment and the use of its beliefs and preachments in the solution of current social, civic, and economic problems" (72).

The changes in religious interest during adolescence are even more radical than the changes in vocational interests. Like childhood vocational interests, childhood concepts of religion are basically unrealistic, and the adolescent may become critical of earlier beliefs. The pattern of changes in religious interest and their effect on behavior are given in Box 8-7.

Interest in Status Symbols

Status symbols are prestige symbols that tell others that the person who has them is superior or has a higher status in the group than other group members. During adolescence, status symbols serve four important functions: they tell others that the adolescent has a high or even a higher socioeconomic status than other members of the peer group; that the adolescent is superior in some achievement that is valued by the group; that the adolescent is affiliated with the group and is an accepted member of it because of appearance or actions similar to those of other group members; and that the adolescent has a near-adult status in society (165).

If, for example, adolescents have cars of their own as soon as they are legally able to drive; if their families have large homes in prestigious neighborhoods; and if they have money to spend without having to work for it, these proclaim the superior socioeconomic status of the adolescent. Boys who belong to the school team in a prestigious sport, such as baseball or football, proclaim to their peers their importance in the school group (41).

Because being grown up or near-adult means so much to almost all American adolescents of today, a new type of status symbol has become popular among them. It is known as engaging in *tabooed pleasures* —forms of recreation that are thought of as symbolic of adults, and which parents and teachers maintain adolescents are "too young" to engage in. The most common tabooed pleasures American adolescents engage in to symbolize their near-adult status

and their identity with the peer group are premarital sex, smoking, drinking, and use of different types of drugs.

Smoking often begins in junior high school or even before. By the time boys and girls reach senior high school, smoking is a widespread practice for different social activities and even in forbidden areas, such as on the school grounds. Adolescents feel that

To an adolescent, smoking is a symbol of maturity. (Photo by Erika.)

they must conform to peer-group norms rather than to adult or institutional authority if they want others to identify them with the peer group and think of them as no longer children but near-adults (134).

Unlike adolescents of earlier generations, *drinking* has become a status symbol for girls as well as for boys. It begins earlier now, during the junior high school years, and sometimes at the end of the elementary school years. At first, most drinking is of beer but the so-called "hard liquor" gradually replaces beer.

Relatively few adolescents are solitary drinkers; drinking is a peer-group activity. Because it is limited mainly to peer activities during the adolescent years, it is unusual for adolescents to become so addicted to drinking that they could be regarded as "alcoholics." However, the taste for liquor is developed during the adolescent years as is the tendency to regard drinking as an important symbol of group belonging. Under such conditions, the basis for chronic alcoholism is, among many girls as well as among many boys, often laid during the adolescent years. Whether they be-

come alcoholics as they grow older will depend upon many conditions in their lives at that time (48,104, 112).

As with drinking, the use of *drugs* begins as a peer-group activity. Even in the higher grades of elementary school and in junior high school, the smoking of marijuana is not unusual. As adolescents progress through high school and into college, the use of drugs at parties and other social get-togethers becomes more frequent and more widespread—for girls as well as boys. Even more important, what starts out as an occasional smoking of marijuana often develops into a persistent pattern, not occasionally but daily. In addition, many adolescents are not satisfied with marijuana and start to use other drugs that are more likely to be habit-forming and harmful to health (60,77). Figure 8-6 shows the ages for the first use of different types of drugs and the relationship of these ages to the first use of wine or beer, hard liquor, or tobacco.

Studies of why adolescents begin to use drugs have revealed that there are reasons other than the

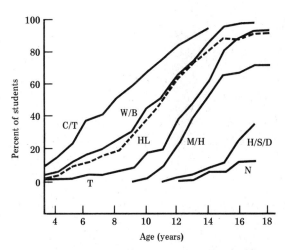

C/T = coffee or tea; W/B = wine or beer; HL = hard liquor; T = tobacco; M/H = marijuana or hashish; H/S/D = hallucinogens, stimulants, or depressants; and N = narcotics.

FIGURE 8-6 Distribution of ages at first use of drugs and their relationship to use of tobacco and liquor. (Adapted from B. A. Hamburg, H. C. Kraemer, and W. Jahnke. A hierarchy of drug use in adolescence: Behavioral and attitudinal correlates of substantial drug use. *American Journal of Psychiatry*, 1975, **132**, 1155–1163. Used by permission.)

status-symbol value drugs have. Many adolescents are motivated by a desire for independence from family restrictions; by a desire to increase their social acceptance by conforming to the pattern of behavior set by leaders in the peer group; or by a desire for adventure (78,88,146). That many adolescents are motivated to use drugs out of boredom is shown by the fact that use of drugs is greater in suburban than in urban areas. This is because most adolescents complain that there is nothing to do in the suburbs (78, 88).

Almost all adolescents will use drugs occasionally, out of curiosity or a desire to conform to the patterns of behavior that are popular among members of the crowd. But there are certain types of adolescents who are likely to become more than occasional users of drugs. Among such types are those who are dissatisfied with their home conditions; those who lack social acceptance in the prestigious crowds of their schools; and those who experience many problems characteristic of adolescence which they have not been able to cope with satisfactorily (71). Boys who belong to gangs tend to be the heaviest users of drugs (51,113). Girls, except those who belong to gangs, use drugs far less than boys. When they do use drugs, they are usually initiated into their use by boys and they limit their use to times when they are with them (51,71).

Gulas and King, from studies of the personality patterns of users and nonusers of drugs during the adolescent years, have come to the conclusion that there are certain personality characteristics that distinguish users from nonusers. These characteristics also differ for adolescents who limit their use of drugs to marijuana and those who use other drugs in addition (57). These personality differences are shown in Figure 8-7.

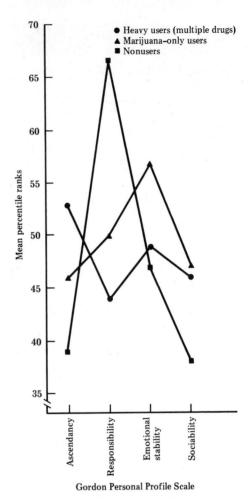

FIGURE 8-7 Some personality characteristics of users of drugs and nonusers. (Adapted from I. Gulas and F. W. King. On the question of pre-existing personality differences between users and nonusers of drugs. *Journal of Psychology*, 1976, **92,** 65–69. Used by permission.)

CHANGES IN MORALITY DURING ADOLESCENCE

One of the important developmental tasks adolescents must master is learning what the group expects of them and then being willing to mold their behavior to conform to these expectations without the constant guidance, supervision, proddings, and threats of punishment they experienced as children. They are expected to replace the specific moral concepts of childhood with general moral principles and to for-

mulate these into a moral code which will act as a guide to their behavior. Equally important, they must now exercise control over their behavior, a responsibility that was formerly assumed by parents and teachers. Mitchell has listed the five fundamental changes in morality adolescents must make (106). These are given in Box 8-8.

By adolescence, boys and girls have reached what Piaget has called the *stage of formal operations* in cognitive ability. They are now capable of con-

FUNDAMENTAL CHANGES IN MORALITY DURING ADOLESCENCE

- The individual's moral outlook becomes progressively more abstract and less concrete.
- Moral convictions become more concerned with what is right and less concerned with what is wrong. Justice emerges as a dominant moral force.
- Moral judgment becomes increasingly cognitive. This encourages the adolescent to analyze social and personal codes more vigorously than during childhood and to decide on moral issues.
- Moral judgment becomes less egocentric.
- Moral judgment becomes psychologically expensive in the sense that it takes an emotional toll and creates psychological tension.

sidering all possible ways of solving a particular problem and can reason on the basis of hypotheses or propositions. Thus they can look at their problems from several points of view and can take many factors into account when solving them (121).

According to Kohlberg, the third level of moral development, *postconventional morality,* should be reached during adolescence. This is the level of self-accepted principles, and it consists of two stages. In the first stage, the individual believes that there should be a flexibility in moral beliefs to make it possible to modify and change moral standards if this will be advantageous to group members as a whole. In the second stage, individuals conform to both social standards and to internalized ideals to avoid self-condemnation rather than to avoid social censure. In this stage, morality is based on respect for others rather than on personal desires (85).

Even with the best foundations, the three major tasks in achieving adult morality—replacing specific concepts with general moral concepts, formulating these newly developed concepts into a moral code as a guideline for behavior, and assuming control over one's own behavior—are difficult for many adolescents. Some fail to make the shift to adult morality during adolescence and must finish this task in early adulthood. Others not only fail to make the shift but

they build a moral code on socially unacceptable moral concepts.

Changes in Moral Concepts

Two conditions make the replacement of specific moral concepts with generalized concepts of right and wrong more difficult than it should be. The first is lack of guidance in learning how to generalize specific concepts. Believing that adolescents have already learned the major principles of right and wrong, parents and teachers frequently put little emphasis on teaching them to see the relationship between the specific principles they learned earlier and the general principles that are essential to control over behavior in adult life. Only in new areas of behavior, such as relationships with members of the opposite sex, do adults feel that there is any real need for further moral training (92).

The second condition that makes the replacement of specific moral concepts with generalized ones difficult has to do with the kind of discipline the adolescent is subjected to at home and in school. Because parents and teachers assume that adolescents know what is right, their major emphasis in discipline is on punishment for what they regard as intentional misbehavior. Little emphasis is placed on explaining to the adolescent why certain things are right and others wrong, and even less is placed on rewarding the adolescent for doing the right thing (20,80).

Building a Moral Code

When they reach adolescence, children will no longer accept in an unquestioning way a moral code handed down to them by parents, teachers, or even their contemporaries. They now want to build their own moral codes on the basis of concepts of right and wrong which they have changed and modified to meet their more mature level of development and which they have supplemented with laws and rules learned from parents and teachers. Some adolescents even supplement their moral codes with knowledge derived from their religious teaching (90).

Building a moral code is difficult for adolescents because of inconsistencies in standards of right and wrong they encounter in daily life. These inconsistencies confuse them and impede their progress in building a moral code which is not only satisfactory to them but which will also lead to socially approved behavior. Sooner or later, most adolescents discover, for example, that peers of different socioeconomic, religious, or racial backgrounds have different codes of right and wrong; that their parents' and teachers' codes are often stricter than those of their contemporaries; and that in spite of the breaking down of the traditional sex-approved roles, there is still a "double standard" which is far more lenient for boys than for girls.

While older children may condemn lying on moral grounds, many adolescents feel that "social lies," or lies told to avoid hurting other people's feelings, are sometimes justified. Much the same sort of confusion is apparent in high school and college students' attitudes toward cheating. Many feel that since it is so widespread, their contemporaries must condone it, and they also claim that it is justified when they are pressured to get good grades in order to be accepted by a college and thus succeed socially and economically in later life. As interest in members of the opposite sex increases, adolescents discover that certain patterns of behavior are not only approved but even applauded for boys while they are harshly condemned for girls.

Inner Control of Behavior

Because parents and teachers cannot watch adolescents as closely as they did when they were children, adolescents must now assume responsibility for control over their own behavior. While it was formerly believed that fear—either of punishment or of social disapproval—was the best deterrent to wrongdoing, today it is recognized that "outer-controlled" sources of motivation are effective only when there is a possiblity that others will find out about the misbehavior and punish those responsible for it.

Studies of juvenile delinquents, for example, have revealed that punishment not only does not deter willful wrongdoing but also often contributes to it. There is also evidence that fear of being shamed loses its effectiveness as a deterrent to misbehavior when there is little likelihood that others will know of the misbehavior, or if individuals feel they will be able to rationalize their actions or project the blame for them on others, and thus avoid punishment or social disapproval (161, 176).

Studies of moral development have emphasized that the only effective way people of any age can control their own behavior is through the development of a *conscience*—an inner force that makes external controls unnecessary. When children

or adolescents learn to associate pleasant emotions with group-approved behavior, and unpleasant emotions with group-disapproved behavior, they will have the necessary motivation to behave in accordance with group standards. Under such conditions, individuals feel guilty when they realize that their behavior is falling below social expectations, while shame is aroused only when they are aware of unfavorable judgments of their behavior by members of the social group. Behavior that is controlled by guilt is thus inner-controlled while that controlled by shame is outer-controlled (7,45).

In morally mature individuals, both guilt and shame are present. However, guilt plays a more important role than shame in controlling the individual's behavior in the absence of external control. Relatively few adolescents reach this level and, as a result, they cannot correctly be called "morally mature" people (90).

SEX INTERESTS AND SEX BEHAVIOR DURING ADOLESCENCE

To master the important developmental tasks of forming new and more mature relationships with members of the opposite sex, and of playing the approved role for one's own sex, young adolescents must acquire more mature and more complete concepts of sex than they had as children. The motivation to do so comes partly from social pressures but mainly from the adolescent's interest in and curiosity about sex.

Because of their growing interest in sex, adolescent boys and girls seek more and more information about it. Few adolescents feel that they can learn all they want to know about sex from their parents (see Figure 8-8). Consequently they take advantage of whatever sources of information are available to them—sex hygiene courses in school or college, discussions with their friends, books on sex, or experimentation through masturbation, petting, or intercourse. By the end of adolescence, most boys and girls have enough information about sex to satisfy their curiosity.

Studies of what adolescents are primarily interested in knowing about sex have revealed that girls are especially curious about birth control, the "Pill," abortion, and pregnancy. Boys, on the other hand, want to know about venereal diseases, enjoyment of

"Well, so much for the birds and the bees, Mom. Now how about teen-age boys?"

FIGURE 8-8 Few adolescents feel that the sex information they receive from parents is adequate. (George Clark. "The Neighbors." Chicago Tribune-New York News Syndicate, Oct. 22, 1971. Used by permission.)

sex, sexual intercourse, and birth control. Their major interest is in sexual intercourse, its context and its consequences (149, 151).

Development of Heterosexuality

The first developmental task relating to sex adolescents must master is forming new and more mature relationships with members of the opposite sex. This is far from easy for both boys and girls, after the years during late childhood when members of the two sexes had their own gangs and interests, and during puberty when both boys and girls developed attitudes of resentment against members of the opposite sex.

Now that they are sexually mature, both boys and girls begin to have new attitudes toward members of the opposite sex, and to develop an interest not only in members of the opposite sex but also in activities in which they are involved. This new interest, which begins to develop when sexual maturation is complete, is romantic in nature and is accompanied by a strong desire to win the approval of members of the opposite sex. Gradually, this desire takes the

place of the desire that dominated in childhood—the desire to win the approval and acceptance of members of the same sex.

Development of interest in members of the opposite sex—*heterosexuality*—follows a predictable pattern. However, there are variations in ages at which the adolescent reaches different stages in this development, partly because of differences in age of sexual maturing and partly because of differences in opportunities to develop this interest. Interest in members of the opposite sex is also markedly influenced by patterns of interest among the adolescent's friends. If they are interested in activities involving members of both sexes, the adolescent must also be able to retain status in the peer group.

There are two separate and distinct elements in the development of heterosexuality. The first is the development of patterns of behavior involving members of the two sexes and the second is the development of attitudes relating to relationships between members of the two sexes.

In past generations, these two aspects of heterosexuality were rigidly prescribed by tradition and little leeway was given to adolescents to deviate from these prescribed patterns of behavior and attitudes. There was, for example, a socially approved pattern of behavior known as "courtship," and any deviation from this pattern, either in behavior or in timing, was frowned upon. Those involved were subjected to social disapproval or scorn.

It was not, for example, considered proper for boys to kiss girls on their first dates. When girls permitted or encouraged this, boys often regarded them as "easy marks"—a label that did not encourage them to consider the girls seriously as future mates.

Similarly, there were socially approved attitudes both boys and girls were expected to have toward members of the opposite sex and toward their relationships with each other. These attitudes were colored by unrealism and were highly romanticized. Instead of seeing boys as boys, similar in some respects and different in others from girls, boys were romanticized to the point where they were not recognizable as boys but rather were thought of as "conquering heroes." The tendency to romanticize girls was even more pronounced. It used to be said that boys in love put their girls on pedestals and literally worshiped them.

These highly romanticized attitudes were also

present in activities in which both sexes were involved. In the past, a date with a girl meant getting dressed up, taking her a gift of candy, flowers, or a book, seeing her under the parental roof, and leaving at a prescribed time. Attitudes toward what young people did on dates were also carefully prescribed. Kissing and petting were considered in bad taste if not actually wrong unless the couple was engaged. Even then, petting was very limited and within the bounds of what was regarded as "proper" and "safe."

New social attitudes toward sex, the ready availability of contraceptive devices, and the legalization of abortion in many states have brought about radical changes in sexual behavior during adolescence and in attitudes toward sex and sexual behavior. While these changes are by no means universal, they are widespread enough to be regarded as "typical" of adolescents today in urban and suburban centers and, to a lesser extent, in small towns and rural communities.

New Patterns of Heterosexuality There are two features that distinguish adolescent heterosexuality today from that of past generations. These are the telescoping of stages in heterosexual behavior, and greater permissiveness. For the most part, adolescents now follow a pattern of development in their heterosexual behavior similar to the traditional pattern, though they pass from one stage of the pattern to another far more quickly than in the past. Kissing on the first date today, for example, is common. In the past, this might readily jeopardize a beginning relationship between a boy and a girl.

When adolescents prefer alternate lifestyles, especially in the later stages of heterosexual behavior, they often have negative attitudes toward marriage, due to unfavorable parent-child relationships or negative perceptions of marriage, based on their parents' marriage. As Stinnett and Taylor have explained: "Many youths turn to alternate life styles in an attempt to find the close relationship which they have not found in their own families" (155).

Dating starts earlier today than in past generations and it quickly develops into a going-steady relationship. It is not unusual, for example, for dating to begin when girls are thirteen years old and the going-steady stage to occur before they are fourteen (91, 149).

Dating serves many purposes in the lives of today's adolescents, the most common of which are explained in Box 8-9. Because dating serves different purposes, it is understandable that adolescents want different types of partners for different types of dating. This is also explained in Box 8-9.

Many young adolescents prefer going steady to playing the field because it gives them a feeling of security to know that they have an available partner for all social activities. Larson et al., after studying boys and girls in high school, concluded that those who were going steady not only feel personally insecure but also have lower educational-occupational aspirations than those who were not going steady at so early an age (91).

Going steady does not necessarily involve plans for the future or a committment to marry. It does, however, sanction advanced forms of sexual behavior (149,151). The usual pattern of sexual behavior in dating and going steady is illustrated in Figure 8-9. Learning the accepted dating code of the peer group is part of adolescent socialization (28). It is an accepted form of behavior, for example, to kiss on the first date and to begin petting then or on a subsequent date. Since adolescents begin to date and go steady earlier today than in the past, they engage in different forms of sexual intimacy at earlier ages, and intercourse is common among couples who go steady.

With the trend toward coeducational dormitories in many colleges and universities, the relaxing of restrictions on visiting hours in segregated dormitories and of requirements for residence in campus dormitories, and the widespread practice among adolescents of traveling together in unchaperoned groups composed of members of both sexes, living together in a premarital relationship is becoming an accepted pattern among older adolescents in college. This is also true of older adolescents who go to work after completing high school and live apart from their parents in order to enjoy a freedom they would not otherwise have. There is also a growing trend toward communal living, patterned after the lifestyle of the so-called Hippie culture (39,149).

The changed pattern of sexual behavior among today's adolescents is not regarded by them as wrong or as promiscuous because usually they have only

Kissing ⟶ Light petting ⟶ Heavy petting ⟶ Coitus

FIGURE 8-9 Pattern of sexual intimacy in dating and going steady.

COMMON REASONS FOR DATING DURING ADOLESCENCE

Recreation

When dating is for recreation, adolescents want their partners to have the social skills members of the peer group consider important: to be good sports and pleasant companions. In the case of boys, having a car or access to one and money to spend are essential.

Socialization

When peer-group members divide into dating couples, boys and girls must date if they are to be accepted members of the peer group and enjoy its social activities. Dating partners must want to participate in social activities and have the social skills, time, money, and independence needed for participation in these activities.

Status

Dating for both boys and girls, especially when it takes the form of going steady, gives them status in the peer group. The more popular the dating partner is with members of the peer group and the more prestigious the socioeconomic status of the dating partner's family in the community, the more this will reflect favorably on the adolescent. Dating under such conditions is primarily a stepping-stone to higher status in the peer group.

Courtship

In the courtship pattern of adolescence, dating plays a dominant role. Because adolescents are in love and hope and plan to marry eventually, they give serious thought to the suitablity of the dating partner as a future mate.

Mate Selection

Adolescents who want to marry when they complete high school and have no plans for higher education look upon dating as an opportunity to try out different dating partners to see if they have the qualities they want in their future mates. Major emphasis is put on compatibility of interests and temperament and on ways of showing affection. This justifies, in their minds, heavy petting and coitus. Many adolescents who are interested in early marriage regard dating as a trial-and-error way to pick out their future mates.

one sexual partner at a time whom, in most cases, they expect to marry at some time in the future. Even when parents object to these relationships, many adolescents continue to maintain them.

There are many reasons for this new pattern of sexual behavior. Among these are the belief that it is the "thing to do" because everyone else does it; that girls and boys who are still virgins by the time they reach senior year in high school are "different," and to adolescents this means "inferior"; that they must comply with pressures from the peer group if they wish to maintain their status in the group; and that such behavior is an expression of a meaningful relationship which fills the need every adolescent has for a close association with others, especially when this need is not filled by family relationships.

New Attitudes toward Sexual Behavior Marked as changes in sexual behavior are, changes in sexual attitudes are even more pronounced. Behavior which, scarcely a generation age, would shock adolescents if it occurred among their peers, and give them feelings of guilt and shame if it occurred in their own lives, now are taken for granted as right and normal, or at least permissible. Even premarital intercourse is regarded as "right" if the individuals involved are deeply in love and committed to each other. Coitus with affection is more acceptable than petting without affection (105).

In the past, girls who engaged in heavy petting and intercourse lost the respect of boys even though they may have been more popular as dating partners than girls who refused to engage in these forms of sexual behavior. Today, adolescent boys maintain that marrying a virgin is unimportant to them, though they tend to lose respect for girls who are too promiscuous and too permissive. Thus, the "double standard" is gradually giving way to a single standard which holds for girls as well as for boys.

Accompanying these changed attitudes are strong ideas about right and wrong in regard to sexual behavior. Behavior which adolescents feel is "right" is accompanied by favorable attitudes, while behavior they feel is "wrong" is accompanied by unfavorable attitudes.

Adolescents of today feel that expressions of love, regardless of the form the expression takes, are good, provided both partners feel strongly about each other. On the other hand, if love is missing and sexual behavior is engaged in only because others do it, or because it is the way for a girl to ensure having a date for social events, or for excitement, they regard this as wrong. They also regard it as wrong for a boy to force a girl to engage in intercourse if she is unwilling or for a girl to use intercourse as a way to force a boy into marriage (39,105,149).

There are also new social attitudes toward premarital pregnancy and toward keeping the child, even when there is no intention on the part of the parents to marry. Today, some parents accept daughters with illegitimate children and share in the care and expenses involved in the care. Other adolescents, when they become aware of pregnancy, marry even though they are still students and have no independent source of support.

Older adolescents in urban and suburban communities have a more permissive attitude toward living together without marriage—*cohabitation*—than those in small towns or rural districts. Older adolescents in college tend to cohabit more frequently than those who go to work when they finish high school. Living together without marriage is also more common and more condoned by peers among older adolescents than among younger adolescents who are still living under the parental roof and have not yet reached the legal age of school leaving.

APPROVED SEX ROLES DURING ADOLESCENCE

The second developmental task relating to sexuality adolescents must master is learning to play approved sex roles. This is even more difficult for many adolescents, especially for girls, than mastering the first developmental task relating to sexuality—learning to get along with age-mates of the opposite sex.

As was pointed out earlier, sex-role typing or learning to play socially approved sex roles is easier for boys than for girls. First, since early childhood boys have been made aware of sexually appropriate behavior and have been encouraged, prodded, or

even shamed into conforming to the approved standards. Second, boys discover with each passing year that the male role carries far more prestige than the female role.

Girls, by contrast, often reach adolescence with blurred concepts of the female role, though their concepts of the male role are clearer and better defined. This is because, as children, they were permitted to look, act, and feel much as boys without constant proddings to be "feminine." Even when they learn what society expects of them, their motivation to mold their behavior in accordance with the traditional female role is weak because they realize that this role is far less prestigious than the male role and even less prestigious than the role they played as children.

Sex education courses in junior and senior high school are important in fostering concepts of the traditional roles of males and females. They emphasize that the feminine role is family-orientated and that women derive satisfaction from being wives, mothers, and homemakers rather than from success in the business and professional worlds (35,154). Many adolescent girls, as a result of such training and pressures from peers, especially peers of the opposite sex, are, as Deutsch and Gilbert have explained, "pulled toward opposing goals, a situation ripe for conflict" (35).

If adolescent girls rebel against the traditional female role, they may be rejected not only by members of the opposite sex but also by other girls. Before early adolescence is over, most girls accept, often reluctantly, the stereotype of the female role as a model for their own behavior and pretend to be completely "feminine," even though they prefer an egalitarian role that combines features of both the male and the female roles. This is a price they are willing to pay, temporarily at least, for social acceptance.

Rosen and Aneshensel have labeled as the *chameleon syndrome* the pretending to be feminine, the willingness, regardless of actual feelings about the traditional female role, to play the role in order to enjoy the social acceptance of members of both sexes and the conforming to the accepted patterns of the environment. They maintain that this is a family-instigated pattern of behavior. According to them, the chameleon syndrome originates in the family—a product of the process in which parents instruct daughters on the behavior and attitudes appropriate to their sex (132).

Because the women's liberation movement has concentrated on achieving equality for women in the business and professional fields and in marriage, it has had little impact, to date, on younger adolescents' attitudes toward sex roles. However, the influence of this movement is beginning to be felt among older adolescents who go to college or begin training for business or a career, or who marry or go to work at the completion of high school. Older adolescent girls no longer meekly accept or pretend to accept the traditional female sex role. Instead, they expect, demand, and achieve a more egalitarian role, whether in school, at work, or in their own homes.

Effects of Sex-Role Typing on Adolescents

Sex-role typing affects the behavior and attitudes of both male and female adolescents but in different ways. Of the many effects, four are so common that they are almost universal in the American culture of today. They are as follows.

Feelings of Masculine Superiority While adolescent boys do not tease and bully girls as they did during the gang-age days of late childhood, they still retain a feeling of superiority. Even though they become interested in girls and spend increasingly more time dating them as adolescence progresses, the feeling of their superiority over girls persists.

The usual ways in which masculine superiority is expressed in adolescence is by expecting to play leadership roles in any social, school, or community activity in which both boys and girls participate. While girls play some leadership roles in these activities, boys generally play the important and prestigious roles.

In addition, boys try to show their masculine superiority by achievements superior to those of girls, whether in academic work, in games and sports, or in greater autonomy in their lives. They insist upon more freedom in all areas of their lives than do girls and, to them, this is a subtle insignia of their superiority.

Sex Bias Closely related to feelings of masculine superiority which develop in connection with sex-role typing is sex bias, or the tendency to devalue female achievements regardless of whether they equal or are superior to male achievements (117). As Etaugh and Rose have explained, "Sex bias is well established in

boys and girls by the early years of adolescence" (44).

Unlike boys in the gang age of late childhood who devalue female achievements mainly by criticizing or ridiculing them, or by boasting of the superiority of their own achievements, adolescent boys are more subtle in their techniques. Because of their interest in dating and desire to establish close, personal relationships with girls, they try to let girls believe that their achievements are inferior mainly by talking in a semiboastful way about their own achievements. Ignoring girls' achievements is thus a subtle way of informing them that their achievements are inferior to those of boys.

Sex bias is rarely an expresssion of the effects of female sex-role typing. While girls may know or certainly suspect that their achievements are equal to or superior to those of boys, they realize that if they verbalize or otherwise express this knowledge it will jeopardize their chances for social acceptance. Consequently, they pretend that their achievements are inferior to those of boys, often to the point where they actually believe it.

Underachievement By adolescence, the pattern of behavior characterized by underachievement in activities in which both boys and girls are involved has become well developed from the foundations laid during the childhood years (37). As Campbell has said, "Girl decliners appear to be accepting the feminine stereotype including that it isn't feminine to be smart" (22).

Awareness of the values boys have for dating partners and for future mates motivates some girls to underachieve in any activities in which both boys and girls are involved. This they do to conform to the traditional stereotype of masculine superiority. In activities in which only girls are involved, as in sex-separated schools, there is no reason for underachievement and, as a result, girls work up to their capacities unless they have some other reason to become underachievers (153).

Among boys, there are as many or even more underachievers than among girls. However, their reasons for underachievement are unrelated to a desire to avoid surpassing girls. According to the traditional stereotype, males are achievers and superior to females in any activity in which members of the two sexes are involved. Male underachievers in areas in which boys and girls both are involved are often a product of boredom or rebellion against parental pressures to succeed, not of any desire to show their inferiority to girls.

Fear of Success Behind some female underachievement is a fear of success—a fear based on the belief that success will militate against social acceptance by boys and place an almost insurmountable barrier in the path of mate selection (69,114). While this fear may only be temporary, until girls achieve their goal of marriage, it may reinforce their tendencies to underachieve, tendencies that can and often do become habitual and lead to life-long underachievement. On the other hand, fear of success, like the tendency to underachieve, is far less common among girls in sex-segregated schools than in coeducational schools.

As is true of underachievement, fear of success is not characteristic of boys. According to the traditional stereotype, success is one of the outstanding characteristics of males. When boys develop a fear of success, it is due to some cause other than wanting to let girls think of them as inferior. It is usually the result of repeated failures in past activities which has undermined self-confidence and led to the belief that they lack the qualities essential for success (175).

FAMILY RELATIONSHIPS DURING ADOLESCENCE

When the relationships of young adolescents with members of their families deteriorate as adolescence progresses, the fault usually lies on both sides. Parents far too often refuse to modify their concepts of their children's abilities as they grow older. As a result, they treat their adolescent sons and daughters much as they did when they were younger. In spite of this, they expect them to "act their age," especially when it comes to assuming responsibilities.

Even more important is the so-called "generation gap" between adolescents and their parents. This gap is partly the result of radical changes in values and standards of behavior that normally occur in any rapidly changing culture, and partly the result of the fact that many young people now have greater educational, social, and cultural opportunities than most of their parents had when they were adolescents. Thus it is more correctly a "cultural gap," not due entirely to differences in chronological age (26,95).

In no area is this generation gap more apparent than in sexual mores. As was pointed out earlier, sex-

ual behavior that is condoned today among adolescents would have been strongly condemned by their parents at that age.

Parents cannot be blamed for all the friction that develops between them and their adolescent children. No one is more irresponsible, more difficult to live with, more unpredictable, or more exasperating than young adolescents—with the possible exception of preadolescents. Their inability or unwillingness to communicate with their parents helps to widen the gap between them (55).

Parents likewise find it difficult to accept their adolescent children's objections to the restraints they regard as necessary; and they may be impatient with their failure to assume responsibilities they feel are appropriate for their age. These sources of irritation generally reach their peak between fourteen and fifteen years, after which there is generally an improvement in parent-child relationships (171).

Equally important, many adolescents feel that their parents do not "understand them" and that their standards of behavior are old-fashioned. This is due more to the cultural gap, explained above, than to differences in age.

Although the sources of friction between adolescents and members of their families are myriad, certain ones are almost universal in American families of today. These may be greater in early than in late adolescence and they may be more common among girls than among boys (26). The most common and most serious sources of friction between adolescents and members of their families are listed in Box 8-10.

Improvements in Family Relationships

As adolescence progresses, the frictional relationship many adolescents have with the members of their families gradually is replaced by a more pleasant and affectionate relationship. This is true of relationships with all family members.

Improvements in adolescent-parent relationships result, first, when parents begin to realize that their sons and daughters are no longer children. As a result, they give them more privileges, while at the same time expecting more in the way of work and assumption of responsibilities. Second, parent-adolescent relationships are eased when parents try to understand adolescents and the new cultural values of the peer group—even if they do not wholeheartedly approve of them—and recognize that today's

BOX 8-10

COMMON CAUSES OF FAMILY FRICTION DURING ADOLESCENCE

Standards of Behavior

Adolescents often consider their parents' standards of behavior old-fashioned and resent having to conform to standards different from those of their peers.

Methods of Discipline

When adolescents regard disciplinary methods used by their parents as "unfair" or "childish," they rebel. The greatest rebellion occurs in homes where one parent is perceived as having more authority than the other. This is especially so when the mother has the greater authority. By contrast, egalitarian marriage relationships tend to be related to a moderate amount of rebellion (82). Figure 8-10 shows the relationship between adolescent rebellion and parental authority.

Relationships with Siblings

The adolescent may be scornful of younger siblings and resentful of older ones, leading to friction with them as well as with parents, whom they may accuse of "playing favorites."

Feeling Victimized

Adolescents often become resentful if the socioeconomic status of their families makes it impossible for them to have the same status symbols—clothes, cars, etc.—their friends have; if they must assume many household responsibilities, such as care of younger siblings; or if a stepparent comes into the home and tries to "boss"

them. This antagonizes parents and adds to an already strained parent-adolescent relationship.

Hypercritical Attitudes

Family members resent adolescents' hypercritical attitudes toward them and the general pattern of family life. See Figure 8-11.

Family Size

In medium-sized families—three to four children—there is more friction than in small or large families. Parents in large families will not tolerate friction while, in small families, they are more permissive and adolescents feel less need to rebel.

Immature Behavior

Parents often develop punitive attitudes when adolescents neglect their school work, shun their responsibilities, or spend their money foolishly. Adolescents resent these critical and punitive attitudes.

Rebellion against Relatives

Parents and relatives become angry if adolescents openly express their feelings that family gatherings are "boring" or if they reject their suggestions and advice.

"Latchkey Problems"

The new and more active social life of adolescents may result in the breaking of family rules concerning time to return home and the people they associate with, especially members of the opposite sex.

---

adolescents are living in a different world from the one in which they grew up. When parents make these adjustments, the parent-adolescent relationship generally becomes more relaxed, and the home a pleasanter place in which to live.

Much the same pattern occurs in the adolescent's relationships with siblings, grandparents, and other relatives. During early adolescence, these relationships are also frictional. Older adolescents now accept their siblings, whom they frequently considered nuisances when they were younger, in a calmer and more philosophical manner. They can understand the behavior of younger siblings better

than they could earlier and their newly acquired poise and self-confidence make them less easily embarrassed or upset by their behavior. When adolescents claim that their siblings are different from them, it reduces sibling rivalry and friction (159).

Often older adolescents develop a parental attitude toward their younger siblings and this eliminates much of the friction. Older siblings are treated more casually by younger ones and there is less envy.

Older adolescents even accept grandparents and other relatives more graciously than they did several years earlier. This difference in their attitude may be the result of their more mature concept of old age,

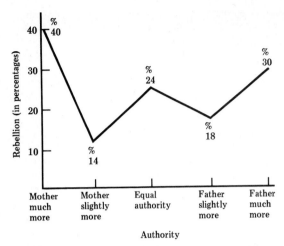

FIGURE 8-10 Relationship between parental authority and rebellion during the adolescent years. (Adapted from J. O. Balswick and C. Macrides. Parental stimulus for adolescent rebellion. *Adolescence,* 1975, **10,** 253–266. Used by permission.)

"I don't cook this right! I don't bake that right! Why don't you get out and do your protesting in the street like other kids!"

FIGURE 8-11 Parental reactions to adolescent criticism. (M. O. Lichty. "Grin and Bear It." Publishers-Hall Syndicate, Nov. 11, 1966. Used by permission.)

although it is far more likely due to the fact that their grandparents and other relatives treat them more like adults than they formerly did. In addition, grandparents and other relatives tend to criticize the behavior and appearance of older adolescents less than they did previously.

Sex Differences in Family Relationships

As a rule, the adolescent's relationships with family members of the female sex are less favorable than those with male family members. While it is true that mothers tend to be more lenient with their sons than their daughters, this is one of the few exceptions to the rule. Because girls are more restricted by their mothers than by their fathers, mother-daughter friction is often intense, at least until the latter part of adolescence.

Grandfathers and other male relatives assume little control over the adolescent's behavior, believing that to be the parents' responsibility. Grandmothers and other female relatives, however, tend to be more outspoken in their criticisms. Also, both boys and girls in adolescence have a more frictional relationship with a stepmother than with a stepfather.

The friendly relationships of same-sex siblings during childhood often deteriorate in adolescence; an older girl may criticize her younger sister's appearance and behavior, for example, and younger siblings tend to resent the privileges their older siblings are granted.

PERSONALITY CHANGES DURING ADOLESCENCE

By early adolescence, both boys and girls are well aware of their good and bad traits, and they appraise these in terms of similar traits in their friends. They are also well aware of the role personality plays in social relationships and thus are strongly motivated to improve their personalities—by reading books or articles on the subject, for example—in the hope of increasing their social acceptance.

Older adolescents are also aware of what constitutes a "pleasing personality." They know what traits are admired by peers of their own sex as well as by peers of the opposite sex. Although different traits are admired as adolescence progresses, and although admired traits differ somewhat from one social group to another, adolescents know what the group with which they are identified admires.

Many adolescents use group standards as the basis for their concept of an "ideal" personality against which they assess their own personalities. Few feel that they measure up to this ideal, and those who do not may want to change their personalities.

This is a difficult, often impossible task. First, the personality pattern, established during childhood, has begun to stabilize and take the form it will maintain with few modifications during the remaining years of life. True, there will be changes with age, but these will be more *quantitative* than qualitative, in that desirable traits will be strengthened, and undesirable traits will be weakened.

Second, many of the conditions that are responsible for molding the personality pattern are not within the adolescent's control since they are a product of the environment in which the adolescent lives and thus will continue to affect the self-concept—the core of the personality pattern—as long as the environment remains stable.

If, on the other hand, adolescents change their environments, as happens when they go away to school or college or to a new place to live or work, environmental changes may bring about personality changes. Adolescents who go away to college, for example, usually show greater social and emotional maturity, and greater tolerance, than those who remain under the parental roof. On the other hand, even in a different environment adolescents tend to seek people who treat them in a manner congruent with their self-concepts and to avoid those who do not. This reinforces their already-established self-concepts and their characteristic patterns of adjustment to life.

Even when the environment does not change, some of the conditions contributing to an unfavorable self-concept will automatically change as group values change. When high value is placed on social acceptance, adolescents who are not popular will feel inadequate. Later, as the closely knit peer groups begin to break up and less value is placed on popularity, adolescents will be able to view themselves from a different frame of reference and thus will feel more adequate. This feeling of adequacy will be greatly increased if older adolescents go steady or get married earlier than other members of the peer group, or if they earn money which enables them to have the autonomy and status symbols which their peers are unable to have.

Many conditions in the adolescent's life are responsible for molding the personality pattern through their influence on the self-concept. Some of these are similar to those present during childhood, but many are the product of the physical and psychological changes which occur during adolescence. The most important of these are given in Box 8-11.

Consequences of Attempts to Improve Personality

How successful adolescents will be in their attempts to improve their personalities depends on many factors. First, they must set ideals that are realistic and attainable *for them*. Otherwise, they will inevitably experience failure and, along with it, feelings of inadequacy, inferiority, and even martyrdom if they project the blame for their failures on others.

Second, they must make a realistic assessment of their strengths and weaknesses. A marked discrepancy between their actual personalities and their ego-ideals will lead to anxiety, uneasiness, unhappiness, and the tendency to use defensive reactions.

Third, adolescents must have stable self-concepts. The self-concept usually becomes increasingly more stable as adolescence progresses. This gives adolescents a sense of inner continuity and enables them to see themselves in a consistent manner, rather than one way now and a different way later. This also increases their self-esteem and results in fewer feelings of inadequacy.

Fourth, and most important of all, adolescents must be reasonably well satisfied with their achievements and eager to make improvements in any area in which they feel deficient. Self-acceptance leads to behavior that makes others like and accept the adolescent. This, in turn, reinforces the adolescent's favorable behavior and feelings of self-acceptance. Attitude toward self thus determines how happy and well adjusted the individual will be.

HAZARDS OF ADOLESCENCE

Physical hazards are now less numerous and less important than psychological hazards, although they do exist. However, they are significant primarily because of their psychological repercussions. Overweight per se, for example, would have relatively little effect on the adolescent's behavior and thus on social adjustments, but it is a hazard because it can result in unfavorable peer attitudes.

BOX 8-11

CONDITIONS INFLUENCING THE ADOLESCENT'S SELF-CONCEPT

Age of Maturing

Early maturers, who are treated as near-adults, develop favorable self-concepts and thus make good adjustments. Late maturers, who are treated like children, feel misunderstood and martyred and thus are predisposed to maladjusted behavior.

Appearance

Being different in appearance makes the adolescent feel inferior, even if the difference adds to physical attractiveness. Any physical defect is a source of embarrassment which leads to feelings of inferiority. Physical attractiveness, by contrast, leads to favorable judgments about personality characteristics and this aids social acceptance.

Sex-Appropriateness

Sex-appropriate appearance, interests, and behavior help adolescents achieve favorable self-concepts. Sex-inappropriateness makes them self-conscious and this influences their behavior unfavorably.

Names and Nicknames

Adolescents are sensitive and embarrassed if members of the peer group judge their names unfavorably or if they have nicknames that imply ridicule.

Family Relationships

An adolescent who has a very close relationship with a family member will identify with this person and want to develop a similar personality pattern. If this person is of the same sex, the adolescent will be helped to develop a sex-appropriate self-concept.

Peers

Peers influence the adolescent's personality pattern in two ways. First, the self-concepts of adolescents are reflections of what they believe their peers' concepts of them are and, second, they come under peer pressures to develop personality traits approved by the group.

Creativity

Adolescents who have been encouraged to be creative in their play and academic work as children develop a feeling of individuality and identity that has a favorable effect on their self-concepts. By contrast, adolescents who have been forced to conform to an approved pattern since earliest childhood lack a feeling of identity and of individuality.

Level of Aspiration

If adolescents have unrealistically high levels of aspiration, they will experience failure. This will lead to feelings of inadequacy and to defensive reactions in which they blame others for their failures. Adolescents who are realistic about their abilities will experience more successes than failures. This will lead to greater self-confidence and self-satisfaction, both of which contribute to better self-concepts.

Physical Hazards

Mortality as a result of illness is far less common during adolescence than in earlier years, although deaths due to automobile accidents increase. Adolescents are generally in good health, but they often discover they can avoid unpleasant situations by "not feeling well." Girls often use their menstrual periods as an excuse for not going to school (119, 130).

Suicide or attempts at suicide are becoming increasingly common among today's adolescents. See Figure 8-12. It has been reported that suicide is the number two cause of death among adolescents in America today (145). Studies of adolescent suicide have disclosed that the median age is sixteen years and that more males commit suicide than females (142,145). Many boys and girls who commit or attempt to commit suicide have been socially isolated for a period of time before and many have experienced family disruptions and school problems (131,142,145).

Physical defects that can be corrected, such as crooked teeth, poor eyesight, or hearing loss, rarely prevent adolescents from doing what their peers do. However, these may become psychological hazards in the case of the adolescent who must wear glasses or a hearing aid, for example. Physical defects which

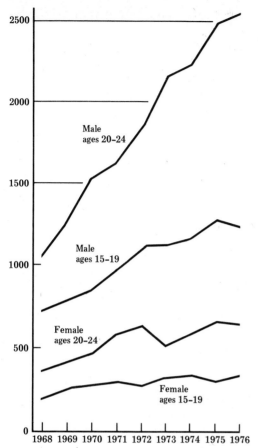

FIGURE 8-12 The growing tendency for adolescents to commit suicide. (Adapted from a nationwide survey of suicides among the young from 1958 to 1975. Washington, D.C.: U.S. Department of Health, Education, and Welfare, 1978. Used by permission.)

prevent the adolescent from doing what peers do, such as chronic asthma and obesity, are physical as well as psychological hazards.

As a result of muscle growth during early adolescence, *strength* increases. Because girls' muscles do not develop as much as boys' do, girls have less strength and tend to feel inadequate when they participate with boys in such sports as swimming and tennis, a feeling that contributes to their growing sense of inferiority.

Clumsiness and *awkwardness* are more serious during adolescence than at any other time during the life span. If their skills and motor development are not

on a par with those of their friends, adolescents cannot take part in the games and sports that play such important roles in their social lives. This has a serious impact on their social adjustments as well as on their self-concepts.

A *sex-inappropriate body build* is far more disturbing to an adolescent than to a child. There are two reasons for this. First, adolescents are judged more by their sex-appropriate appearance than children, and an inappropriate build, such as excessive tallness in girls or excessive thinness in boys, leads to unfavorable social judgments—judgments which affect social acceptance unfavorably. Second, adolescents are well aware of the fact that, once their growth is nearly complete, as it is when adolescence draws to a close, this will be their body build for life. There is nothing, for example, that a too-tall girl can do to make herself look shorter nor can a too-thin boy use padded clothes that will camouflage his lack of the sex-approved mesomorphic build.

To looks-conscious adolescents, perhaps the most serious of all physical hazards in *homeliness*. As was stressed earlier, adolescents who are attractive-looking find this an advantage in their schooling as well as in their social relationships. While beauty aids can, to a limited degree, camouflage homeliness in girls, there is little that adolescent boys can do to camouflage their homeliness. If homeliness is combined with a sex-inappropriate body build, adolescents have an almost insurmountable physical hazard to cope with (1).

Just because physical attractiveness is an asset, there is evidence that adolescents who are *too attractive* have a physical hazard because their peers, especially those of their own sex, become jealous and envious. Girls who are very attractive are often thought of in terms of the stereotype of "beautiful but dumb" while very attractive boys are often accused of being conceited, selfish, and prone to let others do their work for them (38).

Psychological Hazards

The major psychological hazards of adolescence center around the failure to make the psychological transitions to maturity that constitute the important developmental tasks of adolescence. In most cases adolescents fail to make these transitions not because they want to remain immature but because they encounter obstacles in their attempts to achieve mature patterns of behavior. Some of the most common and most serious obstacles adolescents encounter in their attempts to make the psychological transitions to maturity are listed in Box 8-12.

If adolescents are to make good personal and social adjustments, it is important for them to show signs of increasing maturity with each passing year. Some of the areas of immaturity which proclaim their immaturity most loudly are explained below. Performance in these areas determines whether personal and social adjustments will be judged as mature or immature.

Social Behavior In the area of social behavior, immaturity is shown in a preference for childish patterns of social groupings and social activities with peers of the same sex and in a lack of acceptance by peer groups, which in turn deprives the adolescent of the opportunity to learn more mature patterns of social behavior. Young adolescents, who are unsure of themselves and of their status in the peer group, tend to overconform; a persistence of this into late adolescence, however, suggests immaturity. Other common indications of immaturity in the area of social behavior include discrimination against those of different racial, religious, or socioeconomic backgrounds; attempts to reform those with different standards of appearance and behavior; and attempts on the part of adolescents to draw attention to themselves by wearing conspicuous clothes, using unconventional speech, bragging and boasting, and making jokes at the expense of others.

Sexual Behavior Immaturity is especially apparent in the area of sexual behavior. The reason for this is that adjustment from antagonism toward members of the opposite sex, characteristic of late childhood and puberty, to an interest in and the development of feelings of affection for them is a radical one. Adolescents who do not date because they are unattractive to members of the opposite sex, or because they continue to have a childish dislike for them, are regarded as immature by contemporaries. This cuts adolescents off from social contacts with their peers who have made the shift to more mature attitudes and behavior in relation to members of the opposite sex.

Rejection of the socially approved sex role, a continued preoccupation with sex, premarital pregnancy, and early marriage before adolescents have any stable source of support are also regarded as in-

teen—the age of legal maturity—is divided into early adolescence, which extends to seventeen years, and late adolescence, which extends until legal maturity. It is characteristically an important period in the life span, a transitional period, a time of change, a problem age, a time when the individual searches for identity, a dreaded age, a time of unrealism, and the threshold of adulthood.

2. Because mastery of the developmental tasks of adolescence requires major changes in children's habitual attitudes and patterns of behavior, many adolescents reach legal maturity with mastery of some of these developmental tasks unfinished and, as a result, they may carry much unfinished business into adulthood.

3. Even though physical growth is far from complete when puberty ends, its rate slackens in adolescence and much of the change that occurs then is internal rather than external. When physical growth will be complete is influenced by sex and age of maturing, thus causing many concerns for boys and girls.

4. While, traditionally, adolescence is a period of heightened emotionality, a time of "storm and stress," there is little evidence that this is universal or is as pronounced and persistent as is popularly believed.

5. The important social changes in adolescence include increased peer-group influence, more mature patterns of social behavior, new social groupings, and new values in the selection of friends and leaders and in social acceptance.

6. The most important and most universal interests of today's adolescents fall into seven major categories; recreational interests, personal and social interests, educational interests, vocational interests, religious interests, and interest in status symbols.

7. The major changes in morality during adolescence consist of replacing specific moral concepts with generalized moral concepts of right and wrong; the building of a moral code based on individual moral principles; and the control of behavior through the development of a conscience.

8. Sex interests and behavior, which center around heterosexuality, have two separate and distinct elements. First, the development of a pattern of behavior involving members of the two sexes and, second, the development of attitudes relating to relationships between members of the two sexes. These differ from adolescent heterosexuality in the past in two respects: first, the stages in heterosexual behavior are more telescoped today than in the past and, second, there is greater permissiveness in sexual behavior.

9. There are a number of effects of sex-role typing on adolescents, the most important of which are feelings of masculine supremacy, sex bias, underachievement in activities regarded as sex-inappropriate, and fear of success on the part of adolescent girls because of the possibility of facing the stigma of sex-inappropriateness.

10. Relationships between adolescents and members of their families tend to deteriorate in early adolescence though these relationships often improve as adolescence draws to a close, especially among adolescent girls and their family members.

11. While most adolescents are anxious to improve their personalities in the hope of advancing their status in the social group, many of the conditions influencing their self-concepts are beyond their control.

12. Among the physical hazards of adolescence, suicide is becoming increasingly frequent and serious, though other physical hazards, such as awkwardness, a sex-inappropriate body build and homeliness are too common to be overlooked.

13. The major psychological hazards of adolescence center around failure to make the transition to maturity—which is the most important developmental task of adolescence. This failure is often due to obstacles over which adolescents have little or no control.

14. The areas in which immaturity, due to failure to make the transition to more mature behavior, are especially common are social, sexual, and moral behavior and immaturity in family relationships. When immaturity is pronounced, it leads to self-rejection with its damaging effects on personal and social adjustments.

15. Most adults remember adolescence as an unhappy age. Studies of adolescence have revealed that this is truer of early than of late adolescence.

Bibliography

1. Adams, G. R. Physical attractiveness, personality, and social reactions to peer pressure. *Journal of Psychology*, 1977, **96**, 287–296.
2. Adams, J. F. (Ed.). *Understanding adolescence: Current developments in adolescent psychology.* (2nd ed.) Boston: Allyn & Bacon, 1973.
3. Anderson, D. L., G. W. Thompson, and F. Popovich. Adolescent variation in weight, height and mandibular length in 111 females. *Human Biology*, 1975, **47**, 309–319.

4. Anthony, J. The reactions of adults to adolescents and their behavior. In G. Caplan and S. Lebovici (Eds.). *Adolescence: Psychosocial perspectives*. New York: Basic Books, 1969, Pp. 54–78.

5. Alwin, D. F., and L. B. Otto. High school context effects on aspirations. *Sociology of Education*, 1977, **50**, 259–273.

6. Astin, H. The new realists. *Psychology Today*, 1977, **11**(4), 50–53, 105–106.

7. Ausubel, D. P., R. Montemayor, and P. N. Svajian. *Theory and problems of adolescent development*. (2nd ed.) New York: Grune & Stratton, 1977.

8. Balswick, J. O., and C. Macrides. Parental stimulus for adolescent rebellion. *Adolescence*, 1975, **10**, 253–266.

9. Baltes, B., and J. R. Nesselroade. Cultural change and adolescent personality development. *Developmental Psychology*, 1972, **7**, 244–258.

10. Bealer, R. C., and F. C. Willets. The religious interests of American high school youth: A survey of recent research. *Religious Education*, 1967, **62**, 435–444.

11. Beelick, D. B. Sources of student satisfaction and dissatisfaction. *Journal of Educational Research*, 1973, **67**, 19–22, 28.

12. Berry, G. W. Personality patterns and delinquency. *British Journal of Educational Psychology*, 1971, **41**, 221–222.

13. Berscheid, E., E. Walster, and G. Bohrnstedt. The happy American body: A survey report. *Psychology Today*, 1973, **7**(6), 119–131.

14. Bledsoe, J. C., and R. G. Wiggins. Self-concept and academic aspirations of "understood" and "misunderstood" boys and girls in ninth grade. *Psychological Reports*, 1974, **35**, 57–58.

15. Blos, P. The child analyst looks at the young adolescent. *Daedalus*, 1971, **100**, 961–978.

16. Boyce, J., and C. Benoit. Adolescent pregnancy. *New York State Journal of Medicine*, 1975, **75**, 872–874.

17. Boyd, R. E. Conformity reduction in adolescence. *Adolescence*, 1975, **10**, 297–300.

18. Bronfenbrenner, U. Developmental research, public policy, and the ecology of childhood. *Child Development*, 1974, **45**, 1–5.

19. Bruch, H. Obesity in adolescence. In G. Caplan and S. Lebovici (Eds.). *Adolescence: Psychosocial perspectives*. New York: Basic Books, 1969, Pp. 213–225.

20. Bruggen, P., and T. Pitt-Aikens. Authority as a key factor in adolescent disturbance. *British Journal of Medical Psychology*, 1975, **48**, 153–159.

21. Burkett, S. R., and E. L. Jensen. Conventional ties, peer influences, and the fear of apprehension: A study of adolescent marijuana use. *Sociological Quarterly*, 1975, **76**, 522–523.

22. Campbell, P. B. Adolescent intellectual decline. *Adolescence*, 1976, **11**, 629–635.

23. Chaffee, S. H., and A. R. Tims. Interpersonal factors in adolescent television use. *Journal of Social Issues*, 1976, **32**(4), 98–115.

24. Chess, S., A. Thomas, and M. Cameron. Sexual attitudes and behavior patterns in a middle-class adolescent population. *American Journal of Orthopsychiatry*, 1976, **46**, 689–701.

25. Clifford, E. Body satisfaction in adolescence. *Perceptual & Motor Skills*, 1971, **33**, 119–125.

26. Coleman, J., R. George, and G. Holt. Adolescents and their parents: A study of attitudes. *Journal of Genetic Psychology*, 1977, **130**, 239–245.

27. Coleman, J., J. Herzberg, and M. Morris. Identity in adolescence: Present and future self-concepts. *Journal of Youth & Adolescence*, 1977, **6**, 63–75.

28. Collins, J. K., J. R. Kennedy, and R. D. Francis. Insights into a dating partner's expectations of how behavior should ensue during the courtship process. *Journal of Marriage & the Family*, 1976, **38**, 373–378.

29. Cross, J. F., and J. Cross. Age, sex, race, and the perception of facial beauty. *Developmental Psychology*, 1971, **5**, 433–439.

30. Curran, J. P., and S. Lippold. The effects of physical attractiveness and attitude similarity on attraction in dating dyads. *Journal of Personality*, 1975, **43**, 528–539.

31. Dalsimer, K. Fear of academic success in adolescent girls. *Journal of the American Academy of Child Psychiatry*, 1975, **14**, 719–730.

32. Davidsen, J. K., and G. R. Leslie. Premarital sexual intercourse: An application of axiomatic theory construction. *Journal of Marriage & the Family*, 1977, **39**, 15–25.

33. Davies, B. L. Attitudes toward school among early and late maturing girls. *Journal of Genetic Psychology*, 1977, **131**, 261–266.

34. Delong, G. Inquiry in pre- and early-adolescent interests. *Adolescence*, 1975, **10**, 187–190.

35. Deutsch, C. J., and L. A. Gilbert. Sex role stereotypes: Effect on perceptions of self and others and on personal adjustment. *Journal of Counseling Psychology*, 1976, **23**, 373–379.

36. Dion, K., E. Berscheid, and E. Walster. What is beautiful is good. *Journal of Personality & Social Psychology*, 1972, **24**, 285–290.

37. Doherty, E. G., and C. Culver. Sex-role identification, ability, and achievement among high school girls. *Sociology of Education*, 1976, **49**, 1–3.

38. Dormer, M., and D. L. Thiel. When beauty may fail. *Journal of Personality & Social Psychology*, 1975, **31**, 1168–1176.

39. Edwards, J. W., and A. Booth. Sexual behavior in and out of marriage: An assessment of correlates. *Journal of Marriage & the Family*, 1976, **38**, 73–81.

40. Eisenberg, L. A developmental approach to adolescence. *Children*, 1965, **12**, 131–135.

41. Eitzen, D. S. Athletics in the status system of male adolescents: A replication of Coleman's "The Adolescent Society." *Adolescence*, 1975, **10**, 267–276.

42. Erikson, E. H. *Childhood and society*. (Rev. ed.) New York: Norton, 1964.

43. Essman, C. S. Sibling relations and socialization for parenthood. *Family Coordinator*, 1977, **26**, 259–262.

44. Etaugh, C., and S. Rose. Adolescents' sex bias in evaluation of performance. *Developmental Psychology*, 1975, **11**, 663–664.

45. Eysenck, H. J. The development of moral values in children. VII. The contribution of learning theory. *British Journal of Educational Psychology*, 1960, **30**, 11–21.

46. Faust, M. S. Somatic development of adolescent girls. *Monographs of the Society for Research in Child Development*, 1977, **42**(1).

47. Feshbach, N., and G. Sones. Sex differences in adolescent reactions toward newcomers. *Developmental Psychology*, 1971, **4**, 381–386.

48. Fiske, E. B. Study finds use of alcohol is up sharply at colleges. *The New York Times*, March 11, 1978.

49. Frankel, J., and J. Dullaert. Is adolescent rebellion universal? *Adolescence*, 1977, **12**, 227–236.

50. Freud, A. Adolescence as a developmental disturbance. In G.

Caplan and S. Lebovici (Eds.). *Adolescence: Psychosocial perspectives*. New York: Basic Books, 1969, Pp. 5–10.

51. Friedman, C. J., F. Mann, and H. Adelman. Juvenile street gangs: The victimization of youth. *Adolescence*, 1976, **11**, 527–533.

52. Frisch, R. E. Fatness of girls from menarche to age 18 years, with a nomogram. *Human Biology*, 1976, **48**, 353–359.

53. Gesell, A., F. L. Ilg, and L. B. Ames. *Youth: The years from ten to sixteen*. New York: Harper & Row, 1956.

54. Goldberg, L., and J. S. Guilford. Delinquent values: It's fun to break the rules. *Proceedings of the Annual Convention of APA*, 1972, **7**(1), 237–238.

55. Grando, R., and B. G. Ginsberg. Communication in the father-son relationship: The parent-adolescent relationship development program. *Family Coordinator*, 1976, **25**, 465–473.

56. Greenberger, E., R. Josselson, C. Knerr, and B. Knerr. The measurement and structure of psychosocial maturity. *Journal of Youth & Adolescence*, 1975, **4**, 127–143.

57. Gulas, I., and F. W. King. On the question of pre-existing personality differences between users and nonusers of drugs. *Journal of Psychology*, 1976, **92**, 65–68.

58. Gunter, B. G., and H. A. Moore. Youth, leisure, and post-industrial society: Implications for the family. *Family Coordinator*, 1975, **24**, 199–207.

59. Gurel, L. M., J. C. Wilbur, and L. Gurel. Personality correlates of adolescent clothing styles. *Journal of Home Economics*, 1972, **64**(3), 42–47.

60. Hamburg, B. A., H. C. Kraemer, and W. Jahnke. A hierarchy of drug use in adolescence: Behavioral and attitudinal correlates of substantial drug use. *American Journal of Psychiatry*, 1975, **132**, 1155–1163.

61. Hansen, S. L. Dating choices of high school students. *Family Coordinator*, 1977, **26**, 133–138.

62. Harris, M. B. Sex role stereotyping and teacher expectations. *Journal of Educational Psychology*, 1975, **67**, 751–756.

63. Havighurst, R. J. *Developmental tasks and education*. (3rd ed.) New York: McKay, 1972.

64. Heilbrun, A. B. Identification with the father and sex-role development of the daughter. *Family Coordinator*, 1976, **25**, 411–416.

65. Hendry, L. B., and H. Patrick. Adolescents and television. *Journal of Youth & Adolescence*, 1977, **6**, 325–336.

66. Hollander, E. P., B. J. Fallon, and M. T. Edwards. Some aspects of influence and acceptability for appointed and elected group leaders. *Journal of Psychology*, 1977, **95**, 289–296.

67. Horrocks, J. E., and M. Benimoff. Stability of adolescents' nominee status over a one-year period as a friend by their peers. *Adolescence*, 1966, **1**, 224–229.

68. Hutton, S. S. Sex role illustrations in junior high school home economics textbooks. *Journal of Home Economics*, 1976, **68**(2), 27–30.

69. Jackaway, R. Sex differences in the development of fear of success. *Child Study Journal*, 1974, **4**, 71–79.

70. Jepson, D. A. Occupational decision development over the high school years. *Journal of Vocational Behavior*, 1975, **7**, 225–237.

71. Jesser, R. Predicting time of onset of marijuana use: A developmental study of high school youth. *Journal of Consulting & Clinical Psychology*, 1976, **44**, 125–134.

72. Jones, V. Attitudes of college students and their changes: A 37-year study. *Genetic Psychology Monographs*, 1970, **81**, 3–80.

73. Joseph, T. P. Adolescents from the view of the members of an informal adolescent group. *Genetic Psychology Monographs*, 1969, **79**, 3–88.

74. Judd, N., R. H. Bull, and D. Gahagan. The effects of clothing style upon the reactions of a stranger. *Social Behavior & Personality*, 1975, **3**, 225–227.

75. Jurich, A. P., and J. A. Jurich. The lost adolescent syndrome. *Family Coordinator*, 1975, **24**, 357–361.

76. Kagan, J. A conception of early adolescence. *Daedalus*, 1971, **100**, 997–1012.

77. Kandel, D. B. Stages in adolescent involvement in drug use. *Science*, 1975, **190**, 912–914.

78. Kandel, D. B. Similarity in real-life adolescent friendship pairs. *Journal of Personality & Social Psychology*, 1978, **36**, 306–312.

79. Kaplan, H. B. Increase in self-rejection and continuing discontinued deviant responses. *Journal of Youth & Adolescence*, 1977, **6**, 77–87.

80. Kemper, T. D., and M. L. Reichler. Father's work integration and types and frequencies of rewards and punishments administered by fathers and mothers to adolescent sons and daughters. *Journal of Genetic Psychology*, 1976, **129**, 207–219.

81. Kenniston, K. Student activism: Moral development and morality. In W. R. Loeft (Ed.). *Developmental psychology: A book of readings*. Hinsdale, Ill.: Dryden Press, 1972, Pp. 437–456.

82. Kerckhoff, A. C., and J. L. Huff. Parental influence on educational goals. *Sociometry*, 1974, **37**, 307–327.

83. Kernan, J. B. Her mother's daughter? The case of clothing and cosmetic fashions. *Adolescence*, 1973, **8**, 343–350.

84. Klagsbrun, F. Preventing teenage suicide. *Family Health*, 1977, **9**(4), 21–24.

85. Kohlberg, L. *Stages in the development of moral thought and action*. New York: Holt, 1969.

86. Kugelmass, I. N. *Adolescent immaturity: Prevention and treatment*. Springfield, Ill.: Charles C Thomas, 1973.

87. Kulin, H. E. The physiology of adolescence in man. *Human Biology*, 1974, **46**, 133–144.

88. La Driere, M. LaV., R. E. Odell, and E. Pesys. Marijuana: Its meaning to a high school population. *Journal of Psychology*, 1975, **91**, 297–307.

89. Landsbaum, J. B., and R. H. Willis. Conformity in early and late adolescence. *Developmental Psychology*, 1971, **4**, 334–337.

90. Langford, P. E., and S. George. Intellectual and moral development in adolescence. *British Journal of Educational Psychology*, 1975, **45**, 330–332.

91. Larson, D. L., E. A. Spreitzer, and E. E. Snyder. Social factors in the frequency of romantic involvement among adolescents. *Adolescence*, 1976, **11**, 7–12.

92. Lasseigne, M. W. A study of peer and adult influence on moral beliefs of adolescents. *Adolescence*, 1975, **10**, 227–230.

93. Lelyveld, J. The new sexual revolution. *The New York Times*, July 3, 1977.

94. Lerner, R. M., S. A. Karabenick, and M. Meisels. Effects of age and sex on the development of personal space schemata towards body build. *Journal of Genetic Psychology*, 1975, **127**, 91–101.

95. Lerner, R. M., M. Karson, M. Meisels, and J. R. Knapp. Actual and perceived attitudes of late adolescents and their parents. The phenomena of the generation gap. *Journal of Genetic Psychology*, 1975, **126**, 195–207.

96. Littrell, M. B., and J. B. Eicher. Clothing opinions and the social

acceptance process among adolescents. *Adolescence*, 1973, **8**, 197–212.

97. Lorenzi, M. E., L. V. Klerman, and J. F. Jekel. School-age parents: How permanent a relationship? *Adolescence*, 1977, **12**, 13–22.

98. Lynn, D. B. Fathers and sex role development. *Family Coordinator*, 1976, **25**, 403–409.

99. Mahoney, E. R. Gender and social class differences in changes in attitudes toward premarital coitus. *Sociology & Social Research*, 1978, **62**, 279–286.

100. Mahoney, E. R., and M. D. Finch. Body-cathexis and self-esteem: A reanalysis of the differential contribution of specific body aspects. *Journal of Social Psychology*, 1976, **99**, 251–258.

101. Majeres, R. L. Semantic connotations of the words "adolescent," "teenager," and "youth." *Journal of Genetic Psychology*, 1976, **129**, 57–62.

102. Malina, R. M. Adolescent changes in size, build, composition, and performance. *Human Biology*, 1974, **46**, 117–131.

103. Marotz-Baden, R., and I. Tallman. Parental aspirations and expectations for daughters and sons: A comparative analysis. *Adolescence*, 1978, **13**, 252–268.

104. McMorrow, F. Do kids and alcohol mix? *The New York Times*, July 17, 1977.

105. Mirande, A. M., and E. L. Hammer. Premarital sexual permissiveness: A research note. *Journal of Marriage & the Family*, 1974, **36**, 356–358.

106. Mitchell, J. J. Moral growth during adolescence. *Adolescence*, 1975, **10**, 221–226.

107. Mitchell, T. R. Leader complexity and leadership style. *Journal of Personality & Social Psychology*, 1970, **16**, 166–174.

108. Monge, R. H. Developmental trends in factors of adolescent self-concept. *Developmental Psychology*, 1973, **8**, 382–393.

109. Musa, K. E., and M. E. Roach. Adolescent appearance and self-concept. *Adolescence*, 1973, **8**, 385–393.

110. Muson, H. Teenage violence and the telly. *Psychology Today*, 1978, **11**(10), 50–54.

111. Nelson, M. O. The concept of God and feelings toward parents. *Journal of Individual Psychology*, 1971, **22**, 46–49.

112. *New York Times* report. Study finds drinking—often to excess —now starts at earlier age. *The New York Times*, March 27, 1977.

113. O'Hagan, F. J. Gang characteristics: An empirical survey. *Journal of Child Psychology & Psychiatry & Allied Disciplines*, 1976, **17**, 305–314.

114. Olsen, N. J., and E. W. Willemsen. Fear of success—fact or artifact? *Journal of Psychology*, 1978, **95**, 65–70.

115. Omvig, C. P., R. W. Tulloch, and E. G. Thomas. The effect of career education on career maturity. *Journal of Vocational Behavior*, 1975, **7**, 265–273.

116. Onat, T., and B. Ertem. Adolescent female height velocity: Relationship to body measurements, sexual and skeletal maturity. *Human Biology*, 1974, **46**, 199–217.

117. Orcuitt, J. D. The impact of student activism on attitudes toward the female sex role: Longitudinal and cross-sectional perspectives. *Social Forces*, 1975, **54**, 382–392.

118. Osterrieth, P. A. Adolescence: Some psychologic aspects. In G. Caplan and S. Lebovici (Eds.). *Adolescence: Psychosocial perspectives*. New York: Basic Books, 1969, Pp. 11–21.

119. Paige, K. E. Women learn to sing the menstrual blues. *Psychology Today*, 1973, **7**(4), 41–46.

120. Patchen, M., G. Hofmann, and J. D. Davidson. Interracial perceptions among high school students. *Sociometry*, 1976, **39**, 341–354.

121. Piaget, J. The intellectual development of the adolescent. In G. Caplan and S. Lebovici (Eds.). *Adolescence: Psychosocial perspectives*. New York: Basic Books, 1969, Pp. 22–26.

122. Piers, E. V. Adolescent creativity. In J. F. Adams (Ed.). *Understanding adolescence: Current developments in adolescent psychology*. (2nd ed.) Boston: Allyn & Bacon, 1973, Pp. 191–220.

123. Place, D. M. The dating experience for adolescent girls. *Adolescence*, 1975, **10**, 157–174.

124. Prediger, D. J., and N. S. Cole. Sex-role socialization and employment realities: Implications for vocational interest measures. *Journal of Vocational Behavior*, 1975, **7**, 239–251.

125. Rivenbark, W. H. Self-disclosure patterns among adolescents. *Psychological Reports*, 1971, **28**, 35–42.

126. Roberts, J., and J. Ludford. *Skin conditions of youths 12–17 years: United States*. Rockville, Md.: Health Resources Administration, National Center for Health Studies, 1976.

127. Roche, A. F. Differential timing of maximum length increments among bones within individuals. *Human Biology*, 1974, **36**, 145–157.

128. Roche, A. F., and G. H. Davila. Late adolescent growth in stature. *Pediatrics*, 1972, **50**, 874–880.

129. Rodman, H., P. Voydanoff, and A. E. Lovejoy. The range of aspirations: A new approach. *Social Problems*, 1972, **22**, 184–198.

130. Rogers, K. D., and G. Reese. Health studies, presumably normal high school studenst. II. Absence from school. *American Journal of Diseases of Children*, 1965, **109**, 9–27.

131. Ron, R. D., R. Salls, T. Kenny, B. Reynolds, and F. Heald. Adolescents who attempt suicide. *Journal of Pediatrics*, 1977, **90**, 636–638.

132. Rosen, B. C., and C. S. Aneshensel. The chameleon syndrome: A social psychological dimension of the female sex role. *Journal of Marriage & the Family*, 1976, **38**, 605–617.

133. Rosenkrantz, A. L. A note on adolescent suicide: Incidence, dynamics, and some suggestions for treatment. *Adolescence*, 1978, **13**, 209–214.

134. Rudolph, J. P., and B. L. Borland. Factors affecting the incidence and acceptance of cigarette smoking among high school students. *Adolescence*, 1976, **11**, 519–525.

135. Russian, R. B. Idealization during adolescence. *Smith College Studies in Social Work*, 1975, **45**, 211–229.

136. Rutter, M., P. Graham, O. F. D. Chadwick, and W. Yule. Adolescent turmoil: Fact or fiction. *Journal of Child Psychology & Psychiatry & Allied Disciplines*, 1976, **17**, 35–56.

137. Ryan, M. S. *Clothing: A study in human behavior*. New York: Holt, 1966.

138. Savin-Williams, R. C. Age and sex differences in the adolescent image of Jesus. *Adolescence*, 1977, **12**, 353–366.

139. Schachter, F. F., E. Shore, S. Feldman-Rotman, R. E. Marquis, and S. Campbell. Sibling deidentification. *Developmental Psychology*, 1976, **12**, 418–427.

140. Scheck, D. C., and R. Emerick. A young male adolescent's perception of early child-rearing behavior: The differential effects of socioeconomic status and family size. *Sociometry*, 1976, **39**, 39–52.

141. Schulman, M. L. Idealization of engaged couples. *Journal of Marriage & the Family*, 1974, **36**, 139–147.

142. Shaffer, T. S. Suicide in childhood and early adolescence. *Journal of Child Psychology & Psychiatry & Allied Disciplines,* 1974, **15**, 275–291.

143. Siman, M. L. Application of a new model of peer group influence to naturally existing adolescent friendship groups. *Child Development,* 1977, **48**, 270–274.

144. Singh, B. K., B. L. Walton, and J. S. Williams. Extramarital sexual permissiveness: Conditions and contingencies. *Journal of Marriage & the Family,* 1976, **38**, 701–712.

145. Smith, D. F. Adolescent suicide: A problem for teachers. *Phi Delta Kappan,* 1976, **57**, 539–542.

146. Smith, G. M., and C. P. Fogg. Teenage drug use: A search for causes and consequences. *Personality & Social Psychology Bulletin,* 1974, **1**, 426–429.

147. Snyder, E. E. A longitudinal analysis of social participation in high school and early adulthood voluntary associational participation. *Adolescence,* 1970, **5**, 79–88.

148. Sommer, B. B. *Puberty and adolescence.* New York: Oxford University Press, 1978.

149. Sorenson, R. C. *Adolescent sexuality in contemporary America.* New York: World Book, 1973.

150. Sorossky, A. D. The psychological effects of divorce on adolescents. *Adolescence,* 1977, **12**, 123–136.

151. Spanier, G. B. Perceived sex knowledge, exposure to eroticism, and premarital sexual behavior: The impact of dating. *Sociological Quarterly,* 1976, **17**, 247–261.

152. Steele, C. L. Obese adolescent girls: Some diagnostic and treatment considerations. *Adolescence,* 1974, **9**, 81–96.

153. Stein, A. M., and M. M. Bailey. The socialization of achievement orientation in females. *Psychological Bulletin,* 1973, **80**, 345–366.

154. Steinmann, A., and A. P. Jurich. The effects of a sex education course on the sex role perceptions of junior high school students. *Family Coordinator,* 1975, **24**, 27–31.

155. Stinnett, N., and S. Taylor. Parent-child relationships and perceptions of alternate life styles. *Journal of Genetic Psychology,* 1976, **129**, 105–112.

156. Tanner, J. M. Sequence, tempo, and individual variation in the growth and development of boys and girls, aged twelve to sixteen. *Daedalus,* 1971, **100**, 907–930.

157. Tanner, J. M. *Fetus into man: Physical growth from conception to maturity.* Cambridge, Mass.: Harvard University Press, 1978.

158. Thomas, M. J. Realism and socioeconomic status (SES) of occupational plans of low SES Black and white male adolescents. *Journal of Counseling Psychology,* 1976, **23**, 46–49.

159. Thompson, G. G., and E. F. Gardner. Adolescents' perceptions of happy-successful living. *Journal of Genetic Psychology,* 1969, **115**, 107–120.

160. Thornburg, H. D. Peers: Three distinct groups. *Adolescence,* 1971, **6**, 59–76.

161. *Time* magazine report. The youth crime plague. Young, female and more violent. *Time,* July 11, 1977, Pp. 18–28.

162. Tobias, J., and T. LaBlanc. Malicious destruction of property in the suburbs—1975. *Adolescence,* 1977, **12**, 111–114.

163. Tolar, A. The generation gap: Fact or fiction? *Genetic Psychology Monographs,* 1976, **94**, 35–130.

164. *U.S. News & World Report* article. 18-year-old adults: Their unexpected problems. *U.S. News & World Report,* Aug. 20, 1973, Pp. 40–42.

165. *U.S. News & World Report* article. What's in, what's out. The search for status. *U.S. News & World Report,* Feb. 14, 1977, Pp. 38–42.

166. Vener, A. M., M. M. Zaenglein, and C. Stewart. Traditional religious orthodoxy: Respect for authority and nonconformity in adolescence. *Adolescence,* 1977, **12**, 43–56.

167. Viernstein, M. C., and R. Hogan. Parental personality factors and achievement motivation in talented adolescents. *Journal of Youth & Adolescence,* 1975, **4**, 183–190.

168. Waber, D. P. Sex differences in mental abilities, hemispheric lateralization, and rate of physical growth in adolescence. *Developmental Psychology,* 1977, **13**, 29–38.

169. Wagner, H. The increasing importance of the peer group during adolescence. *Adolescence,* 1971, **6**, 53–58.

170. Wagner, H. The adolescent and his religion. *Adolescence,* 1978, **13**, 349–364.

171. Weller, L., and E. Luchterhand. Adolescents' perception of their parents. *Adolescence,* 1977, **12**, 367–372.

172. Whiting, J. W. M., T. K. Landauer, and T. M. Jones. Infantile immunization and adult stature. *Child Development,* 1968, **39**, 54–67.

173. Whiteside, M. Age and sex differences in self-perception as related to ideal trait selections. *Adolescence,* 1976, **11**, 585–592.

174. Wilkinson, M. Romantic love: The great equalizer? Sexism in popular music. *Family Coordinator,* 1976, **25**, 161–166.

175. Winchel, R., D. Fenner, and P. Shaver. Impact of coeducation on ''fear of success'' imagery expressed by male and female high school students. *Journal of Educational Psychology,* 1974, **66**, 726–730.

176. Zube, M. J. Changing concepts of morality. *Social Forces,* 1972, **50**, 385–393.

CHAPTER NINE
EARLY ADULTHOOD: PERSONAL AND SOCIAL ADJUSTMENTS

After reading this chapter, you should be able to:

- Define the subdivisions of adulthood and the names usually applied to them.
- Show how the developmental tasks of early adulthood are concentrated on preparing the individual for adjustment to the new pattern of life and the social expectations characteristic of this age.
- Describe the changes in interests that are common in adulthood and the conditions responsible for these changes.
- Call attention to the conditions responsible for social mobility in early adulthood and the effects of different types of mobility on the personal and social adjustments of young adults.
- Give reasons why many young adults have difficulty in making satisfactory sex-role adjustments.
- Stress why the personal and social hazards of early adulthood stem from a failure to master some or most of the important developmental tasks for that age.

The term *adult* comes from the same Latin verb as the term *adolescence*—*adolescere*—which means "to grow to maturity." However, the word adult is derived from the past participle of that verb—*adultus*—which means "grown to full size and strength" or "matured." Adults are, therefore, individuals who have completed their growth and are ready to assume their status in society along with other adults.

Different cultures have different ages at which children reach the adult status or the age of legal maturity. In most of the older cultures, they reached this status when their puberty growth was complete or nearly complete and when their sex organs had developed to the point where they were capable of procreation. Until recently, children in the American culture were not considered legally adults until they reached the age of twenty-one years. Today, adulthood is legally reached at the age of eighteen. With a gradual increase in longevity, adulthood is now by far the longest period in the total life span.

During the long period of adulthood, certain physical and psychological changes occur at predictable times. Like childhood and adolescence—also long periods during which certain physical and psychological changes occur at predictable times—adulthood is customarily subdivided on the basis of the times at which these changes take place together with the adjustment problems and cultural pressures and expectancies stemming from them. The subdivisions of adulthood are given in Box 9-1.

It is important to note that these subdivisions are not fixed and rigid. Instead, they indicate only the ages at which the *average* man or woman can be expected to begin to show some changes in appearance, bodily functions, interests, attitudes, or behavior and at which certain environmental pressures in our culture give rise to adjustment problems which few men or women escape. As Gould emphasized, "The precise ages at which changes occur are a product of an individual's total personality, life style and subculture" (42).

CHARACTERISTICS OF EARLY ADULTHOOD

Early adulthood is a period of adjustments to new patterns of life and new social expectations. The young

adult is expected to play new roles, such as that of spouse, parent, and breadwinner, and to develop new attitudes, interests, and values in keeping with these new roles. These adjustments make early adulthood a distinctive period in the life span and also a difficult one (74). It is especially difficult because, up until now, most boys and girls have had someone—parents, teachers, friends or others—to help them make the adjustments they are faced with. Now, as adults, they are expected to make these adjustments for themselves. To avoid being considered "immature," they hesitate to turn to others for advice and help when they find the adjustments too difficult to cope with successfully alone.

A brief description of some of the outstanding characteristics of the years of early adulthood are given below. These should serve to show why adjustment to adulthood is usually difficult and why many young adults find the early years of adulthood so difficult that they try to prolong their dependency by retaining the roles of students long after their age-mates have tried to end their dependency on parents and are striving to become independent of help from others.

Early Adulthood Is the "Settling-down Age"

It has been said that childhood and adolescence are the periods of "growing up" and that adulthood is the time for "settling down." In past generations, it was assumed that when boys and girls reached the age of legal maturity, their days of carefree freedom were over and the time had come to settle down and assume the responsibilities of adult life. That meant settling into a line of work that would be the man's career for the rest of his life, while the young woman was expected to assume the responsibilities of homemaker and mother—responsibilities that would be hers for the remainder of her life.

Today, it is recognized that "settling down" too early is often laying the foundations for discontent because of too early choices of careers or life-mates. Consequently, many young men try out different lines of work to see which meets their needs best and which will bring them lifelong satisfaction. While trying out different lines of work, many young men also try out different women to find out if they have the qualities they want for a lifelong spouse.

In the same way, young women of today go through the trying-out process before they are willing to consider settling down. They take jobs to see if they prefer working to marriage or if they want to combine work with marriage. They date and/or go steady with different men before they decide on the one they believe will make a satisfactory life-mate.

This trying out of different life patterns and different individuals to share their life patterns takes time. Consequently, young adults today usually start to settle down later than their parents did and much later than their grandparents did. The average adult of today has chosen a lifestyle and an individual to share that lifestyle by the early thirties, though many do so before then.

When adults of today start to settle down depends upon two factors. First, how soon they are able to find a lifestyle that meets their needs then and which they believe will meet their needs throughout life. A woman who, since the days she played with dolls always wanted to be a wife and mother, will not need long after completing her education to choose

these occupations as her life roles. Similarly, a man who never wanted to be anything but a doctor will not have to go through the trial-and-error process to find a career that meets his needs as will his friends who frankly claimed, as boys, that they did not know what they wanted to do when they reached the end of their schooling.

The second condition that determines when young adults will settle down is the responsibilities they must assume before doing so. The man who has selected medicine as a life career certainly cannot start to settle down to the practice of medicine until the late twenties at the earliest because he must complete college, medical school, internship, and residency before he can hang out his shingle as a full-fledged doctor. By contrast, age-mates who decide they want to go into overall or blue-collar jobs can start to settle down shortly after they complete high school because they will not need a period of formal training for these jobs. The woman who wants to spend her life as wife and mother may have to delay one or both of these roles should she decide to marry a man who must delay marriage because of financial responsibilities related to his education or to the care of aging parents.

Once individuals decide upon the pattern of life they believe will meet their needs, they develop patterns of behavior, attitudes, and values which will tend to be characteristically theirs for the remainder of their lives. Any need to change this pattern in middle or old age will be difficult and emotionally disturbing for them. Some of the discontent and unhappiness in middle and old age can, unquestionably, be traced to settling down before finding a life pattern that offers possibilities for lifelong satisfaction.

Early Adulthood Is the "Reproductive Age"

Parenthood is one of the most important roles in the lives of most young adults. Those who were married during the latter years of adolescence concentrate on the role of parenthood during their twenties and early thirties; some become grandparents before early adulthood ends.

Those who do not marry until they have completed their education or have started their life careers, do not become parents until they feel they can afford to have a family. This is often not until the early thirties. Also, if women want to pursue careers after marriage, they may put off having children until the thirties. For them, then, only the last decade of early adulthood is the "reproductive age." For those who begin to have children early in adulthood or even in the closing years of adolescence and have large families, all of early adulthood is likely to be a reproductive age.

Early Adulthood Is a "Problem Age"

The early adult years present many new problems, different in their major aspects, from the problems experienced in the earlier years of life. With the lowering of the age of legal maturity to eighteen years, in 1970, young adults have been confronted with many problems they are totally unprepared to cope with. While they are now able to vote, to own property, to marry without parental consent, and to do many things young people could not do when the age of legal maturity was twenty-one years, there is no question about the fact that "this new-found freedom is creating unforeseen problems for the youthful adults, and often for their parents, too" (113). The adjustments to the problems of adulthood have been intensified by the shortening of adolescence, which has given individuals less time to make the transition from childhood to adulthood (74,84).

From the beginning of adulthood, the average American of today is preoccupied with problems related to adjustments in the different major areas of adult life. In the years from the beginning of legal adulthood to thirty, most men and women are adjusting to marriage, parenthood, and jobs. In the decade from thirty to forty years, adjustments focus more on family relationships because it is an accepted fact that changing jobs or selecting a new vocation after the mid-thirties is difficult if not impossible. Consequently, most men have made their adjustments to their work earlier and are now concentrating on adjustments related to problems of parenthood (42).

Because the problems young adults must face are difficult as well as time- and energy-consuming, these adjustments will not all be made at the same time, nor will their final forms be accepted simultaneously. It is difficult, if not impossible, for example, for men to adjust to their chosen vocations at the same time they are trying to adjust to marriage. Similarly, when parenthood comes within the first year of marriage, most women, as is true also of men, find adjustments to the problems this new role gives rise to

so difficult that they often fail to make them satisfactorily. Figure 9-1 shows some of the adjustments young men and women must make during the years of early adulthood.

There are many reasons why adjustment to the problems of adulthood is so difficult. Three are espe-

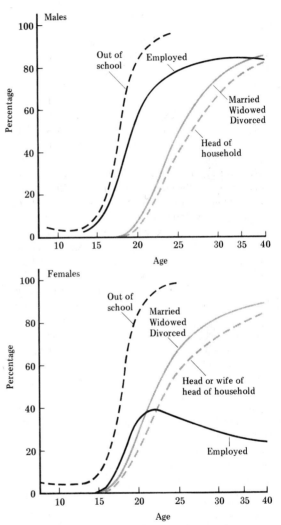

FIGURE 9-1 Pattern of male and female adjustments in different areas during the early years of adulthood. (Adapted from F. K. Stuttleworth. The adolescent years. *Monographs of the Society for Research in Child Development,* 1949, **14**(1). Used by permission.)

cially common. First, very few young people have had any preparation for meeting the types of problems they are expected to cope with as adults. Education in high school and college provides only limited training for jobs, and few schools or colleges give courses in the common problems of marriage and parenthood. Even those who have had baby-sitting experience have limited preparation for parenthood because most baby-sitters are hired only for short times when parents are out of the home and their major responsibility is to keep the children safe and happy until the parents return.

Second, just as trying to learn two or more skills simultaneously usually results in not learning any one of them well, so trying to adjust to two or more new roles simultaneously usually results in poor adjustment to all of them. It is difficult for a young adult to deal with the choice of a career and the choice of a mate simultaneously. Similarly, adjustment to marriage and parenthood makes it difficult for young adults to adjust to work if they marry while they are still students.

Third, and perhaps most serious of all, young adults do not have the help in meeting and solving their problems that they had when they were younger. This is partly their own fault and partly that of their parents and teachers. Most young adults are too proud of their new status to admit that they cannot cope with it. So, they do not seek the advice and help in meeting the problems this new status gives rise to. Similarly, most parents and teachers, having been rebuffed by adolescents who claimed they were capable of handling their own affairs, hesitate to offer help unless they are specifically asked to do so. That is why, as was stressed earlier, the shortening of adolescence in the American culture has made the transition to adulthood especially difficult.

Early Adulthood Is a Period of Emotional Tension

When people are trying to get the lay of a new land in which they find themselves, they are likely to be emotionally upset. This, unquestionably, was in part at the basis of the student riots of the 1960s. As near-adults or young adults, they were still college students on the verge of entering the adult world of work. As they looked out from their ivy-covered towers, they did not like what they saw and wanted to change it.

Now, a decade or more later, it is interesting to see how these angry student rebels have settled down and become a part of the mainstream of American life. Having had opportunities to assess their tactics, most of them have come to the conclusion that the way to bring about the changes they wanted to make as students could best be done from within the established pattern of American life rather than from the outside. As a result, many of them have joined the very establishments they previously tried to overthrow and have settled down as competitive workers, parents, and law-abiding citizens (117).

By the early or mid-thirties, most young adults have solved their problems well enough to become emotionally stable and calm. Should the heightened emotionality characteristic of the early years of adulthood persist into the thirties, it suggests that adjustments to adult life have not been satisfactorily made (22).

When emotional tension persists into the thirties, it is generally expressed in worries. What young adults worry about will depend on what adjustment problems they are facing at the time and how much success or failure they are experiencing in meeting these problems. Their worries may be mainly concentrated on their work, because they feel they are not advancing as rapidly as they had hoped to, or their worries may be concentrated on marital or parenthood problems. When adults feel that they have not been able to cope with the problems in the major areas of their lives, they are often so emotionally disturbed that they contemplate or attempt suicide.

Early Adulthood Is a Period of Social Isolation

With the end of formal education and the entrance into the adult life pattern of work and marriage, associations with the peer groups of adolescence wane and, with them, opportunities for social contacts outside the home. As a result, for the first time since babyhood even the most popular individual is likely to experience social isolation, or what Erikson has referred to as an "isolation crisis" (34).

Many young adults, having become accustomed throughout childhood and adolescence to depending on peers for companionship, experience loneliness when responsibilities at home or at work isolate them from groups of their peers. Those who were most popular during their school and college days, and who devoted much of their time to peer activities, find the adjustment to social isolation in adulthood especially difficult. Whether the loneliness that comes from this isolation will be temporary or persistent depends on how quickly and how satisfactorily the young adult can establish new social contacts to replace those of school and college days.

Isolation is intensified by a competitive spirit and a strong desire to rise on the vocational ladder. To achieve success, they must compete with others—thus replacing the friendliness of adolescence with the competitiveness of the successful adult—and they must also devote most of their energies to their work, which leaves them little time for the socialization that leads to close relationships. As a result, they become self-centered, which contributes to loneliness (34).

Early Adulthood Is a Time of Commitments

As young adults change their role from that of student and dependent, characteristic of adolescence, to that of independent adult, they establish new patterns of living, assume new responsibilities, and make new commitments. While these new patterns of living, new responsibilities, and new commitments may change later, they form the foundations on which later patterns of living, responsibilities, and commitments will be established. In speaking about these early commitments, Bardwick has said (6):

It does not seem possible that people make commitments "for ever." This is too big a responsibility to be borne. Yet some commitments have that quality: if you are a parent you are a parent forever; if you take a DDS, the chances are good that you will be working on people's mouths forever; if you achieved a Ph.D. because you did well in school when you were a kid, the chances are that you will spend your life as a professor.

Early Adulthood Is Often a Period of Dependency

In spite of achieving the status of legal adulthood at age eighteen, with the independence this status carries, many young adults are partially or totally dependent on others for varying lengths of time. This dependency may be on parents, on the educational institution they attend on part or total scholarship, or on the federal government for loans to finance their education.

Some young adults resent this dependency, though they realize it is essential if they are to get the training needed for their chosen careers. Many,

however, take the financial support of their parents, of educational institutions, or of the government for granted, but feel no obligation to be dominated in any way by those who have financed their training for their future careers. They expect and demand the same autonomy that their self-supporting age-mates have.

Other young adults, while rebelling against the dependency a prolonged career training necessitates, become so accustomed to depending on others for financial support that they question their own ability to become economically independent. As a result, they often become "perpetual students," going from one training center to another for more and more training for their careers. To compensate for any feeling of guilt or shame they may have for playing the perpetual student role, they try to convince themselves and others that the more training they get, the greater their chances for reaching the top of the ladder in their chosen careers. As a result, their state of dependency is often prolonged into the late twenties or early thirties.

Early Adulthood Is a Time of Value Change

Many of the values developed during childhood and adolescence change as experience and social contact with people of different ages broaden and as values are considered from a more mature standpoint. Adults who used to consider school a necessary evil may now recognize the value of education as a stepping-stone to social and vocational success and to personal fulfillment. As a result of such changed values, many adults who dropped out of school or college decide to finish their education. Some find studying so stimulating that they continue to take courses even after receiving high school or college diplomas (112).

There are many reasons for value changes in early adulthood, three of which are very common. First, if young adults want to be accepted by members of the adult group, they must accept the values of the adult group just as, during childhood and adolescence, they had to accept the values of their peer group to win acceptance. Many young adults discover that the "sloppy Joe" appearance of their school and college days and rebellious attacks on the establishment must give way to adult-approved appearance and behavior if they want to be accepted in adult economic and social groups.

Second, young adults soon discover that most social groups hold conventional values about beliefs and behavior, just as they do about appearance. While the adolescent peer culture may have regarded premarital sex as acceptable behavior, most adults do not and demand more conventional courtship and marriage as the price of acceptance into the social group.

Third, young adults who become parents not only tend to change their values earlier and more radically than those who are unmarried or childless, but they also shift to more conservative and traditional values. In general, the values of most young adults change from egocentric to social. Members of the "me" generation—those who think mainly of their own happiness and desire for self-indulgence—gradually become more socially conscious and concerned as they assume the roles of spouse and parent (117).

Early Adulthood Is the Time of Adjustment to New Lifestyles

While lifestyles in the American culture have been in a state of flux since the turn of the present century, at no period in the life span is this more true than in early adulthood. And in no area of early adult life are new lifestyles more prevalent than in the areas of marriage and parenthood. Instead of the traditional courtship of the past, many young adults regard premarital sex as an accepted part of the courtship pattern. Similarly, use of contraceptives and resort to abortion when contraception fails are so widespread among young adults, especially those who are in colleges or training schools, that they also are regarded as part of the courtship pattern. Nor is marriage after pregnancy regarded as the "hush-hush" matter it formerly was. Instead, many young couples want as large and as elaborate weddings as they had hoped for before the bride became pregnant.

Of the many adjustments young adults must make to new lifestyles the most common are adjustments to egalitarian rather than traditional sex roles, new family-life patterns, including divorce and one-parent families, and new vocational patterns, especially large and impersonal work units in business and industry.

While it is always hard to adjust to new patterns of life, the adjustments young adults must make today are especially difficult because what preparation they received in childhood and adolescence was usually unrelated to or unsuited to the new lifestyles. For ex-

ample, preparation for marriage received at home or in school was very different from that needed for cohabitation. Similarly, young adults are seldom prepared to cope with the responsibilities involved with being a single parent or a combination parent and worker outside the home.

Early Adulthood Is a Creative Age

Unlike older children and adolescents who want to conform to the appearance, behavior, and speech of their age-mates for fear of being regarded as "inferior," many young adults pride themselves on being different and do not regard this as an indication of inferiority. Because they are no longer shackled by the restrictions placed on their behavior by parents and teachers, young adults are free to be themselves and to do what they want to do.

What form creativity will take in adulthood will depend upon individual interests and abilities, opportunities to do what they want to do, and activities that give the greatest satisfaction. Some young adults find a creative outlet in hobbies while others choose vocations in which they can express their creativity (108).

Even though interest in creative activities starts in the twenties, creative achievements often do not reach their peak until middle age. This is due to the fact that creativity is more often discouraged than encouraged in the early years of life. Thus it is that during early adulthood men and women must not only discover where their creative interests and talents lie but they must also develop their capacities which, in many cases, remained dormant while the patterns of their lives were prescribed by parents and teachers. As they approach middle age, however, men and women should have overcome these obstacles sufficiently to achieve the maximum of which they are capable.

As adolescents, girls are given more opportunity to be creative than boys—since creativity is regarded as more sex-appropriate for females than for males. Therefore, as young women, they tend to be more creative in whatever they do—in their dress, their home decorations, or their hobbies—than men. However, home duties and child-care responsibilities often hamper expressions of creativity. As a result, when they reach middle age, women's creative achievements often lag behind those of men who, earlier in adulthood, were less creative than they (1,55).

AIDS TO MASTERY OF DEVELOPMENTAL TASKS

Physical Efficiency

The peak of physical efficiency is generally reached in the mid-twenties, after which there is a slow and gradual decline into the early forties. Thus during the period when adjustment problems are the most numerous and difficult, the individual is physically able to meet and solve them.

Motor Abilities

Young adults reach the peak of their strength between the ages of twenty and thirty. Maximum speed of response comes between twenty and twenty-five years, after which decline begins at a slow rate. In learning new motor skills, adults in their early twenties are superior to those who are approaching middle age. Furthermore, young adults can count on their ability to perform in a given situation, which they could not do in adolescence when rapid and uneven growth often caused them to be awkward and clumsy.

Mental Abilities

The most important mental abilities needed for learning and for adjusting to new situations, such as recall of previously learned material, reasoning by analogy, and creative thinking, reach their peak during the twenties and then begin a slow and gradual decline. Even though young adults may not learn quite as rapidly as they did earlier, the quality of their learning does not deteriorate.

Motivation

When adolescents reach the age of legal maturity, they have a strong desire to be regarded by the social group as independent adults. This provides them with the motivation to master the developmental tasks needed to be so regarded.

Role Model

Adolescents who go to work when they finish high school or training school have role models to imitate. Being associated with adults gives them the motivation to model their behavior along adult lines so that they themselves will be judged as adults. By contrast, adolescents who remain in school or college after they reach legal maturity are thrown mostly with their age-mates and, as a result, they pattern their behavior along the lines of adolescent rather than adult behavior. So long as the dependency state persists, they have little opportunity or motivation to master the developmental tasks of adulthood.

DEVELOPMENTAL TASKS OF EARLY ADULTHOOD

Social expectations for young adults are clearly defined and familiar to them even before they reach legal maturity. Perhaps at no other age in life do they know as clearly and distinctly what society expects of them.

The developmental tasks of early adulthood (refer to page 10 for a list of these tasks) center around social expectations and include getting started in an occupation, selecting a mate, learning to live with a marriage partner, starting a family, rearing children, managing a home, taking on civic responsibilities, and finding a congenial social group (46).

How well these tasks are mastered in the early years of adulthood will influence the degree of success people will experience when they reach the peak during middle age—whether the peak relates to work, social recognition, or family living—and will determine how happy they will be then as well as during the closing years of their lives.

Success in mastering the developmental tasks of early adulthood is greatly influenced by the kind of foundations laid earlier. However, certain conditions in adult life facilitate the mastery of these tasks, the most important of which are given in Box 9-2.

CHANGES IN INTERESTS IN EARLY ADULTHOOD

Typically, adolescents carry over into the adult years many of their interests. Interests change during the adult years, however. Some of these carry-over interests are no longer appropriate to the adult role while

BOX 9-3

CONDITIONS RESPONSIBLE FOR INTEREST CHANGES IN ADULTHOOD

Changes in Health Conditions

Many adults, as they approach middle age, find that their strength and endurance are not what they formerly were. As a result, they gradually shift to interests that require less strength and endurance, especially in recreations.

Changes in Economic Status

When the economic status of adults improves, they tend to expand the range of their interests to include those they previously could not afford. If, on the other hand, their economic status is strained, due to family responsibilities or lack of vocational advancement, many interests must be abandoned.

Changes in Life Patterns

Young adults must reassess their old interests in terms of the time, energy, money, and companionship they entail to see whether they fit into their new life patterns or give as much satisfaction as they did earlier.

Changes in Values

The new values the individual acquires influence already-existing interests or lead to new ones.

Sex-Role Changes

The pattern of adult women's lives differs markedly from that of adult men's lives, with the result that sex differences in interests become greater than they were earlier.

Changes from Single to Married Status

Because their life patterns differ, unmarried adults develop different interests than those of married adults of the same age level.

Assumption of Parental Role

When young adults become parents, they usually do not have the time, money, or energy to keep up their former interests. Instead, their interests become family-oriented rather than self-oriented. Whether they will resume their former interests when their parental responsibilities end will depend largely on how much they missed opportunities to pursue those interests and partly on the prevailing conditions in their lives.

Changes in Preferences

Likes and dislikes, which have a profound influence on interests, tend to become stronger with age, and this leads to increased stability of interests in adulthood.

Changes in Cultural and Environmental Pressures

Because at every age interests are influenced by pressures from the social group, as social-group values change, so do interests.

---

others do not provide the satisfaction they did earlier. Box 9-3 gives some of the major reasons for changes in interests during early adulthood.

Changes in interests occur most rapidly during adolescence, which is also a period of rapid physical and psychological changes. As these physical and psychological changes slow down, so do interest changes. As Strong pointed out many years ago, at "twenty-five years the adult is largely what he is going to be and even at twenty years he has acquired pretty much the interests he will have throughout life" (106).

Typically, the greatest change in interests during early adulthood is the narrowing down of inter-

ests. Young adults narrow down the range of their interests rather than change them entirely. As a result, they have fewer interests as they approach middle age than they had during adolescence or even during early adulthood.

Furthermore, as duties and responsibilities change, there is normally a shift of emphasis on already-existing interests rather than the establishment of new ones. Most individuals do not acquire new interests as they grow older unless their environments change or they have the opportunity to develop new interests and a strong desire to do so.

Although the range of interests among young adults is extremely wide, certain interests may be regarded as typical for young adults in the American culture of today. These are divided into three categories—personal interests, recreational interests, and social interests.

Personal Interests

Personal interests are those related to the individual. Most young adults carry over from their adolescent years a strong interest in self which results in egocentrism. As work, home, and parental responsibilities increase, egocentric interests gradually give way to more socialized interests.

Appearance By the time they reach adulthood, most men and women have learned to accept their physiques and to make the most of them. Although their physical appearance may not be to their liking, they have learned that little can be done to alter it but that much can be done to improve it. As a result, the adult's major concern with appearance is in improving it. This leads to interest in beauty aids and in dieting and exercise.

Young adults know, from their experiences in childhood and adolescence, that an attractive appearance is a tremendous asset in social relationships while unattractiveness is a liability. They have discovered that self-esteem, self-assertiveness, liking by others, happiness, and physical attractiveness are all closely interrelated, with the last being responsible for the other qualities (53). As Mathes and Kahn have explained (76):

In a social exchange, physical attractiveness is a positive input and can be used to obtain a variety of good outcomes for its possessor. One of the most frequently obtained outcomes is liking. Attractive people are liked more as friends . . . and receive more positive evaluations from others . . . and empathy . . . than unattractive people. . . . As a result of the many good outcomes obtained by attractive people, it seems likely that they are happier and better adjusted than unattractive people. It is also probable that the liking received from others is reflected in a high self-esteem.

Women discover that physical attractiveness aids their status in life, both in business and through marriage. In our present-day culture, physical attractiveness in women is more important than intelligence and education in making a successful marriage and, thus, achieving a higher social status (9,110). By con-

trast, most young adults soon discover that a deviant physical appearance—especially one that conforms to the public stereotype of a "hippie"—is a social liability (22).

Interest in appearance begins to wane during the late twenties when business and family pressures are especially strong. However, this interest is revived at the first signs of aging and becomes stronger as these signs appear with greater frequency and intensity.

Typically, the first indication of aging is gain in weight. Men, as a whole, tend to be less concerned about weight gain than women, though concern varies according to socioeconomic status. Men of the middle and upper socioeconomic groups are more concerned about being overweight than are those of the lower groups. The same is true of women, though in all socioeconomic groups, women are more concerned than men (18,91). Adults with lower IQs tend to be more obese than those with higher IQs and are less concerned about it (9).

In addition to gaining weight, other signs of aging, such as sagging chins, gray hair, and protruding abdomens, become problems for the young adult. Some accept these signs of aging without attempting to correct them. Most, however, recognize the important role appearance plays in business, social, professional, and even family life, and they try to correct the problem—by dieting, for example—and they also use clothes and beauty aids to camouflage the telltale signs of aging.

Clothes and Personal Adornment Interest in clothing and personal adornment remains strong in early adulthood. Because they know that appearance is important to success in all areas of their lives, young adults frequently spend more time and money on clothing and grooming than they can afford. Box 9-4 shows the importance of clothes in personal and social adjustments.

Unlike interest in physical appearance, interest in clothes does not lag as adulthood progresses. Instead, it remains strong and often increases in intensity as both men and women discover that attractive, expensive clothes help them to succeed in any area that is important to them, whether in business, social, or family life. As Bickman has explained, clothes "may seem to be superficial qualities, but they are important determinants of one person's reaction to another" (14).

THE ROLES OF CLOTHES IN EARLY ADULTHOOD

Improvement of Appearance

Young adults select clothes that enhance their good features and camouflage their less attractive ones. When telltale signs of aging begin to appear, they choose clothes that make them look younger than they actually are.

Indication of Social Status

Young adults, especially those who are socially and vocationally mobile, use clothes as status symbols that will identify them with a particular social group.

Individuality

Even though adults want their clothes to identify them with a particular social group, they also want them to have enough individuality to be noticed and admired by the group members.

Socioeconomic Success

Few things are able to proclaim economic success more quickly and in a more subtle way than clothes. Expensive clothes, a large wardrobe, and clothes from name designers and manufacturers all tell that the wearer has enough money to have such clothes.

Sex-Appropriateness

Men and women whose bodies are not as sex-appropriate in appearance as they would like them to be select clothes that enhance their sex-appropriateness.

Symbols of Maturity Most young adults feel the need to impress upon their parents and other adults the fact that they are no longer adolescents but full-fledged adults with the accompanying rights, privileges, and responsibilities that adulthood brings. This arouses an interest in symbols of maturity.

As is true of all status symbols, symbols of maturity must be apparent to others in order to have an impact. Thus young adults are interested in such symbols of maturity as adult styles of grooming and dress, patterns of speech and behavior that proclaim adult status, autonomy in all areas of life, and a name that suggests adult status, rather than a pet name used by

family members or a nickname given by members of the peer group.

Once young men and women have established themselves as adults through their work, their marriage, or parenthood, their need for symbols of maturity wane. Consequently, there is a decreased interest in these symbols.

Status Symbols Status symbols are marks of distinction that set the individual apart from others. They may take any form but, in adulthood, the common status symbols are cars, homes in prestigious neighborhoods, club membership, travel, and material possessions (91).

What are status symbols in one social area will not necessarily be in another area. There are fads in status symbols just as there are fads in clothes and cars. However, most young adults know what status symbols are highly prized in their communities. Knowing that they are indications of social and economic success, the typical young adult is eager to rise as fast as possible in the vocational world in the hope of acquiring the material possessions that will proclaim high status.

While an automobile is a major status symbol for the adolescent, a home is the most important material possession of the young adult. Although a home may be important to older people mainly in terms of comfort, to the young adult it means prestige in the eyes of others. Packard has explained this as follows (91):

One reason the home is replacing the automobile as a favored way for demonstrating status is that a home can be a showcase for "culture." In a home you can display antiques, old glassware, leather-bound books, classical records, paintings. These are things a car can't do.

Money Young adults are interested in money because of what it can do for them *now*, rather than in the future. They believe that if they can have and do the things that other young adults with whom they want to be identified have and do, this will increase their chances for acceptance and solidify the acceptance they have already achieved.

Some of the problems relating to money come from lack of knowledge of how to use money wisely or from values they have carried over from the peer-group standards of adolescence. As adolescents, they

FACTORS INFLUENCING RELIGIOUS INTEREST IN EARLY ADULTHOOD

Sex

Women tend to be more interested in religion than men and to take a more active part in religious observances and church affairs.

Social Class

Members of the middle class are, as a group, more interested in religion than those of the upper and lower classes; they participate more in church functions of all kinds, and they assume leadership roles in different church organizations. Adults who are anxious to improve their social status in the community are more active in religious organizations than those who are satisfied with their status.

Place of Residence

Adults who live in rural and suburban areas tend to show a greater interest in religion than those who live in urban areas.

Family Background

Adults who were brought up in homes where religion played an important role and who became affiliated with a church tend to continue to show a greater interest in religion than those whose early religious experiences were less important to them.

Religious Interests of Friends

Adults are more likely to be interested in religion if their neighbors and friends are active in religious organizations than if their friends have little religious interest.

Spouses of Different Faiths

Husbands and wives of different faiths tend to be less active in religious affairs than those of the same faith.

Concern about Death

Adults who are concerned about death or who have a morbid preoccupation with death tend to be far more interested in religion than those whose attitude is more realistic.

Personality Pattern

The more authoritarian the personality pattern, the more preoccupied young adults are with religion per se and the more intolerant they are of other religions. By contrast, well-adjusted adults are tolerant of other religions and usually participate in religious activities.

---

were concerned primarily with earning enough money for their needs or getting enough from their parents. They showed little interest in the management of family finances and little desire to learn about the costs involved in family living.

Furthermore, as adolescents or even as young adults living with their families before marriage, they had little training in the use of money. Parents may advise younger adolescents on the use of their allowances, but older adolescents usually have complete freedom to use their money as they wish. As a result, they are ill prepared, as young adults, to budget the income they have to live on, and they frequently buy on credit or use installment plans, thus putting themselves in a position where they are always in debt.

Religion   Usually, by the time they reach adulthood, young men and women have resolved the religious doubts that plagued them in adolescence and have

formulated a philosophy of life, based on religion, that is satisfactory to them. Or, they have rejected the family religion as having little or nothing to offer them (26). In either case, young adults tend to be less interested in religion that they were when they were younger. That is why Peacocke has called the early twenties the "least religious period of life" (94). This lack of interest is shown by a decrease in church attendance and by an indifference to other religious observances.

When the responsibilities of parenthood are assumed, there is generally a return to religion, or at least a *show* of interest in it. Parents of young children often feel that it is their duty and responsibility not only to teach their children the fundamentals of their own faith and to see that they receive proper religious instruction in Sunday school, but also to set a good example for them. Consequently, they may revive religious practices which were observed in their own homes, even if these are somewhat modified to fit into the pattern of life today. Regular attendance at church is now part of the parents' life, and they begin to take an active part in some of the church organizations. This does not, however, necessarily mean that they have experienced another period of religious awakening, as often happens in early adolescence.

Many factors determine the strength and form of expression of religious interest among young adults, the most common of which are given in Box 9-5.

Recreational Interests

The term *recreation* means an activity that renews strength and refreshes spirits after toil or anxiety. Like play in childhood, it is activity engaged in for enjoyment, with no ulterior purpose to be achieved. It serves the same purpose as play does in the childhood years. However, the recreational interests of adults are different, in most respects, from the play interests in childhood or even in adolescence.

Young adults in the American culture of today have more leisure time than their parents or grandparents did and more than adults in most other cultures. This is due partly to the shorter workweek and partly to mechanization, which has made running a home less time- and energy-consuming than it formerly was. Furthermore, members of all social classes have more money to spend on recreation today than in the past.

In spite of these opportunities, many young adults do not find their recreational activities satisfactory. One of their major adjustment problems involves learning how to use their free time in an enjoyable way.

There are several major reasons why recreation presents a major adjustment problem. First, while they were in school or college, various forms of recreation were readily available to them, at no cost or at only a minimum cost, and they had many friends with whom to engage in these activities. Second, parents and teachers encouraged them to participate in the readily available forms of recreation as an important part of school and college life. And third, schools and colleges provided them with guidance and supervision in recreation so that they learned how to use their leisure time in a way that gave them satisfaction (60,90,123).

Many factors influence the pattern of adult forms of recreation. Some of the most important of these are given in Box 9-6.

An analysis of the different kinds of recreational interests of American men and women today will show that they are in large part home- or neighborhood-centered and that they differ markedly from the recreational interests of adolescents. Many of these changes in interest are the result of necessity. For example, while the children are still young, many of the family's recreational activities are centered around them. Even when the children reach adolescence, the parents' recreation is largely family-centered.

Talking Talking, especially with those whose interests are similar, is a popular pastime of both young men and young women. It is especially popular among married women whose parental responsibilities keep them in the home for the major part of the day. Much of this talking must be done over the telephone because of the restrictions that children place on the mother's activities. Men, by contrast, do much of their talking to friends outside the home—at work or at meeting places such as bars or recreation centers.

Most young adults talk mainly about personal, day-to-day concerns relating to their families, their work, and social matters. Gossiping about friends and neighbors is common among women, while men are more apt to tell jokes or discuss politics. In discussions with members of the opposite sex, women try to talk about matters of interest to men, while few men try to adapt their conversations to women's interests.

Dancing Dancing, which is one of the most popular forms of recreation in adolescence, is engaged in only infrequently during early adulthood. When home *and* business responsibilities are assumed, young adults have fewer opportunities to dance than they did during their high school and college days. Many adults of all socioeconomic groups dance only infrequently during their early twenties and even less during their thirties. Thus the quality of their dancing deteriorates, and they derive less satisfaction from it than they did during adolescence.

Sports and Games Active participation in sports and athletic events of all sorts decreases during the adult years, not because adults are in poorer health or are less interested in sports, but because they have less time and money to invest in these activities than they did when they were in school or college. Participation reaches a low point as the adult approaches mid-

BOX 9-6

FACTORS INFLUENCING ADULT RECREATION

Health

Healthy young adults engage in a wider variety and in more strenuous forms of recreation than those whose health is not as good. But even the healthiest adults begin to slow down as they approach middle age and spend more time on amusements and on less strenuous forms of recreation.

Time

In spite of a shorter workweek, most young adults find that they have less time for recreation than they had as adolescents because of work or family responsibilities, obligations to community organizations, or the necessity of taking a second job so that they can acquire the status symbols they consider important. They engage in forms of recreation that give them the greatest satisfaction or which are most practical from the point of view of time and money.

Marital Status

Young unmarried men and women not only have more time and money for different forms of recreation than those who are married but also spend more of their recreational time outside the home. In large families, much of the family-centered recreation is also home-centered—watching television and playing games with family members, for example.

Socioeconomic Status

Middle-class adults have more time for recreation, engage in a wider variety of recreational activities,

spend more of their recreational time as spectators, and devote more of their recreational time to activities related to their work, such as reading, than those of the lower classes. Recreational activities of middle-class families are generally home-oriented, while those of lower-class adults involve commercial entertainments outside the home.

Sex

Regardless of marital status, young men and women must make radical changes in their recreational activities. Most of the recreational activities of women with children must be home-centered. Figure 9-2 shows how women's recreational activities in early adulthood are affected by their roles as wives and mothers.

Social Acceptance

Young adults who are popular and have many friends from their school years or from their jobs have opportunities for more socially oriented recreations after they finish their education than have adults who were not popular in school or college or who are living far away from their old schoolmates. Young adults who are completing their education have more opportunities for recreations involving people than have those who have no educational affiliation. Because geographically or socially mobile people have few social contacts and often lack acceptance in their new social groups, their recreations must, of necessity, be primarily solitary or family-oriented.

dle age. This is truer of members of the lower socioeconomic groups than of the middle and upper classes, who have more places such as clubs and recreation centers available to them.

Because they have fewer opportunities for active participation in sports, adults show their interest in this form of recreation by reading and by talking about sports, attending athletic contests, listening to sports events on the radio, or watching them on television. This passive participation in sports increases as adults approach middle age.

Interest in games of strategy and games of chance, which began during adolescence, increases during adulthood. Games of strategy, where winning is dependent on the skill of the player—bridge, for example—appeal more to adults of the middle and upper socioeconomic groups. Games of chance, where winning depends on luck rather than skill, appeal more to members of the lower socioeconomic groups. Women enjoy bingo, while men like poker, though these games are by no means limited to members of one sex or one social class.

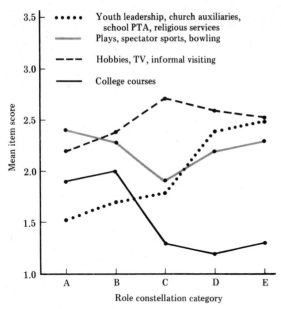

A—Single, working full time

B—Married, living with husband, childless, working at least ½ time

C—Married, living with husband, preschool children only, not working

D—Married, living with husband, preschool and school-age children, not working

E—Married, living with husband, school-age children only, not working

FIGURE 9-2 The pattern of female recreational activity is markedly influenced by the role the woman plays in life. (Adapted from S. S. Angrist. Role constellation as a variable in women's leisure activities. *Social Forces*, 1967, **45,** 423–431. Used by permission.)

Entertaining Limited budgets and parental responsibilities restrict the amount of entertaining by young adults. Entertaining relatives is far more common than entertaining friends and neighbors. Even unmarried adults do relatively little entertaining, and what little they do is more often done outside the home.

Entertainment of friends and neighbors is usually informal. During the summer months, picnics or backyard barbecues, which children also attend, are the favorite forms of entertainment. Home entertainment may also include card parties, where simple refreshments are served, and small dinners or cocktail parties.

Hobbies Many adults do not pursue hobbies until their financial position is such that they have the necessary leisure time. Others, who find their work boring and frustrating, take up hobbies as a form of compensation. Men and women of high intelligence have more hobbies than those of lesser abilities. As a rule, men who are vocationally the most successful pursue more hobbies than those who are less successful.

Hobbies are, for the most part, of a constructive nature. They include such activities as cooking, gardening, painting, sewing, knitting, crocheting, making and repairing furniture, taking pictures and developing films, playing an instrument, and collecting things. Most of these hobbies can be carried out in the home and do not require the companionship or help of others.

Amusements While amusements—activities in which the individual is a passive participant—are enjoyed by people of all ages, they grow in popularity during adulthood. Some of the amusements men and women enjoyed when they were younger, such as going to the movies, become less appealing as they grow older. On the other hand, interest in other amusements, slight during childhood or adolescence, grows stronger in adulthood. Box 9-7 lists some of the most popular amusements among young adults in the American culture of today.

Social Interests

Early adulthood, as Erickson has emphasized when he referred to it as the time of "isolation crisis," is frequently a lonely time for both men and women (34). Young unmarried men often find themselves at loose ends during their leisure time. As is true of unmarried women, their friends of earlier years and their business associates are occupied with family activities or with courtship. As a result, young men miss the kind of social life they enjoyed during adolescence, when there was usually a congenial group to talk to or do things with.

Even young married adults are lonely at times and miss the companionships they enjoyed during the adolescent years. Tied down with the care of young children, limited by a budget that will permit little beyond the necessities of life, and often living in a community away from family and former friends, married adults may be as lonely as those who are unmarried and in a less favorable position to solve the loneliness problem.

BOX 9-7

POPULAR AMUSEMENTS AMONG YOUNG ADULTS

Reading

Because of their many responsibilities, young adults have limited time for reading. As a result, they must become more selective about what they read. Young adults spend more time reading newspapers and magazines than books.

Listening to Music

Young adults listen to records and to music on radio and television, often as a way of relieving feelings of boredom or loneliness. Some prefer popular music, a carry-over from adolescence, while others may develop a taste for classical music.

Movies

Young unmarried adults often go to the movies on dates, as they did in adolescence. Married adults go to the movies less frequently, especially if they have children, in which case they must either hire baby-sitters or limit their choice of movies to those which are suitable for children.

Radio

Many women listen to the radio while doing housework, and men may listen as they drive to and from work. The radio provides both news and entertainment.

Television

Television watching, especially in the evenings, is a favorite amusement of adults with children. The larger the family and the lower the income, the more time is spent watching television. Men, as a group, prefer sports programs while women prefer domestic comedies or reruns of well-known movies.

Havighurst has explained that loneliness during the early adult years occurs because this is a "relatively unorganized period in life which marks the transition from an age-graded to a social-status-graded society" (46). No longer can either men or women count on readily available companionship, as they could during their school or college days. Now they must make their own way, form their own friend-

ships, and establish themselves through their own efforts. As they reach the thirties, adults, whether married or single, have usually made adjustments to these changes and have established a satisfactory and relatively stable social life for themselves.

Of the many changes in social interests and activities young adults must make, the ones described below are the most common and the most difficult. A comparison of the pattern of social interests and activities of adolescence with that of early adulthood, as described below, will show how radically different they are.

Changes in Social Participation Participation in social activities, so important to adolescents because of its prestige value, must, of necessity, be limited during early adulthood. The social life of young adults is for the most part centered in the home, with members of the family replacing friends as companions.

Because the pattern of life is not the same for all, the amount of social participation, as well as the form it will take, varies greatly. On the whole, there is more participation in social activities outside the home as adults approach middle age, during the mid- to late thirties, than there is during the early or even the late twenties. Furthermore, the pattern of social participation and the amount of such participation differ for married adults and for those who are unmarried. The most important factors influencing social participation in early adulthood are listed in Box 9-8.

Participation in social activities among young married adults may be individual or joint activities. When there are children and when it is difficult or impossible to turn over their care to someone else, the parents must, through necessity, have separate social lives. In some cases, separate social lives are the result of lack of similar interests. Whatever the reason, marital satisfaction tends to be greater when there is joint rather than individual participation in social activities (90).

Changes in Friendships The craving for popularity and for a large number of friends, which started to wane during the latter part of adolescence, wanes still further during early adulthood. This is especially true of married men and women, who have each other for companionship and whose lives center around home and family responsibilities. Even unmarried adults, however, are more selective in their choice of friends

BOX 9-8

SOME FACTORS INFLUENCING SOCIAL PARTICIPATION IN EARLY ADULTHOOD

Social Mobility

The more anxious adults are to improve their social status, the more they try to become affiliated with the community organizations that will help them to rise on the social ladder.

Socioeconomic Status

Whether single or married, young adults whose socioeconomic status is favorable are able to participate in more social activities, especially outside the home, than are those whose socioeconomic status is strained.

Length of Residence in the Community

Many young adults who must move to a new community become active participants in community organizations as a way of meeting people and forming friendships.

Social Class

Upper- and middle-class adults belong to more community organizations, are more active in these organizations, and assume more leadership roles in them than lower-class adults. They also have more intimate friends, entertain and visit more, and spend less time with relatives than do members of the lower classes.

Environment

The social life of young adults living in cities may center more around relatives than that of young adults who live in rural and suburban areas, where there is more "neighborliness" and social participation.

Sex

Married men are freer to engage in social activities outside the home than married women, who often must limit their social participation to the home or immediate neighborhood. Unmarried women, however, are often more active in community life than unmarried men.

Age of Sexual Maturing

Men who matured early are more active in community affairs and more often play leadership roles than men who matured late. Women who were early maturers continue to be socially active in adulthood if circumstances in their lives permit.

Birth Order

Firstborns, many of whom suffer from feelings of insecurity, tend to be "joiners" and are more active in community affairs than those who were born later.

Church Affiliation

Adults who are members of a church tend to be more active in church and other community organizations than do those who have no church affiliation.

than they were earlier. As a result, young adults have fewer but more intimate friends than they did when they were younger (121).

As is true at every age, friends in adulthood are selected on the basis of congeniality. Young adults find people whose interests and values are similar to theirs more congenial than those whose interests and values are different. While they are selective in the choice of friends, they are especially so in the choice of intimate same-sex friends (63). The reason for this, as Packard has emphasized, is that "For better or worse, most people feel more at ease with their own kind" (91).

Changes in Social Groupings The same degrees of friendship that existed in adolescence continue into adulthood. Young adults usually have a small group of intimate friends or confidants. Frequently, these are old friends unless young adults have changed so much that they no longer find their old friends congenial.

How many intimate friends young adults have will depend also on how much they are willing to disclose about their interests, problems, and aspirations. Many adults are reticent about discussing their personal affairs with outsiders as they grow older. This is partly because they want to create a favorable im-

While young adults continue their education, the same types of social groupings continue as those which existed in adolescence—especially small groups of intimate friends. (Photo by Erika.)

pression and partly because they do not want to run the risk of having their personal affairs discussed by others.

In addition to intimate friends, most young adults know a number of people whom they see fairly frequently—at parties or other social gatherings. On the outer rim of the friendship circle are many acquaintances whom they know only slightly and with whom they come in contact infrequently.

By the late thirties or mid-forties, most men and women have a circle of friends as large as they want. Because their interests are stabilized by this time, they are less likely to change friends than they were when they were younger. This results in a tightly knit social group, similar to the cliques of early adolescence, which is difficult for outsiders to penetrate. One of the problems of occupational mobility (to be discussed later in this chapter) is the difficulty of establishing new and close friendships when the family must move to a new community or to a new neighborhood in the old community.

Many young adults, but by no means all, have memberships in some voluntary association in their community. These may be affiliated with churches or with different lines of work, or they may be organized primarily for social reasons (64). Figure 9-3 shows the percentage of young adults at different ages who have membership in different voluntary associations. Note that more men belong to such associations than women and that more men and women belong in middle age than at older or younger ages.

Change in Value Placed on Popularity Popularity becomes increasingly less important as adults approach middle age. A few congenial friends mean more than a large group with whom they have less in common and find less congenial.

Social acceptance or the lack of it affects adults much as it does adolescents, but to a lesser extent. The more they are accepted by the group with which they would like to be identified, the more they conform to group pressures. When, on the other hand, they enjoy less than complete acceptance—but if they see the possibility of improving this situation—there will be a high degree of adherence to group

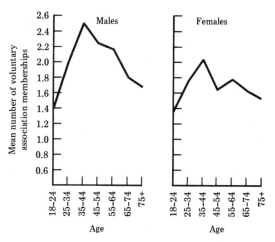

FIGURE 9-3 Pattern of membership in voluntary associations in the community of men and women at different ages during the adult years. (Adapted from S. J. Cutler. Age differences in voluntary association membership. *Social Forces*, 1976, **55**, 43–58. Used by permission.)

Today there is an increasing number of women in leadership roles in business and community organizations. (Sybil Shelton from Monkmeyer.)

standards. If, however, their acceptance is low, they have little motivation to conform to group standards except in public, and then only to forestall the possibility of complete rejection.

Changes in Leadership Status Adults achieve leadership status in different ways. Some are elected to an office in a business or community organization while others are appointed. Some are informal leaders in the community but are influential in that others look up to them and try to follow their patterns of behavior. Some who are elected or appointed to an office in community organizations are not perceived as influential and thus may have less influence in community life than the informal leaders.

Studies of persistence of leadership have revealed that in most cases, "once a leader, always a leader." The experience gained from leadership status in school, the prestige associated with leadership, and the self-confidence that being a leader engenders all contribute to success in adult life.

However, whether individuals will continue to be leaders in adulthood depends largely on their willingness to adapt themselves to the wishes of the group. By the time they reach adulthood, most leaders have learned adaptability. As a result, they are flexible enough to adjust to groups of many different structures. This is especially true of very bright individuals who, during high school and college, participated in many extracurricular activities and played roles of leadership in these activities (31,101).

Studies of men and women who hold executive positions in business and industry, and who play leadership roles in community affairs, have shown that they have many of the qualities necessary for leadership in adolescence, as well as others not essential at that time. In addition, some of the qualities considered important in adolescent leaders, such as success in sports, are less important now. Box 9-9 gives some of the characteristic qualities of adult leaders.

Because of the prestige that accompanies leadership, leaders in one area may find themselves in leadership roles in areas where their abilities and training are limited. The more leadership roles individuals play, the more confident they become of their abilities as leaders and the more leadership skills they acquire. Lack of self-confidence, lack of strong motivation to be leaders, and lack of leadership skills, on the other hand, are fundamentally responsible for the fact that there are fewer women leaders in every area of adult life than one would expect on the basis of the number of women participating in these areas. Even those women who played leadership roles as girls are often prevented from doing so in business, industry, or community affairs because their home responsibilities limit the time they can devote to such activities.

SOCIAL MOBILITY IN EARLY ADULTHOOD

There are two types of mobility that play important roles in the lives of young adults, geographic and social. *Geographic* mobility means going from one place to another. This is done more often for vocational than for social reasons. How it affects young adults will be explained in the following chapter in the discussion of vocational adjustments.

Social mobility means moving from one social group to another. This may be horizontal—moving to another social group on the same level—or vertical —moving to a social group above or below the group at the present level. Most young adults want to be upwardly mobile; few are satisfied to move from one social group to another on the same level; and even fewer are content to move down on the social scale. Geographic mobility almost always accompanies social mobility.

Part of the American dream of today is to have a better education, a better social and economic status, and more material possessions than one's predecessors. Stated simply, people want to move up the social ladder. This they want not only for themselves but also for their children.

The desire to move up the social ladder is especially strong among young adults who discovered, during adolescence, that those who were most popular and who held most of the leadership roles came from the higher socioeconomic groups. They believe that if they, too, can climb up the social ladder the chances of greater popularity and more leadership roles for themselves and for all members of their families will be increased.

Because men and women usually achieve their highest social and economic status in middle adulthood, from thirty years of age on, young adults are motivated to do all they can to rise above their present status as rapidly as possible. The most important conditions leading to upward social mobility in early adulthood are given in Box 9-10.

In general, men rise on the social ladder mainly by their own efforts while women rise mainly through their marriages to upper-status men or those who are able to advance through their own efforts and achievements (23,104). Physical attractiveness is a greater asset in social mobility for women than education while the reverse is true for men (109). First-borns, especially boys, are most likely to be given opportunities to rise above the status of their families. As

Altus has pointed out, firstborns are given "greater opportunities for education which makes rise on the social ladder possible" (2).

SEX-ROLE ADJUSTMENTS IN EARLY ADULTHOOD

Sex-role adjustments during early adulthood are extremely difficult. Long before adolescence is over, boys and girls are well aware of the approved adult sex roles but this does not necessarily lead to acceptance. Many adolescent girls want to play the role of wife and mother when they reach adulthood, but they do not want to be wives and mothers in the traditional sense—being subordinate to their husbands, devoting most of their time to their homes and children, and having few or no outside interests. Their reason for wanting to avoid playing the traditional female role has been explained by Arnott and Bengston (3):

The role of "homemaker" is undervalued in the United States, where occupation is the key to the assignment of role status, and achievement and monetary value tend to provide the criteria for so-cial ranking. In contemporary America, women tend to absorb the same values as the men with whom they are educated, and to use these men as reference persons in comparing role rewards. Educated women in the "homemaker only" role may feel a sense of "relative deprivation" in the distribution of social status. A "homemaker-plus" role (such as the addition of employment to home duties) may promise greater social recognition.

The hope of many of today's young women for an egalitarian marriage is based not on wishful thinking but on the realization that there have been marked changes in the adult pattern of living. For example, wives often work until their husbands finish their education or become established in business, or they take jobs in order to acquire various status symbols that the family would otherwise be unable to afford. Most important of all, young women are aware of the breakdown of the "double standard," not only in sexual and moral behavior, but also in social, business, and professional life.

In fact, the traditional concepts are gradually being modified or even replaced by new, more egalitarian ones—concepts that stress similar behavior patterns for members of the two sexes. These egalitar-

The woman who accepts the egalitarian sex-role concept does not feel guilty about using her abilities and training to give her satisfaction, even if this requires employing someone to take care of her home and children. (Photo by Erika.)

BOX 9-11

CONCEPTS OF ADULT SEX ROLES

Traditional Concepts

Traditional concepts of sex roles emphasize a prescribed pattern of behavior, regardless of individual interests or abilities. They emphasize masculine supremacy and intolerance toward any trait that hints of femininity or any work that is considered "woman's work."

Men

Outside the home the man holds positions of authority and prestige in the social and business worlds; in the home he is the wage earner, decision maker, adviser and disciplinarian of the children, and model of masculinity for his sons.

Women

Both in the home and outside, the role of the woman is other-oriented in that she gains fulfillment by serving others. She is not expected to work outside the home except in cases of financial necessity, and then she does only work that serves others, such as nursing, teaching, or secretarial work.

Egalitarian Concepts

Egalitarian concepts of sex roles emphasize individuality and the egalitarian status of men and women. Roles should lead to personal fulfillment and not be considered appropriate for only one sex.

Men

In the home and outside, the man works with the woman in a companionship relationship. He does not feel "henpecked" if he treats his wife as an equal, nor does he feel ashamed if she has a more prestigious or remunerative job than he does.

Women

Both in the home and outside, the woman is able to actualize her own potentials. She does not feel guilty about using her abilities and training to give her satisfaction, even if this requires employing someone else to take care of the home and children.

ian concepts have found acceptance among all social groups, even those which formerly held firmly to traditional concepts of the male and female roles. The traditional and egalitarian concepts of adult sex roles are given in Box 9-11.

Many young women recognize the low prestige associated with the traditional role of wife and mother, and consequently they have little motivation to learn this role. When they become wives and mothers, they see little opportunity for escape from this role into one they previously found more satisfying and personally rewarding. Conflict between what they would like to do and what they know they must do further weakens their motivation to play the traditionally prescribed sex role (95). The conflicts and frustrations many young women in the American culture experience are heightened by the constant bombardment of advice from the mass media to play a role other than that of the traditional wife and mother. See Figure 9-4.

PERSONAL AND SOCIAL HAZARDS OF EARLY ADULTHOOD

The major personal and social hazards of early adulthood stem from a failure to master some or most of the important developmental tasks for that age, making the individual seem immature as compared with other young adults. Up to age thirty, it is quite common for both men and women to be immature in certain areas of their behavior, while at the same time showing marked maturity in others. Gradually, with new achievements and new expectations from the social group, much of the immaturity that characterized behavior in the early part of this period disappears, resulting in a more even development on a more mature level (46).

Mastering developmental tasks is difficult at any age, and this difficulty is increased when stumbling blocks impede the individual's progress. The most common stumbling blocks to the mastery of the developmental tasks of early adulthood are listed in Box 9-12.

Failure to master the developmental tasks of early adulthood, resulting in a failure to come up to social expectations in different areas of behavior, affects the individual's personal and social adjustments. For example, the young adult who clings to youthful interests and fails to develop more mature ones is

Woman Besieged

FIGURE 9-4 American women today are being bombarded by advice in the mass media to play roles other than that of wife and mother. (Lou Erickson. *The Atlanta Journal and Constitution,* Feb. 13, 1977. Used by permission.)

judged by others as immature, leading to feelings of unhappiness. Similarly, much of the discontent experienced by young adults is due to the fact that they have fewer material possessions than their friends and neighbors have—an attitude that is a carry-over from adolescence.

Some of the most common and most serious hazards to personal and social adjustments during the early adult years are briefly discussed below. While all adults will not necessarily experience all of these hazards, most of them are experienced at one time or another by a majority of young adults.

Physical Hazards

Poor health or physical defects that cannot be corrected or camouflaged are just as hazardous to personal and social adjustments in adulthood as they are in childhood and adolescence. Adults who are handicapped by poor health cannot achieve what they are capable of in their vocational or social lives. As a result, they constantly suffer from frustrations. The more they see those potentially less capable than they achieving successes above theirs, the more frustrated they become. When their frustrations lead to overstrain to compete with their peers who are not physically handicapped, it is likely to lead to stress

which, in time, may and often does bring on heart attacks (40).

Physical defects and poor health are often not as serious hazards to good personal and social adjustments as physical unattractiveness. Adults with sex-inappropriate body builds, or with unattractive physical features that they have been unable to camouflage with beauty aids, or the inability to afford clothes that would compensate to some extent for an unpleasing appearance, face many problems which few can cope with successfully. They find their unattractive appearances detrimental in business, a handicap to a happy and successful marriage, and an almost insurmountable barrier to upward social mobility.

When they compare their achievements in the areas of adult life that are most important, they discover that those who are physically attractive have greater success. For example, attractive women usually make better marriages than those who are unattractive while, for both men and women, physical attractiveness is such an asset in the business world that they can count on getting ahead faster and with less work than their less attractive coworkers. Leadership in different organizations, they discover, usually goes to an attractive person, just as it did during the adolescent years (8,31,66).

BOX 9-12

STUMBLING BLOCKS TO MASTERY OF DEVELOPMENTAL TASKS OF EARLY ADULTHOOD

Inadequate Foundations

The more unfinished business, in the form of unmastered earlier developmental tasks, the individual carries into adulthood, the longer and harder the adjustment to adulthood will be.

Physical Handicaps

Poor health or physical defects that prevent the individual from doing what others of similar age can do make mastery of the developmental tasks of adulthood difficult or impossible.

Discontinuities in Training

When training received at home or in school has little or no relationship to the pattern of life in adulthood, the individual will be ill prepared to meet the demands of adult life.

Overprotectiveness

The adult who was overprotected during childhood and adolescence may find adjustment to adult life extremely difficult. Many parents continue to overprotect their adult sons and daughters, thus adding to their adjustment difficulties.

Prolongation of Peer-Group Influence

The longer young adults continue their education in college or training schools, the longer peer-group influences will prevail and the longer their behavior will conform to peer-group standards and values. Because they have become accustomed to behaving as adolescents, learning to behave as adults is more difficult than it otherwise would be.

Unrealistic Aspirations

Adults who were extremely successful academically, socially, and athletically in high school or college are likely to develop unrealistic concepts of their abilities. As a result, they expect to be equally successful in the adult world. Parental aspirations during adolescence often add to the adjustment problems of adulthood.

Religious Hazards

There are two hazards in the area of religion that cause emotional disturbances for many young adults. The first relates to adjusting to a new religious faith accepted in place of the family faith of childhood. Some young adults accept a new faith because it seems to have more in common with their personal interests and beliefs than their family religion had. Others accept a new faith when they marry to please their spouses or their spouses' families. Whatever the reason for accepting a new faith, there is likely to be a conflict with the childhood faith and a problem of adjusting to the ritual associated with the new faith.

The second and more difficult problem related to religion in early adulthood occurs in mixed marriages when in-laws pressure the couple to adopt one or the other faith. Even when young adults have little interest in religion, they object to having the religious training of their children dictated by grandparents on either side, and they resent the implications that their religions are inferior to those of their mates—an implication inherent in the insistence that the change be made.

Furthermore, when faced with this problem, young adults have to contend with the pressures from their own parents, to whom adherence to the family faith may also be important. Adjustment problems in religion frequently complicate marital adjustments and are often at the basis of "in-law" problems—one of the most difficult problems in the area of marital adjustments.

Social Hazards

Many young adults find hazards in their adjustments to the social groups with which they are now identified. Three of these hazards are especially common and difficult to overcome successfully.

First, young adults find it difficult to become associated with a congenial social group—one of the important developmental tasks of early adulthood. There are several conditions responsible for this difficulty. Women who are tied down by home responsibilities may have neither the time nor the money for the social activities they formerly enjoyed and may be unable to find satisfactory substitutes. This results in discontentment which often affects their marital satisfaction. Men likewise, because of pressure from work and home responsibilities, often find it difficult to become associated with a congenial social group. Like women, they then experience discontent with their lives. How satisfaction with social activities affects marital satisfaction is illustrated in Figure 9-5 which shows satisfaction at different stages in the life span. Even when they have the time and money for social activities, some adults find it difficult to establish warm, friendly relationships with the people with whom they come in contact. This may be due to lack of congeniality, resulting from differences in interests and values, but more often it is due to the competitive spirit many young adults develop in their hopes of climbing the vocational ladder—a spirit which becomes habitual and carries over into their social relationships. That is one of the reasons why, as both Erikson and Havighurst have explained, early adulthood is one of the loneliest periods in the life span (34,46).

The second hazard to good adjustments and satisfaction with social life is dissatisfaction with the role the social group expects the individual to play. Adults who were accustomed to playing leadership roles in adolescence now find it difficult to play the role of follower, should circumstances require this. A man who was a leader in his school or college days is likely to become frustrated, as an adult, when leadership roles in business, industry, or community affairs go to men who have a higher socioeconomic status or greater prestige in the community.

The third hazard to social adjustments is social mobility. Socially mobile people face far more dilemmas than the relatively immobile because they must adjust to new social groups with new values and standards of behavior. Families that are upwardly socially mobile, for example, move to better neighborhoods, give up old associations and values, choose between associations with members of two classes, join new social organizations, and give up most of the social life they enjoyed with former neighbors. This increases the loneliness that is characteristic of early adulthood and often leads to depression (12).

Equally serious, social mobility often causes stress in the family, not only between husband and wife but between parents and children as well. The husband is often critical of his wife if he feels that she is not presenting a favorable image to the new neighbors. Also, parents who are overly anxious to have their children associate with the "better" group in their new neighborhood may become aggressive and punitive in their treatment of them.

Individuals who are forced to move downward in the social hierarchy find that they have little in common with the members of the social class with which they are now identified. As a result, they tend to isolate themselves. Also, their former friends and neighbors are likely to drop them because they

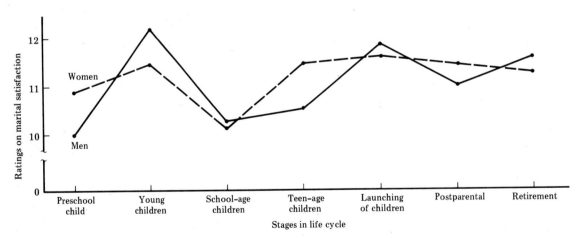

FIGURE 9-5 Satisfaction with social activities affects marital satisfaction among both men and women. (Adapted from W. R. Burr. Satisfaction with various aspects of marriage over the life cycle: A random middle-class sample. *Journal of Marriage & the Family,* 1970, **32,** 29–37. Used by permission.)

no longer live in the same neighborhood or cannot afford the social activities they formerly engaged in.

Sex-Role Hazards

Because of the conflict concerning approved sex roles today, adherence to either traditional or egalitarian concepts presents hazards (11). Adherence to traditional concepts of sex roles has a marked influence on a young adult's personal adjustments. For example, a man may go to any length to prove to himself and others that he is typically masculine. He may overtax his strength, disregarding danger signals of poor health, in the belief that it is unmasculine to worry about one's health, or he may devalue feminine characteristics to the point where he tries constantly to assert his superiority in his relationships with women (40,95,96,107).

Women, as a result of being looked down upon and treated as inferior to men, often develop a typical "minority-group complex"—an emotionally toned belief in their inferiority, not unlike that experienced by members of minority, religious, or ethnic groups. In addition, they are often conditioned to be afraid of success, especially in any activity in which men are involved because success, they believe, would suggest that they were unfeminine (25,28). As Midgley and Abrams have said, "Social constraints and social definition of sex-appropriate behavior have had crippling effects on achievement motivation in women" (79). This is less likely to be true in activities in which only members of the female sex are involved, though many women develop the habit of underachievement as a result of fear of success in activities in which they compete with men (19,50).

Married women often feel "trapped" in a situation they had not anticipated and from which they see little hope of escape. If a wife and mother finds that those for whom she has sacrificed her personal interests do not appreciate her efforts; if she finds the work she must do dull, lonely, confining, and below her abilities and training; and if she finds the romance she had associated with the role of a married woman lacking, she becomes disillusioned and resentful. See Figure 9-6.

This unfavorable attitude is exaggerated by the "lazy-husband syndrome." The wife feels resentful when she sees her husband taking it easy and enjoying himself while she works more or less continuously from morning to night, seven days a week. The lazy-husband syndrome has been described this way (88):

FIGURE 9-6 For many women, the role of "only a housewife" leads to disillusionment and resentment. (Lou Erickson. *The Atlanta Journal and Constitution,* Jan. 28, 1974. Used by permission.)

The picture is one of a husband who has had a "long" eight-hour day at his air-conditioned office and who comes home, calls for a drink, plops exhausted into a chair with the newspaper or in front of the television set, gets up to eat his dinner an hour later, complains that the meat is not well done, pecks his wife on the cheek and goes out with the bowling team, has a beer, comes home, watches some more television, and plops into bed. Meanwhile, his wife, who has been working all day, gets the meal, tries to discipline the children so Daddy can rest, feeds the infant, serves the meal, does the dishes, feeds the dog, bathes the kids, puts them to bed, puts a load of washing through, does some ironing, watches TV for an hour (while darning). . . . This goes on day after day. The husband is happy but the woman becomes vaguely unhappy, tense and fatigued.

When married women work outside the home, they not only experience a work overload but they usually find that their husbands' careers take precedence over theirs if any occupational conflict arises or if there are occupational demands in the husband's career that might interfere with the wife's career, such as moving to another community. Because many employers expect women to adjust their work to family needs, they tend to restrict them to less important jobs with poorer pay and fewer opportunities for advancement. This often has a deleterious effect on marriage because of the resentments women feel about their work overload and discrimination against them (87,103).

Even unmarried women who do not have to divide their time and energies between family and career and who do not suffer from the feeling of being trapped, often find barriers to advancement in their chosen fields of work. They find that men, frequently less able than they, often receive larger salaries and are given positions with greater prestige and responsibility, mainly because the policy of the organization for which they work favors men. They also discover that prejudicial bias in the evaluation of women's work tends to result in barriers to achievement and advancement (82).

In conclusion, it is obvious that the most important hazard to good personal and social adjustments comes from the effects of sex-role stereotypes that influence the attitudes and behavior of both men and women. While any sex-role stereotype may prove to be a barrier to good adjustments, the traditional stereotypes are by far the most hazardous in today's American culture.

Chapter Highlights

1. Adulthood—the longest period of the life span—is usually subdivided into three periods: early adulthood, which extends from eighteen to approximately forty years; middle adulthood or "middle age," which extends from approximately forty to approximately sixty years; and late adulthood or "old age," which extends from approximately sixty years to death.

2. Early adulthood is the settling-down and reproductive age; a problem age and one of emotional tension; a time of social isolation; a time of commitments; and often a time of dependency, of value changes, of creativity, and of adjustments to a new life pattern.

3. There are certain aids to mastering the developmental tasks of early adulthood—physical efficiency, motor and mental abilities, motivation, and a good role model.

4. Because many of the interests carried over from adolescence are no longer appropriate for the adult role, changes in all areas of interests are inevitable. The greatest change is in narrowing down the range of interests.

5. Personal interests in early adulthood include interest in appearance, in clothes and personal adornment; in symbols of maturity and status symbols; in money; and in religion.

6. Even though the recreational activities of adults serve much the same purpose as play activities do in childhood, the recreational interests of adults differ in many respects from the play interests of childhood due to changes in roles and life patterns.

7. The major recreational interests of young adults in the American culture of today include talking, entertaining, hobbies, and amusements which, for the most part, are enjoyed in the home.

8. Social activities in early adulthood are often greatly curtailed because of vocational and family pressures. As a result, many young adults experience what Erikson has called an "isolation crisis"—a time of loneliness due to isolation from the social group.

9. During early adulthood, social participation is often limited and changes in friendships, in social groupings, and in values placed on popularity and leadership status are inevitable.

10. Social mobility in men comes mainly through their own efforts while, in women, it comes mainly through marriage to upper-status men or those who, through their achievements, have been able to climb the social ladder.

11. Most young married women find sex-role adjustment in early adulthood very difficult, especially when they are forced into traditional roles after playing more egalitarian roles before marriage.

12. Difficulties in mastering the developmental tasks of early adulthood are often increased by such stumbling blocks as inadequate foundations, physical handicaps, discontinuities in training, parental overprotectiveness, prolongation of peer-group influence, and unrealistic aspirations.

13. The most common and most important physical hazard of early adulthood is physical unattractiveness because it is detrimental to the individual's personal and social adjustments.

14. Two important religious hazards in early adulthood—adjustment to a new religious faith in place of the childhood family faith and in-law pressure to adopt another faith in mixed marriages—are hazardous to good personal and social adjustments because they cause emotional disturbances.

15. Finding a congenial social group to identify with, especially in social mobility, and acceptance of traditional sex roles are the major psychological hazards most young adults must cope with in their personal and social lives.

Bibliography

1. Alpaugh, P. A., and J. E. Birren. Are there sex differences in creativity across the adult life span? *Developmental Psychology,* 1975, **18,** 461–465.
2. Altus, W. D. Birth order and its sequelae. *Science,* 1966, **151,** 44–49.
3. Arnott, C., and F. L. Bengston. "Only a homemaker." Distributive justice and role choice among married women. *Sociology & Social Research,* 1970, **54,** 495–507.
4. Bachtold, L. M. Women, eminence, and career-value relationships. *Journal of Social Psychology,* 1975, **95,** 187–192.
5. Balswick, J. O., and C. W. Peek. The inexpressive male: A tragedy of American society. *Family Coordinator,* 1971, **20,** 363–368.
6. Bardwick, J. M., Middle age and a sense of future. *Merrill-Palmer Quarterly,* 1978, **24,** 129–138.
7. Baumrind, D. From each according to her ability. *School Review,* 1972, **80,** 161–197.
8. Bennetts, L. Beauty is found to attract some unfair advantages. *The New York Times,* March 18, 1978.
9. Benson, P. L., S. A. Karabenick, and R. M. Lerner. Pretty pleases: The effects of physical attractiveness, race, and sex on receiving help. *Journal of Experimental Social Psychology,* 1976, **12,** 409–415.
10. Bernard, J. Note on changing life styles, 1970–1974. *Journal of Marriage & the Family,* 1975, **37,** 582–593.
11. Bernard, J. Change and stability in sex-role norms and behavior. *Journal of Social Issues,* 1976, **32**(3), 207–223.
12. Bernard, J. Homosociality and female depression. *Journal of Social Issues,* 1976, **32**(4), 213–238.
13. Berscheid, E., E. Walster, and G. Bohrnstedt. The happy American body: A survey report. *Psychology Today,* 1973, **7**(6), 119–123, 126–131.
14. Bickman, L. Social roles and uniforms: Clothes make the person. *Psychology Today,* 1974, **7**(11), 48–51.
15. Bischof, L. J. *Adult psychology.* (2nd ed.) New York: Harper & Row, 1976.
16. Block, J. H. Conceptions of sex role: Some cross-cultural and longitudinal perspectives. *American Psychologist,* 1973, **28,** 512–526.
17. Booth, A. Sex and social participation. *American Sociological Review,* 1972, **37,** 183–193.
18. Borkan, G. H., and A. H. Norris. Fat distribution and the changing body dimensions of the adult male. *Human Biology,* 1977, **49,** 495–514.
19. Breedlove, C. J., and V. C. Cirirell. Women's fear of success in relation to personal characteristics and type of occupation. *Journal of Psychology,* 1974, **86,** 181–190.
20. Burr, W. R. Satisfaction with various aspects of marriage over the life cycle: A random middle-class sample. *Journal of Marriage & the Family,* 1970, **32,** 29–37.
21. Butler, E. W., R. J. McAllister, and E. J. Kaiser. The effects of voluntary and involuntary residential mobility on males and females. *Journal of Marriage & the Family,* 1973, **35,** 219–227.
22. Campbell, A. The American way of mating: Marriage si, children only maybe. *Psychology Today,* 1975, **8**(12), 37–43.
23. Chase, I. D. A comparison of men's and women's intergenerational mobility in the United States. *American Sociological Review,* 1975, **40,** 483–505.
24. Cogswell, B. E. Variant family forms and life styles: Rejection of the traditional nuclear family. *Family Coordinator,* 1975, **24,** 391–406.
25. Condry, J., and S. Dyer. Fear of success: Attribution of cause to the victim. *Journal of Social Issues,* 1976, **32**(3), 63–83.
26. Cox, H. Eastern cults and Western culture: Why young Americans are buying Oriental religions. *Psychology Today,* 1977, **11**(2), 36–42.
27. Cutler, S. J. Age differences in voluntary association membership. *Social Forces,* 1976, **55,** 43–58.
28. Darley, S. A. Big-time careers for the little woman: A dual role dilemma. *Journal of Social Issues,* 1976, **32**(3), 85–98.
29. Deutsch, D. Woman's role: An Adlerian view. *Journal of Individual Psychology,* 1970, **37,** 356–360.
30. Digenan, M. A., and J. B. Murray. Religious beliefs, religious commitments, and prejudice. *Journal of Social Psychology,* 1975, **97,** 147–148.
31. DiMarco, N., C. Kuell, and E. Wims. Leadership style and interpersonal need orientation as moderators of changes in leadership dimension scores. *Personnel Psychology,* 1975, **28,** 207–213.
32. Eisdorfer, C., and M. P. Lawton (Eds.). *The psychology of adult development and aging.* Washington, D.C.: APA, 1973.
33. Elder, G. H. Role orientations, mental age and life patterns in adulthood. *Merrill-Palmer Quarterly,* 1972, **18,** 3–24.
34. Erikson, E. H. *Identity: Youth and crisis.* New York: Norton, 1968.
35. Farley, F. H., K. L. Smart, and C. V. Brittain. Academic achievement motivation and birth order in adults. *Journal of Social Psychology,* 1976, **98,** 283–284.
36. Featherman, D. L., and R. M. Hauser. Sexual inequalities and socioeconomic achievement in the U. S., 1962–1973. *American Sociological Review,* 1976, **41,** 462–483.
37. Fozard, J. L., and S. J. Popkin. Optimizing adult development: Ends and means of an applied psychology of aging. *American Psychologist,* 1978, **33,** 975–989.
38. Frieze, I., J. Parsons, P. Johnson, D. Ruble, and G. Zellerman. *Women and sex roles: A social psychological perspective.* New York: Norton, 1978.
39. Ginzberg, E. When mothers work. *Parents Magazine & Better Homemaking,* 1977, **52**(4), 34, 78–79.
40. Glass, D. C. Stress, competition, and heart attacks. *Psychology Today,* 1976, **10**(7), 54–57.
41. Gordon, F. E., and D. T. Hall. Self-image and stereotype of femininity: Their relationship to women's role conflicts and coping. *Journal of Applied Psychology,* 1974, **59,** 241–243.
42. Gould, R. Adult life stages: Growth toward self-tolerance. *Psychology Today,* 1975, **8**(9), 74–78.
43. Gould, R. L. The phases of adult life: A study in developmental psychology. *American Journal of Psychiatry,* 1972, **129,** 521–531.
44. Grotevant, H. D. Family similarities in interests and orientation. *Merrill-Palmer Quarterly,* 1977, **22,** 61–72.
45. Halas, C. M. Sex-role stereotypes: Perceived childhood socialization experiences and the attitudes and behavior of adult women. *Journal of Psychology,* 1974, **88,** 261–275.
46. Havighurst, R. J. *Developmental tasks and education.* (3rd ed.) New York: McKay, 1972.
47. Hawkins, L. F. Urbanization, families, and the church. *Family Coordinator,* 1969, **18,** 49–53.
48. Hjelle, L. A. Relationship of a measure of self-actualization to

religious participation. *Journal of Psychology,* 1975, **89,** 179–182.

49. Hjelle, L. A., and R. Butterfield. Self-actualization and women's attitudes toward their roles in contemporary society. *Journal of Psychology,* 1974, **87,** 225–230.

50. Hoffman, L. W. Fear of success in 1965 and 1974. A follow-up study. *Journal of Consulting & Clinical Psychology,* 1977, **45,** 310–321.

51. Hoge, D. R. Changes in college students' value patterns in the 1950s, 1960s, and 1970s. *Sociology of Education,* 1976, **49,** 155–163.

52. Ivancevich, J. M., and J. H. Donnelly. Leader influence and performance. *Personnel Psychology,* 1970, **23,** 539–549.

53. Jackson, D. J., and T. L. Huston. Physical attractiveness and assertiveness. *Journal of Social Psychology,* 1975, **96,** 79–84.

54. Jackson, E. F., W. S. Fox, and C. J. Crockett. Religion and occupational achievement. *American Sociological Review,* 1970, **35,** 48–63.

55. Joesting, J. The influence of sex roles on creativity in women. *Gifted Child Quarterly,* 1975, **19,** 336–339.

56. Jones, M. C. Personality antecedents and correlates of drinking patterns of women. *Journal of Consulting & Clinical Psychology,* 1971, **36,** 61–69.

57. Jones, S. B. Geographic mobility as seen by the wife and mother. *Journal of Marriage & the Family,* 1973, **35,** 210–218.

58. Kampler, H. L. Extended kinship ties and some modern alternatives. *Family Coordinator,* 1976, **25,** 143–149.

59. Keller, S. The future role of women. *Annals of the American Academy of Political & Social Sciences,* 1973, **408,** 11–12.

60. Kelly, J. R. Life styles and leisure choices. *Family Coordinator,* 1975, **24,** 185–190.

61. King, K., T. J. Abernathy, I. E. Robinson, and J. O. Balswick. Religiosity and sexual attitudes and behavior among college students. *Adolescence,* 1976, **11,** 535–539.

62. Klobus, P., J. N. Edwards, and D. L. Klemmack. Differences in social participation: Blacks and whites. *Social Forces,* 1978, **56,** 1035–1052.

63. Knapp, C. W., and B. T. Harwood. Factors in the determination of intimate same-sex friendships. *Journal of Genetic Psychology,* 1977, **131,** 83–90.

64. Knoke, D., and R. Thomson. Voluntary association membership trends and the family life cycle. *Social Forces,* 1977, **56,** 48–65.

65. Kobrin, F. E. The primary individual and the family: Changes in living arrangements in the United States since 1940. *Journal of Marriage & the Family,* 1976, **38,** 233–239.

66. Krebs, D., and A. A. Adinolfi. Physical attractiveness, social relations, and personality style. *Journal of Personality & Social Psychology,* 1975, **31,** 245–253.

67. Kreze, A., M. Zelina, J. Julas, and M. Garbara. Relationship between intelligence and relative prevalence of obesity. *Human Biology,* 1974, **46,** 109–113.

68. Laney, G. T. The new morality and the religious communities. *Annals of the American Academy of Political & Social Sciences,* 1970, **387,** 14–31.

69. Laumann, E. D., and J. S. House. Living room styles and social attitudes: The patterning of material artifacts in a modern urban community. *Sociology & Social Research,* 1970, **54,** 321–342.

70. Lavrakas, P. J. Female preferences for male physiques. *Journal of Research in Personality,* 1975, **9,** 324–334.

71. Levine, A., and J. Crumrine. Women and fear of success: A problem in replication. *American Journal of Sociology,* 1975, **80,** 964–974.

72. Levinson, D. J. Growing up with the dream. *Psychology Today,* 1978, **11**(8), 20–31, 89.

73. Lipman-Blumen, J. How ideology shapes women's lives. *Scientific American,* 1972, **226**(1), 34–42.

74. Marini, M. M. The transition to adulthood: Sex differences in educational attainment and age at marriage. *American Sociological Review,* 1978, **43,** 483–507.

75. Mason, K. O., and J. L. Czajka. Change in U.S. women's sex-role attitudes, 1964–1974. *American Sociological Review,* 1976, **41,** 573–596.

76. Mathes, E. W., and A. Kahn. Physical attractiveness, happiness, neurotocism, and self-esteem. *Journal of Psychology,* 1975, **90,** 27–29.

77. McAllister, R. J., E. W. Butler, and E. J. Kaiser. The adaptation of women to residential mobility. *Journal of Marriage & the Family,* 1973, **35,** 197–204.

78. McGahan, P. The neighbor role and neighboring in a highly urban area. *Sociological Quarterly,* 1972, **13,** 397–408.

79. Midgley, N., and M. Abrams. Fear of success and locus of control in young women. *Journal of Consulting & Clinical Psychology,* 1974, **42,** 737.

80. Mims, P. R., J. J. Hartnett, and W. R. Nay. Interpersonal attraction and help volunteering as a function of physical attractiveness. *Journal of Psychology,* 1975, **89,** 125–131.

81. Minuchin, P. The schooling of tomorrow's women. *School Review,* 1972, **80,** 199–208.

82. Mischel, H. N. Sex bias in the evaluation of professional achievement. *Journal of Educational Psychology,* 1974, **66,** 157–166.

83. Money, J., and A. A. Ehrhardt. *Man and woman, boy and girl.* Baltimore, Md.: Johns Hopkins Press, 1973.

84. Montagu, A. Don't be adultish! *Psychology Today,* 1977, **11**(3), 46–50, 55.

85. Neugarten, B. L. Education and the life cycle. *School Review,* 1972, **80,** 209–216.

86. Neugarten, B. L. Continuities and discontinuities of psychological issues into adult life. In D. C. Charles and W. R. Looft (Eds.). *Readings in psychological development through life.* New York: Holt, 1973, Pp. 348–355.

87. Nevill, D., and S. Damico. Role conflict in women as a function of marital status. *Human Relations,* 1975, **28,** 487–498.

88. New York Times article. Lazy husbands said to fatigue wives. *The New York Times,* April 3, 1966.

89. New York Times article. If you feel worthless doing family chores. *The New York Times,* March 29, 1973.

90. Orthner, D. K. Leisure activity patterns and marital satisfaction over the marital career. *Journal of Marriage & the Family,* 1975, **37,** 91–102.

91. Packard, V. *The status seekers.* New York: Pocket Books, 1961.

92. Paige, K. E. Women learn to sing the menstrual blues. *Psychology Today,* 1973, **7**(4), 41–46.

93. Pankratz, L., P. Levendusky, and V. Glaudin. The antecedents of anger in a sample of college students. *Journal of Psychology,* 1976, **92,** 173–178.

94. Peacocke, A. R. The Christian faith in a scientific era. *Religious Education,* 1963, **58,** 372–376.

95. Pleck, J. H. The male sex role: Definitions, problems, and sources of change. *Journal of Social Issues,* 1976, **32**(3), 155–168.

96. Pleck, J. H., and J. Sawyer. *Men and masculinity*. Englewood Cliffs, N. J.: Prentice-Hall, 1974.

97. Rogers, D. L., W. D. Hefferman, and W. K. Warner. Benefits and role performance in voluntary organizations: An exploration of social exchange. *Sociological Quarterly*, 1972, **13**, 183–196.

98. Rosenfeld, R. A. Women's intergenerational occupational mobility. *American Sociological Review*, 1978, **43**, 36–46.

99. Ryan, M. S. *Clothing: A study in human behavior*. New York: Holt, 1966.

100. Schmitz-Scherzer, R., and I. Strodel. Age-dependency of leisure time activities. *Human Development*, 1971, **14**, 47–50.

101. Schriesheim, C. A., and C. J. Murphy. Relationships between leader behavior and subordinate satisfaction and performance: A test of situational moderators. *Journal of Applied Psychology*, 1976, **61**, 634–644.

102. Shields, S. A. Functionalism, Darwinism, and the psychology of women: A study in social myth. *American Psychologist*, 1975, **30**, 739–754.

103. Smith, A. J. How sex bias can ruin a marriage. *Journal of Home Economics*, 1977, **69**(3), 25–27.

104. Sørensen, A. B. The structure of intergenerational mobility. *American Sociological Review*, 1975, **40**, 456–471.

105. Staines, G., C. Tavris, and T. E. Jayaratne. The queen bee syndrome. *Psychology Today*, 1974, **7**(8), 55–60.

106. Strong, E. K. Satisfactions and interests. *American Psychologist*, 1958, **13**, 449–456.

107. Tavris, C., and D. Pope. Masculinity: What does it mean to be a man? *Psychology Today*, 1976, **9**(10), 58–66.

108. Taylor, I. A. Developing creativity in gifted young adults. *Education*, 1974, **94**, 266–268.

109. Taylor, P. A., and N. D. Glenn. The utility of education and attractiveness for females' status attainment through marriage. *American Sociological Review*, 1976, **41**, 484–498.

110. Udry, J. R. The importance of being beautiful: A reexamination and racial comparison. *American Journal of Sociology*, 1977, **83**, 154–160.

111. U.S. News & World Report article. Leisure boom: Biggest ever and still growing. *U.S. News & World Report*, April 17, 1972, Pp. 42–46.

112. U.S. News & World Report article. Big surge in education: Back to school for millions of adults. *U.S. News & World Report*, April 2, 1973, Pp. 73–74.

113. U.S. News & World Report article. 18-year-old adults: Their unexpected problems. *U.S. News & World Report*, Aug. 20, 1973, Pp. 40–42.

114. U.S. News & World Report article. For lots of reasons, more workers are saying "No" to job transfers. *U.S. News & World Report*, Feb. 14, 1977, Pp. 73–74.

115. U.S. News & World Report article. What's in, what's out: The search for status. *U.S. News & World Report*, Feb. 14, 1977, Pp. 38–42.

116. U.S. News & World Report article. Women: Their impact grows in the job market. *U.S. News & World Report*, June 6, 1977, Pp. 58–59.

117. U.S. News & World Report article. Yesterday's rebels grow up. *U.S. News & World Report*, March 27, 1978, Pp. 38–62.

118. U.S. News & World Report article. America's adults: In search of what? *U.S. News & World Report*, Aug. 21, 1978, Pp. 56–59.

119. Vanck, J. Time spent in housework. *Scientific American*, 1974, **231**(3), 116–120.

120. Van Dusen, R. A., and E. B. Sheldon. The changing status of American women: A life cycle perspective. *American Psychologist*, 1976, **31**, 106–116.

121. Verbrugge, L. M. The structure of adult friendship choices. *Social Forces*, 1977, **56**, 576–597.

122. Wicker, A. W., and A. Mehler. Assimilation of new members in a large and a small church. *Journal of Applied Psychology*, 1971, **55**, 151–156.

123. Williams, R. S. Psychological approaches to the study of leisure. *Bulletin of the British Psychological Society*, 1977, **30**, 8–12.

CHAPTER TEN
EARLY ADULTHOOD: VOCATIONAL AND FAMILY ADJUSTMENTS

After reading this chapter, you should be able to:

- Evaluate critically the conditions that contribute to vocational adjustments in early adulthood, especially vocational selection and its stability and adjustment to work conditions in the vocation selected.
- Identify the many different types of family patterns there are in the American culture of today and point out the characteristics of each type.
- Understand the difficulties young adults experience in marital adjustments and the conditions that contribute to these difficulties.
- Explain what adjustments young adults must make to parenthood and some of the conditions that influence these adjustments.
- Examine critically the ages at which marital adjustment is easiest during early adulthood, the conditions that contribute to this adjustment, and the criteria used to assess it.
- List and briefly describe the problems involved in singlehood, divorce, and remarriage.
- Discuss why vocational and marital adjustments are particularly hazardous in early adulthood and show in what areas of adjustment these hazards are most likely to lead to poor personal and social adjustments.

Among the developmental tasks of early adulthood, those relating to occupation and family life are the most numerous, the most important, and the most difficult to master. Even when adults have had some work experience, have married and have become parents, they must still make major adjustments to these roles.

The other developmental tasks of adulthood— finding a congenial social group, adjusting to changes in recreation necessitated by adult patterns of living, and taking on civic responsibilities, as described in the preceding chapter—are easier for adults to master because they acquired a background of training and experience in these areas during childhood and adolescence. Thus these adjustments are mainly revisions of patterns of behavior that have already been established.

In the case of adjustments to be described in this chapter, adults have less of a foundation on which to build. As a result, these adjustments are more difficult, require a longer time to make, and the end results are often far from satisfactory.

Furthermore, sex roles, as discussed in the preceding chapter, are fundamentally important in both the areas of vocation and family life. If adults are to make successful adjustments to marriage and also to parenthood, they must play roles that are mutually satisfying to both spouses, and they must derive satisfaction from playing these roles. In addition, if they are to derive satisfaction from their roles as parents, they must select roles that both parents agree are best for their children, and they must feel confident of their abilities to play these roles successfully.

Sex-role adjustment is fundamental to vocational adjustment, just as it is to marital adjustment. For example, a man cannot be satisfied with a "masculine" vocation that he selected because of parental or social pressure when his real interest is in a vocation that is regarded as "feminine." Work dissatisfaction is not limited to the job; it soon becomes generalized and colors every area of the individual's life.

Women, accustomed during their school and college days to playing egalitarian roles with their male peers, find it hard to adjust to the treatment they receive in industry, business, and the professions. Playing a subordinate role as an adult, after playing an egalitarian or near-egalitarian role during the formative years, makes adjustment to their vocational roles

far more difficult than it would be if they had played subordinate roles earlier.

By far the most important aspect of the problem is the fact that success or failure in making these adjustments will affect the areas of life most closely related to prestige in the eyes of others, their concepts of themselves as individuals, their own happiness and that of every member of their families. For these reasons they can correctly be regarded as the major adjustments of adulthood.

VOCATIONAL ADJUSTMENTS

For most adult men in America today, happiness depends to a large extent upon satisfactory vocational adjustments. The whole pattern of their lives is dependent on how much they earn and how they earn it.

Because an increasing number of women, both single and married, now work outside the home, they too must make vocational adjustments. These are likely to present an even more serious problem for women than for men because many women, in spite of attempts on the part of the federal government to eliminate sex discrimination in the work world, can find employment only in low-paying jobs, which are primarily routine in nature, or in lines of work that require limited ability and training and have little prestige associated with them. Even women of superior competence are discriminated against in the vocational world (69).

Some women adjust to the frustrations and resentments that are inevitable when occupational doors are shut to them or opened only slightly to comply with laws against discrimination. One of the common ways they do this is by helping their husbands to achieve the success they themselves would have liked to achieve but which, because of barriers in their paths, they realize they would never have been able to achieve.

Studies have revealed that adjustments must be made in a number of areas. Each of these adjustments not only depends upon and in turn influences adjustments in other areas but, even more important, the success or failure the individual experiences in these adjustments has a tremendous influence on personal and social adjustments as well as on the degree of life satisfaction. Of the many areas of vocational adjustment adults must make, the ones described below are the most common and most important.

Selection of a Vocation

The first major adjustment is the selection of a vocation. While some adults have made this selection years earlier and have been trained for the work the vocation demands, many young adults, when they graduate from high school, college, or even a professional training school are not sure of what they want to do for the rest of their lives. Even worse, they often find that what they thought they wanted to do is not available or that they lack the training necessary to carry out the work required by the vocation they selected.

Today, there is evidence that selection of a vocation becomes increasingly difficult for each successive generation of young adults. This contributes heavily to the difficulty they have adjusting to their vocations. Box 10-1 gives the most common factors which make vocational choice difficult.

Many young adults who have had little or no training for a particular line of work go through a period of trying out one job after another, often in different lines of work. This "job-hopping" as it is called often goes on during the twenties or even into the thirties. When the selection of a vocation will be made depends on certain factors, the most important of which are the individual's liking for the kind of work selected, evidence of ability to do the work successfully, and necessity, due to financial or other responsibilities. Young men who must support a family, for example, often make a vocational selection earlier than those who have no such financial obligations.

Many young adults claim that they do not want to go into the same line of work as their parents or other relatives. But even though their first vocational choices may have little relation to the occupations of their fathers or mothers, there is evidence that the final choice of a job is more often in that general occupational group than in a different. The exception to this general trend is when young adults have had education and training above that of their parents and thus vocational upward mobility is possible (82,102).

Stability of Vocational Selection

The second major adjustment the young adult must make is the stabilization of the vocational selection. It is not at all uncommon for both men and women to change jobs—job-hopping—during their

BOX 10-1

FACTORS MAKING VOCATIONAL CHOICE DIFFICULT

- The ever-increasing number of different kinds of work from which to choose
- Rapid changes in work skills due to increased use of automation
- Lack of flexibility in working time which is especially difficult for women who must adjust their work schedule to their home responsibilities
- Long and costly preparation which makes career shifts impossible
- Sexual stereotypes of certain occupations— teaching and nursing as "women's work" and aviation and engineering as "men's work"
- Unfavorable stereotypes of some occupations, especially the service occupations
- A desire for a job that will give a sense of identity rather than one that makes the individual feel like a cog in a big machine
- Lack of security in work, especially seasonal jobs, which influences women's vocational selections more than men's
- Ignorance of one's own capacities due to lack of job experience or vocational guidance
- Insufficient education or training for available jobs
- Unrealistic vocational aims carried over from adolescence or even childhood
- Unrealistic values and expectations, especially concerning job prestige and autonomy

twenties and sometimes even into their thirties. However, by the late thirties, as Gould has pointed out, "it is too late to make major changes in a career" (68). This is especially true of a career that requires special training unless the individual is in a position to take time out for this training.

How stable the individual's vocational selection will be will depend largely on three factors. These are job experience, personal interests, and vocational values. Of lesser importance is economic necessity which, today, plays a less dominant role than in the past. This is partly because unemployment insurance enables the worker to live for a period of time on insurance before getting another job, and partly because many wives go to work to help support the family while the husband makes a job or even a career shift.

Adults who have had *job experience* can make far more satisfactory vocational choices than those who lack such experience. Even job experience on a part-time basis during high school or college helps individuals to know what to anticipate in different jobs and gives them an insight into features of a job that will be or will not be to their liking.

When adults choose vocations related to their *personal interests,* as reflected in their choice of academic subjects in high school or college or in their choice of extracurricular activities, they are usually more satisfied with their decisions than those whose choices have little or no relationship to their interests. When personal interests are taken into consideration in the choice of jobs, adults are less likely to change jobs than when factors other than personal interests have motivated their choices.

Vocational values are even more important in vocational stability than job experience and personal interests. Studies of what work means to different people have revealed that, regardless of their occupations, work has different meanings for different people. For some, for example, it may be a source of prestige and social recognition while for others it may be an opportunity for social participation, a way of being of service to others, a source of enjoyment and creative self-expression, or merely a way of earning a living (72,143,151).

However, it is important to realize that both men and women tend to change their vocational values as a result of experience in the work world. As they grow older, they often attach more value to stability of a job and the independence it provides them than they do to more interesting work or higher salaries. This shift in values becomes especially pronounced as adults approach middle age.

Factors Influencing Stability of Vocational Selection   There are a number of factors that influence the stability of vocational selection. Stability has been found to increase with age. Those who change jobs or careers as they approach middle age do so for economic reasons, or because their interests have changed, or because they want a job with more prestige, or a job in some area of the state or country where they and their families prefer to live.

Job changes *within an occupation* are more frequent than occupational changes. Professional workers change jobs least, while those in unskilled or the higher white-collar occupations change most. Skilled workers find it increasingly hard to change their occupations because of the difficulty of acquiring new skills. Individuals who are *successful* in their careers tend to be stable in their vocational choices. When such individuals do change jobs, they usually stay within their original general vocational category, and the change is the result of mature appraisal of talents and predispositions, based on experience.

Women tend to be less stable in their vocational choices than men, mainly because married women, who constitute a large proportion of the female labor force, often must adapt their vocational interests to their home responsibilities or to changes in their husbands' jobs (13,92,144,152).

Adjustment to Work

The third major adjustment is to the job that has been selected. When adults have made a vocational selection, they must adjust to the work itself, to the hours of the work day or work week, to their co-workers and superiors, to the environment in which the work is done, and to the restrictions the work imposes on their personal lives.

For many young adults, especially those who have had little or no work experience during their school or college years, this is often the most difficult of all vocational adjustments. For example, adults who cut classes during their student days when they felt like sleeping late often find getting up to get to work at the appointed time day after day both difficult and frustrating. Similarly, those who, during their student days, avoided the classmates they disliked now find that they cannot avoid the coworkers they dislike.

Unquestionably, the factor that influences adjustments to work most is the worker's attitude. Havighurst, from a study of workers' attitudes toward work, has come to the conclusion that they can be divided into two general categories which he has labeled "society-maintaining work attitudes" and "ego-involving work attitudes." The characteristics of these attitudes are explained in Box 10-2 (72).

Conditions that affect the vocational adjustments of men and women differ in many respects, and are discussed separately below. In general, it will be apparent that the adjustments men must make are

COMMON WORK ATTITUDES

Society-maintaining Work Attitudes

Workers whose attitudes are society-maintaining have little or no interest in their work per se and gain little personal satisfaction from it. Their main interest is in their paychecks. They often regard their jobs as heavy and unpleasant burdens and look forward to their time of retirement.

Ego-involving Work Attitudes

Workers who find their jobs ego-involving derive great personal satisfaction from them. For some, work is a basis of self-respect and a sense of worth. For others, it is a means of gaining prestige, a locus of social participation, or a source of intrinsic enjoyment or creative self-expression, as well as a way of making time pass in a pleasant, routine manner. Because work means so much to workers with such attitudes, they may become preoccupied with it to the exclusion of other interests and dread the time when they will be forced to retire.

men adjust to authority. Many boys and young men in high school and college resent the authority of their teachers and school administrators. They expect to achieve autonomy when they graduate and enter the work world. How well they can adjust to reality in a world where hierarchy of authority exists will influence their adjustments to their work. If they continue to resent the authority of those above them, they will make poor adjustments to their work.

Fourth, adjustments to work are influenced by pay raises or lack of them. Adult men expect to be paid more each year than they were the year before and to move slightly higher up on the vocational ladder. If they get what they regard as reasonable raises and if they see they are climbing up the vocational ladder, even if at a slower rate than they had hoped, they are satisfied or at least partially satisfied. However, even climbing the vocational ladder does not necessarily guarantee good adjustments. This is especially true if workers think their advancement is due to "pull" rather than to ability. Under such conditions, this makes them feel inadequate for the work they are now expected to do.

Sometimes men can advance vocationally only if they are willing to move to another community. By doing so, the entire family is uprooted and must make adjustments to new patterns of living. Because of this, many men today question whether the satisfaction they gain from vocational advancement compensates for the adjustment problems their families must face. As a result, there is a growing trend for workers to say no to job transfers (58,82,164).

less difficult than those women must make but this is, by no means, always the case.

Men's Adjustments   There are a number of conditions, important to them, that influence men's adjustments to their work. First, if the job allows them to play the roles they want to play, they will be satisfied and adjust well to their work. If, for example, a man wants to play the role of leader and has been accustomed to playing this role in school and college, he will be satisfied with his work if he is in a position of authority over others.

Second, satisfaction is attained if men feel that their jobs make use of their abilities and training. Men who are forced, because of limited education and training, to do work which they regard as below the level of their abilities, will derive little satisfaction from their work or from the social group in the community with which they are associated. This dissatisfaction soon spreads to all areas of their lives and has an adverse effect on their personal and social adjustments.

Third, adjustment to work is influenced by how

Women's Adjustments   Just as there are a number of conditions that influence men's adjustments to their work, so there are a number of conditions that influence women's adjustments. Among these, six stand out as especially important.

First, when women are unable to find jobs suited to their abilities, training, and expectations, they feel frustrated. This militates against good adjustments to their work and to their coworkers and superiors. If they are forced to take what are considered "sex-appropriate" jobs—instead of jobs in areas where their interests and abilities lie but which are regarded as "men's work"—their frustrations increase (2,82).

Second, when women feel they are in dead-end jobs, especially as they approach middle age, they often become what Kanter referred to as "bitchy bosses'' and take out their frustrations on their subordinates (83).

Third, when women have formed stereotyped occupational aspirations, which means aspirations below their capacities to avoid rivaling or surpassing male workers, they tend to become frustrated when they discover that their capacities and training justify higher occupational aspirations (86). Whether or not they will raise their aspirations under such conditions will depend partly on whether they feel they can do so successfully and partly on whether they are afraid that serious competition with male coworkers may cost them their jobs.

Fourth, when women are denied leadership roles in their occupations, especially when they have played such roles in school and college, they are not only frustrated but resentful when they see these roles going to men, many of whom, they feel, have less ability and training for them than they have. As Garland and Price have pointed out, there is bias against women in management not only at the beginning of their careers but also when they have superior performance records (60).

Fifth, many women resent having to carry a double work load—one in the work world and one in the home. They may feel guilty because they must neglect many of the homemaking duties other women perform or rely on their children or outside help to assist them. In addition, they may feel guilty if the recreational activities of the family must be curtailed or if they are too busy or too tired when they return from work to take an active part in their children's interests.

As a result of these feelings on the part of working wives, their home lives may be far from satisfactory for the whole family. This adds to the adjustment problems arising from the work itself, as will be discussed at greater length later in the chapter.

Evidence from several national surveys about how women feel about the double load of job and homemaking has led to the following conclusion by Wright (174):

Evidence presented . . . makes it reasonably plain that both work and housekeeping roles have costs and benefits attached to them. Working women enjoy an outside income and some increase in independence as a result of it; they get out of the house and so on. But they also pay for these benefits in reduced free time for themselves, a more hectic pace, and a more complicated life. The life of a housewife, in contrast, is somewhat easier . . . and almost certainly less hectic, but then, their work (that is, housework) is possibly somewhat less satisfying qua *work than the labors of their employed counterparts.*

Sixth, many women long for the job they gave up when they assumed the roles of housewife and mother. The more they think back to the calm and peace of their jobs, their salary checks, and their free time to do as they please, the more restrictive, hectic and frustrating their jobs in the home seem to be. See Figure 10-1. This affects both personal and social adjustments.

FIGURE 10-1   When family members suggest that housework is not "work," many women who gave up jobs in the business world to become homemakers contrast their present jobs with those they gave up. (Bil Keane. "The Family Circus," May 22, 1977. Used by permission.)

Appraisal of Vocational Adjustment

How successfully young adults adjust to their chosen vocations can be judged by three criteria: their achievements on the job, the amount of voluntary "job-hopping" or changing jobs they do and the degree of satisfaction they and their families derive from their work and the socioeconomic status associated with it. Because of their importance, each of these three criteria will be discussed separately and in detail below.

Achievements   The first criterion of an individual's vocational adjustment is the degree of success achieved in the job. The desire to "get ahead" and be successful, so strong in adolescence, usually carries over into adulthood. This motivates young adults to put forth tremendous effort, often at the expense of their health, their families, and their personal interests. Because of this effort, they often reach the peak of their vocational achievements during the mid- to late thirties (24).

Those who have not made satisfactory adjustments to their work and who have not shown at least reasonable success in it by the time they reach middle age are not likely to do so as they grow older. By middle age, the drive for success is often replaced by a drive for security. For many adults, having a safe job

In the assessment of vocational adjustments, achieving one's expectations and deriving satisfaction from the job are important criteria. (Freda Leinwand from Monkmeyer.)

now means more than climbing higher on the vocational ladder.

In spite of the desire to achieve success, it is important to realize that relatively few men and even fewer women realize their vocational aspirations or even their vocational potentials. There are a number of reasons for this. Adults may fail in this regard because of an *environmental obstacle,* such as limited opportunities for the work they can do best in areas where they live; *personal obstacles,* such as limited training or an inability to get along with coworkers; inadequate *motivation* to make the most of their training or abilities; unrealistically high *aspirations,* age, and sex *stereotypes* about the jobs they have selected as their life careers; or *fear of success.*

There are, for example, many stereotypes about male and female success and failure in sex-linked occupations. Women, for example, are not supposed to make as great a success in typically masculine lines of work, such as law and aviation, as in typically feminine lines of work, such as nursing and teaching (51). Similarly, there are stereotypes about age and success. These stereotypes depict those approaching middle age as potentially less employable and less likely to be creative and motivated than those who are younger. This affects not only employment but also advancement, especially for highly demanding and challenging positions (133).

Unquestionably, the most common and most serious obstacle to achieving what they are capable of is fear of success. Some adults may fear vocational success because they feel inadequate to assume heavy job responsibilities. For example, if a man gets a job through "pull," he may realize that he does not have the ability or the training to handle the job successfully. Under such conditions, he may rationalize his poor achievements or he may project the blame on others when he does not do well.

Women's fear of success is far more often the result of a feeling that success will be damaging to their image and may even lead to social rejection. Horner has explained the young woman's fear of success in this way (78):

Most highly competent and otherwise achievement motivated young women, when faced with a conflict between their feminine image and expressing their competencies or developing their abilities and interests adjust their behavior to their internalized sex-role stereotypes. . . . Among women, the anticipation of success, especially against a male competitor, poses a threat to the sense of femininity and self-esteem and serves as a potential basis for becoming socially rejected—in other words, the anticipation of success is anxiety producing and as such inhibits otherwise positive achievement motivation and behavior. In order to feel or appear more feminine, women, especially those high in fear of success, disguise their abilities and withdraw from the mainstream of thought, activism, and achievement in our society.

Voluntary Change of Jobs The second criterion of vocational adjustment is the number of voluntary changes the individual makes in jobs or even in lines or work. Put in another way, the amount of "job-hopping" the individual does can be used as a criterion of success or failure in vocational adjustment.

Some job changes, it is important to note, are involuntary. A factory or business organization may shut down and all workers thrown out of their jobs. Under such conditions, it does not necessarily mean that the worker made a poor adjustment to the job. As a matter of fact, many contented and successful workers lose their jobs in times of economic depression or when the organization for which they work is taken over by another organization that wants to put its own employees in key positions.

Many job changes among women are involuntary. A working wife, no matter how successfully she may have adjusted to her job, may have to give it up and look for another job when her husband's work requires a move to another community. Or, she may have to take a part-time job if she finds her home duties and responsibilities demand more time and energy than she can give to the job she liked and was handling successfully (46,134).

When, on the other hand, workers voluntarily give up their jobs and look for others because they are bored with the work they are doing, dislike the work environment, feel they are progressing too slowly, or for some other reason, it suggests poor vocational adjustment. Either they have unrealistically high aspirations for their achievements or they have unrealistic concepts of what working means.

Changing a line of work and taking time off to train for a new career is even more pronounced evidence of poor vocational adjustment. The older the individual is when change of line of work is made, the stronger the evidence of poor vocational adjustment, because change of career brings with it more hardships for the worker and the entire family than change

of jobs. This is especially true when special training for the new career is essential (105).

Women, as a group, do far less voluntary job-hopping than men and also are less likely to change their careers. Only when it is necessary are they likely to do so, even when the work they are doing is not to their liking nor a challenge to their abilities and training.

There are two common reasons for greater stability in vocations among women than among men. First, there are fewer job opportunities for women than for men. Giving up a job in the hopes of finding another more to their liking may mean a long period of unemployment or a step down the vocational ladder. Second, most women who work outside the home do so because they and their families need the money. Recognizing how difficult it is for women to get jobs, they cling to what they have, regardless of their personal feelings, when they realize how important their earnings are to them and to their families. Men, by contrast, can take more chances because more vocational opportunities are available to them, even in times of economic hardship, than to women.

Satisfaction The third criterion of vocational adjustment is the degree of satisfaction derived from work. In fact, this is usually regarded as the best single criterion.

There are age cycles in vocational satisfaction for both men and women. In their early twenties, most individuals are glad to have a job, even if it is not entirely to their liking, because it gives them the independence they want and makes marriage possible. With the confidence of youth, they believe it will be just a matter of time until they are promoted to a better job or find one that is more to their liking (49,114).

Dissatisfaction usually begins to set in during the mid- to late twenties when young adults have not risen as rapidly as they had hoped to. If family responsibilities make it impossible for them to change jobs, or if it is a time of economic depression when jobs are scarce, their dissatisfaction increases. This period of unrest and dissatisfaction lasts generally until the early or mid-thirties, after which there is usually an increase in satisfaction resulting from greater achievement and better financial rewards. It has been found that most individuals in their thirties like their work, but they do not "love" it. They enjoy the social con-

BOX 10-3

CONDITIONS INFLUENCING VOCATIONAL SATISFACTION

Opportunity to Choose Work

Men and women who can choose jobs in areas in which they are interested and can use their abilities and training are usually better satisfied than those who must take what is available.

Work Meeting Needs and Interests

Jobs involving work that meets the needs and interests of the workers lead to greater job satisfaction than those that fail to meet individual needs and interests.

Vocational Expectations

Adults who expect their work to give them the autonomy they did not have when they were younger, and to rise rapidly on the vocational ladder, will become discouraged and dissatisfied with their jobs if these expectations are not met.

Stimulating versus Nonstimulating Work

The more stimulating the work involved in a job, the greater satisfaction the worker derives from it. Nonstimulating, routine work leads to boredom and this, in turn, leads to job dissatisfaction.

Degree of Career Orientation

Career-oriented workers are willing to work up to their capacities, to try to improve their skills and to make personal sacrifices in terms of time and effort in the hope of achieving success.

Vocational Security

A reasonable amount of job security will contribute to the satisfaction of all workers while uncertainty—if they fear they may be put out of work because of automation or that they may be fired—makes them feel that they are "sitting on the top of a volcano."

Level of Education

Adults with college degrees are usually better satisfied with their jobs than those who have only high school diplomas. The least satisfied are, for the most part, the dropouts from high school or college because they find themselves in dead-end jobs or jobs with little security.

Opportunities for Advancement

Workers who see a possibility of advancement will be far more satisfied with their jobs than those who suspect or know that they are in "dead-end" jobs.

Stereotypes about Jobs

Unfavorable stereotypes about jobs, such as the service jobs or those considered unappropriate for members of the worker's sex, make workers dissatisfied with their jobs when they realize they are regarded unfavorably by the social group.

Occupational Stress

Too much responsibility, a too-heavy work load, feeling unqualified for the job, or necessity for making decisions affecting the lives of others tend to lead to stress on the part of workers and this weakens their satisfaction with their work.

Working Conditions

A reasonable amount of autonomy, the chances for congenial associations with coworkers, lack of discrimination, fair treatment and consideration from superiors, and liberal fringe benefits add to the worker's job satisfaction.

Attitudes of Significant People

The satisfaction of workers is increased when they know that family members are proud of their jobs and satisfied with the salary they receive and when friends and members of the social group regard their jobs favorably.

tacts work gives them, the feeling of being a part of the world of action, the satisfaction they derive from achievement, and, most important of all, the money they can use to live as they want to live (25).

Women, as a group, tend to be far less satisfied with their jobs than men. This is not only because they are usually forced to take jobs below their abilities and training but also because their working often means carrying a work overload and dissatisfaction on the part of the family members because they must do this. Relationships with their husbands are often strained when women work outside the home and

BOX 10-4

TYPICAL FAMILY PATTERNS IN THE AMERICAN CULTURE OF TODAY

Nuclear Families

Because of small living quarters, most American families are nuclear, consisting of parents and children.

Elongated Families

Except in rural and small-town areas, elongated families, consisting of the nuclear family plus relatives who live under the same roof, are relatively uncommon today.

Single-Child Families

Single-child families are more common among adults who marry late than among those who marry early, and among those where the wife is dedicated to her career.

Different-sized Families

In urban and suburban areas, small families, with three or fewer children, are more common than large families with six or more children, or medium-sized families, with three to six children.

Childless Families

Career-oriented and highly educated men and women often decide to have no children so they can advance in their careers and enjoy the good life made possible by their joint earnings.

Young-Parent Families

Adults who assume the parental role in their late teens or early twenties and have their last child before they are thirty are more common among the less-educated adults than among those who attend college and professional training schools.

Overage-Parent Families

Adults who marry late or who voluntarily delay parenthood until the thirties are regarded as "overage" parents.

Families with Working Mothers

Families where mothers work outside the home and turn the children over to caretakers or put them in child-care centers are increasing in all socioeconomic groups, especially in urban and suburban areas.

Single-Parent Families

In a single-parent family, either the mother or the father assumes the responsibility for the care of the children after death, divorce, or the birth of an illegitimate child. An increasing number of fathers are assuming this role.

Reconstituted Families

Following death or divorce, the family may be reconstituted by a stepparent who replaces the missing parent.

Communal Families

In communal families, several nuclear families band together to share the responsibilites for the care of the home and the children and they often share marital partners.

Foster-Parent Families

In foster-parent homes, the parents have no legal responsibility for the children nor do the children bear their names. Their role is primarily that of paid caretaker for children whose parents cannot or will not keep them or whose parents are dead or mistreat them.

Adoptive Families

In adoptive families, some or all of the children have no blood ties with the parents who have legal responsibility for them and give them the family name. They have all the rights and privileges of natural children.

Interreligious Families

Spouses comes from different religious faiths though one often converts to the faith of the other either before or after marriage.

Interracial Families

In an interracial family, the two spouses come from different racial groups.

BOX 10-5

CONDITIONS CONTRIBUTING TO DIFFICULTIES IN MARITAL ADJUSTMENT

Limited Preparation for Marriage

Although sexual adjustments may be easier now than in the past because of more readily available sex information in the home, schools, and colleges, and premarital sexual experience, most couples have received little preparation in the areas of domestic skills, child rearing, getting along with in-laws, and money management.

Roles in Marriage

The trend toward changes in marital roles for both men and women and the different concepts of these roles held by different social classes and religious groups make adjustment problems in marriage more difficult now than in the past, when these roles were more rigidly prescribed.

Early Marriage

Marriage and parenthood before young people have finished their education and are economically independent deprives them of the opportunity to have many of the experiences enjoyed by their unmarried contemporaries or even by their married friends who waited to be financially independent before marrying. This leads to constant envy and resentment which militates against good marital adjustments.

Unrealistic Concepts of Marriage

Adults who have spent their lives in school and college, with little or no work experience, tend to have unrealistic concepts of what marriage means in terms of work, deprivations, financial expenditures, or changes in life patterns. See Figure 10-2.

This unrealistic approach to marriage inevitably leads to serious adjustment problems which often lead to divorce.

Mixed Marriages

Adjustments to parenthood and to in-laws—both of which are important to marital happiness—are much more difficult in interracial or interreligious marriages than when both marriage partners come from the same racial or religious backgrounds.

Shortened Courtships

The courtship period is shorter now than in the past, and thus the couple has less time to solve many of the problems related to adjustment before they are actually married.

Romantic Concepts of Marriage

Many adults have a romantic concept of marriage developed in adolescence. Overly optimistic expectations of what marriage will bring often lead to disenchantment, which increases the difficulties of adjusting to the duties and responsibilities of marriage.

Lack of Identity

If a man feels that his family, friends, and associates treat him as "Jane's husband" or if a woman feels that the social group regards her as "just a housewife" even though she is or has been a successful career woman, they are likely to resent the loss of their identity as individuals which they strove hard to achieve and valued highly before marriage.

---

this increases their vocational dissatisfcation (15,25, 30,97,107).

In spite of the general pattern of vocational satisfaction and dissatisfaction, described above, within every age group there are variations in the vocational satisfaction men and women experience. Box 10-3 gives the most important factors influencing these variations.

The degree of satisfaction derived from jobs has a marked influence on the quality and quantity of young adults' work. Satisfaction increases their moti-

vation to do what they are capable of doing and to learn more about the work so that they can perform it more efficiently. It also increases ego-involvement in their work and this further increases their motivation (63,142). Equally important, vocational satisfaction decreases absenteeism and job turnover (105,111).

Workers who are satisfied with their jobs become dedicated to their work and loyal to their organization. As a result, they play an important role in keeping worker morale at a high level. From the personal point of view, job satisfaction contributes to the

"Remember, two people can live as cheaply as one...but only if you don't do much living."

FIGURE 10-2 Unrealistic concepts about marriage, especially those related to the financial aspects of marriage, can play havoc with marital adjustments. (From Lichy and Wagner. "Grin and Bear It." Field Newspaper Syndicate, May 13, 1978. Used by permission.)

worker's self-satisfaction and this, in turn, contributes to the worker's happiness.

MARITAL ADJUSTMENTS

Just as the ever-increasing number of vocational opportunities makes vocational selection and adjustment difficult, so does the ever-increasing number of family patterns make marital adjustment difficult. This difficulty is increased when one spouse has grown up in a family where the lifestyle differs markedly from that of the other spouse. A woman, for example, whose childhood home life was that of the typical nuclear family may and very likely will find it difficult to adjust to the conditions and problems that arise when she marries a man from an elongated family background.

While there are many family patterns in America today, those that are most common are listed and briefly explained in Box 10-4. A careful study of these patterns will help to emphasize the marital adjustment difficulties that are almost inevitable when husband and wife have been brought up in homes where different family patterns prevailed.

Regardless of the type of family, marital adjustment is one of the most difficult adjustments young adults must make. Although it is difficult everywhere, certain factors in the American culture of today make it particularly hard. The most important of these are given in Box 10-5.

During the first year or two of marriage, the couple normally must make major adjustments to each other, to members of their families, and to their friends. While these adjustments are being made, there are often emotional tensions and this then is understandably a very stormy period. After adjusting to each other, their families, and friends, they must adjust to parenthood. This increases the adjustment problems if it comes while the earlier adjustments are being made.

People who marry during their thirties or in middle age frequently require a longer time for adjustments and the end result is often not as satisfactory as in the case of those who marry earlier. However, those who marry in their teens or early twenties tend to make the poorest adjustments of all as shown by the high divorce rate among those who married at these ages.

The times when adjustments to different aspects of marital life must be made differ according to the age at which men and women marry. However, as Glick has reported, there are certain ages when characteristically important events necessitate major adjustments. These are shown in Figure 10-3, which emphasizes the age at which marriage occurred (65,66).

Of the many adjustment problems in marriage, the four most common and the most important for marital happiness are adjustment to a mate, sexual adjustments, financial adjustments, and in-law adjustments.

Adjustment to a Mate
The first major adjustment problem in marriage is adjustment to a mate. Interpersonal relationships

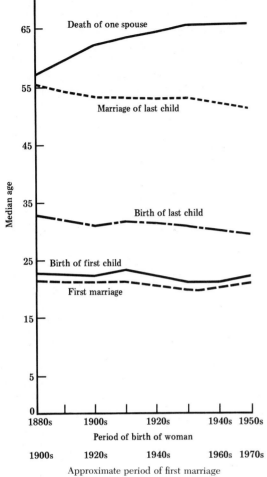

65 — Death of one spouse

55 —

Marriage of last child

45 —

Median age

35 —

Birth of last child

25 — Birth of first child

Birth of first child

First marriage

15 —

5 —

0
1880s   1900s   1920s   1940s 1950s
Period of birth of woman

1900s   1920s   1940s   1960s 1970s
Approximate period of first marriage

FIGURE 10-3 Median age of mothers at the beginning of selected stages of the family life cycle. (Adapted from P. C. Glick. Updating the life cycle of the family. *Journal of Marriage & the Family,* 1977, **39,** 5–13. Used by permission.)

play as important a role in marriage as in friendships and business relationships. However, in the case of marriage, the interpersonal relationships are far more difficult to adjust to than in social or business life because they are complicated by factors not usually present in any other area of the individual's life.

The more experience in interpersonal relationships both the man and the woman have had in the past, the greater social insight they have developed, and the greater their willingness to cooperate with others, the better they will be able to adjust to each other in marriage.

Far more important to good marital adjustment is the ability of husband and wife to relate emotionally to each other and to give and receive love. Men who were trained during childhood to control the expression of their emotions—with the possible exception of anger—may have learned not to show affection, just as they learned not to show fear. This lack of expression of affection, Sattel has pointed out, may take one of two forms: lack of indication of affection or lack of support and appreciation for the wife's efforts and behavior (140). Men may also rebuff expressions of affection from others and thus seem cold and aloof to their wives—an attitude they regard as masculine.

While women have not usually been subjected to similar training, many who felt rejected by family and peers during childhood have learned not to show affection for others as a defense against possible rejection of that affection. A husband and wife who have the habit of not expressing affection will have difficulty establishing a warm and close relationship because each interprets the other's behavior as an indication of "not caring."

Almost as important as ability and willingness to show affection is ability and willingness to communicate. Throughout childhood and adolescence, those who could or would communicate with their peers were more popular than those who tended to be self-bound. Adults who have learned to communicate with others and who are willing to do so avoid many of the misunderstandings that complicate marital adjustment (62).

Adults who were popular throughout childhood and adolescence have acquired the ability to adjust to others and the social insight necessary to make adjustments. They have also learned to give and receive affection from their peers, to communicate with them, and to show that they enjoy being with them and value their friendship. These experiences go a long way toward making marital adjustments easier. However, other factors contribute to the ease or difficulty with which the adult adjusts to a mate in marriage; the most common of these are given in Box 10-6.

The present trend toward "living together" or cohabitation among many adolescents and young

BOX 10-6

FACTORS INFLUENCING ADJUSTMENT TO A MATE

Concept of an Ideal Mate

In choosing a marriage partner, both men and women are guided to some extent by a concept of an ideal mate built up during adolescence. The more the individual must readjust to reality, the more difficult the adjustment to the mate will be.

Fulfillment of Needs

If good adjustments are to be made, a mate must fulfill needs stemming from early experiences. If the adult needs recognition, a sense of achievement, and social status to be happy, the mate must help meet these needs.

Similarity of Backgrounds

The more similar the backgrounds of husband and wife, the easier the adjustment. However, even when their backgrounds are similar, each adult has acquired a unique outlook on life, and the more these outlooks differ, the more difficult the adjustment will be.

Common Interests

Mutual interests in things the couple can do or enjoy together lead to better adjustments than mutual interests that are not easily shared.

Similarity of Values

Well-adjusted couples have more similar values than those who are poorly adjusted. Similar backgrounds are likely to produce similar values.

Role Concepts

Each mate has a definite concept of the role a husband and wife should play, and each expects the other to play that role. When role expectations are not fulfilled, conflict and poor adjustment result.

Change in Life Pattern

Adjustment to a mate means reorganizing the pattern of living, revamping friendships and social activities, and changing occupational requirements, especially for the wife. These adjustments are often accompanied by emotional conflicts.

adults, especially those who are still in college or professional training school, has been found to ease the adjustment problems to a mate. Having lived in a marital relationship with a member of the opposite sex, the individual has learned how to eliminate some of the problems such a relationship gives rise to and how to solve those that do arise. While cohabitation is not a socially accepted pattern of behavior, there is some evidence that it makes for better marriages and eliminates some of the problems that lead to divorce (71,130,159).

Sexual Adjustments

The second major adjustment problem in marriage is sexual adjustment. This is unquestionably one of the most difficult adjustments to marriage, and it is the one most likely to lead to marital discord and unhappiness if it is not satisfactorily achieved. Usually the couple has had less preliminary experience related to this adjustment than to the others, and they may be unable to make it easily and with a minimum of emotional tension.

For women, sexual adjustments tend to be more difficult to make and the end results less satisfactory than for men (35). Rubin has explained why women find sexual adjustments especially difficult: "Socialized from infancy to inhibit and repress their sexuality, women can't just switch to uninhibited enjoyment as the changing culture of their husbands dictate" (137).

The present trend toward accepting premarital intercourse as a part of the dating pattern, as discussed in detail in the chapter on adolescence, has helped to ease the adjustment problem arising from this area of marriage for women (130). Cohabitation, which many young people regard as a form of "trial marriage," has likewise helped to overcome the sexual adjustment problems which most young women and some young men in the past had to solve before making good adjustments to their marriages (8).

Many factors influence sexual adjustments to marriage, the most important of which are given in Box 10-7. While these factors have a greater influence on men and women who have had no premarital sexual experiences, they can and often do affect the early premarital sexual experiences that accompany dating and cohabitation. See also Figure 12-3 which shows satisfaction with sex at different times during the adult years.

BOX 10-7

SOME IMPORTANT FACTORS THAT INFLUENCE SEXUAL ADJUSTMENTS

Attitudes toward Sex

Attitudes toward sex are greatly influenced by the way men and women received sex information during childhood and adolescence. Once unfavorable attitudes have developed, it is difficult if not impossible to eradicate them completely.

Past Sexual Experiences

The way adults and peers reacted to masturbation, petting, and premarital intercourse when men and women were younger and the way they themselves felt about them affect their attitudes toward sex. If a woman's early experiences with petting were unpleasant, for example, this may have colored her attitude toward sex unfavorably.

Sexual Desire

Sexual desire develops earlier in men than in women and tends to be persistent, while that of women is periodic, fluctuating during the menstrual cycle. These variations affect interest in and enjoyment of sex, which in turn affects sexual adjustments.

Early Marital Sexual Experiences

The belief that sexual relations produce states of ecstasy unparalleled by any other experience causes many young adults to be so disillusioned at the beginning of their married lives that later sexual adjustments are difficult or even impossible to make.

Attitudes toward Use of Contraceptives

There will be less friction and emotional conflict if husband and wife agree concerning the use of contraceptives than if they feel differently about this matter.

Effects of Vasectomy

When men have had vasectomy operations, it eliminates any fear of an unwanted pregnancy. This has a favorable effect on women's sexual adjustments but it may make men question their virility.

Financial Adjustments

The third major adjustment problem in marriage is financial. Money or lack of it has a profound influence on adults' adjustments to marriage. Today, as a result of premarital experience in the business world, many wives resent not having control of the money needed to run a home, and they find it difficult to adjust to living on their husbands' earnings after having been accustomed to spending their own money as they wish.

Many men also find financial adjustments very difficult, particularly if the wife worked after they were married and then must stop with the arrival of the first child. Not only is their total income reduced, but the husband's earnings must now cover a wider area of expenses.

The couple's financial situation can pose a threat to their marital adjustments in two important areas. First, friction may develop if the wife expects her husband to share the work load. During the early years of marriage, when expensive labor-saving devices and domestic help are most needed, the family usually cannot afford such luxuries, and the wife may want her husband to help share the burden of running the home. This frequently causes friction, especially when the man considers homemaking "woman's work." If the wife resents the "lazy-husband syndrome," discussed in the preceding chapter, marital adjustments can be adversely affected.

The second common threat that the couple's financial situation poses to good marital adjustments comes from a desire to have material possessions as a stepping-stone to upward social mobility and a symbol of the family's success. If a husband is unable to provide his wife and family with the material possessions they want, they may feel resentful of him, and a frictional attitude develops. Many wives, faced with this problem, take jobs to provide the family with such possessions. Many husbands object to this because they feel that others will think they are unable to provide for their families as well as husbands of non-working wives do (15,107,114,146).

In-Law Adjustments

The fourth major adjustment problem in marriage is to the in-laws. With marriage, every adult acquires a whole new set of relatives—the in-laws. These are people of different ages, ranging from babies to the elderly, who often have different interests and values and sometimes markedly different educational, cultural and social backgrounds. Both husbands and wives must learn to adjust to their in-laws if they are to avoid frictional relationships with their spouses.

It is not at all uncommon, particularly when the married couple is young and inexperienced, for the in-laws to try to exert some control over their lives, especially if they are partially or totally responsible for their support. When, by contrast, the couple is older, more experienced, and better established financially, in-law interference with their lives is less likely to occur (81,128).

In-law adjustments have been made more difficult by a number of factors which are of recent origin and which members of past generations, for the most part, were not forced to cope with. These are listed in Box 10-8.

In-law trouble is especially serious during the early years of marriage and is one of the most important causes of marital breakup during the first year. It is more serious in families where there are no

In-law trouble is especially serious during the early years of marriage and is one of the most important causes of marital breakup at that time. (Suzanne Szasz. Photo Researchers, Inc.)

BOX 10-8

FACTORS INFLUENCING IN-LAW ADJUSTMENTS

Stereotypes

The widely accepted stereotype of the "typical mother-in-law" can lead to unfavorable mental sets even before marriage. Unfavorable stereotypes about the elderly—that they are bossy and interfering—can add to in-law problems.

Desire for Independence

Young married adults tend to resent advice and guidance from their parents, even if they must accept financial aid, and they especially resent such interference from in-laws.

Family Cohesiveness

Marital adjustments are complicated when one spouse devotes more time to relatives than the other spouse wants to; when a spouse is influenced by family advice; or when a relative comes for an extended visit or lives with the family permanently.

Social Mobility

Young adults who have risen above the status of their families or that of their in-laws may want to keep them in the background. Many parents and relatives resent this and hostile relationships with the young couple as well as marital friction are likely to develop.

Care of Elderly Relatives

Caring for elderly relatives is an especially complicating factor in marital adjustments today because of present unfavorable attitudes toward older people and the belief that young people should be independent of relatives, especially when there are children in the family.

Financial Support of In-Laws

When a young couple must contribute to or assume responsibility for the financial support of in-laws, it can and often does lead to a frictional marital relationship. This is because the spouse whose in-laws must be aided financially resents having to make sacrifices of wants or even needs to make this aid possible.

children or only a few children than in large families, where in-law help is often welcome. It is also more common in middle- and upper-class groups than in lower-class groups, where the traditional concept of an elongated family, with relatives as the chief source of companionship, is more widely held (28,84).

Certain factors have been found to contribute to good in-law adjustments. These include approval of the marriage by the parents of both spouses, opportunities for the parents to meet and become acquainted before the marriage, and friendliness on the part of both families when they meet. In-law problems are also eased if the marriage is between persons of the same religion; if the couple has taken a course in marriage, especially the wife; if relationships between the grandparents and grandchildren are good; if the in-laws have similar patterns of social activities; if the in-laws as well as the young couple are happily married; and if husband and wife accept each other's family as their own (26,124,126).

ADJUSTMENT TO PARENTHOOD

It has been said that parenthood is the most important criterion of the individual's transition to maturity and adult responsibility (75,138). While parenthood, unquestionably, brings with it many gratifications, it can also be regarded as a "crisis" in life because it necessitates major changes in attitudes, values, and roles.

With the arrival of a child, the family is temporarily upset and all family members are under varying degrees of stress. Although the arrival of every child in the family is a crisis, the arrival of the firstborn is generally the most upsetting, partly because both parents may feel inadequate for the parental role, partly because they have highly romanticized concepts of parenthood, partly because of the personal, social, and economic privations parenthood brings, and partly because the baby is an intruder who disrupts the affection and intimacy of the husband-wife relationship, transforming it from a dyad to a triad relationship (138).

While both husband and wife must make marked adjustments in the patterns of their lives when they become parents, mothers with professional training and experience often suffer extremely severe crisis shock when they realize that they must give up a role that was highly important to them in favor of one for which they feel inadequate and which, in the eyes of

the social group as well as in the eyes of their husbands, has less prestige than the role they were forced to abandon because they were unable to get adequate help with the care of their babies.

Even though most men do not have to change their roles radically when they become parents, many fathers show a disenchantment with the parental role by becoming less sexually responsive to their wives, worrying about economic pressures, or developing feelings of resentment at being "tied down" or excluded from the mother-child relationship. These unfavorable attitudes can and often do play havoc with men's attitudes toward parenthood and their marital adjustments.

Voluntary Childlessness

In spite of the traditional belief that every woman should be a mother to be truly feminine and that having a large number of children is foolproof evidence of a man's virility, an increasing number of married couples today are voluntarily childless (109, 126,139). While this is true of all socioeconomic levels, it is especially true of those of the higher and better educated groups.

Adults may have many reasons for not having children, some of the most important of which are engrossing careers which they feel will be handicapped by children, unwillingness to give up the "good life" they have established for themselves, interracial or interreligious marriages which they believe will be handicaps to their children, or fear that their incomes will never be large enough to give their children the advantages they would want them to have (7,166).

Other adults voluntarily limit the number of children they have. Many adults feel, from childhood experiences or from the experiences of their friends, that one child is likely to be far less disrupting to the marital relationship than two or more. Furthermore, women who do not want to give up their careers or their personal and social interests, often limit their children to one, feeling that by so doing they can still have the gratifications of parenthood and the gratifications of personal interests (37,87,166).

Single Parenthood

While there have always been single-parent families when one parent died and the other was left alone to care for the children, the number of one-parent families has increased greatly in recent years (162). There are two reasons for this; first, many more

BOX 10-9

SOME IMPORTANT FACTORS INFLUENCING ADJUSTMENT TO PARENTHOOD

Attitudes toward Pregnancy

The woman's attitude toward parenthood is colored by her physical and emotional condition during pregnancy. In most cases, if her attitude has been unfavorable, it improves after the baby's birth.

Attitudes toward Parenthood

Adults adjust better to parenthood if they want children because they feel they are essential to a happy marriage, rather than because of family or social pressures.

Age of Parents

Young parents tend to take their parental responsibilities lightly and not allow them to interfere too much with their other interests and pleasures. Older parents tend to be more anxious and concerned. Thus younger parents often make better adjustments.

Sex of Children

Adults' attitudes toward parenthood are more favorable if they have a child or children of the sex they prefer.

Number of Children

When adults have the number of children they consider "ideal," their adjustment to parenthood will be better than if they have more or fewer children than they want.

Parental Expectations

If parents have a "dream-child" concept, their adjustment to parenthood will be affected by how well the child measures up to this ideal.

Feelings of Parental Adequacy

Conflicts about child-training methods lead to confusions and to feelings of anxiety about doing the job well. This has an unfavorable effect on the adult's adjustment to parenthood.

Attitudes toward Changed Roles

Parenthood means that both the man and the woman must learn to play family-centered rather than pair-centered roles. See Figure 10-4. How men and women react to these role changes will have a profound influence on their adjustments to parenthood.

The Child's Temperament

Children who are easy to manage and who are responsive and affectionate make parents feel rewarded for the time and effort they spend on them. This has a favorable effect on parents' attitudes toward their parental roles.

---

one-parent families are the result of divorce than of death and, second, an increasing number of illegitimate babies are cared for by their mothers instead of being made available for adoption, as in the past.

Another change is in the make-up of the one-parent family. In the past, it was usually the mother who was left to take care of the children. Should the mother die and the care of the children be left to the father, he generally had a female relative—mother or aunt—come to live with him to take care of the children or he had a paid housekeeper.

Today, many fathers are in charge and they do not call on relatives or employ housekeepers to take charge of the children. Instead, they assume this responsibility themselves, in addition to their jobs, just as women do when they are heads of one-parent fam-

ilies. Both employ baby-sitters or send their young children to day-care centers. Evidence points to the fact that fathers, as a group, make as good single parents as mothers, though there is no question about the fact that every child needs and should have two parents (52,61,172).

Variations in Adjustment to Parenthood

Whether in a single- or two-parent family, there are marked variations in the adjustments men and women must make to parenthood. Some of the most important factors that influence adjustment to parenthood are listed and briefly explained in Box 10-9. Some of these factors affect women more than men; others have a greater influence on men.

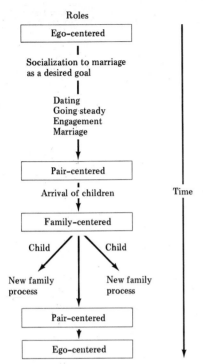

Roles

Ego-centered

|

Socialization to marriage
as a desired goal

|

Dating
Going steady
Engagement
Marriage

↓

Pair-centered

Arrival of children

Family-centered

Child ╱ ╲ Child

New family   New family
process   process

↓

Pair-centered

↓

Ego-centered

Time

FIGURE 10-4 Role changes are inevitable with marriage, parenthood, and the growing up and departure of one's children. (Adapted from S. Clavan. The family process: A sociological model. *Family Coordinator,* 1969, **18,** 312–317. Used by permission.)

ASSESSMENT OF MARITAL ADJUSTMENT

No one specific pattern of living is favorable to marital adjustment. The success of a marriage depends on whether it provides satisfaction for the whole family, not just one or two of the members. For example, a man who needs to succeed in his career in order to be happy but who feels that family duties and responsibilities are keeping him from achieving success will be dissatisfied with his marriage, and the marriage will suffer.

Ages of Best Adjustment

Marital adjustments are easier at some periods during married life than at others. As Paris and Luckey have pointed out, "There are identifiable periods in the lives of most married people that may be less happy than others" (120). The most readily identifiable periods are the first few years of marriage, when the couple must make adjustments to their new roles as spouses and parents; the period when the children reach the "troublesome teens" and tend to rebel against parental authority; and the "empty-nest" period, which requires readjustment to a childless home and loss of the parental role. Figure 10-5 shows parental satisfaction at different stages in the life cycle.

Conditions Contributing to Marital Adjustment

There are a number of conditions that contribute to marital adjustment, six of which are especially important. The first is the timing of parenthood. If the first child arrives within the first year of marriage, before the young couple has had time to learn to adjust to one another or to put their finances in a reasonably satisfactory condition, there likely will be stress and tension.

The second factor is attaining a stable financial condition. If young people can have the home and status symbols they want, through joint earnings, they will be far better adjusted to marriage than they would be if, due to parenthood, they had to live on the husband's earnings alone and deprive themselves of many of the things they wanted or felt were essential to their happiness. Many young people, as was pointed out earlier (refer to Figure 10-2), have unrealistic concepts of what it costs to live. As a result, their expectations about their financial ability to have what they regard as essentials to happiness are likewise unrealistic. When faced with financial reality, they often find marital adjustments difficult.

The third condition is unrealistic expectations about marriage. Young people who marry after finishing school or after a period of cohabitation are often unaware of the problems and responsibilities marriage will bring. Having had their daily living problems assumed by dormitories or their families, they are unaware of what they will have to do when they are no longer taken care of by their schools, colleges, or parents. Large weddings also add to the adjustment problems caused by unrealistic expectations. As one bride put it, "It is a big step from the wedding veil to the garbage pail."

The fourth condition is number of children. When husbands and wives agree about an "ideal number" of children and when they have children of this number, their adjustments to marriage will be far better than when one spouse feels that there are too

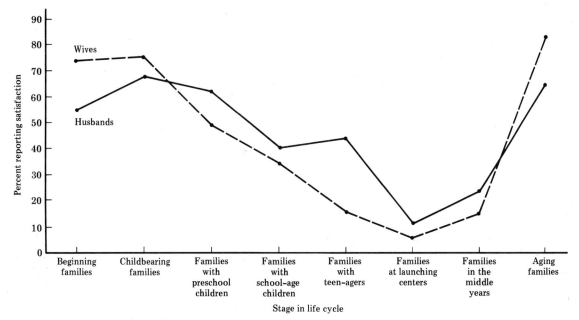

FIGURE 10-5 Parental satisfaction at different stages in the life cycle. (Adapted from B. C. Rollins and H. Feldman. Marital satisfaction over the family life cycle. *Journal of Marriage & the Family,* 1970, **32,** 20–28. Used by permission.)

many children or when circumstances prevent them from having the desired number of children.

The fifth factor is ordinal position in the family. This is important because it results in the individual's learning to play certain roles that are later transferred to the marital situation. The more similar the new situation is to the old one, the better the adjustment to it will be.

It has been found that both men and women who were reared in homes with siblings make better adjustments to marriage than those who were only-children. For men, the best position is that of the oldest brother with younger sisters; for women, the best position is that of a younger sister with older brothers. Should the husband be the younger brother of older sisters, and the wife the older sister of younger brothers, there is likely to be a frictional marital relationship; the wife will try to "boss" her husband as she did her younger brothers. When both spouses were the oldest children in their homes, there is likely to be a highly frictional relationship, with each trying to dominate the other (70). Refer to page 37.

The sixth condition is in-law relationships. Favorable in-law relationships are important to marital adjustments at any time but especially so in the early years of marriage and when parents are learning to adjust to the "empty nest" stage of their own marriage which comes with the marriage of their children. As will be pointed out in the discussion of middle age, one of the major adjustment problems parents must face when their children marry is the acquisition of new interests to replace those that were concentrated on their children. In addition, good relationships with inlaws give young people and their children a feeling of family solidarity and stability which is especially important at holiday seasons if there are children in the family.

Because of the importance of the different variables that affect marital adjustment, Miller has suggested a theoretical model of variables to assess marital satisfaction. This is shown in Figure 10-6. In it Miller shows some of the conditions that contribute to marital satisfaction that can be used to assess the degree of satisfaction achieved (104).

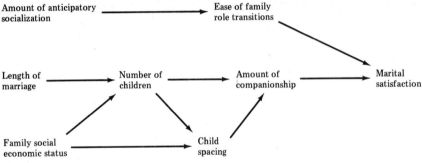

FIGURE 10-6 Theoretical model of variables antecedent to marital satisfaction. (Adapted from B. C. Miller. A multivariate developmental model of marital satisfaction. *Journal of Marriage & the Family,* 1976, **38,** 643–657. Used by permission.)

Criteria of Marital Adjustment

The success of marriage is reflected in a number of interpersonal relationships and behavior patterns. While these may vary, to some extent, for different people and for marriages at different ages, they can, for the most part, be used to assess the adjustment of any marriage. The most important of these criteria are given and explained in Box 10-10.

ADJUSTMENT TO SINGLEHOOD

According to the old cliche, in many communities there is no place for the bachelor or for the single woman except as an extra man at a dinner party or as a baby-sitter for married relatives. It is also popularly assumed that men and women who do not marry will be lonely, unhappy, and thwarted in their normal desires for sex, parenthood, affection from an admired member of the opposite sex, and the prestige that marriage and family living provide. Furthermore, because early adulthood is a lonely time during which radical adjustments must be made in every area of life, many adults feel that marriage will help them to make these adjustments.

There is no question about the fact that in a culture in which marriage is the normal pattern for adult life, most adults want to marry and come under strong pressure from parents and peers to do so. During their twenties, the goal of most unmarried women, whether working or not, is marriage. If they have not married by the time they reach their thirtieth birthdays, they tend to shift their goals and values toward a new lifestyle oriented toward work, success, and personal pleasures (1).

Thirty has been called a "critical age" for an unmarried woman. As Campbell has put it, "For women, age thirty is still the Great Divide" (29). The reason for this is that the woman's life is often characterized by stress as she reaches her thirtieth birthday and is still unmarried. This stress usually reaches a peak at thirty and then gradually decreases as she makes adjustments to new goals and a new pattern of living. For many women, a desire for marriage and a family decrease after thirty as they realize they are not likely to achieve their goals. Furthermore, many become disillusioned with the thought of marriage as they see the unhappy and unfavorable experiences of some of their contemporaries (149).

How women feel about being unmarried varies according to the communities in which they live. Those who live in rural, small-town, or suburban areas are far more handicapped by singlehood than are those who live in urban areas. As one young women put it, "I would never live single in the suburbs again. It's deadly boring, and people make you feel as though you should apologize for being single. Here (in the city), I feel alive" (153).

Single men do not, as a rule, experience the stress that single women do. They know that if they want to marry they can do so. Many men remain single throughout their twenties or even thirties because they want to enjoy the freedom of singlehood or because they want to devote their time and energy to becoming established in their careers. Some may

BOX 10-10

CRITERIA OF SUCCESSFUL MARITAL ADJUSTMENT

Happiness of Husband and Wife

A husband and wife who are happy together derive satisfaction from the roles they play. They also have a mature and stable love for each other, have made good sexual adjustments, and have accepted the parental role.

Good Parent-Child Relationships

Good parent-child relationships reflect successful marital adjustment and contribute to it. If parent-child relationships are poor, the home climate will be marked by friction, which makes marital adjustment difficult.

Good Adjustment of Children

Children who are well adjusted, well liked by their peers, and successful and happy in school are proof of their parents' good adjustment to marriage and parental roles.

Ability to Deal Satisfactorily with Disagreements

Disagreements between family members, which are inevitable, generally end in one of three ways: There is a temporary truce with no solution, one person gives in for the sake of peace, or all family members try to understand the others' point of view. In the long run, only the latter leads to satisfactory adjustments though the first two help to reduce the tension that friction gives rise to.

"Togetherness"

When marital adjustments are successful, the family enjoys spending time together. If good family relationships are built up during the early, formative years, men and women will retain close ties with their families after they grow up, marry and establish homes of their own.

Good Financial Adjustments

In many families, one of the most common sources of friction and resentment centers around money. Regardless of the income, a family that learns to budget its expenses so as to avoid constant debts and to be satisfied with what it can afford to have and do is better adjusted than one in which the wife constantly complains about the husband's earning power or takes a job to supplement his earnings.

Good In-Law Adjustments

Husbands and wives who get along well with their in-laws, especially parents-, brothers- and sisters-in-law, are far less likely to have frictional relationships.

---

have obligations to parents or they may be conditioned against marriage by unpleasant family conditions or by the experiences of their friends. This conditioning may even start in childhood.

Reasons for Singlehood

Whether voluntary or involuntary, most unmarried adults have what they regard as valid reasons for remaining single. Some of these are environmental in origin and some are personal. The most common reasons are given in Box 10-11.

While reasons for remaining single may hold for any time during adulthood, for the most part they are likely to affect behavior only during the twenties. After that, the reasons are either modified or changed. A man, for example, who remained single during his twenties because he felt he had financial obligations to care for elderly parents or to help educate younger brothers and sisters, may now be in a financial position to both carry out such obligations and to marry. Or, a woman who elected not to marry because of a strong drive to rise in her chosen career, may now decide that she can combine marriage with her career and still rise on the vocational ladder.

Effects of Singlehood

Not all unmarried women, by any means, are willing to resign themselves to being single, nor are they all willing to allow themselves to be lonely because of lack of companionship with members of the opposite sex. They may become active in church and community-service or social organizations where they will come in contact with members of both sexes; they may join clubs where members of both sexes engage in various sports or social activities; they may spend their vacations at places where they are

REASONS WHY YOUNG ADULTS REMAIN SINGLE

- An unattractive or sex-inappropriate appearance
- An incapacitating physical defect or prolonged illness
- Lack of success in the search for a mate ✓
- Unwillingness to assume the responsibilities of marriage and parenthood
- A desire to pursue a career that requires working long and irregular hours or much traveling
- Residence in a community where the sex ratio is unbalanced
- Lack of opportunity to meet eligible members ? of the opposite sex
- Responsibilities for aging parents or younger siblings
- Disillusionment as a result of unhappy earlier family experiences or unhappy marital experiences of friends
- Sexual availability without marriage
- An exciting lifestyle
- Opportunity to rise on the vocational ladder
- Freedom to change and experiment in work and lifestyle
- Belief that social mobility is easier when single than married
- Strong and satisfying friendships with members of the same sex
- Homosexuality

likely to meet eligible men; or they may become part of a commune of single men and women and cohabit with men they like but whom, at the present, they either do not want to marry or who do not want to marry them.

It is usually easier for a man to adjust to being single than for a woman. A single man is in great social demand and has little time to feel lonely. Furthermore, unless he is single because of responsibilities for family members, he is usually financially able to pursue a pattern of life that is to his liking.

Finding a satisfactory outlet for the sex drive, which is especially strong during early adulthood, is the most difficult problem the unmarried person faces. The unmarried man usually finds sexual gratification either by engaging in autoerotic practices or by having intercourse with women of his acquaintance or with prostitutes. Although women, like men, engage in autoerotic practices, they have less opportunity for sexual encounters, which are still not condoned for women in all segments of society, and they must always face the possibility of pregnancy. However, with the growing trend toward cohabitation, many young women who are single and feel sexually thwarted move to areas, such as large cities, where unconventional behavior will be unacknowledged or uncriticized. And, with improved methods of contraception and the legalization of abortion, the single woman who becomes pregnant and does not want to marry the father of her child or he, for one reason or another, does not want to or cannot marry her, can submit to an abortion and thus eliminate the social stigma that is still attached to illegitimacy (149, 153,162,163).

HAZARDS OF VOCATIONAL AND MARITAL ADJUSTMENTS DURING EARLY ADULTHOOD

Vocational and marital adjustments are particularly hazardous during the early years of adulthood. Young adults have fewer foundations on which to make adjustments than in other areas of their lives, and they receive little guidance and help, as they did when making adjustments during childhood and adolescence.

Society has recognized these difficulties and attempts have been made to eliminate some of the potential hazards of vocational and marital adjustments. For example, the growing trend toward introducing vocational guidance in schools, often as early as the elementary school years, is based on the belief that adults will make better vocational adjustments if they go into a line of work that fits their needs and abilities and for which they have been at least partially trained while in school and college than if they enter the work world with no such preparation. Similarly, courses in sex education and family living, while far from universal in schools and colleges, are designed to ease the transition into marriage and parenthood.

Even this preparation has been found to be so far from adequate that many community agencies have been set up to provide vocational counseling and advice for dissatisfied workers, and many businesses and industries are attempting to cope with the causes of persistent worker dissatisfaction, especially boredom. Others are encouraging the more able among their dissatisfied workers to return to school or college, at night or on weekends, to prepare for jobs that are better suited to their abilities and will thus give them more satisfaction. Still other agencies are providing day care for children, thus enabling their mothers to take full-time jobs and have an opportunity to rise on the vocational ladder.

Because marital adjustments are even more serious and far-reaching in their effects on the adult's personal and social life than vocational adjustments, marriage clinics and private marriage counselors are widely available today even in small communities. Since some of the most serious marital hazards are the result of poor parent-child relationships, widespread attempts are being made to help parents cope with child-rearing problems and thus improve their marital relationships.

Even though marital and vocational adjustments are closely interrelated and influence each other, the hazards associated with each are distinct and will be discussed separately.

Vocational Hazards

While there are many vocational hazards at all ages, during the years of early adulthood there are two that are not only especially common but hazardous both to good personal and social adjustments. They are job dissatisfaction and unemployment. Of the two, job dissatisfaction is more common than unemployment, except during periods of economic depression.

Job Dissatisfaction Although workers at all levels—white-collar, blue-collar, and professional—may become dissatisfied with their jobs, women and members of minority racial and religious groups are more apt to experience job dissatisfaction because they are subjected to discrimination and may feel they have little hope of advancing, regardless of the quality of their work (60,69,165,170).

The most common causes of job dissatisfaction are boredom, lack of autonomy, lack of congeniality with coworkers, restrictions on free time, a job that makes the worker feel like a cog in a big machine, slow advancement up the vocational ladder, and an antiwork attitude carried over from childhood and adolescence. See Figure 10-7. Dissatisfaction is espe-

cially common among those who feel their jobs are below their abilities.

Job dissatisfaction is expressed in many ways, the most common of which are given in Box 10-12.

Besides affecting performance in the present job, dissatisfaction with work has many serious long-term consequences. First, motivation is lowered to the point where workers may become habitual under-

"This is the part of the job I hate . . . doing the work!"

FIGURE 10-7 An antiwork attitude is a common vocational hazard in adulthood. (George Clark. "The Neighbors," Chicago Tribune-New York News Syndicate, Apr. 11, 1973. Used by permission.)

achievers, working constantly below their capacities. As a result, they will be overshadowed when they compete with other, better motivated workers who exert more effort to succeed. When women become underachievers because they fear success, as Horner has pointed out, a high price is "paid by the individual in negative and interpersonal consequences and by the society in a loss of valuable human and economic resources" (78).

A second long-term consequence of job dissatisfaction is that workers may verbalize their complaints and gain the reputation of being "gripers" or "troublemakers"—a reputation they may carry from one job to another.

A third consequence of job dissatisfaction is that it may affect attitudes toward work and toward those who have authority (58,83). Much of the agressive hostility of workers that makes them "strike-prone" stems from the habitual dissatisfaction they experience from their work.

Many adults try to compensate for job dissatisfaction by pursuing an avocation that does give them satisfaction or by enjoying a happy home life and realizing that they are providing well for their families. A man may become active in community organizations, for example, or he may engage in a creative activity, such as painting or writing.

Unemployment A second and less common vocational hazard is unemployment, the severity of which depends on three conditions. First, if unemployment is voluntary, the effects will be far less severe than if it is involuntary. For example, an adult who gives up a job in order to find a better one is less affected by unemployment than a worker who is fired.

Second, the length of unemployment determines how severe a psychological hazard it will be. If it lasts a relatively short time, workers are far less seriously affected than if it is prolonged to the point where their whole standard of living must be radically revised and they begin to consider themselves no longer employable.

The third and most important factor is what workers believe to be the cause of their employment. Some people tend to blame themselves for unemployment and to think of themselves as failures. They develop defensive attitudes that militate against good adjustments to any jobs they may obtain in the future. Other workers place the blame on an antagonistic supervisor. A worker who does not take the blame personally escapes many of the psychological effects that interfere with subsequent vocational adjustments.

Marital Hazards

Many hazards center around conditions that contribute to poor marital adjustments, which are in turn a hazard to good personal and social adjustments. As Renne has explained: "Relations with the spouse are so central a feature of an individual's social and emotional life that an unhappy marriage may impair the capacity of both partners for satisfactory relations with their children and others outside the family" (128).

Adjustment to a Mate Good adjustment to a mate may be difficult when husband and wife have different racial, religious, or social backgrounds and thus have different interests, values, and frames of reference. This usually leads either to lack of communication or to quarreling, both of which are hazardous to good marital relationships. An equally serious obstacle to good marital adjustment is a highly romanticized concept of a mate built up before marriage—a concept that may have to be radically changed afterward. This is a more common hazard of first marriages than of subsequent ones because the individual has learned to be more realistic about a mate.

When adjustments to a mate are poor, many men abuse their wives, even to the extent of beating them. When wife abuse is severe and frequent, it is not uncommon for wives to run away from their homes, leaving their husbands and often their children. While wife abuse and runaway wives are to be found in all socioeconomic groups, there has been an increase in recent years in the higher socioeconomic groups (158). Running away from husband, children, and home is rarely a sudden decision, done on the impulse of the moment. As Casady has pointed out, "Husbands don't pick up the danger signals their wives send out" (32).

Competitiveness A more common and perhaps more serious marital hazard is the competitive spirit many young adults develop in their attempts to achieve vocational success. While the competitive spirit is more characteristic of men than of women, women who hope to be successful in their social lives likewise learn to compete with others. This can make it difficult for them to establish warm, intimate relationships, which are even more essential to good adjustment to a mate—particularly sexual adjustments—than to good adjustment to friends. Erikson has said that young adulthood is characterized by "a crisis of intimacy vs. isolation" (50). Those who can establish warm, intimate relationships with others, especially with their spouses, children, in-laws, and other relatives are happier and make better personal and social adjustments than those who isolate themselves from family members as a carry-over of the competitiveness they learned in their attempts to climb the vocational ladder.

Competitiveness often occurs when wives hold down jobs and are as successful or even more successful than their husbands. While many men claim they are "proud" of their wives' successes, they are often envious and jealous. This leads to a strain in the marital relationship (25,102,162).

Sexual Adjustments   Poor sexual adjustments, which are more hazardous during the early years of marriage than later, can result when either husband or wife has an unfavorable attitude toward sex because of earlier, unpleasant sexual experiences; when one spouse—usually the husband—attaches greater importance to sex than the other; when the wife is overly aggressive, which may result in the husband's impotence; or when the couple have unrealistic expectations about the role sex should play in marriage. As Bischof has explained, "As the adjusted adult husband and wife well know, marriage is not one long sexual orgy, but marriage is mortgages, PTA meetings, parental pressures, and the like" (12).

There are other causes of deterioration in sexual adjustments during the early years of marriage. The family may, through economic necessity, be forced to live in crowded quarters which often results in quarreling among family members, especially among children. This affects all family members but especially mothers who are constantly subjected to this emotional stress (16).

Many women, even when they do not have an outside job, are overworked as a result of caring for a large number of children. If they work outside the home and receive little help from other family members, they are constantly tired, and this affects their sexual responsiveness (15,57,107). When children have a curious or unfavorable attitude toward their parents' sexuality, it is likely to make their parents self-conscious about their sexuality and this has a detrimental effect on sexual responsiveness, especially among women (35,57,99).

Many adults find that their satisfaction with the sexual aspect of marriage declines during the time when parenthood plays a dominant role in their lives (27,35). This affects not only their relationships with each other but also their relationships with their children, and the home climate may deteriorate.

Adults whose sexual adjustments to their mates are unsatisfactory may engage in autoerotic practices, homosexuality, or extramarital realtionships. While any or all of these may give temporary satisfaction, they are often hazardous in the long run. Autoerotic practices and homosexuality usually lead to guilt and shame while those who have extramarital relationships live in constant fear of discovery, which they know will further strain the marital relationship, even to the point of separation or divorce.

Economic Status   An economic status below the expectations of either or both mates is a hazard to good marital adjustments, especially when the family is large and money worries are constant. Marital adjustments are also threatened when the woman has chosen her husband because she believed he could help her rise above her status. As Elder has explained (48):

A woman's prospect for social ascent through marriage is dependent on her access to men of higher status and on the exchange value of her personal resources for marriage. . . . One of the oldest forms of exchange in hypergamous marriage involves the women's attractiveness and the man's higher social status or potential status.

This is a potential hazard to good marital adjustment not only because the woman's hopes may not be realized but also because she selected her husband without considering other areas important to good marital adjustment.

When the socioeconomic status of the wife's family is decidedly higher than that of the husband's family, or vice versa, it can and often does cause friction not only between husband and wife but also with in-laws. The in-laws tend to feel that the spouse is inferior to them and act in accordance, thus antagonizing the spouse (122,169).

Another source of marital discord is the working wife. If the wife works because it is essential to supplement the family income, the husband feels inadequate and inferior, feelings that are often expressed in resentments against the wife. Should she, on the other hand, work because of a strong interest in her career or to obtain the status symbols she wants for herself and her family, the husband may resent the implication that he is unable to satisfy his wife's wants or he may resent having to share some of the home responsibilities that is inevitable in a home where the wife works outside the home. The husband-wife stress often spreads to the children and results in a generally frictional home climate.

Role Changes As was pointed out earlier in this chapter, the birth of a child is often a time of crisis in marriage. This is because of the radical role changes that must be made not only with the birth of the first child but also with the birth of any subsequent children. While this change to the parental role may be difficult and therefore more traumatic than other marital role changes, it is by no means the only one that must be made (3). How difficult it will be is influenced to some extent by the size of the family (109).

For *women,* one of the most hazardous role changes involves the woman's relegation of major decision making to her husband and her assumption of the role of housewife if she held a responsible position in the business or professional world before marriage. As Ferree has explained, "In the present conditions of our society, full-time housework is becoming a job that is difficult to enjoy" (54).

However, it is important to understand that it is the woman's *attitude* toward the role changes she must make with marriage and parenthood that determines how successfully she adjusts to marriage. If, for example, she enjoys the role of housewife and mother, giving up a career will not be hazardous to marital adjustments. Instead, she may find volunteer work a satisfactory substitute, especially if she feels that it will contribute to the family's upward social mobility in the community.

When, on the other hand, women find it increasingly difficult to find satisfaction in the housewife and mother roles, they may return to school or college to get extra training to fit them for interesting jobs when the children no longer need their undivided attention. More and more women are returning to school and college during the thirties, finding the student role more stimulating and interesting than their home roles. Furthermore, they regard this training as a stepping-stone to more interesting jobs and careers during the forties and fifties when their home roles will be greatly reduced as their children grow up and leave home (176).

Men must also make *role* changes in marriage. How great these changes are will depend partly on the man's concept of a husband's role and partly on the particular family situation—if the wife is overburdened with household responsibilities, for example, or must take a job to supplement the family income.

Relationships with In-Laws Poor relationships with in-laws may affect any family member, but since the woman's life is more family-centered than the man's, any friction with in-laws affects her more than it does her husband and thus is more hazardous to her marital adjustment than to his (81,124).

While any marriage can be threatened by poor in-law relationships, mixed marriages are most hazardous in this respect. Regardless of whether husband and wife come from different religious, racial, or socioeconomic backgrounds, there is usually opposition to the marriage on the part of parents and other family members on one or both sides.

With the trend toward increase in divorce during the early adult years, another potential source of friction with in-laws comes when the couple is divorced. In-laws can stir up trouble between husband and wife before divorce and can make adjustments after divorce not only difficult for them but also for the children. This is especially likely to happen when the in-laws live nearby and have been a regular unit of the family for holidays and other important celebrations (4,148).

Parenthood The role change to parenthood can and does represent a major hazard to marital adjustment even when children are planned, although it is far more hazardous in the case of unwanted pregnancies, either before or after marriage. In discussing the hazardous nature of marital relationships following a premarital pregnancy, Dame et al. have explained: "Premarital pregnancy imposes additional strains, both emotional and realistic, upon a marriage at a time when the couple has many adjustments to make. Therefore it constitutes a severe hazard unless both partners have considerable ego strength" (42).

The marital relationship will be strained if a husband resents it if his wife devotes more time to their children than to him. (Photo by Erika Stone.)

Parenthood is especially hazardous at certain times during a marriage (27,131). As may be seen in Figure 10-5, parental satisfaction drops sharply as children grow older, reaching its lowest point when they are in their teens and when they begin to leave home. The slight sex difference that has been reported is in favor of men, especially when children reach their teens and tend to be more critical of their mothers than of their fathers.

Parenthood involves several common potential hazards to good marital adjustment (20,129). First, the mother must devote more time to her children than to her husband, and the marital relationship will be strained if he resents this. Second, clashes over child-training methods—with one parent blaming the other for being too strict, while the other retaliates with accusations of overpermissiveness—will further strain the marital relationship.

Third, parents who have more children than they wanted and who are overworked and overburdened financially become disenchanted with marriage and with their relationships to each other.

Not having a child or children of the desired sex is a fourth common hazard to good marital relationships. The husband may blame his wife for not giving him the son he wanted, for example, or he may

feel that not having a son is an indication of his lack of virility—a belief that can contribute to impotence.

Fifth, an older child or adolescent who becomes hypercritical of parents can cause a good deal of friction in the home, which can seriously damage marital relationships. Figure 10-8 shows how readily a mother can become irritated by a child's criticism and attempts at reform.

Sixth, when parents have high aspirations for their children and make personal sacrifices to enable them to achieve these aspirations, they will be disappointed and resentful if children fail to live up to these aspirations. If, on the other hand, children do live up to parental aspirations, they may be ashamed of their parents whom they come to regard as their social inferiors (22). In either case, parent-child friction can lead to poor marital adjustments.

Hazards of Singlehood

The stronger a woman's desire to marry, the more hazardous remaining single will be for her. This is due in part to the unfavorable stereotype of the unmarried woman and in part to a feeling of inadequacy at not being able to attract a member of the opposite sex and of being "out of things" when her friends talk about their families (29).

"You know, Mom, if you took vitamins like the lady in the commercial, you'd never be tired."

FIGURE 10-8 The hypercritical attitude and attempts at reform by a child or adolescent often have a damaging effect on family and marital adjustments. (George Clark. "The Neighbors," Chicago Tribune-New York News Syndicate, Mar. 30, 1973. Used by permission.)

Except for occasional periods of loneliness, remaining single is not hazardous for men. Most men are able to marry if they wish, and their eligibility increases with each passing year as they become vocationally more successful. Even those who have financial obligations for aging parents are usually able to support a family of their own as well as take care of their parents.

Hazards of Divorce

Divorce is the culmination of poor marital adjustment and comes when husband and wife have been unable to find any other satisfactory solution to their problems. Many unhappy marriages, it is important to realize, do not end in divorce because of religious, moral, economic, or other reasons and many marriages end in annulment, separation, either legal or informal, and desertion.

Since the end of World War II, the divorce rate has been increasing in the United States. Every year, during the last decade, it has reached new highs (116). This is shown in Figure 10-9. The peak year for separation is the first year of marriage, and, for divorce, the third year (56,116). Figure 10-10 shows the periods in the adult life span when divorce is most frequent. Notice that the peak comes during the twenties and thirties.

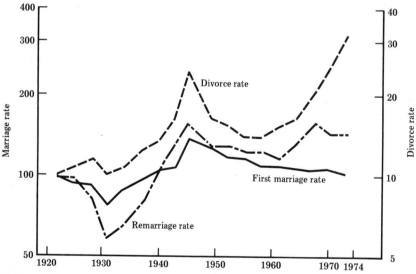

FIGURE 10-9 There has been a marked increase in the divorce rate in the United States since the end of World War I. (Adapted from A. J. Norton and P. C. Glick. Marital instability: Past, present, and future. *Journal of Social Issues*, 1976, **32**(1), 5–20. Used by permission.)

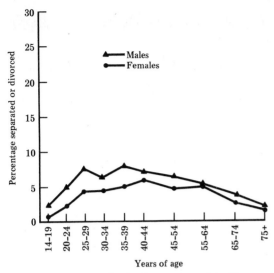

FIGURE 10-10 Periods during the adult life span when divorce occurs most frequently and least frequently. (Adapted from U.S. Census Report. Marital Status, 1972. Used by permission.)

Conditions Affecting the Stability of Marriage There are many conditions that affect the stability of marital life which may and often do lead to divorce. The most important of these are given in Box 10-13. Not one of the conditions alone, it is important to realize, is likely to lead to desertion, separation, or divorce. Instead, a constellation of causes is far more apt to be responsible.

Furthermore, although all these conditions contribute to poor marital adjustment, they are not the actual cause of divorce. It has been found, for example, that there are slightly more divorces in families where the wife works than in families where she is a full-time homemaker. However, when such a marriage ends in divorce, it may not be the wife's working but rather the low economic status of the family that caused the marital unhappiness (17,116,132).

It has also been found that the cause of divorce varies from one period in marriage to another. Drinking, for example, is the cause of only 9 percent of divorces during the first year of marriage, as contrasted with 43 percent after twenty-five years of marriage. Similarly, adultery is rarely given as the cause for separation in the first year of marriage, but is the cause for one-third of all separations in the eleven- to fifteen-year period (80,132). Those who marry because the woman has become pregnant are much more

likely to seek a divorce early in marriage than later (59).

Certain people who have made poor personal adjustments seem to be "divorce-prone." Many poorly adjusted adults feel that marriage will be the solution to their emotional problems. It rarely is. Not only do they become more poorly adjusted with the assumption of new responsibilities, but they also create such an unhealthy atmosphere in the home that divorce may be the only solution.

Effects of Divorce The traumatic effect of divorce is usually greater than that of death because of the bitterness and emotional tension preceding it and because of the social attitudes toward divorce. These complicate postdivorce adjustments (171). Hozman and Froiland have pointed out that there are five phases of adjustment to divorce. These are: first, denial that there is a divorce; second, anger, in which the individuals strike out at those involved in the situation; third, bargaining on the part of children in an attempt to bring their parents back together; fourth, depression, when the full impact of the divorce on the family is recognized; and, fifth, acceptance of the divorce (80).

Landis has pointed out that divorce necessitates certain adjustments on the part of every member of the family. The most important of these adjustments are, according to Landis (90):

Adjustment to the knowledge that divorce will take place
Adjustment to the divorce itself
Adjustment to the use by one parent of the child against the other parent
Adjustment to peer group attitudes
Adjustment to changed feelings
Adjustment to living with one parent
Adjustment to remarriage
Adjustment to implications of family failure

The effects of divorce are especially serious in the case of the children of the family. Children whose parents are divorced or remarried are embarrassed because they are "different." This is very damaging to their self-concepts unless they live in a neighborhood where most of their playmates' families are also divorced or remarried.

Children are most hurt by divorce when their loyalties are divided and when they suffer from anxiety because of the uncertainties that divorce brings to their lives. This uncertainty is especially serious in the

BOX 10-13

CONDITIONS AFFECTING STABILITY OF MARRIAGE

Number of Children

There are more divorces among childless couples and those with few children than among couples with big families, mainly because the former can manage better after divorce than the latter. Figure 10-11 shows how children contribute to the stability of marriage.

Social Class

Desertion is more common among the lower social classes, and divorce among the upper-middle and upper classes.

Similarity of Background

Divorce is much more common among couples who have different cultural, racial, religious, or socioeconomic backgrounds than among those whose backgrounds are more similar. This is especially true of couples with different religious backgrounds.

Time of Marriage

The divorce rate is very high among couples who marry early, before they are vocationally and economically established. There are three reasons for this: First, young people know that it will be relatively easy for them to remarry; second, those who marry early are likely to be plagued by financial problems, which make marital adjustment difficult; and third, young people often have overly romantic concepts of marriage, which inevitably lead to disenchantment.

Reason for Marriage

Those who are forced to marry because of pregnancy have a higher-than-average divorce rate.

Time at Which the Couple Become Parents

The shorter the interval between marriage and the birth of the first child, the higher the divorce rate. Couples who become parents early have not had time to adjust to marriage, which complicates their adjustment to parenthood.

Economic Status

The lower the economic status of the family, the higher the rate of desertion and divorce. This is true of couples of all ages.

Parental Model

Marital success or failure tends to run in families. Children of happily married parents are far less likely to be divorced than children of unhappily married or divorced parents.

Ordinal Position in Childhood Family

Men who were only-children have the highest divorce rate, while women who were only-children have the lowest. This can be attributed to the fact that only boys tend to be spoiled, while only girls learn to assume responsibilities. Firstborn men, who also assumed responsibilities when they were young, have a low divorce rate; firstborn women, who may have been domineering toward younger siblings, have a high divorce rate.

Maintenance of Identity

Adults who can maintain their identity after marriage, and who have opportunities for self-actualization, are far less likely to be divorced than those whose own lives are completely submerged in that of their spouses.

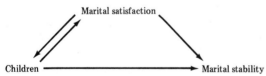

FIGURE 10-11 How children contribute to the stability of marriage. (Adapted from A. Thornton. Children and marriage stability. *Journal of Marriage & the Family*, 1977, **39**, 531–540. Used by permission.)

case where custody of the children is fought by parents and when they are shifted back and forth from one parent to another (150).

On the other hand, there is evidence that children whose parents are "emotionally divorced," even though living together under the same roof, suffer even more than those whose parents are legally divorced. There is evidence that the effects of continued home conflict is more harmful to the children than divorce itself (6,90,150).

While many men and women may benefit from divorce in the sense that it gives them an opportunity to build a new life more to their liking, they face many problems that far outweigh the benefits of divorce (23,171). As Hetherington et al. have pointed out, like the myth of romantic love, the myth of romantic divorce as a cure-all for marital problems just is not true. They go on further to explain, "When many couples divorce, they expect less stress and conflict, the joys of greater freedom, and the delights of self-discovery. With this happily-ever-after attitude, few are prepared for the traumas and stresses they will find in reaching for these goals" (74).

Studies of the effects of divorce on family members have shown that these effects are most pronounced during the first year following the divorce. During the second year after divorce, adjustments are gradually made and the problems that plagued family members, especially husbands and wives, are gradually solved (23,74,171).

While all adults face certain individual problems in divorce, there are some problems that are almost universal for all men and women who are divorced. These problems, however, are often very different for men and women and the solutions to them are likewise different. Of the many universal problems, the most common and most serious are given in Box 10-14.

Hazards of Remarriage

Remarriage may follow the death of a spouse or a divorce. Among young adults in America today, remarriage is more often after divorce than after death because death of a spouse in early adulthood is relatively infrequent in today's America except during periods of war. Refer to Figure 10-9 which shows the increasing tendency toward remarriage since the 1930s.

Because of changed social attitudes toward remarriage after divorce, many adults try to solve their adjustment problems by marrying soon again. It has been reported that approximately three-fourths of those who are divorced remarry within five years (36, 40,74). For widows, the median length of time between death of a spouse and remarriage is 3.5 years and, for widowers, 1.7 years. Women's chances of remarriage decrease sharply after they are thirty-five years old (36).

For those who do not remarry or who remarry only after a long interval, divorce often adds economic strains to the other adjustment problems. This is especially true for women who often must take jobs and hire someone to care for their homes and children.

In spite of the fact that many men and women believe that remarriage will solve most of the problems that divorce brings, there is evidence that many remarriages are not as successful as first marriage. This is shown by the high divorce rate among those who remarry. This suggests that individuals are conditioned toward instability after divorce. There is evidence, however, that widows have more stable remarriages than divorced women (45).

Adjustments in Remarriage Just as is true of a first marriage, so it is true of remarriage that many adjustments must be made by both men and women. These adjustments tend to be more difficult in remarriage than in a first marriage, partly because men and women are older and all adjustments become increasingly difficult with age, partly because adjustments in remarriage mean breaking habits of action, often of many years' duration, and establishing new habits, and partly because remarriage usually involves the children and in-laws from the first marriage and this increases the adjustment problems.

While adjustment problems in every marriage are individual, some are almost universal and, hence, common. This is true of remarriage just as it is of first marriage. In remarriage, there are two problems that are universal.

First, in remarriage, all men and women must adjust to a new mate. The chances of transferring the adjustments made in a previous marriage to the new marriage are slim. As a result, both men and women must break old adjustments and establish new ones. This is especially true of sexual adjustments and adjustments to roles the mate will expect to play (123). A man, for example, who learned to adjust to the role played by a home-making wife, where all home responsibilities were assumed by her, may find it difficult to adjust to the role played by a working wife who expects him to assume some of the home responsibilities.

Second, in remarriage, many men and women must adjust to the role of stepparent. While remarriage may provide two parents and a home for the children, both the stepparent and the stepchildren usually find their roles exceedingly difficult. How successfully children adjust to stepparents is greatly

BOX 10-14

COMMON PROBLEMS DIVORCED MEN AND WOMEN FACE

Economic Problems

After divorce, the husband and wife are both on reduced incomes because the husband's income must now support two households. Often the wife must take a job to supplement her alimony and child support.

Practical Problems

Even when the husband assumed few household responsibilities before divorce, the wife must now assume all household responsibilities. The practical problems of daily living—food preparation, bed-making, cleaning, marketing, etc.—formerly assumed by the woman, must, after divorce, be assumed by the man.

Psychological Problems

Both men and women, after divorce, tend to suffer from feelings of rootlessness and lack of identity. This is especially true of women whose identity was formerly associated with that of their husbands.

Emotional Problems

Few men and women are happy and carefree after divorce though many are relieved that the stresses and strains of an unhappy marriage have ended. In many women, feelings of guilt, shame, resentment, anger, and anxiety about the future are so dominant that they bring about personality changes.

Social Problems

Because social life in the adult American culture is built around couples, divorced women tend to be left out and, as Hetherington et al. have put it, "are locked into a child's world" (74). Their social lives are limited mainly to relatives and friends of the same sex. Divorced men usually fare better but even they find that, because social life is centered around couples, they too are often left out.

Problems of Loneliness

Having been accustomed, since childhood, to the constant companionship of family members and then of a spouse, divorced men and women are lonely when they find themselves deprived of the constant companionship of a person of similar interests and values. Men, when the custody of the children is given to their wives, tend to be especially lonely over weekends and at holiday times.

Problems of Divided Child Custody

When custody of the children is divided between divorced parents, each experiences adjustment problems for themselves and for the children. After being with one parent, for example, the other parent often encounters rebellion on the part of the children against home rules and responsibilities.

Sexual Problems

After divorce, both men and women are deprived of regular sexual outlets unless they remarry shortly after divorce or establish a cohabitation arrangement. While men may be able to solve their sexual problems with affairs or cohabitation, women with children often find such solutions impractical. Furthermore, the time interval between divorce and remarriage tends to be longer for women than for men, as was pointed out earlier, and this prolongs their sexual problems.

Problems of Changed Self-Concepts

Regardless of which spouse was responsible for the problems that led to divorce, both spouses tend to experience feelings of failure because their marriages went on the rocks and feelings of resentment against each other. These feelings inevitably color their self-concepts unfavorably and lead to personality changes.

---

influenced by their ages at the time of remarriage. Older children have already made adjustments to one pattern of life and are often resistant to change, especially if they have developed an unfavorable attitude toward the stepparent for some reason. Younger chil-

dren, by contrast, may welcome a stepparent who brings greater stability to their lives (14,45).

Children of any age who have been accustomed to the affection and attention of a parent may resent the transference of some of this to the stepparent. This resentment will be increased if stepparents try to assign children new roles and use disciplinary methods that differ radically from those they have been accustomed to (14). While children may resent both stepmothers and stepfathers, their resentment against stepmothers tends to be greater than against stepfathers (127,173). There are two reasons for this. First, stepfathers play a far less important role in the home than do stepmothers and, second, there are fewer negative attitudes toward stepfathers, from traditional beliefs and stereotypes, than toward stepmothers. As Visher and Visher have explained, "Stepfathers do not have to overcome such a negative press as do stepmothers" (167).

In addition to resentment against stepparents, many children are embarrassed about having a stepparent if they live in a neighborhood or community where divorce and remarriage are relatively infrequent. Their embarrassment may come from unfavorable peer attitudes toward stepparents or from the fact that children of remarried parents have different surnames than their parents have if it is the mother who has remarried. This complicates the problems of adjustment to the new pattern of family life, especially if the stepparent has never been a parent before.

SUCCESS OF ADJUSTMENT TO ADULTHOOD

Successful adjustment to adult life can be measured in terms of three criteria: achievements, satisfaction, and personal adjustments as reflected in the individual's personality. All three are so closely interrelated that one alone is inadequate to assess the individual's adjustment.

Achievement

Normally, adulthood is a time of achievement. Adults usually reach the peak of their achievements between the ages of thirty and thirty-nine years. Thirty-five is often regarded as the "crisis year"—meaning that if individuals have not shown significant achievements by then, it is unlikely that they ever will.

However, it is important to realize that the age at which adults reach their peaks depends on the area in which they attain distinction. The peak in athletic abilities, for example, has been found to come in the mid-twenties, though it varies somewhat with the different types of athletic activities. Those who are involved in science, mathematics, music, writing, philosophy, and inventing usually reach their peak during their thirties or early forties (44, 94).

Satisfaction

The degree to which adults are successful in adjusting to the important problems they face in adult life will determine the degree of their satisfaction. This, in turn, will affect their happiness (29).

During their twenties, young adults are apt to be somewhat pessimistic about the future and, as a result, many are dissatisfied and unhappy. However, as they approach the thirties, they usually become more optimistic and more realistic. As a result, they are better satisfied with their lives and, hence, happier. In fact, this decade in the life span is often regarded as one of the happiest periods in life (93).

Personal Adjustments

The success with which adults adjust to the problems of adult life has an effect on their self-concepts and, through them, on their personalities. The more successfully they adjust, the more favorable their self-concepts will be and the more self-confidence, assurance, and poise they will have. One of the major problems many adults face is personal attractiveness and the role it plays in vocational, social, and marital life. By the age of thirty, most adults are better satisfied with their looks because they have learned to use beauty aids successfully. Consequently, they are better satisfied with themselves and, hence, happier (11,101).

Feelings of inadequacy, on the other hand, are the usual accompaniments of failures in adjustment. This is true also when there is a large discrepancy between the perceived and ideal self. Under such conditions, adults tend to be anxious, dissatisfied, and unhappy. This is often expressed in suicidal tendencies.

By the time men and women reach adulthood, their personality patterns are fairly well established. As Thorndike pointed out, many years ago: "A person's nature at 12 is prophetic of his nature in adult years. . . . The child to whom approval is more cherished than mastery is likely to become a man who seeks applause rather than power, and similarly throughout" (155).

Thus, it should be apparent that the personality

pattern influences the kind of adjustments men and women make to adult life, rather than the reverse.

While there is unquestionably a cause-and-effect relationship working both ways, it is stronger in the direction of the personality's influence on adjustments. Adults who make good adjustments have integrated personality patterns in which the core is a stable, realistic self-concept, whereas those who make poor adjustments have poorly integrated personality patterns with unstable, unrealistic self-concepts.

Chapter Highlights

1. Vocational and family adjustments in early adulthood are especially difficult because most young adults have limited foundations on which to build their adjustments due to the newness of the roles these adjustments require.
2. The major problems in vocational adjustment in early adulthood consist of selection of a vocation, achieving stability in the selection made, and adjustment to work situations. How successfully men and women make these adjustments can be judged by their achievements, voluntary changes of jobs, and the satisfaction derived from the jobs.
3. The ever-increasing number of family-life patterns makes marital adjustment difficult, especially when the family-life pattern that fits the individual's needs differs from that approved by the social group.
4. A number of conditions contribute to difficulties in marital adjustment, the most common of which are limited preparation for marriage, early marriages, unrealistic and romanticized concepts of marriage, mixed marriages, shortened courtships, lack of identity in marriage, and marked role changes.
5. Among the common adjustment problems in marriage, adjustment to a mate, sexual adjustments, and financial and in-law adjustments are the most common and most difficult.
6. Parenthood may be regarded as a "crisis" in the individual's life because it necessitates changes in attitudes, values, and roles. This is especially true for women who must give up careers for which they have trained and in which they have been successful.
7. Of the many factors influencing adjustment to parenthood, the most important are attitudes toward pregnancy and parenthood, age of parents, sex of children, parental expectations, feelings of parental adequacy, attitudes toward changed roles necessitated by parenthood, and the child's temperament.
8. In assessing marital adjustment, seven criteria may be applied: happiness of husband and wife, good parent-child relationships, good adjustments of children, ability to deal satisfactorily with disagreements, "togetherness," good financial adjustments, and good in-law adjustments.
9. The effects of singlehood in early adulthood are, today, far less serious and far less damaging to good personal and social adjustments of both men and women than was true in the past.
10. Among the most common and most serious vocational hazards of early adulthood are job dissatisfaction and unemployment.
11. The most common and most serious marital hazards of early adulthood center around adjustment to a mate, competitiveness in the marital relationship, sexual adjustments, acceptance of the family economic status and role changes, relationships with in-laws, and adjustment to parenthood.
12. Hazards of divorce are intensified when there are children, especially when the children are old enough to comprehend the radical changes divorce brings into their lives.
13. Among the most common problems divorced men and women face are economic, practical, psychological, emotional, social, loneliness, sexual, divided child custody and changes in self-concepts.
14. There are two adjustment problems in remarriage that are almost universal in the American culture of today: first, adjustment to a new mate, and, second, adjustment to the role of stepparent.
15. Success of adjustment to adulthood can be assessed by three criteria: achievement in the vocation and life pattern chosen by the individual, degree of satisfaction derived from chosen vocation and life pattern, and success of personal adjustments.

Bibliography

1. Adams, M. *Single blessedness: Observations on the single status in married society.* New York: Basic Books, 1976.
2. Albrecht, S. L., H. M. Bahr, and B. A. Chadwick. Public stereotyping of sex roles, personality characteristics and occupations. *Sociology & Social Research,* 1977, **61,** 223–240.
3. Aldous, J. The making of family roles and family change. *Family Coordinator,* 1974, **23,** 231–235.
4. Anspach, D. F. Kinship and divorce. *Journal of Marriage & the Family,* 1976, **38,** 323–330.

5. Baird, L. S. Relationship of performance to satisfaction in stimulating and nonstimulating jobs. *Journal of Applied Psychology,* 1976, **61**, 721–727.

6. Bane, M. J. Marital disruption and the lives of children. *Journal of Social Issues,* 1976, **32**(1), 103–117.

7. Bean, F. D., and L. H. Aiken. Intermarriage and unwanted fertility in the United States. *Journal of Marriage & the Family,* 1976, **38**, 61–72.

8. Bell, R. R., S. Turner, and L. Rosen. A multivariate analysis of female extramarital coitus. *Journal of Marriage & the Family,* 1975, **37**, 375–384.

9. Berk, B. Face-savings at the singles dance. *Social Forces,* 1977, **24**, 530–544.

10. Bernard, J. Note on changing life styles, 1970–1974. *Journal of Marriage & the Family,* 1975, **37**, 582–593.

11. Berscheid, E., E. Walster, and G. Bohrnstedt. The happy American body: A survey report. *Psychology Today,* 1974, **7**(6), 119–123, 126–131.

12. Bischof, L. J. *Adult psychology.* (2nd ed.) New York: Harper & Row, 1976.

13. Blum, S. H. The desire for security in vocational choice: A comparison of men and women. *Journal of Psychology,* 1975, **91**, 277–281.

14. Bohannan, P., and R. Erickson. Stepping in, *Psychology Today,* 1978, **11**(8), 53–54, 59.

15. Booth, A. Wife's employment and husband's stress: A replication and refutation. *Journal of Marriage & the Family,* 1977, **39**, 645–650.

16. Booth, A., and J. N. Edwards. Crowding and family relations. *American Sociological Review,* 1976, **41**, 308–321.

17. Brandwein, R. A., C. A. Brown, and E. M. Fox. Women and children last: The social situation of divorced mothers and their families. *Journal of Marriage & the Family,* 1974, **36**, 498–514.

18. Broderick, C. B. Fathers. *Family Coordinator,* 1977, **26**, 269–275.

19. Bronfenbrenner, U. The origins of alienation. *Scientific American,* 1974, **231**(2), 53–61.

20. Bronfenbrenner, U. Nobody home: The erosion of the American family. *Psychology Today,* 1977, **10**(12), 40–47.

21. Bronfenbrenner, U. Who needs parent education? *Teachers College Record,* 1978, **79**, 767–787.

22. Brook, J. S., M. Whiteman, E. Peisach, and M. Deutsch. Aspiration levels of and for children: Age, sex, race, and socioeconomic correlates. *Journal of Genetic Psychology,* 1974, **124**, 3–16.

23. Brown, C. A., R. Feldberg, E. M. Fox, and J. Kohen. Divorce: Chance of a new lifetime. *Journal of Social Issues,* 1976, **32**(1), 119–133.

24. Burke, R. J. Occupational stresses and job satisfaction. *Journal of Social Psychology,* 1976, **100**, 235–244.

25. Burke, R. J., and T. Weir. Relationship of wives' employment status to husband, wife, and pair satisfaction and performance. *Journal of Marriage & the Family,* 1976, **38**, 279–287.

26. Burke, R. J., and T. Weir. Marital helping relationships: The moderators between stress and well being. *Journal of Psychology,* 1977, **95**, 121–130.

27. Burr, W. R. Satisfaction with various aspects of marriage over the life cycle: A random middle-class sample. *Journal of Marriage & the Family,* 1970, **32**, 29–37.

28. Byrne, S. The erosion of the American family. *Psychology Today,* 1977, **10**(12), 41–47.

29. Campbell, A. The American way of mating: Marriage si, children only maybe. *Psychology Today,* 1975, **8**(12), 37–43.

30. Campbell, D. P., and K. L. Klein. Job satisfaction and vocational interests. *Vocational Guidance Quarterly,* 1975, **24**, 125–131.

31. Cantor, N. L., and D. M. Gelfand. Effects of responsiveness and sex of children on adults' behavior. *Child Development,* 1977, **48**, 232–238.

32. Casady, M. Runaway wives: "Husbands don't pick up the danger signals their wives send out." *Psychology Today,* 1975, **8**(12), 42.

33. Centers, R. Attitude similarity-dissimilarity as a correlate of heterosexual attraction and love. *Journal of Marriage & the Family,* 1975, **37**, 305–312.

34. Cherry, N. Persistent job changing: Is it a problem? *Journal of Occupational Psychology,* 1976, **49**, 203–221.

35. Chilman, C. S. Some psychosocial aspects of female sexuality. *Family Coordinator,* 1974, **23**, 123–131.

36. Cleveland, W. P., and D. T. Gianturco. Remarriage probability after widowhood: A retrospective method. *Journal of Gerontology,* 1976, **31**, 99–103.

37. Cochrane, S. H., and F. D. Bean. Husband-wife differences in the demand for children. *Journal of Marriage & the Family,* 1976, **38**, 297–307.

38. Cogswell, B. E. Variant family forms and life styles: Rejection of the traditional nuclear family. *Family Coordinator,* 1975, **24**, 391–406.

39. Cohen, D. J., E. Dibble, and J. M. Grawe. Parental style. *Archives of General Psychiatry,* 1977, **34**, 445–457.

40. Conroy, R. C. Widows and widowhood. *New York State Journal of Medicine,* 1977, **77**, 357–360.

41. Cummings, T. G., and J. Bigelow. Satisfaction, job involvement and intrinsic motivation: An extension of Lawler and Hall's factor analysis. *Journal of Applied Psychology,* 1976, **61**, 523–528.

42. Dame, N. G., G. H. Finck, R. G. Mayos, R. S. Reiner and B. O. Smith. Conflicts in marriage following premarital pregnancy. *American Journal of Orthopsychiatry,* 1966, **36**, 468–475.

43. Dean, G., and D. T. Gurak. Marital homogamy the second time around. *Journal of Marriage & the Family,* 1978, **40**, 559–570.

44. Dennis, W. Creative productivity between the ages of 30 and 80 years. *Journal of Gerontology,* 1966, **21**, 1–8.

45. Duberman, L. *The reconstituted family: A study of remarried couples and their children.* Chicago: Nelson-Hall, 1975.

46. Duncan, R. P., and C. C. Perrucci. Dual occupation families and migration. *American Sociological Review,* 1976, **41**, 252–261.

47. Eiduson, B. T., J. Cohen, and J. Alexander. Alternatives to child rearing in the 1970s. *American Journal of Orthopsychiatry,* 1973, **43**, 720–731.

48. Elder, G. H. Appearance and education in marriage mobility. *American Sociological Review,* 1969, **34**, 519–533.

49. Enderlein, T. E. Causal patterns related to post high school employment satisfaction. *Journal of Vocational Behavior,* 1975, **7**, 67–80.

50. Erikson, E. H. Identity and the life cycle: Selected papers. *Psychological Issues Monographs,* Vol. 1, No. 1. New York: International Universities Press, 1967.

51. Feather, N. F., and J. G. Siman. Stereotypes about male and female success and failure at sex-linked occupations. *Journal of Personality,* 1976, **44**, 16–37.

52. Fein, R. A. Men's entrance to parenthood. *Family Coordinator,* 1976, **25**, 341–348.

53. Feldberg, R., and J. Kohen. Family life in an anti-family setting: A critique of marriage and divorce. *Family Coordinator,* 1976, **25**, 151–159.

54. Ferree, M. M. The confused American housewife. *Psychology Today,* 1976, **10**(4), 76–80.

55. Fleming, J. D. What mother knows best. If one baby's nice, what's wrong with two? *Psychology Today,* 1975, **8**(2), 43.

56. Framo, J. L. The friendly divorce. *Psychology Today,* 1978, **11**(9), 78–79, 100–102.

57. Frank, E., C. Anderson, and D. Rubinstein. Frequency of sexual dysfunction in "normal" couples. *New England Journal of Medicine,* 1978, **299**, 111–115.

58. Fry, P. S. Changes in youth's attitudes toward authority. The transition from university to employment. *Journal of Counseling Psychology,* 1976, **23**, 66–74.

59. Furstenberg, F. F. Premarital pregnancy and marital stability. *Journal of Social Issues,* 1976, **32**(1), 67–86.

60. Garland, H., and R. H. Price. Attitudes toward women in management and attributes for their success and failure in a managerial position. *Journal of Applied Psychology,* 1977, **62**, 29–33.

61. Gasser, R. D., and C. M. Taylor. Role adjustment of single parent fathers with dependent children. *Family Coordinator,* 1976, **25**, 397–401.

62. Gilbert, S. J. Self-disclosure, intimacy and communication in families. *Family Coordinator,* 1976, **25**, 221–231.

63. Glenn, N. D., P. A . Taylor, and C. N. Weaver. Age and job satisfaction among males and females: A multivariate, multisurvey study. *Journal of Applied Psychology,* 1977, **62**, 189–193.

64. Glenn, N. D., and C. N. Weaver. A multivariate, multisurvey study of marital happiness. *Journal of Marriage & the Family,* 1978, **40**, 269–282.

65. Glick, P. V. A demographer looks at American families. *Family Coordinator,* 1975, **24**, 15–26.

66. Glick, P. C. Updating the life cycle of the family. *Journal of Marriage & the Family,* 1977, **39**, 5–13.

67. Gottfredson, G. D. Career stability and redirection in adulthood. *Journal of Applied Psychology,* 1977, **62**, 436–444.

68. Gould, R. Adult life stages: Growth toward self-tolerance. *Psychology Today,* 1975, **8**(9), 74–78.

69. Hagen, R. L., and A. Kahn. Discrimination against competent women. *Journal of Applied Social Psychology,* 1975, **5**, 362–376.

70. Hall, E. Ordinal position and success in engagement and marriage. *Journal of Individual Psychology,* 1965, **21**, 154–158.

71. Hassett, J. A new look at living together. *Psychology Today,* 1977, **11**(7), 82–83.

72. Havighurst, R. J. Body, self, and society. *Sociology & Social Research,* 1965, **49**, 261–267.

73. Hetherington, E. M., M. Cox, and R. Cox. Divorced fathers. *Family Coordinator,* 1976, **25**, 417–429.

74. Hetherington, E. M., M. Cox, and R. Cox. Divorced fathers. *Psychology Today,* 1977, **10**(11), 42–46.

75. Hobbs, D. F., and S. P. Cole. Transition to parenthood: A decade replication. *Journal of Marriage & the Family,* 1976, **38**, 723–731.

76. Hoffman, L. W. Changes in family roles, socialization, and sex differences. *American Psychologist,* 1977, **32**, 644–657.

77. Horenstein, D., and B. K. Houston. The effects of vasectomy on postoperative psychological adjustment and self-concept. *Journal of Psychology,* 1975, **89**, 167–173.

78. Horner, M. S. Toward an understanding of achievement-related conflicts in women. *Journal of Social Issues,* 1972, **28**(2), 157–175.

79. House, J. Divorced women: How they fare financially. *Journal of Home Economics,* 1976, **68**(3), 36–38.

80. Hozman, T. L., and D. J. Froiland. Families in divorce: A proposed model for counseling the children. *Family Coordinator,* 1976, **25**, 271–276.

81. Johnson, E. S., and B. J. Bursk. Relationships between the elderly and their adult children. *Gerontologist,* 1977, **17**, 90–96.

82. Kanter, R. M. The impact of hierarchical standards on the work behavior of women and men. *Social Problems,* 1976, **23**, 415–430.

83. Kanter, R. M. Why bosses turn bitchy. *Psychology Today,* 1976, **9**(12), 88–90.

84. Kempler, H. L. Extended kinship ties and some modern alternatives. *Family Coordinator,* 1976, **25**, 143–149.

85. Kezur, D. The development of maternal attachment. *Smith College Studies in Social Work,* 1978, **48**, 183–208.

86. Klemmack, D. L., and J. N. Edwards. Women's acquisition of stereotyped occupational aspirations. *Sociology & Social Research,* 1973, **57**, 510–525.

87. Knox, D., and K. Wilson. The difference between having one and two children. *Family Coordinator,* 1978, **27**, 23–25.

88. Kobrin, F. E. The primary individual and the family: Changes in living arrangements in the United States since 1940. *Journal of Marriage & the Family,* 1976, **38**, 233–239.

89. Lamb, M. E. Fathers: Forgotten contributions to child development. *Human Development,* 1975, **18**, 245–266.

90. Landis, J. T. Social correlates of divorce or nondivorce among the unhappily married. *Marriage & Family Living,* 1963, **25**, 178–180.

91. Lantz, H., M. Schultz, and M. O'Hara. The changing American family from the preindustrial to the industrial period: A final report. *American Sociological Review,* 1977, **42**, 406–421.

92. Lau, A. W., and N. M. Abrahams. Stability of vocational interests within nonprofessional occupations. *Journal of Applied Psychology,* 1971, **55**, 143–150.

93. Lee, G. R. Age at marriage and marital satisfaction: A multivariate analysis with implications for marital stability. *Journal of Marriage & the Family,* 1977, **39**, 493–504.

94. Lehman, H. C. The psychologist's most creative years. *American Psychologist,* 1966, **21**, 363–369.

95. Leifer, M. Psychological changes accompanying pregnancy and motherhood. *Genetic Psychology Monographs,* 1977, **95**, 55–96.

96. Levenson, H., B. Burford, B. Bonno, and L. Davis. Are women still prejudiced against women? A replication and extension of Goldberg's study. *Journal of Psychology,* 1975, **89**, 67–71.

97. Lofquist, L. H., and R. V. Davis. Vocational needs, work reinforcers, and job satisfaction. *Vocational Guidance Quarterly,* 1975, **24**, 132–139.

98. London, M., R. Crandall, and G. W. Seals. The contribution of job and leisure satisfaction to quality of life. *Journal of Applied Psychology,* 1977, **62**, 328–334.

99. Masters, W. H., and V. E. Johnson. *Human sexual responsiveness.* Boston: Little, Brown, 1966.

100. Masters, W. H., and V. E. Johnson: *Human sexual inadequacy.* Boston: Little, Brown, 1970.

101. Mathes, E. W., and A. Kahn. Physical attractiveness, happiness,

neurotocism, and self-esteem. *Journal of Psychology*, 1975, **90**, 27–30.

102. McClendon, McK. J. The occupational status attainment process of males and females. *American Sociological Review*, 1976, **41**, 52–64.

103. Mendes, H. A. Single fathers. *Family Coordinator*, 1976, **25**, 439–444.

104. Miller, B. C. A multivariate developmental model of marital satisfaction. *Journal of Marriage & the Family*, 1976, **38**, 643–657.

105. Mobley, W. H. Intermediate linkages in the relationship between job satisfaction and employee turnover. *Journal of Applied Psychology*, 1977, **62**, 237–240.

106. Monahan, T. P. An overview of statistics on interracial marriage in the United States, with data on its extent from 1963–1970. *Journal of Marriage & the Family*, 1976, **38**, 223–231.

107. Mueller, C. W., and B. G. Campbell. Female occupational achievement and marital status: A research note. *Journal of Marriage & the Family*, 1977, **39**, 587–593.

108. Mueller, C. W., and H. Pope. Marital instability: A study of its transmission between generations. *Journal of Marriage & the Family*, 1977, **39**, 83–93.

109. Nevill, D., and S. Damico. Family size and role conflict in women. *Journal of Psychology*, 1975, **89**, 267–270.

110. New York Times article. Husband and wife work in 47.1% of marriages. *The New York Times*, March 7, 1977.

111. Nicholson, N., C. A. Brown, and J. K. Chadwick-Jones. Absence from work and job satisfaction. *Journal of Applied Psychology*, 1976, **61**, 728–737.

112. Nilson, L. B. The social standing of a married woman. *Social Problems*, 1976, **23**, 581–592.

113. Nilson, L. B. The social standing of a housewife. *Journal of Marriage & the Family*, 1978, **40**, 541–548.

114. Nord, W. R. Job satisfaction reconsidered. *American Psychologist*, 1977, **32**, 1026–1035.

115. Norman, R. D. Sex differences in preferences for sex of children: A replication after 20 years. *Journal of Psychology*, 1974, **88**, 229–239.

116. Norton, A. J., and P. C. Glick. Marital instability: Past, present, and future. *Journal of Social Issues*, 1976, **32**(1), 5–20.

117. Notz, W. W. Work motivation and the negative effects of extrinsic rewards: A review with implications for theory and practice. *American Psychologist*, 1975, **30**, 884–891.

118. Orthner, D. K., T. Brown, and D. Ferguson. Single-parent fatherhood: An emerging family life style. *Family Coordinator*, 1976, **25**, 429–437.

119. Ory, M. G. The decision to parent or not: Normative and structural components. *Journal of Marriage & the Family*, 1978, **40**, 531–539.

120. Paris, B. L., and E. B. Luckey. A longitudinal study of marital satisfaction. *Sociology & Social Research*, 1966, **50**, 212–222.

121. Patty, R. A., and M. M. Ferrell. A preliminary note on the motive to avoid success and the menstrual cycle. *Journal of Psychology*, 1974, **86**, 173–177.

122. Pearlin, L. I. Status inequality and stress in marriage. *American Sociological Review*, 1975, **40**, 344–357.

123. Peters, J. W. A comparison of mate selection and marriage in the first and second marriages in a selected sample of remarried divorced. *Journal of Comparative Family Studies*, 1976, **7**, 483–490.

124. Pieper, E. Grandparents can help. *The Exceptional Parent*, 1976, **6**(2), 6–10.

125. Pierce, R. C., and D. A. Chiriboga. Dimensions of adult self-concept. *Journal of Gerontology*, 1979, **34**, 80–85.

126. Polit, D. F. Stereotypes relating to family-size status. *Journal of Marriage & the Family*, 1978, **40**, 105–114.

127. Rallings, E. M. The special role of stepfather. *Family Coordinator*, 1976, **25**, 445–449.

128. Renne, K. S. Correlates of dissatisfaction in marriage. *Journal of Marriage & the Family*, 1970, **32**, 54–67.

129. Rheingold, H. L. To rear a child. *American Psychologist*, 1973, **28**, 42–46.

130. Ridley, C. A., D. J. Peterman, and A. W. Avery. Cohabitation: Does it make for a better marriage? *Family Coordinator*, 1978, **27**, 129–136.

131. Rollins, B. C., and H. Feldman. Marital satisfaction over the family life cycle. *Journal of Marriage & the Family*, 1970, **32**, 20–28.

132. Rose, V. L., and S. Price-Bonham. Divorce adjustment: A woman's problem. *Family Coordinator*, 1973, **22**, 291–297.

133. Rosen, B., and T. H. Jerdee. The nature of job-related age stereotypes. *Journal of Applied Psychology*, 1976, **61**, 180–183.

134. Rosenfeld, R. A. Women's intergenerational occupational mobility. *American Sociological Review*, 1978, **43**, 36–46.

135. Rosenthal, K. M., and H. F. Keshet. The not-quite stepmothers. *Psychology Today*, 1978, **12**(2), 83–86, 100–101.

136. Rossi, A. S. A biosocial perspective on parenting. *Daedalus*, 1977, **106**(2), 1–31.

137. Rubin, L. B. The marriage bed. *Psychology Today*, 1976, **10**(3), 44–50, 91.

138. Russell, C. S. Transition to parenthood: Problems and gratifications. *Journal of Marriage & the Family*, 1974, **36**, 294–301.

139. Russo, N. F. The motherhood mandate. *Journal of Social Issues*, 1976, **32**(3), 143–153.

140. Sattel, J. W. The inexpressive male: Tragedy of sexual politics? *Social Problems*, 1976, **23**, 469–477.

141. Schooler, C. Childhood family structure and adult characteristics. *Sociometry*, 1972, **35**, 255–269.

142. Schrank, R. How to relieve worker boredom. *Psychology Today*, 1978, **12**(2), 79–80.

143. Schuler, R. S. Role perceptions, satisfaction, and performance: A partial reconciliation. *Journal of Applied Psychology*, 1975, **60**, 683–687.

144. Shinan, E. H. Sexual stereotypes of occupations. *Journal of Vocational Behavior*, 1975, **7**, 99–111.

145. Simon, W. E., and L. H. Primavera. Attitudes toward ideal family size: Some preliminary data. *Psychological Reports*, 1976, **38**, 1282.

146. Sloane, L. College education and job satisfaction. *The New York Times*, April 20, 1977.

147. Sørensen, A. B., and S. Fuerst. Black-white differences in the occurrence of job shifts. *Sociology & Social Research*, 1978, **62**, 537–557.

148. Spicer, J. W., and G. D. Hampe. Kinship interaction after divorce. *Journal of Marriage & the Family*, 1975, **37**, 113–119.

149. Spreitzer, E., and L. E. Riley. Factors associated with singlehood. *Journal of Marriage & the Family*, 1974, **36**, 533–542.

150. Stack, C. B. Who owns the child? Divorce and child custody decisions in middle class families. *Social Problems*, 1976, **23**, 505–515.

151. Steers, R. M. Effects of need for achievement on the job performance-job attitude relationship. *Journal of Applied Psychology*, 1975, **60**, 678–681.

152. Stein, B., A. Cohen, and H. Gadon. Flextime: Work when you want to. *Psychology Today,* 1976, **10**(1), 40–43, 80.

153. Stein, P. J. Singlehood: An alternative to marriage. *Family Coordinator,* 1975, **24**, 489–503.

154. Taylor, P. A., and N. D. Glenn. The utility of education and attractiveness for females: Status attainment through marriage. *American Sociological Review,* 1976, **41**, 484–498.

155. Thorndike, E. L. Note on the shifts of interest with age. *Journal of Applied Psychology,* 1940, **30**, 55.

156. Thornton, A. Children and marital stability. *Journal of Marriage & the Family,* 1977, **39**, 531–540.

157. Tietze, C., and S. Lewit. Legal abortion. *Scientific American,* 1977, **236**(1), 21–27.

158. Todres, R. Runaway wives: An increasing North American phenomenon. *Family Coordinator,* 1978, **27**, 17–21.

159. Trost, J. Attitudes toward and occurrence of cohabitation without marriage. *Journal of Marriage & the Family,* 1978, **40**, 393–400.

160. Udry, J. R. The importance of being beautiful: A reexamination and racial comparison. *American Journal of Sociology,* 1977, **83**, 154–160.

161. U.S. News & World Report article. "Blue collar blues:" Just a catch phrase or a real threat? *U.S. News & World Report,* Dec. 25, 1972, 55–58.

162. U.S. News & World Report article. The American family: Can it survive today's shocks? *U.S. News & World Report,* Oct. 17, 1975, 30–46.

163. U.S. News & World Report article. The ways "singles" are changing U.S. *U.S. News & World Report,* Jan. 30, 1977, 59–60.

164. U.S. News & World Report article. For lots of reasons, more workers are saying "no" to job transfers. *U.S. News & World Report,* Feb. 14, 1977, 73–74.

165. U.S. News & World Report article. Women: Their impact grows in the job market. *U.S. News & World Report,* July 6, 1977, 58–59.

166. Veevers, J. E. Voluntary childlessness: A neglected area of family study. *Family Coordinator,* 1973, **22**, 199–205.

167. Visher, E. B., and J. S. Visher. Common problems of stepparents and their spouses. *American Journal of Orthopsychiatry,* 1978, **48**, 252–262.

168. Wallerstein, J. S., and J. B. Kelly. The effects of parental divorce: Experiences of the preschool child. *Journal of the American Academy of Child Psychiatry,* 1975, **14**, 600–616.

169. Warheit, G. J., D. E. Holzer, R. A. Bell, and S. A. Arey. Sex, marital status, and mental health: A reappraisal. *Social Forces,* 1976, **55**, 458–470.

170. Weintraub, E. The real cause of workers' discontent. *The New York Times,* Jan. 21, 1973.

171. Weiss, R. S. The emotional aspect of marital separation. *Journal of Social Issues,* 1976, **32**(1), 135–145.

172. Wente, A. S., and S. B. Crockenberg. Transition to fatherhood: Lamaze preparation, adjustment difficulty and the husband-wife relationship. *Family Coordinator,* 1976, **25**, 351–357.

173. Wilson, K. L., L. A. Lurcher, D. C. McAdams, and R. L. Curtis. Stepfathers and stepchildren: An exploratory analysis from two national surveys. *Journal of Marriage & the Family,* 1975, **37**, 526–536.

174. Wright, J. D. Are women *really* more satisfied? Evidence from several national surveys. *Journal of Marriage & the Family,* 1978, **40**, 301–313.

175. Yost, E. D., and R. J. Adamek. Parent-child interaction and changing family values: A multivariate analysis. *Journal of Marriage & the Family,* 1974, **36**, 115–121.

176. Zatlin, C. E., M. Storandt, and J. Botwinick. Personality and values of women continuing their education after thirty-five years of age. *Journal of Gerontology,* 1973, **28**, 216–221.

CHAPTER ELEVEN
MIDDLE AGE: PERSONAL AND SOCIAL ADJUSTMENTS

After reading this chapter, you should be able to:

- Understand why middle age is divided into two subdivisions, when they occur, and the characteristics of each.
- Describe the developmental tasks of middle age that should prepare men and women for successful adjustment to old age.
- Appreciate why adjustments to physical changes are among the most difficult middle-aged people must make.
- Recognize some of the common characteristics of the menopause syndrome in women, and the climacteric syndrome in men, and what criteria can be used to assess the success of adjustment to the changes these stages bring.
- Show how middle-aged people can adjust to mental changes and changes in interests.
- Account for some of the conditions responsible for changes in social attitudes and activities in middle age and explain what conditions most often contribute to good social functioning at this time.
- Acknowledge the most common personal and social hazards of middle age and understand why they are regarded as hazards.

Middle age is generally considered to extend from age forty to age sixty. The onset is marked by physical and mental changes, as is the end. At sixty, there is usually a decline in physical vigor, often accompanied by a lessening of mental alertness. Although many adults experience these changes later now than in the past, the traditional boundary lines are still recognized. The increasing trend toward voluntary or involuntary retirement at age sixty rather than age sixty-five also justifies considering sixty to be the boundary line between middle and old age.

Because middle age is a long period in the life span, it is customarily subdivided into *early middle age,* which extends from age forty to age fifty, and *advanced middle age,* which extends from age fifty to age sixty. During advanced middle age, physical and psychological changes that first began during the early forties become far more apparent.

As is true of every other period in the life span, individuals differ in the ages at which the physical changes that mark off middle age from early adulthood at one end, and old age, at the other, occur. According to the old saying, just as apples ripen at different times, so do humans—with some ripening in July and others not until October.

Middle age in the American culture of today is an especially difficult time in the life span. How well individuals adjust to it will depend on the foundations laid during earlier stages in the life span but especially on the adjustments they made to the roles and social expectations of adult society. Good mental health, acquired in adulthood, will go a long way toward easing the adjustments to the new roles and new social expectations of middle age.

CHARACTERISTICS OF MIDDLE AGE

Like every period in the life span, middle age is associated with certain characteristics that make it distinctive. Ten of the most important of these characteristics are listed below and briefly explained.

Middle Age Is a Dreaded Period

The first characteristic of middle age is that it is a dreaded period in the life span. It is recognized that, next to old age, it is the most dreaded period in the total life span and the one adults will not admit that they have reached until the calendar and the mirror force them to do so. As Desmond has pointed out, "Americans slump into middle age grudgingly, sadly and with a tinge of fear" (21).

Men and women have many reasons—reasons that seem valid to them—for dreading middle age. Among these are the many unfavorable stereotypes about middle-aged people, the traditional beliefs concerning the mental and physical deterioration that are believed to accompany the cessation of the reproductive life, and the emphasis on the importance of youth in the American culture as compared with the reverence for age found in many other cultures. These all influence adult attitudes unfavorably as they approach this period in their lives. While dreading middle age, most adults become nostalgic about their younger years and wish that they could turn back the hands of the clock. Figure 11-1 shows how a middle-aged women is likely to react to reminders of her younger years.

Middle Age Is a Time of Transition

The second characteristic of middle age is that it is a time of transition. Just as puberty is a time of

FIGURE 11-1 Many middle-aged people become nostalgic about their younger years. (Adapted from the cover drawing by Amos Sewell. *The Saturday Evening Post,* Jan. 26, 1957. Used by permission.)

transition from childhood to adolescence and then to adulthood, so middle age is the time when men and women leave behind the physical and behavioral characteristics of adulthood and enter a period of life when new physical and behavioral characteristics will prevail. It has been said that this is the time when men undergo a change in virility and women a change in fertility. In discussing the transitional nature of middle age, Bardwick has said, "Americans seem to deal with aging by changing roles, especially in work, and by changing partners" (4).

Transition always means adjustment to new interests, new values, and new patterns of behavior. In middle age, sooner or later all adults must make adjustments to physical changes and must realize that the behavioral patterns of their younger years have to be radically revised. Adjustment to changed roles is even more difficult than adjustment to changed physical conditions and changed interests. Why these adjustments are difficult will be explained later in the chapter.

Refer to Figure 10-4 which shows the pattern of role changes in adult life. Note that for both men and women there must be a change to a pair-centered relationship as compared with the family-centered relationship during the early years of adulthood when the main roles of men and women in the home are those of parents.

In addition to role changes in the home, men must adjust to the changes that impending retirement and physical conditions necessitate in their work. For women, the adjustments must be either to changing the role of housewife and mother for that of a worker in business, industry, or one of the professions or of an "isolate" in a formerly busy home as the "empty nest" period in home life sets in.

Every important role change is likely to result in a crisis of minor or major severity. During middle age, Kimmel has identified three common and almost universal developmental crises which are as follows.

First, the parenthood crisis characterized by the "Where did we go wrong?" syndrome. This crisis occurs when children fail to come up to parental expectations and the parents then question whether they have used the right methods of child training, blaming themselves for their children's failures to come up to their expectations.

Second, the crisis arising from dealing with aging parents, and "I hate to put Mother there" reaction. Many middle-aged parents, in trying to cope

BOX 11-1

CATEGORIES OF STRESS IN MIDDLE AGE

- *Somatic stress,* which is due to physical evidences of aging.
- *Cultural stress,* stemming from the high value placed on youth, vigor, and success by the cultural group.
- *Economic stress,* resulting from the financial burden of educating children and providing status symbols for all family members.
- *Psychological stress,* which may be the result of the death of a spouse, the departure of children from the home, boredom with marriage, or a sense of lost youth and approaching death.

with the problems of aging parents, feel guilty when they either cannot or do not want to have their aging parents live in their homes.

Third, the crisis that comes from trying to deal with death, especially that of a spouse. This, according to Kimmel, is characterized by a "How can I go on?" attitude which colors the individual's personal and social adjustments unfavorably until the crisis can be solved to the individual's satisfaction (49).

Middle Age Is a Time of Stress

The third characteristic of middle age is that it is a time of stress. Radical adjustments to changed roles and patterns of life, especially when accompanied by physical changes, always tend to disrupt the individual's physical and psychological homeostasis and lead to a period of stress—a time when a number of major adjustments must be made in the home, business, and social aspects of their lives (65).

Marmor has divided the common sources of stress during middle age that lead to disequilibrium into four major categories (61). What these categories are and what is characteristic of each are explained in Box 11-1.

There is evidence that there are sex differences in the ages at which men and women experience middle-aged stress. Most women, for example, experience a disruption in homeostasis during their forties, when normally they go through the menopause and their last children leave home, thus forcing them to make radical readjustments in the pattern of their entire lives. For men, by contrast, the climacteric comes later—generally in the fifties—as does the imminence of retirement with its necessary role changes (43,61,65).

Middle Age Is a "Dangerous Age"

The fourth characteristic of middle age is that it is commonly regarded as a "dangerous age" in the life span. The usual way of interpreting "dangerous age" is in terms of the male who wants to have a last fling in life, especially in his sex life, before old age catches up with him. As Archer has pointed out (3):

To those around him, it may seem that the mid-life man is pursuing a diffuse, almost promiscuous sampling of new activities and experiences. The period may be dramatized by episodic escapes into extramarital relationships, or by a form of alcoholism. For some men, the crisis of the mid-life decade can end in a relatively permanent disruption and constriction of their lives.

Middle age can be and is dangerous in other respects also. It is a time when individuals break down physically as a result of overwork, overworry, or careless living. The incidence of mental illness rises rapidly in middle age among both men and women, and it is also a peak age for suicides, especially among men. These matters will be discussed later.

The threats to good adjustment that make middle age dangerous are intensified by sex differences in the time when upsets in physical and psychological homeostasis occur. The so-called "middle-age revolt" of men usually coincides with the upsets in homeostasis caused by the menopause in women. This not only strains the husband-wife relationship, sometimes leading to separation or divorce, but it often predisposes both men and women to physical and mental illness, alcoholism, drug addiction, and suicide.

Middle Age Is an "Awkward Age"

The fifth characteristic of middle age is that it is known as an "awkward age." Just as adolescents are neither children nor adults, so middle-aged men and women are no longer "young" nor are they yet "old." As Franzblau has put it, the middle-aged person "stands between the younger 'Rebel Generation' and the 'Senior Citizen Generation'—both of which are continuously in the spotlight and suffer from the dis-

comforts and embarrassments associated with both age groups" (29).

Feeling that they have no recognized place in society, middle-aged people try to be as inconspicuous as possible. A *Time* magazine report has said that the middle-aged population in the American culture of today is "cloaked in a conspiracy of silence. It is a generation that dares not, or prefers not, to speak its name—middle age" (95).

The desire of middle-aged men and women to be inconspicuous is reflected in their clothing. Most middle-aged people try to dress as conservatively as possible and yet adhere to the prevailing styles (86). This conservatism rules their choice of material possessions, such as homes and cars, and their patterns of behavior—whether it is the way they entertain or the way they dance (77). The more inconspicuous they are, the less out of place they feel in a society that worships youth.

Middle Age Is a Time of Achievement

The sixth characteristic of middle age is that it is a time of achievement. According to Erikson, it is a crisis age in which either "generativity"—the tendency to produce—or "stagnation"—the tendency to stand still—will dominate. According to Erikson, during middle age, people either become more and more successful or they stand still and accomplish nothing more (26). If middle-aged people have a strong desire to succeed, they will reach their peak at this time and reap the benefits of the years of preparation and hard work that preceded it.

Women, like men, who have worked throughout the years of early adulthood, generally reach their peak during middle age. However, this peak, until very recently, was far below that of male workers. Women who spent their early adulthood in homemaking and reentered the vocational world after their children were grown and on their own, find that they, too, are forced to reach their peak in middle age because employers regard them as "too old" as they approach the sixties.

Middle age should be a time not only for financial and social success but also for authority and prestige. Normally, men reach their peak between forty and fifty years, after which they rest on their laurels and enjoy the benefits of their hard-won successes until they reach the early sixties when they are regarded as "too old" and usually must relinquish their

If middle-aged individuals have a strong desire to succeed, they will usually reach the peak of their achievements during these years. (Bruce Roberts from Photo Researchers.)

jobs to younger and more vigorous workers. Earnings normally reach a peak in middle age as shown in Figure 11-2.

Middle age is the period when leadership roles for men and women in business, industry, and community organizations are the reward for achievement. Most organizations, especially the older ones, elect

presidents who are in their fifties and older. The fifties are also the years when individuals are granted recognition from the various professional societies (55).

Because leadership roles are generally held by middle-aged persons, they regard themselves as the "command generation." As *Time* (95) has explained:

Middle-aged men and women, while they by no means regard themselves as being in command of all they survey, nevertheless recognize that they constitute the powerful age group vis-à-vis other age groups; that they are the norm-bearers and the decision-makers; and they live in a society which, while it may be oriented towards youth, is controlled by the middle-aged.

Neugarten has explained this attitude on the part of middle-aged people: "The successful middle-aged person often describes himself as no longer 'driven' but as now the 'driver'—in short, 'in command'" (69).

Middle Age Is a Time of Evaluation

The seventh characteristic of middle age is that it is mainly a time of self-evaluation. Because middle age is when men and women normally reach their peaks of achievement, it is logical that it also would be the time when they would evaluate their accomplishments in light of their earlier aspirations and the expectations of others, especially family members and friends. Archer has pointed out, "It is in the twenties that we commit ourselves to an occupation and to a marriage. During the late thirties and early forties, it is common for men to review those early commitments" (3).

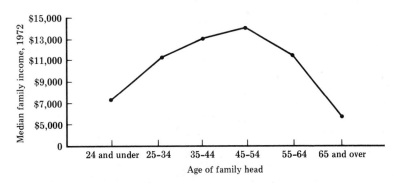

FIGURE 11-2 Earnings normally reach their peak during middle age. (U. S. Bureau of the Census statistics for 1972.)

As a result of this self-evaluation, Archer has further pointed out, "The mid-years seem to require the development of a different, generally more realistic sense of who one is. . . . In growing up, everyone nurtures fantasies or illusions about what one is, and what one will do. A major task of the mid-life decade involves coming to terms with those fantasies and illusions" (3).

Middle Age Is Evaluated by a Double Standard

The eighth characteristic of middle age is that it is evaluated by a double standard, a standard for men and a standard for women. In spite of the growing trend toward egalitarian roles for men and women in the home, in business, industry, the professions, and in social life, there still exists a double standard regarding aging. While this double standard affects many aspects of the lives of middle-aged men and women, two are especially common.

The first relates to physical changes. When men's hair becomes gray, when they develop lines and wrinkles on their faces and a middle-aged pouch in place of a once-slender waistline, they are usually regarded as "distinguished." Similar physical changes in women are judged as unattractive with major emphasis on the "middle-age spread."

The second area in which the double standard is apparent is in the approved way for members of the two sexes to age. There are two different philosophies about how people should adjust to middle age: one, that they should stay young and active and, two, that they should grow old gracefully, deliberately slowing down and taking life comfortably—this is the "rocking-chair" philosophy. Women, on the whole, are more likely to adopt the rocking-chair philosophy than men, though this holds true more for women of the lower class than for the upper-middle and upper classes (30,80).

Middle Age Is the Time of the Empty Nest

The ninth characteristic of middle age is that it is the time of the empty nest—the time when the children no longer want to live under the parental roof. Except in cases where men and women marry later than the average age, or postpone having their children until they are well established in their careers, or have large families spread out over a decade or more

of time, middle age is the "empty nest" stage in marital lives.

For most American families of today, the empty-nest stage begins in the forties, though, with late marriage and parenthood, or with large numbers of children, it may not begin until the mid- or late fifties. Figure 10-3 shows the median age of mothers in America today as compared with earlier decades when their last children leave home. Note that with today's smaller families, the empty-nest period in marital lives comes earlier.

After years of living in a family-centered home, most adults find it difficult to adjust to a pair-centered home. Refer to Figure 10-4. This is because, during the child-rearing years, husbands and wives often grew apart and developed individual interests. As a result, they have little in common after mutual interests in their children wane and when they are thrown together to adjust to each other the best they can.

Unquestionably, the empty-nest period of middle age is far more traumatic for women than for men. This is especially true of women who have devoted their adult years to homemaking and who have few interests or resources to fill their time when their homemaking jobs lessen or come to an end. Many experience a "retirement shock" similar to that experienced by men when they retire.

Middle Age Is a Time of Boredom

The tenth characteristic of middle age is that it is often a time of boredom. Many, if not most, men and women experience boredom during the late thirties and forties. Men become bored with the daily routine of work and with a family life that offers little excitement. Women, who have spent most of their adulthood caring for the home and raising children, wonder what they will do for the next twenty or thirty years (45). The unmarried woman who has devoted her life to a job or career is bored for the same reasons men are. Archer (3) has explained the boredom men experience in this way:

By the time you are 40 everyone—including you— knows that you can do whatever you are doing. And at that point some men get bored. Some begin looking for new territory. In most men, however, this impulse is checked by the sense that one has passed the last chance to change directions, to choose new goals.

DEVELOPMENTAL TASKS OF MIDDLE AGE

Tasks Relating to Physical Changes

These include the acceptance of, and adjustment to, the physical changes that normally occur during middle age.

Tasks Relating to Changed Interests

The middle-aged person often assumes civic and social responsibilities and develops an interest in adult-oriented leisure-time activities in place of family-oriented activities, which prevailed during early adulthood.

Tasks Relating to Vocational Adjustments

These tasks revolve around establishing and maintaining a relatively stable standard of living.

Tasks Relating to Family Life

The important tasks in this category include relating oneself to one's spouse as a person, adjusting to aging parents, and assisting teen-age children to become responsible and happy adults.

Box 11-2 (39). The first two of these categories will be discussed in this chapter, and the second two in the following chapter.

Like the developmental tasks of other periods, those of middle age are not all mastered at the same time or in the same way by all people. Some are more likely to be mastered during the early years of middle age, and some in the latter part of the period. This, however, will vary for different individuals.

The age at which middle-aged people married, the time when they became parents, and the number of children they have all influence the age at which they must adjust to the developmental tasks relating to family life, to civic and social responsibilities, and to adult leisure-time activities. Those who married when they were still in their teens may have no children at home when they reach middle age. Consequently, they can take a more active part in civic and social life; their leisure-time activities can be adult- rather than family-oriented; and they are free to spend more time together than they were able to do when there were children living at home.

Most of the developmental tasks of middle age prepare the individual for successful adjustment to old age; thus the mastery of these tasks is important for success and happiness not only in middle age but also in the later years of life.

At no age is boredom conducive to happiness or even contentment. Consequently, middle age is often one of the unhappy periods of life. In a study of pleasant and unpleasant memories over a span of years, adults rated middle age, especially the years from forty to forty-nine, as the least pleasant. Only the years after sixty did they find nearly as unpleasant (66). These ratings are shown in Figure 1-7.

DEVELOPMENTAL TASKS OF MIDDLE AGE

Certain problems of adjustment are characteristic of middle age in today's culture. Some of these problems are more difficult for men, and others are more difficult for women. The major problems that American men and women must meet and adjust to satisfactorily during middle age involve the developmental tasks for this period. Havighurst has divided these tasks into four major categories, which are given in

ADJUSTMENTS TO PHYSICAL CHANGES

One of the most difficult adjustments middle-aged men and women must make is to changed appearance. They must recognize that the body is not functioning as adequately as it formerly did and may even be "wearing out" in certain vital areas. They must accept the fact that their reproductive capacity is waning or coming to an end and that they may be losing some of their sex drive and sexual attractiveness. Like pubescent children who have childhood ideals of what they want to look like when they grow up and who must then adjust to the reality of their appearance when it does not come up to their expectations, so middle-aged people must adjust to the changes which they dislike and which, even worse, are telltale signs of aging.

The adjustment to physical changes is made doubly hard by the fact that the individual's own unfavorable attitudes are intensified by unfavorable social attitudes toward the normal changes that come with advancing years. The most important physical changes to which the middle-aged person must adjust are discussed below.

Changes in Appearance

Having known, since early adolescence, the important role appearance plays in social judgments, social acceptance, and leadership, middle-aged people rebel against threats to the status they fear they may lose as their appearance deteriorates.

For the man, there is the added handicap of competition with younger, more vigorous, and more energetic men who tend to judge his capacity to hold down his job in terms of his appearance. For both men and women, there is the ever-present fear that their middle-aged looks will militate against their ability to hold their spouses or to attract members of the opposite sex. Figure 11-3 shows how some middle-aged people react to the attitude of members of the social group toward their appearance.

"All this started on a bus when two young soldiers offered him their seats!"

FIGURE 11-3 A person's recognition of others' attitudes toward his or her middle-aged appearance often causes one to have an unfavorable attitude toward oneself. (George Clark. "The Neighbors." Chicago Tribune-New York News Syndicate, Apr. 20, 1967. Used by permission.)

As a general rule, men in our culture show signs of aging sooner than women. This may be explained by the fact that women, who know how much their attractiveness to members of the opposite sex depends on their physical appearance, quickly cover up the signs of middle age.

The signs of aging also tend to be more apparent among members of some socioeconomic groups than others. In general, men and women of the higher socioeconomic groups appear younger than their years, while those of the lower socioeconomic groups look older than they actually are. This may be explained partially by the fact that those of the more favored groups work less, expend less energy, and are better nourished than those who must earn their living by hard manual work. Furthermore, those who come from the less well-to-do groups are unable to afford the beauty aids and clothing that cover up the telltale signs of aging.

The most obvious—and, to most men and women, the most troublesome—telltale signs of aging are given in Box 11-3.

Changes in Sensory Abilities

Gradual deterioration of sensory abilities begins in middle age. The most troublesome and most marked changes are in the eyes and ears. The degenerative and functional changes in the eye result in a decrease in pupil size, acuity, and glare resistance and in a tendency toward glaucoma, cataracts, and tumors. Most middle-aged people suffer from presbyopia, or farsightedness, which is a gradual loss of accommodative power of the eye resulting from a decrease in the elasticity of the lens. Between the ages of forty and fifty, the accommodative power of the lens is usually insufficient for close work, and the individual must wear glasses.

Hearing is likely to be impaired, with the result that most middle-aged people must listen more attentively than they formerly did. Sensitivity to high pitches is lost first, followed by progressive losses down the age scale. Because of hearing loss, many middle-aged people start to talk very loudly, and often in a monotone.

There is also a decrease in the sense of *smell* and *taste* with advancing age. This is especially true for men. The reason for this is that in men there is an increase in hair in the nose, thus affecting the ability of the smell stimuli to penetrate to the sense organs for smell at the base of the nose. Because taste is

BOX 11-3

TELLTALE SIGNS OF AGING

Weight Gain

During middle age, fat accumulates mainly around the abdomen and on the hips.

Loss and Graying of Hair

The middle-aged man's hairline begins to re- cede, the hair becomes thinner, and baldness on the top of the head is very common. Hair in the nose, ears, and eyelashes becomes stiffer, while facial hair grows more slowly and is less luxuriant. Women's hair becomes thinner, and there is an increase of hair on the upper lip and chin. Both men and women have a predomi- nance of gray hair by fifty, and some have white hair before middle age ends.

Skin Changes

The skin on the face, neck, arms, and hands be- comes coarser and wrinkled. Bags appear under the eyes, and dark circles become more permanent and pronounced. Bluish-red discol- orations often appear around the ankles and on the mid-calf.

Body Sag

The shoulders often become rounded, and there is a general sagging of the body which makes the abdomen appear prominent and causes the person to look shorter.

Muscle Changes

Most middle-aged people's muscles become soft and flabby in the areas of the chin, upper arms, and abdomen.

Joint Problems

Some middle-aged people develop problems in their joints and limbs that cause them to walk with difficulty and to handle things with an awkwardness rarely found in younger adults.

Changes in Teeth

The teeth become yellowed and must often be replaced with partial or complete dentures.

Changes in Eyes

The eyes look less bright than they did when the individual was younger, and there is a tend- ency for mucous to accumulate in the corners of the eyes.

greatly dependent on smell, it too is weaker as age progresses.

To date, studies of the effect of aging on *touch, temperature,* and *pain* sensations have not been made extensively enough to give conclusive evidence about the effects of aging on them. There is, however, a suggestion that, because the skin becomes thinner with age, these sensitivities are stronger than they are in younger adults.

Changes in Physiological Functioning

The changes in the exterior of the body are paralleled by changes in the internal organs and in their functioning. These changes are, for the most part, the direct or indirect result of changes in the body tissues. Like old rubber bands, the walls of the arteries become brittle as middle age progresses, and this leads to circulatory difficulties. Increase in blood pressure, especially among those who are over- weight, may lead to heart complications.

There is increasing sluggishness in the function- ing of most of the glands of the body. The pores and skin glands rid the skin of waste materials more slowly, with the result that there is an increase in body odors. The different glands connected with the digestive process likewise function more slowly, with a consequent increase in the number and severity of digestive disorders.

To add to this problem, many middle-aged men and women wear dentures, which increase the difficulty of chewing. In addition, few individuals re- vise their eating habits in accordance with the slow- ing down of their activities, and this likewise adds a burden to the functioning of the digestive system. Constipation is very common in middle age.

Changes in Health

Middle age is characterized by a general de- cline in physical fitness and some deterioration of health is common. Beginning in the mid-forties, there is an increase in disability and invalidism which pro- gresses rapidly from then on (80,99). This trend is shown in Figure 11-4.

Common health problems in middle age in- clude the tendency to fatigue easily; buzzing or ring- ing in the ears; muscular pains; skin sensitivity; gen- eral aches and pains; gastrointestinal complaints such as constipation, acid stomach, and belching; loss of appetite; and insomnia.

How middle age affects the individual's health

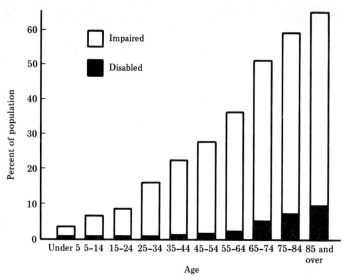

FIGURE 11-4 Disability and invalidism increase with advancing age. (Adapted from N. W. Shock. *Trends in gerontology*. [2nd ed.] Stanford, Calif.: Stanford University Press, 1959. Used by permission.)

depends on many factors, such as heredity, past health history, the emotional stresses of life, and willingness to adjust the pattern of living to changed physical condition. For example, aggressive, ambitious men may be able to avoid health problems during early adulthood, but after forty they are more likely to have heart attacks than men who have a relatively calm outlook and less taxing jobs (73).

Sexual Changes

By far the most difficult physical adjustment men and women must make in middle age is to changes in their sexual capacity. Women go through the *menopause,* or *change of life,* at which time the menstrual periods cease, and they lose their childbearing ability. Men experience the *male climacteric.*

Both the menopause and the male climacteric are surrounded by mystery for most men and women, and there are many traditional beliefs which heighten the dread people feel as they approach the period in life when these physical changes occur. The years during which the woman goes through the menopause, for example, are often referred to as "critical" (17,29).

Far more is known today about the causes and effects of the sexual changes that occur during middle

age than in the past. Furthermore, there is growing evidence that these changes are a normal part of the life pattern and also that marked psychological changes during middle age are more the result of emotional stress than of physical disturbances. This is true of men as well as of women (17,53).

Sexual Changes in Women General bodily and emotional changes occur at the time of the menopause but are not necessarily caused by it or related to it. Cessation of menstruation is therefore only one aspect of the menopause.

The average age for cessation of the menstrual flow is around forty-nine years, though this varies widely among women, depending on hereditary endowment, general health conditions, and variations in climate. There is some evidence, though far from conclusive at the present time, that smoking, especially when excessive, brings on an earlier onset of the menopause (14).

Early puberty usually means late menopause, and vice versa. Loss of the childbearing function is not an overnight phenomenon, any more than the development of this function at puberty is. It takes several years for the reproductive apparatus to cease its normal functioning, the rate depending on the rate of

BOX 11-4

THE MENOPAUSAL SYNDROME

Cessation of Menstruation

The woman may experience a sudden cessation of menstruation; regular periods with a gradual diminution of the menstrual flow; increased irregularity, with the periods coming further and further apart; or shorter cycles with profuse flow.

Generalized Atrophy of the Reproductive System

There is a generalized atrophy of the genital tract, with the result that neither mature ova nor the ovarian hormones, estrogen and progestin, are produced.

Decline in Feminine Appearance

As production of the ovarian hormones diminishes, the typically feminine secondary sex characteristics become less pronounced. Facial hair becomes coarser, the voice deepens, the curves of the body flatten out, the breasts appear flabby, and pubic and axillary hair become scantier.

Physical Discomforts

The most common physical discomforts experienced during the menopause are flushes, involving the head, neck, and upper thorax; sweating that accompanies or immediately follows the flush; hot flashes, typified by tingling over the entire body; headaches; fatigue; nervousness and irritability; heart palpitations; restlessness; and frigidity.

Weight Gain

Just as many pubescent children go through a "fat" period, many women gain weight during the menopause. Like the fat acquired during puberty, it is concentrated mainly around the abdomen and hips, making the woman seem heavier than she actually is.

Knobbiness

The joints, especially those of the fingers, often become painful with the decline in ovarian functioning. This causes them to become thickened, or "knobby."

Personality Changes

Many women experience personality changes during the menopause. They become depressed, hostile, and self-critical and have wide mood swings. With the restoration of endocrine balance as the menopause ends, these changes normally disappear.

---

decline of ovarian functioning. The menopause is regarded as officially over when there has been no menstruation for a year.

During the period when the endocrine interactional system is becoming adjusted to lessened ovarian functioning, certain physical symptoms normally occur. These are the result of the estrogen deprivation which comes from the decline in the functioning of the ovaries. In addition, other symptoms are due partly to estrogen deprivation but are mainly the result of environmental stress and thus are psychological in origin (51,97). The physical and psychological characteristics of the menopausal syndrome are given in Box 11-4.

For a number of years, doctors have used estrogen replacement therapy to slow down the menopausal changes and to ward off the physical discomforts that often accompany these changes. However, recent medical reports of the higher incidence of uterine cancer in women who have received estrogen replacement therapy than in the general population have made many doctors stop using it and have caused many women to wonder if menopausal discomforts and telltale signs of aging are not less serious than the risks of developing uterine cancer.

Sexual Changes in Men The male climacteric is very different from the menopause. It comes later, usually during the sixties or seventies, and progresses at a very slow rate. With the general aging of the entire body comes a very gradual weakening of the male sexual and reproductive powers. It is hard to determine exactly when hormonal imbalance begins in men because there is no definite indication of this change, as occurs in the female with the cessation of menstruation. Testosterone secretion may begin to decline in men at any age, but the magnitude of the deficiency increases with advancing years.

BOX 11-5

THE MALE CLIMACTERIC SYNDROME

Decline in Functioning of the Sex Organs

After fifty, there is a gradual decline in gonadal activity, although men in their seventies and eighties occasionally father children.

Decline in Sexual Desire

A decline in sexual desire parallels the decline in sex-organ functioning. This is due partly to the decline in gonadal functioning and partly to psychological causes, such as unfavorable marital relationships or business, economic, or family worries.

Decline in Masculine Appearance

With the decline in gonadal activity, the man loses some of his typically masculine characteristics and takes on some that are more feminine. The voice, for example, becomes somewhat higher in pitch, there is less hair on the face and body, and the body becomes slightly more rounded, especially the abdomen and hips.

Anxiety about Virility

The man whose appearance and behavior seem less masculine may become concerned about his virility. This often leads to impotence.

Physical Discomforts

Many middle-aged men complain of depression, anxiety, irritability, tingling sensations in their extremities, headaches, insomnia, digestive disturbances, nervousness, flushes, fatigue, and many minor aches and pains. Some of these conditions are real whereas others are imaginary.

Decline in Strength and Endurance

This decline is due in part to poor health and in part to gonadal deficiency. Because of the high social value placed on strength and endurance, men may feel they are losing their virility when decline in these areas sets in.

Personality Changes

Concern about loss of virility causes some middle-aged men to behave almost like the adolescent who is "sowing his wild oats." This can be a dangerous period for men, during which they may have extramarital affairs, engage in other behavior that leads to the breakup of the family, or cease caring about their business responsibilities.

While the climacteric in men actually comes during the period of old age, rather than during the middle years of life, many men in their forties or fifties have symptoms similar to those which women develop during the menopause. These occur in the absence of any demonstrable organic change and thus are emotional or social rather than physical in origin. They are the result of business, social, or family pressures, and the fact that they are not relieved by testosterone therapy may be regarded as proof of their psychological origin (3,53).

However, there is evidence that men experience a climacteric syndrome during middle age, just as women do. As Lear has said, "The male climacteric syndrome is a cluster of physiologic, constitutional and psychological symptoms occurring in some men aged approximately 45 to 60, associated with hormonal changes and often closely resembling the female climacteric syndrome" (53).

The major characteristics of the male climacteric are given in Box 11-5. Compare these with the characteristics of the menopausal syndrome, listed in Box 11-4.

ASSESSMENT OF ADJUSTMENT TO PHYSICAL CHANGES

Adjustments to physical changes are generally made gradually and reluctantly, but once men and women accept these changes, they make better adjustments to their roles as "middle-aged." It is important to realize, however, that middle-aged men and women make adjustments more quickly and less reluctantly if they can camouflage some of the telltale signs of aging.

Revolt against the loss of youth, as it becomes apparent in loss of physical and sexual vigor, often develops into a *generalized* revolt against work, the spouse, friends, and former pleasures. A middle-aged individual who reacts this way has not been willing to accept the inevitable changes that accompany aging and, as a result, has made poor adjustments to them.

By far the most difficult adjustment men and women must make is to changes in sexual functioning. This adjustment is much harder for women than for men, and fewer of them make it successfully. While many girls have difficulty adjusting during puberty, a larger number of women experience stress and strain in their attempts to adjust to the change in the pattern of life that comes with the menopause (17,43).

Adjustments by Women How successfully women make the adjustment to the physical and psychological changes that accompany the menopause is influenced greatly by their past experiences, especially their willingness to accept the feminine sex role. Those who made poor adjustments earlier have psychological reactions to the menopause that are similar to those experienced during puberty, especially a tendency to overeat and hence to become fat.

While most women are prepared for the physical changes that come with the menopause, few are prepared for the psychological changes that occur at this time, some of which are unrelated to the menopause, such as those involving changes in life roles. Unfortunately, these changes usually coincide with the menopause, and this intensifies the difficulties the woman experiences in adjusting to the physical changes (51,97).

Adjustments by Men How well men adjust to the climacteric is likewise influenced by previous experiences and the success of adjustments in other areas. Men who are successful in business, who enjoy high prestige in the community, and who are well adjusted to their families accept the changes in appearance, the lessened physical strength, and the beginning of the waning of sexual desire as a normal part of aging and adjust philosophically to them.

By contrast, men who are not happy in their vocational or in their family lives, or in both, tend to revolt against the physical changes that accompany middle age. This revolt, as was pointed out earlier, is at the basis of the so-called "dangerous age"—common but by no means universal among middle-aged men.

ADJUSTMENT TO MENTAL CHANGES

There is a traditional belief that as physical abilities decline, so do mental abilities. As was pointed out earlier, scientific interest in middle age is of such recent origin that few longitudinal studies have been made; however, there is evidence that this traditional belief is not valid (5,79).

Terman and Oden's study of a group of men and women followed from preschool years to middle life has shown that mental decline does not set in during middle age among those with high intellectual abilities (93). A follow-up study made fifty years after the original study likewise showed little intellectual decline among the members of the group (60). In specific mental abilities, such as problem solving and verbal ability, little or no decline was reported in middle age among those whose initial abilities were high (48).

A study reported by Kangas and Bradway has indicated that intelligence may even increase slightly in middle age, especially among those of higher intellectual levels. While this study was made on only a small group—forty-eight subjects—they were tested over a span of years: at the preschool level, during junior high school and young adulthood, and finally when they were between thirty-nine and forty-four years of age. No follow-up into the latter part of middle age has been reported to date (47).

Like members of the Terman and Oden group, those with higher IQs showed less intellectual change than those with lower IQs. Men showed a slight gain in IQ scores as they grew older, while women showed a slight decline. Because men must be mentally more alert in order to compete vocationally than women must be in order to carry out their roles as homemakers, these findings suggest that use of mental abilities is an important factor in determining whether there will be mental decline in middle age (47,51).

That many men and women are anxious to remain mentally alert is evidenced by the growing interest in cultural pursuits as a form of recreation and by the increasing numbers who are completing their education or supplementing the education they received during their school and college years. This will be discussed later in connection with recreational interests.

ADJUSTMENT TO CHANGED INTERESTS

While there are changes in interests during middle age, they are far less marked than the changes that occurred during the earlier years of life. As Ryan has pointed out, "Whatever the chronological age, the interests, attitudes, and habits of earlier years will remain fundamentally the same" (86).

The changes in interests that take place now are the result of changes in duties and responsibilities, in health, and in roles in life. Men's concentration on vocational advancement plays an important role in narrowing down the range of interests they had when they were younger. The more successful men are, the more time and attention they must give to their vocations and the less time they have to devote to other interests and activities.

Women experience far more pronounced role changes in middle age than men, and consequently there are more marked changes in their interests. The woman who played the role of mother during her earlier years of adulthood finds, when she faces the child-free days of middle age, that she has the time to pursue interests and activities she was forced to forgo earlier. Furthermore, because her husband usually spends more time and energy on his occupation than he did earlier, she must develop new interests to replace those she formerly shared with him.

New interests may be established in middle age but men and women are more likely to cling to the old ones they found satisfying than to change to new ones unless there are changes in their environments and patterns of life and unless they have opportunities to develop new interests and the motivation to do so.

This tendency to cling to old interests rather than establish new ones is frequently interpreted as indicative of the mental rigidity popularly associated with middle-aged and elderly people. There is little evidence from studies of middle-aged people that such is the case. Rather, the evidence points more in the direction of *values*. Middle-aged people know

---

BOX 11-6

CHARACTERISTIC CHANGES IN INTERESTS IN MIDDLE AGE

- Interests are more commonly narrowed down than expanded with advancing age.
- There is a shift in emphasis on already-present interests as when interest in the fashionable quality of clothes shifts to interest in clothes that make the wearer look younger.
- There is a shift toward interests that are more solitary in nature, such as hobbies, reading, and television watching.
- Many middle-aged people develop increased interests in cultural pursuits such as reading, painting, and attending lectures and concerts.
- There is a lessening of sex differences in interests with men showing more interest in so-called women's activities, such as reading for pleasure, than in so-called men's activities, such as engaging in sports or watching sports contests.
- There is a tendency for men and women to engage in shared interests, such as hobbies and cultural pursuits, instead of engaging in interests with members of their own sex.
- There is an increased interest in activities leading to self-improvement, such as attending lectures and concerts and taking courses, and a decreased interest in activities that are purely for enjoyment, such as going to the movies or playing cards. This applies more to the upper-middle and upper-class middle-agers than to those of the lower classes.

---

from experience what gives them satisfaction, and they see little reason to change just for the sake of change (51,79).

The characteristic changes in interests during middle age are given in Box 11-6. These changes may affect the interests of men or of women or of both. In most cases, these changes take place gradually and are spread over the age span of the middle years.

In the sections below are given brief descriptions of the common interests of middle-aged men and women in the American culture of today together with an explanation of what causes changes in these interests and what effects they have on the behavior of men and women at this age level.

Appearance and Clothes

Interests in *appearance,* which begins to wane after marriage and especially during the early years of parenthood, intensifies when the external physical changes which accompany advancing age become noticeable. Both men and women use diets, exercise, cosmetics, or clothing either to reverse those changes or to hide them. As a result, many middle-aged men and women look younger than they are. This makes them more satisfied with their appearance (8).

Middle-aged people are well aware that *clothes* are important to their image. As Douty has pointed out, "Clothing may not be consciously perceived but its effect can be just as strong as though it were" (22). Men recognize the importance of clothing and grooming to business success. As they advance toward the peak of achievement in middle age, they become far more clothes-conscious than they were when they were younger and their status in the business world was lower. Women, by contrast, are less clothes-conscious in middle age than in early adult-

hood, though they, like men, recognize the importance of clothes and grooming to success in both the business and social worlds (86).

Money

Regardless of how much or how little money they may have, middle-aged men and women are interested in money though the emphasis of their interest may be different. Also, the interest men have in money during middle age is often radically different from that of middle-aged women.

Unless his wife, children, or relatives make heavy demands on him, the middle-aged *man* is less concerned about how much money he earns than he was when he was younger. Stability of work, job satisfaction, and prestige are more important to him than earnings. And because most men in the skilled-artisan field, in business, and in professional fields are reaching the peak of their achievements during middle age, many of the money worries they had when they were younger are lessened.

For those in the unskilled and semiskilled groups, employment is less stable as workers become middle-aged. In addition, the slowing down of middle-aged workers' speed as well as the difficulties they often experience in learning new techniques frequently force them to accept jobs at wages below those of their earlier peak years. For them, money becomes a source of real concern.

Poor health, debts carried over from earlier years, or economic responsibilities for elderly relatives tend to heighten money worries for middle-aged men of all occupational groups, except those whose incomes are more than adequate to meet their needs. And with worry comes a focusing of attention on money.

The middle-aged *woman* is often more interested in money than the middle-aged man. Not only will money provide her with many of the material possessions she wants, such as clothes, a car, and a home that will compare favorably with those of her friends or come up to her own standards, but it also means security to her. Worry about financial security in case of the death or illness of the breadwinner or if there should be a divorce plagues many middle-aged women of today. This concern heightens their interest in money.

In middle age there is usually a change in attitude toward the use of money. As a result of having

Diet, exercise, cosmetics, and well-selected clothing help middle-aged people—especially the more affluent ones—to delay or conceal the signs of aging. (Ray Ellis from Photo Researchers.)

budgeted their incomes to meet family needs and because they realize the necessity for having money put aside in case of emergencies and for their old age, many adults regard extravagance as wrong. This attitude strengthens as the person grows older and is more the result of a different value system than of conservatism, which is typically associated with advancing age (16).

Status Symbols

Because middle-aged people like to think of themselves as the "command generation"—the group that exercises the most power—they want certain material possessions that will proclaim their status to others. As Packard has pointed out, "The status arises from the evaluations many people have in the backs of their heads as to the social worth of such things—address, home, etc.—as status symbols" (77).

Although most middle-aged people have known since adolescence how important a role status symbols play in the judgments others make of them, many were unable to afford these status symbols earlier, when the family income was smaller and the children were a heavy drain on the family budget. When the financial strains of early adulthood lessen, middle-aged people become keenly interested in status symbols.

While any material possession of value can be used as a status symbol, a home, a car, and clothing are most valuable because they are most visible. A home is generally considered the most important status symbol because others are impressed more by its cost than by the cost of a car or clothing. If it has a "proper" address, its status-symbol value is enhanced. Furthermore, it offers opportunities for the use of other status symbols such as expensive furnishings, antiques, and art objects.

The more anxious the individual is to move up the social ladder, the more important status symbols become. When socially mobile middle-agers move to new neighborhoods or new communities, neighbors and business associates appraise them on the basis of their status symbols before accepting or rejecting them. The more status symbols they have and the more valuable and visible they are, the better their chances of gaining acceptance.

Religion

Many middle-aged men and women show a greater interest in church and church-related activities than they did when they were younger, though this interest may be for reasons other than religious ones. For example, many middle-aged people, especially women, who have more free time and fewer family responsibilities than they formerly had, find that religious activities fill their needs, whether religious or social. Increased interest in religion may also develop after the death of a family member or a close friend.

Many middle-aged men and women find that religion is a much greater source of comfort and happiness than it was during their younger years. On the whole, middle-aged people are less worried by religious questions, less dogmatic in their beliefs, less sure that there is only one true religion, and more skeptical about the devil and hell and about miracles than college students. They are not religiously disturbed at this time in their lives, and they are more tolerant in their attitudes toward other religions than they were when they were younger (42,57,89).

Community Affairs

Middle-aged men and women, who feel that they are in command of community life as well as their homes and businesses, also regard middle age as a time for service. The middle-aged man is well established in his work, and the average woman's home responsibilities have decreased. Thus they can devote more time to community affairs; they may serve on committees, on church or professional boards, or in leadership roles in different community organizations, for example. In addition, most middle-aged people can now afford to belong to various clubs and lodges.

During middle age, men and women have different reasons for joining community organizations and for taking an active part in them. Middle-aged people participate in different formal community organizations to enjoy themselves, to be of service to the community, to help others, or to advance socially, culturally, or professionally. For example, middle-aged men or women may serve on school boards, be active in their churches or in the Red Cross, or participate in the activities of local or community associations.

Loneliness is by no means the only reason middle-aged men and women join community organizations and take part in their activities. In many cases, it is the best opportunity they have for social contacts and, if they want to be socially mobile, to have an opportunity to get to know the people they want to be identified with. Furthermore, they regard being active in community organizations as prestigious, especially if they play leadership roles.

Interest in active participation in community organizations is not consistent through the years of middle age. As Figure 9-3 shows, the peak of interest in active participation comes during the forties rather than during the fifties and it comes slightly earlier in the forties for women than for men.

The decline in interest in active participation in community organizations during the fifties may be due in part to the decline in health and energy that tends to set in at this time or to the fact that older middle-agers sense or know that the membership in these organizations wants younger leaders and that, as a result, there is a tendency to plan the activities of the organizations for the young adults rather than for those who are middle-aged (2,19).

Recreations

One of the major developmental tasks of middle age is learning how to use leisure time in a satisfying way. This is an especially difficult task because men and women now have more leisure time than they did in early adulthood and because there is an ever-increasing number of recreational activities open to middle-aged people.

The recreational interests of the middle-aged differ in many respects from those of young adults, as described in detail in Chapter 9. However, there are four especially important changes that occur in recreational interests in middle age. First, interest in strenuous recreation wanes rapidly and the individual prefers quieter activities. Second, there is a shift from interest in recreational activities involving large groups to those involving only several people. When middle-aged people do participate in activities involving groups, it is usually in connection with a community organization such as a club, a lodge, or a civic or church group. Third, recreational activities of middle age tend to be adult-oriented rather than family-oriented, like those of early adulthood. And fourth, there is a narrowing down of recreational interests in middle age. Middle-aged men and women tend to concentrate on the activities that give them the greatest pleasure and to abandon those which they find less interesting now but which they engaged in earlier for the sake of their children.

Certain forms of recreation are universally popular among middle-aged American men and women today. These are shown in Box 11-7. Note how many of them fall into the category of "amusements," which require minimum effort.

Sex Differences in Recreations   There are more marked sex differences in recreational interests in middle age than there were in the earlier years of adulthood. Two of these sex differences are especially pronounced and universal.

First, men of all social classes concentrate more of their recreational time on sports than women do, especially as spectators at athletic contests; they enjoy fishing and boating, and they may spend some of their time gardening, doing carpentry, and making home repairs.

Women, on the other hand, have a greater interest in formal and informal associations with other people than men have, they devote more time to reading than men do, and the manual tasks they undertake are more artistic than utilitarian in nature.

Second, recreational interests are greatly influenced by the roles middle-aged men and women play. In the case of men, the pattern of their recreational interests is influenced by their vocations. If they are in a line of work, such as medicine, which is demanding on their time, they will not only have less time for recreation than men in less demanding occupations but they will also have less energy for recreation and, as a result, tend to concentrate on amusements.

Middle-aged women's recreational interests are influenced by their roles in the home. If, for example, they still have children at home, their recreational activities will tend to be home-centered rather than community-centered. Refer to Figure 9-2 which shows how the pattern of female recreational activities is influenced by the roles women play.

SOCIAL ADJUSTMENTS

Middle age often brings with it a renewed interest in social life. As the couple's family responsibilities decrease and as their economic status improves, they are better able to engage in social activities than they were during early adulthood, when family responsibilities and adjustment to work made an active social life difficult. Many middle-aged people, but especially women, find that an active social life alleviates the loneliness they experience when their children are grown and have homes of their own.

Middle-aged people enjoy entertaining friends

POPULAR RECREATIONAL ACTIVITIES OF THE MIDDLE-AGED

Sports

Middle-aged men and women spend increasingly more time watching sports than participating in them. The sports they do engage in are the less strenuous ones—swimming, boating, fishing, golfing, and bowling.

Reading

As a general rule, middle-aged people spend more time reading newspapers and magazines than books and they are more selective about what they read than they were earlier. Many prefer reading about world events to crime and sex.

Movies

Going to the movies is less popular in middle age than it was earlier, partly because many movies are slanted to the interests of adolescents and young adults and partly because middle-aged men and women got out of the habit of going to the movies when their children were young. However, they enjoy watching movies on television, especially well-known movies.

Radio and Television

Many middle-aged women listen to the radio while doing housework, and many men listen while driving to and from work. Many prefer news or discussion programs, rather than programs of popular music, as they did earlier. Middle-aged people also enjoy television, but most have become more selective about their viewing.

Entertaining

Middle-aged people have more time and money for entertaining than they did earlier. Middle-aged friends of the same sex also like to get together informally to talk or play cards, for example.

Taking Trips

Now that they have fewer parental responsibilities and increased income, middle-aged people are able to take more trips to visit friends or relatives or to sightsee.

Hobbies

The hobbies of middle-aged people are mainly of a constructive nature—gardening, sewing, painting, cooking, and woodworking, for example.

Taking Courses

Middle-aged people take courses for enjoyment rather than for vocational advancement. They like the intellectual stimulation, the social contacts, and the opportunity to get away from the home that adult education provides.

---

at dinners or parties, although much of the social life of middle age centers around gathering of members of the same sex. These activities reach their peak in the late forties and early fifties and then begin to decline as the individual approaches the sixties. A decrease in energy at this time puts a stop to a too active social life. Furthermore, as the individual looks ahead to retirement and decreased income, entertaining and active participation in community organizations lose much of their appeal. As a result, men and women in the fifties tend to spend much of their leisure time with family members, intimate friends, and with their children's newly established families (42,59,82).

However, the pattern of social activities in middle age is greatly influenced by the *social-class* status of the individual. Those of higher status are more active during middle age than are those of lower status, most of whom belong to no community groups, rarely attend meetings of those organizations to which they belong, and have few friends except their close neighbors. Most of their social contacts are with family members or neighbors. As Packard has said, they are "socially isolated" (78).

There are also *sex* differences in social activities during middle age. Men have more friends and acquaintances than women, but women have a more affectionate and a closer relationship with their friends than men have. Men belong to more community organizations than women, but women devote more time and effort to the activities of the organizations with which they are affiliated than men do. Women have more social contacts with family members and relatives than with outsiders, while the reverse is true of men (11,19).

Single, widowed, and divorced men and women tend, as a rule, to be equally as active socially as those who are married. No longer are widowed and divorced women as unwelcome in the social activities of their friends and neighbors as they formerly were. Instead, they are often as welcome as men in similar positions. This matter will be discussed in more detail in the following chapter.

Assessment of Social Adjustments in Middle Age

Social adjustments at every age are determined by two factors: first, how adequately people play the social roles that are expected of them and, second, how much personal satisfaction they derive from playing these roles. One of the important developmental tasks of middle age is achieving civic and social responsibility. How successfully middle-aged people master this task will affect not only their social adjustments but also their personal adjustments and happiness.

However, the success with which middle-aged people master this developmental task may be determined by physical or social factors over which they have little or no control. Poor health or a physical disability may prevent them from engaging in social or civic activities they would otherwise enjoy.

Studies of social adjustments at middle age have shown that there are certain factors conducive to good social functioning at this age. The most important of these and how they contribute to good social functioning are given and briefly explained in Box 11-8.

On the whole, middle-aged people make better social adjustments than younger ones because they must depend more on people outside the home for companionship than they did earlier.

A study of patterns of social relationships among middle-aged couples has revealed that close-knit social networks are most common when the husband and wife have grown up and lived in the same area. Loose social networks, by contrast, are more common among those who have moved from place to place, especially upwardly mobile middle-class couples (102).

Because middle-aged people derive more satisfaction from social contacts where there is a close personal relationship than from the greater social distance that characterizes acquaintanceships, they usually prefer the former to the latter. This is true of men as well as of women and of those from the higher social classes as well as those from the lower classes.

PERSONAL AND SOCIAL HAZARDS OF MIDDLE AGE

The major personal and social hazards of middle age stem from the tendency of many men and women to accept the cultural stereotype of the middle-aged person as fat, forty, and balding. Because of a lack of scientific information about middle age, cultural stereotypes and many traditional beliefs have persisted. They can have serious effects on the attitudes of middle-aged persons and members of the social group toward them.

However, while serious to good personal and social adjustments is acceptance of cultural stereotypes and traditional beliefs, they are by no means the only hazards. Some of the important personal and social hazards that make adjustment especially difficult for middle-aged people in the American culture of today are discussed below.

Personal Hazards

There are a number of personal hazards middle-aged people encounter in their adjustments to their new roles and new lifestyles. Of these, six are especially common and serious.

Acceptance of Traditional Beliefs Acceptance of traditional beliefs about middle age has a profound influence on attitudes toward the physical changes that come with advancing age. The menopause, for example, is often referred to as a "critical" period, and this can heighten a women's dread of it. As Parker has said (80):

This [term] carries the implication of danger—that woman is on the brink of disaster, that her health, her happiness, and her very life is in jeopardy. It further implies that this is not merely a time of crisis that can be met forthwith and dissolved, but rather years when she must feel her way along a narrow ledge of safety, at any moment of which by one false step she might fall into the abyss of a mental breakdown or serious physical illness.

Because hair on the head, face, body, arms, and legs is traditionally associated with virility in men, the thinning of the hair in middle age is likely to be a source of great concern to them. Even the beginning of baldness disturbs them because they believe that it is indicative of a decline in their sexual powers. In reality, *anxiety about virility* is one of the chief causes of such decline, and the balding middle-aged man who worries about his sexual powers merely accelerates the rate of their decline.

Idealization of Youth Many middle-aged people, particularly men, are in constant rebellion against the restrictions age places on their usual patterns of behavior. A man may refuse to adhere to a diet his doctor prescribes or to restrict his activities for the sake of his health. Like the pubescent child, the middle-aged man rebels against restrictions on behavior, but for a different reason. Rebellion stems from a recognition of the value that society attaches to youth and thus he is rebelling against restrictions that mean he is growing old. This may bring on middle-aged ailments of minor or major seriousness. As Steincrohn has pointed out (92):

If you relax more often, if you slow up, don't believe that you will grow old prematurely. The grim reaper won't swish his scythe at you and cut you off long before you reach the 70s and 80s. On the contrary, the reaper seems to have patience for the relaxers and is impatient with the overdoers.

Women who make the poorest adjustments to middle age are those who have attached a great deal of importance to a youthful appearance and masculine admiration. When they are forced to recognize that they are no longer as attractive as they once were and that they cannot attract and hold masculine attention, they may openly rebel against middle age.

When adjustment to middle age is poor, as shown by constant rebellion against the physical changes that inevitably come with aging, interest in clothing is intensified. Men and women concentrate mainly on selecting clothes which will make them look younger than they are. Bright colors, extreme styles, and a large wardrobe become as important to the middle-aged man or women who is trying to defy age as they are to the adolescent.

Rebellion against middle age is often heightened by magazine articles, television advertisements, and so on, that stress what the middle-aged person can and should do to camouflage the telltale signs of aging. Ryan, however, has suggested that these changes in appearance are not necessarily unattractive. According to her (86):

Some of these changes may make the individual more, rather than less, attractive. Often the first and most obvious change is in the color of the hair which usually turns to gray and then to white. This frequently is a positive factor: many people are more attractive with white hair. Also, as individuals grow older, the face becomes more lined and wrinkled. This, again, is not necessarily a detriment. These lines may give a pleasing character to a face which was bland and uninteresting with the smoothness of youth.

Role Changes Changing roles is never easy, especially after one has played certain prescribed roles over a period of time and has learned to derive satisfaction from them. Furthermore, too much success in one role is likely to lead to rigidity and may make adjustment to another role difficult.

Also, a person who has played a narrow range of roles is likely to be less flexibile than one who has played a wider range and has learned to derive satisfaction from different roles. The person who has played many roles finds it easier to shift to a new one. To make a good adjustment to new roles, the individual must, as Havighurst has explained, "withdraw emotional capital from one role and invest it in another one" (39).

Changing Interests A serious hazard to good personal adjustments in middle age comes from the ne-

BOX 11-9

COMMON CONDITIONS MILITATING AGAINST GOOD SOCIAL ADJUSTMENTS IN MIDDLE AGE

The "Rocking-Chair" Philosophy

Middle-aged people who subscribe to the philosophy that aging people should be inactive and remain on the sidelines contribute little to the enjoyment of others in social situations.

Unattractive Appearance

Middle-aged men and women who allow their appearance to deteriorate and make little or no effort to improve it are more likely to be neglected or rejected in social situations than those whose clothing and grooming make them look more youthful and attractive.

Lack of Social Skills

Middle-aged people who never learned the social skills of their peers when they were younger, or who allowed their earlier-learned social skills to become rusty during early adulthood, feel ill at ease in social situations and either withdraw from them or play onlooker roles.

Preference for Family Contacts

Men and women who find family members more congenial than outsiders and family activities more enjoyable than community activities will not be motivated to broaden their social horizons to include outsiders and community activities.

Financial Problems

Middle-aged people who are plagued by financial problems stemming from unemployment, support of elderly parents, or education of children are unable to participate in many of the social activities of their friends or to belong to community organizations. As a result, they become socially isolated.

Family Pressures

While most middle-aged people have fewer family responsibilities than they had when their children were young, some are still under pressure to help both financially and through personal aid grown children, grandchildren, or dependent elderly parents. This reduces not only money for social activities but also time to engage in them.

Desire for Popularity

Some middle-aged men and women, especially those who married early and were deprived of the social experiences their unmarried contemporaries enjoyed, now want an active social life as evidence of their popularity. This can be hazardous if, in the effort to achieve this goal, men and women break up the established patterns of their lives, seek adventure and excitement outside the home, and neglect their work.

Social Mobility

Socially mobile people often find it difficult if not impossible to break into the close-knit social networks of other middle-aged people in their new neighborhoods or communities. As a result, they must play the role of involuntary isolate or affiliate themselves with any group that will accept them, regardless of congeniality of interests or values.

---

cessity for changing interests as physical strength and endurance decrease and as health deteriorates. Unless middle-aged men and women can develop new interests to replace those they must give up, or unless they have developed enough interests in their earlier years to be able to abandon some of them without feeling their loss too seriously, they are likely to become bored and wonder how they can spend their leisure time.

Like adolescents who become bored when they have too few interests and activities to fill their time, middle-aged people, both men and women, are likely to try to "stir up some excitement." Usually they do this by seeking out extramarital relationships.

While these may be temporarily satisfying, they are likely to lead to feelings of guilt and shame, to anxiety about being "caught," and to serious problems with the spouse and other family members if they are discovered. This will be discussed in more detail in the following chapter.

Status Symbols Women's increased interest in status symbols, discussed earlier in this chapter, which is a common characteristic, can be a hazard to good personal and social adjustments if families cannot afford the status symbols they want. In such cases, there are three common reactions on the part of women who crave these symbols. First, they may complain and nag their husbands for not providing the money for these symbols; second, they may overspend and plunge the family into debt; or, third, they may go to work to earn the money themselves. All of these patterns of response to the craving for status symbols tend to lead to frictional relationships with spouses, especially the third pattern, which many men feel reflects unfavorably on their ability to provide for their families.

Unrealistic Aspirations Middle-aged people who have unrealistic aspirations concerning their achievements—often carried over from adolescence—face a serious hazard to good personal adjustments when they realize that they have fallen short of their goals and that time is fast running out.

While this hazard is more likely to have a direct effect on men than on women, women are indirectly affected when their husbands fail to achieve the financial and vocational success they had expected. Even though women who work tend to have more realistic aspirations than men, as was explained in Chapter 10, they may also realize that they have not reached their goals and that time is running short.

Failure to reach any goal can lead to feelings of inferiority and inadequacy, feelings that tend to become generalized and result in a failure complex. People who develop such complexes have a defeatist attitude toward everything they undertake. As a result, their achievements fall even further below their aspirations.

Social Hazards

Social adjustments in middle age are less affected by traditional beliefs and stereotypes than personal adjustments. However, social adjustments are affected to some extent by traditional beliefs such as "You can't teach an old dog new tricks"—the new "tricks" being new social skills—or "Once a leader, always a leader." For example, middle-aged men and women who were not leaders in school or college may feel that they now have no hope of achieving leadership roles in either the vocational or social worlds.

There are other important conditions that influence social adjustments in middle age. These are given and explained in Box 11-9. Note that many of these conditions are carry-overs from earlier stages in the life span, especially adolescence and early adulthood. That is why those who have not made good so-cial adjustments during the earlier years of their lives are not likely to do so as they grow older.

Making poor social adjustments in middle age is hazardous because, with advancing age, most men and women must rely more and more on the companionship of outsiders, as their spouses become ill or die and as their grown children become increasingly preoccupied with their own lives. Middle-aged persons who do not master the important developmental task of achieving adult civic and social responsibility are likely to be lonely and unhappy in their old age and may find that it is too late then to make good social adjustments.

Chapter Highlights

1. Because middle age is an especially difficult time in the American culture of today, adjustment to it is greatly dependent on the foundations laid earlier.
2. There are ten important characteristics of middle age, the most significant of which are that it is a dreaded age, a time of transition and of stress, a time of achievement and of evaluation, and the time of the empty nest and boredom.
3. Adjustment to physical changes in middle age are especially difficult in the areas of appearance, physiological functioning, and sexuality.
4. The female menopausal syndrome is due partly to estrogen deprivation and partly to environmental stress which is psychological in origin.
5. The male climacteric syndrome is due to a combination of physiological and psychological conditions that often lead to changes in attitudes, behavior, and self-evaluations.
6. The success of adjusting to physical changes in middle age is aided by camouflaging the telltale signs of aging.
7. There is little evidence, to date, that mental decline universally begins in middle age, especially among those of high intellectual ability.
8. Changes in interests in middle age are far less pronounced than those occuring during the earlier years and are, for the most part, the result of role changes.
9. Middle-aged men, as a group, have a greater interest in clothing and appearance than middle-aged women, as a group, because they recognize its importance to vocational success.
10. Middle-aged men's interest in money is different from that of middle-aged women, though it is

usually greater in women than in men who regard it as essential to security and to having the status symbols they crave.

11. Interest in religion in middle age is usually greater than in early adulthood and is often based on personal and social needs.

12. There are four important changes in recreational interests in middle age: first, interest in strenuous recreations wanes; second, there is a shift from recreational activities involving large groups to those involving only several people; third, recreational activities are adult- rather than family-oriented as they were in early adulthood; and, fourth, there is a narrowing down of recreational interests.

13. Social interests and activities in middle age are greatly influenced by social-class status, sex, and marital status.

14. The most important personal hazards of middle age include acceptance of traditional beliefs about middle age, idealization of youth, unrealistic aspirations, and changes in roles, in interests, and in value placed on status symbols.

15. Among the common hazards that affect social adjustments in middle age are acceptance of the "rocking chair" philosophy about middle age, an unattractive appearance, lack of social skills, preference for family contacts, financial problems, family pressures and obligations, a desire for popularity as expressed in immature patterns of behavior, and social mobility.

Bibliography

1. Amundsen, D. W., and C. J. Diers. The age of menopause in classical Greece and Rome. *Human Biology*, 1970, **42**, 79–86.
2. Angrist, S. S. Role constellation as a variable in women's leisure activities. *Social Forces*, 1967, **45**, 423–431.
3. Archer, D. The male change of life. *Yale Alumni Magazine*, March 1968. Pp. 33–35.
4. Bardwick, J. M. Middle age and a sense of future. *Merrill-Palmer Quarterly*, 1978, **24**, 129–138.
5. Bayley, N. Research in child development: A longitudinal perspective. *Merrill-Palmer Quarterly*, 1965, **11**, 183–208.
6. Beard, R. J. The menopause. *British Journal of Hospital Medicine*, 1975, **12**, 631–637.
7. Bellini, G. Plastic surgery: Why? When? Where? How? *Harper's Bazaar*, Aug. 1973, Pp. 59,88.
8. Berscheid, E., E. Walster, and G. Bohrnstedt. The happy American body: A survey report. *Psychology Today*, 1974, **7**(6), 119–123, 126–131.
9. Bielby, D. Del V., and D. E. Papalia. Moral development and perceptual role-taking egocentrism: Their development and interrelationship across the life span. *International Journal of Aging & Human Development*, 1975, **6**, 293–308.
10. Bischof, L. J. *Adult psychology*. (2nd ed.) New York: Harper & Row, 1976.
11. Booth, A. Sex and social participation. *American Sociological Review*, 1972, **37**, 183–193.
12. Borland, D. C. Research on middle age: An assessment. *Gerontologist*, 1978, **18**, 379–386.
13. Bourque, L. B., and K. W. Back. Life graphs and life events. *Journal of Gerontology*, 1977, **32**, 669–674.
14. Brody, J. E. Smoking linked to earlier onset of menopause. *The New York Times*, July 7, 1977.
15. Brozan, N. Middle age needn't be like dark ages. *The New York Times*, March 29, 1973.
16. Chew, P. *The inner world of the middle-aged man*. New York: Macmillan, 1976.
17. Clausen, J. A. Glimpses into the sexual world of middle age. *International Journal of Aging & Human Development*, 1976, **7**, 99–106.
18. Clavan, S. The family process: A sociological model. *Family Coordinator*, 1969, **18**, 312–317.
19. Cutler, S. J. Age differences in voluntary association membership. *Social Forces*, 1976, **55**, 45–58.
20. Dennis, W. Creative productivity between the ages of 20 and 80 years. In B. L. Neugarten (Ed.). *Middle age and aging: A reader in social psychology*. Chicago: University of Chicago Press, 1968, Pp. 108–114.
21. Desmond, T. C. America's unknown middle-agers. *The New York Times*, July 29, 1956.
22. Douty, H. I. Influence of clothing on perception of persons. *Journal of Home Economics*, 1963, **55**, 197–202.
23. Eisdorfer, C., and M. P. Lawton (Eds.). *The psychology of adult development and aging*. Washington: APA, 1973.
24. Entine, A. D. Mid-life counseling: Prognosis and potential. *Personnel & Guidance Journal*, 1976, **55**, 112–114.
25. Erikson, E. H. *Childhood and society*. (Rev. ed.) New York: Norton, 1964.
26. Erikson, E. H. Identity and the life cycle: Selected papers. *Psychological Issues Monographs*, Vol. 1, No. 1. New York: International Universities Press, 1967.
27. Feibleman, J. K. The leisurely attitude. *Humanitas*, 1972, **8**, 279–285.
28. Forbes, G. B. The adult decline in lean body mass. *Human Biology*, 1976, **48**, 161–173.
29. Franzblau, R. N. *The middle generation*. New York: Holt, 1971.
30. Frenkel-Brunswik, E. Achievements and reorientation in the course of the life span. In B. L. Neugarten (Ed.). *Middle age and aging: A reader in social psychology*. Chicago: University of Chicago Press, 1968. Pp. 77–84.
31. Fried, B. *The middle-age crisis*. New York: Harper & Row, 1967.
32. Geriatric Focus article. A new look at the "crisis" of middle age. *Geriatric Focus*, 1970, **9**(1), 7–9.
33. Gould, R. The phases of adult life: A study in developmental psychology. *American Journal of Psychiatry*, 1972, **129**, 521–531.
34. Greenleigh, L. Facing the challenge of change in middle age. *Geriatrics*, 1974, **29**(11), 61–68.
35. Harper's Bazaar article. The menopause that refreshes. *Harper's Bazaar*, Aug. 1973. Pp. 87, 134.
36. Havighurst, R. J. The leisure activities of the middle-aged. *American Journal of Sociology*, 1957, **63**, 152–162.

37. Havighurst, R. J. The social competence of middle-aged people. *Genetic Psychology Monographs*, 1957, **56**, 297–375.

38. Havighurst, R. J. Body, self, and society. *Sociology & Social Research*, 1965, **49**, 261–267.

39. Havighurst, R. J. *Developmental tasks and education*. (3rd ed.) New York: McKay, 1972.

40. Havighurst, R. J., and K. Feigenbaum. Leisure and life styles. In B. L. Neugarten (Ed.). *Middle age and aging: A reader in social psychology*. Chicago: University of Chicago Press, 1968. Pp. 347–353.

41. Havighurst, R. J., B. L. Neugarten, and S. S. Tobin. Disengagement and patterns of aging. In B. L. Neugarten (Ed.). *Middle age and aging: A reader in social psychology*. Chicago: University of Chicago Press, 1968. Pp. 161–172.

42. Hawkins, L. F. Urbanization, families and the church. *Family Coordinator*, 1969, **18**, 49–53.

43. Horrocks, J. E., and M. C. Mussman. Middlescence: Age related stress periods during adult years. *Genetic Psychology Monographs*, 1970, **82**, 119–159.

44. Hunt, B., and M. Hunt. *Prime time*. New York: Stein & Day, 1974.

45. Jacoby, S. What do I do for the next 29 years? *The New York Times*, June 17, 1973.

46. Johnston, W. M. *The years after fifty*. College Park, Md.: McGrath Publishing, 1970.

47. Kangas, J., and K. Bradway. Intelligence at middle age: A thirty-eight-year follow up. *Developmental Psychology*, 1971, **5**, 333–337.

48. Kesler, M. S., N. W. Denney, and S. E. Whitely. Factors influencing problem-solving in middle-aged and elderly adults. *Human Development*, 1976, **19**, 310–320.

49. Kimmel, D. C. *Adulthood and aging: An interdisciplinary developmental view*. New York: Wiley, 1974.

50. Kivett, V. R. Religious motivation in middle age: Correlates and implications. *Journal of Gerontology*, 1979, **34**, 106–115.

51. Kivett, V. R., J. A. Watson, and J. C. Busch. The relative importance of physical, psychological, and social variables on locus of central orientation in middle age. *Journal of Gerontology*, 1977, **32**, 203–210.

52. Kuhlen, R. G. Developmental changes in motivation during the adult years. In B. L. Neugarten (Ed.). *Middle age and aging: A reader in social psychology*. Chicago: University of Chicago Press, 1968. Pp. 115–136.

53. Lear, W. M. Is there a male menopause? *The New York Times*, Jan. 28, 1973.

54. Lehman, H. C. *Age and achievement*. Princeton, N.J.: Princeton University Press, 1953.

55. Lehman, H. C. Age at time of first election to presidents of professional organizations. *Scientific Monthly*, 1955, **80**, 293–298.

56. Lehman, H. C. The most creative years of engineers and other technologists. *Journal of General Psychology*, 1966, **108**, 263–277.

57. LeShan, E. *The wonderful crisis of middle age*. New York: Warner, 1973.

58. Livson, F. B. Patterns of personality development in middle-aged women: A longitudinal study. *International Journal of Aging & Human Development*, 1976, **7**, 107–115.

59. Lopata, H. Z. The life cycles of the social role of the housewife. *Sociology & Social Research*, 1966, **51**, 5–22.

60. Maeroff, G. A rare look at the gifted; fifty years later. *The New York Times*, Nov. 7, 1975.

61. Marmor, J. The crisis of middle age. *American Journal of Orthopsychiatry*, 1967, **37**, 336–337.

62. Masters, W. H., and V. E. Johnson. *Human sexual response*. Boston: Little, Brown, 1966.

63. Masters, W. H., and V. E. Johnson. *Human sexual inadequacy*. Boston: Little, Brown, 1970.

64. McCall's article. The empty days. *McCall's*, Sept. 1965, Pp. 78–81, 140–146.

65. McClelland, J. Stress and middle age. *Journal of Home Economics*, 1976, **68**(5), 16–19.

66. Meltzer, H., and D. Ludwig. Age differences in memory optimism and pessimism in workers. *Journal of Genetic Psychology*, 1967, **110**, 17–30.

67. Mischel, W. Continuity and change in personality. *American Psychologist*, 1969, **24**, 1012–1018.

68. Morgan, R. F. The adult growth examination's preliminary comparisons of physical aging in adults by sex and race. *Perceptual & Motor Skills*, 1968, **27**, 595–599.

69. Neugarten, B. L. The awareness of middle age. In B. L. Neugarten (Ed.). *Middle age and aging: A reader in social psychology*. Chicago: University of Chicago Press, 1968. Pp. 93–98.

70. Neugarten, B. L. (Ed.) *Middle age and aging: A reader in social psychology*. Chicago: University of Chicago Press, 1968.

71. Neugarten, B. L., and R. J. Kraines. "Menopausal syndrome" in women of various ages. *Psychosomatic Medicine*, 1965, **27**, 266–273.

72. Neugarten, B. L., V. Wood, R. J. Kraines, and B. Loomis. Women's attitudes toward the menopause. In D. C. Charles and W. P. Looft (Eds.). *Readings in psychology through life*. New York: Holt, 1973. Pp. 380–390.

73. New York Times article. "Go-getters" called more susceptible to heart attacks. *The New York Times*, Jan. 8, 1966.

74. New York Times article. Leisure use called factor in marriage. *The New York Times*, May 11, 1966.

75. Notelovitz, M. Gynecologic problems of menopausal women: Part 2. Treating estrogen deficiency. *Geriatrics*, 1978, **33**(9), 35–37, 41.

76. Nydeqger, C. N. Middle age: Some early returns—a commentary. *International Journal of Aging & Human Development*, 1976, **7**, 137–141.

77. Packard, V. *The pyramid climbers*. New York: McGraw-Hill, 1962.

78. Packard, V. *A nation of strangers*. New York: McKay, 1972.

79. Papalia, D. E., and D. Del V. Bielby. Cognitive functioning in middle and old age adults: A review of research based on Piaget's theory. *Human Development*, 1974, **17**, 424–443.

80. Parker, E. *The seven ages of women*. Baltimore, Md.: Johns Hopkins Press, 1960.

81. Peck, R. C. Psychological developments in the second half of life. In B. L. Neugarten (Ed.). *Middle age and aging: A reader in social psychology*. Chicago: University of Chicago Press, 1968. Pp. 88–92.

82. Phillips, D. L. Social participation and happiness. *American Journal of Sociology*, 1967, **72**, 479–488.

83. Piaget, J. Intellectual evolution from adolescence to adulthood. *Human Development*, 1972, **15**, 1–12.

84. Rose, L. (Ed.). *The menopause book*. New York: Hawthorn, 1977.

85. Rosenberg, S. D., and M. P. Farrell. Identity and crisis in middle-aged men. *International Journal of Aging & Human Development,* 1976, **7,** 153–170.

86. Ryan, M. S. *Clothing: A study in human behavior.* New York: Holt, 1966.

87. Schmeck, H. M. Mid-life viewed as crisis period. *The New York Times,* Nov. 20, 1972.

88. Schmitz-Scherzer, R., and I. Strodel. Age dependency of leisure time activities. *Human Development,* 1971, **14,** 47–50.

89. Sheehy, G. *Passages: Predictable crises of adult life.* New York: Dutton, 1976.

90. Sherman, J. A. *On the psychology of woman: A survey of empirical studies.* Springfield, Ill.: Charles C Thomas, 1971.

91. Simon, A. W. *The new years: A new middle age.* New York: Knopf, 1968.

92. Steincrohn, P. J. Exercise after 40? Forget it. In C. B. Vedder (Ed.). *Problems of the middle-aged.* Springfield, Ill.: Charles C Thomas, 1965. Pp. 18–24.

93. Terman, L. M., and M. H. Oden. *The gifted group at mid-life: Thirty-five year follow-up of the superior child.* Vol. 5. Stanford, Calif.: Stanford University Press, 1959.

94. Thompson, L. J. Stress in middle life from the psychiatrist's viewpoint. In C. B. Vedder (Ed.). *Problems of the middle aged.* Springfield, Ill.: Charles C Thomas, 1965, Pp. 116–120.

95. Time magazine article. The springs of youth. *Time,* Aug. 16, 1965, P. 73.

96. Tomlinson-Keasey, D. Formal operations in females from eleven to fifty-six years of age. *Developmental Psychology,* 1972, **6,** 364.

97. Treloar, A. E. Menarche, menopause, and intervening fecundability. *Human Biology,* 1974, **46,** 89–107.

98. Troll, L. E. *Early and middle adulthood: The best is yet to be — maybe.* Monterey, Calif.: Brooks/Cole, 1975.

99. U.S. Department of Health, Education, and Welfare. *Facts on older Americans.* Washington, D.C., 1973.

100. U.S. News & World Report article. Leisure boom: Biggest ever and still growing. *U.S. News & World Report,* April 17, 1972, 42–45.

101. U.S. News & World Report article. Big surge in education: Back to school for millions of adults. *U.S. News & World Report,* April 2, 1973, 73–74.

102. Udry, J. R., and M. Hall. Marital role segregation and social networks in middle-class, middle-aged couples. *Journal of Marriage & the Family,* 1965, **27,** 392–395.

103. Vahanian, G. Ethic of leisure. *Humanitas,* 1972, **8,** 347–365.

104. Vedder, C. B. (Ed.). *Problems of the middle-aged.* Springfield, Ill.: Charles C Thomas, 1965.

105. Winokur, G. Depression in the menopause. *American Journal of Psychiatry, 1973,* **130,** 92–93.

106. Zatlin, C. E., M. Storandt, and J. Botwinick. Personality and values of women continuing their education after thirty-five years. *Journal of Gerontology,* 1973, **28,** 216–221.

CHAPTER TWELVE
MIDDLE AGE: VOCATIONAL AND FAMILY ADJUSTMENTS

After reading this chapter, you should be able to:

- Understand that vocational adjustment problems affect middle-aged women as well as middle-aged men, and recognize some of the changed work conditions that contribute to these problems.
- Describe some of the factors influencing vocational adjustment in middle age and know the criteria used to assess vocational adjustments at this age.
- Explain the impact of the "empty nest" on family patterns in middle age and point out the types of adjustment problems this change gives rise to.
- Describe the problems single men and women face in middle age.
- List and describe the common vocational and marital hazards of middle age.
- Assess the adjustments men and women make to middle age, using four criteria to do so.
- Demonstrate why preparation during middle age for the next stage in the life span eases some of the adjustment problems that are inevitable in old age.

Adjustments that center around work and the family are even more difficult in middle age than personal and social adjustments, discussed in the preceding chapter. Establishing and maintaining a comfortable standard of living, for example, has become increasingly difficult in recent years. As a result of increased use of automation and because of the trend toward merging small companies with larger ones, many middle-aged persons are thrown out of work. They may find that the jobs for which their training and experience have fitted them no longer exist and that they lack the training and experience for jobs that do exist; thus they are forced into the ranks of the unemployed.

Adjustments to changed patterns of family life are equally difficult. It is never easy to adjust to playing the role of adviser to grown or nearly grown children after many years of caring for them and supervising their activities. These difficulties are intensified and prolonged when parents must subsidize a child's early marriage or extended education.

Many middle-aged men and women find it difficult to relate to their spouses as persons, as they did during the days of courtship and early marriage, after having played the role of coparent for many years while their children were growing up. This adds to the stresses many middle-aged people experience and militates against good personal and social adjustments.

While far from universal, problems of singlehood, divorce, and widowhood plague many middle-aged men and women. As is true in the years of early adulthood, these adjustments interfere with the personal and social lives of the middle-aged and complicate other adjustments they must make at this time.

For many middle-aged men and women, perhaps the most difficult adjustment they must make is to the care of aged parents. After years of freedom from responsibility for them, having to take over responsibility for them just at a time in their lives when they must face many personal, vocational, and social adjustments makes the situation doubly burdensome.

For many men, adjustment problems arising in relation to work are the most serious while, for women, those involving family relationships are the hardest to cope with. For women who carry jobs in addition to home responsibilities, family-relationship problems are usually intensified.

In addition to these areas of adjustment, the middle-aged person is faced with a totally new problem, that of adjusting to impending old age. Like all adjustments for which the individual has had no previous experience, this one is often difficult and gives rise to strong emotional tension.

VOCATIONAL ADJUSTMENTS

In the past, as has been pointed out before, relatively few people lived to middle age, and even fewer were vocationally active during this entire period. Furthermore, changes in vocational patterns and in working conditions took place at a much slower rate than they do now. Thus relatively few workers were affected by such changes, and those who were affected suffered only slightly.

All this has changed, especially since World War II, when many of today's middle-aged workers were just entering the labor force. Even more important, many more middle-aged workers are affected by these changes in working conditions now than in the past. According to U.S. Department of Labor reports, there were 33.7 million middle-aged men and women working in 1972; it is estimated that by 1990, there will be 45.9 million (111).

Because of the radical changes that have taken place in all aspects of American life since World War II, the vocational adjustments of middle-aged men and women are complicated by a number of new conditions in the working environment. Some of the most important of these are listed and briefly explained in Box 12-1.

Sex Differences in Vocational Adjustment

Now that ever-increasing numbers of women are entering the work world during middle age, vocational adjustment problems are no longer experienced mainly by men. Women have many of the same problems men do and also many that are unique to themselves.

Normally, the height of vocational success for *men* comes during the forties and early fifties. Not only does the worker reach the peak of his status in the organization at this time, but his income reaches its peak also. Middle-aged men, as a group, are better

CHANGED WORKING CONDITIONS THAT AFFECT MIDDLE-AGED WORKERS

Unfavorable Social Attitudes

While older workers used to be respected for the skills they had acquired through years of experience, today the tendency is to regard them as too old to learn new skills or keep pace with modern demands, as uncooperative in their relations with coworkers, and as subject to absenteeism and accidents because of failing health.

Hiring Policies

Because of the widespread belief that maximum productivity can be achieved by hiring and training younger workers and because employers want to spend the minimum amount for retirement pensions, middle-aged workers have greater difficulty getting jobs than younger ones, although this varies for different kinds of work. Thus changing jobs becomes increasingly more hazardous with each passing year.

Increased Use of Automation

Automated work requires a higher level of intelligence, more training, and greater speed than work that is not automated. This has an adverse effect on middle-aged men and women of lower levels of intelligence, with training for specific lines of work only, or whose health causes them to work more slowly than younger workers.

Group Work

Training in the home, neighborhood, and school puts more stress on social adjustments now than in the past; thus younger workers can usually get along better with their superiors and coworkers than can middle-aged workers.

Role of the Wife

As the man becomes more successful, the wife must act as a sounding board for his business problems, she must be an asset to him at social functions related to his work, and she must become active in community affairs.

Compulsory Retirement

With compulsory retirement now coming in the mid- to late sixties, the chances of promotion after fifty are slim, and the chances of getting a new job are even slimmer, except at a lower level and with lower pay.

Dominance of Big Business

Many small business and industrial organizations are now being taken over by bigger ones. Middle-aged workers whose companies merge with others may find that there is no place for them in the new organizations or that their jobs are on lower levels than before. This is especially true of jobs in the managerial level.

Relocation

With the consolidation of small businesses into big corporations, many workers are forced to relocate as factories and offices are moved near the parent company. Middle-aged workers who must move in order to keep their jobs often have more difficulty in adjusting to the new location than younger workers have. Furthermore, such moves tend to be traumatic experiences for middle-aged wives and teenage children.

---

satisfied with their jobs than younger men, partly because they are glad to have jobs and partly because they normally have better jobs than they had when they were younger (118).

However, some middle-aged men who have achieved status vocationally are still dissatisfied with their work. Under such conditions, some of them look around for jobs more to their liking and others not only change jobs but even change lines of work (2).

Vocational instability in the early forties stems from a number of causes, the most important of which are the general restlessness characteristic of this period of life; the ending of responsibility for the support of the children, which frees the worker from a burden he has carried for many years; and the realization that if he wants to change jobs, he must do it now or never.

As the number of middle-aged *women* in the professions, business, and industry increases, so do their adjustment problems. One of the major problems involves full equality with men in terms of hir-

BOX 12-2

CONDITIONS INFLUENCING VOCATIONAL ADJUSTMENTS IN MIDDLE AGE

Satisfaction with Work

Middle-aged men and women who like their work will make far better vocational adjustments than those who have stayed on jobs they disliked because of earlier family responsibilities and who now feel "trapped."

Opportunities for Promotion

Each year, as workers approach the age of compulsory retirement, their chances for promotion grow slighter and they are likely to be pushed aside to make way for younger workers. This has an adverse effect on vocational adjustments.

Vocational Expectations

As retirement becomes imminent, middle-aged workers assess their achievements in light of earlier aspirations. This assessment, whether favorable or unfavorable, has a profound effect on vocational adjustments.

Increased Use of Automation

Certain aspects of automation militate against good vocational adjustment on the part of middle-aged workers, such as boredom and lack of pride in their work, the possibility of losing their jobs to younger workers, increased speed required on the job, which makes many older workers nervous, and an unwillingness to retrain because of the imminence of retirement.

Attitude of Spouse

If a wife is dissatisfied with her husband's status at work, his pay, or the fact that his work takes him away from home and she is lonely—now that the children are grown—the husband too may become dissatisfied. Women whose husbands object to their working and constantly complain about their being out of the home may also experience job dissatisfaction.

Attitude toward "Big Business"

Workers who take pride in being associated with big, prestigious companies will make better adjustments to their work than those who regard themselves merely as little cogs in big machines.

Attitudes toward Coworkers

Middle-aged workers who resent the treatment they receive from their superiors or their subordinates and who regard younger workers as shiftless and careless will have less favorable attitudes toward their work than those who are on friendlier terms with their coworkers.

Relocation

How workers feel about moving to another community in order to keep their present jobs or be promoted to better ones will have a profound influence on their vocational adjustments.

---

ing, promotion, and salary. Most women, regardless of their training and ability, find it more difficult to get jobs and to be promoted than do men. This is true in all except "women's fields," such as elementary school teaching, nursing, and beauty culture, where women encounter less competition from men than in other lines of work.

Because of these conditions, not only do many middle-aged women derive less satisfaction from their work, but they also have less desire to remain in the same job or to get another job as middle age advances. Some few, especially those in the higher levels of work, decide not only to change jobs but even careers in mid-life. This usually requires a period of several years of retraining which, for most women, is financially impossible unless they have ac-

cumulated savings or unless their husbands can pay for the training (26).

Factors Influencing Vocational Adjustment in Middle Age

Good vocational adjustment in early adulthood will not necessarily guarantee the same in middle age because the conditions contributing to good adjustment at one age often differ from those at another. Box 12-2 gives some of the conditions that influence the vocational adjustments of middle-aged men and women.

Assessment of Vocational Adjustment

Vocational adjustment in middle age, like that in early adulthood, can be assessed in terms of the success men and women achieve in their work and the degree of satisfaction they derive from it. Unless both of these conditions are taken into consideration, an assessment of their vocational adjustments will not be accurate.

Achievements Many middle-aged workers enjoy a degree of success that gives them the income, the prestige, the authority, and the autonomy they had hoped for. Others, also trained and experienced, find themselves in less rewarding jobs below their capacities. Still others may be successful in that they have made the most of their abilities and training, but regard themselves as failures because they have not achieved the success they had hoped for when they were younger. This lack of satisfaction with their achievements makes them discontented with their jobs and with themselves as workers.

Women, far more often than men, fail to achieve the vocational success they are capable of during middle age. This is just as true of women who have worked continuously since they finished their education as of women who left their jobs after they were married and then returned to work after their home and parental duties diminished. This failure is due not to lack of ability and training but to prejudice against women in positions of responsibility.

Satisfaction Among industrial workers, the forties are the "critical age" for job satisfaction. This age comes slightly later for workers in business and the professions. By the end of the fifties and early sixties, there is usually a sharp drop in vocational satisfaction (95). This is shown in Figure 12-1.

About five years before the compulsory retirement age, whether it is sixty, sixty-two, sixty-five, or seventy, there is usually a sharp drop in the satisfaction *men* experience in their work. (Refer to Figure 12-1.) The reason for this drop is that men now feel that they have little chance for advancement, no matter how hard they may work or how faithful they may be about keeping absenteeism to a minimum.

Job satisfaction also wanes as middle age progresses because men begin to feel the pressures of work as a result of their general slowing down and increased tendency toward fatigue, both of which are natural accompaniments of aging. In addition, they resent the attitudes of some younger workers who not only can do the work more easily than they but who often seem to be counting the days until the older

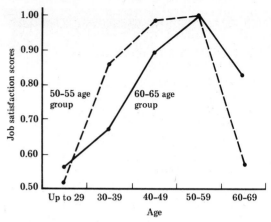

FIGURE 12-1 Job satisfaction reaches its peak in the mid-fifties and then declines abruptly. (Adapted from S. D. Saleh and J. L. Otis. Age and level of job satisfaction. *Personnel Psychology*, 1964, **17**, 425–430. Used by permission.)

men retire and they can take their places. None of these factors contributes to job satisfaction.

Middle-aged *women*, even more than men, fail to derive the satisfaction they should from their work. And, like men, their dissatisfaction increases with each passing year until they welcome the compulsory retirement age. Their dissatisfaction is due to many of the same factors that cause dissatisfaction in men, but it is intensified by their resentment at not being given equal opportunities for advancement when their abilities justify it. Members of *minority groups,* both men and women, also experience job dissatisfaction for this reason.

The most important conditions leading to vocational satisfaction in middle age are given in Box 12-3. When satisfaction is high, workers will do all they possibly can to keep their work up to previous standards, even though they may have to press themselves to do so; they will be loyal to their employers and not take unnecessary time off from work; they will try to bolster the morale of their coworkers; and they will not complain, even when things are not to their liking.

ADJUSTMENT TO CHANGED FAMILY PATTERNS

The pattern of family life undergoes marked changes during the period of middle age. As Cavan has

CONDITIONS CONTRIBUTING TO VOCATIONAL SATISFACTION IN MIDDLE AGE

- Achievement or near achievement of a vocational goal set earlier.
- Satisfaction on the part of family members, especially the spouse, with the worker's vocational achievements.
- Opportunities for self-actualization on the job.
- Congenial relationships with coworkers.
- Satisfaction with treatment from management and direct superiors.
- Satisfaction with the provisions made by management for illness, vacations, disability, retirement, and other fringe benefits.
- Feelings of security about the job.
- Not being forced to relocate to hold a job, advance in it, or get a new job.

pointed out, "The most obvious change is the withdrawal of . . . children from the family, leaving husband and wife as the family unit" (13). This change is usually more difficult for women to adjust to than for men because women's lives are centered around the home and family members during the early adult years. Then, during the "shrinking circle stage," as Lopata has called it, the middle-aged housewife no longer derives all her satisfaction and prestige from her roles as wife and mother, and the replacements she finds for these roles, whether as a worker outside the home or as a participant in community activities, are rarely as satisfying (53).

Adjustment to changed family patterns in middle age is often complicated by a number of factors that are either directly or indirectly related to family life. The most important of these are given in Box 12-4.

Some of these factors affect men and women differently, and some are more important early in middle age than later. For example, because the woman has had to center her interests mainly around the home, her habit of being family-oriented is more firmly fixed than her husband's and is more difficult to break in middle age. Also, the impact of the menopause occurs earlier and more suddenly than the impact of the male climacteric, and women must make

a more radical adjustment to the physical and psychological changes that accompany loss of the reproductive function.

While both men and women must make role changes as their children grow up and leave home, these changes are easier for men to make than for women, partly because the father's role is far less time- and energy-consuming than the mother's and partly because men can compensate for radical changes in family life by deriving added satisfaction from their work, which most women cannot do.

Finally, men and women become disenchanted with marriage for different reasons. The man may be disenchanted with his marriage if he feels that his lack of vocational success is the result of the strains of family life or the unfavorable attitudes of family members toward his work. A woman is more likely to become disenchanted with marriage if she feels useless now that her maternal responsibilities have lessened or are over or if she feels that her husband is more concerned about his work than about his home and family. Thus in the case of both men and women during middle age, disenchantment with marriage is due more to conditions within the family than to the relationship between husband and wife, though this tends to intensify the effects of changed family patterns.

Some of the adjustment problems that middle-aged men and women must face in their family lives are individual in nature while others are more or less universal and a product of the culture in which the person lives. The most important of these are discussed below.

Adjustment to Changed Roles

When the children leave home—to go to college, to marry, or to pursue a career—parents must face the adjustment problems of what is commonly referred to as the period of the "empty nest" (53). In many homes, this period is almost as long as the whole period during which the children were living in the home. When the empty nest period occurs, it means a change of roles for both parents and a branching out from the family which, in most cases, is more difficult for women than for men.

Whether the empty nest period will begin in the forties or fifties will depend on the size of the family and when the children leave home. If they go away to school or college, they will leave home earlier than if they remain at home while they are still students or while they are working until they marry. Figure 10-3

CONDITIONS COMPLICATING ADJUSTMENT TO CHANGED FAMILY PATTERNS IN MIDDLE AGE

Physical Changes

The physical and psychological disturbances that accompany the menopause and the male climacteric often intensify the other adjustment problems of middle age which, in turn, heighten these physical and psychological disturbances.

Loss of Parental Role

Like all habits, that of centering one's life around one's home and children is hard to break. Middle-aged people who are able to occupy their time with activities they find satisfying will be able to adjust to the loss of the parental role.

Lack of Preparation

While most middle-aged people are prepared for the physical changes that accompany middle age, few are prepared for the role changes that take place in both their family and vocational lives. See Figure 12-2. Adjustment problems are greatly intensified if role changes and physical changes occur simultaneously.

Feelings of Failure

Middle-aged people whose marriages have not turned out as they had hoped, or whose children have not come up to their expectations, often blame themselves and feel that they have been failures.

Feelings of Uselessness

The more child-centered the home was earlier, the more useless the middle-aged person will feel when parental responsibilities diminish or come to an end.

Disenchantment with Marriage

Disenchantment with marriage is often caused or intensified by unforeseen changes in the marital situation, such as the husband's loss of a job or lack of success or the failure of children to come up to parental expectations.

Care of Elderly Relatives

Most middle-aged people resent having to care for an elderly relative because they do not want to be tied down, as they were when their children were young, and because they fear that strained relationships with the spouse or adolescent children will result.

---

shows the median age of mothers at the time of marriage of the last child. Note that in the 1970s it was fifty-two.

Refer to Figure 10-4 for a graphic illustration of the pattern of role changes that middle-aged men and women must make when their parental responsibilities are over. Note that the pattern for middle-aged men and women is that of a pair-centered relationship as compared with the family-centered relationship of early adulthood.

Role changes necessitated by the empty nest period of family life affect women far more than men though men are not spared the effects of these role changes. According to tradition, the empty nest is a traumatic and unhappy period in life for the typical woman, though far less so for the typical man (34).

According to evidence, the empty nest is far from universally an unhappy period in the lives of middle-aged men and women. As Campbell has put it, "Raising a family seems to be one of those tasks, like losing weight or waxing the car, that is less fun to be doing than to have done" (12).

In one survey it was found that 83 percent of "empty nest mothers," forty to forty-nine years of age, said they were "very happy" compared with 57 percent of women of the same age who still had children at home. For women in the fifty to fifty-nine age group of this study, 71 percent of the empty nest mothers claimed to be "very happy" as compared with 46 percent who still had children in the home (42).

Role changes necessitated by the empty nest period of middle age affect women and men differently. As Horn has put it, the departure of children is a "cruel blow" to some parents, especially those who are widowed or divorced (42). Otherwise, the effects are often positive (34). Whether the effects will

"Enjoy them every minute, Deary. Before you can turn around they'll be grown."

FIGURE 12-2 For an overworked, harassed mother, preparation for the "empty nest" stage when parental responsibilities are over is difficult. (Adapted from Bil Keane. "The Family Circus." The Register and Tribune Syndicate, March 31, 1978. Used by permission.)

be positive or negative will depend, to a large extent, upon marital relationships (36).

From an extensive survey of the effects of the empty nest, Harkins has come to the conclusion that, like retirement, the transition to the empty nest stage is usually only transitory and the effect is often slight (36):

The results lend further credence to prior studies indicating that the empty nest is not a particularly stressful period in most women's lives and hence is not a major source of threats to psychological and physical well-being. The only threat to well-being is having a child who does not become successfully independent when it is expected.

The difficulties of adjusting to the departure of children from the home and to the role changes that this necessitates are increased for parents who have few outside interests and have built their lives around their children. Overly protective and possessive parents are especially prone to make their children the center of their lives.

As their married children become increasingly involved in their own families, it becomes clear to parents that they feel more love and concern for their children than their children feel for them. This intensifies the parents' adjustment problems, especially those of the mother.

Adjustment to Spouse

With the ending of parental responsibilities, the husband and wife once again become dependent upon each other for companionship. Whether they will adjust successfully to this changed pattern of family relationships is greatly influenced by how well adjusted they were when parental roles took precedence over husband-wife roles.

Only when the husband and wife can establish a close relationship, similar to the one they had during the early years of marriage, can they find happiness in marriage during middle age (35). Refer to Figure 10-4 which shows how middle-aged people must adjust to a pair-centered relationship after having adjusted to a family-centered relationship during the years when parenthood dominated their lives.

Establishing such a relationship is often difficult and, even more important, it may take time as husbands and wives adjust to their new roles (91). Marital satisfaction, it has been found, reaches a low point when children are leaving home and when radical role changes must be made. As those role changes are made, marital satisfaction increases (91). Refer to Figure 10-5 for a graphic illustration of this pattern.

Sexual Adjustments

There is ample evidence that sex is as important to marital satisfaction in middle-age today as it is in early adulthood (18,58,84). As Figure 12-3 shows, there is a sharp rise in sexual satisfaction in the postparental years after low points during the years of school-aged and teen-aged children. As children begin to leave home—the "launching stage"—sexual satisfaction between the parents increases (10).

Sexual satisfaction is greater for both men and women when intercourse can be carried to its completion, but it has been reported that women, during middle age, can enjoy coitus without orgasm more than they could during the early years of marriage (58,114). Men, on the other hand, must be able to complete the sexual act to be satisfied (58,84).

While poor sexual adjustment does not necessarily lead to marital unhappiness and divorce, it has

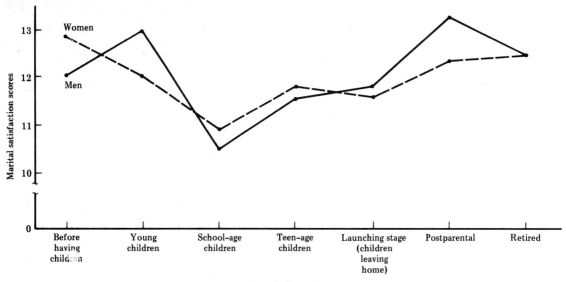

FIGURE 12-3 Sexual satisfaction is as important to good marital adjust-ment in middle age as it is during early adulthood. The graph shows how this phase of marital satisfaction varied for a sample of couples at various stages of their married life. (Adapted from W. R. Burr. Satisfaction with vari-ous aspects of marriage over the life cycle: A random middle-class sample. *Journal of Marriage & the Family,* 1970, **32,** 29–37. Used by permission.)

been found to be an important factor contributing to the disenchantment that so often occurs during mid-dle age (81,83,84). Thus poor sexual adjustment is a serious interference with good marital adjustment.

Causes of Poor Sexual Adjustment There are a num-ber of causes of poor sexual adjustment during mid-dle age, five of which are especially common, though by no means universal.

First, one of the major causes of poor sexual ad-justment in middle age is differences in the sex drive at this time. Studies of the pattern of development of the sex drive have shown that the male's sex drive is stronger in adolescence and reaches its peak earlier than the female's sex drive. The woman's sex drive and interest in sex, by contrast, become stronger as she approaches middle age. The fact that husband and wife are at different stages of development of the sex drive, combined with differences in interest in sexual behavior, may result in marital discord (18,53, 58).

Second, poor sexual adjustments often result when men become concerned with the loss of their sexual vigor. They may develop feelings of inade-quacy or go to the opposite extreme and have sexual relations with younger women to prove to themselves that they are still virile (7,81,84).

Third, during the forties and early fifties, many women lose their earlier inhibitions and develop more interest in sex. Because this occurs at the time when the man's interest in sex is declining, middle-aged women may be sexually unsatisfied and un-happy.

Fourth, some middle-aged women, knowing that it is their last chance, decide to have a child. This often complicates their adjustments to their husbands, who may not want a baby now that they have won freedom from their parental responsibilities or who may be embarrassed at having a baby the age of their grandchildren.

Fifth, the middle-aged woman who derives little satisfaction from intercourse or who feels that it is no longer interesting to her husband or a necessary part of her marriage may take the initiative in stopping it. This intensifies an already-existing belief that she is no longer needed or wanted, a belief that neither adds to her own happiness nor contributes to her husband's.

Effects of Good Sexual Adjustments   In spite of the difficulties involved, there is evidence that many middle-aged men and women make satisfactory sexual adjustments (10,35,58). As may be seen in Figure 12-3, after a drop in sexual interest during early adulthood when the children are young, satisfaction increases as the children grow up and begin to leave home. A woman's decline in satisfaction from sex during middle age is due primarily to the attitude and behavior of her husband. By contrast, a man's lessening of sexual satisfaction may be due more to conditions within himself than to those related to his wife or his home life (10,18,58).

Adjustments to In-Laws

While adjusting to in-laws is one of the major adjustment problems of young adults (refer to Box 10-8 for a list of factors influencing these adjustments), there are two new kinds of in-law adjustments that must be made during middle age. These are, first, adjustments to children's spouses and, second, adjustments to the care of aging parents (7).

Because many young people today are marrying while still in their late teens or early twenties, *adjustment to a child's spouse* on the part of the parents usually must be made while the parents are still in their forties or, at the latest, in their early fifties. Because middle-aged parents of today usually got married at about the same ages that their own children are marrying, caring for their own aged parents is also likely to occur in their forties or early fifties. If, however, adjustments to both older and younger in-laws must be made simultaneously, it is doubly hard.

Even when middle-aged parents are happy for their children to marry and establish homes of their own, they often encounter difficulties in establishing good relationships with their children's spouses. While adjusting to children's spouses is an age-old problem, it is more difficult today than in the past for reasons explained in Box 12-5.

The second in-law adjustment problem—that of *caring for aging parents*—is less common today

---

BOX 12-5

CONDITIONS CONTRIBUTING TO DIFFICULTIES IN ADJUSTING TO CHILDREN'S SPOUSES

- Short courtships that give parents little time to get to know their future in-laws or their families.
- Spouses from other communities, states, or even countries. This deprives both sets of parents of opportunities to get to know their future in-laws before marriage.
- Few parents of today are consulted about their children's choice of spouse; they often consider the choice "unsuitable."
- The expectation on the part of the middle-aged couple that they will continue to have the same relationship with their children that existed before marriage and that their relationship with a son- or daughter-in-law will be the same as their relationship with their own children.
- The necessity for married children to live with their parents or in-laws.
- The tendency of the middle-aged couple to offer too much advice to a son- or daughter-in-law.
- Dissimilarity of sociocultural background of in-laws, leading to criticisms and strained relationships.
- Elopement, which leads to parental embarrassment and resentment.
- Disapproval of spouse because of willingness to cohabit for a year or more before marriage.
- Disapproval because marriage was forced due to premarital pregnancy.
- Residential propinquity, which encourages frequent contacts and parental overprotectiveness and interference.
- Psychological dependency of a married daughter on her parents, which may make her husband resent them.
- A lack of grandchildren, which may be a disappointment to the middle-aged parents and which may also give the married children more independence and thus cause them to neglect their parents, which adds to parental resentment.
- Disapproval of son-in-law's occupation or that daughter-in-law works after marriage.

Caring for an aging parent in the home is more likely to be a happy experience for all family members if the aging parent is male. (David Strickler from Monkmeyer.)

than in the past. This is because most aging people can survive on social security, welfare payments, or pensions without depending on their children for financial support. In addition, there are homes for retired people—single, widowed, or couples—and nursing homes for those whose health is such that they cannot care for themselves in their own homes or be cared for in the homes of their children.

However, when circumstances are such that aging parents *must* be cared for by their children, the problem is far more complicated today than in the

past because the typical family of today is the nuclear family—parents and children. When aging parents, for whatever reason, must be cared for in the homes of their children, the most important conditions influencing the middle-aged child's adjustment to this problem are given in Box 12-6.

Middle-aged persons who carry the burden of parent care are often deprived of opportunities to develop new interests and to engage in social activities outside the home. While caring for an elderly parent may help fill the gap created when children leave

CONDITIONS AFFECTING ADJUSTMENT TO CARE OF AGED PARENTS

Role Reversal

Most elderly parents do not find it easy to relinquish the authority and autonomy they enjoyed in their own homes, even to a grown child, especially not to an in-law.

Place of Residence

The adjustment to care of elderly parents is eased if the parents can remain in their own homes and receive only financial aid from their children, rather than moving in with them or living in a home for the aged.

Degree of Responsibility

Many middle-aged people become resentful if the care of elderly parents represents a heavy financial burden or greatly restricts their activities.

Relationship of Aging Parent to Middle-aged Person

Although both husbands and wives are more resentful about caring for an in-law than a parent, the wife is especially resentful because she has the major responsibility for this care.

Role Played by Elderly Parents

When elderly parents are physically able to help with household chores and do not disrupt the family routine, the adjustment will be better than if they expect to be waited on or if they interfere in the lives of other family members.

Sex of Elderly Parent

Regardless of whose home the elderly parent lives in, men cause less work and interfere less than women.

Earlier Experiences with Elderly Parent

Middle-aged people whose earlier experiences with their own parents or with their parents-in-law have been favorable make far better adjustments to the care of these relatives than those whose earlier experiences have been unfavorable.

Attitudes toward Elderly Parents

Adjustments to the care of elderly parents depend greatly on attitudes toward these relatives, attitudes that may range from loathing to loving. Attitudes depend partly on earlier experiences with the elderly parents and partly on their current behavior and attitudes.

home, the satisfaction derived from this companionship may be far from adequate and may even intensify parental loneliness.

Adjustment to Grandparenthood

With the present trend toward early marriage, many men and women today become grandparents before middle age ends. In fact, some men and women become grandparents before middle age begins.

Grandparents as a group play less important roles in the lives of their children and grandchildren than they did in the past. The reason for this is not only that many families live farther apart today than they formerly did but also because many middle-aged women take jobs, after their children marry, and, as a result, they are not available as baby-sitters for grandchildren. Because today's grandparents have fewer contacts with their grandchildren, they have less influence over them than was true of past generations.

However, the relationships of grandparents with their children and their grandchildren depend on the role they play in their grandchildren's lives. Neugarten and Weinstein have distinguished five roles that modern grandparents can and do play in the American culture (72). These are listed and briefly explained in Box 12-7.

Most grandparents claim that they prefer a "pleasure without responsibility" relationship with their grandchildren. While they are willing to help out in emergencies and to baby-sit occasionally, they prefer playing with them and taking them to the zoo or to a movie, to assuming actual care for them (53,82,89). In fact, they often find that they derive greater enjoyment from doing things with their grandchildren than they did when they played the role of parents (89).

The "fun-seeking" grandparental role is characterized by informality and playfulness; the grandparent tries to be a "pal" to the grandchild. (Suzanne Szasz.)

The older the grandchildren, the more trying most grandparents find them after a short time. This is illustrated in Figure 12-4. Consequently, middle-aged people prefer shorter contacts with their grandchildren and fewer responsibilities (72,82,89). As grandchildren approach the teens, their relationships with their grandparents tend to worsen, partly because they often have intolerant attitudes toward middle-aged and elderly people and partly because grandparents frequently disapprove of the dress, grooming, and behavior of today's teenagers.

ADJUSTMENT TO SINGLEHOOD

By middle age, most unmarried men and women have adjusted to being single and are reasonably happy with the pattern of life they have established for themselves. Refer to Box 10-11 for a list of reasons why adults remain single. Some, however, have not made a satisfactory adjustment to being single and decide to marry during middle age.

Most *women* are realistic enough to know that, after they pass forty, their chances for marriage grow slimmer every year. This, it has been found, is far more true in the case of single women than of widows and divorcees. After forty-five, it has been reported, the single woman's chances of marriage are 9 out of 100, as compared with 50 out of 100 for divorcees and 18 out of 100 for widows (19,96). Knowing how slim her chances of marriage are, the middle-aged single woman adjusts her life pattern accordingly and often centers her life around her work.

Most *men* who are single in middle age are so by preference. They find it socially advantageous to be bachelors, and they know they can marry whenever they no longer derive satisfaction from being single. Furthermore, if they have high aspirations for vo-

FIGURE 12-4 For many middle-aged people, the grandparent role is often more trying than pleasurable. (M. O. Lichty. "Grin and Bear it." Publishers-Hall Syndicate, Nov. 14, 1972. Used by permission.)

"They got some idea that asking us to sit with our grandchildren makes us feel 'needed' . . . All I get is a feeling of being 'used'! . . ."

cational success, they may prefer to devote their time and energy to working and getting ahead.

Just as marriage creates many problems for men and women in middle age, so does being single. Furthermore, single women, like those who are married, tend to have more difficult problems during middle age than men do. The most complex problems that single men and women must cope with during middle age are discussed below.

Problems of Single Women Problems related to employment and vocational advancement are even more serious for middle-aged women than for men. If a woman should lose her job she has even less chance of finding another one than a middle-aged man in the same position. Also, women who hold their jobs through middle age are far less often promoted to positions of prestige and responsibility than men, and they must face an earlier retirement age in many companies.

As a result of these practices, working is not al-ways a satisfactory substitute for marriage—with the security marriage normally brings. Worries about economic security and frustrations arising from the realization that promotion will be denied her more because of her sex than because of lack of ability make middle age a less happy period for women than early adulthood, when job security was taken for granted and there was always the possibility of marriage.

To add to her adjustment problems, it is usually the single woman in a family who is expected to assume the responsibility of caring for an elderly parent. This often creates a financial burden in addition to the physical and emotional burden of caring for an elderly person while holding down a job.

Assuming responsibilities for the care of an aging parent generally means that the middle-aged single woman must limit her social life. As a result, she often cuts herself off from social contacts and activities in community organizations so drastically that when the care of the parent ends with the parent's death, she finds herself far lonelier than the middle-aged widow or divorcée who may have her children or the friends she acquired during the years of her marriage to fall back on for companionship.

Problems of Single Men The single man is usually in a more favorable position in middle age than the single woman. Because he has not had the responsibilities of a family through the early adult years, he has been able to devote as much time as he wished to his work, and he has been free to move to areas where greater opportunities were available. Although success in the business world depends on hard work and a willingness to adapt oneself to new situations, the middle-aged man is usually better rewarded for his past efforts than the middle-aged woman who has followed the same pattern of hard work and personal sacrifice in earlier years, and he is more likely to be promoted. The middle-aged bachelor is therefore generally at the peak of his career, and he has little reason to be concerned about unemployment.

Furthermore, a single man is not handicapped by the problems of caring for elderly parents unless no other family members can assume the responsibility. When he must take on this burden, he usually provides financial aid rather than sacrificing his time and efforts to take care of their needs. Consequently, he is free to lead the kind of life he wants, and he has relatively few of the adjustment problems that the middle-aged single woman must face.

ADJUSTMENT TO LOSS OF A SPOUSE

The loss of a spouse, whether as a result of death or divorce, presents many adjustment problems for the middle-aged man or woman, but especially for the woman. The middle-aged *woman* whose husband dies, or who is divorced, experiences extreme feelings of loneliness. This is intensified by frustrations of the normal sexual desires, which are far from dormant, and by economic problems that are inevitable when the family breadwinner no longer provides for the family.

The *man* whose wife dies, or who is divorced, experiences a disruption in his pattern of living unless a relative can manage the home for him. A woman who is widowed or divorced in middle age often must give up her home, go to work, and live very differently from the way she did when her husband was alive or before her divorce. The woman alone also encounters social complications which men do not face. She may be reluctant to go out by herself, and the problem of entertaining is likewise awkward.

The effects of loss of a spouse differ according to the cause of the loss: death or divorce. These will be discussed separately.

Loss by Divorce Loss of a spouse as a result of divorce affects middle-aged people very differently, depending primarily upon who wanted the divorce. A woman whose husband divorced her to marry someone else will have different reactions from those of a woman who found her marriage intolerable and, as a result, initiated the divorce herself. This matter will be discussed in more detail later in connection with the hazards of middle age.

The problems middle-aged men and women face when they are divorced are similar, in most respects, to those faced by young adults and described in detail in Box 10-14. However, there are two problems that are especially serious for middle-aged women—social activities and economic well-being.

For divorced women, *social* problems are even harder to cope with than they are for those who are widowed. Not only may the divorced woman be excluded from social activities, but, even worse, she often loses old friends. While some will remain her friends, many will ostracize her or rally around her husband. As Goode has explained (74):

The divorcee is often anathema to married couples because she embodies tensions they may be feeling
but are trying to overlook. Wives, suspicious of her motives, misinterpret her most casual gestures toward their husbands. Husbands, meanwhile, assume she is in a perpetual state of tumescence.

The second major problem many middle-aged women face after divorce is *economic.* Unless they have readily marketable skills that they have kept up-to-date during their years of child-rearing, they will find it difficult to get jobs that pay enough to enable them to support themselves and any children who are still at home unless they receive adequate alimony from their ex-husbands. However, today there is a growing tendency for alimony to be given by the courts for fixed and short periods, rather than for life or until the wife remarries. This can and usually does have a devasting effect on middle-aged women (117).

Loss by Death Except when death follows a long and terminal illness (evident to and acknowledged by all that death was inevitable) most middle-aged men and women go through a predictable course of grief. This course, as Conroy has pointed out, has four stages: first, numbness, when the individual is unable to grasp the reality of the death of the loved one; second, pining, characterized by recollections of past experiences and the strong wish that they could continue; third, depression, resulting from acceptance of death during which the individual goes into solitude and often resorts to some form of escape, such as pills or alcohol; and, fourth, recovery, in which the individual accepts the death of the loved one and tries to build a new pattern of life with interests and activities to fill the void (20).

Death in middle age is far more common among men than among women. Therefore, widowhood is primarily a woman's problem. The problems of widowhood in middle age, as listed and briefly explained in Box 12-8, are similar in some respects to those of divorced men and women, as given in Box 10-14. But in many respects they are different and often more long-lasting and far-reaching in their effects (51,54,99).

That many middle-aged women do not make satisfactory adjustments to widowhood is shown by the fact that, as a group, they are considered high risks for mental illness and for the use of escape measures, such as drugs and alcohol. These effects, it has been found, are not due to grief per se so much as to circumstances associated with widowhood, such as ec-

BOX 12-8

COMMON PROBLEMS OF WIDOWHOOD

Economic Problems

Some widows are financially better off than they were during their married lives, but they are the exception to the rule. Unless a man has built up a sizable estate and has carried large life insurance policies, the widow finds herself in greatly reduced economic circumstances when her husband's earnings come to an end. With ever-increasing inflation, what widows receive in inheritance is frequently far from adequate for their needs. Even when a widow starts to work in middle age, she usually cannot earn enough to maintain the standard of living she has become accustomed to.

Social Problems

Because social life among the middle-aged, as is true of young adults, is pair-oriented, a widow soon discovers that there is no place for her among married couples unless there happens to be a widower who is invited to social gatherings to pair off with her. Most of a widow's social life is centered around activities with other women. If she is economically handicapped, a widow is unable to participate in many community social organizations, such as clubs.

Family Problems

If there are children still at home, a widow must play the roles of both mother and father, and must face all the problems of one-parent homes described earlier. Then, too, there are often problems related to members of the husband's family, especially if they were not congenial with the wife during the husband's lifetime.

Practical Problems

Trying to run a household alone, after being used to the help of a husband with fixing appliances, cutting the grass, shoveling snow, etc., presents many practical problems for every widow. Unless she has children who can help her with these tasks or is able to do them herself, she will be forced to pay for outside help—an added strain on an already-strained budget.

Sexual Problems

Because the sex drive is far from dormant during middle age, widows who enjoyed a satisfactory sexual life during their married years now feel frustrated and deprived. Some cope with this problem by having affairs with single or married men, by cohabiting, or by remarriage. Others continue to feel frustrated and deprived, or engage in autoerotic sexual practices.

Residential Problems

Where a widow will live depends usually upon two conditions: first, her economic status and, second, whether she has anyone to live with her. Many widows are forced to give up their homes because their economic condition does not enable them to maintain them. In such cases, they must move into smaller quarters or live with married children. If their health prevents them from living alone, they may be forced to move into a retirement home, or pay for a companion to live with them in their own homes, or live with a married child.

onomic status, loneliness, opportunities for outside interests, and place of residence (20,38,68).

Remarriage Middle-aged men and women who lose their spouses due to divorce or death make reasonably satisfactory adjustments to being single after a period of time. However, most tend to be lonely and find the single status unsatisfactory. Consequently, they decide to remarry or to cohabit.

Some middle-aged men and women, especially those who live in urban areas, prefer cohabitation to remarriage after divorce or death of a spouse. They like the temporary nature of the arrangement; it prevents the cutting off of alimony or funds from the pensions of former husbands; and, in some cases, money from inheritance funds set up by former husbands. In addition, cohabiting allows for greater personal independence, even to the point of maintaining their own homes, while, at the same time, meeting the sexual and social needs of both men and women (75, 109).

Most middle-aged men and women in the American culture of today prefer to follow the traditional pattern and remarry. For men, whether di-

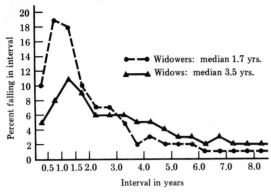

FIGURE 12-5 Distribution of intervals between death of spouse and remarriage. Note that a large percentage of remarriages comes within several years after loss of spouse. (Adapted from W. P. Cleveland and D. T. Gianturco. Remarriage probability after widowhood: A retrospective method. *Journal of Gerontology*, 1976, **31,** 99–103. Used by permission.)

vorced or widowed, this is relatively easy. There are plenty of women of their own ages and younger who are both ready and willing to marry either a widower or a divorced man.

Such, however, is not true for women. Perhaps the most serious problem that loss of a spouse presents to women stems from the fact that their chances for remarriage become slimmer as they grow older (19). Figure 12-5 shows how women's chances for remarriage decrease as age progresses.

And, since women can expect to live longer than men, this means a long period of loneliness, complicated by financial, social, and other problems. This is why widows, as a group, are a high risk for mental illness and for addiction to psychological pain killers, such as drugs and alcohol (20,38,117).

ADJUSTMENT TO APPROACHING RETIREMENT

Even though most business and industrial organizations, as well as firms of professional workers, do not require their workers to retire until the government mandatory age of seventy, they have voluntary retirement at sixty, sixty-two, or sixty-five years. They encourage their workers to take advantage of the financial benefits made available to them if they elect to retire before the compulsory age of seventy. This

means that middle-aged men, and to a less extent, middle-aged women, must adjust to impending retirement.

In recent years, many business and industrial organizations have come to realize that they have an obligation to help their employees adjust to the problems of retirement since they are largely responsible for creating these problems. At first, the main emphasis was on making provisions for an adequate income after retirement. However, it soon became apparent that preparation for retirement should take into account other, and often more difficult problems, such as how to spend leisure time and how to become involved in community volunteer services (46, 56,105,110).

Unquestionably one of the most common and most serious adjustment problems to retirement relates to family members. Although some wives— and sometimes children who are still living at home —look forward to the retirement of the family breadwinner, others have grave reservations about how retirement will affect the pattern of their lives (29). This is illustrated in Figure 12-6.

While the problems of adjusting to approaching retirement are difficult for all men, they are made more so when family attitudes are unfavorable. This, unfortunately, is one of the major areas in preretirement counseling that is ignored or given little attention (29,46,105).

To date, relatively little has been done to help women adjust to retirement. It is assumed that, because they have carried home responsibilities throughout their working lives, either as single or as married women, they will not have difficulty in filling their time when they retire and will, in fact, welcome the freedom from pressure that carrying a double load entails. In addition, because many single career women have been active in community organizations for years, it is assumed that this interest will help them fill the void caused by retirement. How women adjust to retirement will be discussed in detail in Chapter 14.

ADJUSTMENT TO APPROACHING OLD AGE

It is a well-known psychological fact that people adjust more quickly and more easily to problems if they are prepared for them beforehand than if they must face and cope with them without any foreknowledge

"I hate to think of when he retires. It's going to be like one long weekend with no Monday morning to look forward to."

FIGURE 12-6 How family members, especially wives, feel about men's impending retirement affects their attitudes and, in turn, their adjustments. (Dan Tobin. "The Little Woman." King Features Syndicate, August 17, 1977. Used by permission.)

or expectation. While few counseling services, as in the case of preparation for retirement, have tried to prepare middle-aged people for approaching old age, there is much advice given in the mass media, and many doctors try to encourage their middle-aged patients to prepare, physically at least, for a healthy old age.

Middle-aged people who have unfavorable attitudes toward old age literally shut their eyes and ears to anything relating to it. They do not, for example, want to watch television programs about health measures to keep one fit, nor do they want to talk about the time when they will be unable to maintain their homes and follow the same living pattern they now enjoy.

Because middle-aged men and women so often dread old age as a result of its unfavorable stereotypes, they are usually inadequately prepared to make the necessary adjustments to this age. Thus, many of them find old age to be one of the most unsatisfactory periods of life. This matter will be discussed in detail in Chapter 14.

Most of the problems of old age, it has been found, originate in middle age or even earlier (112). Therefore if men and women are to adjust successfully to old age, they must make preparations for it earlier in life. The problems most likely to arise in old age and suggestions about how middle-aged people can prepare to meet them are given in Box 12-9.

VOCATIONAL AND MARITAL HAZARDS OF MIDDLE AGE

Vocational and marital adjustments during middle age are the most difficult to make and thus the most hazardous. Satisfactory adjustments in these areas are even more important to happiness than personal and social adjustments, and failure to make them is at the basis of much middle-aged dissatisfaction. Members of both sexes are faced with these hazards, though the effects may be slightly different.

Vocational Hazards

While many vocational hazards of middle age are similar to those of early adulthood, described in Chapter 10, some are particularly characteristic of this period. Of these, eight are especially common and serious.

Failure to Reach Earlier Goals Failure to reach a goal set earlier is an ego-deflating experience for middle-aged people because they know that this is the peak time for achievements and that they are unlikely to attain their goals in old age. Their reactions to the failure to reach their goals will affect their attitudes toward themselves and the kind of personal and social adjustments they make now and when they reach old age. In discussing the effects of failure to achieve an earlier-set goal, Bischof has pointed out (7):

Middle age is a "time of truth." Dreams and aspirations may have carried the man well through his 20s, 30s, and into his 40s. . . . When a man gets to be 50 or so he settles his brains, if he is wise, to the realities of life. He must learn to cooperate with the inevitable. Whatever it was he had in his younger days that gave him the confidence to plan or to dream may not have been adequate for the advancement he sought in his occupation. Many men when faced with this time of truth may seek solace in at least one of two ways; compensation or rationalization.

BOX 12-9

AREAS OF PREPARATION FOR OLD AGE

Health

Preparation for old age should include health measures that will prevent or mitigate the effects of the chronic or debilitating diseases of old age. This includes diet, excercise and regular medical check-ups.

Retirement

Middle-aged people who have prepared for vocational retirement, or for termination of the parental role by acquiring new interests and engaging in new activities, adjust better to old age than those who have made no such preparation.

Use of Leisure Time

In preparation for old age, middle-aged people should pursue hobbies and acquire interests that will be satisfactory in old age when they must give up more strenuous leisure-time activities.

Financial Independence

Middle-aged people should learn to live on incomes equivalent to what their social security and pension incomes will be when they retire. In addition, they should try to set aside a nest egg for emergencies even if it means foregoing some of the expenditures for status symbols and pleasures their friends enjoy.

Social Contacts

Because social contacts with contemporaries become increasingly difficult in old age, middle-aged men and women should form friendships with neighbors and members of community organizations who are younger than they to avoid becoming socially isolated, thus assuring themselves of a continuation of social contacts in old age.

Role Changes

Middle-aged men and women must prepare for the role changes that are inevitable in old age, whether in business, in the home, or in community activities. It is especially important that they learn gradually to relinquish leadership roles, to play the role of follower, and to adapt to this change.

Life Patterns

Middle-aged people should recognize that circumstances in old age, such as poor health or reduced income, may force them to move from their homes and to change their life patterns. Those who are unprepared to make such changes will have difficulty in adjusting to a new pattern of life and will be unhappy.

Not all men and women cling to their early aspirations. Some revise them because they have become more realistic, while others do so because their values have changed. Whatever motivates this revision, it is important because it eliminates the potential hazard stemming from failure to come up to earlier aspirations and expectations. In a forty-year follow-up of Terman's "gifted group," Oden pointed out that some of the "C men"—those least successful vocationally—fell below their expectations because of value changes as they grew older. As she explained, "It should not be overlooked that a few of the C men have deliberately chosen not to seek 'success,' expressing a preference for a less competitive way of life with greater opportunity for personal happiness and freedom from pressure to pursue their avocational interests" (76).

Decline in Creativity Even though their level of productivity may remain the same or even improve, many middle-aged workers show a decline in vocational creativity. This makes middle-aged workers less satisfied with their achievements and they are no longer acclaimed for their creativity, as they were earlier.

This decline may not be due to a lessening of mental abilities or to mental rigidity, as is widely believed, but rather to the fact that middle-aged workers have less time for creative work than they did before as a result of the added responsibilities and pressures that come with success. As has already been pointed out, those who were successful earlier are usually assigned leadership roles when they reach middle age. This leaves them little free time for the mental "play" essential to creativity (7,23).

Boredom While boredom is also a vocational hazard during early adulthood, it affects middle-aged workers more than younger workers because their chances of finding more stimulating jobs grow slimmer with each passing year. Boredom is especially common among industrial workers who find that automation is increasingly replacing individual workmanship. As Packard has pointed out (78):

The repetitive arm movement he makes hour after hour is excruciatingly boring. His father, he recalls, was poor, but a craftsman who was proud of the barrels he made. Here the machine has all the brains, all the reason for pride. Perhaps the rules also forbid him to talk to workers nearby, or to get a drink of water except at the break period.

"Bigness" The tendency toward "bigness" in business, industry, and the professions is a vocational hazard to many of today's middle-aged workers. Having been accustomed to working in a friendly, informal atmosphere where they knew their coworkers and where coffee breaks and other leisure occasions were times for comradeship, working in the large, impersonal atmosphere characteristic of many of today's

work environments makes them feel like little cogs in big machines. Even professional workers feel that, in the large professional complexes characteristic of cities today, they have little opportunity to get to know their patients or clients and, as a result, the friendly interaction they used to enjoy is a thing of the past. For many professional workers, as is true of workers in other areas, this takes away much of the enjoyment they formerly experienced in their work.

Feeling of Being "Trapped" Many middle-aged workers who are not happy in their work feel that they are "trapped" for the rest of their working lives and will never be able to free themselves until they reach retirement age. Younger workers who are dissatisfied or bored with their jobs know that, sooner or later, they can usually find other work more to their liking. Most middle-aged people, however, feel that they must stay in a job or even a line of work they dislike because it is either too late or because ongoing family responsibilities prevent their taking time out to retrain for a new line of work (40). One middle-aged man put it this way when interviewed about his attitude toward his work (106):

Sure I feel trapped. Why shouldn't I? Twenty-five years ago, a dopey 18-year-old college kid made up his mind that I was going to be a dentist. So now here I am, a dentist. I'm stuck. What I want to know is: who told that kid he could decide what I was going to do with the rest of my life?

Unemployment Unemployment is always serious though more so in times of economic recession than in times of prosperity. Young adults who are fired or who give up their jobs can, normally, count on getting new ones in a relatively short time. However, finding a new job becomes increasingly difficult with each passing year, and the period of unemployment grows increasingly longer, as may be seen in Figure 12-7 (86). In times of reasonably good business it has been estimated that it takes about one year to get a new job after being fired—not always because of inefficiency but often because of consolidations and mergers. And, because people still equate being fired with incompetency, a new job is often less important and has less responsibility than the old one (64).

Four groups of middle-aged workers are especially vulnerable to unemployment: those with low IQs, women, men of minority groups, and executives

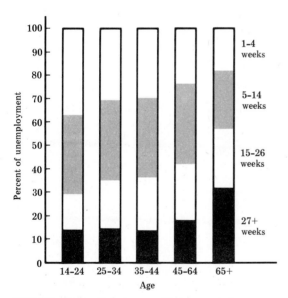

FIGURE 12-7 For the working population as a whole, the period of unemployment increases with each passing year. (From the Report of the President's Council on Aging, 1961.)

Middle-aged workers who take pride in their work are less likely than other middle-aged workers to feel bored or trapped in their jobs. (Bruce Roberts from Photo Researchers.)

or those in middle-management level jobs. In the case of *workers with low IQs*, Anman has explained that with the increased use of automation "we are eliminating the 80 IQ jobs but haven't yet determined what to do with the 80 IQ jobless" (1).

Women, even during periods of prosperity, and *men of minority groups* are more subject to unemployment than men who are not minority-group members, and they are far more likely to be laid off during periods of economic recession or depression. Middle-aged women who want to reenter the business world after their children are grown, and who try to prepare for this by learning new skills or brushing up on old ones, often find that the available jobs go to younger women (26,28).

When *executives* or *men in middle-manage-*

ment positions are fired or demoted because of management shifts or mergers with other organizations, they are far less likely to get new jobs than are those on lower levels. Men in the forty-five to fifty-five age group are more in demand than those over fifty-five, but there are some in the latter age bracket who are fortunate enough to land new jobs, even at lower pay and with less prestige (2).

Unemployment is a serious psychological hazard for any worker, regardless of age, sex, race, or minority-group status. Those who have been unemployed for a long time often develop feelings of inadequacy and of being unwanted, which result in either overaggressiveness or extreme passivity, both of which are handicaps to possible future employment. Walters contends (115):

I am confirmed in my belief that widespread unemployment—and underemployment—at middle age is one of this country's most serious social problems. . . . The shattering effect on individual lives is cause enough for action. Alcoholism, Depression, Mental Illness, Suicide. Even for those who overcome or avoid these and eventually find work again, the experience takes its toll. . . . Another compelling reason for action to alleviate joblessness at middle age is the effect it is having on the morale of many Americans. Many of the victims are terribly bitter, totally disillusioned.

Unfavorable Attitudes toward Job Unfavorable attitudes toward their jobs can have detrimental effects on the achievements and personal adjustments of middle-aged workers. Like students who dislike school or college, dissatisfied workers often become underachievers and complainers who, in turn, undermine the morale of those around them.

If workers are dissatisfied because they feel trapped in jobs they dislike or because they think their race, sex, or some other condition over which they have no control is blocking their path to success, they will develop feelings of martyrdom and these will intensify unfavorable attitudes. This militates against their holding the jobs they already have and makes getting and holding new jobs far more difficult than it otherwise might be.

Geographic Mobility Some middle-aged workers are faced with the necessity of moving to another community, often miles away from where they now live, to hold onto a job or to get another one if they are unemployed. While many business and industrial organizations shift their workers more during the twenties and thirties, executives and middle-management personnel are sometimes shifted during middle age. This is especially likely to happen if they are slated to climb the company ladder or if there is a merger of the company for which they have been working with another company.

Most middle-aged people resist moving, especially if they still have teenage children at school or if their wives have jobs or are active in community organizations. Knowing how seriously their children's social lives will be affected if they are uprooted at such a critical age, and how hard it will be for their wives to get jobs in the new community or to play roles in the new community organizations, makes many middle-aged men try to find some solution to this dilemma.

Unfortunately, many have no alternative but to move. While they may be willing to forgo a raise if it means moving to a new community, there is sometimes no alternative if their company relocates after a merger or if, having become unemployed, the only jobs available are in other communities (118).

Marital Hazards

Although some of the marital hazards of middle age are similar to those of early adulthood, most stem from changes in the pattern of family life that occur at this time and thus are unique to middle age. Furthermore, marital hazards are often more serious now than they were in early adulthood because the chances of establishing good adjustments grow slimmer as time passes and as the children leave home, lowering the adult's motivation to provide a happy family atmosphere.

While marital hazards have a greater direct impact on middle-aged women than on middle-aged men, since the woman's life has been centered around her home and family for many years, they have an important indirect effect on the man's vocational life. As has been pointed out before, not only do the attitudes of different family members, especially those of the wife, influence the man's attitude toward his work and thus his vocational adjustments, but his adjustment to his family life also affects the quality of his work and his dedication to it. A man whose family life is stressful and unhappy, for example, finds it difficult to give his wholehearted attention to his work and may become a vocational underachiever. Also, because competing with other workers requires more concentrated effort in middle age than earlier, the middle-aged man whose home life is unhappy is doubly disadvantaged in this respect.

A number of hazards to the good personal and social adjustments of middle-aged men and women develop from conditions within their marriage. The most important of these are discussed below.

Role Changes   As has been pointed out earlier, role changes are a serious hazard for the woman. When the children leave home, she finds herself in much the same position that the typical man does at retirement —unemployed. Few women, however, receive preparation for this, as many men now do from their employers. As one woman has put it, "Freshman have their advisers to help them to adjust to the changes that college life brings, but who helps the parent emeritus?" (113).

While most mothers want their children to be independent when they are developmentally ready, to have homes and families of their own, and to be successful in their work, many put roadblocks in their children's paths when the time actually comes for them to be on their own. Instead of gladly relinquishing the burden they have carried for years, many mothers cling to it because they fear that their lives will now seem empty and futile. For such women, the ending of the parental role is a traumatic experience, and neurotic difficulties are often the aftermath (25, 79).

Boredom   Just as vocational workers become bored with jobs that are highly repetitive, due to automation, or with jobs in which there is little or no chance for advancement, so women who have devoted their adult lives to homemaking often become bored in middle age. By then, the novelty of housekeeping has long since worn off, motivation decreases as family size shrinks when children leave home, and feelings of standing still begin to play a dominant role. All of these add to the boredom that results from repetition.

As middle-aged women see their husbands climb the vocational ladder and then compare this with their own work in the home, they not only become bored but, even worse, they become discontented and dissatisfied because they see little or no chance for advancement in the roles they keep playing year after year. Refer to Figure 12-8.

Just as boredom in a vocation leads to underachievement and discontent, so it does in homemak-

"The trouble with housework is there's so little room for advancement."

FIGURE 12-8   Middle-aged women often suffer from boredom resulting from the monotony of housework and the realization that there is no chance for advancement in the housewife role (Don Tobin. "The Little Woman." King Features Syndicate, January 17, 1977. Used by permission.)

ing roles. Many middle-aged women of today, recognizing that there are opportunities in the vocational world, decide to learn new skills or to brush up on any they once had that have become rusty by attending training schools or colleges (97). Other women who lack money for this, or lack support and encouragement from their husbands, just continue to be bored and, as a result, make poor personal, marital, and social adjustments.

Opposition to a Child's Marriage   A serious problem sometimes arises when a teenage or even a grown child marries someone their middle-aged parents do not approve. If they oppose the marriage, it militates against their making satisfactory adjustments to the child's departure from the home. Such opposition generally creates a barrier between the parents and the child, with the result that contacts with the child are few and relationships with grandchildren and with their child's in-laws are strained and, therefore, unfavorable.

ATTITUDES MILITATING AGAINST THE ESTABLISHMENT OF GOOD RELATIONSHIPS WITH A SPOUSE

Husband's Attitudes

- Dissatisfaction with sexual adjustments
- If he is successful vocationally, the feeling that his wife has not kept pace with him in his upward climb
- If he is unsuccessful vocationally, the feeling that his wife has been of no help and may even have handicapped him
- The feeling that he and his wife have little in common because she has refused to be interested in the things that are important to him
- A critical attitude toward his wife's management of the home and the family finances and a belief that her child-training methods have been too permissive
- Dissatisfaction with his wife's appearance
- The feeling that his wife dominates him and treats him like a child

Wife's Attitudes

- Dissatisfaction with sexual adjustments
- Disillusionment with her husband because of his lack of vocational success
- The feeling of being a slave to the home or to an elderly relative
- The belief that her husband is stingy about money for clothes and recreation
- The belief that her husband does not appreciate the time and effort she has devoted to homemaking
- The feeling that her husband is more interested in his career than in her
- The feeling that her husband spends too much time and money on members of his own family
- The suspicions that he is involved with another women

Inability to Establish Satisfactory Relationships with the Spouse as a Person One of the important developmental tasks of middle age is that of establishing satisfactory relationships with a spouse. This is especially difficult for the woman because of the problems she faces in making satisfactory adjustments to the new role she must play now that the children have left home. This hazard to good marital adjustment affects men as well.

Many men and women make this adjustment successfully and are even happier in their marriage than they were during the child-rearing years, but for others it is a hazardous transition. The most important attitudes on the part of husband and wife that militate against the establishment of good relationships are given in Box 12-10. Many of these unfavorable attitudes have been developing over the years, and by middle age they are often so deep-rooted that they are impossible to eradicate.

Sexual Adjustments Failure to achieve a good relationship with the spouse inevitably has an adverse effect on sexual relationships during middle age. This is a hazard to good marital adjustments and contributes greatly to disenchantment with marriage during this period.

A *woman* who is disenchanted with her marriage may try to compensate for this by devoting her time and energies to helping her grown children, by becoming active in community affairs, or by having an extramarital relationship with a man who she feels appreciates her more than her husband does.

The middle-aged *man* whose sexual life is unsatisfactory may likewise turn to extramarital affairs, or he may feel guilty because he has failed to give his wife sexual gratification. Wallin and Clark have explained (114):

Women's lack of sexual gratification has repercussions for their husbands as well as for themselves. In a culture that stresses the equality of marital partners and the right of both to sexual enjoyment, it is to be expected that husbands will tend to suffer some guilt in urging an activity they know is not pleasurable to their wives. Added to the guilt, and accentuating it, may be feelings of inadequacy engendered in husbands by the thought that the fault is or could be theirs.

A serious hazard to good sexual adjustments during middle age is the unfavorable attitude of younger members of the family—especially teenagers—toward sexual behavior on the part of their parents (18,84). As McKain has said, "Most children have never thought of their parents in the role of husband

and wife. Instead, they have seen them only as mother and father—a self-sacrificing, asexual, and narrow role" (61).

The awareness that their children have such attitudes tends to make middle-aged parents self-conscious about their sexual behavior or to regard it as something to be ashamed of "at their age." This is unquestionably hazardous to good sexual adjustments.

Caring for an Elderly Parent Caring for an elderly parent in their home is a serious hazard for many middle-aged couples because it interferes with their adjustment to each other after the children begin to leave home. It also interferes with good sexual adjustments.

To complicate the situation, the elderly relative is usually the mother of one of the spouses. If she does not want to change her role from that of head of a household to that of a dependent, she may try to dominate, as she did in her own home. This leads to friction with all family members and results in a generally stressful home climate.

Loss of Spouse Loss of a spouse due to death or divorce during middle age is hazardous to good personal and social adjustments because of the many problems, discussed in detail earlier, that result from death or divorce. Loss of a spouse in middle age is more likely to be due to divorce than to death while the reverse is true in old age. Refer to Figure 10-10, which shows how divorce reaches a peak in early middle age.

Because of this, divorce or threat of divorce is one of the most serious marital hazards of middle age. In contrast to younger people, who usually seek a divorce because of sexual incompatibility, parental interference, or disenchantment with marriage and parenthood, most middle-aged people divorce because the husband or wife has been unfaithful, because they feel their spouse has become irresponsible or is constantly nagging, or because they no longer have anything in common (8,83,93).

Because divorce in middle age is "major surgery" for both men and women, they do not rush into it impulsively, as many young adults often do (106). However, there is evidence that divorce in middle age is the result of conditions that have worsened and persisted over the years until they finally became intolerable. Dame et al. have explained (22):

One factor in the ultimate breakdown of some of the marriages was "grudges" which had been cherished on both sides for many years. Several husbands were preoccupied with unanswered questions about possible sexual activity of their wives either before or after the marriage. . . . Many of the wives held grudges about their suffering during pregnancies and their husbands' attitudes toward them at that time. . . . The actual turning point for the wife depends on many factors—release from the confining care of small children, the end of a shared endeavor (such as building and furnishing a home), a sense that life is slipping by or encouragement from another woman.

Remarriage Remarriage in middle age is likely to be hazardous, especially when it follows divorce. Such marriages are more likely to end in divorce than those of younger people who remarry after having been divorced (47,73). While financial problems plague younger adults who remarry following divorce, problems of adjustment to each other and to a new pattern of living are more likely to interfere with the success of remarriage in middle age. It is always difficult for middle-aged people to change their roles and follow new patterns of living (19,90,96).

Because changing patterns established over a period of years is always difficult and because many middle-aged people have become accustomed to the homes they have lived in for years, some people try to avoid the adjustment problems of remarriage by cohabitation. This is far from widespread at the present time and is limited mainly to middle-agers in the large cities where the chances of gossip and ostracism are slight as compared with suburban or smaller communities (75).

ASSESSMENT OF ADJUSTMENT TO MIDDLE AGE

Middle age should be a time of "payoff" and of new-found freedom, not only from the cares and responsibilities of the home, but also from economic problems and worries. It should also be a time for redefining oneself as a person rather than as just "Mother" or "Father," and it should be a time of contentment and satisfaction derived from a feeling that the years have been well spent.

But for far too many people, unfortunately,

middle age is a time of regrets, of disappointments, and of general unhappiness. They may be plagued by financial problems, vocational worries, career failures, or marital difficulties of long standing which flare up into serious problems at this age. Even worse, middle-aged people often feel that they are failures and that it is now too late to achieve all they had hoped to. As Erikson has pointed out, "In middle life and beyond we begin to see not so much what we wanted to do but what we actually have done" (27).

The high suicide rate among middle-aged people is evidence that this is far too often a time of poor adjustment (107). In one study it was found that the suicide rate starts to climb between the ages of thirty-six and forty years, reaching its peak between forty and sixty years. It then declines in the sixties, only to rise again at seventy. Suicide is more common among men than among women, and money problems are the major cause (41). Rates of suicide at different ages are shown in Figure 12-9.

Four criteria can be used to determine how well middle-aged men and women have adjusted to this period of the life span: first, their achievements; second, their emotional states; third, the effects of their adjustments at this age on their personalities; and fourth, how happy or unhappy they are. Each of these criteria will be discussed in detail below.

Achievements

The first criterion of adjustment is achievement. The closer middle-aged people come to achieving the goals they set for themselves earlier, the better satisfied and, hence, the better adjusted they will be. Even when middle-aged people have been as successful as could reasonably be expected, considering their abilities and training, they often feel that they have been failures because they have clung to aspirations developed in youth or even in childhood. As Whitman has explained (116):

Many middle-aged men and women feel like failures when they aren't failures at all. They are merely using the wrong tape measure. They look at themselves in their 40s and 50s and take their measures by the standards of childhood dreams and ambitions. These standards are as ill-fitting to their present stature as the trousers or the dresses they wore when they were youngsters. Childhood dreams are wonderful for children: but when we keep clinging to them in our middle years, they can make failures of us all. This is not because the childhood dreams are wrong—it is rather that we misunderstand their function. . . . Somewhere in the middle years we must let go of the dream. We must, in our maturity, recognize the dream for what it really is: a childhood spur to get us on our way, a goal.

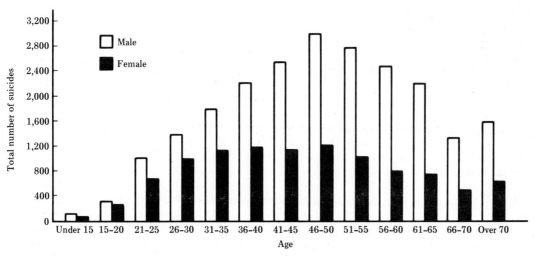

FIGURE 12-9 The suicide rate is highest among middle-aged persons. From data based on the Medical Examiner's records for New York City over a thirty-year period. (Adapted from J. Hirsh. Suicide. *Mental Hygiene, N.Y.,* 1959, **43,** 516–525. Used by permission.)

Because many middle-aged people are not realistic about their potentials, they become discouraged when their achievements fall below their expectations. As Montagu has put it: "It's a very hard thing to be an "ordinary Joe," as it were. One is faced with a great many frustrations and unrealized ideals and dreams; one has to settle for something far less than what one had anticipated in first starting out" (67).

When discouraged because their achievements have fallen below their expectations, it lowers the motivation of individuals to do what they are capable of and, as a result, they become underachievers.

Emotional States

The second criterion of how well men and women are adjusting to middle age is their emotional states or how stressful they are. As Billig and Adams have pointed out, "There has been an increasing awareness that middle age can bring anxiety and insecurity" (6). Stress, they explain, may be shown in many ways, the most common of which are conflicts with members of the family and a tendency to make great demands on them; excessive demands by middle-aged persons on those who work under them; a glorification of youthful patterns of behavior, especially as evidenced in sexual relations with younger people; and intense anxieties.

Middle-aged men and women have also been found to worry more than younger people. There is some evidence that emotional stress is more common during the early part of middle age than it is during the latter part. This can be explained by the fact that, during the forties, changes in living patterns, role changes, and changes in self-concepts resulting from physical and role changes generally come upon men and women suddenly. Although changes are always difficult and thus are generally accompanied by stress, they are especially disturbing and emotion-provoking for those who have not made adequate provision for them (35).

By the mid-fifties, most individuals are fairly well adjusted to middle age and are no longer upset by it. They have adjusted their roles, their interests, and their activities in accordance with the physical and psychological changes they have undergone. Life then moves along smoothly until the onset of old age (6). As worries subside during the latter part of middle age, the individual is calmer and, thus, happier.

Effects on Personality

The way in which physical and role changes affect the self-concepts of middle-aged people is the third criterion of how well they are adjusting to middle age. When they are making satisfactory adjustments, their self-concepts will be positive: they will feel that they are still useful members of society and that they can still make worthwhile contributions, whether they be familial, social, or vocational. By contrast, poorly adjusted individuals develop negative self-concepts, characterized by feelings of worthlessness and uselessness.

Personality disorganization in middle age is related to poor social and emotional adjustment, much of which stems from poor adjustment in the earlier years. There is little evidence to indicate that middle age, per se, is responsible for the mental illnesses that occur at this time. On the other hand, there is adequate evidence that those who break under the strain of adjustments in middle age have a history of unresolved problems which have interfered with good adjustments. The stresses of middle age then prove to be too much for them to cope with, and mental illness severe enough to require institutionalization may set in (21,71,92).

Happiness

The fourth criterion of how successfully men and women are adjusting to middle age is the happiness or life satisfaction they experience. Happiness in middle age, as at all ages, comes when the individual's needs and desires *at that time* are met and satisfied. People who are well adjusted, in the sense that they are able to satisfy their needs and desires quickly and adequately within the controls and outlets provided by the cultural group with which they are identified, will be far happier than those who have been unable or who are unwilling to make the essential adjustments.

Success in a chosen vocation, which brings with it prestige, financial rewards, and improved social status for the family, goes a long way toward making middle age a satisfying period of life for *men* and helps to compensate for the lack of satisfaction they may derive from other areas of their lives. For *women,* whose lives have usually been centered around the home, satisfaction in middle age depends mainly on the success with which they are able to adjust to the changes they must make in the homemak-

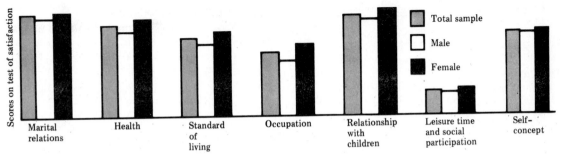

FIGURE 12-10 The degree of satisfaction middle-aged men and women derive from different areas of their lives varies markedly. (Adapted from M. P. Hayes and N. Stinnett. Life satisfaction of middle-aged husbands and wives. *Journal of Home Economics,* 1971, **63**, 669–674. Used by permission.)

ing role (35). These adjustments are easier if the husband is successful vocationally and the wife is able to enjoy her newfound freedom, rather than being forced to go to work herself (92).

Figure 12-10 shows how markedly the degree of satisfaction experienced by middle-aged men and women varies (39). Note that women tend to be better satisfied than men and that they derive greater satisfaction from their marital relations and their children than from their occupations and leisure-time and social activities. Note also that they are reasonably well satisfied with their self-concepts, further suggesting that they are able to make the good adjustment that is essential to happiness. Refer also to Figure 10-5 which shows how satisfaction with family life varies at different times during the family-life cycle.

To be happy in middle age, as at all ages, the person must be realistic and realize that life has its problems as well as its rewards. If the rewards are adequate to compensate for the problems, the scale will be balanced in favor of happiness. As Levine has pointed out (52):

What the mind loses in alertness, it makes up for it in the assurance of reflective thinking. If the muscles grow sensitive to fatigue, they learn to respond more selectively to stimuli. If the bodily functions show signs of impairment, they flash intermittently the amber lights of caution. And if the fires of passion are being damped, one comes to prize the release from their tyrannical domination.

Chapter Highlights

1. Vocational adjustments of middle-aged men and women are complicated by such factors as unfavorable social attitudes, hiring policies, increased use of automation, group work, increasing importance of the role of wives, compulsory retirement, dominance of big business, and necessity for relocation.
2. Vocational adjustment in middle age can be assessed by two criteria—achievement and satisfaction—with satisfaction usually a more important contributor to adjustment than achievement.
3. Middle age has been called the "shrinking circle stage" of family life because the most important change at this time is a reduction of family members living under the same roof.
4. The "empty nest period"—a time of radical role changes for both men and women—is less traumatic than is popularly believed though, for many women, it requires far greater adjustment in life patterns than it does for men.
5. Poor sexual adjustments in middle age are due to many causes. The five most common causes are differences in the male and the female sex drives; male concern about loss of sexual vigor; increased female interest in sex; female desire to have one more child; and female initiative in putting a stop to sexual intercourse.
6. There are two new forms of in-law adjustment most middle-aged people must make—adjustment to their children's spouses and adjustment to the care of each other's aging parents.

7. Middle-aged men and women play different grandparent roles. The five most common are the formal role, the fun-seeking role, the surrogate-parent role, the "reservoir of family wisdom" role, and the distant-figure role.

8. Adjustment to singlehood in middle age is more difficult for women, as a group, than for men, as a group, because single women, more often than single men, are expected to assume responsibility for the care of elderly parents.

9. Adjustment to the loss of a spouse is different when the loss is due to death than when due to divorce though, in both cases, the adjustment is more difficult for women than it is for men.

10. The most common problems of widowhood are economic, social, familial, practical, sexual, and residential.

11. Chances for remarriage after death of a spouse or divorce grow slimmer with each passing year for women, especially those who live in small towns or rural areas while, for men, chances for remarriage are good, regardless of where they live.

12. While adjustment to approaching retirement and approaching old age should be important developmental tasks for all middle-aged men and women, they are made more difficult than they should be because of unfavorable social attitudes that militate against adequate preparation for these tasks.

13. Among the important vocational hazards of middle age are failure to reach earlier goals, decline in creativity, boredom, the growing tendency toward "bigness" in business and industry, feelings of being "trapped" in a job, unemployment, unfavorable attitudes toward present job, and geographic mobility in order to advance or to retain present job.

14. Among the common and most serious marital hazards in middle age are the necessity for making role changes, boredom (especially on the part of women), inability to establish satisfactory relationships with the spouse as a person, opposition to a child's marriage, sexual maladjustments, care of an elderly parent, loss of a spouse, and remarriage.

15. The success with which men and women adjust to middle age can be assessed by four criteria: achievements, emotional states, the effects of the physical and psychological changes on personality, and the degree of satisfaction or happiness the middle-aged person experiences.

Bibliography

1. Anman, F. A. Retraining: How much of an answer to technological unemployment? *Personnel Journal*, 1962, **41**, 505–507.
2. Barmash, I. New jobs for old hands. *The New York Times,* May 29, 1977.
3. Becker, H. S. Personal changes in adult life. In B. L. Neugarten (Ed.). *Middle age and aging: A reader in social psychology.* Chicago: University of Chicago Press, 1968. Pp.148–156.
4. Belbin, E., and R. M. Belbin. New careers in middle age. In B. L. Neugarten (Ed.). *Middle age and aging: A reader in social psychology.* Chicago: University of Chicago Press, 1968. Pp. 341–346.
5. Bernard, J. No news but new ideas. In P. Bohannon (Ed.). *Divorce and after.* Garden City, N.Y.: Doubleday, 1970. Pp. 3–29.
6. Billig, O., and R. W. Adams, Emotional conflicts of the middle-aged man. In C. B. Vedder (Ed.). *Problems of the middle-aged.* Springfield, Ill.: Charles C Thomas, 1965. Pp. 121–133.
7. Bischof, L. J. *Adult psychology.* (2nd ed.) New York: Harper & Row, 1976.
8. Bohannon, P. (Ed.). *Divorce and after.* Garden City, N.Y.: Doubleday, 1970.
9. Brozan, N. Middle age needn't be like dark ages. *The New York Times,* March 29, 1973.
10. Burr, W. R. Satisfaction with various aspects of marriage over the life cycle: A random middle-class sample. *Journal of Marriage & the Family,* 1970, **32**, 29–37.
11. Cameron, P. Stereotypes about generational fun and happiness vs. self-appraised fun and happiness. *Gerontologist,* 1972, **12**, 120–129, 190.
12. Campbell, A. The American way of mating: Marriage si; Children only maybe. *Psychology Today,* 1975, **8**(12), 37–43.
13. Cavan, R. S. Family tensions between the old and middle-aged. In C. B. Vedder (Ed.). *Problems of the middle-aged.* Springfield, Ill.: Charles C Thomas, 1965. Pp. 82–91.
14. Cherlin, A. Remarriage as an incomplete institution. *American Journal of Sociology,* 1978, **84**, 634–650.
15. Christrup, H. A. preretirement program that works. *Journal of Home Economics,* 1973, **65**(4), 20–22.
16. Clavan, S. The impact of social class and social trends on the role of grandparent. *Family Coordinator,* 1978, **27**, 351–357.
17. Clayton, P. J., J. A. Halikas, and W. L. Maurice. The depression of widowhood. *British Journal of Psychiatry,* 1972, **120**, 71–77.
18. Cleveland, M. Sex in marriage: At 40 and beyond. *Family Coordinator,* 1976, **25**, 233–240.
19. Cleveland, W. P., and D. T. Gianturco. Remarriage probability after widowhood: A retrospective method. *Journal of Gerontology,* 1976, **31**, 99–103.
20. Conroy, R. C. Widows and widowhood. *New York State Journal of Medicine,* 1977, **77**, 357–360.
21. Crisp, A. T., and R. G. Priest. Psychoneurotic profiles in middle age. *British Journal of Psychiatry,* 1971, **119**, 385–392.
22. Dame, N. G., G. H. Finck, B. S. Reiner, and B. O. Smith. The effect on the marital relationship of the wife's search for identity. *Family Coordinator,* 1965, **14**, 133–136.
23. Dennis, W. Creative productivity between the ages of 20 and 80 years. In D. C. Charles and W. R. Looft (Eds.). *Readings in*

psychological development through life. New York: Holt, 1973. Pp. 283–295.

24. Desmond, T. C. America's unknown middle-agers. *The New York Times,* July 29, 1958.

25. Deutscher, I. The quality of postparental life. In B. L. Neugarten (Ed.). *Middle age and aging: A reader in social psychology.* Chicago: Univesity of Chicago Press, 1968. Pp. 263–268.

26. Dullea, G. More women risk the big switch: Changing careers in mid-life. *The New York Times,* July 11, 1977.

27. Erikson, E. H. Identity and the life cycle: Selected papers. *Psychological Issues Monographs,* Vol. 1, No. 1. New York: International Universities Press, 1967.

28. Evans, O. They got their degrees—often the hard way—and then what? *The New York Times,* July 16, 1972.

29. Fengler, A. P. Attitudinal orientations of wives toward their husbands' retirement. *International Journal of Aging & Human Development,* 1975, **6**, 139–152.

30. Franzblau, R. N. *The middle generation.* New York: Holt, 1971.

31. Frenkel-Brunswik, E. Adjustments and reorientation in the course of the life span. In B. L. Neugarten (Ed.). *Middle age and aging: A reader in social psychology.* Chicago: University of Chicago Press, 1968. Pp. 77–84.

32. Fried, B. *The middle-age crisis.* New York: Harper & Row, 1967.

33. Gebhard, P. Postmarital coitus among widows and divorcees. In P. Bohannon (Ed.). *Divorce and after.* Garden City, N.Y.: Doubleday, 1970. Pp. 89–106.

34. Glenn, N. D. Psychological well-being in the postparental stage: Some evidence from national surveys. *Journal of Marriage & the Family,* 1975, **37**, 105–110.

35. Gorney, S., and C. Cox. *How women can achieve fulfillment after forty.* New York: Dial Press, 1973.

36. Harkins, E. B. Effect of empty nest transition on self-report of psychological and physical well-being. *Journal of Marriage & the Family,* 1978, **40**, 549–556.

37. Harper's Bazaar article. Childbirth after 40: New freedom from risk. *Harper's Bazaar,* Aug. 1973. Pp. 32, 57, 86.

38. Harvey, C. D., and H. M. Bahr. Widowhood, morale, and affiliation. *Journal of Marriage & the Family,* 1974, **36**, 97–106.

39. Hayes, M. P., and N. Stinnett. Life satisfactions of middle-aged husbands and wives. *Journal of Home Economics,* 1971, **63**, 669–674.

40. Heddesheimer, J. Multiple motivations for mid-career changes. *Personnel & Guidance Journal,* 1976, **55**, 109–111.

41. Hirsch, J. Suicide. *Mental Hygiene, N.Y.,* 1959, **43**, 516–525.

42. Horn, J. Happiness is—an empty nest. *Psychology Today,* 1976, **9**(8), 22, 100.

43. Johnson, W. M. *The years after forty.* College Park, Md.: McGrath Publishing, 1970.

44. Kahana, E., and B. Kahana. Theoretical and research perspectives on grandparenthood. *Aging & Human Development,* 1971, **2**, 261–268.

45. Kalish, R. A. Of children and grandfathers: A speculative study on dependency. *Gerontologist,* 1967, **7**, 65–69.

46. Kalt, N. C., and M. H. Kohn. Pre-retirement counseling: Characteristics of programs and preferences of retirees. *Gerontologist,* 1975, **15**, 179–181.

47. Kerckhoff, R. K. Marriage and middle age. *Family Coordinator,* 1976, **25**, 5–11.

48. Kimmel, D. C. *Adulthood and aging: An interdisciplinary developmental view.* New York: Wiley, 1974.

49. Lee, G. R. Age at marriage and marital satisfaction: A multivariate analysis with implications for marital stability. *Journal of Marriage & the Family,* 1977, **39**, 493–504.

50. LeShan, E. *The wonderful crisis of middle age.* New York: McKay, 1973.

51. Levin, S. On widowhood: Discussion. *Journal of Geriatric Psychiatry,* 1975, **8**, 57–59.

52. Levine, A. J. A sound approach to middle age. In C. B. Vedder (Ed.). *Problems of the middle-aged.* Springfield, Ill.: Charles C Thomas, 1965. Pp. 40–43.

53. Lopata, H. Z. The life cycle of the social role of the housewife. *Sociology & Social Research,* 1966, **51**, 5–22.

54. Lopata, H. Z. On widowhood: Grief, work, and identity reconstruction. *Journal of Geriatric Psychiatry,* 1975, **8**, 41–55.

55. Lowenthal, M. F., and D. Chirboga. Transition to the empty nest: Crisis, challenge, or relief? *Archives of General Psychiatry,* 1972, **28**, 8–14.

56. Manion, U. V. Preretirement counseling: The need for a new approach. *Personnel & Guidance Journal,* 1976, **55**, 119–121.

57. Marmor, J. Crisis of middle age. *American Journal of Orthopsychiatry,* 1967, **37**, 336–337.

58. Masters, W. H., and V. E. Johnson. *Human sexual response.* Boston: Little, Brown, 1966.

59. McConnell, A., and B. Anderson. *Smile after 50: How to have the time of your life.* New York: McGraw-Hill, 1978.

60. McDaniels, C. Leisure and career development in mid-life: A rationale. *Vocational Guidance Quarterly,* 1977, **25**, 344–350.

61. McKain, W. C. A new look at older marriage. *Family Coordinator,* 1972, **21**, 61–69.

62. Mead, M. Grandparents as educators. *Teachers College Record,* 1974, **76**, 240–249.

63. Meltzer, H. Attitudes of workers before and after 40. *Geriatrics,* 1965, **20**, 425–432.

64. Menk, C. W. What are the chances of being fired? *The New York Times,* June 18, 1978.

65. Miller, A. A. Reaction of friends to divorce. In P. Bohannon (Ed.). *Divorce and after.* Garden City, N.Y.: Doubleday, 1970. Pp. 63–86.

66. Monk, A. Factors in the preparation for retirement by middle-aged adults. *Gerontologist,* 1971, **11**, 348–351.

67. Montagu, A. Don't be adultish. *Psychology Today,* 1977, **11**(3), 46–50, 55.

68. Morgan, L. A. A re-examination of widowhood and morale. *Journal of Gerontology,* 1976, **31**, 687–695.

69. Morgan, M. I. The middle life and the aging family. *Family Coordinator,* 1969, **18**, 296–298.

70. Neugarten, B. L., and D. C. Garra. Attitudes of middle-aged persons toward growing older. In C. B. Vedder (Ed.). *Problems of the middle-aged.* Springfield, Ill.: Charles C Thomas, 1965. Pp.12–17.

71. Neugarten, B. L., R. J. Havighurst, and S. S. Tobin. Personality and patterns of aging. In B. L. Neugarten (Ed.). *Middle age and aging: A reader in social psychology.* Chicago, Ill.: University of Chicago Press, 1968. Pp. 173–177.

72. Neugarten, B. L., and K. K. Weinstein. The changing American grandparent. *Journal of Marriage & the Family,* 1964, **26**, 199–204.

73. New York Times article. Divorce rise laid to "20-year-slump." *The New York Times*, Dec. 9, 1970.

74. Newsweek article. The divorced women—American style. *Newsweek*, Feb. 13, 1967, 64–70.

75. Newsweek article. Living together. *Newsweek*, Aug. 1, 1977, 46–50.

76. Oden, M. H. The fulfillment of promise: 40-year follow-up of the Terman Gifted Group. *Genetic Psychology Monographs*, 1968, **77**, 3–93.

77. Ogle, J. Sex after forty. *Harper's Bazaar*, Aug. 1973, 86–87.

78. Packard, V. *The pyramid climbers.* New York: McGraw-Hill, 1962.

79. Parker, E. *The seven ages of woman.* Baltimore, Md.: Johns Hopkins Press, 1960.

80. Parkes, C. M. The first year of bereavement: A longitudinal study of the reactions of London widows to the death of their husbands. *Psychiatry*, 1970, **33**, 444–476.

81. Pfeiffer, E., A. Verwoerdt, and G. C. Davis. Sexual behavior in middle life. *American Journal of Psychiatry*, 1972, **128**, 1262–1267.

82. Pieper, E. Grandparents can help. *The Exceptional Parent*, 1976, **6**(2), 6–10.

83. Pineo, P. C. Disenchantment in the later years of marriage. In B. L. Neugarten (Ed.). *Middle age and aging: A reader in social psychology.* Chicago: University of Chicago Press, 1968. Pp. 258–262.

84. Pocs, O., A. Godow, W. L. Tolone, and R. H. Walsh. Is there sex after 40? *Psychology Today*, 1977, **11**(1), 54–56, 87.

85. Powers, E. A. The effect of the wife's employment on household tasks among postparental couples: A research note. *Aging & Human Development*, 1971, **2**, 284–287.

86. *Report of the President's Council on Aging.* Washington, D.C.: U.S. Government Printing Office, 1961.

87. Rickles, N. K. The discarded generation: The woman past fifty. *Geriatrics*, 1968, **23**, 112–116.

88. Rico-Venasco, J. and L. Mynko. Suicide and marital status: A changing relationship. *Journal of Marriage & the Family*, 1973, **35**, 239–244.

89. Robertson, J. F. Grandmotherhood: A study of role conceptions. *Journal of Marriage & the Family*, 1977, **39**, 165–174.

90. Rollin, B. The American way of marriage: Remarriage. *Look*, 1971, **35**, 62, 64–67.

91. Rollins, B. C., and H. Feldman. Marital satisfaction over the family life cycle. *Journal of Marriage & the Family*, 1970, **32**, 20–28.

92. Rose, A. M. Factors associated with the life satisfaction of middle-class, middle-aged persons. In C. B. Vedder (Ed.). *Problems of the middle-aged.* Springfield, Ill.: Charles C Thomas, 1965. Pp. 59–67.

93. Rose, V. L., and S. Price-Bonham. Divorce adjustment: A woman's problem? *Family Coordinator*, 1973, **22**, 291–297.

94. Ross, A. M., and J. N. Ross. Employment problems of older workers. In C. B. Vedder (Ed.). *Problems of the middle-aged.* Springfield, Ill.: Charles C Thomas, 1965. Pp. 68–74.

95. Saleh, S. D., and J. L. Otis. Age and level of job satisfaction. *Personnel Psychology*, 1964, **17**, 425–430.

96. Schlesinger, B. Remarriage: An inventory of findings. *Family Coordinator*, 1968, **17**, 248–250.

97. Scott, R., and L. Holt. The new wave: A college responds to women returnees. *Phi Delta Kappan*, 1976, **58**, 338–339.

98. Silverman, P. R. The widow as a caregiver in a program of preventive intervention with other widows. *Mental Hygiene, N. Y.*, 1970, **54**, 540–547.

99. Silverman, P. R., and A. Cooperband. On widowhood: Material help and the elderly widow. *Journal of Geriatric Psychiatry*, 1975, **8**, 9–27.

100. Somerville, R. M. The future of family relationships in the middle and older years: Clues in fiction. *Family Coordinator*, 1972, **21**, 487–498.

101. Spence, D., and T. Lonner. The "empty nest": A transition within motherhood. *Family Coordinator*, 1971, **20**, 369–375.

102. Sussman, M. B., and L. Burchinal. Kin family networks: Unheralded structure in current conceptualization of family functioning. In B. L. Neugarten (Ed.). *Middle age and aging: A reader in social psychology.* Chicago: University of Chicago Press, 1968. Pp. 247–254.

103. Thomas, L. E. Why study mid-life career change? *Vocational Guidance Quarterly*, 1975, **24**, 37–40.

104. Thompson, L. J. Stress and middle life from the psychiatrist's viewpoint. In C. B. Vedder (Ed.). *Problems of the middle-aged.* Springfield, Ill.: Charles C Thomas, 1965. Pp. 116–120.

105. Thurnher, M. Goals, values, and life evaluations at the preretirement stage. *Journal of Gerontology*, 1974, **29**, 85–96.

106. Time magazine article. The command generation. *Time*, July 29, 1966, 50–54.

107. Time magazine article. On suicide. *Time*, Nov. 25, 1966, 48–49.

108. Troll, L. E. *Early and middle adulthood: The best is yet to be—maybe.* Monterey, Calif.: Brooks/Cole, 1975.

109. Trost, J. Attitudes toward and occurrence of cohabitation without marriage. *Journal of Marriage & the Family*, 1978, **40**, 393–400.

110. Ullmann, C. A. Preretirement planning: Does it prevent postretirement shock? *Personnel & Guidance Journal*, 1976, **55**, 115–118.

111. U. S. News & World Report article. When nation will have 113 million workers. *U. S. News & World Report*, April 30, 1973, 60–62.

112. Vedder, C. B. (Ed.). *Problems of the middle-aged.* Springfield, Ill.: Charles C Thomas, 1965.

113. Wade, B. Freshman have advisers but who helps the parent emeritus? *The New York Times*, Sept. 24, 1972.

114. Wallin, P., and A. L. Clark. A study of orgasm as a condition of women's enjoyment of coitus in the middle years of marriage. *Human Biology*, 1963, **35**, 131–139.

115. Walters, P. Middle-aged, jobless, despairing. *The New York Times*, March 27, 1977.

116. Whitman, H. Let go of the dream. In C. B. Vedder (Ed.). *Problems of the middle-aged.* Springfield, Ill.: Charles C Thomas, 1965. Pp. 199–202.

117. Williams, R. Alimony: A short good-bye. *Psychology Today*, 1977, **11**(2), 71–77, 92.

118. Wright, J. D., and R. F. Hamilton. Satisfaction and age: Some evidence for the "job change" hypothesis. *Social Forces*, 1978, **56**, 1140–1158.

119. Yee, W., and M. D. Van Arsdol. Residential mobility, age, and the life cycle. *Journal of Gerontology*, 1977, **32**, 211–221.

120. Zatlin, C. E., M. Storandt, and J. Botwinick. Personality and values of women continuing their education after thirty-five years. *Journal of Gerontology*, 1973, **28**, 216–221.

CHAPTER THIRTEEN
Old Age: Personal and Social Adjustments

After reading this chapter, you should be able to:

- Explain why the period of old age is subdivided into two periods, the characteristics of each, and social attitudes regarding both periods.
- Describe how most of the developmental tasks of old age relate more to the individual's personal life than to the lives of others.
- Recognize the major adjustments that the elderly must make to physical, motor, and psychological changes, and the effects these changes have on their attitudes and behavior.
- Give reasons why there are changes in interests in old age, and list the areas of interest in which these changes are most pronounced, and the forms they take.
- Discuss the interest in and concern about death that are characteristic of the elderly in the American culture of today.
- Identify and explain the potential physical hazards of old age.
- Evaluate the serious effects on personal and social adjustments of the common psychological hazards of old age.

Old age is the closing period in the life span. It is a period when people "move away" from previous, more desirable periods—or times of "usefulness." As people move away from the earlier periods of their lives, they often look back on them, usually regretfully, and tend to live in the present, ignoring the future as much as possible (72).

Age sixty is usually considered the dividing line between middle and old age. However, it is recognized that chronological age is a poor criterion to use in marking off the beginning of old age because there are such marked differences among individuals in the age at which aging actually begins.

Because of better living conditions and better health care, most men and women today do not show the mental and physical signs of aging until the mid-sixties or even the early seventies. For that reason, there is a gradual trend toward using sixty-five—the age of retirement in many businesses—to mark the beginning of old age.

The last stage in the life span is frequently subdivided into *early old age,* which extends from age sixty to age seventy, and *advanced old age,* which begins at seventy and extends to the end of life. People during the sixties are usually referred to as "elderly"—meaning somewhat old or advanced beyond middle age—and "old" after they reach the age of seventy—meaning, according to standard dictionaries, advanced far in years of life and having lost the vigor of youth.

CHARACTERISTICS OF OLD AGE

Like every other period in the life span, old age is characterized by certain physical and psychological changes. The effects of these changes determine, to a large extent, whether elderly men and women will make good or poor personal and social adjustments. The characteristics of old age, however, are far more likely to lead to poor adjustments than to good and to unhappiness rather than to happiness. That is why old age is even more dreaded in the American culture of today than middle age.

Old Age Is a Period of Decline

As has been stressed repeatedly, people are never static. Instead, they constantly change. During the early part of life the changes are evolutional in

that they lead to maturity of structure and functioning. In the latter part of life, by contrast, they are mainly involutional, involving a regression to earlier stages. These changes are the natural accompaniment of what is commonly known as "aging." They affect physical as well as mental structures and functionings.

The period during old age when physical and mental decline is slow and gradual and when compensations can be made for these declines is known as *senescence*—a time of growing old or of aging (5). People may become senescent in their fifties or not until their early or late sixties, depending upon the rate of physical and mental decline.

The term "senility" is used to refer to the period during old age when a more or less complete physical breakdown takes place and when there is mental disorganization. The individual who becomes eccentric, careless, absentminded, socially withdrawn, and poorly adjusted is usually described as "senile." Senility may come as early as the fifties, or it may never occur because the individual dies before deterioration sets in.

Decline comes partly from physical and partly from psychological factors. The *physical* cause of decline is a change in the body cells due not to a specific disease but to the aging process. Decline may also have *psychological* causes. Unfavorable attitudes toward oneself, other people, work, and life in general can lead to senility, just as changes in the brain tissue can. Individuals who have no sustaining interests after retirement are likely to become depressed and disorganized. As a result, they go downhill both physically and mentally and may soon die. How the individual copes with the strains and stresses of living will also affect the rate of decline.

Motivation likewise plays a very important role in decline. The individual who has little motivation to learn new things or to keep up to date in appearance, attitudes, or patterns of behavior will deteriorate much faster than one whose motivation to ward off aging is stronger. The new leisure time, which comes with retirement or with the lessening of household responsibilities, often brings boredom which lowers the individual's motivation.

There Are Individual Differences in the Effects of Aging

Individual differences in the effects of aging have been recognized for many centuries. Cicero, for example, in his *De Senectute,* stressed this in his reference to the popular belief that aging makes people difficult to live with. According to him, "As it is not every wine, so it is not every disposition that grows sour with age" (105).

Today, even more than in the past, it is recognized that aging affects different people differently. Thus it is impossible to classify anyone as a "typically" old person or any trait as "typical" of old age. People age differently because they have different hereditary endowments, different socioeconomic and educational backgrounds, and different patterns of living (96,98,99). These differences are apparent among members of the same sex, but they are even more apparent when men and women are compared because aging takes place at different rates for the two sexes (10,111).

As differences increase with age, they predispose individuals to react differently to the same situation. For example, some men think of retirement as a blessing, while others regard it as a curse (3,13).

As a general rule, physical aging precedes mental aging, though sometimes the reverse is true, especially when the individual is concerned about growing old and lets go mentally when the first signs of physical aging appear (107).

Old Age Is Judged by Different Criteria

Because the meaning of age is vague and undefined to young children, they tend to judge age in terms of physical appearance and activities. To them, children are smaller than adults and must be cared for while adults are big and can take care of themselves. Old people have white hair and no longer go to work every day (135). See Figure 13-1.

By the time children reach adolescence, they judge old age in much the same way as adults do, namely in terms of the person's appearance and what the person can and cannot do. Knowing that these are the two most common criteria used to judge their ages, many elderly people do all they can to camouflage the telltale physical signs of aging by wearing clothes like those worn by younger people, and trying to keep up a pace that often overtaxes their strength and energy. This is their attempt to create the illusion that they are not yet elderly or old.

There Are Many Stereotypes of Old People

In the American culture of today, there are many stereotypes of old people and many traditional

2-27

1975, The Register and Tribune Syndicate

"He's retired. That means he graduated from work."

FIGURE 13-1 One of the criteria children use in judging an adult's age is what the person does. (Bil Keane. "The Family Circus." Register and Tribune Syndicate, February 27, 1975. Used by permission.)

beliefs about their physical and mental capacities. These stereotypes and traditional beliefs have come from many sources, the four most common of which are as follows:

First, folklore and fairy tales, handed down from one generation to another, tend to depict the aged unfavorably. Although it is true that some of these picture old people as kindly and understanding, many depict them as wicked and cruel, especially women.

Second, the elderly are often characterized unfavorably in different forms of the mass media. Shakespeare, for example, made 132 references to the physical and behavioral changes accompanying old age (150). In describing senility, he wrote:

Last scene of all,
That ends this strange eventful history,
Is second childishness, and mere oblivion,
Sans teeth, sans eyes, sans taste, sans everything.

Shakespeare also wrote of the elderly person's appearance:

His youthful hose, well saved, a world too wide
For his shrunk shank; and his manly voice,

Turning again toward childish treble, pipes
And whistles in his sound.

One of the few cheerful literary references to old age is provided by Browning:

Grow old along with me!
The best is yet to be,
The last of life, for which the first was made.

Images of the elderly in poetry today likewise tend to be negative. Sohngen and Smith have concluded, from their study of modern poetry, that the emphasis is on physical, social, and emotional losses. As they put it, "Images of age found in the most readily available poems are similar to the negative stereotypes of popular culture (141).

Fiction has been no more favorable to the elderly than poetry. The tendency there, as in poetry, is to depict the elderly in negative terms (10,140). However, there is some evidence that, in recent years, fiction for children has been portraying the aged in a less negative way than in the past (25).

Television has made its contribution to stereotypes of the elderly. Because of the constant emphasis on the beauty and strength of youth, the elderly are made to seem unattractive and ineffectual by comparison. While television does not directly emphasize the negative aspects of age, indirectly it does so by its unfavorable comparisons with the young (116).

Third, jokes and different forms of humor contribute to the unfavorable stereotypes of the elderly. For the most part, the foolishness rather than the wisdom of age is emphasized. This, understandably, leads to negative attitudes that reinforce the already-existing unfavorable stereotypes (49,124,152).

Fourth, stereotypes have been reinforced by scientific studies of the aged. Because the subjects in most of these studies, as was emphasized earlier, have been persons in institutions whose physical and mental decline was primarily responsible for their institutionalization, it is not surprising that the results of these studies support the popular stereotype. And yet studies of representative samplings of noninstitutionalized elderly people have provided little evidence to justify this stereotype.

The common stereotype of the aged is that of men and women who are worn out physically and mentally, who are unproductive, accident-prone, crotchety and hard to live with, and who, because their days of usefulness are over, should be pushed

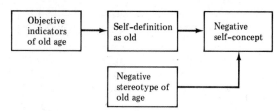

FIGURE 13-2 Unfavorable attitudes toward personal aging combined with unfavorable social attitudes toward aging result in a negative self-concept. (Adapted from T. H. Brubaker and E. A. Powers. The stereotype of "old": A review and alternative approach. *Journal of Gerontology*, 1976, **31**, 441–447. Used by permission.)

aside to make way for younger people. According to this stereotype, "Young is beautiful and old is ugly," as Berry had explained (12). This unfavorable stereotype, it should be apparent, makes it difficult to see aging as anything but a negative phase in the life span (32).

Equally important, the concepts people have of their own old age, built up in the early years of life and based more on cultural stereotypes than on personal experiences with the elderly, affect their attitudes not only toward elderly people but also toward themselves as they grow older. Because these effects are negative, it contributes to their dread of old age and to a negative self-concept. Figure 13-2 shows how this is done.

Social Attitudes toward Old Age

Stereotypes about old age have a pronounced influence on social attitudes toward both old age and old people. And because most stereotypes are unfavorable, social attitudes likewise tend to be unfavorable. As Bennett has pointed out, "It is hard to glamorize aging or give it sex appeal" under such conditions (9).

How unfavorable social attitudes are has been emphasized by a nationwide survey of social images of the elderly in different areas of behavior as compared with self-images of the elderly. Figure 13-3, based on the results of this survey, emphasizes the difference between the social image of the elderly—the image on which social attitudes are based—and the images the elderly have of themselves—self-images (15). Note that, for the most part, the elderly have a more favorable image of themselves than the social group has of them.

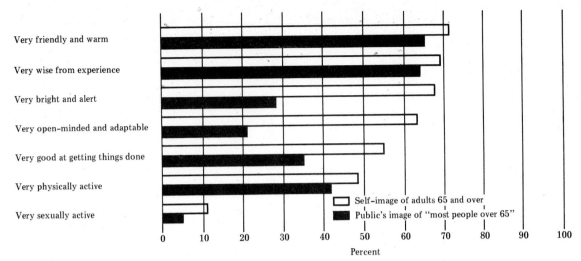

Self-image of adults 65 and over

Public's image of "most people over 65"

FIGURE 13-3 A comparison of the self-images and the public's images of elderly people. (Adapted from E. V. Beverley. The beginning of wisdom about aging. *Geriatrics*, 1975, **30**(7), 116–119, 122–123, 127–128. Used by permission.)

The significance of unfavorable social attitudes toward the elderly is that it affects the way elderly people are treated. Instead of the reverence and respect for the elderly, characteristic of many cultures, social attitudes in America result in making the elderly feel that they are no longer useful to the social group and, hence, are more of a nuisance than an asset (10,27,58,85).

Unfavorable social attitudes toward the elderly are fairly universal in the American culture today, but they tend to be stronger among certain racial groups and social classes than among others. People who come from countries where respect for the elderly is customary usually treat elderly people with more consideration and respect than do those whose families have lived in America for several generations and who have absorbed the prevailing American social attitude toward the elderly. Members of the upper social classes, knowing that the elderly hold the purse strings to family fortunes, tend to treat elderly members of their social group with more respect than do those of the middle or lower classes, who often must be financially responsible for elderly family members and, as a result, resent them (146).

The Elderly Have a Minority-Group Status

In spite of the fact that the number of old people in America today is growing, they occupy a min-ority-group status—a status that excludes them to some extent from interaction with other groups in the population and which gives them little or no power. This minority-group status is primarily the result of the unfavorable social attitudes toward the aged that have been fostered by the unfavorable stereotypes of them.

This "second-class citizenship" puts the elderly on the defensive and has a marked effect on their personal and social adjustments. It makes the latter years of life far from "golden" for most people, and it causes them to be victimized by some members of the majority group. As Langer has stressed (103):

If the aged are victimized in general, they are also victimized in particular. Their illness, loneliness, and terrors make the aged easy prey to a growing army of charlatans in whom their vulnerability arouses instincts not of sympathy but of greed. An ingenious array of frauds, from quack medicines to uninhabitable homesites, and from dancing lessons to fake furnace repairs has been revealed.

The elderly in America today are not only taken advantage of by unscrupulous business people but they are also the victims of crimes ranging from purse snatching to rape. This is especially true of elderly women who create the impression that they are not strong or agile enough to defend themselves. As a result of the crimes against them, many elderly people hesitate to leave their homes or to do so without a younger person along to protect them (65).

Aging Requires Role Changes

Just as middle-aged people must learn to play new roles, so must the elderly. Refer to Figure 10-4 for a graphic illustration of the role changes that must be made in old age. In the American culture of today, where efficiency, strength, speed, and physical attractiveness are highly valued, elderly people are often regarded as useless. Because they cannot compete with young people in the areas where highly valued traits are needed, the social attitude toward them is unfavorable.

Furthermore, it is expected that old people will play a decreasingly less active role in social and community affairs, as well as in the business and professional worlds. As a result, there is a marked reduction

Feeling useless and unwanted, many elderly people develop feelings of inferiority and resentment—feelings that are not conducive to good personal and social adjustments. (Photo by Erika.)

in the number of roles the elderly person is able to play, and there are changes in some of the remaining roles. While these changes are due in part to the individual's preferences, they are due mainly to social pressures.

Because of unfavorable social attitudes, few rewards are associated with old-age roles, no matter how successfully they are carried out. Feeling useless and unwanted, elderly people develop feelings of inferiority and resentment—feelings that are not conducive to good personal or social adjustments. As Busse and Pfeiffer have pointed out, "It is difficult to maintain a positive identity when one's usual props for such an identity, such as one's social and occupational roles, have been taken away" (36).

Poor Adjustment is Characteristic of Old Age

Because of the unfavorable social attitudes toward the elderly that are reflected in the way the social group treats them, it is not surprising that many elderly people develop unfavorable self-concepts. These tend to be expressed in maladjustive behavior of different degrees of severity (111). Those who have a history of poor adjustments tend to become more maladjusted as age progresses than those whose earlier personal and social adjustments were more favorable (149).

Elderly people tend, as a group, to be more subject to maladjustments than those who are younger. Butler has pointed out (38).

The elderly are disproportionately subject to emotional and mental problems. The incidence of psychopathology rises with age. Functional disorders—notably depressions and paranoid states—increase steadily with each decade, as do organic brain diseases after age 60 . . . Suicide also increases with age, and the rate of suicide is highest in elderly white men.

Explaining why this is so, Butler gives the following reasons: increased loss of status in a society dominated by the young, a desire to protect their finances for their wives, and a desire to escape partial helplessness or pain (38).

The Desire for Rejuvenation Is Widespread in Old Age

The minority-group status accorded to most elderly persons has naturally given rise to a desire to re-

FIGURE 13-4 Many older women regard beauty aids as a way to regain their youthful attractiveness. (Dan Tobin. "The Little Woman." King Features Syndicate, Oct. 22, 1973. Used by permission.)

"I keep hoping Herbert will look at me and say, 'How beautiful,' but all he ever says is 'how much?'"

main young as long as possible and to be rejuvenated when the signs of aging appear. See Figure 13-4. Among the ancients, elixirs or potions, alchemy, witchcraft, and sorcery were used to achieve these ends. Later, there were searches for "fountains of youth" that were believed to have the magical powers of turning the aged into young men and women. As Sue commented (144):

Today many people are still looking for ways to slow down aging by resorting to food fads or the extravagent use of vitamins. Others have undergone face lifts to remove the telltale signs of aging and have used cosmetic preparations to cover up wrinkles. All these procedures are reflections of humankind's historic preoccupation with youth. These "cures" may not differ so much from inhaling the breath of young girls or joining Ponce de Leon's historic search for the fountain of youth.

Today, medicine is taking over the task of trying to ward off old age. Because a deficiency of sex hormones plays such an important role in aging, attempts

have been made to rejuvenate aging people by means of sex-hormone therapy, such as Gerovital, the so-called "youth drug" (97). However, medical science is questioning the safety of this technique, especially estrogen for women, which may be a cause of uterine cancer.

Recent experiments have shown that it is impossible to make aging people young again (35, 62). The administration of hormones can, however, build up an aging person's health and vigor and thus slow down the rate of aging.

DEVELOPMENTAL TASKS OF OLD AGE

For the most part, the developmental tasks of old age relate more to the individual's personal life than to the lives of others. See page 10 for a list of these tasks (75). Old people are expected to adjust to decreasing strength and gradually failing health. This often means marked revisions in the roles they have played in the home and outside. They are also expected to find activities to replace the work that consumed a major part of their time when they were younger.

Meeting social and civic obligations is difficult for many older people as their health fails and as their income is reduced by retirement. As a result, they are often forced to become socially inactive. Failing health and reduced income likewise require the establishment of new living arrangements which are often radically different from those of earlier years.

Sooner or later, most old people must adjust to the death of a spouse. This is far more likely to be a problem for women than for men. Because the death of a spouse often means reduced income and hazards associated with living alone, it may necessitate changes in living arrangements.

As grown children become increasingly involved in their own vocational and family affairs, the elderly can count less and less on their companionship. This means that they must establish affiliations with members of their own age group if they are to avoid the loneliness that plagues the elderly when their contacts with the larger social group are cut off because of retirement and because they gradually reduce their contacts with community organizations.

Although most older people learned during childhood and adolescence to get along with their age-mates successfully, during most of their adult

One of the problems unique to old age is making new friends to replace those who have died, moved away, or are invalided. Homes for the elderly offer excellent opportunities to solve this problem. (David Strickeler from Monkmeyer.)

lives they have had to be affiliated with individuals of all age groups. Regressing to this earlier pattern of social life is often difficult because it means that the individual must now become affiliated with a group that is largely rejected by society. Having known since childhood and adolescence that affiliation with a rejected group brings little prestige, old people have little motivation to become involved with such a group.

Certain problems of adjustment resulting from these developmental tasks are unique to old age. The most common of these are given in Box 13-1.

ADJUSTMENT TO PHYSICAL CHANGES IN OLD AGE

While it is unquestionably true that physical changes do occur with aging and that these changes are, for the most part, in the direction of deterioration, individual differences are so marked that no two people of the same age are necessarily at the same state of deterioration. Furthermore, within the same individual there are variations in the rate of aging of different parts of the body. The organs of reproduction, for example, age sooner than the other organs.

The major physical changes that occur in old age are described below and an attempt is made to point out why they may be regarded as "major" changes.

Changes in Appearance

Bischof has said that aging means "proceeding from bifocals to trifocals and dentures to death" (21). This suggests that the most obvious signs of aging are changes in the face. Even though women can use cosmetics to cover up some of the telltale signs of aging on the face, many cannot be camouflaged, as changes in other areas of the body can.

The hands also give away a person's age. Like the face, they change more with aging than the rest of the body, and these changes are also less subject to camouflage.

Box 13-2 gives the changes in appearance that normally occur during old age. While not all people show all these signs of aging, nor do all of them appear simultaneously, sooner or later they will become apparent if the individual lives long enough.

Internal Changes

Although internal changes are not as readily observable as external ones, they are nevertheless as pronounced and as widespread. Changes in the *skeleton* are due to hardening of the bones, deposits of mineral salts, and modifications of the internal structure of the bones. As a result of these changes, the bones become brittle and are subject to fractures and breaks, which are increasingly slow to heal as age progresses.

Changes in the *nervous system* are especially marked in the case of the brain. In old age, there is a loss in brain weight, the lateral ventricles tend to be dilated, and the ribbon of cortical tissue is narrowed (138).

Central nervous system changes come early in the aging period; they are reflected first in a decrease in the speed of learning and later in a decline in intellectual powers (138).

The *viscera* go through a marked transformation with advancing age. Atrophy is particularly marked in the spleen, liver, testes, heart, lungs, pancreas, and kidneys. Perhaps the most marked change of all is in the heart. In the early years of life, the heart is positioned more nearly in the center of the chest than it is in advanced age. It increases in bulk with age and continues to grow even after the body has ceased to do so. Therefore, the ratio of heart weight to body weight decreases gradually with age. As a result of an increase in fibrous tissue from deposits of fat and calcium and because of changes in the quality of the elastic tissue, the valves gradually become less soft and pliable. The gastrointestinal tract, the urinary tract, and the smooth-muscle organs generally are the least and last affected by aging.

Changes in Physiological Functions

There are also changes in the functioning of the organs. Regulation of body *temperature* is influenced by impairment of the regulatory devices. Old people cannot tolerate extremes of temperature, either hot or cold, because of the decreased vascularity of the skin. Reduced metabolic rate and lessened muscular vigor also make regulation of body temperature difficult.

When an old person becomes short of breath as a result of unusual exertion, it takes longer to restore *breathing* and *heart action* to normal than it did when younger. *Pulse rate* and *oxygen consumption* are more varied among the elderly than among younger people (41). Elevated *blood pressure* due to the increased rigidity of the walls of the aorta and central arteries is quite common in old age. Elderly people *excrete less urine,* and there is less creatine in their urine than in that of younger adults.

In old age, there is a decline in the amount of *sleep* needed and in the quality of sleep. By age sixty

or seventy the daily amount is reduced an hour or two, and brief periods of rest and sleep generally replace the longer periods of sleep of the younger person. Most old people suffer from insomnia, especially women.

Digestive changes are perhaps the most marked of the changes in the regulatory functions. Difficulties in eating are due partly to loss of teeth, which is fairly universal in old age, and also to the fact that the senses of smell and taste become less acute, making even the best food seem somewhat tasteless (1).

Gradual atrophy of the glands lining the walls of the stomach and bowels results in a decrease in the ferments and juices that aid in *digestion*. Thus the old person needs more fluids to lubricate and to dissolve food elements.

Strength and the *ability to work* decrease as muscular flabbiness and general weakness make it more difficult for old people to use their muscles. The ability to do strenuous work for a short period of time diminishes with age, while the ability to withstand a long, steady grind increases. It also takes the older person longer to recover from physical *fatigue* and from fatigue caused by continued mental work or nervous strain. As a result, most old people learn to cut down on any work that requires either strength or speed.

Sensory Changes

All the sense organs function less efficiently in old age than they did when the individual was younger. However, because sensory changes are slow and gradual in most cases, the individual has an opportunity to make adequate adjustments to them. Furthermore, glasses and hearing aids can almost completely compensate for impaired vision or hearing loss.

The eyes and ears, which are the most useful of all the sense organs, are also the most seriously affected by old age, although changes occur in the functioning of all the sense organs (11,114,125,139). Box 13-3 gives the changes in sensory functioning in old age.

Sexual Changes

The male climacteric comes later than the menopause and requires more time. Generally there is a decline in sexual potency during the sixties, which continues as age advances. Like the menopause, it is accompanied by a decline in gonadal

BOX 13-3

COMMON CHANGES IN SENSORY FUNCTIONING IN OLD AGE

Vision

There is a consistent decline in the ability to see at low levels of illumination and a decline in color sensitivity. Most old people suffer from presbyopia—farsightedness—which is due to the diminishing elasticity of the lenses.

Hearing

Old people lose the ability to hear extremely high tones, as a result of atrophy of the nerve and end organs in the basal turn of the cochlea, although most can hear tones below high C as well as younger people. Men tend to experience greater hearing loss in old age than women.

Taste

Marked changes in taste in old age are due to atrophy of the taste buds in the tongue and the inner surface of the cheeks. This atrophy becomes progressively more widespread with advancing age.

Smell

The sense of smell becomes less acute with age, partly as a result of the atrophy of cells in the nose and partly because of the increased hairiness of the nostrils.

Touch

As the skin becomes drier and harder, the sense of touch becomes less and less acute.

Sensitivity to Pain

The decline in the sensitivity to pain occurs at different rates in different parts of the body. There is a greater decline, for example, in the forehead and arms than in the legs.

functioning, which is responsible for the changes that occur during the climacteric (94,95).

The male climacteric has two common effects. First, there is a waning of the secondary sex characteristics. The voice, for example, becomes higher in pitch; the hair on the face and body becomes less luxuriant; and the heavy musculature gives way to a general flabbiness. In general, older men are less "masculine" than they were in the prime of life, just as women are less "feminine" after the menopausal changes have taken place.

Second, the male climacteric affects sexual functioning. However, even though sexual potency has declined, there is not necessarily a decline in sexual desire or in the ability to have intercourse. There is evidence that cultural influences are more important in the waning of the sex drive than physical changes. Cultural influences produce anxieties, which in turn affect attitudes toward sex and sexual behavior. Men and women often refrain from continuing sexual relations in old age or from remarrying because of unfavorable social attitudes toward sex among older people and because of doubts about their sexual capacities. To avoid having their pride hurt, men especially are likely to refrain from sexual activity as they grow older (109).

The strength of the sex drive in old age will depend largely upon the individual's general health and the kind of sexual adjustments made earlier in life. Those who made poor sexual adjustments when they were younger have been found to lose the sex drive earlier than those who made better adjustments (39,44,120).

CHANGES IN MOTOR ABILITIES IN OLD AGE

Most old people are aware that they move more slowly and are less well coordinated in movements than they were when they were younger. These changes in motor abilities are due partly to physical causes and partly to psychological causes.

The *physical causes* of changes in motor abilities include a decrease in strength and energy, which is a normal accompaniment of the physical changes that take place with age; lack of muscular tone; stiffness of the joints; and tremors of the hands, forearms, head, and lower jaw.

The *psychological causes* of changes in motor abilities stem from the awareness of "slipping" and from feelings of inferiority experienced when comparisons are made with younger people in terms of strength, speed, and skills. Emotional tension, stemming from these psychological causes, may hasten the changes in motor abilities or decrease the motivation to attempt to do what might still be done (43).

There is evidence that practice and activity will ward off, to some extent at least, decline in motor abilities. Those who continue to exercise are, on the whole, speedier and better coordinated than those who fail to do so (142,145). As Spirduso has claimed, from the results of a study in which the effects of practice were noted, "Certainly these results strongly support vigorous sports participation as a significant factor in retarding the onset of aging" (142). However, even under the most favorable conditions and with the strongest motivation, few individuals can hope that their motor abilities will continue at the same level they reached when they were younger.

While all motor abilities decline to some extent, some decline earlier and more rapidly than others. The changes in motor abilities that have the most important effect on personal and social adjustments are given in Box 13-4.

CHANGES IN MENTAL ABILITIES IN OLD AGE

As Baltes and Schaie have commented, "During the past few decades, the psychology of intellectual aging has been beset by a stereotype of decline" (6). Psychologists, from the results of their studies, have confirmed the popular belief that, with the trend toward decline in other areas, there would automatically be decline in mental abilities as well.

Today, these popular beliefs and stereotypes are not only being questioned by scientists but scientific attention is being directed toward improving techniques to measure the so-called mental decline that supposedly occurs with the onset of old age. These studies are also looking for individual differences in mental changes between people of the same chronological ages but with different intellectual abilities.

To date, evidence points to the fact that changes in mental abilities are less than has been believed and that there are marked individual differences in these changes. The popular stereotype of mental decline as one of the outstanding characteristics of old age is gradually being weakened, but it still exists and will do so until further evidence disproves it entirely or certainly changes it radically.

Causes of Changes in Mental Abilities

In the past it was assumed that mental deterioration inevitably accompanied physical deterioration.

That physical decline does contribute to mental decline has been shown by the fact that sex-hormone treatment of elderly women can result in improvement in the ability to think, to learn new material, to memorize, and to remember—and in increased willingness to expend intellectual energy (97). On the other hand, some pathological conditions, such as hypertension, lead to intellectual loss with aging, although, as Wilkie and Eisdorfer have emphasized, such loss is not part of the "'normal' aging process" (154).

Lack of environmental stimulation also affects the rate of mental decline. In mental as in motor learning, continuation of practice through the years slows down the rate of decline (19,102). Those who continue to work as they reach the latter years of life have more normal brain functioning and do better on intelligence tests than those who are idle (6,59).

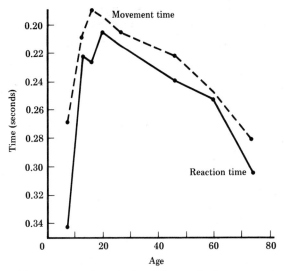

FIGURE 13-5 Speed of reaction and of movement decline sharply as age advances. (Adapted from J. Hodgkins. Influence of age on the speed of reaction and movement in females. *Journal of Gerontology*, 1962, **17**, 385–389. Used by permission.)

What may be interpreted as poor comprehension resulting from intellectual decline may be due primarily to poor hearing. As hearing decreases, many elderly people fail to grasp what others say and their responses suggest that they are not as mentally alert as they formerly were (69).

How Great Is Mental Decline in Old Age?

It is important to recognize that the mental decline associated with old age may not be as great as popularly supposed or as reported in earlier studies. As has been pointed out, there is a growing belief that what is assumed to be a decline in mental ability may be the result of discrepancies in the choice of groups at different age levels for comparisons and of the differences between education now and at the time the elderly groups were schoolchildren. Schaie et al. (129) have emphasized the importance of this:

Conventional cross-sectional studies confound historical (generational) with individual (ontogenetic) change components. Since such designs sample individuals differing not only in age but also in terms of generation-related environmental backgrounds, the resulting age differences provide most inappropriate evidence for ontogenetic <u>change</u>.

Other conditions may account, to some extent, for the apparent mental decline that accompanies age. Most old people, for example, are not familiar with testing, are not sympathetic toward it, and refuse to be tested. This biases the samplings used for studies and usually means that institutionalized persons must be used for studies of old-age groups, thus giving an unfair sampling of the old-age population and an inaccurate picture of how mental abilities are affected by aging (83).

In addition, since it is known that speed of action slows down with advancing age, tests of mental ability that emphasize the time element are unfair to elderly subjects. In measuring mental abilities, the ability to cope with mental tasks must be considered free from the influence of speed and other factors that may obscure mental abilities.

Because of the contradictory evidence available today about decline in mental abilities, Horn and Donaldson have warned (82):

There are results which caution against the view that all of the abilities which are believed to be involved in intelligence necessarily decline or decline in the same way; some abilities may decline little or not at all. Also, there are results which caution against supposing that decline necessarily occurs for all subjects or necessarily sets in as early as might be supposed from considerations of cross-sectional data alone.

The only way to measure the amount of decline precisely is to have an accurate record of the individual's abilities at their peak and then to determine from this standard the percentage of decline that sets in at different ages. To date, as has been stressed earlier, few studies have been made using the longitudinal method; most have been made using samples from different age levels—the cross-sectional method (4, 64). One longitudinal study reported decline to be far less than is popularly believed (6). See Figure 13-6.

Variations in Mental Changes

As in all other areas of decline, there are marked individual variations in mental decline. There is no one age at which the decline begins and no specific pattern of decline that is characteristic of all old people.

In general, those of higher intellectual levels experience relatively less decrease in mental efficiency than those of lower levels. Studies of gifted individuals carried out over a long period of time, for exam-

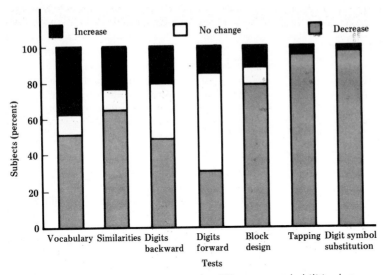

FIGURE 13-6 Changes in test scores for different mental abilities between the ages of sixty-four and eighty-four years. (Adapted from J. E. Blum, J. L. Fosshage, and L. F. Jarvik. Intellectual changes and sex differences in octogenarians: A twenty-five year longitudinal study of aging. *Development Psychology*, 1972, **7**, 178–187. Used by permission.)

ple, have provided evidence that mental decline sets in later than is popularly believed (8,117).

Just as there are differences in the rate of mental decline among different individuals of the same chronological age, so there are also differences within the same individual in the rate of decline of different mental abilities. Even when the element of speed is eliminated and the tests are given as power tests to measure different mental abilities, declines of varying degrees have been found (84). This is illustrated in Figure 13-6. In summarizing the results of their studies, Schaie et al. have reported (129):

In abilities heavily dependent upon educational and acculturation output systems (such as Verbal Meaning, Reasoning, Numbers, etc.) there was a negligible amount of genuine longitudinal change. The strong cross-sectional age decrements reported in the conventional literature for these abilities simply are a consequence of whatever cultural change factors produce higher and higher intellectual performance in successive generations. . . . Abilities mediated by formal education systems should not show any pronounced aging decrements.

An analysis of different mental abilities, as measured by tests, has revealed the characteristic changes

that occur with advancing age and the apparent reasons for these changes. These are given in Box 13-5.

CHANGES IN INTERESTS IN OLD AGE

Like the physical, psychological, and lifestyle changes in old age, changes in interests are inevitable. A number of conditions are responsible for this, the most important of which are given in Box 13-6.

There is a close correlation between the number of interests people at all ages have and the success of their adjustments. This, in turn, determines how happy or unhappy they will be. In old age, this is just as true as at other ages in the life span.

It is important to recognize, however, that adjustments in old age are markedly influenced by whether changes in interests are voluntary or involuntary. If elderly people want to change their interests because of health, financial situation, or any other reason, they will be better satisfied than if they must give up activities because of unfavorable attitudes on the part of the social group.

Like the interests of people at every age level,

MENTAL CHANGES IN OLD AGE

Learning

Older people are more cautious about learning, need more time to integrate their responses, are less capable of dealing with new material that cannot readily be integrated with earlier experiences, and are less accurate than younger people.

Reasoning

There is a general reduction in the speed with which the individual reaches a conclusion in both inductive and deductive reasoning. This is partly the result of the tendency to become increasingly cautious with age.

Creativity

Older people tend to lack the capacity for, or interest in, creative thinking. Thus significant creative achievements are less common among older people than among younger ones.

Memory

Old people tend to have poor recent memories but better remote memories. This may be due partly to the fact that they are not always strongly motivated to remember things, partly to lack of attentiveness, and partly to not hearing clearly and distinctly what others say.

Recall

Recall is affected more by age than recognition. Many older people use cues, especially visual, auditory, and kinesthetic ones, to aid their ability to recall.

Reminiscing

The tendency to reminisce about the past becomes increasingly more marked with advancing age. How much the individual reminisces depends mainly on how pleasant or unpleasant the elderly find their living conditions now.

Sense of Humor

A common stereotype of the elderly is that of humorless people. While it is true that their comprehension of the comic tends to decrease with advancing age, their appreciation for the comic that they can comprehend increases.

Vocabulary

Deterioration in vocabulary is very slight in old age because elderly people constantly use words most of which were learned in childhood or adolescence. Learning new words in old age is more infrequent than frequent.

Mental Rigidity

Mental rigidity is far from universal in old age, in contradiction to the stereotype of the elderly as mentally rigid. When mental rigidity sets in during middle age, it tends to become more pronounced with advancing age partly because the elderly learn more slowly and with more difficulty than they did earlier and partly because they believe that old values and ways of doing things are better than new ones. This is not mental rigidity in the strict use of the term but a carefully reasoned decision.

those of the elderly differ markedly. However, certain interests may be regarded as typical of old age: personal interests, recreational interests, social interests, religious interests, and interest in death. These are discussed below.

Personal Interests

Personal interests in old age include interest in self, interest in appearance, interest in clothes, and interest in money.

Interest in Self People become increasingly more preoccupied with themselves as they grow older.

They may become egocentric and self-centered to the point where they think more about themselves than about others and have little regard for others' interests and wishes.

Even when they are in good physical condition, older people are often preoccupied with their health and with the bodily processes. They tend to complain about their health and to exaggerate any ailment they may have. They also show their preoccupation with themselves by talking endlessly about their pasts, expecting to be waited on, and wanting to be the center of attention.

This self-centeredness contributes to the unfa-

SOME COMMON CONDITIONS AFFECTING CHANGE OF INTERESTS IN OLD AGE

Health

Changes in health and energy are reflected in an increased interest in sedentary pursuits and a decreased interest in activities requiring strength and energy.

Social Status

Older people of the higher social groups usually have a wider range of interests than those of the lower groups. Many of these are carry-overs of interests developed earlier in life.

Economic Status

Older people who have inadequate money to meet their daily needs often have to give up many of the interests that are important to them and concentrate on the ones they can afford, regardless of whether they are meaningful to them or meet their needs.

Place of Residence

Where elderly people live has a marked influence on whether their earlier interests will persist or change. If they live in their own homes with family members, their interests are far more likely to remain static than if they go to live with married children or in a retirement home.

Sex

Women, as a group, have more interests in old age than do men, just as they do throughout adulthood. Because of the few interests they developed when they were younger, many older men, after retirement, find it difficult to cultivate interests to occupy their time.

Marital Status

Just as unmarried men and women in early adulthood and middle age have more time and money to cultivate interests than do those who are married, so do the unmarried in old age. Some of their interests may be new but most are carry-overs from younger years.

Values

As values change, so do interests at every age. In old age, value changes are common and usually toward conservatism. This affects the relative value they place on their interests. Older people, for example, may come to value social contacts rather than hobbies as compensation for the loneliness caused by loss of a spouse.

---

vorable social attitude toward old people that is so prevalent today. Younger people, who are aware of the social expectation of cooperativeness and unselfishness, often find the self-centeredness of old people completely contradictory to their standards of socially acceptable behavior.

Interest in Appearance Although some old people are as concerned about their appearance as they were when they were younger, many show little interest in how they look. They may cease to care about their clothes or become careless about grooming. While few are dirty and slovenly in appearance, most elderly people do not take the time and trouble to make the most of their looks or to camouflage the telltale signs of physical aging as well as they could.

There are a number of explanations for decline in interest in appearance with advancing age. The

more *socially active* people are, the more incentive they have to be careful about their looks. Socially withdrawn people, by contrast, have far less motivation to keep up their appearance.

The *economic status* of the elderly is an important factor in the degree of interest they have in appearance. When every penny must be counted and when some of the necessities of life must be skimped on, money to improve one's appearance is considered a luxury that cannot be afforded.

Place of residence also plays an important role in determining how great an interest the elderly have in their appearance. Those who live alone have far less interest than those who live with grown children or in homes for the retired elderly.

The *sex* of the elderly influences their attitudes toward appearance. Old men, as a group, tend to be more interested in their appearance than old women.

This is in direct contrast to the situation earlier and may be explained partly by habit and partly by economic conditions. Many older men, and older women who worked during early adulthood or middle age, have developed the habit of careful grooming because it was important to them in their work. This habit often persists after retirement. Older women, who spent their younger years mainly in the home, tend to be less careful of their appearance in old age just as they were when they were younger.

The sex difference in interest in appearance may also be due in part to economic conditions. It costs less for men to be well groomed than for women, who not only need more up-to-date and a larger assortment of clothes than men but who also must buy beauty aids in the form of cosmetics, permanent waves, etc. Many men, after retirement, have a wardrobe left from their working years that will continue to serve them well. This does not apply to former working women because constant changes in fashion soon make their wardrobes out of style.

Interest in Clothes   Interest in clothes depends to some extent upon how socially active the elderly are, partly on their economic status, and partly on how willing they are to accept the fact that they are growing old and must adjust to it. Some elderly people continue to wear styles they wore earlier and refuse to dress according to the current fashion, even when it means that they must have their garments made to order.

Other older people, by contrast, are very fashion-conscious and may choose clothes that are designed for those young enough to be their children or even their grandchildren. They are rebelling against old age and are trying to convince themselves and others that they are younger than they really are.

Limited incomes prevent many elderly people from having as great an interest in their clothes and appearance as they might otherwise have. They simply do not have enough money to buy new clothes except when it is absolutely necessary.

Lack of income also contributes to the social withdrawal of many elderly people. If they cannot afford to be well dressed, they tend to shun social activities for fear that they will be embarrassed by their shabby and out-of-date appearance. This is especially true of women because women's clothing styles change faster than those of men.

Older people's interest in clothing is also affected by the difficulty they have finding ready-made clothes that are stylish and yet fit their aging figures. When short skirts are in vogue, for example, it is hard for an older women to find a ready-made dress, skirt, or coat of a length that she considers appropriate for her age. Also, clothing intended for elderly women is often poorly designed, uninteresting, and made in prints or colors that are unflattering to the older woman's skin and hair. The problem of finding ready-made clothes that are becoming affects elderly men also, but less than it affects women (80,126,134).

Interest in Money   Interest in money, which starts to wane during middle age, generally is revived and becomes more intense as old age progresses. Retirement or unemployment may leave the elderly with greatly reduced incomes or with no income at all unless they are eligible for social security or welfare relief. This focuses their attention on money and stimulates their interest in how they can get more money or make ends meet with what they have.

When the income of elderly people is drastically reduced, their interest in money is focused not on what they want to buy and on the purchase of status symbols, as is often true in the earlier years, but on how they can maintain their independence—how they can live where and how they want to without relying on relatives or charity.

In order to maintain the pattern of life they prefer, even when simpler than what they had grown accustomed to, many older people are forced to cut down their expenditures for clothes and grooming aids, for social activities and recreations, and for membership in different community organizations. Travel and vacations away from home, except when visiting friends or relatives, often becomes impossible for many elderly people (60).

Recreational Interests

Elderly men and women tend to remain interested in the recreational activities they enjoyed in early adulthood, and they change these interests only when necessary (50). Changes that do occur consist mainly of a gradual narrowing down of interests, rather than a radical change in pattern, and a shift toward more sedentary forms of recreation.

Causes of Changed Recreational Activities   While it is more unusual than usual for older people to cultivate new recreational interests, they often devote

Elderly men and women tend to cling to the recreational interests they developed when they were younger, changing them only when failing health or some other obstacle forces them to do so. (Irene Bayer from Monkmeyer.)

their time to recreations that interested them when they were younger but which they had to put aside because of the pressures of work or family life or for some other reason. A woman, for example, who enjoyed painting when she was younger but had to give it up during the busy years of homemaking and child rearing, may become interested in it again in old age.

Some changes in recreational activities are inevitable. However, most of these changes are made as a result of necessity, not choice. The most important conditions affecting the recreational patterns of the elderly are given in Box 13-7. Note that most of them are not related to interests but to conditions in their lives over which they have little or no control.

Common Recreational Activities in Old Age Common recreational activities of older people include reading, writing letters, listening to the radio, watching television, visiting friends and relatives, sewing,

embroidering, gardening, traveling, playing cards, going to the theater or movies, and taking part in the activities of civic, political, or religious organizations (15). Figure 13-7 shows the recreational activities of the elderly as reported in a nationwide survey.

In general, the number and variety of activities engaged in declines with advancing age, even though an interest in them may persist. Therefore, it is incorrect to judge the older person's recreational interests in terms of the number engaged in (76,147).

Social Interests

With advancing age, most people suffer increasing social loss or *social disengagement* —a process of mutual withdrawal of the aged from the social environment (89). Social disengagement, as Birren has explained, involves four elements of "load shedding": less involvement with other people, a reduction in the variety of social roles played, a greater use

COMMON CONDITIONS RESPONSIBLE FOR CHANGES IN RECREATIONAL ACTIVITIES

Health

As health gradually fails and as physical disabilities such as poor eyesight set in, the individual acquires an interest in recreational activities that require a minimum of strength and energy and can be enjoyed in the home.

Economic Status

Reduced income after retirement may force the cutting down on or elimination of recreational activities, such as movie going, that cost money. This is especially true of people in the lower socioeconomic groups.

Education

The more formal education a person has, the more intellectual recreational activities, such as reading, will be cultivated. Because these require little energy, they can be enjoyed in old age. Those with limited education must often depend mainly on television for recreation.

Marital Status

Elderly people who have been accustomed to engaging in recreations with their spouses must make radical changes in their patterns after the loss of a spouse through divorce or death. A woman accustomed to playing cards or going to community clubs with her husband may have to cultivate new recreational interests when she is left alone.

Sex

Women tend to cultivate a wide range of recreational interests throughout life, many of which are sedentary in nature and thus can be carried into old age. Men, by contrast, tend to limit their recreational interests to sports, which they must give up when their health fails. Thus they have a paucity of recreational interests in old age and may depend mainly on television.

Living Conditions

Elderly persons who live in a home for the aged have recreations provided for them that are suited to their physical and mental abilities. Those who live in their own homes or with a married child have fewer opportunities for recreation, especially if their economic status is poor or if failing health or transportation problems prevent them from participating in community-sponsored recreational activities.

---

of mental ability, and less participation in physical activity (20).

Social disengagement in old age is commonly expressed in a narrowing down of the sources of social contact and a decline in social participation. For most older people this means a radical change in the pattern of social life they established during early adulthood and carried on, with only minor changes, through middle age.

Kinds of Social Disengagement Social disengagement may be voluntary or involuntary. In the case of *voluntary* social disengagement, elderly people withdraw from social activities because they feel that such activities no longer meet their needs. As their interest in themselves increases, their interest in others decreases until their social interests are limited to their immediate families.

The more socially isolated elderly people are, the more ingrown they become and the fewer opportunities they have to keep up to date. As a result, they become boring to others. This further adds to their social isolation.

Involuntary social disengagement comes when elderly people want and need social contacts but are deprived of the opportunities to have them because of conditions over which they have little or no control. When, for example, many of their contemporaries have died or have moved away or are physically or economically unable to do things with them, elderly people no longer have the companionship they formerly enjoyed.

Elderly people may also lack the strength or the means of transportation to see their friends. If their income is limited, they may not be able to participate in church or other community activities, and they often find it difficult or impossible to keep up with the pace set by their younger relatives or friends. Equally

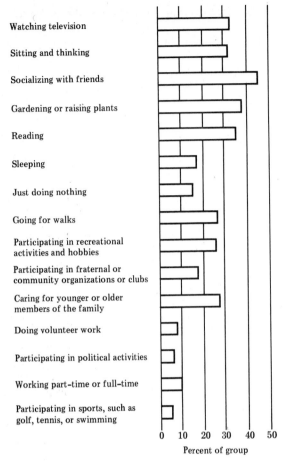

Watching television

Sitting and thinking

Socializing with friends

Gardening or raising plants

Reading

Sleeping

Just doing nothing

Going for walks

Participating in recreational activities and hobbies

Participating in fraternal or community organizations or clubs

Caring for younger or older members of the family

Doing volunteer work

Participating in political activities

Working part-time or full-time

Participating in sports, such as golf, tennis, or swimming

0   10   20   30   40   50

Percent of group

FIGURE 13-7 Common recreational activities in which the elderly spend "a lot of time." (Adapted from E. V. Beverley. The beginning of wisdom about aging. *Geriatrics,* 1975, **30**(7), 116–119, 122–123, 127–128. Used by permission.)

serious is the unfavorable social attitude toward the elderly which contributes its share to their involuntary social disengagement. In discussing attitudes toward older people in social situations, Kalish has said (87):

We Americans like to invest our efforts, money, time, and emotional involvements in people who will pay off. Society is contrived so that older people are very unlikely to pay off. Since they will probably not be productive in the ways we wish, they will not be able to be independent as they were when they were younger, they will be less meaningful, and they have limited futures.

SOURCES OF SOCIAL CONTACT AFFECTED BY AGING

Close, Personal Friendships

Close, personal friendships with members of the same sex, many of which date back to adolescence or the early years of marriage, often end when one of the friends dies or moves away, and it is unlikely that the old person will be able to establish another such relationship.

Friendship Cliques

These cliques are made up of couples who banded together when they were younger because of mutual interests stemming from the husbands' business associations or because of the wives' mutual interests in their families or community organizations. As men retire and women's home and community activities dwindle, the members have little left in common and gradually drift apart.

Formal Groups or Clubs

As leadership roles in formal groups and clubs are taken over by younger members and as the activities are planned mainly around their interests, older people feel unwanted in these organizations and discontinue their membership in them.

Sources of Social Contact Of the different sources of possible social contact in old age, three are greatly affected by aging (156). These are listed in Box 13-8. The serious thing about this is that once these sources of social contact are broken they are rarely mended or replaced.

Women, as a rule, retain their friendships longer than men, mainly because their friends, for the most part, come from their neighborhoods, while men's friends are largely work associates who live in scattered areas of the community and who are not brought together by their common interest in work after retirement (122). Thus many retired men are forced to rely mainly on their wives for companionship and to play "homebody" roles, which they find damaging to their masculine egos. Only when the man has a group of intimate friends, many of whom are his contemporaries and have been his friends since childhood, can he rely to any extent upon social contacts outside the home. Even then, these contacts may be infrequent because of problems relating to health or transportation. Furthermore, because men tend to die earlier than women, many elderly men suffer ongoing losses of old friends (132).

As a result of shrinkages of sources of social contact, the family circle usually constitutes the nucleus of older people's social lives. The older they are, the more they must rely on members of their families for companionship. This is especially true of men, many of whose friends die before they do (156).

Social Participation With advancing age, participation in social activities declines and its scope narrows. As may be seen in Figure 9-3, there is a rapid decline in membership and activity in community organizations after sixty or, for men, after retirement. There is less attendance at the meetings of community organizations and a tendency to take a less active part in the running of the organizations (48,148).

There are many reasons for decline in social participation with advancing age. While *declining health* is generally believed to be the main reason, this is not always the case. Other reasons are as important and sometimes even more important. The extent of *participation in social activities when younger* has a marked influence on participation in old age. Studies of social participation at different ages have shown that those who are active in adolescence and early adulthood continue to be active in middle and old age, except when such obstacles as poor health, economic privations, or family responsibilities prevent them from being so (47,147).

At every age, *socioeconomic status* plays an important role in the amount of participation in community and social organizations. Members of the upper groups dominate the organized life of the community and supply it with leadership. Because members of the lower groups usually did not belong to these organizations when they were younger, they hesitate to join them when they are older. Not only do members of the lower socioeconomic groups belong to fewer social organizations and take a less active part in them, but they also have fewer friends outside the family than members of the middle and upper groups.

Because many community organizations are *occupation-oriented,* as is true of the different business clubs and trade unions, older people who are re-

tired usually no longer belong to these organizations. Thus their participation is limited mainly to the non-occupationally oriented organizations. This partly accounts for the fact that elderly people tend to discontinue their membership in community organizations or to become less active in them.

A *change in the individual's status,* due either to loss of a spouse or to retirement, is likely to affect friendships and social participation. For example, fewer men and women are widowed during their sixties than during their seventies, and thus the social life of people in their sixties is usually dominated by married couples. During the seventies, by contrast, more are widowed, and most men are retired. As a result, men and women in their seventies whose spouses have died have more opportunities for friendships and social activities (119).

The same principle holds true in the case of retirement. Men or women who retire earlier than others of their age groups or than their friends are deviant in the sense that they do not fit into the social life dominated by those who still work. After most of their friends retire, they find that there is more time for socialization and shared interests.

One of the advantages of institutional living for the elderly is that it provides opportunities for contacts with contemporaries which they usually do not have if they live in their own homes or in the homes of grown children (147). The social advantages of institutional living for the elderly will be discussed further in the following chapter.

Religious Interests

Although it is popularly believed that people turn to religion as life draws to a close, there is little evidence to support this belief. While elderly people may become more religious as death approaches, or if they are seriously disabled, the average elderly person does not necessarily turn to religion in the sense that it becomes a new interest or a new focal point of attention.

An analysis of research studies relating to attitudes toward religion and religious practices in old age has provided some evidence of greater interest in religion with advancing age and some evidence of declining interest. Instead of a turn to or away from religion in old age, most people carry on the religious beliefs and habits formed earlier in life (23,24,61). As Covalt has pointed out (46):

The attitude of most older people about religion is probably most often that with which they grew up or which they have accepted as they achieved intellectual maturity. Patterns of worship and of church attendance have remained much the same or have been modified by circumstances which, to the individual, are logical modifications.

However, certain changes in religious interests and attitudes are typical of older people in the American culture of today. The most common of these changes and the effects they have on personal and social adjustments during old age are given in Box 13-9.

There is evidence that the *quality* of church membership plays a more important role in the individual's adjustments in old age than membership per se. Those who joined voluntarily when they were younger and who have been active participants tend to be better adjusted in old age than are those whose interest and activity in religious organizations have been limited (24). Religion, as Moberg has explained, is only one factor in the adjustment to old age, but it is an important one (113).

The relationship between church attendance and personal adjustment in old age may be affected more by the social experiences the church offers than by the religious experiences. The church offers opportunities for social life and companionship, thus satisfying the older person's need to belong and to feel useful, and it minimizes feelings of loneliness. In addition, religion alleviates anxieties about death and the afterlife. As Moberg has pointed out, "A sense of serenity and decreased fear of death tend to accompany conservative religious beliefs" (113).

Whatever the reasons for interest in religion, attendance at church, and participation in religious organizations, there is evidence that these contribute to good adjustment in old age (24,71,113). There is also evidence, as Covalt has pointed out, that "The religious have a reference group that gives them support and security: the nonreligious are more likely to lack such social support" (46).

Interest in Death

During childhood, adolescence, and—to a lesser extent—early adulthood, interest in death revolves more around life after death than around what causes a person to die. As a result of religious training in the home, Sunday school, church, or synagogue,

BOX 13-9

SOME COMMON EFFECTS OF RELIGIOUS CHANGES DURING OLD AGE

Religious Tolerance

With advancing age, the individual adheres less strictly to religious dogmas and adopts a more lenient attitude toward the church, the clergy, and people of different faiths.

Religious Beliefs

Changes in religious beliefs during old age are generally in the direction of acceptance of the traditional beliefs associated with the individual's faith.

Religious Observances

Decline in church attendance and participation in church activities in old age is due less to lack of interest than to factors such as failing health, lack of transportation, embarrassment about not having proper clothing or being able to contribute money, and feeling unwanted by the younger members of the church organizations. Women continue to participate in church activities more than men do because of the opportunities they offer for social contacts.

many young people have distinct concepts of heaven or hell and about the afterlife (81).

As people become older, they usually become less interested in life after death and more concerned about death per se and about their own death. This is especially true of elderly people whose physical or mental condition has begun to deteriorate. When health fails, they tend to concentrate on death and to become preoccupied with it. This is in direct contrast to younger people to whom death seems very far away and is thus of little concern to them.

When interest in death shifts from interest in the afterlife, characteristic of the younger years, to interest in the individual's own death, characteristic of the old-age stage of the life span, research studies have shown that this interest takes many forms. To categorize this material, it will be presented below in relation to five major questions that almost all elderly people ask themselves or others at some time or other (40,58,66,73,86,92,121).

However, it is important to note that, even when these questions dominate interest in death among the elderly, they may and often do still fear death because of the uncertainty about whether there is an afterlife and what it will be like.

"When Will I Die?"   The first question about death that is of profound interest to many elderly people is, "When will I die?" While they know that no one can predict this with any degree of accuracy—not even the ablest doctors or life insurance actuaries—they try to estimate approximately how much longer they have to live on the basis of the longevity of family members and the present state of their health.

Even elderly people who have no fear of death may want to know how much time they have left because of what they regard as "unfinished business" in their lives—a trip they had always planned to take or a project they want to complete. Many older people want their doctors to be frank about impending death so that they can tend to this unfinished business or settle their affairs.

"What Is Likely to Cause My Death?"   The second question about death that concerns many elderly people is: "What is likely to cause my death?" While statistics show that heart disease, cancer, strokes, and accidents are the most common causes of death among the elderly, many die from other causes (58, 92).

Interest in the question of what will cause death in the individual's case centers around four major areas of concern. First, elderly people wonder whether they can do anything to ward off their deaths, even for a short time. For example, if they know they are in danger of having a stroke because of high blood pressure, they may try to lower it by relaxing, by carefully prescribed diets, by losing weight, and by taking medication prescribed by their doctors.

The second concern about what will cause death stems from the desire to take care of unfinished business, as discussed above. Knowing the probable cause of their death will give them some idea of the time remaining for them to accomplish or complete their unfinished business because some diseases progress more rapidly than others.

Financial consideration is the third concern relating to the probable cause of death. If, for example, people have reason to suspect that they may die as a

result of a heart attack, which comes quickly and is not likely to involve a long period of invalidism, they may adopt an "eat, drink, and be merry" philosophy about their money, as opposed to those who believe their death will be a slow and lingering process and will involve great medical expenses for them and for their families.

Fourth, many elderly people want to know what the cause of their deaths will be because this determines whether their last days will be debilitating and painful or whether they have a good chance of remaining mentally alert and physically active until the end. This is important because it will influence their decisions about what medical treatment they will seek, whether they will be willing to undergo an operation, or whether they will consider committing suicide.

"What Can I Do to Die as I Wish to Die?"   The third question about death that many elderly people ask is: "What can I do to die as I wish to die?" In the past, most men and women accepted the belief that death is a matter of "God's will" and that the individual should have no voice in the matter.

Today there is a growing tendency, fostered by those who believe in euthanasia and backed by the theories of some members of the medical, psychological, psychiatric, and legal professions, as well as by some members of the clergy, to believe that people should have some say about how they will die and even when they will die.

Proponents of euthanasia, or "mercy killing," believe that those who are suffering from a painful, incurable disease, or who are hopelessly injured, should be put to death or be allowed to die peacefully, by doing nothing to prolong their lives, such as performing surgery, or by giving artificial respiration or blood transfusions (22,74). However, such solutions to the problem of the hopelessly ill or injured are the subject of heated legal, religious, and medical debate—a debate which, at the present time, has reached no conclusion.

Elderly people who believe that they have the right to determine how they will die are urged to make a "living will" in which they spell out their wishes in this matter. A living will differs from a traditional will in three major respects. First, it contains information about how the individual wishes to die and what is to be done with the body after death rather than what is to be done with the individual's material possessions, as is characteristic of traditional wills. Second, the contents of a living will are always known to the next of kin or a person appointed as an executor so that they will be able to carry out the individual's wishes. And, third, a living will is not a legal document as a traditional will is and, as a result, does not have the same binding quality as a traditional will (22).

"Am I Justified in Taking My Life?" The fourth question that some elderly people ask themselves is whether they are justified in taking their lives if, for one reason or other, they find life has become unbearable. In spite of strong religious prohibitions and unfavorable social attitudes toward suicide, elderly people who believe they have the right to die in dignity and peace and be spared a long, debilitating illness that may sap the energies and financial resources of family members sometimes feel they are justified in taking their own lives while still physically and mentally able to do so. They believe, however, that they are justified in this only *after* a careful and accurate medical diagnosis has shown that there is no hope of recovery.

Even if earlier moral and religious training emphasized the wrongful nature of suicide, their personal beliefs may be strong enough to counteract any feeling of guilt about committing such an act. More and more people in the American culture of today are accepting the belief that there are times when suicide is justified (73,121).

How Can I Have a "Good" Death? The fifth question many elderly people ask is how can they have a "good" death. While a "good" death may have different meanings for different people, most elderly people agree that it can be considered "good" if, as Schulz has pointed out, three important personal needs are met. The first of these needs is control of pain. While modern medicine is unable to control all pain, every elderly person wants to have as painless a death as possible.

The second important need is maintenance of dignity by giving an elderly person about to die an opportunity to participate in decision making. This may relate to whether or not to operate or whether or not to continue to use life-saving measures when there is adequate medical evidence that the patient will never again be physically or mentally normal.

The third important need of all elderly people who are approaching death is affection and love from those who are caring for them. These are shown by willingness to listen, understand, sympathize, and give assurance that their wishes will be followed (133).

Sex Differences in Interest in Death Because psychological research relating to interest in and attitudes toward death is of such recent origin, few studies have investigated sex, socioeconomic, religious, or other differences. The few references there are to sex differences suggest that elderly men have different interests in death than elderly women.

For the most part, *men* focus their attention on their own deaths—what will cause them, when they will occur, etc. While they may be interested in the deaths of their wives, children, close friends, and relatives, their interest is primarily egocentric.

In the case of *women,* interest in death is likewise egocentric in the sense that their concern is how death will affect them and the pattern of their lives. Their interest, however, is concentrated on their husbands' deaths rather than on their own. Many engage in what has been called a "rehearsal for widowhood." In this rehearsal, their concern is focused on how they will manage financially when their husbands die, where they will live, what they will do with their time, etc. While some women, unquestionably, are interested in their own deaths, more, it has been reported, are interested in the deaths of their husbands (58,92).

HAZARDS TO PERSONAL AND SOCIAL ADJUSTMENTS IN OLD AGE

At few times during the life span are there more potentially serious hazards to good personal and social adjustment than there are in old age. This is due partly to the physical and mental decline that makes the elderly more vulnerable to potential hazards than they were earlier, and partly to lack of recognition of these potential hazards on the part of the social group. The result is that few attempts are made to warn the elderly or to prepare them for these hazards as they grow older.

For example, elderly people are seldom prepared for the hazard of accidents, which are so common in old age, nor are they taught how to avoid

BOX 13-10

COMMON PHYSICAL HAZARDS CHARACTERISTIC OF OLD AGE

Diseases and Physical Handicaps

Elderly people are most commonly afflicted by circulatory disturbances, metabolic disorders, involutional mental disorders, disorders of the joints, tumors (both benign and malignant), heart disease, rheumatism, arthritis, visual and hearing impairments, hypertension, gait disorders, and mental and nervous conditions. Figure 11-4 shows the marked increase in physical disability with age.

Malnutrition

Malnutrition in old age is due more to psychological than to economic causes. The most common psychological causes are lack of appetite resulting from anxiety and depression, not wanting to eat alone, and food aversions stemming from earlier prejudices. Even when their food intake is not deficient qualitatively or quantitatively, many older people do not get the full value from their food because of malabsorption resulting from digestive or intestinal disturbances or failure of the endocrine system to function as it formerly did.

Dental Disorders

Sooner or later, most elderly people lose some or all of their teeth. Those who must wear dentures often have difficulty in chewing foods that are rich in proteins, such as meat, and may concentrate on those high in carbohydrates. Chewing difficulties also encourage the swallowing of larger and coarser food masses, which may lead to digestive disorders. Ill-fitting dentures or the absence of teeth often causes lisping and slurring, which interferes with the older person's speech and causes embarrassment.

Sexual Deprivation

Sexual deprivation or unfavorable attitudes toward sex in old age affect the old person in much the same way that emotional deprivation affects the young child. Happily married elderly people are healthier and live longer than those who never married, who have lost a spouse, or who become sexually inactive.

Accidents

Older people are generally more accident-prone than younger ones. Even when the accidents are not fatal, they frequently leave the individual disabled for life. Falls, which may be due to environmental obstacles or to dizziness, giddiness, weakness, or defective vision, are the most common accidents among older women, while older men are most commonly involved in motor vehicle accidents, either as drivers or as pedestrians. Accidents caused by fire are also common in old age. Figure 13-8 shows the common causes of burns among the elderly.

---

them. Similarly, few are given help in learning how to use their increased amount of leisure time in ways that are compatible with their declining strength and energy and their decreased incomes.

During the past decade or so, doctors have become increasingly active in their campaign to encourage middle-aged or even younger patients to take off weight in order to avoid the potential danger of heart trouble as they grow older. Unfortunately, many middle-aged people fail to follow such advice or even to recognize that they may avoid trouble in the future if they change their pattern of living gradually, rather than having to change it abruptly and radically later on, when it may be too late to repair the damage done earlier.

Just as there is no conclusive evidence that preparation for retirement always guarantees good adjustment to it, so there is no justification for believing that preparation for old age will always lead to good personal and social adjustments during this period. However, there is ample evidence that the person who is prepared for the personal and social changes that take place during old age is better able to adjust to them than one who has received no such preparation.

In the following discussion of the physical and psychological hazards of old age, it should be apparent how important a role preparation can play and how greatly increased the hazards are when preparation is minimized or completely absent.

Physical Hazards

All the common hazards to physical well-being at earlier ages not only are more common during old

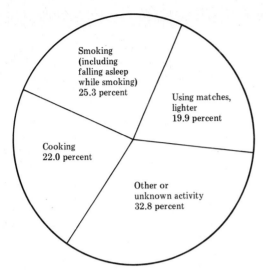

FIGURE 13-8 Most frequent activities associated with burns among the elderly, age sixty-five and older. (Adapted from E. V. Beverley. Reducing fire and burn hazards among the elderly. *Geriatrics*, 1976, **31**(5), 106–110. Used by permission.)

age but also affect a larger proportion of individuals. In addition to these common hazards, there are some that are largely limited to the old-age groups. What these hazards are, and their causes and effects, are briefly explained in Box 13-10.

In addition to real physical hazards, there are imaginary ones. Many older people suffer from imaginary illness and concentrate on any ache or pain they may have, thus exaggerating it out of all proportion. Talking about aches, pains, medicine, and doctors is a favorite pastime of many old people. It serves as a means of attracting attention to themselves and of winning sympathy from others (51).

Many old people learn to cope with their physical ailments, while others do not. Some complain and feel sorry for themselves, and this may destroy any motivation they otherwise might have had to cope with their conditions successfully. Still others make practical use of their disorders as a way of controlling others. As Kassel has pointed out, "Their disabilities have become status symbols, a means whereby they can obtain attention and control their families" (90).

An often-overlooked hazard associated with the impaired physical condition of the older person is the financial drain it represents. Even Medicare, Medicaid, and health insurance policies often do not cover all expenses, such as the cost of hiring someone to take care of the household or the cost of expensive dental work.

These health costs often prevent elderly people from doing things they would like to do, such as joining a club, taking a trip, or visiting a relative or friend. They may even have to cut down on expenditures for clothing and grooming aids, both of which, as was pointed out earlier, are essential morale builders.

Grown children or other relatives may become resentful if they must share in the burden of elderly people's health costs. If this happens, it will jeopardize the major source of social contact for the elderly. Furthermore, older people may become extremely money-conscious and cut down on expenses unnecessarily because they fear greater future expenditures for illness or disability. This becomes a hazard to good social adjustments if it cuts off social contacts (15,17,75).

Psychological Hazards

There are also a number of psychological hazards characteristic of old age. While these may occur at other ages, as is true of the physical hazards, psychological hazards are not only more likely to occur during old age than during the younger years of the life span but their impact on personal and social adjustments is greater.

Of the many psychological hazards characteristic of old age, the following are the most common and the most serious.

Acceptance of Cultural Stereotypes of the Elderly The first psychological hazard is acceptance of the traditional beliefs and cultural stereotypes of the aged. This is hazardous because it encourages the elderly to feel inadequate and inferior. Even worse, it tends to stifle their motivation to do what they are capable of doing.

For example, elderly people who believe that they are too old to learn new skills, because "you can't teach an old dog new tricks," will be at a disadvantage if they seek full or part-time employment after retirement, or if they are encouraged to pursue a new hobby to fill their leisure time. If the elderly accept the traditional belief that all old people should withdraw from life, their health will be impaired because of lack of exercise. Similarly, reminiscing or "living in the past" is a trait that bores other people and sets up roadblocks to good social adjustments.

While both men and women are influenced by the cultural beliefs and stereotypes of aging, women tend to be more affected than men. This is primarily because the social group judges elderly women in a negative way as physically unattractive, usually in poor health, and financially strapped as a result of widowhood. This negative stereotype of elderly women affects their personal and social attitudes and, in turn, their personal and social adjustments (118).

Effects of Physical Changes of Aging The second psychological hazard of old age stems from feelings of inferiority and inadequacy that come with physical changes. The loss of an attractive, sex-appropriate appearance may lead both men and women to feel rejection by the social group.

Loss of hearing interferes with communication with other people. In addition, many older people have difficulty in speaking because of missing teeth or poorly fitted dentures. This also proves to be a barrier to communication and to social relationships (112).

Changes in Life Patterns The necessity for establishing a different, more appropriate pattern of life is the third psychological hazard many elderly people face. They may, for example, no longer need as large a home now that their children are grown and have homes of their own. However, many older people cling to their homes and possessions and to the lifestyle associated with them. Streib has explained why giving up homes and cherished possessions is so traumatic to many older people (143).

Part of our depression at the loss of possessions is due to our feeling that we must now go without certain goods that we expected the possessions to bring in their train. Yet in every case there remains, over and above this, a sense of the shrinkage of our personality, a partial conversion of ourselves to nothingness, which is a psychological phenomenon by itself.

Tendency to "Slip" Mentally The fourth psychological hazard is the suspicion or realization that mental decline has started to set in. Many elderly people suspect or realize that they are becoming somewhat forgetful, that they have difficulty learning new names or facts, and that they cannot hold up under pressure as well as they used to. They may come to think that they are "slipping" mentally, and this encourages them in their belief that they are too old to

learn anything new. Instead of adjusting their activities to conform to their mental state, they withdraw from *all* activities that might involve competition with younger people, and thus they experience all the problems, described earlier, that social disengagement brings (67).

Feelings of Guilt about Idleness The fifth psychological hazard is guilt about not working while other people still are. Many older people of today, who grew up in a more work-oriented society, feel guilty after retirement or after their home responsibilities have diminished. They want to do something useful, but may shy away from community activities planned for older citizens because they regard them as "make-work" or forms of recreation rather than real work. This they do even when they want the companionship these activities will provide.

Because most elderly people need to feel useful if they are to be happy and well adjusted, attempts are made to get them interested in doing volunteer work in their communities. Volunteer work, it is claimed, is a suitable substitute for the retired person's former occupation because it presents a personal challenge for the individual, thus generating self-respect, while at the same time winning social approval and esteem (14).

Elderly men, on the whole, tend to be less willing to engage in volunteer community work than women. This is partly because they have become accustomed to being paid for their services and thus resist "working" for nothing and partly because they associate volunteer work with the feminine role. The cultural stereotype of the volunteer as a dilettante who dabbles in this work to kill time has a strong influence on the attitudes of those who have lived a work-oriented life and who shun any substitute that does not conform to their earlier values (16).

Reduced Income The sixth psychological hazard is the result of reduced income. After retirement, many elderly people are unable to afford the leisure-time activities they consider worthwhile, such as attending lectures or concerts or participating in various community activities. If they must rely upon television for entertainment, they often find that the majority of the programs are youth- or young-adult oriented. As such, they offer little of interest to the elderly.

Women, even more than men, find a reduced income a hazard to their personal and social adjustments. It is especially serious during widowhood if the husbands' former pensions end with their deaths. This matter will be discussed in more detail in the following chapter.

Social Disengagement   The seventh and by far the most serious psychological hazard in old age is social disengagement. As was explained earlier, this may be voluntary, but far more often it is involuntary—due to poor health, limited financial resources, or other conditions over which the elderly have little or no control.

Perhaps the best way to emphasize the hazardous nature of social disengagement is to point out the benefits that social belonging and participation in social activities bring to the elderly. Studies of members in different types of voluntary associations or in senior citizen centers have revealed that active participation in these groups contributes greatly to psychological well-being as shown in an increase in life satisfaction (33,47,100).

Some elderly people gain adequate satisfaction from social contacts with family members and relatives and, consequently, do not experience the ill effects of social disengagement (31). Some substitute indirect social contacts, as through telephone conversations, for direct, face-to-face social interactions but they are rarely as satisfying as direct interactions (31).

Because social contacts are especially important for women after their husbands retire or die, social disengagement becomes a serious hazard to personal and social adjustments (100). This matter will be discussed more fully in the following chapter.

The elderly who are disengaged, either voluntarily or involuntarily, become socially isolated. As a result, they lack the social support they had in times of trouble or stress when they were younger. This is especially serious if they are widowed or have few family members to turn to with their problems.

Chapter Highlights

1. Old age, which begins at approximately sixty years, is characterized by certain physical and psychological changes that are far more likely to lead to poor adjustments and unhappiness than to good adjustments.
2. There are marked individual differences in the effects of aging, with physical aging, as a general rule, preceding psychological aging.
3. There are certain problems of adjustment unique

to old age, such as increased physical and economic dependency on others, establishing new social contacts, developing new interests and activities to occupy increased leisure time, learning to treat grown children as adults, and being victimized because of the inability to defend oneself.

4. Physical changes include changes in appearance, changes in the different internal physical systems, changes in physiological functioning, and sensory and sexual changes.
5. The most common changes in motor abilities include changes in strength and speed, an increase in time needed to learn new skills, and a tendency to become awkward and clumsy.
6. While there are many causes of changes in mental abilities, lack of environmental stimulation and lack of motivation to remain mentally alert are among the most common and most serious.
7. Changes in interests are due to many conditions, the most common of which are deterioration in health and economic status, changes in place of residence and in marital status, and changes in values.
8. Personal interests of the elderly include self, appearance, clothes, and money.
9. Changes in recreational activities in old age are due more to changes in health, economic and marital status, and living conditions, than they are to changes in recreational interests.
10. Social disengagement, characteristic of old age, may be voluntary or involuntary, though voluntary social disengagement tends to be far less common than involuntary social disengagement.
11. Of the different sources of social contact, those most seriously affected by aging are close personal friendships, cliques, and formal groups or clubs.
12. Interest in religion is often concentrated on concern with death which, at this age, becomes a personal matter instead of an abstract, theoretical one as it often is during the earlier years of life.
13. Potential hazards to good personal and social adjustments are due partly to the physical and mental decline characteristic of old age, which makes the elderly especially vulnerable, and partly to lack of recognition of potential hazards on the part of the social group.
14. Among the common physical hazards characteristic of old age are diseases, physical handicaps, malnutrition, dental disorders, accidents, and sexual deprivation.
15. Psychological hazards include acceptance of cultural stereotypes of the elderly, feelings of inferiority and inadequacy resulting from physical

changes, changes in life patterns, a tendency to "slip" mentally, feelings of guilt about idleness, especially on the part of men after retirement, and reduced income that necessitates changes in living patterns.

Bibliography

1. Abraham, S., M. D. Carroll, C. M. Dresser, and C. L. Johnson. *Dietary intake of persons 1–74 years of age in the United States.* Washington, D.C.: U.S. Department of Health, Education, and Welfare, No. 6, March 30, 1977.

2. Adamowicz, J. K. Visual short-term memory and aging. *Journal of Gerontology,* 1976, **31,** 39–46.

3. Andres, R. Defining and evaluating the myriad influences on human aging. *Geriatrics,* 1975, **30**(3), 36, 39–40.

4. Arenberg, D. A longitudinal study of problem solving in adults. *Journal of Gerontology,* 1974, **29,** 650–658.

5. Armstrong, P. W. More thoughts on senility. *Gerontologist,* 1978, **18,** 315–316.

6. Baltes, P. B., and K. W. Schaie. On the plasticity of intelligence in adulthood and old age: Where Horn and Donaldson fail. *American Psychologist,* 1976, **31,** 720–725.

7. Barrett, J. H. *Gerontological psychology.* Springfield, Ill.: Charles C Thomas, 1972.

8. Bayley, N. Research in child development: A longitudinal perspective. *Merrill-Palmer Quarterly,* 1965, **11,** 183–208.

9. Bennett, R. Attitudes of the young toward the old: A review of research. *Personnel & Guidance Journal,* 1976, **55,** 136–139.

10. Bennett, R., and J. Eckman. Attitudes toward aging: A critical examination of recent literature and implications for future research. In C. Eisdorfer and M. P. Lawton (Eds.). *The psychology of adult development.* Washington, D.C.: APA, 1973. Pp. 575–597.

11. Bergman, M., V. G. Blumenfeld, D. Cascardo, B. Dash, H. Levitt, and M. K. Margulies. Age-related decrement in hearing for speech: Sampling and longitudinal studies. *Journal of Gerontology,* 1976, **31,** 533–538.

12. Berry, J. Counseling older women: A perspective. *Personnel & Guidance Journal,* 1976, **55,** 130–131.

13. Beverley, E. V. Exploring the many faceted mysteries of aging. *Geriatrics,* 1975, **30**(3), 159–161, 164–166.

14. Beverley, E. V. Values and volunteerism. *Geriatrics,* 1975, **30**(6), 122–127, 129, 133, 137.

15. Beverley, E. V. The beginning of wisdom about aging. *Geriatrics,* 1975, **30**(7), 116–119, 122–123, 127–128.

16. Beverley, E. V. The double-barreled impact of volunteer service. *Geriatrics,* 1975, **30**(7), 132–134, 136, 140–141.

17. Beverley, E. V. Creative approaches to the fulfilling use of leisure time. *Geriatrics,* 1975, **30**(12), 86, 90, 92–94.

18. Beverley, E. V. Reducing fire and burn hazards among the elderly. *Geriatrics,* 1976, **31**(5), 106–110.

19. Beverley, E. V. Lifelong learning—a concept whose time has come. *Geriatrics,* 1976, **31**(8), 114, 118, 120, 124, 126–127.

20. Birren, J. E. *The psychology of aging.* Englewood Cliffs, N. J.: Prentice-Hall, 1964.

21. Bischof, L. J. *Adult psychology.* (2nd ed.) New York: Harper & Row, 1976.

22. Black, P. McL. Focusing on some of the ethical problems associated with death and dying. *Geriatrics,* 1976, **31**(1), 138–141.

23. Blank, M. L. Recent research findings on practice with the aging. *Social Casework,* 1971, **52,** 382–389.

24. Blazer, D., and E. Palmore. Religion and aging in a longitudinal panel. *Gerontologist,* 1976, **16,** 82–85.

25. Blue, G. F. The aging as portrayed in realistic fiction for children, 1945–1975. *Gerontologist,* 1978, **18,** 187–192.

26. Blum, J. E., J. L. Fosshage, and L. F. Jarvik. Intellectual changes and sex differences in octogenarians: A thirty-five year longitudinal study of aging. *Developmental Psychology,* 1972, **7,** 178–187.

27. Borges, M. A., and L. J. Dutton. Attitudes toward aging: Increasing optimism found with age. *Gerontologist,* 1976, **16,** 220–224.

28. Botwinick, J. Who are the aged? *Geriatrics,* 1974, **29**(7), 124–126, 129.

29. Botwinick, J. *Aging and behavior.* (2nd ed.) New York: Springer, 1978.

30. Brinley, J. F., T. J. Jovick, and L. M. McLaughlin. Age, reasoning, and memory in adults. *Journal of Gerontology,* 1974, **29,** 182–189.

31. Brown, A. S. Satisfying relationships for the elderly and their patterns of disengagement. *Gerontologist,* 1974, **14,** 258–262.

32. Brubaker, T. H., and E. A. Powers. The stereotype of "old": A review and alternative approach. *Journal of Gerontology,* 1976, **31,** 441–447.

33. Bull, C. N., and J. B. Aucoin. Voluntary association participation and life satisfaction: A replication note. *Journal of Gerontology,* 1975, **30,** 73–76.

34. Bultena, G. L., and E. A. Powers. Denial of aging: Age identification and reference group orientations. *Journal of Gerontology,* 1978, **33,** 748–754.

35. Busse, E. W. Theories of ageing. In E. W. Busse and E. Pfeiffer (Eds.). *Behavior and adaption in late life.* Boston: Little Brown, 1969. Pp. 11–32.

36. Busse, E. W., and E. Pfeiffer. Functional psychiatric disorders in old age. In E. W. Busse and E. Pfeiffer (Eds.). *Behavior and adaption in late life.* Boston: Little, Brown, 1969. Pp. 183–235.

37. Butler, R. N. Age: The life review. *Psychology Today,* 1971, **5**(7), 51, 89.

38. Butler, R. N. Psychiatry and the elderly: An overview. *American Journal of Psychiatry,* 1975, **132,** 893–900.

39. Butler, R. N., and M. I. Lewis. *Sex after sixty: A guide for men and women in their later years.* New York: Harper & Row, 1976.

40. Cameron, P., L. Stewart, and H. Biber. Consciousness of death across the life span. *Journal of Gerontology,* 1973, **28,** 92–95.

41. Campbell, E. J., and S. S. Lefrak. How aging affects the structure and function of the respiratory system. *Geriatrics,* 1978, **33**(6), 68–73.

42. Clayton, V. Erikson's theory of human development as it applies to the aged: Wisdom as contradictive cognition. *Human Development,* 1975, **18,** 119–128.

43. Clement, F. J. Longitudinal and cross-sectional assessments of age changes in physical strength as related to sex, social class, and mental ability. *Journal of Gerontology,* 1974, **29,** 423–429.

44. Cleveland, M. Sex in marriage: At 40 and beyond. *Family Coordinator,* 1976, **25,** 233–240.

45. Cook, F. L., W. G. Skogan, T. B. Cook, and G. E. Antunes. Criminal victimization of the elderly: The physical and economic consequences. *Gerontologist,* 1978, **18,** 338–349.

46. Covalt, N. K. The meaning of religion to older people. In C. B.

Vedder and A. S. Lefkowitz (Eds.). *Problems of the aged.* Springfield, Ill.: Charles C Thomas, 1965. Pp. 215–224.

47. Cutler, S. J. Membership in different types of voluntary associations and psychological well-being. *Gerontologist,* 1976, **16**, 335–339.

48. Cutler, S. J. Aging and voluntary association participation. *Journal of Gerontology,* 1977, **32**, 470–479.

49. Davies, L. J. Attitudes toward old age and aging as shown by humor. *Gerontologist,* 1977, **17**, 220–226.

50. De Carlo, T. J. Recreation participation patterns and successful aging. *Journal of Gerontology,* 1974, **29**, 416–422.

51. Dovenmuehle, R. H., E. W. Busse, and G. Newman. Physical problems of older people. In E. B. Palmore (Ed.). *Normal aging.* Durham, N.C.: Duke University Press, 1970. Pp. 29–39.

52. Durfak, J. A. Relationship between attitudes toward life and death among elderly women. *Developmental Psychology,* 1973, **8**, 146.

53. Dye, D., M. Goodman, M. Roth, N. Biex, and K. Jensen. The older adult volunteer compared with the nonvolunteer. *Gerontologist,* 1973, **13**, 215–218.

54. Eisdorfer, C., and M. P. Lawton (Eds.). *The psychology of adult development.* Washington, D.C.: APA, 1973.

55. Ellison, J. *Life's second half: The pleasures of aging.* Old Greenwich, Conn.: Devin-Adair, 1978.

56. Erber, J. T. Age differences in recognition memory. *Journal of Gerontology,* 1974, **29**, 177–181.

57. Feifel, H. (Ed.). *New meanings of death.* New York: McGraw-Hill, 1977.

58. Fischer, D. H. *Growing old in America.* New York: Oxford University Press, 1977.

59. Fisher, J. Competence, effectiveness, intellectual functioning, and aging. *Gerontologist,* 1973, **13**, 62–68.

60. Friedsam, H. J., and C. A. Martin. Travel by older people as a use of leisure. *Gerontologist,* 1973, **13**, 204–207.

61. Geriatric Focus article. Church attendance may decline with age but religious interest and concern increases. *Geriatric Focus,* 1965, **4**(11), 2–3.

62. Geriatric Focus article. Implantation of synthetic sex hormones. *Geriatric Focus,* 1971, **10**(2), 1, 5.

63. Giambra, L. M. Daydreaming about the past: The time setting of spontaneous thought intrusions. *Gerontologist,* 1977, **17**, 35–38.

64. Gilbert, J. G. Thirty-five-year follow-up study of intellectual functioning. *Journal of Gerontology,* 1973, **28**, 68–72.

65. Goldsmith, J. Why are the aged so vulnerable to crime and what is being done for their protection? *Geriatrics,* 1976, **31**(4), 40–42.

66. Goleman, D. We are breaking the silence about death. *Psychology Today,* 1976, **10**(4), 44–47, 103.

67. Goodrow, B. A. Limiting factors in reducing participation in older adult learning opportunities. *Gerontologist,* 1975, **15**, 418–422.

68. Graney, M. J. Happiness and social participation in aging. *Journal of Gerontology,* 1975, **30**, 701–706.

69. Granick, S., M. H. Kleban, and A. D. Weiss. Relationships between hearing loss and cognition in normally hearing adult persons. *Journal of Gerontology,* 1976, **31**, 434–440.

70. Greulich, R. C. Prolonging life span: Present and future possibilities. *Geriatrics,* 1978, **33**(8), 88–89.

71. Guinan, St. M. Aging and religious life. *Gerontologist,* 1972, **12**, 21.

72. Haas, K. B. The golden years myth. *Phi Delta Kappan,* 1976, **57**, 650–657.

73. Hall, E., and P. Cameron. Loving death: Our failing reverence for life. *Psychology Today,* 1976, **9** (11), 104–108, 113.

74. Haug, M. Aging and the right to terminate medical treatment. *Journal of Gerontology,* 1978, **33**, 586–591.

75. Havighurst, R. J. *Developmental tasks and education.* (3rd ed.) New York: McKay, 1973.

76. Havighurst, R. J. Social roles, work, leisure, and education. In C. Eisdorfer and M. P. Lawton (Eds.). *The psychology of adult development.* Washington, D.C.: APA, 1973. Pp. 598–618.

77. Havighurst, R. J., and G. Glasser. An exploratory study of reminiscence. *Journal of Gerontology,* 1972, **27**, 245–253.

78. Hayflick, L. The strategy of senescence. *Gerontologist,* 1974, **14**, 37–45.

79. Henretta, J. C., and R. T. Campbell. Status attainment and status maintenance: A study in stratification in old age. *American Sociological Review,* 1976, **41**, 981–992.

80. Hoffman, A. M., and I. M. Bader. Clothing—Common denominator between the young and the old. *Gerontologist,* 1974, **14**, 437–439.

81. Hogan, R. A. Adolescent views of death. *Adolescence,* 1970, **5**, 55–56.

82. Horn, J. L., and G. Donaldson. On the myth of intellectual decline in adulthood. *American Psychologist,* 1976, **31**, 701–719.

83. Horn, J. L., and G. Donaldson. Faith is not enough: A response to the Baltes-Schaie claim that intelligence does not wane. *American Psychologist,* 1977, **32**, 369–376.

84. Jarvik, L. F., and C. Eisdorfer (Eds.). *Intellectual functioning in adults: Psychological and behavioral influences.* New York: Springer, 1973.

85. Kahana, E., J. Liang, B. Felton, T. Fairchild, and Z. Harel. Perspectives of aged on victimization, "ageism," and their problems in urban society. *Gerontologist,* 1977, **17**, 121–129.

86. Kahoe, R. B., and R. F. Dunn. The fear of death and religious attitudes and behavior. *Journal for the Scientific Study of Religion,* 1976, **14**, 379–382.

87. Kalish, R. A. Of social values and dying: A defense of disengagement. *Family Coordinator,* 1972, **22**, 81–94.

88. Kalish, R. A. *Late adulthood: Perspectives of human development.* Monterey, Calif.: Brooks/Cole, 1975.

89. Kalish, R. A., and F. W. Knudtson. Attachment versus disengagement: A life span conceptualization. *Human Development,* 1976, **19**, 171–181.

90. Kassel, V. Polygyny after 60. *Geriatrics,* 1966, **21**, 214–218.

91. Kastenbaum, R. *Old age on the new scene.* New York: Springer, 1978.

92. Kastenbaum, R., and R. Aisenberg. *The psychology of death.* New York: Springer, 1976.

93. Kent, D. P., and M. B. Matson. The impact of death on the aged family. *Family Coordinator,* 1972, **21**, 29–36.

94. Kent, S. Impotence: The facts versus the fallacies. *Geriatrics,* 1975, **30**(4), 164, 169–171.

95. Kent, S. Neuroendocrine changes that come with age do not spell the end of sexual fulfillment. *Geriatrics,* 1975, **30**(3), 184–186, 188.

96. Kent, S. How do we age? *Geriatrics,* 1976, **31**(3), 128–130, 134.

97. Kent, S. A look at Gerovital—the "youth" drug. *Geriatrics,* 1976, **31**(12), 95–96, 101–102.

98. Kent, S. Scientists count brain cells to figure theory of aging. *Geriatrics,* 1976, **31**(4), 114–115, 119, 122–123.

99. Kent, S. Why do we grow old? *Geriatrics,* 1976, **31**(2), 135, 138–139.

100. Kline, C. The socialization process of women: Implications for a theory of successful aging. *Gerontologist,* 1975, **15**, 486–492.

101. Kohlberg, L. Stages and aging in moral development—some speculations. *Gerontologist,* 1973, **13**, 497–502.

102. Labouvie-Vief, G., and G. N. Gonda. Cognitive strategy training and intellectual performance in the elderly. *Journal of Gerontology,* 1976, **31**, 327–332.

103. Langer, E. Growing old in America: Frauds, quackery swindle the aged and compound their troubles. *Science,* 1963, **140**, 470–472.

104. Leaf, A. Getting old. *Scientific American,* 1973, **229**(3), 45–52.

105. Leon, E. F. Cicero on geriatrics. *Gerontologist,* 1963, **3**, 128–130.

106. Lofland, L. H. *The craft of dying: The modern face of death.* Beverly Hills, Calif.: Sage Publications, 1978.

107. Maddox, G. L., and E. B. Douglass. Aging and individual differences: A longitudinal analysis of social, psychological, and physiological indicators. *Journal of Gerontology,* 1974, **29**, 555–563.

108. Markson, E. W., and G. Levitz. A Guttman Scale to assess memory loss among the elderly. *Gerontologist,* 1973, **13**, 337–340.

109. Masters, W. H., and V. E. Johnson. *Human sexual response.* Boston: Little, Brown, 1966.

110. Masters, W. H., and V. E. Johnson. *Human sexual inadequacy.* Boston: Little, Brown, 1970.

111. Medvedev, Z. A. Aging and longevity: New approaches and new perspectives. *Gerontologist,* 1975, **15**, 196–201.

112. Meyerson, M. D. The effects of aging on communication. *Journal of Gerontology,* 1976, **31**, 29–38.

113. Moberg, D. O. Religiosity in old age. In B. L. Neugarten (Ed.). *Middle age and aging: A reader in social psychology.* Chicago: University of Chicago Press, 1968. Pp. 497–508.

114. Nash, M. M., and J. M. Wepman. Auditory comprehension and age. *Gerontologist,* 1973, **13**, 243–247.

115. Neugarten, B. L. Grow old along with me! The best is yet to be. *Psychology Today,* 1971, **5**(7), 45–48, 79–81.

116. Northcott, H. C. Too young, too old—age in the world of television. *Gerontologist,* 1975, **15**, 184–186.

117. Owens, W. A. Age and mental abilities: A longitudinal study. In D. C. Charles and W. R. Looft (Eds.). *Readings in psychological development through life.* New York: Holt, 1973. Pp. 243–254.

118. Payne, B., and F. Whittington. Older women: An examination of popular stereotypes and research evidence. *Social Problems,* 1976, **23**, 488–504.

119. Petrowsky, M. Marital status, sex and the social networks of the elderly. *Journal of Marriage & the Family,* 1976, **38**, 749–756.

120. Pocs, O., A. Godow, W. L. Tolone, and R. H. Walsh. Is there sex after 40? *Psychology Today,* 1977, **11**(1), 54–56, 87.

121. Portwood, D. A right to suicide? *Psychology Today,* 1978, **11**(8), 66–76.

122. Powers, E. A., and G. L. Bultena. Sex differences in intimate friendships of old age. *Journal of Marriage & the Family,* 1976, **38**, 739–747.

123. Reich, W. T. Ethical issues related to research involving elderly subjects. *Gerontologist,* 1978, **18**, 326–337.

124. Richman, J. The foolishness and wisdom of age: Attitudes toward the elderly as reflected in jokes. *Gerontologist,* 1977, **17**, 210–219.

125. Roberts, J., and M. Rowland. *Refraction status and motility defects of persons 4–74 years.* Hyattsville, Md.: U.S. Department of Health, Education, and Welfare, National Center for Health Statistics, 1978.

126. Ryan, M. S. *Clothing: A study in human behavior.* New York: Holt, 1966.

127. Sacher, G. A. Longevity, aging, and death: An evolutionary perspective. *Gerontologist,* 1978, **18**, 112–119.

128. Schaie, K. W. External validity in the assessment of intellectual development in adulthood. *Journal of Gerontology,* 1978, **33**, 695–701.

129. Schaie, K. W., G. V. Labouvie, and B. U. Buech. Generational and cohort-specific differences in adult cognitive functioning: A fourteen year study of independent samples. *Developmental Psychology,* 1973, **9**, 151–161.

130. Schaier, A. H., and V. G. Cicirelli. Age difference in humor comprehension and appreciation in old age. *Journal of Gerontology,* 1976, **31**, 577–582.

131. Schiffman, S., and M. Pasternak. Decreased discrimination of food odors in the elderly. *Journal of Gerontology,* 1979, **34**, 73–79.

132. Schonberg, W. B., and H. C. Potter. Friendship fluctuations in senescence. *Journal of Genetic Psychology,* 1976, **129**, 333–334.

133. Schulz, R. *The psychology of death, dying, and bereavement.* Reading, Mass.: Addison-Wesley, 1978.

134. Schuster, J. D., and D. H. Kelly. Preferred style features in dresses for physically handicapped elderly women. *Gerontologist,* 1974, **14**, 106–109.

135. Seefeldt, C., R. K. Jantz, A. Galper, and K. Serock. Using pictures to explore children's attitudes toward the elderly. *Gerontologist,* 1977, **17**, 507–512.

136. Sinick, D. Counseling the dying and their survivors. *Personnel & Guidance Journal,* 1976, **55**, 122–123.

137. Smith, A. D. Aging and interference with memory. *Journal of Gerontology,* 1975, **30**, 319–325.

138. Smith, B. H., and P. K. Sethi. Aging and the nervous system. *Geriatrics,* 1975, **30**(3), 109–112, 115.

139. Snyder, L. H., J. Pyrek, and K. C. Smith. Vision and mental function of the elderly. *Gerontologist,* 1976, **16**, 491–495.

140. Sohngen, M. The experience of old age as depicted in contemporary novels. *Gerontologist,* 1977, **17**, 70–78.

141. Sohngen, M., and R. G. Smith. Images of old age in poetry. *Gerontologist,* 1978, **18**, 181–186.

142. Spirduso, W. W. Reaction and movement time as a function of age and physical activity level. *Journal of Gerontology,* 1975, **30**, 435–440.

143. Streib, G. F. Are the aged a minority group? In B. L. Neugarten (Ed.). *Middle age and aging: A reader in social psychology.* Chicago: University of Chicago Press, 1968. Pp. 35–46.

144. Sue, D. W. Aging. *Personnel & Guidance Journal,* 1976, **55**, 100.

145. Surburg, P. R. Aging and effect of physical-mental practice upon acquisition and retention of a motor skill. *Journal of Gerontology,* 1976, **31**, 64–67.

146. Thorson, J. A. Attitudes toward the aged as a function of race and social class. *Gerontologist,* 1975, **15**, 343–344.

147. Toseland, R., and J. Sykes. Senior citizen center participation and other correlates of life satisfaction. *Gerontologist*, 1977, **17**, 233–241.

148. Trela, J. E. Social class and association membership. An analysis of age-graded and non-age-graded voluntary participation. *Journal of Gerontology*, 1976, **31**, 198–203.

149. Urban, H. B., and D. J. Lago. Life-history antecedents in psychiatric disorders of the aging. *Gerontologist*, 1973, **13**, 502–508.

150. Vest, W. E. William Shakespeare, gerontologist. *Geriatrics*, 1954, **9**, 80–82.

151. Warren, L. R., J. W. Wagener, and G. E. Herman. Binaural analysis of the aging auditory system. *Journal of Gerontology*, 1978, **33**, 731–736.

152. Weber, T., and P. Cameron. Humor and aging—a response. *Gerontologist*, 1978, **18**, 73–79.

153. White, K. L. Life and death and medicine. *Scientific American*, 1973, **229**(3), 23–33.

154. Wilkie, F., and C. Eisdorfer. Intelligence and blood pressure in the aged. *Science*, 1971, **172**, 959–962.

155. Wingrove, C. R., and J. P. Alston. Age, aging, and church attendance. *Gerontologist*, 1971, **11**, 356–358.

156. Wood, V., and J. F. Robertson. Friendship and kinship interaction: Differential effect on the morale of the elderly. *Journal of Marriage & the Family*, 1978, **40**, 367–375.

CHAPTER FOURTEEN
Old Age: Vocational and Family Adjustments

After reading this chapter, you should be able to:

- Realize how older people feel about their jobs, what vocational opportunities are available to them, and how successfully they perform their work.
- Understand the difficulties many older people experience in adjusting to retirement and the conditions that influence these adjustments.
- Appreciate the adjustments older people must make to the many changes in family life and how successfully or unsuccessfully they make these adjustments.
- Recognize the many adjustment problems elderly men and women face with the loss of a spouse, and with remarriage.
- Explain why some elderly men and women in the American culture of today prefer cohabitation or singlehood to marriage, and the problems these patterns give rise to.
- Demonstrate the conditions in living arrangements that meet the needs of the elderly and stress the advantages and disadvantages of institutional living and geographic mobility.
- Identify the vocational and family-life hazards that are characteristic of old age and describe how they affect personal and social adjustments.
- List and explain the four criteria commonly used to assess the success or failure of adjustments to old age on the part of both men and women.

Two of the most difficult developmental tasks of old age relate to areas that are especially important for all adults—work and family life. Elderly people face adjustment problems in these areas that are similar in some respects to those they faced earlier but that are unique in many ways. For example, not only must they adjust to working conditions but they must also adjust to the realization that their usefulness to their employers is lessened as they grow older and that, as a result, their status in the work group decreases. Furthermore, they have the problem of adjusting to retirement which, for most elderly people, comes soon after old age sets in.

In the family, older men and women must adjust to depending on each other for companionship; to the lack of contact with, and influence over, their children; and often to the loss of a spouse. Unmarried elderly people often face adjustment problems that are more serious than the ones confronting those who are married or who have lost a spouse.

Vocational and family adjustments in old age are complicated by economic factors which play a far more important role now than they did earlier. Although government aid, in the form of social security, old-age benefits, Medicaid, and the gradual spread of retirement benefits from business and industry alleviate the elderly person's financial problems to some extent, they by no means solve them. This is especially true during periods of spiraling inflation.

VOCATIONAL ADJUSTMENTS IN OLD AGE

Older men are more interested in steady work than in advancement which they realize is not likely to be forthcoming. As a result, they are usually more satisfied with their jobs than younger men. Even knowing that retirement is imminent does not affect their attitudes toward their work if they enjoy what they are doing and are anxious to work. Refer to Figure 12-1, which shows the typical pattern of job satisfaction.

Even women who did not work during early adulthood, when they were preoccupied with housework and child care, often return to work during middle age and find it a satisfactory compensation for diminished home and family responsibilities. However,

they tend to be less satisfied with their jobs than men, primarily because the only jobs available to middle-aged women who reenter the labor force are even less interesting and less challenging than those available to middle-aged men who shift to other jobs during middle age. As a result, older women are less satisfied with the jobs they have and are less disturbed at the thought of retirement than older men.

Attitudes toward Work

Attitudes toward work are important at all ages but especially so during old age when they affect not only the quality of work performed but also the attitudes toward impending retirement. In old age, as is true of other ages during the adult life span, people have different reasons for wanting to work. However, as Havighurst has pointed out, attitudes toward work, which are at the basis of the desire to work, fall roughly into two categories. What these two categories are and the characteristics of each are given in Box 10-2 (60).

Workers can have either of these two attitudes toward any job. If they have a society-maintaining attitude toward their work, their leisure time will be more important to them than time on the job. If, on the other hand, they have an ego-involving attitude, the time they spend on the job will take on greater significance for them and leisure time will decrease in significance.

The prevailing cultural attitude toward work also influences the older worker's attitude toward it.

For the work-oriented older person, it is important to have a job that provides both status and feelings of usefulness. (Ray Ellis from Rapho/Photo Researchers.)

BOX 14-1

CONDITIONS LIMITING EMPLOYMENT OPPORTUNITIES FOR OLDER WORKERS

Compulsory Retirement

Because most industries, businesses, and governmental bureaus require workers to retire at certain fixed ages, ranging from sixty to seventy years, they do not want to hire men or women who are approaching the mandatory retirement age because of the time, energy, and expense that would be involved in training them for the jobs.

Hiring Policies

When the personnel departments of business and industry are in the hands of younger people, the older worker's difficulties in finding employment are greatly increased.

Pension Plans

There is a close correlation between the existence of a pension plan in business and industry and the failure to make use of workers over sixty-five years of age.

Social Attitudes

The widespread belief that older workers are accident-prone, that they are too slow to keep pace with younger workers, and that retraining them to use modern techniques is too costly militates against employing older workers.

Fluctuations in Business Cycles

When business conditions are poor, older workers are generally the first to be laid off and are then replaced by younger workers when the situation improves.

Kind of Work

The period of employment of workers in executive positions is limited by retirement policies. Skilled, semiskilled, and unskilled workers find that their strength and speed decrease with age and that their usefulness to their employers also decreases as a result. Only when workers own their own businesses or are in a profession can they continue to work as long and as much as they wish.

Sex

Women more than men generally find it more difficult to hold their jobs or to get new ones as they grow older. Part-time work in offices or stores and domestic work are among the few vocational opportunities open to older women.

Those who grew up when the cultural attitude toward work was generally more favorable than it is today have a very different attitude toward work than young people now. This colors their attitude toward their own work and increases the difficulties they have adjusting to not being able to get employment if they are physically able to work. For work-oriented older men, having jobs that give them status and make them feel useful is essential to good mental health. Remunerative work is essential to good adjustment for such individuals because, as was pointed out in the preceding chapter, many of them look with disdain on volunteer work and regard it as "unmasculine" (11).

Vocational Opportunities for Older Workers

Unfortunately, when older men and women lose their jobs, often through no fault of their own, they find that there are very few job opportunities open to them even if they are eager to work and are able to do so. This is true also of those who would like to change jobs because they are dissatisfied with the jobs they now have. The most important reasons for these difficulties are explained in Box 14-1.

As was explained in Chapter 12, during middle age vocational opportunities decrease rapidly. By the mid- to late fifties, getting a new job is very difficult and often impossible. If older workers are fortunate enough to get a job, they are, for the most part, monotonous, dead-end jobs far below the level of their abilities and training. Consequently, they do not find them satisfying. Relatively few jobs open to elderly people are highly skilled or involve responsibility. In business and industry, only the worst jobs are usually available to the older workers.

This all means that, on the whole, older workers are overrepresented at the bottom of the earning scale and underrepresented at the top. Consequently it is not surprising that many older workers derive little satisfaction from their jobs.

Even workers who are able to hold onto the jobs they have had for a number of years discover that promotions are slow or minimal as they grow older and that jobs with greater responsibility are given to younger workers. While they may not lose their jobs, they feel that they are marking time until they reach retirement age and that their usefulness to their employers is of far less value than formerly.

Appraisal of Older Workers

Studies of the advantages and disadvantages of hiring older workers reveal that these differ according to the kind of work to be done. Some jobs are more appropriate for older workers, and some for younger workers. Jobs in which judgment and experience are required or in which quality is more important than speed are more appropriate for older workers. Even in work where speed and ability to adjust to new tasks are essential, as in skilled, unskilled, and clerical work, the older worker usually compensates for loss of speed and difficulties of adjustment by steadiness and ability to work without supervision.

Studies of older workers have emphasized qualities that contribute to their success in their work. Older workers, for example, because of their experience, tend to do things with *less waste motion* than younger, less experienced workers. This compensates for their slower work speed. They are also less inclined to be *preoccupied with problems* related to their personal lives than younger workers whose interests are often centered around romance and their families.

Older workers, it has been reported, are *less restless* and less likely to be *dissatisfied* with their jobs or to want to change them than are younger workers. While the volume of their work may be less than that of younger workers, the *quality* is generally higher. They make *fewer mistakes*, partly because their judgment is better and partly because they work at a slower speed.

There is greater *conscientiousness* among older workers because of their more mature attitudes and their desire to keep their jobs. As a result, they are generally more *dependable*. *Absenteeism*, due to illness or disinclination to work, is highest among younger workers, especially those under twenty years of age, while older workers are far less prone to taking time off.

Disabling illnesses and injuries, popularly believed to make older workers less desirable employment risks, are far less frequent among them than is thought and are less frequent among older workers than among younger ones. Even workers up to seventy-four years of age are affected by chronic disabilities in only about half the cases, and these are not serious enough to militate against their working abilities.

Accident proneness is likewise far less common among older workers than is popularly believed. The argument that older workers get along less well with coworkers than those who are younger has likewise been found not to be true. While some older workers unquestionably make poorer *adjustments to their fellow workers* than others do, the percentage who have such difficulty is not appreciably greater than the percentage of younger workers who have trouble getting along with coworkers. In summary, then, it should be apparent that the unfavorable social attitudes toward older workers are unjustified by the facts (2,9,30,38, 101,117).

ADJUSTMENT TO RETIREMENT

Retirement, Schwartz has said, may be the termination of a pattern of life or a transition to a new pattern of life (106). It always involves role changes, changes in interests and values, and changes in the whole pattern of the individual's life. To show how widespread these changes are, a summary by Gordon will highlight their extensiveness (54):

Retirement is . . .
. . . *not setting an alarm clock.*
. . . *reactivating your public library card.*
. . . *starting a second career—if anyone wants you.*
. . . *wondering how long you can keep going if inflation does too.*
. . . *dispensing with dress-up clothes.*
. . . *taking the grandchildren places on weekdays.*
. . . *wondering why your former colleagues don't phone once in a while.*
. . . *waiting for the postman to bring some excitement into your day.*
. . . *taking a course you want instead of have to.*
. . . *reading a book all the way through at one sitting.*
. . . *getting special low rates on the bus, at the movies, in the hotels.*

. . . *trying to keep out of your loved one's way.*
. . . *going to matinees.*
. . . *traveling in the off season.*
. . . *taking a coffee break any old time—and frequently.*
. . . *receiving all sorts of invitations to serve as a volunteer.*
. . . *replaying the past, playing in the present, preparing for the future.*
. . . *looking at the obituary column and being gratified at not finding your name there.*
. . . *reading the newspaper all the way through.*
. . . *getting better acquainted with your neighbors.*
. . . *making the best out of the rest of your life.*
. . . *anticipation followed by deprivation, stagnation, institutionalization*
OR
anticipation followed by participation, recreation, exultation.

Kinds of Retirement

Retirement may be voluntary or compulsory, regular or early. Some workers retire *voluntarily*, often before the age of compulsory retirement. This they do because of health or a desire to spend the remaining years of their lives doing things that are more meaningful to them than their jobs. For others, retirement is involuntary or *compulsory*. The organization for which the individual works sets an age at which *all* its workers must retire, regardless of whether they want to or not. Those who would prefer to remain on the job but are forced out at the compulsory retirement age often show resentment and, as a result, have little motivation to make good adjustments to retirement (3,122). Figure 14-1 shows how workers who are forced to retire at a compulsory retirement age tend to go downhill both physically and psychologically.

While most workers retire at the regular compulsory retirement age, there is a growing trend to take an early retirement. Those who take *early* retirement may do so, as in the case of voluntary retirement, for health reasons or because they want to spend the remaining years of their lives doing things that are more meaningful and more enjoyable to them than their jobs. Sometimes early retirement is compulsory because management wants to make changes and forces its older workers out to make way for new ones, and sometimes it is voluntary. Some workers may resent being forced out of their jobs and into retirement before the compulsory retirement age but others are

'And in appreciation of years of dedicated loyal service, we present this gold watch with which you can time your descent'

Figure 14-1   For most workers, forced retirement means the beginning of physical and mental decline. (Lou Erickson. *The Atlanta Journal,* June 24, 1977. Used by permission.)

satisfied to do so. Their satisfaction depends not so much on their desire to continue working as on their financial situation in the form of a pension and whether or not they have outside interests (7,44,67). How well workers adjust to compulsory *regular* retirement depends mainly on how well prepared they are for it (13,48).

Attitudes toward Retirement

Until recently, retirement was a problem that affected relatively few workers. Today, however, with the widespread acceptance of compulsory-retirement policies and the growing tendency for men and women to live longer than ever before, retirement is becoming one of the major social problems of our culture. Each year, the gap between the total life span and the span of the working life for men and women is widened. As a result, the length of the retirement period grows longer and longer for more people. Figure 14-2 shows the increase in leisure time and the decrease in work time from 1855 to 2000.

To the younger person, whose days are so often overly crowded with duties and responsibilities, the

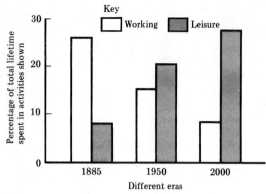

Figure 14-2 Increase in leisure time and decrease in work time—actual and projected. (Adapted from J. W. Still. Boredom: The psychological disease of aging. *Geriatrics*, 1957, **12**, 557–560. Used by permission.)

years of retirement or semiretirement seem like a golden period of life. By middle age, thoughts of retirement grow increasingly strong, not only because men and women find the burden of work becoming heavier and heavier as their strength and energy diminish but also because they realize that they are waging a losing battle in their competition with younger workers (61).

When retirement actually comes, however, it may seem far less desirable than it did earlier. Elderly people may find that their pensions are insufficient to enable them to live as they had planned and hoped to live. As a result, they are forced to try to find jobs to supplement their incomes (43). This means that, for most elderly people, there is a marked difference between the expectations and the realities of retirement. As Beverley has explained, on the basis of material gathered from a nationwide survey of attitudes of elderly people, "Retirement looks better to the younger group than to those already in it. The value placed on leisure time appeared to increase in direct proportion to income and education" (13).

Havighurst has divided elderly people into two general categories on the basis of their attitudes toward retirement. The first category he labeled the *transformers*—those who are able and willing to change their lifestyles by reducing their activities by choice and by creating for themselves new and enjoyable lifestyles. This they do by dropping old roles and undertaking new ones. They seldom relax and do

nothing but, instead, they develop hobbies, travel, and become active in community affairs.

The second category, the *maintainers*, Havighurst has explained, hold onto work by pursuing part-time assignments after retirement and by supplementing this with other activities to fill their time. They, like the transformers, seldom relax and do nothing, but what they do is a continuation of what they have done for years—some form of work for which they are paid as they were throughout their working years (60).

Conditions Affecting Adjustment to Retirement

Certain conditions aid adjustment to retirement while others militate against it. The worker's attitude toward retirement, unquestionably, has a profound effect on adjustment. This attitude may range from delight at the thought of freedom from the responsibilities work entails to despair at the thought of having to give up something as meaningful as work. As Back has explained, "The more retirement is looked on as a change to a new status, and the less it is perceived as the giving up of a prized status, the better the transition will be accomplished (6).

In general, if conditions make it possible for elderly people to remain in their communities and if they have enough money to live just about as they lived before retirement, they will make better adjustments than if they must make radical changes in the pattern of their lives (8,67,71). However, other conditions are also important. Some of the most important of these are given in Box 14-2.

Sex Differences in Adjustment to Retirement

Women, on the whole, adjust better to retirement than men. There are several reasons for this. First, the role change is not as radical because, for the most part, women always played the domestic role, whether they were married or single, throughout their working years, in addition to their working roles.

Second, because work provides fewer psychological benefits and social supports for women, retirement is less traumatic for them than for men (65). Third, because few women have held executive positions, they do not feel that they have suddenly lost all their power and prestige.

Unmarried women, as a group, adjust better to retirement than housewives because they have more

BOX 14-2

CONDITIONS AFFECTING ADJUSTMENT TO RETIREMENT

- Workers who retire voluntarily adjust better than those who are forced to retire, especially if they want to continue to work.
- Poor health at the time of retirement facilitates adjustment while good health is likely to militate against it.
- Most workers find that tapering off is better than abruptly ending patterns of work and living established many years earlier.
- Preretirement counseling and planning aid adjustment. Refer to page 374 for conditions emphasized in preretirement counseling.
- Workers who develop interests in substitute activities that are meaningful to them and which provide many of the satisfactions they formerly derived from work will not find adjustment to retirement as emotionally disturbing as those who fail to develop substitute interests.
- Social contacts, like those provided in many homes for the aged, aid in adjusting to retirement. Remaining in their own homes or in the homes of relatives usually cuts retired people off from social contacts.
- The less change in the pattern of living retirement necessitates, the better the adjustment will be.
- A good economic status, which makes it possible to live comfortably and enjoy meaningful recreations, is essential to good adjustment to retirement.
- A happy marital status aids adjustment to retirement while a frictional one militates against it.
- The more the workers like their work, the poorer their adjustment to retirement. There is an inverse relationship between work satisfaction and retirement satisfaction.
- Place of residence affects adjustment to retirement. The more the community offers for companionship and activities for the elderly, the better they will adjust to retirement.
- The attitudes of family members toward retirement have a profound effect on workers' attitudes. This is especially true of the attitudes of spouses. Refer to Figure 12-6.

social resources to fall back on to fill their free time. In addition, they are more dependent on extrafamilial contacts and, as a result, have a ready-made social group to identify with during the leisure time that retirement brings (46).

Men, on the other hand, have less readily available means of deriving satisfaction to replace that which their work provided than have women. As a result, retirement is more traumatic for them and they adjust less well to the role changes necessitated by retirement.

ADJUSTMENTS TO CHANGES IN FAMILY LIFE IN OLD AGE

The pattern of family life, established in early adulthood, starts to change with the onset of middle age. These changes are made more pronounced by retirement, with the accompanying reduced income, or by the death of a spouse in old age.

Of the many adjustments centering around family relationships that the elderly person must make, the five most important involve relationships with a spouse, changes in sexual behavior, relationships with offspring, parental dependency, and relationships with grandchildren.

Relationships with Spouse

The first important adjustment centering around family relationships elderly people must make is establishing good relationships with their spouses. With the role change from worker to retiree, most men spend much more of their time at home than they ever did before. If their relationships with their wives are good, this will contribute to the happiness of both. When, however, their relationships are strained, friction is increased by constant contacts.

Because many retired men feel lost and do not know what to do with their free time, they tend to be depressed and unhappy. They may show their feelings by being critical, faultfinding, and irritable in their treatment of their wives. Many of them resent any suggestion that they assume some of the household responsibilities on the grounds that that is "woman's work."

How well husbands and wives will adjust to each other in old age when retirement forces them together more than at any previous time in their marriage will depend primarily on how many interests they have in common. This, in turn, will depend largely on how compatible they have been earlier, especially in middle age, when their children left home and thus freed them from parental responsibilities and child-oriented recreations.

Middle- and upper-class adults, on the whole, spend more of their leisure time with spouses and have more recreational interests in common with them than those of the lower-class groups. Because they have developed a pattern of "togetherness" in their recreational activities, it is easier for them to apply this pattern to all areas of their lives when retirement forces men to spend the major part of their time in the home.

Changes in Sexual Behavior

The second important adjustment centering around family relationships elderly people must make are changes in sexual behavior. These adjustments are made difficult by the popular belief that impotence and lack of interest in sex are natural accompaniments of aging. They are believed to be due to the neuroendocrine changes that occur with physical aging (68,69).

There is evidence that changes in sexual behavior among the elderly are due more to psychological than to physical causes. An antagonistic relationship and incompatability with the spouse, for example, influence the kind of sexual behavior the elderly engage in (25,84). Unfavorable social attitudes toward sexuality among the elderly also influence sexual behavior. As Kent has said (70):

It is difficult to maintain a high degree of sexual activity in a society that discourages physical intimacy among older people. In our culture, erotic values are associated with youth and physical beauty, which acts as a deterrent to feelings of attractiveness and desire in the aged.

There is evidence that many middle-aged women, freed from the fear of pregnancy, develop a new interest in sex. This interest, when uninhibited by unfavorable attitudes, continues into old age. While it is true that both men and women experience a diminishing of their sexual powers that parallels the decline in other bodily functions, there is a much stronger interest in sex and a greater desire for sexual activity in old age than is popularly believed to exist (21). There is also an increase in thinking about sex in old age

(27). Figure 12-3 shows the rise in sexual satisfaction in old age. Thus, today it is recognized that the sexual needs of the elderly are too widespread to be considered pathological. Instead, they are recognized as normal (21,25,84).

Sexual Activity in Old Age Studies of the sexual behavior of elderly people have revealed that men and women in their sixties, and even seventies, have intercourse, though it is spaced further apart than in the earlier years, and the man's preliminary orgastic phase is longer (96,100). Decline in sexual activity with advancing age is illustrated in Figure 14-3.

When the individual is in reasonably good health, there is a diminishing of sexual activity rather than a sudden cessation of it. As Rubin has pointed out, there is "no automatic cut off to sexuality at any age" (104). Those who terminate sexual intercourse in old age usually do so because of the physical illness of one of the spouses or because the husband experiences difficulties in achieving orgasm, which affects his desire to continue coitus.

Factors Influencing Sexual Behavior There are many factors that influence the sexual interests and behav-

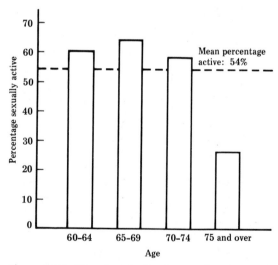

Figure 14-3 There is a decline in sexual activity with advancing age. (Adapted from G. Newman and C. R. Nichols. Sexual activities and attitudes in older persons. In E. B. Palmore (Ed.). *Normal aging.* Durham, N.C.: Duke University Press, 1970, Pp. 277–281. Used by permission.)

ior of the elderly. The most important of these are given in Box 14-3. Note that psychological factors play as important a role as physical factors.

Studies of sexual interests and activities in old age have revealed marked sex differences. As men grow older, they are sexually *interested* more than sexually active. For women, by contrast, interest and activity remain static, but at a much lower level than in men (21,100,104). As Masters and Johnson have commented, "There is no time limit drawn by the advancing years to female sexuality" (84).

Effects on Marital Adjustment In old age, as at other ages, sexual activity has a marked influence on marital adjustments, which in turn affect sexual activity. However, it is not the quantity or quality of sexual activity per se that influences marital adjustments, but whether the sexual activity meets the needs of both partners. When an elderly women finds that coitus does not meet her sexual needs, she may seek substitute sources of satisfaction in masturbation or erotic dreams and daydreams, and this will affect her attitude unfavorably.

The psychological effects of unfavorable social attitudes toward sexual behavior in old age are far more serious than is generally recognized. Guilt feelings, emotional stress due to thwarted sexual desires, and feelings of inadequacy may lead to impotence. As a result, there is a decrease in the frequency of coitus and an increase in other sexual outlets. This is especially damaging psychologically to elderly men for whom potency is a symbol of their masculinity.

Diminishing sexual power can have a serious effect on marital adjustments during old age. If the man believes that his growing impotence is the result of his wife's lack of sexual responsiveness and if she, in turn, blames him for not satisfying her sexual needs, their relationship will be strained, particularly if they are already experiencing difficulties in adjustment as a result of a lack of common interests and boredom on the husband's part stemming from retirement (21,25,37,84).

Relationships with Offspring

The third important adjustment centering around family relationships elderly people must make are changes in relationships with their offspring. Elderly people in America today can count less on their grown children for companionship and help than was true in the past. This is partly because members of the

---

BOX 14-3

COMMON FACTORS AFFECTING SEXUAL BEHAVIOR IN OLD AGE

Pattern of Earlier Sexual Behavior

People who derived enjoyment from sexual behavior and were sexually active during the earlier years of their marriage continue to be sexually more active in old age than those who were less active earlier.

Compatibility of Spouses

When there is a close bond between husband and wife built on mutual interests and respect, the desire for intercourse is much stronger than when a frictional relationship exists.

Social Attitudes

Unfavorable social attitudes toward sex in old age make many elderly men and women feel that interest in sexual matters not only is "not nice" but may even be perverted.

Marital Status

Married people are likely to continue sexual activity into old age. Those who are single or divorced or whose spouses have died usually do not have a strong enough sex drive to make them seek new sex partners.

Preoccupation with Outside Problems

When either or both spouses are preoccupied with financial, family, or other problems, it tends to weaken sexual desire. If they eat or drink excessively in order to escape from these problems, their sexual desires are further weakened.

Overfamiliarity

Being together too much over a long period of time tends to deaden a couple's sexual desire in old age.

Impotence

Many men who find themselves impotent on one occasion, regardless of the condition that gave rise to it, withdraw from further sexual activity to avoid the ego-shattering experience of repeated episodes of sexual inadequacy.

modern generation have less feeling of obligation to their parents than in the past and partly because the geographic mobility so prevalent today separates families often by great distances.

For the most part, the relationships of elderly people with their offspring are far less satisfactory than many believed possible, even during middle age, when these relationships may have begun to deteriorate. Figure 14-4 shows the drop in parental satisfaction that occurs during old age; this drop is more pronounced for men than for women.

When parents are willing to shift their attitudes toward their children to suit the children's age and developmental level, the chances are that the parent-child relationship will be a wholesome one as the years go on, and that the elderly person will find much satisfaction in the companionship of sons and daughters. However, parents who have been unwilling over the years to adjust their attitudes to meet the changing needs of growing children are likely to face a lonely old age (66). The strain in the parent-child relationship that began in adolescence is more likely to grow worse rather than better as time goes on.

For the most part, elderly women are more absorbed in their relationships with their children than elderly men are. This is a continuation of the parent-child relationship that started at the time of the child's birth. Because women have a closer relationship with their grown children than men have, there is usually more friction between women and their children than between men and their children. However, if the parent-child relationship has been satisfactory up to the age of fifty or fifty-five, it is unlikely that new alienations will develop after that (73).

Parental Dependency

The fourth important adjustment centering around family relationships elderly people must make is the possibility of parental dependency. Role reversals, as has been stressed before, are very difficult for older people to make successfully. One role reversal that is especially difficult is that of becoming dependent on grown children. Many elderly people, even when they depend on their children for financial support and companionship, are unable or unwilling to relinquish their role of authority over their children.

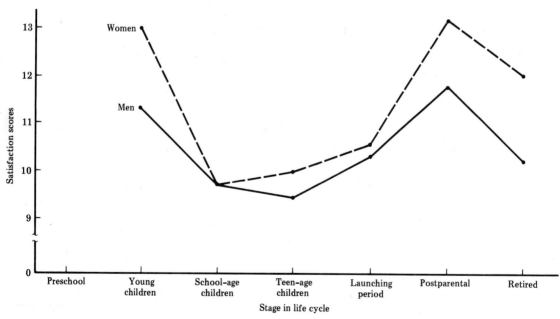

Figure 14-4 Parents' satisfaction with their children at different stages of their married life. (Adapted from W. R. Burr. Satisfaction with various aspects of marriage over the life cycle: A random middle-class sample. *Journal of Marriage & the Family,* 1970, **32**, 29–37. Used by permission.)

They continue to treat them as they did when they were young. Grown children resent this, especially when they are supporting their parents and taking care of their physical and social needs.

Elderly parents who are happily married and have interests of their own are emotionally less dependent on their children than those whose marriages are unhappy or who have failed to develop interests to occupy the time formerly devoted to parental roles.

Financial dependency on their children is a bitter pill for most parents to swallow. This is especially true of men who have played the role of provider for the major part of their lives. Those who accept the role of financial dependency without resistance have usually come from countries where the cultural background differs from that which prevails in America today (15).

Relationships with Grandchildren

The fifth important adjustment centering around family relationships elderly people must make is the type of relationships they will have with their grandchildren. The common patterns of relationships with grandchildren and the common roles grandparents play when their grandchildren are young have been listed and explained in Box 12-7.

By the time men and women reach old age, their grandchildren may be teenagers or young adults. In this case, the grandparents are no longer called upon to help with their care. How much they see the grandchildren and the kind of contacts they have with them will depend partly on how close they live to one another and partly on how well they get along when they are together.

If the grandparents live far away from the grandchildren, as is often the case today, they will have only occasional contacts with them, unless the grandparents go to live in the parents' homes. Even then, the grandchildren eventually go away to college or establish homes of their own and thus many have fewer contacts with the grandparents than they did when they were younger.

As a result of rapidly changing values, attitudes, patterns of dress and behavior, and moral standards, grandparents often find that there is a gap between them and their grandchildren that is too great to bridge. They disapprove of their grandchildren, and the grandchildren in turn regard them as old-fashioned.

When grandparents verbalize their disapproval of their grandchildren, a frictional relationship develops not only between them and the grandchildren but also between them and their own children, whom the grandparents may criticize for not having brought the grandchildren up "properly." This frictional relationship is much more likely to develop if grandparents live under the same roof with their grandchildren than if their contacts with them are only occasional and brief.

When conflicts develop about the grandchildren's behavior, they more often involve the mother and the grandmother than the father and the grandfather. Grandfathers, on the whole, have fewer and more remote contacts with grandchildren than grandmothers do, and they are far less likely to be called on for help in an emergency. As a result, grandmothers generally are more interested and absorbed in the lives of their grandchildren than grandfathers are. While the grandfather may be proud of the achievements of his grandchildren and feel that they reflect favorably on the family, the reactions of grandmothers are usually more personal and more emotionally toned.

Adult grandchildren or those who are approaching middle age often have feelings of responsibility toward their grandparents, even if they had frictional relationships with them when they were younger. These feelings of responsibility may take the form of financial aid or merely as companions or gift-givers (102).

Assessment of Adjustment to Changes in Family Life

People who feel generally happily married find that their marriages become more satisfying to them as they grow older. With time, mutual interests are developed; the children grow up and leave home, thus drawing the partners closer together; illness or retirement on the part of the husband may make the wife feel useful again, as she did when the children were young; and the death of demanding and dominating parents-in-law may remove a source of friction between husband and wife.

Satisfaction with marriage among older people is increased if their children are successful and happily married and if they have good relationships with their grandchildren, even if their contacts with them are infrequent.

Studies of marital happiness in old age have revealed that most older people feel that their marriages have been very satisfactory, that their lives are calmer now that their parental responsibilities are over, and that they have a new freedom to do as they please. Refer to Figure 10-5, which shows how the curve of satisfaction with the present stage in the family life cycle rises during old age. This is true for husbands as well as wives. As Stinnett et al. have commented, this suggests that "progressive marital disenchantment over the life cycle may be a myth" (114).

ADJUSTMENT TO LOSS OF A SPOUSE IN OLD AGE

Unquestionably one of the major adjustments elderly people must make is to the loss of a spouse. Loss of a spouse may be due to death or divorce, though it is far more likely to be due to the former. Because it is customary for women to marry men their own age or older and because men, on the average, die sooner than women, widowhood in old age is far more common for women than for men.

People in their sixties and seventies do get divorced, but far less frequently than younger people. Refer to Figure 10-10. No matter how unsatisfactory marriage may be to elderly people, most of them do not contemplate ending it in a divorce court. When they do decide to get a divorce in old age, it is generally not a new decision, but rather something they have contemplated since the early days of marriage but have put off for their children's sake or for economic reasons.

It has been estimated that 50 percent of sixty-year-old women are widows, while 85 percent of women age eighty-five are widows (5,22,82). There are no statistics available concerning the number of men of comparable ages who are widowers, but there is reason to believe that because widowers at every age remarry more than widows do, the percentages would be far less. Refer to Figure 12-5, which shows the chances for remarriage at different ages. Thus widowhood is a greater problem for women than for men during old age (58,81).

Adjustment to the death of a spouse or to divorce is difficult for men and women in old age because at this time *all* adjustments are increasingly difficult to make. Some of the problems that divorce gives rise to are listed and explained in Box 10-14, and those arising during widowhood, in Box 12-8.

However, all of these are likely to be more difficult to adjust to in old age than when they occur earlier.

Because the adjustment problems to loss of a spouse are different for men than for women at all ages, not in old age alone, the adjustment problems faced by men and by women will be discussed separately.

Adjustment Problems for Men

When men lose their wives shortly after retirement, it greatly increases their difficulties in adjusting to retirement because they must adjust to widowhood —a major adjustment for most men—simultaneously. While it is true that men are far less likely to have serious economic problems than women, due to their pensions, social security, and other sources of income—or to have social problems, because widowers are in great social demand—other problems are often very difficult for them to adjust to. Of these, three are especially common and especially serious.

First, because old age is a period during which interests narrow, elderly men who are left alone find it difficult to compensate for their loneliness by developing new interests as readily as they did when they were younger. Being alone during long hours of leisure, and with few absorbing interests, increases their loneliness and adjustment problems to retirement.

Second, even though widowers may not always have been satisfied with their marriages, they still could count on their wives to provide companionship, to take care of their physical needs and to manage their homes. Few widowers are prepared to live as singles and manage their lives as singles do.

Third, the problem of where to live is a thorny one for many widowers and, in most cases, one of their major adjustment problems. The reason for this is that men, as a group, are more reluctant than women to become dependent on their grown children and live in their homes, unless it is absolutely necessary. They also resist going to homes for the aged, partly because it implies loss of independence and partly because they claim they do not like to be surrounded by people who constantly remind them of their own advancing age. Therefore, they often solve both the loneliness and dependency problems of widowhood by remarriage (5,91).

Adjustment Problems for Women

For women, the adjustment problems of widowhood are very often complicated by decreased income unless their husbands carried life insurance policies or had pensions that provided for the widow of the decreased. While most widows today can count on their deceased husbands' social security benefits, these benefits provide less income than was available while their husbands were alive (22).

The major adjustment problems widows face are influenced by income. A greatly decreased income can play havoc. Three of the problems that are emphasized by decreased income are especially important.

First, a decreased income may and frequently does necessitate giving up interests that otherwise might have been retained. Interests in cultural activities, such as concerts and lectures, going to the movies or other places of amusement, or belonging to clubs, often have to be given up.

Second, a decreased income affects a widow's social life. While many social activities of women do not involve their spouses, as was explained earlier in relationship to early adulthood and middle age, they nonetheless often require money for entertaining and for clothes that must compare favorably with the clothes of their friends (62).

Third, decreased income often means moving into smaller and less desirable living quarters, such as going to live with a married child, or living in an institution. Any of such new patterns of living requires adjustment and further complicates the adjustment to the other problems that widowhood brings (4,57,91, 110).

Because the chances of remarriage are far less for widows than for widowers, some women try to solve the loneliness problem by getting pets, usually dogs or cats. While a pet undoubtedly provides some of the companionship lonely people crave and encourages them to get out of their homes where they will have opportunities to meet and talk to other people, it rarely leads to the establishment of new friendships, and this becomes more difficult with each passing year (79).

Studies of the effects of widowhood almost unanimously point to the conclusion that widowhood is a more serious problem for women than it is for men, and that women adjust less well to the loss of their spouses than do men. They also point to the fact that the long-term effects of widowhood come more from socioeconomic deprivation than from widowhood per se. For that reason, loss of a spouse may be regarded mainly as a "woman's problem" (33,58, 62,91).

REMARRIAGE IN OLD AGE

One of the ways older people try to solve the problems of loneliness and sexual deprivation brought on by the loss of a spouse is by remarrying. Remarriage is more common now than in the past, partly because social attitudes toward remarriage in old age are more favorable than they formerly were, especially when loss of a spouse was due to divorce, and partly because there are more older people alive today than in the past. However, as was stressed earlier—refer to Figure 12-5—the opportunities for remarriage are less for women than for men with each passing year (31).

Age Differences in Remarriage

While elderly people may marry people of approximately the same age—see Figure 14-5—there is a greater tendency to marry those who are younger. Older men, it has been reported, usually select younger women when they remarry. Up to middle age, women usually marry older men or men of approximately the same age. After that, a reverse trend appears, and there is a tendency for older women to marry younger men. This tendency increases with age. It is not unusual for a man to be fifteen or twenty years younger than the woman in her second or third marriage (50,86,120).

While both men and women in their later years do marry individuals of approximately similar age, the number of those who marry younger people is surprisingly large. When this happens, the normal problems of remarriage are complicated by age differences that militate against congeniality of interests and similarity of values. This, it is important to note, is true of any age, not of old age alone.

Adjustment Problems of Remarriage

While marriage at any age brings with it problems of adjustment, remarriage always has certain characteristic problems. This is especially true of remarriage in old age.

Among the common problems are adjusting to the new spouse, to the new set of relatives, to a new home in the same community, and sometimes to a new community. And, as is true of younger people's marriages, it is the woman rather than the man who is expected to make most of these adjustments.

In addition to these problems, there is likely to be discouragement if not open criticism of the remarriage on the part of the children of either the man or

Figure 14-5 Remarriage among the elderly is becoming more frequent and more socially acceptable than it formerly was. (Ray Mellen. *The Atlanta Journal,* April 14, 1977. Used by permission.)

the woman. For the most part, the children are grown and in homes of their own, and do not have to face the problems of having a stepparent as younger children do when their parents remarry. However, many children's attitudes are colored by self-interest. They do not want to lose the help of their mothers as babysitters, nor do they want to lose out on any inheritance. (110).

While some remarriages in old age do not work out satisfactorily for those involved or for members of their families, remarriage late in life is reported to be usually very successful (77). Certain conditions have been found to contribute to good adjustment to re-

marriage in old age; the most important of these are given in Box 14-4.

COHABITATION IN OLD AGE

Without question, remarriage is the common and socially approved solution to the problems of loneliness and sexual deprivation caused by the loss of a spouse. This is true for people of all ages, especially in small-town and rural communities. It is true despite the growing trend toward cohabitation in some areas, especially in the large urban centers, where a more impersonal attitude and interest in other people exists.

Some older people try to solve the problems engendered by loss of a spouse by living together without marriage. This is called *cohabitation.* Unlike many young people, who usually live together to determine whether they are compatible before actually marrying, older people are more often motivated by practical financial considerations.

For example, if a women's inheritance from her dead spouse is in the form of a trust fund that will end if she remarries, or if her social security or other sources of income will cease with her remarriage, it might be impossible for her to marry a retired man and live on his social security and pension benefits. However, if the couple's combined incomes would make a comfortable lifestyle possible, they may accept living together without marriage as a solution to their problems.

Older couples who live together face the possibility of the strong disapproval of grown children, relatives, friends, and neighbors. Some cope with this problem by moving to another community where new friends and neighbors will not know of their marital status. Others remain in their home community, ignoring the attitudes of others and maintaining that the enjoyment and satisfaction they derive from their chosen lifestyle more than compensates for its disadvantages (32,59,91).

ADJUSTMENT TO SINGLEHOOD IN OLD AGE

The popular belief that an old person who has never married will face an unhappy, lonely old age is not borne out by real experiences. The single man has learned over the years to develop interests and become involved in activities to compensate for the lack of companionship of a family of his own. As a result, he is less likely to face a lonely old age than the man who married, whose interests centered around his home and family, and who now, in old age, may find himself without wife and children.

The modern, older single woman builds up a life of her own, just as a man does. As a result, she has much to keep her happy and occupied in old age. Even though she is retired, she usually has the benefit of a pension or social security, in addition to what she has saved, to enable her to live and do much as she pleases. And because she never had to devote her leisure time to a family, she has had an opportunity to establish many interests that will keep her from being lonely when she reaches retirement age (14).

LIVING ARRANGEMENTS FOR THE ELDERLY

Patterns of living vary much more in old age than in middle age, when the pattern is well standardized. Five patterns are common among the elderly today: a married couple living alone; a person living alone in his or her own home; two or more members of the same generation living together in a nonmarital relationship, such as brothers and sisters or friends; a widow or widower living with a married child and/or perhaps grandchildren; and an elderly person living in a home for the aged or in a club or hotel (12,107, 115). Which pattern of living the elderly individual selects will depend upon a number of conditions; the most important of these are given in Box 14-5.

Needs in Living Arrangements

The needs and wants of elderly people vary greatly; therefore living arrangements must vary as well. However, almost all elderly people have certain physical and psychological needs that must be met by their living arrangements if the arrangements are to maintain health and happiness (76). These are given in Box 14-6.

Types of Living Arrangements

Today, the growing realization of the importance of living arrangements suited to the physical and psychological needs of the elderly has resulted in the growth of new living quarters, planned specifically for the elderly. Some of these quarters are financed by the federal government for those with low incomes and are, therefore, open to all those whose incomes fall below the limit specified by the government, regardless of their religion, race, or other factors. Other quarters are financed by private builders or are sponsored by religious, civic, or social groups. For the most part, these groups do not discriminate though they usually require personal interviews and letters of recommendation to ensure that individuals will share common interests and backgrounds, thus contributing to harmonious relationships.

While different age limits may prevail, the usual minimum age ranges from fifty-five to sixty years for one spouse. The other spouse, generally the wife, can be of any age. Some living quarters for the elderly, such as retirement homes, have a maximum age limit—usually 80 years. One reason for these age limits is to avoid accepting those who may, within a short period of time, become incapacitated by illness or accident. Another reason is because when homes or apartments for the elderly must be bought instead of rented, it will be fairer to keep the elderly from making an investment from which they may get only a very short use.

Among the forms of living arrangements for the

BOX 14-5

SOME CONDITIONS INFLUENCING CHOICE OF LIVING ARRANGEMENTS FOR THE ELDERLY

Economic Status

If they are financially able to do so, most elderly people continue to live in their homes or move to smaller, more convenient homes of their own in the same or in a comparable neighborhood. If, however, their economic status has deteriorated, elderly people may be forced to move into less desirable living quarters or into the home of a married child.

Marital Status

While both spouses are alive, their living arrangements are usually determined by their economic status and their health. Older single men and women, as is true of widows and widowers, as a rule live alone, with family members or friends, in clubs, or in institutions for the elderly.

Health

When their health makes it impossible for elderly people to maintain their own homes, they must live with a relative or friend, or in an institution.

Ease of Caring For

Because apartments are, as a rule, easier to care for than homes—with or without gardens—many elderly people nonetheless are forced to move into an apartment if their health makes it impossible for them to care for their own homes or when economic conditions make it impossible for them to hire domestic help for this purpose.

Sex

Widows usually live in homes of their own or with a married child, while widowers are more likely to live in a club, a hotel, or an institution for the elderly.

Children

If they have children, elderly people usually live either near one of them or with one of them. Widows who are childless, and elderly singles, usually live in institutions if they are unable to maintain their own dwellings.

Desire for Companionship

Elderly people in good health and who want companionship may move either to a new home of their own near a married child or relative or to a retirement community, where they can count on social contacts with contemporaries. If their health is poor, they may prefer living in a home for the elderly—where they have contact with contemporaries—to living with a married child, where opportunities for such contact is limited.

Climate

Because elderly people are more affected by the cold than younger people, those who live in the colder areas of the country often migrate to the so-called "sun belts" of the country after retirement. The warmer climate not only eliminates or minimizes some of the physical discomforts of old age—arthritis, sinus, etc.—but it also makes socialization possible for the elderly throughout the year instead of their being housebound for weeks at a time as often occurs in the colder areas.

---

elderly in America today are apartments in buildings limited to those sixty years of age and older; condominiums which only those fifty-five to sixty years of age may purchase; institutions for the elderly, such as retirement and nursing homes (to be discussed in the following section); retirement settlements consisting of individual houses, apartments, or both, located in an area of a city or a suburban community which is situated near shopping centers, with places for dining out and amusement; and retirement communities which are self-contained communities limited to those who are fifty-five to sixty years of age. Many of these retirement communities are located in the so-called "sun-belt" areas of the country and are commonly called the "paradises for the aged."

Regardless of the type of living arrangement, all try to meet the major physical and psychological needs of those who live in them. Refer to Box 14-6 for a listing of these needs. Major emphasis is placed on features that will ensure safety, on opportunities for

PHYSICAL AND PSYCHOLOGICAL NEEDS IN LIVING ARRANGEMENTS FOR THE ELDERLY

Physical Needs

- The house temperature should be comparatively even from floor to ceiling because poor circulation makes the elderly especially sensitive to chilling.
- Elderly people need large windows to ensure plenty of light because of the gradual impairment of vision.
- Provisions should be made for safety. The elderly should have to climb few steps, floors should be unwaxed or covered with wall-to-wall carpeting, and danger areas should be lighted at all times.
- There should be adequate space for indoor and outdoor recreation, a condition best met in multiple-housing developments or in institutions.
- Noise should be controlled, especially during the night. This can be done by locating sleeping quarters in a quiet part of a house or an apartment.
- Elderly people should have labor-saving devices, especially for cooking, dishwashing, and cleaning.
- The living quarters should be on one floor to avoid possible falls on steps.

Psychological Needs

- Elderly people should have at least one small room of their own so that they can have some privacy.
- Living arrangements should include space for sedentary recreations, such as reading and television watching.
- There should be provision for storage of cherished possessions.
- Elderly people should live close to stores and community organizations so that they can be independent in their activities.
- Elderly people should be near relatives and friends so that frequent contacts are possible.
- Provisions should be made for recreation and amusement, especially during the winter months when going outdoors is difficult and being housebound becomes monotonous and boring.
- Provision should be made for transportation to shopping areas, places of amusement, hairdressers, and churches.

---

companionship with those who have similar backgrounds, and on opportunities for recreation, such as areas for individual gardens, a large library with the most recent books, planned and supervised sessions for handicrafts, holiday celebrations, dancing, movies, concerts, bingo games, and religious services of a nondenominational character.

Institutional Living for the Elderly

When health, economic status or other conditions make it impossible for them to continue living in their own homes, and if there is no family member who can or will offer them a place to live, elderly people must take up residence in an institution for the aged. Homes for the elderly fall roughly into two categories, retirement homes and nursing homes. In a *retirement home* personal living quarters may be small —individual apartments or single rooms. As a rule, there is a dining room, recreation rooms and lounges located in an area accessible to all. The facilities are similar to those in a club or residential hotel in which the living quarters, rooms for recreation, and meals are taken care of for permanent residents. In a *nursing home,* the physical needs of the elderly are taken care of by trained personnel and arrangements can be made for hospitalization if necessary.

While many elderly people rebel against giving up their own homes and going into an institution— either a retirement home or a nursing home—there are certain advantages to this type of living. These advantages are listed in Box 14-7. Like anything else, however, there are disadvantages to this type of living. These, likewise, are listed in Box 14-7.

How well elderly people adjust to institutional living depends on many conditions, four of which are both common and essential. First, when men and women enter an institution voluntarily (instead of being forced to do so by circumstances) they will be happier and have a stronger motivation to adjust to the radical changes that institutional living brings.

Second, the more accustomed men and women become to being with other people and to

ADVANTAGES AND DISADVANTAGES OF INSTITUTIONAL LIVING FOR THE ELDERLY

Disadvantages

- It is more expensive than living in one's own home.
- Like all institutional food, it is usually less appealing than home-cooked food.
- Choice of food is limited and often repetitious.
- Close and constant contact with some people who may be uncongenial.
- The location is often some distance away from shops, amusements, and community organizations.
- Location is usually at some distance from family and friends.
- Living quarters tend to be considerably smaller than in former homes.

Advantages

- Maintenance and repairs are provided by the institution.
- All meals are available at reasonable costs.
- Provision is made for suitable recreations and amusements.
- Opportunities are available for contacts with contemporaries with similar interests and abilities.
- Greater chance for acceptance by contemporaries than when with younger people.
- Eliminates loneliness because people are always available for companionship.
- Holiday celebrations for those who have no family are provided.
- Opportunity for prestige based on past accomplishments that would not occur in groups of younger people.

taking part in shared activities, the more they will enjoy the social contacts and recreational opportunities provided by institutions.

Third, elderly people will adjust better to living in an institution if it is close enough to where they lived before so that they can maintain contact with family members and friends. Going to an institution that is far away from the former home is usually a traumatic experience and militates against good adjustment to institutional living and to happiness.

Fourth, and perhaps most important, regardless of where elderly people live, it is important that they feel they are still part of the family and not cut off from contacts with their children and relatives. As their friends die or otherwise become unable to provide companionship, elderly people depend increasingly on their families. As Brody and Spark have emphasized, "The importance of 'family' to the child has been universally accepted. The need of the aged person for 'family' is no less vital. . . . The lack of family, for the infant and aged alike, can be a major deprivation" (20).

They further point out if the elderly are deprived of contacts with their families when they are subjected to what Havighurst has labeled the "insults of aging"—death of a spouse, retirement, and decreasing physical and mental capacities (60)—they will be less able to cope with this deprivation than they would have been earlier. For that reason, they claim, "as his [the elderly person's] dependence increases, those on whom he is dependent hopefully should be able to accept the additional demands" (20).

GEOGRAPHIC MOBILITY IN OLD AGE

Because people often must move from the homes where they have lived for the major part of their adult lives in order to attain suitable living quarters for their old age, there is much mobility among the elderly. Elderly people may have to move from place to place for ten or fifteen years until they finally find living quarters that meet their needs, whether they be in the home of a grown child, in a retirement community, or in an institution.

There are many reasons for mobility in old age. Among the most important are changes in economic conditions following retirement, failing health, loneliness, a desire to be close to members of the family, a more favorable climate, or changes in marital status. Widows and widowers are more likely to move and move more often than those whose spouses are still alive (126).

In recent years, there has been a migration of elderly people to more favorable climates, especially to Florida, Arizona, and California. As a result, these

Elderly people are more likely to make good adjustments to institutional living if they enter the institution voluntarily. (Hella Hammid from Rapho/ Photo Researchers.)

states have had a proportionally greater increase in the number of older residents than other areas of the country.

There are many reasons for this new trend toward migration to "paradises for the aged." The most important of these reasons are a warmer climate, which is favorable for those in poor health and which eliminates the possibility of being cut off from social contacts during the winter months; the breakdown of three-generation family units; improved transportation; inflationary pressures, which make lower living costs necessary; and opportunities for contact with those of the same age group and with similar interests (43).

In addition to migrating to warmer areas, many first-generation Americans return to their former homelands when they retire, and others who have enjoyed travel abroad during their adult years decide to retire to a foreign country where, until recently, they could live better on their retirement pensions and social security than they could here. With rampant inflation in most foreign countries and with the devalu-

ation of the dollar, however, this trend has been reversed. Many elderly people are finding that they cannot live as well abroad as they can in their own country. Thus they are gradually returning.

VOCATIONAL AND FAMILY-LIFE HAZARDS OF OLD AGE

Because of the importance of work and family to older people, anything that prevents good adjustments in these areas may be regarded as a potential hazard to good personal and social adjustments. Of even greater significance is the fact that vocational and family-life hazards increase as the social horizons of the elderly narrow and as their interests are increasingly concentrated on their work and their families.

While hazards are associated with every age in the life span, as has been pointed out repeatedly, the difference between the hazards of old age and those of the younger ages is that elderly people have little or no control over the conditions that are primarily responsible for these hazards. Younger people, for example, who feel that marriage is not complete without children in the home, can control the situation by having children of their own or by adopting them. Elderly people, by contrast, cannot control what their children do, where they will live, or how they will treat their elderly parents. Nor are social pressures or feelings of filial obligation always strong enough to make a grown child voluntarily offer elderly parents a place in their home should poor health or economic necessity make it impossible for them to continue living in their own homes.

Because the conditions that give rise to the vocational and family-life hazards of old age are usually beyond the individual's control, and because adjustments in these areas are even more important to satisfaction and happiness in old age than the personal and social adjustments described in the preceding chapter, they may be regarded as the major hazards of this period.

Vocational Hazards

How important a role vocational hazards play in the personal and social adjustments of elderly people is greatly influenced by their attitudes toward work. As was pointed out earlier, the majority of old people in America today grew up during a time when work was more highly valued as a source of personal satisfaction and social esteem than it is now. As a result, many elderly people today place an extremely high value on work.

There are two important vocational hazards in old age—prevention from working and retirement. These are hazardous to self-esteem and may even lead to feelings of uselessness and martyrdom. As such, they are therefore hazardous to good personal and social adjustments.

Prevention from Working The first serious vocational hazard in old age is prevention from working when one wants to work. There are three reasons why older people may be prevented from working. First, a lack of vocational opportunities for the older worker. Few industrial and business organizations will employ older workers, and even if they are hired, they are most likely to be laid off when business conditions are poor and are least likely to be called back when conditions improve. This is especially true of women and blacks.

Second, unemployment becomes more serious

as workers grow older. Not only is it harder for them to get new jobs but the effects of unemployment on personality are far more serious and far-reaching. The reason for this is that younger workers know that their chances of obtaining future employment are good, even if they must take a temporary setback in wages. Older workers, by contrast, have a far less hopeful outlook. They know that most businesses and industrial organizations have strict policies against hiring older workers and that if they are lucky enough to get a job, it is likely to be far below their capacities, the pay will be less than before, and the job itself may be only temporary or on a part-time basis. Box 14-8 shows some of the most common conditions contributing to the seriousness of unemployment in old age.

Because unemployment lasts longer for older

workers than for younger workers (see Figure 12-7), it causes them more psychological damage. Studies of the mental effects of unemployment on older workers have revealed how serious they are. Measures of the mental efficiency and attitudes of employed and unemployed older people have shown that those who engage in regular, gainful occupations are, on the whole, mentally superior to those who are unemployed. Lack of practice, lack of motivation, and unfavorable attitudes are important contributing factors to the deterioration that comes with unemployment. Being unable to get work contributes to feelings of uselessness. Should they be able to get work, it is likely to be on a lower level than the work they previously did and this is humiliating (2,30,117).

The third condition creating difficulties for the elderly who want to work is the necessity of retiring at a certain age. Those who resist retirement, and who thus refuse to prepare themselves psychologically for it by becoming involved in new interests and activi-

ties, will make poorer adjustments than those who are better prepared for the changes that retirement brings.

Even worse, older people who believe that the organizations for which they formerly worked cannot get along without them and will eventually call them back into service have little motivation to try to adjust to retirement. See Figure 14-6. This unfavorable attitude prolongs the adjustment period to retirement.

Retirement The second serious vocational hazard in old age is retirement. Even when they are prepared for retirement, older people face what Erikson has called an "identity crisis" not unlike the one they faced in adolescence when they were treated sometimes as a child and sometimes as an adult (40). The identity crisis that comes with retirement results from the necessity of making radical role changes—from that of a worker to that of a person of leisure. Furthermore, suddenly changing the habits and patterns established over a lifetime is often very traumatic for the elderly person. Monk has explained why this is so (89):

Retirement entails a loss of status and prestige, a "roleless" situation where appropriate, or at least clearly defined, social positions and role expectations are notoriously absent. . . . Once a person is unable to perform his occupational roles, his former claims to prestige, competence, and social position are no longer valid, thus precipitating the likelihood of an identity breakdown.

An unfavorable attitude toward retirement affects the individual's health, often causing physical decline and premature death. As Horowitz has pointed out, "'Retirement shock' is the new sickness of the aged" (63). The effects of retirement shock are most serious immediately after retirement, when the individual must adjust to changes in routine and to the breaking off of social relationships. It is especially serious for men who lose their wives about this time.

Another vocational hazard of old age, usually overlooked and ignored in studies of the effects of retirement, is the effect of retirement on family members of the retiree, especially the spouses. When husbands retire, the whole pattern of their spouses' lives must, of necessity, also change. The reason is that, instead of going to work daily, the husbands are around the house all the time, making extra work in the form of extra meals or otherwise waiting on them, and they more often than not are both uncooperative and critical because they are bored or feel martyred because

"Ever since he retired he's been waiting for the company to call him back to straighten it out."

Figure 14-6 Retired workers who feel that their business or industrial organizations cannot get along without them make poor adjustments to retirement. (Dale McFeatters. "Strictly Business." Publishers-Hall Syndicate, February 22, 1973. Used by permission.)

they have no work. Many wives resent the extra work their husbands' retirement brings and feel that they, too, should be allowed to retire.

Family-Life Hazards

When the working life of men and women comes to an end, they tend to focus their interests and attention on their homes and family life. Because of this concentration of interest and attention, conditions which previously may have been only minor hazards tend to become major hazards, threatening their physical as well as their psychological well-being.

Because the pattern of family life differs greatly for different people throughout the life span, the changes in this pattern that old age brings will also differ greatly. However, there are certain family-life hazards that are common, four of which are especially common and serious.

Sexual Deprivation The first family-life hazard in old age is sexual deprivation. The change in the pattern of family life in old age may and often does result in sexual deprivation at a time when the sex drive is far from dormant.

Elderly people who are sexually deprived may engage in substitute forms of sexual expression, some of which met their needs earlier. Most of these are frowned on by others and may lead to unfavorable social and self-judgments. The most common substitute sources of sexual satisfaction during old age are given in Box 14-9.

Loneliness The second almost universal family-life hazard to good adjustment in old age is loneliness. Even when grown children live nearby, the elderly person's contacts with them may be only occasional, and their companionship far less than was the case when the three-generation household was more usual than it is today.

One of the most common causes of loneliness in old age is loss of a spouse. While many elderly people acknowledge the possibility of the death of a spouse and make plans for it, relatively few realize the problems involved and are prepared to meet them or to adjust to the loneliness that it brings. Women, as a group, are generally better prepared psychologically for the death of a spouse than men. Heyman and Gianturco have explained the reason for this (62):

BOX 14-9

COMMON SUBSTITUTE SOURCES OF SEXUAL SATISFACTION IN OLD AGE

Masturbation

There is evidence that masturbation is widely practiced by elderly men and women who have few if any other sexual outlets, particularly those who are becoming senile.

Erotic Dreams and Daydreams

Erotic dreams and daydreams are a common substitute source of sexual satisfaction among elderly women who are widowed or divorced and also among those who are married but whose husbands are unable, because of failing health or impotence, to engage in sexual activities. This substitute source of sexual satisfaction is more common in women than in men.

Thinking about Sex

Many elderly men who are sexually deprived not only think about sex but talk about it with their contemporaries. In addition, they like to look at pornographic pictures and tell off-color jokes. Elderly women seldom engage in this form of substitute satisfaction.

Sexual Recrudescence

Elderly men may be sexually attracted to young girls or women, and some may want to marry girls young enough to be their granddaughters. Occasionally they may rape children or adults. Older women may play with dolls, assume a mothering role with someone else's child, or become infatuated with men young enough to be their grandsons.

The elderly widow seems psychologically prepared to accept the death of the spouse through death rehearsal and lessening of social pressures, and she adjusts by maintaining a high rate of social activities. Religious convictions appear to be particularly important sources of strength.

Living Arrangements The third major family-life hazard in old age involves living arrangements. These may be physically or psychologically hazardous or both. *Physically*, it may be hazardous for elderly people to remain in the homes they have occupied since the early years of marriage because these homes are likely to be too large for them to take care of without overtaxing their strength or straining their limited financial resources to provide domestic help.

Remaining in their old homes may be *psychologically* hazardous to good adjustment by being a constant reminder of happier times or by requiring such a large portion of income to maintain that cutting down must be done in other areas, such as clothes, travel, or participation in community activities.

If elderly people move to places that are better suited to their needs, the physical hazards may be reduced but the psychological hazards may increase. If, for example, their health or financial situations force them to live with a married child or in an institution, they may resist the change and thus adjust poorly to their new environment. Moving to an area where climatic conditions are more favorable may likewise reduce physical hazards but increase psychological ones if the move creates loneliness.

Another common psychological hazard that may occur when elderly people move, even if they stay in the same community, is not being able to keep all their cherished possessions. If they go to live in smaller homes of their own, or in the homes of married children or other relatives, or in institutions, they may have to give up much of the furniture, china, pictures, and other material possessions that served as status symbols for many years. They may also have to give up hobbies, such as gardening, if their new homes do not provide opportunities for such pursuits. This may leave them with a feeling of uselessness which will complicate the adjustments they must make to new living arrangements.

Role Changes The fourth major family-life hazard in old age, and unquestionably one of the most serious, is the necessity for making role changes. As has been stressed repeatedly, role changes are always difficult and emotion-provoking. They become increasingly more difficult with each passing year. The more radical the change and the less prestige there is associated with the new role, the more the change will be resisted and the more disturbed the individual will be if forced by circumstances to make the change.

The man or woman who has been accustomed to playing the role of head of the household or of fam-

"Did you have to say I was washing the dishes?"

Figure 14-7 For men who have held positions of responsibility, authority, and prestige, playing the role of helpers to their wives in retirement is often an embarrassing experience. (Lichty and Wagner. "Grin and Bear It." Publishers-Hall Syndicate, November 26, 1978. Used by permission.)

ily breadwinner will find it difficult to live as a dependent in the home of a grown child. Similarly, the man who has achieved a position of prestige and responsibility in the vocational world will find it very difficult to become his wife's "helper" when he retires, a role that implies lack of authority and masculinity. See Figure 14-7. This militates against good adjustment not only to retirement but also to family life. In time it may have a profoundly unfavorable effect on the self-concept, thus leading to poor personal and social adjustments.

ASSESSMENT OF ADJUSTMENTS TO OLD AGE

How successfully men and women will adjust to the problems arising from the physical and mental changes that accompany aging and from the changes in status that occur at this time will be influenced by many factors, some of which are beyond their control. The most important of these factors are given and briefly explained in Box 14-10.

There are many criteria that can be used to assess the kind of adjustment elderly people make, four of which are especially useful. They are quality of behavior patterns, changes in emotional behavior, personality changes, and life satisfaction or happiness. Each of these criteria will be discussed below.

BOX 14-10

SOME FACTORS INFLUENCING ADJUSTMENT TO OLD AGE

Preparation for Old Age

Those who have not prepared themselves psychologically or economically for the changes that old age inevitably brings often find adjusting to these changes a traumatic experience.

Earlier Experiences

The difficulties experienced in adjusting to old age are often the result of earlier learning of certain forms of adjustment that are not appropriate to this period of the life span.

Satisfaction of Needs

To be well adjusted in old age, men and women must be able to satisfy their personal needs and live up to the expectations of others within the framework of life provided for them.

Retention of Old Friendships

The more old friendships the elderly are able to retain, the better adjusted and happier they will be. Moving to other areas or outliving their friends militates against this.

Grown Children

Attitudes of grown children toward their elderly parents and frequent associations with them contribute to good personal and social adjustment on the part of the elderly.

Social Attitudes

One of the greatest handicaps to good adjustment in old age is society's unfavorable attitude toward the elderly.

Personal Attitudes

A resistant attitude toward aging and to adjustment to the changes aging brings is a serious obstacle to successful adjustment in old age.

Method of Adjustment

Rational methods include accepting the limitations of age, developing new interests, learning to give up one's children, and not dwelling on the past; *irrational* methods include denying the changes that come with age and trying to continue as before, becoming preoccupied with the pleasures and triumphs of bygone days, and wanting to be dependent on others for bodily care.

Health Conditions

Chronic illness is a greater handicap to adjustment than temporary illnesses, even though the latter may be more severe while they last than the former.

Living Conditions

When elderly people are forced to live in places that make them feel inferior, inadequate, and resentful, this has an unfavorable effect on the kind of adjustments they make to old age.

Economic Conditions

It is especially difficult for elderly people to adjust to financial problems because they know that they will have little or no opportunity to solve them, as they could when they were younger.

Quality of Behavior Patterns

The first criterion that can be used to assess the kind of adjustments elderly people make is the quality of their behavior. As was pointed out earlier, there are two different and contrasting theories of successful aging: the activity theory and the disengagement theory. According to the *activity theory*, men and women should maintain the attitudes and activities of middle age as long as possible and then find substitutes for the activities they must give up—substitutes for work when they must retire, substitutes for the clubs and associations they are forced to give up for

financial or other reasons, and substitutes for friends or relatives they lose through death or moves to other communities.

According to the *disengagement theory*, men and women curtail, either voluntarily or involuntarily, their involvement in the activities of middle age. They cut down their direct contacts with people, for example; they feel carefree to do as they please and when they please; they are little influenced by the opinions of others; and they do things that are important to them, regardless of how the social group feels about them. It is, however, important to realize that disengagement is not an overnight occurrence nor does it affect all areas of the individual's life simultaneously. Instead, it is a gradual process.

Studies of well-adjusted and poorly adjusted old people have shown that those whom others consider well-adjusted have traits one would expect in a person who has followed the activity theory, while those who seem poorly adjusted have characteristics associated with the disengagement theory (34,93,94). The characteristics of well-adjusted and poorly adjusted elderly people are summarized in Box 14-11.

In general, there is evidence that those who made good adjustments when they were younger will make good adjustments when they are old. As Cicero pointed out in his *De Senectute,* "Those with simple desires and good dispositions find old age easy to take. Those who do not show wisdom and virtue in their youth are prone to attribute to old age those infirmities which are actually produced by former irregularities." How the individual meets the stresses of adolescence and adjusts to them will influence adjustment to old age because patterns of adult attitudes and behavior are set then.

The cultural milieu in which the elderly lived during the formative years of their lives also affects the kind of adjustments they make to old age. Because this is a youth-conscious country in which social attitudes toward old age are often negative and unfavorable, it is difficult for those who have grown up here to accept old age gracefully. Although the elderly are called "senior citizens," they have none of the prestige associated with this status that elderly people have in countries where they are respected because of their wisdom and experience.

Changes in Emotional Behavior

The second criterion that may be used to assess the kind of adjustments elderly people make is the change that takes place in their emotional behavior. Studies of elderly people have shown that they tend to be apathetic in their affective life. They are less responsive than they were when they were younger and show less enthusiasm. Typically, their emotional responses are more specific, less varied, and less appropriate to the occasion than those of younger people. It is not unusual for the elderly person to show signs of regression in emotional behavior, such as negativism, temper tantrums, and excitability characteristic of a child (36,74,98).

Many elderly people have little capacity to

BOX 14-11

COMMON CHARACTERISTICS OF GOOD AND POOR ADJUSTMENT IN OLD AGE

Good Adjustment

- Strong and varied interests
- Economic independence, which makes independence in living possible
- Many social contacts with people of all ages, not just the elderly
- The enjoyment of work which is pleasant and useful but not overtaxing
- Participation in community organizations
- The ability to maintain a comfortable home without exerting too much physical effort
- The ability to enjoy present activities without regretting the past
- A minimum of worry about self or others
- Enjoyment of day-to-day activities regardless of how repetitious they may be
- Avoidance of criticism of others, especially members of the younger generation
- Avoidance of fault-finding, especially about living conditions and treatment from others

Poor Adjustment

- Little interest in the world of today or the individual's role in it
- Withdrawal into the world of fantasy
- Constant reminiscing
- Constant worry, encouraged by idleness
- A lack of drive, leading to low productivity in all areas
- The attitude that the only activities available are "make-work" activities and, therefore, a "waste of time"
- Loneliness due to poor family relationships and lack of interest in contemporaries
- Involuntary geographic isolation
- Involuntary residence in an institution or with a grown child
- Constant complaining and criticizing of anything and everything
- Refusal to take part in activities for the elderly on the grounds that they are "boring"

---

express warm and spontaneous feelings toward others. They become "miserly" with their affections in that they are afraid to express positive feelings toward others because they have discovered, from past experience, that it is unlikely that such feelings will be returned and their efforts will then have been fruitless. The more self-bound elderly people become, the more passive they are emotionally.

While the affective emotions of the elderly are, on the whole, less intense than they were earlier, their resistant emotions may become very strong. For example, old people are likely to be irritable, quarrelsome, crotchety, and contrary. Fears and worries, disappointments and disillusions, and feelings of persecution are far more common than the pleasanter emotional states (47,93,98).

Recovery from emotional experiences also takes longer as the individual grows older. While the child, the young adult, or the middle-aged person may find a release for emotional energy in play or work, the elderly person usually has no such outlet and may remain anxious and depressed for a long time.

Personality Changes

The third criterion that may be used to assess the kind of adjustments elderly people make is the degree and extent of change in personality. It is popularly believed that *all* old people, regardless of their younger personality patterns, develop into ogrelike creatures who are mean, stingy, quarrelsome, demanding, selfish, self-centered, egotistical, and generally impossible to live with. Furthermore, it is popularly believed that if old people live long enough, their personalities will become childlike in the closing years of life—"senile"—requiring that they be treated like children.

As long ago as Plato's time, it was recognized that the personality pattern, prior to old age, influenced people's reactions to old age. This, in turn, determined how much change will take place in their personalities when they become old. This point of view has now been substantiated by modern studies of personality which emphasize that although changes in personality do occur, they are *quantitative* rather than qualitative. This means that the fundamental pattern of personality, set earlier in life, becomes more set with advancing age (93,111).

Although the elderly may, for example, become more rigid in their thinking, more conservative in their actions, more prejudiced in their attitudes toward others, and more self-centered, these are not new traits that developed as they aged. Instead, they are exaggerations of lifelong traits that have become

more pronounced with the pressures of old age. When pressures are too severe to adjust to and personality breakdowns occur, there is still evidence that the predominant traits, developed earlier, will be dominant in the pattern the breakdown takes (34).

Causes of Personality Changes   Changes in personality in old age come from changes in the core of the personality pattern, the *self-concept*. How much this self-concept will change and in what direction the change occurs determines the quality and quantity of change in the personality pattern.

Changes in the self-concept are due mainly to subjective awareness of aging on the part of the elderly. This is often accentuated by their acceptance of the cultural stereotype of old age and by their recognition of social attitudes toward them and the treatment they receive from members of the social group because of their age.

When the elderly become aware of the physical and psychological changes that are taking place within them, they begin to think of themselves as "old." As a result, they are likely to think and behave as old people are supposed to. In time, they develop personality patterns that conform to social expectations.

The treatment the elderly receive from members of the social group because of their age also contributes to changes in their self-concepts. Because this treatment tends to be unfavorable, the effect on the self-concepts of the elderly likewise tends to be unfavorable.

In spite of the fact that the number of old people is increasing rapidly, they still constitute a "minority group" in our culture. They suffer from subordination to the younger members of society, and they are discriminated against and made to feel unwanted, as all minority-group members are. Because of their minority-group status, many old people develop personality traits that are typical of members of minority groups, such as hypersensitivity, self-hatred, feelings of insecurity and uncertainty, quarrelsomeness, apathy, regression, introversion, anxiety, overdependency, and defensiveness (93,94).

It is important to recognize that *not all* older people develop "minority-group" personality patterns. Even those who do develop such patterns do not develop all the traits characteristic of such patterns or in equal strength. Personality differences occur in old age as in every other period of life. However, those who are institutionalized, especially when against their wishes, have poorer attitudes toward themselves and more marked characteristics of the minority-group personality than those who live outside institutions.

Effects of Radical Changes A radical change in the self-concept at any age and for any reason is likely to lead to a breakdown in the personality structure of minor or major severity. Advancing age and its pressures bring an increase in personality breakdowns and in the number of individuals committed to mental institutions (1,94).

In the milder forms, these breakdowns consist of such disorders as disturbances of memory; falsifications of memory; faulty attention; disturbances of orientation concerning time, place, and person; suspiciousness; disturbances in the ethical domain; hallucinations and delusions—especially of persecution—and such common neuroses as anxiety, preoccupation with bodily functions, chronic fatigue, compulsion and hysterical disorders, neurotic depressions, and sex deviations.

Personality breakdown of a more serious kind, as in mental disease, increases greatly with advancing age. After sixty-five, for example, there is a marked upward trend in serious emotional disorders. In the sixties, psychoses with cerebral arteriosclerosis and senile dementia predominate, and these increase steadily to the end of life. After seventy, senile psychoses are most prevalent (19,24).

When a breakdown in personality occurs in old age it may lead to criminal behavior or suicidal tendencies. While the criminal tendencies are, on the whole, of a minor sort—larceny, theft, and alcoholism—they lead to embarrassments for families (109). Suicidal tendencies, while less pronounced than during middle age, are still prevalent enough to indicate personality maladjustment. Marshall maintains that as income status from social security, pensions, etc., improves the suicide rate in old age declines (83).

There is evidence that most personality breakdowns in old age are not the result of brain damage but rather of social conditions which give rise to feelings of insecurity. These are especially serious when there is a history of poor adjustment. Many old people have shown similar maladaptive behavior under stress when they were younger. Then, under the pressure of problems relating to the death of a spouse or to retirement, for example, they experience a breakdown in the personality pattern, which is already weakened by past experiences (19,34,93).

Happiness

The fourth criterion that may be used to assess the kind of adjustment elderly people make is the degree of self-satisfaction or happiness they experience. According to Erikson, old age is characterized by either ego-integrity or despair (40). When the achievements of the elderly have come up to the standards they set for themselves earlier, so that the gap between their real selves and their ideal selves is small, they experience ego-integrity and are reasonably happy and satisfied with themselves and their achievements.

On the other hand, elderly people who feel that they have fallen short of their earlier expectations experience despair because they realize that with each passing day their chances for attaining their goals grow slimmer and slimmer. This is one cause for suicide among men in old age (88). Refer to Figure 12-9, which shows suicide rates at different ages.

Even those who have been successful or reasonably successful may become dissatisfied in old age. As the sands of time run out, they too experience despair, though not to the same extent as those who believe themselves to be failures or near-failures. As Erikson has commented, "Despair is there for everyone, no matter how much he has accomplished (40).

Causes of Happiness in Old Age As is true of other times in the life span, happiness in old age depends upon fulfillment of the "three A's of happiness"—acceptance, affection, and achievement. When any one of these is unfulfilled, it is difficult if not impossible for the elderly to be happy. When, for example, they feel that they are neglected by their grown children or other family members, when they feel that their past achievements have fallen far short of their hopes and expectations, or when they develop a "nobody loves me" complex, it is inevitable that they would be unhappy.

Studies of happiness and unhappiness in old age have revealed that they are usually carry-overs of attitudes formed earlier as a result of the success or failure of their past adjustments. At no other time in life do unsuccessful past adjustments make present adjustments as difficult as in old age and the adjustments that must be made at this time are more difficult than any faced earlier.

This means that unless the elderly have made reasonably good adjustments in the past and have been able to maintain a high degree of ego-integrity, they have far less chance for happiness now than they did earlier. However, it is important to recognize that people derive happiness from different things and from different experiences as they grow older. To the adolescent, for example, happiness means freedom from cares and responsibilities, popularity with members of both sexes, and engaging in enjoyable activities. To the elderly, happiness means something quite different. Barrett has described what makes elderly people happy in this way (9):

The older person who is financially secure, able to utilize his free time constructively, happy in his social contacts and able to contribute services to others will find the later longevous period of life truly rewarding. He will retain a superior self-concept, remain highly motivated, rarely become neurotic or psychotic and live out his life happily. He will not suffer from psychosocial deprivation, nor will he become senescent. When one is adequately prepared for retirement, these may truly be the "golden years."

Variations in Happiness in Old Age   Because happiness does not have the same meaning for those who are old as it does for the younger, the elderly cannot expect to experience the same kind or the same degree of happiness as they did earlier. However, what people do is more important to their happiness in old age than what they are. In general, happy old people are more alert and ready to engage in new activities than are unhappy old people (87).

Middle- and upper-class people, on the whole, tend to be more active in community life than lower-class people. As a result, elderly people in the upper and middle classes tend to be happier in old age than those from the lower classes who, because of their social inactivity, feel lonely and useless (75).

Life satisfaction, as shown in the degree of happiness they experience, tends to be greater for women than for men up to age sixty-five. After that, the reverse is true (93). This may be due, in part, to the freedom from responsibilities men experience when they retire while women's responsibilities continue or

Elderly people who are happy tend to be more alert and ready to engage in new activities than those who are unhappy. (Irene Bayer from Monkmeyer.)

even increase when their husbands are at home most of the time, and, in part, to the fact that physical characteristics of aging, as was pointed out earlier, are less socially approved in women than in men.

Conditions Contributing to Happiness   Regardless of social class, sex, or any other variable, certain conditions can be counted on to contribute to happiness in old age. The most important of these are given in Box 14-12.

Even though all these conditions contribute to happiness in old age, it is not essential that they all be present in order for the elderly person to be happy. Furthermore, because people have different needs, what brings happiness to one in old age may not bring happiness to another. On the other hand, because the pattern of life that brings happiness in old age is usually similar to the pattern that brought happiness earlier, an essential to happiness in the closing years of life is the opportunity to continue the lifestyle

BOX 14-12

SOME IMPORTANT CONDITIONS CONTRIBUTING TO HAPPINESS IN OLD AGE

- A favorable attitude toward old age developed as a result of earlier pleasurable contacts with elderly people
- Happy memories of childhood and adulthood
- Freedom to pursue a desired lifestyle without outside interference
- A realistic attitude toward, and acceptance of, the physical and psychological changes that aging inevitably brings
- Acceptance of self and present living conditions even if these fall below expectations
- An opportunity to establish a satisfying, socially acceptable pattern of life
- Continued participation in interesting and meaningful activities
- Acceptance by, and respect from, the social group
- A feeling of satisfaction with present status and past achievements
- Satisfaction with marital status and sex life
- Reasonably good health without chronic health problems
- Enjoyment of recreational activities planned for the elderly
- Enjoyment of social activities with relatives and friends
- Productive activities whether in housework or volunteer services
- A financial situation adequate to meet needs and wants

---

that previously led to happiness. Havighurst stressed this point when he said (60):

Persons with an active, achieving, and outward-directed life style will be best satisfied with a continuation of this style into old age with only slight diminution. Other persons with a passive, dependent, home-centered life style will be best satisfied with disengagement. . . . Undoubtedly there is a disengaging force operating on and within people as they pass 70 and 80. But they will still retain the personality-life style characteristics of their middle years.

Chapter Highlights

1. Vocational adjustments in old age are markedly influenced by workers' attitudes, the two most common types of which are "society-maintaining" work attitudes—attitudes characterized by little or no interest in work per se but in the pay checks—and "ego-involving" work attitudes—attitudes characterized by great personal satisfaction, self-respect, and a sense of worth.

2. Employment opportunities for older workers are limited by such factors as compulsory retirement, hiring practices, pension plans, social attitudes toward the elderly, business cycles, sex of the worker, and kind of work.

3. Retirement, which involves role changes as well as changes in interests, values, and life patterns, may be voluntary or compulsory, early or regular.

4. Attitudes toward retirement are influenced by a number of conditions, the three most important of which are the economic status of the individual, attitudes of significant people, especially family members, toward the individual's retirement, and the satisfaction the retiree derives from substitute activities.

5. Changes in family-life patterns, made more pronounced by retirement, reduced income, or death of a spouse, require five major adjustments—relationships with a spouse, changes in social behavior, relationships with offspring and with grandchildren, and role reversal or parental dependency on offspring.

6. Adjustment to loss of a spouse, by death or divorce, in old age necessitates different types of adjustment for men and for women with those for men complicated by loneliness and need for dependency and, for women, by decreased income.

7. There are many adjustment problems with remarriage in old age, the most common of which are adjustment to a new spouse, to a new set of relatives, and often to a new home or a new community.

8. Cohabitation in old age, which has been increasing in recent years especially in large urban centers, is usually motivated by practical and financial considerations as compared with the desire to determine compatibility, the usual motivation for cohabitation in younger people.

9. Single men and women tend, in old age, to be better adjusted and happier than those who lose a mate because, over the years, they have established interests and friendships that take the place

of the family relationships that are so absorbing to married individuals.

10. There are five common patterns of living arrangements for the elderly in the American culture of today: an elderly married couple lives alone; an elderly person, whether male or female, lives alone in his or her own home; two or more elderly people—brother and sister, brothers, sisters, or friends—live together in a nonmarital relationship; an elderly widow or widower lives with a married child; an elderly person lives in a home for the elderly, in a hotel, or in a club.

11. Geographic mobility in old age, often necessitated by economic, health or family conditions, or by changes in marital status as happens with divorce or death of a spouse, is more often involuntary than voluntary.

12. The two most common and most serious vocational hazards in old age are exclusion from work due to lack of vocational opportunities or unemployment even though one wants to work, and retirement, especially when it is involuntary, or early, due to conditions over which the individual has no control, or is unprepared for.

13. The most common family-life hazards of old age are sexual deprivation, loneliness, especially when there is loss of a spouse due to divorce or death, changes in living arrangements that are often involuntary, and the necessity for making role changes due to changes in health, economic status, or living conditions.

14. There are four criteria commonly used to assess adjustments to old age on the part of both men and women: the quality of behavior patterns, whether active or characterized by voluntary or involuntary disengagement; changes in emotional behavior; personality changes; and self-satisfaction or happiness.

15. Happiness in old age is characterized by continued activity, while unhappiness is influenced by disengagement, either voluntary or involuntary.

Bibliography

1. Allison, R. S. The varieties of brain syndrome in the aged. In M. P. Lawton and F. G. Lawton (Eds.). *Mental impairment in the aged.* Philadelphia: Philadelphia Geriatric Center, 1965. Pp. 1–66.
2. Alston, J. P., and C. J. Dudley. Age, occupation, and life satisfaction. *Gerontologist,* 1973, **13,** 58–61.
3. Andrews, F. Resentment at having to retire. *The New York Times,* Jan. 14, 1977.
4. Arling, G. The elderly widow and her family, neighbors and friends. *Journal of Marriage & the Family,* 1976, **38,** 757–768.
5. Atchley, R. C. Dimensions of widowhood in later life. *Gerontologist,* 1975, **15,** 176–178.
6. Back K. W. The ambiguity of retirement. In E. W. Busse and E. Pfeiffer (Eds.). *Behavior and adaptation in late life.* Boston: Little, Brown, 1969. Pp. 93–114.
7. Barfield, R. E., and J. N. Morgan. Trends in planned early retirement. *Gerontologist,* 1978, **18,** 13–18.
8. Barfield, R. E., and J. N. Morgan. Trends in satisfaction with retirement. *Gerontologist,* 1978, **18,** 19–23.
9. Barrett, J. H. *Gerontological psychology.* Springfield, Ill.: Charles C Thomas, 1972.
10. Beverley, E. V. Turning the realities of retirement into fulfillment. *Geriatrics,* 1975, **30**(1), 126, 131–132, 134, 139.
11. Beverley, E. V. The retirree's vacation dilemma—what to do with more time but less money. *Geriatrics,* 1975, **30**(3), 171–172, 174, 176, 181.
12. Beverley, E. V. How to choose the right milieu for your later years. *Geriatrics,* 1975, **30**(4), 150–154, 157–160.
13. Beverley, E. V. The beginning of wisdom about aging. *Geriatrics,* 1975, **30**(7), 116–119, 122–123, 127–128.
14. Beverley, E. V. Living happily with oneself—and with others. *Geriatrics,* 1975, **30**(7), 129, 132, 136, 141–142.
15. Beverley, E. V. Confronting the challenge of dependency in old age. *Geriatrics,* 1976, **31**(7), 112–115, 118–119.
16. Bischof, L. J. *Adult psychology.* (2nd ed.) New York: Harper & Row, 1976.
17. Bock, E. W., and I. L. Webber. Suicide among the elderly: Isolating widowhood and mitigating alternatives. *Journal of Marriage & the Family,* 1972, **34,** 24–31.
18. Brand, F. N., and R. T. Smith. Life adjustment and relocation of the elderly. *Journal of Gerontology,* 1974, **29,** 336–340.
19. Britton, J. H. and J. O. Britton. *Personality changes in aging.* New York: Springer, 1972.
20. Brody, E. M., and G. M. Spark. Institutionalization of the aged: A family crisis. *Family Process,* 1966, **5,** 76–90.
21. Brody, J. E. For healthy people, sexual interest and activity continue throughout life. *The New York Times,* July 5, 1978.
22. Brozan, N. Elderly women: Conference throws spotlight on their economic woes. *The New York Times,* May 26, 1978.
23. Burck, G. That ever expanding pension balloon. *Fortune,* Oct. 1971. Pp. 100–103, 130–134.
24. Busse, E. W., R. H. Dovenmuehle, and R. G. Brown. Psychoneurotic reactions of the aged. In E. B. Palmore (Ed.). *Normal aging.* Durham, N.C.: Duke University Press, 1970. Pp. 75–83.
25. Butler, R. N., and M. I. Levis. *Sex after sixty: A guide for men and women in their later years.* New York: Harper & Row, 1976.
26. Cameron, P. Stereotypes about generation fun and happiness vs. self-appraised fun and happiness. *Gerontologist,* 1972, **12,** 120–123, 190.
27. Cameron, P., and H. Biber. Sexual thought throughout the life span. *Gerontologist,* 1973, **13,** 144–147.
28. Carp, F. M. Impact of improved housing on morale and life satisfaction. *Gerontologist,* 1975, **15,** 511–515.
29. Clayton, P. J., J. A. Halikas, and W. L. Maurice. The depression of widowhood. *British Journal of Psychiatry,* 1972, **120,** 71–77.
30. Clemente, F., and J. Hendricks. A further look at the relation-

ship between age and productivity. *Gerontologist*, 1973, **13,** 106–110.

31. Cleveland, W. P., and D. T. Gianturco. Remarriage probability after widowhood: A retrospective method. *Journal of Gerontology*, 1976, **31,** 99–103.

32. Conner, K. A., E. A. Powers, and G. L. Bultena. Social interaction and life satisfaction: An empirical assessment of late-life patterns. *Journal of Gerontology*, 1979, **34,** 116–121.

33. Conroy, R. C. Widows and widowhood. *New York State Journal of Medicine*, 1977, **77,** 357–360.

34. Costa, P. T., and R. R. McCrae. Age differences in personality structure: A cluster analytic approach. *Journal of Gerontology*, 1976, **31,** 564–570.

35. Darnley, F. Adjustment to retirement: Integrity or despair. *Family Coordinator*, 1975, **24,** 217–226.

36. Dean, L. R. Aging and the decline of affect. *Journal of Gerontology*, 1962, **17,** 440–446.

37. Dean, S. R. Geriatric sexuality: Normal, needed, and neglected. *Geriatrics*, 1974, **29**(7), 134–137.

38. Dennis, W. Creative productivity between the ages of twenty and eighty years. In D. C. Charles and W. R. Looft (Eds.). *Readings in psychological development through life*. New York: Holt, 1973. Pp. 283–295.

39. Dovenmuehle, R. H., J. B. Reckless, and G. Newman. Depressive reactions in the elderly. In E. B. Palmore (Ed.). *Normal aging*. Durham, N.C.: Duke University Press,1970. Pp. 90–97.

40. Erikson, E. H. Identity and the life cycle: Selected papers. *Psychological Issues Monographs*, Vol. 1, No. 1. New York: International Universities Press, 1967.

41. Fengler, A. P. Attitudinal orientations of wives toward their husbands' retirement. *International Journal of Aging & Human Development*, 1975, **6,** 139–152.

42. Fillenbaum, G. G., and G. L. Maddox. Work after retirement: An investigation into some psychologically relevant variables. *Gerontologist*, 1974, **14,** 418–424.

43. Fine, M. Interrelationships among mobility, health and attitudinal variables in an urban elderly population. *Human Relations*, 1975, **28,** 451–474.

44. Flint, J. Early retirement is growing in U.S. *The New York Times*, July 10, 1977.

45. Foley, A. R. Preretirement planning in a changing society. *American Journal of Psychiatry*, 1972, **128,** 877–881.

46. Fox, J. H. Effects of retirement and former work life on women's adaptation to old age. *Journal of Gerontology*, 1977, **32,** 196–202.

47. Fox, J. H., J. L. Topel, and M. S. Huckman. Dementia in the elderly—a search for treatable illnesses. *Journal of Gerontology*, 1975, **30,** 557–564.

48. George, L. K., and G. L. Maddox. Subjective adaptation to loss of the work role: A longitudinal study. *Journal of Gerontology*, 1977, **32,** 456–462.

49. Gerber, I., R. Rusalem, N. Hannon, D. Battin, and A. Arkin. Anticipatory grief and aged widows and widowers. *Journal of Gerontology*, 1975, **30,** 225–229.

50. Geriatric Focus article. Remarriage late in life usually *very* successful. *Geriatric Focus*, 1969, **8**(20), 1–5.

51. Glamser, F. D. Determinants of a positive attitude toward retirement. *Journal of Gerontology*, 1976, **31,** 104–107.

52. Glamser, F. D., and G. F. DeJong. The efficacy of preretirement preparation programs for industrial workers. *Journal of Gerontology*, 1975, **30,** 595–600.

53. Gordon, S. K. The phenomenon of depression in old age. *Gerontologist*, 1973, **13,** 100–105.

54. Gordon, T. Retirement is . . . *Phi Delta Kappan*, 1976, **37,** 643.

55. Goudy, W. J., E. A. Powers, and P. Keith. Work and retirement: A test of attitudinal relationships. *Journal of Gerontology*, 1975, **30,** 193–198.

56. Graney, M. J. Happiness and social participation in aging. *Journal of Gerontology*, 1975, **30,** 701–706.

57. Gubrium, J. F. Marital desolation and the evaluation of everyday life in old age. *Journal of Marriage & the Family*, 1974, **36,** 107–113.

58. Harvey, C. D., and H. M. Bahr. Widowhood, morale, and affiliation. *Journal of Marriage & the Family*, 1974, **36,** 97–106.

59. Hassett, J. A new look at living together. *Psychology Today*, 1977, **11**(7), 82–83.

60. Havighurst, R. J. Successful aging. *Gerontologist*, 1961, **1,** 8–13.

61. Haynes, S. G., A. J. McMichall, and H. A. Tyroler. Survival after early and normal retirement. *Journal of Gerontology*, 1978, **33,** 269–278.

62. Heyman, D. K., and D. T. Gianturco. Long-term adaptation by the elderly to bereavement. *Journal of Gerontology*, 1973, **28,** 359–362.

63. Horowitz, J. This is the age of the aged. *The New York Times*, May 16, 1965.

64. Hutchison, I. W. The significance of status for morale and life satisfaction among lower-income elderly. *Journal of Marriage & the Family*, 1975, **37,** 287–293.

65. Jaslow, P. Employment, retirement and morale among older women. *Journal of Gerontology*, 1976, **31,** 212–218.

66. Johnson, E. S. "Good" relationships between older mothers and their daughters: A causal model. *Gerontologist*, 1978, **18,** 301–306.

67. Kell, D., and C. V. Patton. Reaction to induced early retirement. *Gerontologist*, 1978, **18,** 173–179.

68. Kent, S. Neuroendocrine changes that come with age do not spell the end of sexual fulfillment. *Geriatrics*, 1975, **30**(3), 184–186, 188.

69. Kent, S. Impotence: The facts versus the fallacies. *Geriatrics*, 1975, **30**(4), 164, 169–171.

70. Kent, S. Sex after 45: Continued sexual activity depends on health and the availability of a partner. *Geriatrics*, 1975, **30**(11), 142–144.

71. Kimmel, D. C., K. F. Price, and J. W. Walker. Retirement choice and retirement satisfaction. *Journal of Gerontology*, 1978, **33,** 575–585.

72. Kuypers, J. A. Changeability of life style and personality in old age. *Gerontologist*, 1972, **12,** 336–342.

73. Lahniers, C. E. Perceptions of aging parents in the context of disengagement theory. *Genetic Psychology Monographs*, 1975, **92,** 299–320.

74. Lakin, M., and C. Eisdorfer. Affective expression among the aged. In E. B. Palmore (Ed.). *Normal aging*. Durham, N.C.: Duke University Press, 1970. Pp. 243–250.

75. Larson, R. Thirty years of research on the subjective well-being of older Americans. *Journal of Gerontology*, 1978, **33,** 109–125.

76. Lawton, M. P., E. M. Brody, and P. Turner-Massey. The relationship of environmental factors to changes in well-being. *Gerontologist*, 1978, **18**, 133–137.

77. Lee, G. R. Marriage and morale in later life. *Journal of Marriage & the Family*, 1978, **40**, 131–139.

78. Levin, S. On widowhood: Discussion. *Journal of Geriatric Psychiatry*, 1975, **8**, 57–59.

79. Levinson, B. M. *Pets and human development*. Springfield, Ill.: Charles C Thomas, 1972.

80. Lipman, A., and R. Slater. Homes for old people: Toward a positive environment. *Gerontologist*, 1977, **17**, 146–156.

81. Lopata, H. Z. *Widowhood in an American city*, Cambridge, Mass. New York: Schenkman, 1973.

82. Lopata, H. Z. On widowhood: Grief, work and identity reconstruction. *Journal of Geriatric Psychiatry*, 1975, **8**, 41–45.

83. Marshall, J. R. Changes in aged white male suicide: 1948–1972. *Journal of Gerontology*, 1978, **33**, 762–768.

84. Masters, W. H., and V. E. Johnson. Sexual response: The aging female and the aging male. In B. L. Neugarten (Ed.). *Middle age and aging: A reader in social psychology*. Chicago: University of Chicago Press, 1968. Pp. 269–279.

85. Masters, W. H., and V. E. Johnson. *Human sexual inadequacy*. Boston: Little, Brown, 1970.

86. McKain, W. C. A new look at older marriage. *Family Coordinator*, 1972, **21**, 61–69.

87. Medley, M. L. Satisfaction with life among persons sixty-five years and older: A causal model. *Journal of Gerontology*, 1976, **31**, 448–455.

88. Miller, M. Toward a profile of the older white male suicide. *Gerontologist*, 1978, **18**, 80–82.

89. Monk, A. Factors in the preparation for retirement by middle-aged adults. *Gerontologist*, 1971, **11**, 348–351.

90. Montgomery, J. E. Magna Carta of the aged. *Journal of Home Economics*, 1973, **65**(4), 6–13.

91. Morgan, L. Å. A re-examination of widowhood and morale. *Journal of Gerontology*, 1976, **31**, 687–695.

92. Morison, R. S. Dying. *Scientific American*, 1973, **229**(3), 55–62.

93. Neugarten, B. L. Personality changes in late life: A developmental perspective. In C. Eisdorfer and M. P. Lawton (Eds.). *The psychology of adulthood and development*. Washington, D.C.: APA, 1973, Pp. 311–335.

94. Neugarten, B. L. Adult personality: A developmental view. In D. C. Charles and W. R. Looft (Eds.). *Readings in psychological development through life*. New York: Holt, 1973. Pp. 356–366.

95. New York Times article. Job survey finds aged work well. *The New York Times*, Sept. 22, 1972.

96. Newman, G., and C. R. Nichols. Sexual activities and attitudes in older persons. In E. B. Palmore (Ed.). *Normal aging*. Durham, N.C.: Duke University Press, 1970. Pp. 277–281.

97. Newsweek article. Living together. *Newsweek*, Aug. 1, 1976, Pp. 46–50.

98. Nordlicht, S. Stress, aging, and mental health. *New York State Journal of Medicine*, 1975, **75**, 2135–2137.

99. Palmore, E. B., and V. Kivett. Changes in life satisfaction: A longitudinal study of persons aged 46–70. *Journal of Gerontology*, 1977, **32**, 311–316.

100. Pfeiffer, E., A. Verwoerdt, and H-S. Wang. Sexual behavior in aged men and women. In E. G. Palmore (Ed.). *Normal aging*. Durham, N.C.: Duke University Press, 1970. Pp. 299–303.

101. Powers, E. A., and W. J. Goudy. Examination of the meaning of work to older workers. *Aging & Human Development*, 1971, **2**, 38–45.

102. Robertson, J. F. Significance of grandparents: Perceptions of young adult grandchildren. *Gerontologist*, 1976, **16**, 137–140.

103. Rowe, A. R. Scientists in retirement. *Journal of Gerontology*, 1973, **28**, 345–350.

104. Rubin, I. The "sexless older years": A socially harmful stereotype. In D. C. Charles and W. R. Looft (Eds.). *Readings in psychological development through life*. New York: Holt, 1973. Pp. 367–379.

105. Schuckit, M. A. Geriatric alcoholism and drug abuse. *Gerontologist*, 1977, **17**, 168–174.

106. Schwartz, A. N. Retirement: Termination or transition. *Geriatrics*, 1974, **29**(5), 190–192, 195–198.

107. Sears, D. W. Elderly housing: A need determination technique. *Gerontologist*, 1974, **14**, 182–187.

108. Sheppard, H. L. Will our current retirement policies be realistic in the future? *Geriatrics*, 1976, **31**(5), 38, 42, 46.

109. Shichor, D., and S. Kobrin. Criminal behavior among the elderly. *Gerontologist*, 1978, **18**, 213–218.

110. Silverman, P. R., and A. Cooperband. On widowhood: Mutual help and the elderly widow. *Journal of Geriatric Psychiatry*, 1975, **8**, 9–27.

111. Slater, P. E., and P. A. Scarr. Personality in old age. *Genetic Psychology Monographs*, 1964, **70**, 229–269.

112. Snow, R. B., and R. J. Havighurst. Life style types and patterns of retirement of educators. *Gerontologist*, 1977, **17**, 545–552.

113. Spreitzer, E., and E. E. Snyder. Correlates of life satisfaction among the aged. *Journal of Gerontology*, 1974, **29**, 454–458.

114. Stinnett, N., L. M. Carter, and J. E. Montgomery. Older persons' perceptions of their marriages. *Journal of Marriage & the Family*, 1972, **34**, 665–670.

115. Struyk, R. J. The housing situation of elderly Americans. *Gerontologist*, 1977, **17**, 130–139.

116. Taylor, J. L. Retirement? It's a second chance. *Phi Delta Kappan*, 1976, **57**, 652–653.

117. Thompson, G. B. Work versus leisure roles. An investigation of morale among employed and retired men. *Journal of Gerontology*, 1973, **28**, 339–344.

118. Toseland, R., and J. Rasch. Factors contributing to older persons' satisfaction with their communities. *Gerontologist*, 1978, **18**, 395–402.

119. Toseland, R., and J. Sykes. Senior citizen center participation and other correlates of life satisfaction. *Gerontologist*, 1977, **17**, 233–241.

120. Treas, J., and A. Van Hilst. Marriage and remarriage rates among older Americans. *Gerontologist*, 1976, **16**, 132–136.

121. Trost, J. Attitudes toward and occurrence of cohabitation without marriage. *Journal of Marriage & the Family*, 1978, **40**, 393–400.

122. U.S. News & World Report article. Forced retirement: An issue that's riling older Americans. *U.S. News & World Report*, July 4, 1977, P. 75.

123. Vinick, B. H. Remarriage in old age. *Family Coordinator*, 1978, **27**, 359–363.

124. Weiss, W. U., and R. S. Waldrop. Some characteristics of individuals who remain in an institution for the aged. *Developmental Psychology*, 1972, **6**, 182.

125. Whitehead, J. A. *Psychiatric disorders in old age*. New York: Springer, 1974.

126. Yee, W., and M. D. Van Arsdol. Residential mobility, age, and the life cycle. *Journal of Gerontology*, 1977, **32**, 211–221.

INDEX

INDEX

Page numbers in *italic* indicate illustrations.

Age:
  awkward, 336
  of best marital adjustment, 312
  dangerous, 336
  maternal, *306*
  paternal, 311, 324
  of puberty, 199–201, 208
  self-concept and, 254
Aggressiveness of early childhood, 126
Aging:
  individual differences in effects of, 390–391,
    415
  signs of, 273, 340, 341
  (*See also* Elderly parents; Old age)
Alienation syndrome in adolescence, 234
Amniocentesis, 44–46
Amusements:
  of babyhood, 94
  of early adulthood, 278, 279
  of late childhood, 173–174
Anger, 91, 123, 124, 165
Anoxia, 58
Antagonism, sex (*see* Sex antagonism)
Appearance:
  attitude toward, 5
  changes in, 340, 344, 352, 397
  in early childhood, 143
  interest in, 228, 229
    in adolescence, 236
    in early adulthood, 273
    in late childhood, 159, 180
    in middle age, 340, 347, 353
    in old age, 404
  postmenopausal, 343
  at puberty, 213
  self-concept and, 254
  sex-appropriate, 213, 255
  social acceptance and, 20, 22, 143, 169, 188,
    215–216
Aristotle on puberty, 197
Arms, control of, 85
Ascendant behavior, 126
Aspiration, 141, 254, 258, 354
Associates of early childhood, 127
Associative play, 125
Attachment behavior:
  in babyhood, 98, 107
  in early childhood, 126, 145
Attachment objects, 92, 126

Attitudes:
  toward age periods, 22
  toward developmental change, 4–5
  toward education, 180, 238–239
  effects of discipline on, 134
  effects of puberty on, 205–207
  toward job, 379
  toward menstruation, 214
  toward old age, 392–393
  toward older workers, 423
  parental (*see* Parental attitude)
  toward parenthood, 183, 311
  toward pregnancy, 311
  toward retirement, 425–426
  toward school, 180, 238–239
  toward sexual behavior, 247–248
  of significant people: in infancy, 72–73
    in prenatal period, 37–41, 47–49
  toward spouse, 381
  toward work, 298, 422
Attractiveness (*see* Appearance)
Authoritarian discipline, 133, 134, 183–184
Automation, effect on middle-aged worker, 360,
  361
Autonomy, 22, 237–238
Awkward age, 336
Awkwardness, 143, 188, 208, 255

Babbling, 88
Baby talk, 104
Baby teeth, 83, 117
Babyhood:
  characteristics of, 79–81
  defined, 79
  developmental foundations in, 5
  developmental tasks of, 10, 81–82
  discipline in, 97
  emotional behavior in, 89–91
  family relationships in, 98–99
  happiness in, 107–108
  hazards of, 81, 101–107
  moral development in, 96–97
  motor control in, 85
  muscle control in, 85
  personality development in, 99–101
  physical development in, 79, 82, 83
  physiological function in, 82–84
  play interests in, 92–95

Illness:
  in childhood, 142, 187
  imaginary, 414
  in old age, 413–414
  in puberty, 211
Imaginary playmates, 128, 146
Imitation, 126
Imitative age, 115
Imitative play, 94
Immaturity, adolescent, 255–257
    effects of, 257–258
Immunizations, 158
Impotence, 429
Income, reduced, in old age, 45–46
Independence, 22, 108, 237–238, 309
Individual differences in effects of aging, 390–
    391, 415
Individuality, 71, 80, 142
Infancy:
  activity in, 63–64
  adjustments of, 55–61
  care in, 59–61, 71
  characteristics of, 53–55
  consciousness in, 65
  defined, 53
  emotions of, 65–66
  hazards of, 55, 67–74
  learning capacity in, 65
  parental attitudes in, 59, 70–71
  personality in, 66–67
  physical development in, 61–63
  sensory capacities in, 65, 66
  subdivisions of, 53
  vocalization in, 64–65
Infant mortality, 55, 57, 67, 68
Infants:
  characteristics of, 61–67
  effects of maternal stress on, 47
Inferiority, feelings of, 186
In-law relationships:
  in marital adjustment, 308–310, 313, 320
  in middle age, 367–369
In-laws, financial support of, 309
Institutional living for elderly, 437–438
  advantages and disadvantages of, 438
Instrument birth, 56, 57, 67
Intelligence:
  curiosity in, 123
  decline of, 345–346
  and personality development, 186

Intelligence:
  and physical development, 116, 158–159
  play interests and, 129
  prematurity and, 69
  speech skills and, 122
  (*See also* Mental ability)
Interests:
  in achievement, 237
  of adolescence, 234–242
  in appearance, 180, 236, 273, 347, 404
  in clothes, 136–137, 180, 236, 273, 347, 405
  in death, 410–412
  in early adulthood, 271–278
  in early childhood, 134–137
  educational, 180, 238
  effects of, 178–179
  hazards in, 189
  in health, 180
  heterosexual, 208
  in human body, 135–136, 180
  in independence, 180, 237–238
  in late childhood, 178–180
  in middle age, 346–349, 352–353
  in money, 238, 274–275, 347–348, 405
  in old age, 402–412
  recreational, 235–236, 276–277, 349, 350,
    405–407
  in religion, 134–135, 180, 239–240, 275–
    276, 348, 409–410
  in self, 136, 403–404
  sex-appropriate, 182
  sexual, 136, 180, 244–245
  social, 236, 237
  in status symbols, 180, 240
  vocational, 239, 297
Interracial family, 303
Interreligious family, 303
  (*See also* Mixed marriage)
Intimacy versus isolation, crisis of, 319
Isolation (*see* Social isolation)

Jealousy, 123, 124
Job attitudes, unfavorable, 379
Job changes, 296–297, 301
Job dissatisfaction, 317–318
Job experience and vocational choice, 297
Job opportunities for older workers, 423
Job satisfaction:
  conditions contributing to, 363

Parental attitudes:
 prenatal, 48
 punitive, 251, *252*
 and self-concept, 141
 unfavorable, 47–49, 72–73, 83
Parental care, hazards of, 371, 382
Parental dependency, 430–431
Parental expectation, 183, 311
Parental model for successful marriage, 324
Parental satisfaction, *313*, 430
Parenthood:
 adjustment to, 310–311
 assumption of, 272
 effect on marital adjustment, 310, 319–321, 324
 empty-nest period of, 363–365
 new parent blues in, 72
 period of, 266–267
 preparation for, 60
 religious interest in, 275–276
 single, 310–311
Parties, adolescent, 237
Partunate period, 53
Paternal age in developmental irregularities, 42
Paternal attitude:
 toward newborn, 59
 prenatal, 39–41, 48
Peer acceptance, sociometric status and, 169–170
Peer-group influence:
 in adolescence, 230–231, 254
 in early childhood, 126, 141
 and sex-role sterotypes, 179
Peer groups:
 drinking in, 241
 drug use in, 241–242
 leaders of, 233–234
Penis, growth of, 202, 210
Period:
 of change, 223–224
 of embryo, 38, 43
 of fetus, 38, 43
 of gestation, 58–59
 of heightened emotionality, 166
 of neonate, 53
 of partunate, 53
 transitional, 223
 of zygote, 38, 43
Permanent teeth, 117, 159
Permissive discipline, 133, 134, 183

"Perpetual students," 269
Personal hazards of middle age, 351–354
Personal interests, 236–238, 273–276, 403–404
Personality:
 admired traits in, 169, *184*, 185, 252–253
 adult, 327–328
 beginnings of, 66–67
 breakdown of, in old age, 446
 disorganization of, in middle age, 384
 of drug users, *242*
 effects of discipline on, 134
 effects of maternal attitude on, 67
 improvement of, 253
 of leaders, 234
 ordinal position and, 141, 185
 and religious interests, 275
Personality changes:
 in male climacteric, 344
 in menopause, 343
 in old age, 446–447
Personality development:
 during adolescence, 252–254
 in babyhood, 100, 106
 in early childhood, 141–142, 149–150
 hazards to, 106–107, 149–150, 189
 in late childhood, 184–186
 of twins, 34
Pets as substitute companions, 128, 146
Phylogenetic functions, 6
Physical appearance (*see* Appearance)
Physical causality, concepts of, 175
Physical changes:
 during adolescence, 226–228
  concern about, 228–229
 in middle age, 339–345, 364
 in old age, 396–400
 at puberty, 201–204
  acceptance of, 213
  effects of, 204–207
  preparation for, 212–213
Physical defects, 186, 187, 254–255
Physical development:
 in babyhood, 79, 82, 83
 in early childhood, 116, 117
 of infants, 61–63
 in late childhood, 158–*160*
 laws of, 6–7
 prematurity and, 69
 of twins, 34

Physical discomfort:
  in male climacteric, 344
  in menopause, 343
Physical handicaps, 413
Physical hazards:
  of adolescence, 254–255
  of babyhood, 101–103
  of early adulthood, 286
  of early childhood, 142–144
  of late childhood, 187–188
  to newborns, 67–68
  of old age, 413–414
  of prenatal period, 41–45
  of puberty, 211
Physical needs in living arrangements for elderly,
    437
Physical proportions (see Body proportions)
Physiological functions:
  in babyhood, 82–84, 103
  in early childhood, 116–117
  in middle age, 341
  of newborn, 62
  in old age, 398
Piaget:
  on cognitive development, 95, 130, 174, 222,
    242–243
  on moral development, 96, 132, 174, 176
Pituitary gland in pubertal change, 200
Pituitary imbalance, 211
Plateau in development of infant, 54, 71
Play:
  age of, 158
  associative, 125
  in babyhood, 92–95, 105
  collecting as, 172
  constructive, 171–172
  cooperative, 125
  in early childhood, 128–130
  exploratory, 94
  exploring as, 172
  hazards in, 105, 146–147, 189
  imitative, 94
  in late childhood, 171–174
  make-believe, 94
  parallel, 93, 125
  patterns of, 94, 129–130
  sensorimotor, 94
  solitary, 146, 171
  toy stage of, 115, 128–130, 147
  variations in interest in, 129

Play equipment, 129
Play skills, 87, 159, 161
Playmates, 125, 127, 169
  imaginary, 128, 146
Polar body, 30
Popularity:
  change in values in, 281
  desire for, in middle age, 353
Possessions, loss of, in old age, 415
Postconventional morality, 243
Postmaturity, 58, 59, 67
Postnatal care, 59–61, 71
Postnatal life:
  adjustment to, 55–61
  hazards to, 67–74
Postpubescent stage, 198
Prayer, concept of, 135
Precocious puberty, 211
Preconventional morality, 132
Pregang age, 115
Pregnancy, premarital, 248
  (See also Prenatal period)
Prejudice, 126, 168, 231
Premarital intercourse, changed attitudes to-
    ward, 247
Premarital pregnancy, changed attitudes toward,
    248
Prematurity:
  criteria of, 58
  hazards of, 43, 59, 67–68
  long-term effects of, 68, 69
Prenatal development, periods of, 37, 38
Prenatal environment, 56
  unfavorable, 67
Prenatal period, 29–49
  characteristics of, 29–30
  hazards during, 41–49
  length of, 37
  unfavorable attitudes in, 47–49
Preoperational stage, 130
Preparation:
  for marriage, 226
  for old age, 374–376
  for parenthood, 60
  for puberty, 212
  for retirement, 374, 375, 376
Prepubescent stage, 198
Preschool age, 115
  sex-role typing in, 138
Primary sex characteristics, 202–203